ELECTRIC POWER

ELECTRIC POWER

Deregulation and the Public Interest

Edited by
JOHN C. MOORHOUSE

Foreword by
Harold Demsetz

Pacific Studies in Public Policy

PACIFIC RESEARCH INSTITUTE FOR PUBLIC POLICY
San Francisco, California

ISBN 0-936488-02-6 (paper)
      0-936488-11-5 (cloth)

Library of Congress Catalog Card Number 85-63556

Printed in the United States of America

Pacific Research Institute for Public Policy
177 Post Street
San Francisco, California 94108

Library of Congress Cataloging-in-Publication Data

Electric power.

   (Pacific studies in public policy)
   Bibliography: p.
   Includes index.
   1. Electric utilities—Government policy—
United States.   I. Moorhouse, John C., 1943–
II. Series.
HD9685.U5E527   1986   338.4′736362′0973   86-63556
ISBN 0-936488-11-5 (alk. paper)
ISBN 0-936488-02-6 (pbk.: alk. paper)

CONTENTS

**PART II   ENVIRONMENTAL, FUEL, AND SOCIAL
REGULATION OF UTILITIES**

PART III   THE BEHAVIOR OF UTILITY
COMMISSIONS

10

The Performance of Utility Commissions
—Peter Navarro

11

Information, Incentives, and Regulation
—E. C. Pasour, Jr.

PART IV   REGULATORY REFORM

12

Competition Between Electric Utilities
—Walter J. Primeaux, Jr.

LIST OF FIGURES

LIST OF TABLES

FOREWORD

Academic writings about the regulation of economic activity tend to suffer considerably from what I have elsewhere termed the nirvana approach, which implicitly frames any relevant choice as being between an ideal and a flawed form of organization. In pre-1970 literature, and to a lesser extent recently, the nirvana approach cast industry regulation in the role of the ideal and the unregulated market in the role of the flawed (due to problems associated with scale economies and natural monopoly in the provision of electricity). Theorists viewed unregulated utilities as able to enjoy considerable monopoly power at the expense of both consumers and efficiency. They saw regulation as the appropriate corrective to this, satisfying consumer interests without sacrificing scale economies.

The motivation for much of this belief derived from blackboard economics—the ability economists have to shift demand and cost curves or to write their mathematical equivalents on a blackboard unconstrained by the fact that the humans and human decisions backing these formal constructs could not be so easily manipulated. Economists assumed regulators would make decisions designed to achieve efficiency, not in response to political pressures. They represented markets as single firms with monopoly power, not by entrepreneurs and investors motivated to wrest profit away from existing firms.

In reaction to the nirvana approach and blackboard economics, I wrote "Why Regulate Utilities?" The essence of the article, referenced in this volume, was to argue that scale economies granted no sure entitlement to monopoly power, even theoretically, and that the choice between the disciplines of the market and of regulation needs to be based on more careful considerations of how these two arrangements work in fact and off the blackboard. Conceivably—perhaps even plausibly—unregulated markets work better than regulated markets even when scale economies are important.

During the 1960s economists knew a great deal about the operation of markets when many firms simultaneously compete but not much about competition to take a market away from an existing dominant firm and even less about the actual functioning of regulation. The past twenty years, beginning with pioneering work by scholars such as Buchanan, Tullock, and Stigler, has brought forward much new theory and evidence. The notion of properly motivated, effectively administered regulation has been abandoned. By now we know that regulation follows the dictates of political pressures, and these often reflect desires to redistribute wealth rather than increase it.

Scholars, or at least some of them, have also become attracted to the theory of contestable markets put forth by Baumol, Panzar, and Willig. This theory develops in greater depth one of the schemes in "Why Regulate Utilities?"—competition for the market as a substitute for competition in the market. As a result of these developments, confidence has increased that competition can discipline firms in markets characterized by scale economies and confidence has decreased that regulation can achieve blackboard objectives. This is as it should be. But care must be exercised not to adopt another nirvana approach by merely reversing the roles of flawed and unflawed, assuming that the market works perfectly but not so regulation.

The proper balance between free markets and economic regulation surely depends on how both operate in fact. Theories cannot demonstrate this; they can only guide us in our search for facts that will help us make judgments. This volume examines a considerable array of facts and presents cogent theories for assessing these facts. The danger of merely reversing the nirvana approach is avoided by the variety of ideas, evidence, and points of view presented here.

The reader is left to a private assessment of which theories and facts seem most convincing, but the case for reduced regulation seems to me strengthened by much of what is contained in these pages. I had not fully anticipated the severity of some of the regulatory problems. The conflicts between state and federal regulation, among classes of electricity users, between electricity users and the owners and employees who produce it, and among government agencies with specialized interests of their own—tax revenues, safety, abundant energy supplies, and environmental quality—all interact to create a confusing and unpredictable regulatory system. It is impossible to have much confidence that a connection exists between the old blackboard analysis of regulation and the actual regulatory system. On the other hand, market competition—even when limited to interproduct and regional rivalry—seems to have greater potential for protecting consumer interests than one might think before reading this book.

The reader, who will find new and challenging material here, also will learn much about the regulation of electric utilities, but will not have all puzzles resolved. Some questions are suggested by the research itself. An example that struck me—which also seems to reveal the inadequacy of our theory of regulation—is the contrasting assessment of regulatory outcomes during two different periods. In a study of the period 1912 to 1920, Jarrell assesses regulation as favoring electricity producers. Wenders, examining regulation from about 1970 on, concludes that regulation favors residential electricity users. What accounts for this shift in regulatory outcome, assuming these studies correctly reflect the regulatory impact during the periods studied?

We can speculate about this. The cost of organizing residential users in order to exert political pressure may be too large when energy costs are a small fraction of household budgets. This would explain Jarrell's findings for the earlier period. But when energy costs begin to absorb a larger part of the household budget, as was true during the late 1970s, the costs of organizing households may become worth bearing. This would explain Wender's findings. I leave it to the reader to judge this explanation or conjure another if this one is unappealing.

The studies in this excellent volume cover a wide variety of subjects, including the practical possibility of competitive franchising, the evaluation of different approaches to regulatory principles, the study of conflicts among the surprisingly large number of regulatory bodies with an interest in how electric utilities are regulated, and the study of the actual consequences regulation has had in this industry. Readers will learn much that is essential for informed judgments about the past and the future of regulation in this industry. Just as important, they will discover new puzzles, new hints at solutions, and plenty to speculate about.

Harold Demsetz
Department of Economics
University of California
at Los Angeles

INTRODUCTION

The Uncertain Future of the Electric Power Industry

John C. Moorhouse

The 1970s witnessed a series of events that disrupted domestic energy markets. Sharp increases in oil prices worldwide, price controls and contrived fuel shortages at home, comprehensive environmental regulation, accelerating inflation, and unusually high costs of raising capital each contributed to what became known as "the energy crisis." The interdependence of energy markets coupled with inflexible and outmoded utility regulation meant that the electric power industry participated fully in this crisis. A rolling brownout is as much the result of regulatory failure as are gasoline lines and natural gas shortages. Indeed, new circumstances led the electric power industry to enlarge our vocabulary during the 1970s with terms such as blackout, rolling brownout, power shedding, interruptible service, and lifeline rates.

While recent decontrol of domestic oil prices, the breakdown in OPEC pricing discipline, and the phased deregulation of natural gas prices have restored a marked degree of stability to oil and gas markets, the electric power industry faces an ongoing financial crisis and an uncertain future. Since 1972 the construction of one hundred nuclear and a half-dozen coal-fired generating plants has been canceled.[1] Within the last three years, over 40,000 megawatts of electric

---

1. "Are Utilities Obsolete?" *Business Week*, 21 May 1984, p. 122.

generating capacity has been scrapped or canceled.[2] In 1984 the Washington Public Power Service System defaulted on $2.5 billion in debt service payments, and Cleveland Electric Illuminating Company, Public Service of Indiana (PSI), and Consumer Power Company (Michigan) each abandoned costly plants in various stages of completion. (PSI's $7 billion Marble Hill plant was 50 percent built when scrapped.) Other utilities such as Georgia Power and Duke Power (North Carolina) have found it prudent to sell existing generating capacity to improve their finances. And at least one investor-owned utility, Long Island Lighting Company, considered bankruptcy.[3] Experts estimate that the construction cost of abandoned generating capacity may reach $60 billion.[4]

Duke Power's experience with its Catawba Nuclear Station is instructive. Construction of the two-unit plant began in 1974 at an estimated cost of $1.2 billion. After many delays, the plant was completed in 1984 at a cost of $3.9 billion—more than triple the original estimate. By the end of 1984, the plant had yet to generate one kilowatt hour of electricity. In the meantime, as construction costs mounted, Duke sold off 75 percent of the future plant's generating capacity to two leagues of electric cooperatives and a consortium of municipal power companies for $3.1 billion. These buyers in turn financed their purchase by borrowing $1.6 billion from the Rural Electrification Administration at heavily subsidized interest rates and by selling $1.5 billion in tax-exempt municipal bonds. While this was unfolding, Duke applied for substantial rate hikes to pay for its share (25 percent) of the plant and canceled construction of its Cherokee and Perkins nuclear plants. The Duke example reflects many industry problems: construction delays, cost overruns, canceled projects, heavy subsidies, and rate hikes. Taxpayers, consumers, and Duke stockholders are the losers. The reader should bear in mind, moreover, that Duke Power is consistently ranked among the best-managed and most efficient investor-owned utilities in the nation.[5]

Constrained by outmoded regulation in a changed economic environment, electric utilities find it difficult to raise the capital required

2. William W. Berry, "The Case for Competition in the Electric Utility Industry," *Public Utility Fortnightly* 110, no. 6 (16 September 1982):13.

3. "Generators of Bankruptcy," *Time*, 23 July 1984, p. 81.

4. "Are Utilities Obsolete?" *Business Week*, 21 May 1984, p. 126.

5. David Givens, "Last of Duke's N-Plants Nears Completion," *Winston-Salem Journal*, 22 July 1984, p. G1.

to build new capacity and replace obsolete plants. Under such conditions, utilities have opted to cancel projects, scrap partially completed power stations, and in general reduce the level of capital investment. Not surprisingly the financial exigencies of the industry are mirrored in the bond and stock markets. Bond ratings for electric utilities have declined since the mid-1970s. Not only does the rating decline signify more risk, it implies higher borrowing costs and additional financial pressures. Similarly, electric utility stocks, once considered a conservative investment, have sold well below book value since 1976.[6] To finance construction by selling stock under such circumstances would dilute existing stockholder equity. Furthermore, because current bond and stock prices are based on the market's assessment of the industry's future financial performance, both indices presage continuing uncertainty. While the consequences of this might only be apparent to investors now, Navarro argues persuasively that present financial inadequacy will bring higher electric rates and less reliable service in the future.[7]

It is all too easy to blame unfavorable circumstances and mismanagement for the wasted capital resources and financial straits in which many electric utilities find themselves. Undoubtedly managers have made mistakes, but the problems are industrywide, so that an explanation based on systematic mismanagement begs the question. A better explanation must include the climate created by regulation within which long-run investment decisions are made.

Regulation reduces the role of entrepreneurship and hard-headed business decision making; it substitutes for these virtues the arts of public relations and bureaucratic administration. The corporate officers of electric utilities are not businesspeople in the normal sense. How could they be? They operate in an environment where direct competition is illegal, product prices are set, and rates of return are guaranteed. Under regulation, those successful as utility heads have, of necessity, become adroit at placating regulators and packaging decisions for public consumption. We should not be surprised, for example, that when utility managers are encouraged with government subsidies to build nuclear plants, they respond even if some projects

6. See René H. Malès, "Electric Utility Issues," in S.F. Singer, ed., *Free Market Energy* (New York: Universe, 1984), chap. 11, p. 284; and Peter Navarro, "Electric Utility Regulation and National Energy Policy," *Regulation* 5 (January/February 1981):22.

7. Peter Navarro, "Save Now, Freeze Later," *Regulation* 7 (September/October 1983):31.

make little economic sense in the long run. Nor should these managers be judged harshly when they are asked to meet conflicting regulatory goals and operate under conditions of risk directly induced by the regulatory process.

ELECTRIC UTILITY REGULATION

Many contemporary critics of utility regulation attribute the decline of service standards, the remarkable phenomenon of abandoning new plants, the possibility of isolated bankruptcies, and the general financial plight of the industry to the inflexibility of regulation when faced with change.[8] They are, of course, correct. However, something even more fundamental is at work here: namely, the incoherence of traditional utility regulation. Internal contradictions and problems associated with pursuing conflicting regulatory goals were largely masked during the postward period, that is, a period that in retrospect seems to have created an unusually favorable economic climate for electric utilities.

Rapid growth in demand coupled with technological innovation permitted electric utilities to exploit scale economies and declining unit costs throughout the 1950–1970 period. Rate cuts fostered higher sales. Indeed, the primary tasks of state utility commissions then were to approve rate cuts and issue licenses for new plants—a situation conducive to the "quiet life" for regulators. Industrial and residential customers enjoyed a 40-percent drop in real electricity prices between 1960 and 1970.[9] A reasonably stable economic environment and low rates of inflation meant that new plants could be financed at favorable terms. The steady growth in the rate base due to new capacity meant that utilities experienced growing revenues, and stockholders shared in the regular earnings growth. It was a golden era for the electric utilities, their customers, and their regulators—if by golden era we mean circumstances under which regulation was not a binding constraint on the pricing and investment policies of investor-owned utilities. The era gave rise to the widely accepted idea that the public-interest regulation of this natural monopoly worked and worked well.

8. Evidence of declining service standards include the increases in the number of brownouts in 1983 and the growing number of utilities that seek to offer interruptible service to residential customers.

9. *Statistical Yearbook of the Electric Utility Industry* 1982 (Washington, D.C.: Edison Electric Institute, 1983):Table 84, p. 89.

The Traditional View of Regulation

The central task of utility regulation has always been seen as protecting the consumer from the high prices and reduced output that accompany monopoly power. The conventional argument to support regulation is that electric utilities are "natural monopolies" because they enjoy economies of scale, that is, unit costs that decline throughout the relevant production range as output increases. Scale economies in producing, transmitting, and distributing electricity thus preclude competition because a single firm can supply the entire market demand at lower costs than could two or more firms supplying the market. Given its cost structure, an established firm could undercut its rivals and drive them from the market. Indeed, even attempted entry represents a waste of resources either because it involves unnecessary duplication of facilities or because such investment would not be viable in the face of undercutting. Secure from competition, the monopolist would exploit consumers if not for utility regulation. As Kahn defines it, "The essence of regulation is the explicit replacement of competition with government orders as the principal institutional device for assuring good performance."[10]

The traditional tools of utility regulation center on determining the three Rs: rate base, rate of return, and rate (price) structure. Beyond that, regulators grant exclusive service-area franchises, approve construction of new plants, and monitor operating costs. Conventional cost-plus utility regulation has remained much the same over the last fifty years. Writing in 1974, Trebing observes, "The form and content of commission regulation was essentially fixed by the late 1920s, and it has changed little in the intervening years."[11] This is not to suggest that during the so-called golden era regulation lacked its critics. As Trebing continues, "The inability to accommodate change meant a widening gap between what the commissions perceived as socially relevant and the problems that confront society in the real world. For their part, commissions devoted more and more attention to the mechanics of regulation and the procedural rights of litigants."[12]

10. Alfred E. Kahn, *The Economics of Regulation*, vol. 1 (New York: John Wiley & Sons, 1970), p. 20.

11. Harry M. Trebing, "Realism and Relevance in Public Utility Regulation," *Journal of Economic Issues* 8 (June 1974):212.

12. Ibid., p. 212.

Early Criticism of Utility Regulations

Initial criticism focused not on the necessity for regulation but on its practice. At the time critics advocated merely fine tuning the three Rs.

The Rate Base. It was widely recognized that commission use of historic costs for determining the rate base (the value of capital invested in land, plant, and equipment) systematically understated capital costs. The alternatives of using either current reproduction or replacement costs, however, present an almost insurmountable problem of estimation. Moreover the U.S. Supreme Court's suggested use of "fair value. . . . [based] on the probable earnings capacity of the property" is a dead end because it is circular.[13] The fair value of a utility depends on its expected future earnings. But in turn, the future earnings depend on the electricity prices approved by the regulatory commission. Yet the purpose of determining the rate base is precisely to enable the regulators to arrive at a set of adequate and equitable prices for electricity. Since the rate base depends on electricity prices and those prices depend on the rate base, the fair-market standard is perfectly circular—and hence meaningless. Wilcox and Shepherd characterize the debate over the appropriate standard for defining the rate base as "a morass of empty dispute."[14] Even today's sophisticated asset pricing models have not changed the situation. One result of the confusion is that state commissions use a variety of accounting standards for evaluating the rate base and a variety of criteria for including (or excluding) capital expenditures in the rate base. Furthermore it is not clear that the standards and criteria chosen are applied with much precision and rigor.

The Rate of Return. Arriving at an economically appropriate rate of return on invested capital has proven no less troublesome for regulators than defining the rate base. Utilities raise capital in both the debt and equity markets. In 1982 long-term debt represented 50 percent of the capitalization of investor-owned electric utilities.[15] Determining the revenue needed to enable an electric utility to raise additional

13. *Smith* v. *Ames*, 169 U.S. 466. See Clair Wilcox and William G. Shepherd, *Public Policies Toward Business*, 5th ed. (Homewood, Ill.: Irwin, 1975), especially chaps. 14 and 15.

14. Wilcox and Shepherd, *Public Policies Toward Business*, p. 367.

15. *Statistical Yearbook of the Electric Utility Industry 1982*, p. 2.

funds in the debt market is complicated by the tendency regulatory commissions have of relying on embedded debt service based on historic costs. Thus if current bond yields are 12 percent, but embedded debt service rates average 8 percent, regulators are unlikely to permit the utility to earn sufficient revenues to fully service new debt. The problems are even more complex when considering rates of return on equity.

The two principal approaches to arriving at rates of return are: the return necessary to attract capital and the comparable-return standard. The former method requires regulators to estimate future demands for electricity, translate that into capital requirements, and then set the lowest rate of return necessary to attract the required capital. Though this sounds straightforward, the approach is fraught with difficulties. To begin with, regulators are not noted for their acuity in forecasting future demands. The techniques and information are simply not available to the typical commission. Second, in a very real sense, if the goal is to attract new capital, it does not matter what rate of return the regulators set.

Assume the true cost of capital is knowable and known and, for whatever reasons, regulators set the allowed rate of return below the true cost. The market will quickly translate the allowed rate of return into an expected dividend stream and price the utility stock accordingly so that it earns a market rate of return. The problem in this situation is that the utility will be forced to issue a larger number of shares in order to raise a given amount of capital. This in turn will dilute the equity of existing stockholders. Thus the rub is the equitable treatment of existing stockholders and not the difficulty of attracting new capital. The opposite case of allowing a rate of return in excess of the cost of capital would confer a windfall gain on existing stockholders at the expense of consumers. Finally even if a rate of return that preserved present stockholder equity were set, no guarantee exists that the rate would provide an incentive to the utility to pursue the optimal (market) investment path.

The comparable return standard, which calls upon regulators to set a rate of return equal to those earned by comparably risky investments in competitive markets, is no surer a method. Assume that fluctuations in electricity demand and input prices represent a relatively high degree of risk for utilities. Does the comparable-return standard imply guaranteeing utilities a high rate of return to compensate for the risk? Or might it imply that withdrawal of capital from the industry is optimal precisely because it is so risky? This method offers no answer because it is not grounded on a market test.

Ideally the actual earnings of a utility should be related to its efficiency. That is, assume one knew the profit rate of a well-managed, efficient electric utility. If that rate were above the market rate (for comparably risky ventures), the market signal is for expanding net investment and vice versa. Once the rate of return is guaranteed by a regulator, however, this undermines the incentive to be efficient and ceases to provide a meaningful benchmark for investment. In other words the rate of return for a utility must be independently arrived at as a function of that operation's efficiency. That rate then played against market returns provides an incentive for pursuing an optional investment strategy. Setting the allowed rate equal to the comparable returns quite literally destroys any possibility of applying a relevant market test to the utility's economic performance.

Moreover the comparable-returns standard also incorporates an element of circularity. Because the regulatory process is itself a source of risk, defining the underlying independent risk associated with supplying electricity becomes a difficult task—somewhat akin to unscrambling an omelet. Not only is the regulation-induced risk undesirable in itself, it complicates the valuation process.[16] Beyond these problems, the task of gauging allowances for depreciation and obsolescence, the risk associated with financial leverage, and the treatment of federal and state taxation add to the complexity of determining an optimal rate of return on equity. As Weiss summarizes the difficulties, "Altogether, it is not easy to regulate rates of return so that utilities will have an incentive to give adequate service and at the same time have no incentive to waste capital resources. Neither problem arises in a competitive market or even in an unregulated monopolistic one."[17]

The Rate Structure. The third R is the rate structure—the vector of prices charged for electricity. The level of prices should be set to generate sufficient revenue to yield the "allowed rate of return" on the "appropriate rate base," and the structure of prices should be based on cost of service to insure efficiency and equity. Traditionally prices

---

16. Myron J. Gordon and John S. McCallum, "Valuation and the Cost of Capital for Regulated Industries: Comment," *Journal of Finance* 27 (December 1972):1141–46.

17. Leonard W. Weiss, *Case Studies in American Industry*, 3d ed. (New York: John Wiley & Sons, 1980), p. 118.

are set for different user classes (industrial, commercial, and residential) and for different consumption quantities within each class. What emerges is price discrimination among user classes and declining block rates within each class. As explained more fully in the next section, growth in the rate base can benefit the firm under regulation. One way to achieve this is to engage in cross-subsidization among user classes in order to boost electricity demand. By charging high rates where demand is relatively inelastic (initial blocks of residential use), the utility can charge lower prices to customers with elastic demand (the industrial user who could readily turn to alternative energy sources). This system of price discrimination coupled with declining block rates generates adequate revenue and fosters demand growth.

It is easy for utilities to rationalize the rate structure based on cost of service because they exercise great discretion in allocating capital costs. Without going into detail, the arbitrary designation of capital costs permits utilities to carefully tailor prices according to elasticities of demand while appearing to base them on costs.[18] Because the resultant prices bear little relation to marginal cost of service, they generate production and consumption inefficiencies.

Three other problems arise with traditional utility regulation. First, it has long been recognized that cost-plus regulation reduces the incentive to be efficient. Monitoring input use and labor productivity is difficult, even unpleasant. Under a regime where costs can readily be passed on to consumers, the attraction of perks and the quiet life lead to slack and escalating operating costs.

Second, vertical integration—wherein suppliers of fuel, equipment, and land become wholly owned subsidiaries—affords utilities an opportunity to pay nonmarket prices for inputs because, in many cases, input purchases do not involve genuine arm's-length dealing. High input prices generate attractive profits for the nonregulated subsidiaries while, at the same time, the artificially high input costs can be passed on to consumers by the regulated parent company. Thus vertical integration becomes a strategy for tapping potential monopoly profits, that is, a strategy for bypassing regulatory constraints on profits.

Third, regulation distorts the input mix of electric utilities. In a seminal article published in 1962, Averch and Johnson demonstrate that under certain conditions guaranteed rates of return lead utilities to

---

18. Wilcox and Shepherd, *Public Policies Toward Business*, pp. 411–13.

adopt inefficient capital-intensive means of production.[19] (This is now called the A-J effect, after the authors who pointed it out.) So long as the regulated rate of return is even slightly above the cost of capital, utilities can increase total profits by raising capital intensity. This follows because under regulation allowed profit depends only on the amount of capital employed. In contrast, profits for nonregulated businesses represent a return to the whole enterprise; thus, profit-maximizing behavior reinforces the efficient use of all inputs. A-J effects manifest themselves in a number of ways: the substitution of capital for fuel and labor; the provision of excessive reserve capacity; the reluctance of utilities to adopt peak-load pricing; the unwillingness to join integrated regional power pools; and the increased attractiveness of building nuclear power plants (because they are the most capital-intensive means of generating electricity).[20]

The Averch-Johnson article stimulated much research in the 1960s— most pinpointing evidence of inefficiencies induced by guaranteed rates of return.[21] While more recent research, which explicitly takes uncertainty into account, concludes the A-J effects are difficult to isolate, the broad insights of Averch and Johnson are still accepted as valid.[22]

The severe limitations of traditional utility regulation were well understood by the mid-1960s. Summarizing the understanding at that time, Coase argues, "It is becoming increasingly evident that as we surmount one difficulty [of regulatory policy] other problems emerge. We cross one mountain ridge only to find our way barred by others looming just ahead."[23] Schmalensee adds that "much of the criticism of [rate-of-return regulation] after the 1920s argues that regulation evolved to fit a particularly confining niche in the political ecology,

19. Harvey Averch and Leland L. Johnson, "Behavior of the Firm Under Regulatory Constraint," *American Economic Review* 52 (December 1962):1052–69.

20. Alfred E. Kahn, *The Economics of Regulation,* vol. 2, (New York: John Wiley & Sons, 1970), pp. 49–59.

21. See Léon Courville, "Regulation and Efficiency in the Electric Utility Industry," *Bell Journal of Economics and Management Science* 5 (Spring 1974):53–74; H. Craig Peterson, "An Empirical Test of Regulatory Effects," *Bell Journal of Economics* 6 (Spring 1975):111–26; Robert M. Spann, "Rate of Return Regulation and Efficiency in Production: An Empirical Test of the Averch-Johnson Thesis," *Bell Journal of Economics and Management Science* 5 (Spring 1974):38–52.

22. See Michael A. Crew and Paul R. Kleindorfer, "Public-Utility Regulation and Reliability with Applications to Electric Utilities," in M.A. Crew, ed., *Issues in Public-Utility Pricing and Regulation* (Lexington, Mass.: Lexington Books, 1980), pp. 51–75.

23. Ronald H. Coase, "The Theory of Public Utility Regulation," *The Economics of the Regulation of Public Utilities* (Evanston, Ill.: Northwestern University, 1966), p. 96.

a niche that should not have been created."[24] Thus academicians, at least, were questioning the then-prevailing orthodoxy that utility regulation worked reasonably well on behalf of consumers. Yet despite the careful analysis, most scholars and industry experts concluded that something like traditional regulation was necessary and the attendant problems could somehow be mitigated by marginal adjustments in the regulation. With one notable exception, few advocated sweeping reform.[25] We can attribute this to the fact that the golden era of growth in the industry reduced the visibility of regulatory problems precisely because it accommodated both waste and falling real prices for electricity. The 1970s changed this.

THE 1970s: A NEW ECONOMIC ENVIRONMENT

Clearly the impetus behind the current call for significant regulatory reform in the electric power industry is twofold. First is the demonstrated inability of regulation to cope with the adverse economic changes of the 1970s. And second is the very real success of deregulation in airlines, ground transportation, telecommunications, financial markets, domestic oil and, to a more limited degree, natural gas.[26] In assessing the second point first, analogy is not a substitute for analysis, so it is quite possible that the successful deregulation of one market holds few real lessons for predicting the outcome of deregulation in another market. Fundamental structural features in the relevant markets can differ so much that facile comparisons become highly misleading. The point remains, however, that the favorable results of recent deregulation have engendered an intellectual climate that promotes looking with a fresh view at the old verities of "natural monopoly" and its regulation. More significantly, changing economic conditions during the 1970s placed a burden on regulated utilities.

Inflation

The electric power industry was particularly hard hit by accelerating inflation. As measured by the consumer price index (CPI), the rate of inflation was 5.5 percent in 1970; by 1980 it had risen to 12.4

24. Richard Schmalensee, *The Control of Natural Monopoly* (Lexington, Mass.: Lexington Books, 1979), p. 54.
25. See Harold Demsetz, "Why Regulate Utilities?" *Journal of Law and Economics* 11 (April 1968):55–65.
26. See, for example, David R. Graham and Daniel P. Kaplan, "Airline Deregulation IS Working," *Regulation* 6 (May/June 1982):26–32.

percent. During this decade, the price level more than doubled.[27] In addition the nominal price of fuel rose over 500 percent during the period 1970–1980 (in real terms fuel prices doubled).[28] Much of the responsibility for the sharp increase in the producers price index for fuel can be attributed to the success of the OPEC cartel. Because fuel costs make up approximately 40 percent of the total operating costs of generating electricity, fuel-price increases push costs up.

The industry felt the burden of general inflation in several ways. First, inflation boosted construction and operating costs. Second, because anticipated inflation quickly becomes embedded in nominal interest rates (in the form of an inflation premium), the cost of borrowing capital to finance increasingly costly construction projects rose sharply. Moody's average yield on utility bonds went to 13.50 percent in 1982 from 7.48 percent in 1972 (having reached a peak of 17.56 percent in September 1981).[29] Since higher interest costs only apply to incremental capital investment, the adverse impact of inflation on stockholders during the early 1970s was somewhat cushioned by the transfer of wealth from bondholders to stockholders. That is, those who made long-term loans to utilities at single-digit interest rates suffered substantial capital losses as those rates rose.

Third, the uncertainty caused by unanticipated changes in the rate of inflation itself led to the downgrading of utility bond ratings that, in turn, raised the risk premium on loans to electric power companies. Fourth, the inflationary boost in costs put a premium on obtaining timely approval from regulators of electric rate (price) increases. But as the number of rate cases climbed, backlogs developed, and the phenomenon called *regulatory lag* emerged.[30] Regulators were not prepared to deal with the influx of requests for rate increases expeditiously. Often regulators only granted partial rate hikes. That then prompted the utilities to return more quickly with new requests. Electricity prices did rise, and by historic standards they rose rapidly. Yet even the doubling of electricity prices during the decade did not keep up with soaring costs.

27. *The Economic Report of the President* (Washington, D.C.: U.S. Government Printing Office, February 1984), p. 283.
28. *Economic Report of the President*, p. 286.
29. *Statistical Yearbook of the Electric Utility Industry 1982*, p. 85.
30. See Paul L. Joskow, "Inflation and Environmental Concern: Structural Change in the Process of Public Utility Price Regulation," *Journal of Law and Economics* 17 (October 1974):291–328.

By the mid-1970s consumer advocates discovered the issue of rising electric rates. In this instance their "Johnny-one-note" theme was that electricity price increases are anticonsumer. They were duly heard at commission hearings, which not only slowed the proceedings, it also applied group-interest (political) pressure on regulatory commissions. To the extent that consumer advocacy led to rate suppression, electricity consumers in the mid-1970s benefited, but at the expense of future consumers, and in addition energy consumption was artificially encouraged. Thus the prescriptions and pressure tactics of many consumer advocates had outcomes that sharply contrasted with their rhetorical cloak of conservation and concern for future generations. Inflation not only contributed directly to regulatory lag, it also interacted with that lag to generate massive construction cost overruns and to squeeze utility profits. In short inflation politicized utility regulation.

Predictably the response of regulators was ad hoc. In retrospect, the policies they adopted seem more concerned with easing political pressures than dealing with the fundamental problems of adjusting the rate base or allowed rates of return during a period of inflation. To ease the growing financial burden, many state commissions permitted construction work in progress (CWIP) to be included in the rate base for the purposes of setting electricity prices. In addition automatic fuel adjustment (AFA) clauses were adopted permitting utilities to raise electric rates periodically without prior regulator approval. The increases were based on fuel costs—which, as noted above, were rising even more rapidly than the general price index. AFA clauses clearly distort fuel use and the input mix in the generation of electricity. Just when market signals were increasing the incentive to reduce fuel consumption, regulatory policy was encouraging its use by allowing utilities to pass on higher fuel costs more rapidly than other costs.[31]

To placate concern that higher electricity prices would hurt the poor, many state regulatory commissions adopted "lifeline rates," which lowered the price on the initial block of electricity qualifying families used. In addition requirements to be met before service could be discontinued due to nonpayment of utility bills were stiffened. The fact

31. See Frank A. Scott, Jr., "Fuel Adjustment Clauses and Profit Risk," in M.A. Crew, ed., *Issues in Public-Utility Pricing and Regulation* (Lexington, Mass.: Lexington Books, 1980), pp. 77–92; John F. Stewart, "Economic Efficiency and Automatic-Cost Adjustment Mechanisms: Theory and Empirical Evidence," in M.A. Crew, ed., *Regulatory Reform and Public Utilities* (Lexington, Mass.: Lexington Books, 1982), pp. 167–82.

that the implicit loss of revenue was made up by charging other customers higher prices was never widely publicized. It was a policy ideally suited to the politics of the situation. On the one hand, lifeline rates appeared responsive to the concerns of consumer advocates, and, on the other hand, the policy occasioned no real opposition from utilities because it did not cost them anything. Thus the structure of electricity prices was used to redistribute income among customers—albeit in a circuitous and wasteful manner.

Environmental Regulation

The Clean Air Act of 1963 and subsequent amendments (1965, 1967, 1970, and 1977) imposed additional costs on electric utilities.[32] Though addressing a genuine problem, the act adopted an approach to environmental regulation that was unnecessarily cumbersome and costly. Rather than setting acceptable air and water emission levels and providing tax incentives so that each manufacturer could adopt the least costly method of reducing pollution to meet areawide emission targets, the Environmental Protection Agency (EPA) mandated the specific techniques to be used in meeting the plant-by-plant emission standard. From the viewpoint of electric utilities, site approval, requirements for comprehensive environmental impact statements, and the installation of expensive stack scrubbers meant further construction delays and higher operating costs. In some cases literally dozens of permits from federal, state, and local authorities were required before beginning to build a power plant.

Crandall argues that the nature and form of recent environmental regulation can only be fully understood in the context of interregional politics.[33] The hidden agenda of the 1977 Amendments to the Clean Air Act is to slow the industrial decline of the Northeast and reduce the competitive advantage of low-sulfur western coal. An alliance of eastern members of Congress and environmentalists accomplished these ends with two seemingly innocuous provisions in the 1977 Amendments. The first requires that all plants adopt the "best available control technology" regardless of whether they burn high-sulfur

32. See Richard L. Gordon, *Reforming the Regulation of Electric Utilities* (Lexington, Mass.: Lexington Books, 1982), especially chap. 5.
33. Robert W. Crandall, "The Use of Environmental Policy to Reduce Economic Growth in the Sun Belt: The Role of Electric Rates," in M.A. Crew, ed., *Regulatory Reform and Public Utilities* (Lexington, Mass.: Lexington Books, 1982), pp. 125–40. Also see Peter Navarro, "The Politics of Air Pollution," *The Public Interest* 59 (1980):36–44.

eastern coal or low-sulfur western coal. This meant that all utilities were required to install costly stack scrubbers. Since sulfur is the main source of pollution from the combustion of coal and the low-sulfur content of western coal provided its chief competitive advantage (to offset higher average transportation costs), this requirement tends to offset the advantage of using western coal. Thus if not for the political pressure of eastern mine owners and the United Mine Workers, electric utilities could have met environmental standards more effectively and at lower cost by using more western coal.

The second provision, referred to as the "prevention of significant deterioration standard," in effect applies more stringent emission standards to new-site pollution (emissions from new plants). This provides a perverse incentive to operate older, less-efficient plants because it is often less costly to keep them certified than to build new ones. At the same time, the real purpose of the provision was to slow the relocation of productive capacity from the Northeast to the South and West. Pieties of EPA administrators aside, these regulations serve politics, not environmental quality or economic efficiency.

Finally the Power Plant and Industrial Fuel Use Act (1978) requires electric utilities to convert oil- and natural-gas burning plants to coal-fired plants. Though there are many complex exemptions from this particular regulation, the act reverses an earlier policy intended to encourage electric utilities to convert from coal to cleaner burning fossil fuels to meet the requirements of the original Clean Air Act. Many utilities made such conversions between 1965 and 1972. For example Virginia Electric and Power and Florida Power found themselves whipsawed by changing federal environmental and fuel use regulations. Having converted some plants from coal to oil in the early 1970s, both found it necessary, in the late 1970s, to reconvert in order to meet a newer set of rules. Other utility companies found themselves caught between federal conversion rules and local opposition to the use of coal.[34]

Moreover the fuel-use regulations place an uneven burden of compliance among utilities. For some firms it is simply impractical (costly) to convert relatively small oil- or gas-burning boilers into coal-fired boilers. Caught in a tangle of federal, state, and local utility and environmental regulations that often pursue inconsistent objectives—low consumer prices, less pollution, and fuel-specific energy conserva-

---

34. Gordon, *Reforming the Regulation*, p. 199.

tion—electric utilities find investment planning increasingly difficult. Clearheaded business planning is now less important than skilled political maneuvering. Regulatory rules themselves have become less a set of operational constraints than the endogenous outcome of strategic behavior in the political arena.

THE CONTEMPORARY CRITIQUE OF UTILITY REGULATION

Even as the events of the 1970s revealed the inadequacies of utility regulation, scholars were marshaling an analytic assault on traditional regulatory practice that incorporates exclusive franchises, cost-plus pricing, and guaranteed rates of return. There are three major thrusts to these critiques. The first raises questions about the extent of the scale economies underlying the natural monopoly of electric utilities. The second tentatively argues that, in the absence of exclusive franchises and rate regulation, the monopoly power of utilities is not sustainable because potential entry could make these contestable markets. The third suggests that the whole issue of scale economies and natural monopoly is irrelevant because franchise bidding replaces competition in the market with competition for the market.

In his classic 1975 article, Weiss argues that the postwar technological trend toward building even larger optimal-scale generating plants ended in 1966. Thus any further growth in the demand for electricity would accommodate entry and competition in electricity generation. "Most important regions could support enough generating plants to permit extensive competition if the plants were under separate ownership and had equal access to transmission and distribution."[35] Weiss is aware of the problems involved in introducing competition at the generating stage, but he does think such a policy reform is worth exploring.

In the late 1960s the conventional wisdom in the industry was that new plants burning fossil fuels had to have a generating capacity of from 1,000 to 1,500 megawatts and the optimal capacity for nuclear plants might be even larger. But as Berlin, Cicchetti, and Gillen observe, thermal efficiency is not the whole story; reliability plays a role. "The effect of unit size on reserve requirements is a rather straightforward problem. The contingency to be guarded against is

---

35. Leonard W. Weiss, "Antitrust in the Electric Power Industry," in A. Phillips, ed., *Promoting Competition in Regulated Markets* (Washington, D.C.: Brookings Institution, 1975), p. 136.

that a particular unit will not be available when needed. If generating capacity consists of a large number of small units, risk is spread over each of those units. [How large should the units be?] . . . The forced outage rate for fossil-fueled plants over 600 mw is more than twice that of plants below 600 mw. "[36] Within certain bounds the implication is clear: smaller plants are more reliable than large-scale plants. When dynamic reliability is played off against static design efficiency (scale economies), the optimal scale for plants appears to be much smaller than originally thought.

None of this implies that competition is viable. If economies of scale at the firm level mean that a single firm can operate a number of small plants more efficiently than a number of independent firms can, competition cannot effectively replace regulation even at the bulk generating stage. Recent research suggests optimism on this score, however. Interconnection, power pooling, and coordination among independent utilities reduces system economies of scale from the 8,000–10,000 mw level to 1,600–3,800 mw level.[37] Moreover, as Stewart argues, load factor is far more important in determining realized unit costs than are scale economies.[38] And load factor can be kept relatively high by interconnection. Thus the benefits of competition can be introduced without a major loss in productive efficiency.

The further advantage of small plants connected by a power grid is that the law of large numbers reduces reserve requirements. This follows not simply because smaller plants are inherently more reliable, but because networking facilitates less costly scheduling of maintenance, load diversity, and lower marginal costs in meeting daily demand fluctuations.[39] Finally, while economies of scale in transmission and distribution lead many scholars to advocate continued regulation in these areas, even here some evidence exists that these economies are smaller than is generally thought.[40]

36. Edward Berlin, Charles J. Cicchetti, and William J. Gillen, *Perspective On Power* (Cambridge, Mass.: Ballinger Publishing Company, 1974), p. 9.

37. Edison Electric Institute, *Alternative Models of Electric Power Deregulation* (Washington, D.C.: Edison Electric Institute, 1982), pp. II3–II6.

38. John Stewart, "Plant Size, Plant Factor, and the Shape of the Average Cost Function in Electric Power Generation: A Nonhomogeneous Capital Approach." *Bell Journal of Economics* 10, no. 2 (Autumn 1979):549–65.

39. See Paul L. Joskow and Richard Schmalensee, *Markets for Power* (Cambridge: MIT Press, 1983), especially chaps. 3–6.

40. See David A. Huettner and John H. Landon, "Electric Utilities: Scale Economies and Diseconomies," *Southern Economic Journal* 44 (April 1978):883–912; and Weiss, "Antitrust in the Electric Power Industry," pp. 135–73.

Another group of scholars argue that economies of scale are neither necessary nor sufficient to cause natural monopoly.[41] Making the critical dynamic distinction between fixed costs (costs that are not zero at a zero rate of output) and sunk costs (capital invested in plant and equipment that has no alternative use or opportunity cost), they observe that only sunk costs give an existing firm the cost advantage necessary to insulate it from competition. Without significant sunk costs, potential entry undermines monopoly pricing. Such markets are said to be contestable.

As Sharkey states, "The need for this form of regulation may be less than commonly imagined . . . . There may be firms producing closely related products that would be willing and able to enter into competition with, and ultimately replace, the incumbent firm if that firm does not produce at the lowest possible cost or produce the set of outputs desired by consumers. The appropriate question is therefore whether or not potential competition of inactive firms can be more effective in promoting efficiency than direct regulation of the market."[42] Similarly Panzar and Willig find that "contrary to conventional wisdom, a regulated monopoly may be vulnerable to entry by uninnovative competitors even if it is producing and pricing efficiently and earning zero economic profits."[43]

While it is far from obvious that electricity markets can be legitimately classified as contestable, multiproduct production, uncertain demand, risk aversion, and interproduct (interfuel) substitution are all conducive to potential entry.[44] Coursey, Isaac, and Smith conclude that "the most significant result of this [their] research is that the behavioral predictions of the contestable market hypothesis are fundamentally correct. It is simply not true that monopoly pricing is a 'natural' result of a market merely because firms in the market exhibit decreasing costs and demand is sufficient to support no more than a single firm."[45] At a minimum the theory of contestable markets sug-

---

41. The seminal work here is William J. Baumol, John C. Panzar, and Robert D. Willig, *Contestable Markets and the Theory of Industry Structure* (New York: Harcourt Brace Jovanovich, 1982).

42. William W. Sharkey, *The Theory of Natural Monopoly* (New York: Cambridge University Press, 1982), p. 145.

43. John C. Panzar and Robert D. Willig, "Free Entry and the Sustainability of Natural Monopoly," *Bell Journal of Economics,* 8 (Spring 1977):1.

44. See Sharkey, *Theory of Natural Monopoly,* especially chap. 5., and Don Coursey, R. Mark Isaac, and Vernon L. Smith, "Natural Monopoly and Contested Markets: Some Experimental Results," *Journal of Law and Economics* 27 (April 1984):112.

45. Coursey, Isaac, and Smith, "Natural Monopoly and Contested Markets," p. 111.

gests the desirability of repealing legislated barriers to entry, that is, the exclusive franchise provisions of electric utility regulation.

Demsetz launched another much earlier attack on exclusive franchises.[46] He questioned the logical link between scale economies and natural monopoly. In essence, Demsetz argues that the link represents a non sequitur. If natural monopoly is taken to mean the power to charge prices in excess of marginal cost, to reduce output, and to lower quality service, then the presence of scale economies does not necessarily lead to natural monopoly. This follows because the logical alternative to competition within a market is not regulation but competitive franchise bidding for the right to serve the market. Thus even if scale economies mean that the total market demand can most efficiently be produced by a single firm, that does not imply monopoly performance if competition for the right to operate the production facilities exists.

Subsequent studies question the practicality of firms competing by offering alternative contract terms to all consumers in a market.[47] The transaction costs of contract negotiations could be quite high. Presumably the franchise (operating rights) would be awarded to the firm that signed up the largest number of customers or the greatest volume of sales, but then the question of the optimal length of the franchise arises. Too short a contract period increases transaction costs because contracting and bidding must take place more often, and it reduces the incentive to participate in the bidding process because the value of winning the franchise is positively related to the length of the grant. On the other hand if the franchise term is too long, provisions must be made for price adjustments, for enforcing contract terms, and for insuring optimal investment toward the end of the franchise when the risk of nonrenewal is high.[48] Though these may be real obstacles, Demsetz's idea remains an intriguing one. Historic examples of franchise bidding abound here and abroad, and answers to the questions raised by critics do exist.

CONCLUSION

The welfare propositions of the earlier critics of electric utility regulation come from static equilibrium theory. Given the limitations of

46. Demsetz, "Why Regulate Utilities?" pp. 55–65.
47. Oliver E. Williamson, "Franchise Bidding for Natural Monopolies—In General and with Respect to CATV," *Bell Journal of Economics* 7 (Spring 1976):73–104.
48. Schmalensee, *Control of Natural Monopolies*, pp. 68–73.

that paradigm, it is not surprising that critics largely failed to understand the fundamental shortcomings of regulation, accepted it as necessary, and devoted most of their attention to its marginal improvement. However, the high capital costs, impossibility of stockpiling inventory, and uncertain demand that characterize the industry render static analysis inappropriate.

First, only dynamic methods can reveal the nature of utility investment decisions, optimal pricing paths, and intergenerational allocations. The practical problems of electric utilities involve providing optimal reserve capacity, determining the level and schedule for maintenance, investing in innovation, and estimating how current prices affect future consumption. Static analysis addresses none of these issues. Second, by raising the necessary conditions for achieving static equilibrium to a set of normative criteria for assessing market failure, these critics focus on the structural features of the market and miss the nature of the market process. As a result they underestimate the role of potential entry, interfuel competition, decentralized self-generation, cogeneration, direct competition (for heavy industrial user) between electric utilities, and bulk wheeling as dynamic regulators of performance. Third, failure to incorporate uncertainty, risk bearing, and the presence of imperfect information into their calculus means that many analysts do not fully comprehend the impossibility of simulating competitive performance using traditional regulatory means.

The information costs for regulators to achieve even a semblance of competitive performance are prohibitive. Indeed the methods of regulation themselves preclude the goal. For example setting a guaranteed rate of return on an arbitrarily defined rate base comparable to returns on other assets eliminates any possibility of assessing the underlying economic efficiency of utilities, of tying reward (profit) to overall performance, and of accurately measuring either capital costs or operating costs. In short regulation simultaneously leads to waste and to the destruction of the facts necessary to accurately measure that waste. The only information the market generates about electric utilities is their stock prices—the discounted value of expected future dividends. Unfortunately the dividend stream is a regulatory artifact having little to do with potential performance.

To examine this more clearly, let us approach the regulatory process from a slightly different perspective. Exclusive franchises, established by regulation, strengthen monopoly by outlawing competition in the sale of electricity. Yet if scale economies in fact lead to natural monopoly, granting exclusive franchises is at best redundant. Any given service area contains a large pool of revenue that consumers would willingly give up rather than go without electricity. (The amount of the revenue is measured by the area under the demand curve for electricity.) A monopolist can tap this pool, that is, earn monopoly profits, by setting prices in excess of marginal cost on a take-it-or-leave-it basis since consumers have no alternative supplier. In this scenario the only thing standing between the rapacious monopolist and the pool of revenue is regulation.

What emerges in this situation is a strategic game between utilities and regulators. The strategy of the regulators is to minimize political opposition to their decisions. For utilities the strategy is to maximize the revenue extracted from the pool. Earned revenue can take two forms—payment to cover costs, whether the costs are necessary or not, and allowed profits. The tactics utilities use amount to finding a satisfactory trade-off between obtaining revenue in the form of profits (much preferred, dollar for dollar) and obtaining revenue under the guise of covering costs—where the latter finance corporate amenities, high morale, slack, and the quiet life.

For example, to curb monopoly pricing, regulators set prices based on cost of service. The tactical counterploy is for utilities to pad operating expenses. Potential monopoly profits become corporate amenities under regulation. When regulators set an allowed rate of return, utilities reduce reported profits by transferring some realized profits to nonregulated subsidiaries and adopting inefficient capital-intensive production to increase profit levels while complying with the profit-rate constraint. If regulators attempt to adjust allowed rates of return by a risk factor, utilities can influence that over time by varying their debt-to-equity ratio. In addition, much gameplaying occurs in the proceedings before regulatory commissions, for example, in the timing and size of requests for rate increases. The list of tactics and countertactics is long. Far from assuring good performance, the regulatory process fosters strategic posturing—a behavioral pattern making it exceedingly difficult to assess good performance.

This perception is reinforced by the politicization of utility regulation. No longer is the role of regulation defined in technical and economic terms; it is now viewed as a method for balancing legitimate interests. Once responsive (possibly too responsive) to the interests of the industry, regulators now seem bent on absorbing the wisdom of consumer advocates and professional environmentalists. In the name of fairness and conservation, consumption is subsidized, and regulation becomes a means of redistributing income. Equitable regulatory decisions are said to be more likely if "public-interest" spokespersons were appointed to commissions or if commissioners were elected. Only in the political arena does the pursuit of conflicting goals and "the good-person theory of administration" survive. The politicization of utility regulation is not a new phenomenon; all that has changed is the relative effectiveness of pressure groups. The electric power industry has moved from an era of growth, increased annual earnings, and excessive capacity and service reliability to a new era of lower growth, sharply reduced investment, plant abandonment, and possible isolated bankruptcies. The point is that traditional utility regulation failed in both eras. These, then, are the issues addressed in this book.

THE PLAN OF THE BOOK

The recent dismal performance of the electric power industry, according to the canons of economic efficiency, equity, and innovation, has led a growing number of scholars to think about new models of electric utility regulation. Exciting new research findings raise questions about the applicability of the natural-monopoly model to electric utilities, the long-run consequences of incoherent electric pricing regulation, and the possibility of deregulating the industry and permitting competition to determine electricity prices and patterns of investment.

The purpose of the book is to offer an audience of specialists and nonspecialists a collection of integrated, readable essays that analyze the role of electric utility regulation in the energy crisis, the long-run consequences of continued regulation, and the alternatives to traditional regulation. The authors have relied on a rapidly developing literature, to which they have contributed, in such areas as the public-choice theory of utility commission behavior, investment modeling, optimal environmental regulation, and deregulation of the electric power industry. At present, the best work in these areas has been published in a variety of technical academic journals. By pulling together the strands of an emerging thesis now implicit in the literature, this book capitalizes on the growing awareness of the regulatory problems besetting electric utilities.

The book is in four parts. Part I offers an overview of the methods and scope of electric utility regulation and the problems inherent in traditional regulation. The latter include, for example, the use of out-moded methods of cost accounting, the short-run bias in utility commission planning, the pursuit of conflicting regulatory goals, regulatory lags, the imposition of a static regulatory framework on an industry characterized by heavy capital investment, and the inability to foster innovation. Part I also analyzes the underlying assumptions of the natural-monopoly model used to justify regulation of electric utilities. Finally, Part I seeks to demonstrate how the interaction of regulation, tax laws governing utilities, and inflation jeopardizes the ability of electric utilities to make sound long-term investment decisions.

Part II treats the impact of three additional regulatory constraints on the electric power industry—environmental regulation, fuel use and fuel conversion dictates, and pricing guidelines designed to redistribute income—and reviews their roles in hampering the industry's responsiveness to change. The discussion emphasizes the interdependence of energy markets. Part III explains how utility commissions operate and evaluates their performance. Part IV reviews several alternatives to the traditional approach of fully regulating the investment, output standards (including service rationing), and pricing structure of electric utilities.

The major theme of this book is that replacing market competition with government decrees "as the principal institutional device for assuring good performance" has proven unwise. If the energy crisis of the middle and late 1970s seems a dim memory, the fact remains that the electric power industry continues to face an uncertain future.

PART I

ELECTRIC UTILITY REGULATION

Part I: ELECTRIC UTILITY REGULATION

John C. Moorhouse

In a discussion of regulatory reform or deregulation of the electric power industry, the choice is not between simulated competition induced by costless government intervention versus unfettered natural monopoly. Rather the central issue is which is more costly, regulatory or market failure. Both fall short of the perfect (static) competition so celebrated in textbooks and so unattainable in this imperfect world. All too often the discussion of the issues is biased, due to an implicit assumption that the argument is over once it is demonstrated that the electric power industry is not perfectly competitive. Following this, the automatic conclusion is that government regulation will correct the market failure. In fact this argument demonstrates little. Rather the comparison must be between two imperfect policies: regulation of or workable competition among electric utilities and other suppliers of energy. Part I addresses this broad issue.

Chapter 1 provides a careful and comprehensive review covering the logical arguments for and against traditional electric utility regulation. Hammond argues that the single-product model of natural monopoly (based on economies of scale) is limited as a way of addressing the economics of electric generation, transmission, and distribution. New research on multiple-product firms suggests that scale economies might not be sufficient to sustain monopoly power. Potential entry and interproduct competition can dissipate monopoly and render these markets contestable. Hammond goes on to analyze the problems associated with the traditional triad of rate-base, rate-of-return, and rate-structure regulation. Chapter 1 concludes that the standard treatment of electric utilities as natural monopolies is inappropriate and that current regulation leads to significant allocative and dynamic inefficiencies.

Chapter 2 addresses the issue of competition among electric utilities. The argument reduces to assessing the benefits of competition versus those technical efficiencies arising from economies of scale, vertical integration, and power pooling. Maintaining these purported technical efficiencies is seen as requiring regulation. Assessing relative benefits is an empirical question, and economists have done empirical work estimating the significance of scale economies in the production, transmission, and distribution of electricity. Zardkoohi's contribution in this chapter is a careful critique of existing studies. While finding strong evidence that the present regulatory framework has reduced competition and generated inefficiencies, Zardkoohi does not believe the existing evidence is compelling enough to make the case for complete deregulation.

In Chapter 3 Kafoglis presents a unique and masterful overview of the federal, state, and local taxation of electric utilities. The chapter reviews the levels and types of taxation and, more importantly, the interaction among various taxes and state and federal utility regulation. The latter discussion highlights numerous policy conflicts. For example, federal tax policy designed to stimulate investment via accelerated depreciation allowances conflicts with state regulation on fair rates of return. Some state utility commissions have mandated that tax savings resulting from accelerated depreciation must "flow through" to consumers in the form of reduced electric rates. The effect is to subsidize current consumers at the expense of future consumers because the flow-through means that no reserves are built up to cover future tax obligations. Because of this, federal authorities and utility companies support "normalization" of tax benefits. Another example of conflicting policies includes the way fuel adjustment clauses, provided for by state regulatory commissions, frustrate efforts by the federal government to conserve oil and natural gas by levying taxes on their use by utilities. Though the issues are complex, Kafoglis carefully spells out the effects our incoherent tax policies have on electric utilities.

Chapter 4 addresses the problem of regulatory lag during an inflationary period. Utilities cannot pass through their higher operating costs to consumers without the approval of regulators. If regulatory commissions delay their response to requests for rate hikes, inflation can put electric utilities in a cost squeeze. McCormick presents original statistical estimates of the financial burden resulting from regulatory lag for the period 1960 to 1982. Somewhat surprisingly he finds little evidence to suggest that regulatory lag during inflationary periods imposed a significant financial burden on utilities or that it influenced the pattern of debt accumulation by electric utilities. We can explain the results, in part, by the fact that automatic fuel adjustment clauses, adopted by many state regulatory commissions, permit utilities to raise rates in response to higher fuel costs. Moreover fuel costs on average constitute upwards of 40 percent of an electric utility's operating costs. We can interpret this to mean that regulators recognized the problem of regulatory lag and attempted to deal with it via automatic fuel adjustment clauses. Furthermore McCormick does find evidence that regulatory lag has led to a redistribution of wealth from utility bondholders to stockholders. Indeed he concludes that "a regulatory lag problem may still exist but be swamped by [this] wealth redistribution."

1

AN OVERVIEW OF ELECTRIC UTILITY REGULATION

Claire Holton Hammond

INTRODUCTION

The electric industry recently celebrated its one hundredth anniversary to mark the opening of the first central electric power station in New York City in 1882. In these first hundred years U.S. utilities have evolved into a highly complex and important industry. Today 3,450 electric systems supply light, heat, and power to over 95 million residential, commercial, industrial, and governmental users across the nation—and in parts of Canada and Mexico.

From its earliest days the industry has been regulated. At first local governments exercised control over the small, local-service electric utilities by the granting of operating licenses and franchises. Then in the early years of this century, electric utilities developed into intercity systems, and states began to establish public utility commissions to regulate electric companies. Today state commissions regulate electric utilities in every state that has private utilities.

Federal intervention began in 1920 with the formation of the Federal Power Commission (FPC). In 1977 the FPC was reorganized into the Federal Energy Regulatory Commission (FERC) within the Department of Energy. The FERC regulates interstate transmission of electricity, wholesale electricity sales, and transactions and agreements among utilities.

The most frequently cited argument given to support this extensive economic regulation is that electric markets are natural monopolies. Under this assumption, traditional economic theory has generally led to the conclusion that the prudently regulated industry will outperform the unregulated industry. In recent years this rationale has been the subject of increasing debate. Given accumulating evidence on the poor performance of regulated industries in general, and electric utilities in particular, economists and others question whether the current regulated market structure is superior to its alternatives including different methods of regulation and partial or total deregulation.

This chapter lays the groundwork for a careful consideration of arguments for regulatory reform and deregulation in later chapters. First the chapter provides an overview of the natural-monopoly model, emphasizing the definition of natural monopoly and the standard economic arguments for and against regulation. A critical discussion of rate-of-return regulation—the predominant form of industry regulation—follows.

THE NATURAL MONOPOLY MODEL

Almost since the beginning of the electric industry, there has been a pervasive belief that electric utilities are natural monopolies in their service areas. Although no standard definition of the term *natural monopoly* exists, the crucial defining factor almost universally cited, especially with reference to the electric industry, is the existence of persistent economies of scale.

Two other factors are brought in along with economies of scale. One argument is grounded in the view that electricity is a necessity. Thus its production must be by (regulated) monopoly, it is said, because any supply interruption resulting from the vicissitudes of competition would cause unacceptable social disruption. A second argument is based on the fact that electricity is a highly capital-intensive industry. As such it requires a stable revenue base to support the necessary large investments in plant and equipment. This stability can be provided by (regulated) monopoly structure.

These criteria, however, play only a minor role in debates over whether electric markets are natural monopolies. Many industries not considered natural monopolies produce vital products or services (e.g., medical services) or are highly capital-intensive (e.g., mining).[1] In the following discussion I focus on economies of scale as the critical determinant of natural monopoly.

We say economies of scale exist for a firm when per-unit costs of production in the long run fall as output increases. Almost all firms experience economies of scale over some output levels, arising from work-force specialization and the technical advantages of larger scale production. For most firms, however, economies of scale are exhausted at low levels of output relative to the output quantity supplied in their market as a whole. For these industries it is economically feasible for more than one firm to produce in the market while reaping all the advantages of economies of scale. Such industries might be classified as competitive or oligopolistic industries, depending on the number and relative size of the relevant firms.

It is possible that economies of scale hold for the entire range of potential market output levels determined by market demand. In this case a unit-cost advantage always exists for the firm that gains a larger market share and increases its production scale. As firms compete in such an industry, over time—either through merger or attrition—one firm will emerge that will simultaneously produce at the lowest per-unit cost while supplying the entire market. This firm is then called a *natural monopoly: monopoly* because it is the single seller in its market and *natural* because it became the single seller not as a result of government fiat, control over scarce inputs, or unfair practices, but because it outcompeted its rivals by being the first or the most competent to exploit accessible economies of scale.

The call for regulation follows directly from this definition of natural monopoly. If we leave the competitive process unfettered, a monopoly results. If we prevent the single monopoly firm from emerging, per-unit costs of production will be higher than they would be with a single seller. The traditional solution to this dilemma has been to allow one firm to monopolize the industry in the interest of saving on per-unit costs, while regulating that firm's behavior to avoid any abuse of its monopoly power at the same time.

This theory of natural monopoly presents policymakers with two

1. Walter J. Primeaux, Jr., "Some Problems with Natural Monopoly," *Antitrust Bulletin* 24 (Spring 1979):63–85. Primeaux debunks several other so-called indicators of natural monopoly.

tasks. First, they must determine if industries are natural monopolies. Second, once a natural monopoly is identified, they must determine ways to regulate it so that the performance of the regulated industry will surpass that of the unregulated industry. Both tasks are enormously complex, as we shall see in exploring the definition of natural monopoly more fully in the next section.

Multiproduct Natural Monopoly

The understanding that extensive economies of scale represent the crucial element of a natural monopoly has led to a large number of studies on the nature of costs in the electric industry. This standard approach, that of basing natural-monopoly status largely on empirical evidence of economies of scale, has recently come under a fundamental criticism. Baumol finds that linking the definition of natural monopoly to persistent economies of scale can lead to mistaken conclusions in the case of multiproduct firms.[2] He shows that the presence of scale economies is neither a necessary nor sufficient condition for natural monopoly in a multiple-output industry. Instead economies of joint production, like economies of scope and cost complementarity, are the critical factors.[3]

Economies of scope exist if a multiproduct firm can pool inputs so that it can produce its outputs more cheaply than if they were produced by two or more specialty firms. Cost complementarity arises when increasing the production of one product decreases the cost of producing other products. When these conditions hold, the industry is a natural monopoly because production of a given set of outputs by a single firm is less costly than production by any combination of smaller firms. Note that it is entirely possible for a multiproduct industry to be a natural monopoly because of extensive economies of joint production even if all economies of scale have been exhausted.[4]

The distinction between natural monopoly and economies of scale

---

2. William J. Baumol, "On the Proper Cost Test for Natural Monopoly in a Multiproduct Industry," *American Economic Review* 67 (December 1977):809–22.

3. A superior definition of natural monopoly, which follows from Baumol's analysis, is that a market is a natural monopoly if multifirm production is more costly than single-firm production.

4. See William W. Sharkey, *The Theory of Natural Monopoly* (Cambridge: Cambridge University Press, 1982), pp. 54–83 and William J. Baumol, John C. Panzar, and Robert D. Willig, *Contestable Markets and the Theory of Industry Structure* (New York: Harcourt Brace Jovanovich, 1982).

for multiproduct firms has important implications for defining the electric industry as a natural monopoly. First, an electric utility is inherently a multiproduct firm. Electric utilities face varying demands over time, and costs of production vary accordingly. Electricity is unstorable, and the producer meets demands at any one time by operating generating units in increasing order of running costs. Thus the cost of producing an additional kilowatt hour of electricity when the system is running well below capacity (say, at 3 A.M. in December) consists largely of additional fuel costs, whereas the cost of producing the same electricity when the system is close to capacity (say, at 4 P.M. in August) includes the costs of putting more expensive capacity as well as additional fuel into operation. In the empirical studies of cost functions, it has been accepted practice to aggregate the different products of an electric utility into a single-output measure (typically, kilowatts per hour). Since determining a natural-monopoly situation is much more complex for a multiproduct firm than for a single-product firm, such an aggregation may lead to spurious results on the nature of economies of scale.[5]

Furthermore since the electric industry is by nature a multiproduct industry, concentrating on economies of scale in order to determine if it constitutes a natural monopoly is not enough. Instead some measure of the economies of joint production is required, along with evidence of economies of scale, to correctly determine natural-monopoly status.

The appropriate test for natural monopoly in the multiproduct electric industry thus becomes more difficult to administer than once thought. Arguments for regulation based largely on economies of scale are weakened; evidence showing economies of joint production is at least as important. Arguments calling for deregulation due to evidence that economies of scale have been exhausted in electric power are also undermined since it is entirely possible for economies of joint production to be such that single-firm production is cheaper than multifirm production even without economies of scale. For multiproduct industries, we cannot restrict our attention to evidence of economies of scale in either granting or rescinding natural-monopoly status.

5. See John F. Stewart, "Plant Size, Plant Factor, and the Shape of the Average Cost Function in Electric Power Generation: A Nonhomogenous Capital Approach," *Bell Journal of Economics* 10 (Autumn 1979):549–65. See also John W. Mayo, "Multiproduct Monopoly, Regulation, and Firm Costs," *Southern Economic Journal* 51 (July 1984):208–18.

Why Regulate Natural Monopolies?

When a natural monopoly exists, the question that follows is, What, if anything, do we do about it and why? One answer has been to grant a monopoly franchise in order to capture the gains of single-firm production and to regulate the firm in order to avoid the problems of monopoly. This has been the prescription to date for perceived natural monopoly in the electric-power industry. But this solution begs the question of what problems of monopoly require regulation.

It is perhaps easiest to understand what is wrong with monopoly by comparing it to what is right with its antithesis, perfect competition. In essence perfectly competitive markets—characterized by many well-informed buyers and sellers of a standardized product with free entry into and exit from the industry—result in efficient resource allocation. Monopoly, for the most part, results in inefficient allocation.

In a competitive market the price charged to each consumer is bid down to the marginal cost of production. Price equality and marginal cost is the fundamental requirement for efficient allocation of scarce resources. Price reflects the marginal value of a good to consumers. When price and marginal cost are equal, consumers cannot be made better off by reallocation of resources into or away from the industry. When price is greater than marginal cost, the value consumers place on additional units of the product or service, as measured by the price they are willing to pay, is greater than the value of resources used in producing additional units. Thus consumer welfare would be improved if more of the good were produced.

In addition to marginal-cost pricing, competition propels economic profits toward zero. Every resource used in production, including capital and entrepreneurial skill and risk-taking, tends to earn a return just equal to what is necessary to keep the resource in this use. If profits rise above zero, due to increases in demand, for example, new firms attracted by these profits will bid the price down until profits return to zero.

Perfect competition also leads to production efficiency in that any given level of output is produced at minimal unit cost. Any competitive firm not producing at minimum cost, or not continually searching for cost-cutting innovations, will eventually be underpriced and driven from the market by more adept competitors.

Profit-maximizing behavior by a monopolist, however, leads to radically different results. The monopolist faces the entire market demand and can increase sales only by reducing the product's price. (For the competitive firm, the necessary price reduction is imperceptible since each firm is only a fraction of the market.) The monopolist finds that the profit-maximizing level of output occurs where price is greater than marginal cost of production, and the result is inefficient resource allocation. Consumers value the product greater than the cost of producing the marginal unit, but it is not profitable for the firm to increase output. Consumer welfare is lower than it would be under a competitive market structure. Valuable consumption that would take place if the market could be organized competitively is simply lost to society with monopoly pricing. Decreasing this so-called deadweight loss of monopoly is the primary rationale for regulating natural monopolies.

Other kinds of resource inefficiencies are also attributed to monopoly structure. Due to lack of competition, monopolists are likely to earn economic profits in the long run. This easy profitability may dull the monopolist's incentives to produce at minimum cost and to innovate quickly and efficiently. Furthermore firms may waste significant amounts of resources in obtaining or defending their monopoly positions.[6]

Why Not Regulate Natural Monopolies?

Many economists take exception to the ideas that natural-monopoly firms are inherently inefficient and that direct regulation necessarily enhances efficiency. This section describes several shortcomings in the standard arguments supporting natural-monopoly regulation.

Possibilities for Efficient Performance by Monopolies. Economists generally regard monopoly as anathema, but some make exceptions to this evaluation. Posner, for example, argues in his classic 1969 article that the familiar problems attributed to monopoly structure are overrated.[7] He notes that if a monopolist can make price discriminations by charging different prices to different customers or to the

6. See Richard A. Posner, "The Social Costs of Monopoly and Regulation," *Journal of Political Economy* 83 (August 1975):807–27.

7. Richard A. Posner, "Natural Monopoly and Its Regulation," *Stanford Law Review* 21 (February 1969):548–643.

same customer for different quantities, this can reduce and possibly eliminate the monopoly deadweight loss. Additionally, though the monopolist does not wrestle with the discipline of competition, it can still have strong incentives for production efficiency. This occurs because any savings on costs are translated into profits that are not eroded by competition.

Bailey also questions the inevitability of inefficient monopoly behavior.[8] She contends that if a natural-monopoly market is readily contestable—characterized by easy and unrestrained entry and exit—then competitive performance can result. The natural-monopoly firm is disciplined to produce and price efficiently by competition for the privilege of being the sole market supplier and by the ever-present threat of losing its monopoly position to a more efficient enterprise. For electric utilities, the policy implication is that if electric markets can be made contestable (by easing entry conditions), then utility regulation may not be necessary.

The possibility of eliminating regulation of contestable, natural-monopoly markets is tempered by recent theoretical work establishing the possibility that even an efficient natural monopoly may be unable to set prices that preclude entry.[9] In this case the natural monopoly is said to be unsustainable. Without entry barriers (e.g., permanent monopoly franchises), entry will occur. Total costs of production will be higher as firms lose the cost advantages of single-firm production by sharing the natural-monopoly market. In spite of this reservation, the theory of contestable natural-monopoly markets remains an intriguing one. At the very least it challenges existing notions about the advantages of permanent exclusive monopoly franchises. Certainly the question of whether contestable electric markets would lead to optimal and sustainable electric prices merits careful empirical study.

Costs of Regulation. Rational decision making requires that in determining what to do about natural monopoly, policymakers carefully compare the potential regulatory benefits against its costs and effec-

8. Elizabeth E. Bailey, "Contestability and the Design of Regulatory and Antitrust Policy," *American Economic Review* 71 (May 1981):178–83. See also Harold Demsetz, "Why Regulate Utilities?" *Journal of Law and Economics* 11 (April 1968):55–65.

9. See, for example, John C. Panzar and Robert D. Willig, "Free Entry and the Sustainability of Natural Monopoly," *Bell Journal of Economics* 8 (1977):1–22 and William J. Baumol and Robert D. Willig, "Fixed Costs, Sunk Costs, Entry Barriers and Sustainability of Monopoly," *Quarterly Journal of Economics* 96 (1981):405–32.

tiveness. Increasingly people are concluding that the costs of regulation outweigh the benefits.

One base for this negative evaluation is that regulation had virtually no effect on prices or profits during the period of declining costs enjoyed by the industry until the 1960s. The most influential study for electric utilities, published by Stigler and Friedland in 1962, finds that regulation had no effect on electric rate levels or owners' wealth over the years 1887–1937.[10]

Since the inflationary late 1960s and 1970s, regulation has been criticized as being too cumbersome and backward looking to cope with rising costs. Rate increases have lagged behind cost increases and this has resulted, it is argued, in the poor financial condition found in the industry today.[11]

Specific costs and problems attributable to the type of regulation used in the electric industry (known as rate-of-return regulation) will be discussed later in this chapter. At this point, let's review some of the generic costs associated with regulation.

Regulation costs include not only the administrative and operating costs of the regulatory agency, but also the compliance costs borne by the regulated firms. Schmalensee notes that an additional cost arises from rigid and unpredictable regulations that increase the social cost of risk bearing and therefore the cost of capital.[12] Evidence on the linkage between an unfavorable regulatory climate and poor bond ratings for electric utilities suggests this cost is not trivial.[13]

In addition to regulatory costs, theorists suggest that regulatory agencies may not have strong incentives to regulate effectively. One such argument arises from the capture theory of regulation which pro-

10. George J. Stigler and Claire Friedland, "What Can Regulators Regulate? The Case of Electricity," *Journal of Law and Economics* 5 (October 1962):1–16. Their conclusions for rate levels were supported for 1940 and 1950 by Raymond Jackson, "Regulation and Electric Utility Rate Levels," *Land Economics* 45 (August 1969):372–76, and for 1962 by Thomas G. Moore, "The Effectiveness of Regulation of Electric Utility Prices," *Southern Economic Journal* 36 (April 1970):365–75. For criticisms of these studies, see Louis DeAlessi, "An Economic Analysis of Government Ownership and Regulation: Theory and Evidence from the Electric Power Industry," *Public Choice* 19 (Fall 1974):1–42.

11. See, for example, Paul L. Joskow and Paul W. MacAvoy, "Regulation and the Financial Condition of the Electric Power Companies in the 1970s," *American Economic Review* 65 (May 1975):295–301.

12. Richard Schmalensee, *The Control of Natural Monopoly* (Lexington, Mass.: D.C. Heath Co., 1979), pp. 36–37.

13. See Peter Navarro, "Electric Utility Regulation and National Energy Policy," *Regulation* 5 (January/February 1981):20–27.

poses that the regulated firm eventually captures its regulating agency and uses it to further its own purposes in lieu of the public interest.[14] This happens, it is argued, because the firms necessarily possess superior technical knowledge on which the agency depends for its decisions, and also because regulatory agencies are more likely to get the direct approval they seek from the firms they regulate than from the far-flung public.

Critics point to current regulation for muddling the two goals of efficiency and equity. Most utility regulatory commissions operate with the mandate to set "fair and reasonable" rates. No unique or widely held definition of fairness exists, however. This void opens the door to arbitrary and capricious regulatory judgments, with the outcome that equity questions absorb tremendous regulatory resources, leaving efficiency considerations with a dangerously minor role in policymaking.

Trebing examines the fairness concept as developed and applied under current public utility regulation.[15] Virtually all the problems that come before a commission, from allowing rate increases to subsidizing low-income users to approving sites for new capacity, involve equity issues. Commissions typically handle these issues on a case-by-case basis. Therefore equity norms vary from one decision to the next, according to the biases of a particular commission at a particular time.

Nevertheless Trebing describes several general characteristics and effects of equity as applied under the commission system: Commissions tend to balance conflicting claims, maintain a large amount of discretion in their equity judgments, minimize substantial harm to any one interest group, and fail to adequately explore the ramifications of their regulatory actions in terms of equity. Thus the regulatory approach to equity is ambiguous and mutable. The paradox of the regulatory approach is that while equity gets more regulatory attention than appropriate, this attention is neither careful nor systematic. Such

14. For capture theories and their variations, see George Stigler, "The Theory of Economic Regulation," *Bell Journal of Economics and Management Science* 2 (Spring 1971):3–21; Richard A. Posner, "Theories of Economic Regulation," *Bell Journal of Economics and Management Science* 5 (Autumn 1974):335–58; and Sam Peltzman, "Toward a More General Theory of Regulation," *Journal of Law and Economics* 19 (August 1976):211–40.

15. Harry M. Trebing, "Equity, Efficiency, and the Viability of Public Utility Regulation," in Werner Sichel and Thomas G. Gies, eds., *Applications of Economic Principles in Public Utility Industries* (Ann Arbor: University of Michigan, 1981), pp. 17–52.

a focus obscures the issues involved and increases the vulnerability of the total regulatory process to special-interest control and bias. Patterns of cross-subsidization among consumer groups emerge, driving a wedge between the true economic costs of consumption by different consumer classes and the costs they actually bear. Moreover attempts to balance the burden of costs between shareholders and consumers take up enormous amounts of regulatory time so that both groups become dissatisfied and are left with a continuing sense of unfair treatment.

Given the difficulties and conflicts inherent in targeting equity and efficiency goals at the same time, some economists argue that the sole or, at least, dominant objective of public utility regulation should be economic efficiency. Efficiency should come first not because equity is unimportant, but because "there is no systematic, nonarbitrary way to factor concern with distributive justice into regulatory decision making . . . . In the interests of administrative feasibility and rationality . . . the system should be aimed at efficient resource use."[16]

Dynamic Considerations.   Regulatory agencies have been accused of being unwilling and unable to respond appropriately to market changes. A monopoly franchise is granted in response to a set of supply and demand conditions that exist for a particular time. As that time passes, market conditions change, possibly to the extent that a regulated monopoly situation is no longer warranted. For example, demand may increase such that several firms can now supply the expanded market as cheaply as one firm could initially. In this case encouraging competition is clearly efficient.[17] Yet the institutions regulating monopolies are not likely to push for their own extinction due to changing market circumstances. Instead regulatory agencies tend to ignore or downgrade the importance of these changes or to treat them as temporary anomalies.

Opponents of regulation thus warn that over time society will miss opportunities for more competitive market structures and will be left bearing the costs of regulation long after the need for regulation has passed. This social burden of unneeded future regulation, they argue,

16. Schmalensee, *Control of Natural Monopoly*, p. 24. Trebing agrees, as does Alfred E. Kahn, *The Economics of Regulation*, vol. 1 (New York: John Wiley & Sons, 1970).

17. Philip Fanara, Jr., James E. Suelflow, and Roman A. Draba, "Energy and Competition: The Saga of Electric Power," *Antitrust Bulletin* 25 (Spring 1980):125–42.

outweighs any benefits from the regulation of currently existing monopolies.

The effect of regulation on technological change is another dynamic issue subject to controversy. On the one hand, critics accuse regulation of retarding innovation and technological change. One purpose of regulation is to prevent regulated firms from earning excess profits. If successful in this goal, regulation diminishes the firm's incentive to innovate by prohibiting it from capturing the full gains of cost-cutting innovations. Furthermore exclusive franchises protect regulated firms from the threat of entry by innovative new firms, again lessening incentives for research and development as well as for adopting new technologies. On the other hand the lengthy periods of time that occur between the adoption of cost-reducing innovations and downward adjustments in regulated prices means that the regulated firm can retain profits generated by innovation, often for significant amounts of time.

We do not, in fact, know the overall effect of regulation on technological change in the electric industry. It is difficult both to determine an appropriate measure of technological change and to hypothesize the rate of technological change that would have existed in the absence of regulation. Joskow and Schmalensee report that most of the research and development and most of the new ideas for electricity use and cheaper ways to produce, transmit, and distribute it have come from electrical equipment manufacturers, not from regulated utilities.[18] Capron argues that this occurs because of a "regulation-induced conservative bias [that leads] regulated firms to avoid large, high-risk ventures."[19]

Wilder and Stansell studied the determinants of research and development expenditures among privately owned electric utilities for the years 1968 and 1970 to find that outlays are positively associated with profitability, but with an elasticity of less than one.[20] They also find an insignificant difference between research and development outlays in firms under state regulation and those that are not state

18. Paul L. Joskow and Richard Schmalensee, *Markets for Power* (Cambridge: MIT Press, 1983), p. 87.

19. William M. Capron, ed., *Technological Change in Regulated Industries* (Washington, D.C.: Brookings Institution, 1971), p. 8.

20. Ronald P. Wilder and Stanley R. Stansell, "Determinants of Research and Development Activity by Electric Utilities," *Bell Journal of Economics and Management Science* 5 (Autumn 1974):646–50.

regulated. A similar study for 1970 and 1972 by Delaney and Honeycutt supports the neutral effect of regulation on research and development activity.[21] In a different kind of study, Nelson estimates the rate of technological change in the electric industry using data on average age of plants for forty privately owned utilities from 1951–78.[22] He, too, finds a negligible effect of regulation on rate of technological change, and he estimates that tighter regulation would only have reduced the rate of technological change by 1 to 2 percent over the study period. Though suggestive, these studies represent only the beginnings of the work that must be done to settle the question of what effect regulation has on technological change.

REGULATION OF ELECTRICITY

Despite regulatory costs and a propensity for ineffectiveness, policymakers have chosen to regulate electric utilities. The basis for this regulation is the perception that electric markets are natural monopolies. It is not clear, in light of changing definitions of natural monopoly for multiproduct industries, that electric utilities are in fact natural monopolies. Nevertheless they are regulated as if they were. The purpose of this section is to describe the regulatory framework of the industry and to critically analyze the primary method of regulation used—rate-of-return regulation.

Regulatory Framework

As stated, the electric industry is extensively regulated. In general federal authorities regulate wholesale transactions and activities among utilities, and state authorities regulate activities relating to retail customers.

Federal Regulation. The Federal Energy Regulatory Commission (FERC) has authority under the Federal Power Act of 1935 and the Public Utility Regulatory Policies Act of 1978 to regulate wholesale power sold by privately owned utilities and to require, upon com-

21. James B. Delaney and T. Crawford Honeycutt, "Determinants of Research and Development Activity by Electric Utilities: Comment," *Bell Journal of Economics* 7 (Autumn 1976):722–25.
22. Randy A. Nelson, "Regulation, Capital Vintage and Technological Change in the Electric Utility Industry," *Review of Economics and Statistics* 66 (February 1984):59–60.

plaint, mandatory interconnection and wheeling among utilities.[23] The FERC also has authority over power pooling and other cooperative activities. Court decisions have held that the FERC must consider competitive effects in its regulatory decision making.[24]

The Nuclear Regulatory Commission (NRC) has authority under the 1970 Amendments to the Atomic Energy Act to license and regulate the construction and operation of all nuclear power plants. It has a mandate to consider antitrust issues in its licensing deliberations and can require accommodations for wheeling and joint ownership with smaller utilities as conditions for licensing.[25] The Securities and Exchange Commission (SEC) has authority, under the Securities and Exchange Act of 1933 and the Public Utility Holding Company Act of 1935, over the corporate structure of utilities, dissemination of utility financial information, and acquisitions by utilities of nonutility-related services.

State Regulation.   State public utility commissions regulate the activities of independently owned utilities, some cooperatives, and publicly owned utilities. The primary function of state commissions is to regulate the rates and quality of service of retail electricity sold to consumers. State regulatory commissions also regulate accounting procedures; delimit the boundaries of exclusive service territories; sanction entry and exit of utilities in their jurisdictions; and oversee the siting, construction, and safety of electric facilities.

The primary goal of state regulation is to regulate retail prices and services such that efficient production results with all the gains of

23. Wheeling is "the provision of transmission service to enable one electric supplier to receive power from a remote source using the lines of an intervening utility. . . . It allows the purchaser to obtain power from nonadjacent sources without the necessity of constructing its own transmission facilities." Joe D. Pace and John H. Landon, "Introducing Competition Into the Electric Utility Industry: An Economic Appraisal," *Energy Law Journal* 3 (1982):14.

24. Descriptions of FERC (formerly FPC) regulation are found in Joe Pace and John Landon, "Introducing Competition into the Electric Utility Industry," pp. 26–32; and Stephen Breyer and Paul W. MacAvoy, *Energy Regulation by the Federal Power Commission* (Washington, D.C.: Brookings Institution, 1974).

25. Nuclear power appears in trouble: new orders are down and old orders are being canceled. Some of these problems have been attributed to regulation. See Paul L. Joskow, "Problems and Prospects for Nuclear Energy in the U.S.," in Gregory A. Daneke, ed., *Energy, Economics, and the Environment: Toward a Comprehensive Perspective* (Lexington, Mass.: Lexington Books, 1982), pp. 231–54; and Martin B. Zimmerman and Randall P. Ellis, "What Happened to Nuclear Power: A Discrete Choice Model of Technology Adoption," *Review of Economics and Statistics* 65 (May 1983):234–42.

economies of large size but without the inefficiencies of high monopoly prices. To accomplish this goal commissions engage in what is known as rate-of-return regulation. The cardinal principle of rate-of-return regulation is that utilities should be allowed to charge rates just high enough to cover all costs of production, including a "fair and reasonable" return on net capital investments (known as a firm's rate base).

Rate-of-return regulation, while relatively simple to understand in theory, is exceedingly complex to carry out in practice. Public utility commissions face enormous problems that effectively force them away from their objectives and circumscribe effective regulatory practices. The end result may be that rate-of-return regulation constitutes an inferior and unacceptable substitute for the imperfect free market.

Rate-of-Return Regulation

Rate-of-return regulation of electric utilities varies from state to state in detail and emphasis. Sufficient similarities exist, however, to outline a profile of typical commission procedures and to describe their effects. State regulatory commissions grant utilities in their jurisdictions exclusive monopoly franchises for specified retail service areas. In return the utility is expected to supply reliable service and to meet demand as it arises. The utility is proscribed from expanding or abandoning its service area or building new facilities without permission. Finally, and most important, the commission fixes the rates the utility can charge.

The rate-setting function is performed via the mechanism of rate hearings. Two basic tasks are involved: estimating the revenue the utility requires to cover its costs and structuring a set of rates that enables the utility to earn just its revenue requirements. Required revenues are estimated for a test year, chosen because it is the most recent year for which complete data are available, using the formula:

Required revenues = operating expenses + (rate of return)(rate base)

Firms submit operating expenses consisting largely of fuel costs, labor costs, annual depreciation, and taxes. These operating expenses receive varying amounts of commission scrutiny, before the commission sets the rate of return. The rate of return is a composite percentage of the interest rate received by the firm's bondholders and the commission-determined fair return on investment. The rate base is the value of plant and equipment used in production. The utility submits the assets to be included for commission approval, and they are valued according to a method chosen by the regulators—usually original cost minus accumulated depreciation.

After the revenue requirements are fixed, the utility files a tariff schedule designed to ensure that actual revenues equal required revenues. Once a set of tariffs has been approved, the utility cannot change its rates without permission. If the utility experiences a shortfall in revenues because actual costs are greater than test-year costs, it files for a rate increase. If instead actual costs are below estimated levels, the firm normally retains the excess profits earned during the commonly lengthy period before a new rate hearing is held.

The objective of this form of regulation is to replicate the performance of competitive markets subject to considerations of fairness and administrative ease. This requires that the commission accomplish, with limited and dated information, what a competitive market does automatically—efficient pricing, production, and investment, and normal rates of profit in the long run. This objective is exceedingly ambitious; problems beset the regulators virtually every step of the way.

The Test Year.   Commissions determine future rates by looking at costs in a previous year. If costs of production are falling over time, as they were in the electric industry until the mid-1960s, the result is utility rates and profits that are too high. Utility commissions' response in this situation has been to rely on "Dear John letters and jawboning" for inducing utilities to lower rates rather than to accelerate the formal rate-hearing process.[26]

When operating costs are rising, however, as they were during the inflationary 1970s, utility rates and profits based on previous year's costs will be too low. Utilities react by filing for rate increases. The administrative costs of frequent rate reviews in periods of rapid inflation can easily overload the capabilities of the commissions. In response to the rising fuel costs of the 1970s, many commissions implemented automatic fuel adjustment mechanisms that allow electric rates to increase automatically when fuel costs do without a formal rate hearing. Automatic fuel adjustment clauses do not completely remedy the problems of historical test years. They do permit

---

26. Joskow and MacAvoy, "Regulation and Financial Condition," p. 296.

fuel costs to be automatically passed through to customers, but other costs may be rising as well. In addition such adjustments lessen incentives to economize on fuel and create a bias toward fuel-intensive technologies.[27]

Operating Expenses. Rate-of-return regulation is designed to allow the utility to just cover its operating costs. One effect this rule has is to reduce the incentive to produce efficiently—the utility is neither forced by the threat of competition to minimize cost nor rewarded for producing efficiently. Cost savings are passed on to customers in the form of lower rates. This problem has been recognized almost since the beginning of utility regulation, yet few commissions routinely scrutinize utility costs for excessive salaries, unneeded staff, undue promotional activities, and other inflated costs. Commissioners operating within the constraints of limited information and budgets and aware of their lack of expertise are uniformly reluctant to overturn utility management decisions on cost levels. The result is undoubtedly wasted scarce resources and electric rates higher than they would be under competition.[28]

It has been argued that regulatory lag—the time between rate hearings—can mitigate the dulling effect of regulation on efficient production.[29] If prices are fixed for several years, utilities have incentives for efficiency during this period because cost reductions translate directly into utility profits. How well regulatory lag works to effect this result is arguable. If costs are falling for external reasons such as input price decreases or technological advances, the utility may opt to conceal excess profits through waste in order to avoid customer complaints and a possible rate review. When costs are rising, the utility

27. See Michael A. Crew and Paul R. Kleindorfer, *Public Utility Economics* (New York: St. Martin's Press, 1979), pp. 176–77. Several commissions have also begun moving to forecasts of operating expenses for future test years. See Schmalensee, *Control of Natural Monopoly*, p. 115, and Paul L. Joskow, "Inflation and Environmental Concern: Structural Change in the Process of Public Utility Price Regulation," *Journal of Law and Economics* 17 (October 1974):291–328.

28. Utilities may also have incentives to overstate costs using adroit accounting methods involving, for example, depreciation. See William G. Shepherd and Claire Wilcox, *Public Policies Toward Business*, 6th ed. (Homewood, Ill.: Irwin, 1979), pp. 300–2; and Bruce L. Jaffee, "Depreciation in a Simple Regulatory Model," *Bell Journal of Economics and Management Science* 4 (Spring 1973):338–42.

29. See William J. Baumol and Alvin K. Klevorick, "Input Choices and Rate-of-Return Regulation: An Overview of the Discussion," *Bell Journal of Economics and Management Science* 1 (Autumn 1970):162–90.

will be forced to initiate more frequent rate hearings. As soon as a rate review becomes probable in the near future, the utility no longer has much incentive to product efficiently since it must justify its requested rate increase with evidence of high costs.[30] Finally any salutary effects of regulatory lag on production efficiency must be weighed against the pricing inefficiencies introduced by having infrequent rate adjustments to changing cost conditions.

The Rate Base.   The firm is allowed to earn profits on its rate base. Over the years disputes have arisen regarding the appropriate assets for use in earning profits and legal rules and precedents have evolved in most states that specify the acceptable items. These rules ease the administrative burden but do not guarantee that the rate base is correctly defined. For example, electric utilities are slowly becoming diversified into other product areas including fuel exploration, real estate, and energy conservation. With production in unregulated markets, a utility may be able to claim nonutility assets in its utility rate base and thereby justify higher electricity prices while reaping an advantage in the form of lower capital expense for its unregulated division. In addition if utilities operate in more than one state or produce products subject to different regulatory authorities, the utility may be able to thwart regulatory purposes by assigning assets (and operating costs) to jurisdictions that have weaker regulation.[31]

Valuation of the rate base also poses a significant problem. Most regulatory commissions value the rate base at the original cost of installing the plant and equipment minus accumulated depreciation. This procedure is a well-known departure from the competitive marketplace where assets are automatically valued at their replacement cost— the current cost, given today's technologies, of providing the services of the old asset. Commissions rely on the original-cost method largely because it is straightforward, uses readily available data, and follows conventional accounting techniques.

Until the *Hope Natural Gas Case* of 1944 (*FPC* v. *Hope Natural Gas Co.*, 320 U.S. 591) utilities, commissions, and the courts engaged in lengthy debates over how to compute the "fair" value of assets that required consideration of original and reproduction costs

30. Stephen Breyer, *Regulation and Its Reform* (Cambridge: Harvard University Press, 1982), pp. 38–40.

31. Roger Sherman, "Electric Utility Regulation and Performance After Diversification," (Paper for Southern Economic Meetings, Washington, D.C., November 1982).

(the current cost of constructing the identical plant and equipment). This case ended the legal confusion by giving commissions the right to value assets at original cost only. Some utilities still consider reproduction costs in their valuation procedures, but in practice this is essentially the original-cost method plus an adjustment.[32]

Relying on historical costs of assets has implications for utility profitability and efficient pricing, especially during inflationary times. When assets are long lived and when plant construction costs are rising, the original cost of assets diverges by an increasing amount from current replacement costs. Prices based on the historical rate base will consequently be too low to provide adequate cash flow for replacing obsolete facilities and building additional capacity. This implies shortages and higher electricity costs in the future. The inefficiently low price also results in excessive electricity consumption, retards investment in new technology, and forces utilities to finance replacement facilities by borrowing funds or selling more shares, thereby diluting the value of existing equity.

At the same time, since conventional accounting techniques use historical costs of assets in measuring a firm's profits, the utility may be reporting adequate, even healthy, accounting profits. Paradoxically, respectable accounting profits do not necessarily imply revenues sufficient to cover the costs of capital.[33]

In response to these problems, several commissions are turning to replacement cost procedures, at least partially, in determining rate-base value. This is difficult to do administratively as it invites almost endless controversy over the cost and configuration of the hypothetical new plant that would be built.[34] The problem of insufficient revenues can also be addressed in what may be a more fruitful approach by adjusting the allowed rate of return.

Rate of Return. The utility is permitted to earn a fair rate of return on the investments included in its rate base. The obvious question confronting a commission, then, is how to determine the fair rate of

---

32. See Kahn, *Economics of Regulation*, pp. 35–41, for a history of the issue.

33. See Schmalensee, *Control of Natural Monopoly*, pp. 114–15; Ezra Solomon, "Alternative Rate of Return Concepts and Their Implications for Utility Regulation," *Bell Journal of Economics and Management Science* 1 (Spring 1970):65–81; and Stewart C. Myers, "The Application of Finance Theory to Public Utility Rate Cases," *Bell Journal of Economics and Management Science* 3 (Spring 1972):58–97.

34. On this see Breyer, *Regulation and Its Reform*, pp. 38–40 and Kahn, *Economics of Regulation*, pp. 109–16.

return. In theory the answer is straightforward. Regulators trying to duplicate performance of competitive markets should allow utilities to earn a rate of return equal to the cost of capital on new investment. In practice determining the appropriate rate of return is a formidable task embroiling commissions and utilities in time-consuming disputes.

Standard practice is to calculate the allowed rate of return as the weighted average cost of the debt and equity capital listed on the utility's books at the time of the rate hearing. Commissions typically use the embedded cost of debt capital—actual interest payments paid on debt divided by the book value of the utility's outstanding debt (mostly bonds)—plus their estimate of the cost of equity capital. Estimating the cost of equity capital is the source of most conflict, but using embedded debt costs is not without problems.

The use of embedded debt costs enables the utility to earn enough income to make interest payments it has already promised. Basing allowed rate of return on previously incurred debt costs, however, increases the probability that allowed rate of return will not equal the cost of capital on new investment—a concept that looks to the future, not to the past. As interest rates on new bonds have risen in recent years, the use of embedded debt costs has consistently understated the true cost of capital to electric utilities. In 1981, for example, embedded cost of debt was 9.3 percent while the average yield on new utility bonds ranged from 14.9 to 16.2 percent.[35] Since electric utilities borrow a large part of their capital—49.4 percent on average over the last decade—the use of embedded debt cost has been an important source of revenue erosion. With interest payments increasing as a percentage of revenues, utility bond ratings have fallen, implying higher costs of debt capital in the future.

In estimating the rate of return to equity capital, commissions follow the standards set by the courts in the 1944 *Hope Natural Gas* case. According to the *Hope* decision, "the return to the equity owner should be commensurate with returns on investments in other enterprises having corresponding risks. That return, moreover, should be sufficient to assure confidence in the financial integrity of the enterprise so as to maintain its credit and attract capital."[36]

35. Edison Electric Institute, *Statistical Yearbook of the Electric Utility Industry 1982* (Washington, D.C.: Edison Electric Institute, 1983), pp. 84–85, and U.S. Department of Energy, *Statistics of Privately Owned Electric Utilities in the U.S., 1981 Annual* (Washington, D.C.: U.S. Dept. of Energy, June 1983), p. 19.

36. *FPC* v. *Hope Natural Gas Company*, p. 603.

The most widely accepted approach for meeting the so-called comparable earnings and capital attraction standards of the *Hope* decision is to base the allowed rate of return on the accounting rate of return earned by equity holders in industries judged by the commission to face similar risks. Economists have roundly criticized this method largely because of the difficulties inherent in selecting firms facing "corresponding risks."

If a commission looks at rates of return earned by other regulated firms and other commissions do likewise, no appropriate benchmark exists for setting the rate of return; rate setting becomes circular. Another problem is that accounting rates of return for regulated firms reflect previous regulatory policy, not just market forces.

Even if the commission looks beyond regulated firms, it cannot be sure that the reported rate of return for a particular firm or industry is the competitive rate or that the firms face comparable risks. Risks vary over time, and a utility's risk is influenced by the extent to which its regulators are willing to protect it from business failure. In this sense no unregulated firm—by nature susceptible to bankruptcy—is similar to regulated utilities.

Finally accounting rates of return are backward looking. They report average returns on past investments, whereas what is needed is a way of estimating the cost of capital for future investments. In sum the procedures that have evolved for implementing the rate-of-return regulation mandated by the *Hope* decision result in allowed rates of return that diverge from the true cost of equity capital.

Advances in finance theory in the 1960s resulted in a general theory of corporate risk known as the capital asset pricing model. Myers shows in articles published in 1972 how the capital asset pricing model can be used to measure risk of regulated utilities more rigorously and thereby determine an appropriate allowed rate of return.[37]

According to this theory, the relevant cost of capital for a firm is a function of both the expected return to the investor and the riskiness (or variability) of this return. An investor can avoid some of the risks associated with a particular firm by a diversified portfolio. It is impossible, however, to diversify away all risks, especially the risk associated with the stock market as a whole. To be induced to invest

37. Myers, "The Application of Finance Theory" and "On the Use of β in Regulatory Proceedings: A Comment," *Bell Journal of Economics and Management Science* 3 (Autumn 1972):622–27. For an overview of the capital asset pricing model, see Eugene F. Fama, "Efficient Capital Markets: A Review of Theory and Empirical Work," *Journal of Finance* 25 (May 1970):383–417.

in risky stocks, therefore, the investor must be paid a risk premium over and above earnings on a risk-free asset. If the returns paid by a particular firm vary less, on average, than the stock market as a whole, the risk premium for that firm will be less than the average premium for all stocks. If the returns are more variable than the stock market returns, the risk premium required by investors will be more than the average premium for all stocks.

In applying this theory, the commission determines the cost of equity capital to the utility by determining the rate of return to risk-free assets, the stock market risk premium, and the variability of the utility's stocks relative to the market as a whole (known as the firm's β coefficient).

Since the development of the capital asset pricing model, some commissions have cautiously begun using it in rate hearings.[38] Use of capital market procedures is not, however, without its critics, who argue that while this approach is theoretically superior to the traditional, ad hoc methods still used by most commissions, it is also subject to estimation problems.[39] For example, investor's expected rates of return are undoubtedly affected by regulatory policy, yet this is difficult to account for. In addition risk premiums and expected returns are necessarily estimated using ex post stock market data. No guarantee is possible, given changing economic conditions, that the market cost of capital anticipated by investors in a previous year provides a good estimate for the future.

Regulatory Bias.   Rate-of-return regulated electric utilities have been accused of producing electricity inefficiently because they use more capital than necessary, maintain excessive levels of reliability, and favor adopting capital-intensive technologies like nuclear generation. These charges stem directly from a theory which holds that rate-of-return regulation biases the behavior of firms in specific and undesirable ways. The basic hypothesis, originally developed by Averch

38. See Richard H. Pettway, "On the Use of β in Regulatory Hearings," *Bell Journal of Economics* 9 (Spring 1978):239–48, and Robert L. Hagerman and Brian T. Ratchford, "Some Determinants of Allowed Rates of Return on Equity to Electric Utilities," *Bell Journal of Economics* 9 (Spring 1978):46–55.

39. Breyer, *Regulation and Its Reform*, pp. 44–47, William J. Breen and Eugene M. Lerner, "On the Use of β in Regulatory Proceedings," *Bell Journal of Economics and Management Science* 3 (Autumn 1972):612–21; and Hayne E. Leland, "Regulation of Natural Monopolies and the Fair Rate of Return," *Bell Journal of Economics and Management Science* 5 (Spring 1974):3–15.

and Johnson in 1962, and known as the Averch-Johnson (A-J) effect, is that if the allowed rate of return is greater than the cost of capital and if the commission effectively constrains the firm to earn its allowed rate of return and no higher, then the profit-maximizing regulated firm will have an incentive to inefficiently substitute capital for other inputs in its production process.[40]

Substantial theoretical work expands and refines the A-J thesis, but certain studies more directly suggest the charges advanced against regulation of electric utilities.[41] Spence, and Crew and Kleindorfer demonstrate that rate-of-return regulation may lead to excessive product quality and reliability if these features are capital intensive (as they are for electricity).[42] Magat, Smith, and Westfield each theorize that over time the regulated firm will choose to implement technological changes that support overcapitalization but are not necessarily efficient.[43]

No persuasive evidence substantiating these expanded A-J effects for electric utilities has turned up. Courville, Peterson, Spann, and Hayashi and Trapani find evidence of overcapitalization by electric utilities in the 1960s, while Boyes and Smithson reported evidence covering a similar time frame that does not support the A-J hypotheses. Baron and Taggart find evidence that utilities were employing inefficiently low levels of capital in 1970.[44]

40. Harvey Averch and Leland L. Johnson, "Behavior of the Firm Under Regulatory Constraint," *American Economic Review* 52 (December 1962):1052–69.

41. For a review of the literature on the A-J effect, see Baumol and Klevorick, "Input Choices and Rate-of-Return Regulation."

42. A. Michael Spence, "Monopoly, Quality, and Regulation," *Bell Journal of Economics* 6 (Autumn 1975):417–29, and Michael A. Crew and Paul R. Kleindorfer, "Reliability and Public Utility Pricing," *American Economic Review* 68 (March 1978):31–40.

43. Wesley A. Magat, "Regulation and the Rate and Direction of Induced Technological Change," *Bell Journal of Economics* 7 (Autumn 1976):478–96; V. Kerry Smith, "The Implications of Regulation for Induced Technological Change," *Bell Journal of Economics and Management Science* 5 (Autumn 1974):623–32; and Fred M. Westfield, "Innovation and Monopoly Regulation," in Capron, *Technological Change*, chap. 2, pp. 13–43.

44. Léon Courville, "Regulation and Efficiency in the Electric Utility Industry," *Bell Journal of Economics and Management Science* 5 (Spring 1974):53–74; H. Craig Peterson, "An Empirical Test of Regulatory Effects," *Bell Journal of Economics* 6 (Spring 1975):111–26; Robert M. Spann, "Rate of Return Regulation and Efficiency in Production: An Empirical Test of the Averch-Johnson Thesis," *Bell Journal of Economics and Management Science* 5 (Spring 1974):38–52; Paul M. Hayashi and John M. Trapani, "Rate of Return Regulation and the Firm's Equilibrium Capital-Labor Ratio: Further Empirical Evidence on the Averch-Johnson Hypothesis," *Southern Economic Journal* 42 (January 1976):384–98; William J. Boyes, "An Empirical Examination of the Averch-Johnson Effect," *Economic Inquiry* 14 (March 1976):24–

Several factors might explain the ambiguous evidence concerning A-J effects and utilities. Certainly data and specification problems lessen the ability of researchers to capture the existence of A-J effects.[45] More fundamentally the underlying assumptions of the A-J model might not hold for electric utilities. The regulatory lag between electric rate hearings opens the possibility for the firm to earn an actual rate of return different than the allowed rate of return. In this event, as previously argued, the utility may have incentives to economize on all costs, including capital costs, because cost minimization translates directly into greater profits, or fewer losses, for the firm.

In addition the usual practice of calculating the allowed rate of return by applying embedded debt costs and a fair rate of return on equity to the historical book value of the firm's assets encourages the probability—especially in times of inflation—that allowed returns will be below capital costs. When this occurs, the possibility of a negative A-J effect arises in which utilities would be characterized by under-capitalization, reserve capacity insufficient to ensure adequate reliability, and a bias away from capital-intensive nuclear capacity towards fuel-intensive technologies.[46]

The idea that rate-of-return regulation holds the potential for biasing utilities' input choices is compelling. Nevertheless for lack of better evidence on the direction and strengths of these effects, it is difficult to assess current regulation and regulatory reform proposals. Clearly, though, the A-J debate is a further illustration of how extremely difficult it is to mimick the competitive market via regulatory fiat. Firms react and adjust to regulatory constraints in ways not fully anticipated.

Rate Structure.   Finally we come to the most important step of the regulatory procedure, yet the one traditionally receiving the least commission attention: designing efficient electric rates. The funda-

35; and Charles W. Smithson, "The Degree of Regulation and the Monopoly Firm: Further Empirical Evidence," *Southern Economic Journal* 44 (January 1978):568–80; David P. Baron and Robert A. Taggart, Jr., "A Model of Regulation Under Uncertainty and a Test of Regulatory Bias," *Bell Journal of Economics* 8 (Spring 1977):151–67.

45. See Paul L. Joskow and Roger C. Noll, "Regulation in Theory and Practice: An Overview," in G. Fromm, ed., *Studies in Public Regulation* (Cambridge: MIT Press, 1981), pp. 10–14.

46. Joskow and MacAvoy, "Regulation and Financial Condition," p. 297, make this argument.

mental requirement for efficient resource allocation is equality of price and marginal cost. In competitive markets, as noted, the self-interest of price-taking firms guarantees this result. For regulators trying to simulate the efficiency of competitive markets, it follows that they should maintain a parallel, if not identical, pricing goal. Efficiency has not, however, been the primary pricing goal of electric utility regulators. Rather they have set rates so that actual revenues earned would equal the commission-determined required revenues.

A variety of rate structures are potentially compatible with any given level of revenue requirements, but the commissions have traditionally relegated responsibility for choosing the appropriate rate structure to the utilities themselves. Regulated utilities, meanwhile, have virtually no incentive to consider marginal cost in designing their rate structures. Moreover any tinkering of rates by commissions has been motivated, until very recently, by equity and not efficiency concerns. As a result electric rates have historically borne little resemblance to patterns of marginal cost.

Utilities tend to view rate setting as more of an art than a science, and they have evolved a large number of processes for designing rates. Yet we can describe a typical rate-setting procedure for electric utilities. After the commission has determined the revenue level the utility can earn, the rate designer allocates the revenue requirement among the utility's customers. Customers are divided into classes that are reasonably homogeneous with regard to the electric service they demand and the level, time, and duration of their maximum demands. The usual customer classifications are commercial, industrial, and residential. Rates are then set so that each customer class contributes its fair share and so that the revenues from all classes equal the full historical cost of production including the allowed return on embedded investment. Note that with this system, individual consumers within a class may pay more or less than the full costs of their consumption.

To cover the costs of production, a relatively standardized system of volume discounts has evolved. Generally residential and small customers are subject to declining block tariffs. These usually consist of a flat monthly charge to cover the costs of billing and customer service and then declining rates per unit for increased electricity consumption to cover fuel, operating, maintenance, and capacity costs (e.g., 8 cents per kilowatt hour for the first 50 kilowatt hours consumed per month; 4 cents for the next 100 kilowatt hours per month, and so forth). Large industrial and commercial users are often subject to two-part tariffs. These include a declining capacity charge for the maximum load demanded in the previous month (e.g., $4 per kilowatt for the first 200 kilowatts demanded; $3 per kilowatt for next 200 kilowatts demanded, and so forth) and a declining charge per kilowatt hour consumed to cover all other costs.[47]

The key features of both pricing schemes are that price falls as usage rises and large industrial and commercial users face cheaper prices than residential users. In judging the efficiency of these rate structures, the fundamental question is whether existing rate differences reflect true-cost differences. Because of how these rates have developed, the answer is no, they do not.

In the early years of the industry, electricity was sold at a constant rate per kilowatt hour. Then, in order to promote product use and increase profits, utilities began to price discriminate roughly according to the inverse of demand elasticity. For example, industrial users, with more alternative sources of power and thus higher demand elasticities, were charged lower rates to encourage usage. Households, believed to have a fairly inflexible demand for lighting purposes and a relatively flexible demand for appliances, were charged higher rates for their initial, presumably inflexible, usage and lower rates to induce greater consumption via appliances. Thus, as Shepherd and Wilcox lament, "electricity became a patchwork of special deals; some customers squeezed better terms from the utility, while other customer groups became 'creamy' markets. Regulation came after these deals took form and has tended only to ratify them."[48]

This does not mean that rate differences bear no relation to cost differences. Residences often cost more to supply than industrial users, and some declining charges are warranted when certain production costs are the same for large and small users. Nevertheless since utilities are motivated to vary rates according to demand elasticities and to charge what the traffic will bear, and since regulators generally focus their attentions on profit levels instead of on rate structures, we can be sure that a large portion of rate differences are not cost based. The overall conclusion must be that electric rates do not adequately reflect marginal costs. Consequently electric rates give erroneous signals to consumers about the costs of their consumption and lead to inefficient resource allocation.

---

47. For a detailed tariff description, see Crew and Kleindorfer, *Public Utility Economics,* pp. 162–70.

48. Shepherd and Wilcox, *Public Policies Toward Business,* p. 332.

The easiest way to illustrate this is by pointing out the peak-load problem facing electric utilities. Demand for electricity varies by hour and season. Because electricity is essentially nonstorable, utilities cannot meet peak demand with electricity produced in off-peak periods. Instead they must build enough capacity to meet peak demands even if these only last for short periods. This implies an unused capacity in off-peak periods and marginal costs that vary with shifts in demand. In the short run an additional kilowatt hour generated off-peak will cost less than the same amount generated at peak because utilities use their most efficient capacity for their base load, holding their older or less efficient units for peak use. In the long run new installations are based on predictions of future peak demand. Thus an additional kilowatt hour demanded at peak is responsible for the costs of installing as well as operating any required new capacity, while an additional kilowatt hour demanded off-peak is only responsible for the operating expenses necessary to produce that kilowatt hour, assuming sufficient capacity is available.

Because marginal costs vary with time, efficient pricing requires that electric rates also vary with time. Off-peak users should be charged lower rates than peak users. This would encourage shifting consumption to off-peak times, when more efficient capacity can be used, thus lowering the costs of electric production. At the same time, this pricing would tend to reduce the need for future capacity expansion.

The basic theory of marginal cost pricing (often called peak-load pricing or time-of-day pricing) in industries facing variable demand was developed in the 1950s. Since then scholars have provided an enormous quantity of related empirical and theoretical work, expanding our ability to measure demand variations, measure marginal costs in situations of fluctuating demand, and design efficient pricing schemes for these situations.[49] France and other European countries successfully implemented peak-load pricing schemes for their largely nationalized electric industries in the 1950s and 1960s. In the United States, however, virtually all declining block and most two-part tariffs ignored demand variations until the mid-1970s. Even today declining block rates for increasing consumption are typically available regard-

---

49. For an overview of peak-load pricing, see Crew and Kleindorfer, *Public Utility Economics,* pp. 23–117; on problems of peak-load pricing, see John T. Wenders, "Peak Load Pricing in the Electricity Industry," *Bell Journal of Economics* 7 (Spring 1976):232–41; on measuring electricity demand, see Lester D. Taylor, "The Demand for Electricity: A Survey," *Bell Journal of Economics* 6 (Spring 1975):74–110.

less of whether the household is consuming during a peak summer afternoon or an off-peak winter night. Similarly an industrial user's capacity charge is usually based on its maximum capacity use during the previous month regardless of whether it came during the system's peak or off-peak period.

In the early 1970s inflation problems, environmental concerns, and the energy crisis pressured utility commissions into focusing on electric rate structures to find ways to soften necessary rate increases and lessen the need for capacity expansion.[50] Several commissions investigated peak-load pricing, and a few began implementing them. The federal government also encouraged peak-load pricing by financing experiments in several states. Marginal cost pricing got an additional boost with the passage of the Public Utilities Regulatory Act of 1978. The act requires electric utilities to submit marginal cost data to the FERC on a regular basis and also requires that state commissions hold public hearings to consider pricing according to seasonal and daily demand differences.

The use of peak-load pricing techniques in electricity rate regulation is spreading. Though this is a step in the right direction for regulatory policy, regulators and utilities have a long way to go before electric rates approach efficiency. Many practical problems arise with implementing marginal cost pricing of electricity.[51] Two of the thorniest issues will illustrate the difficulties involved.

Once a commission or utility has been persuaded to adopt some form of marginal cost pricing, implementation problems generally fall into two categories: correct measurement of marginal cost and procedures for using marginal costs in rate design once calculated. Measuring marginal cost is complicated by the traditional backward focus rate-of-return regulation has.

Regulators and utilities can erroneously develop peak-load prices based on historical demand peaks and designed to cover historical costs. This is not marginal cost pricing. Because it is the cost of additional consumption, marginal cost necessarily looks to the future, not the past. As Pfannenstiel points out, "There is a difference be-

---

50. Paul L. Joskow, "Electric Utility Rate Structures in the United States: Some Recent Developments," in W. Sichel, ed., *Public Utility Ratemaking in an Energy Conscious Environment* (Boulder, Colo.: Westview Press, 1979), pp. 1–22.

51. For an in-depth treatment, see Jackalyne Pfannenstiel, "Implementing Marginal Cost Pricing in the Electric Utility Industry," in Sichel and Gies, eds., *Applications of Economic Principles*, pp. 53–72.

tween marginal cost pricing and peak-load, or time-of-day, pricing. The former implies the latter, while the reverse is not necessarily true. In other words, marginal costs do vary by time of day, so a rate structure based on marginal cost would also be a peak-load pricing structure. However, time-of-day rates can be, and have been developed independent of any marginal cost study. The peak periods would generally be defined by examination of historical load curves, and the rate levels would be set so as to recover the [historically based] revenue requirement."[52]

If marginal costs are correctly measured—that is, by estimating expected future demand and anticipated fuel, operating, and capacity costs—then utilities and regulators encounter a different problem. Marginal cost pricing is likely to yield revenue levels different from cost levels. If economies of scale in production exist, average costs decrease as output of the industry increases. Because of the relationship between average and marginal, when average costs are falling, marginal costs must be less than average costs. Marginal cost pricing in this situation will not enable the firm to cover its costs. Without adjustment, the firm incurs economic losses and will eventually shut down.

Economists have developed several methods of reconciling revenues to costs without seriously departing from marginal cost pricing principles. One such solution advocated is Ramsey pricing.[53] This involves adjusting rates according to the inverse of demand elasticity so that rates diverge from marginal cost by a greater percentage for consumers with less elastic demands. Aside from some theoretical problems, Ramsey pricing can founder on one practical obstacle— demand elasticities are notoriously difficult to estimate. Other problems are involved in correctly applying marginal cost pricing. All of them underscore, once more, the virtual impossibility of replicating competitive market performance via regulation.

52. Pfannenstiel, "Implementing Marginal Cost Pricing," p. 60.

53. See William J. Baumol and David F. Bradford, "Optimal Departures from Marginal Cost Pricing," *American Economic Review* 60 (June 1970):265–83. On possibly adjusting existing block and two-part tariffs to reflect marginal cost more closely and allow the utility sufficient revenues, see Hayne E. Leland and Robert A. Meyer, "Monopoly Pricing Structures with Imperfect Discrimination," *Bell Journal of Economics* 7 (Autumn 1976):449–62, and Robert D. Willig, "Pareto-Superior Non-Linear Outlay Schedules," *Bell Journal of Economics* 9 (Spring 1978):56–69. For a review of other methods, see Pfannestiel, "Implementing Marginal Cost Pricing," pp. 67–68, and Breyer, *Regulation and Its Reform*, pp. 52–55.

CONCLUSIONS

This chapter reviewed the foundations of economic regulation in electric utilities. Utilities have been regulated because electric market monopolies were considered inevitable. Conventional theory holds that such natural monopolies warrant intervention to prevent high monopoly prices and profits and to check monopolist tendencies toward wasteful and stagnant production methods. The type of regulation chosen for electric utilities tries to rectify monopoly performance by constraining profits to competitive levels.

This chapter criticizes the institution of electricity regulation on three levels. To clarify the critique, let us use the analogy of a patient with a disease. The traditional diagnosis of electric markets is that they are natural monopolies. To bring these markets to fuller health (i.e., efficiency), society has used regulation as the treatment of choice, with rate-of-return regulation the brand of medicine prescribed. The original diagnosis may be faulty, however; it is far from clear that multiproduct electric markets are natural monopolies. Even if they are, the best treatment for the resulting market failure may be no treatment at all. In other words regulation could be a cure worse than the disease itself. At the very least the brand of regulation ought to be changed.

Whether electric markets can correctly be classified as natural monopolies depends on whether single-firm electricity production is cheaper than multifirm production. Since electric utilities are multiproduct in nature, determining natural monopoly status is a complicated task, and the correct diagnosis depends on evidence of economies of joint production, not just economies of scale.

If electric markets are natural monopolies, the relevant issue for policymakers should not be whether natural monopolies result in market imperfections—they undoubtedly do. Instead policymakers are better advised to concentrate on comparing the disadvantages of regulation with those of unimpeded natural monopoly. They should weigh regulatory failure against market failure in order to make the least harmful of two imperfect choices.

Finally rate-of-return regulation is a woefully inadequate solution to natural-monopoly conditions. It attempts to force competitive performance by reducing profits to competitive levels. Yet the fundamental superiority of competitive markets lies not in their tendency toward zero profits, but in marginal cost pricing. By targeting profits instead of prices, rate-of-return regulation insures its own failure. Moreover it does not do even an acceptable job of limiting profits to competitive levels. Rate-of-return regulation is cumbersome and backward looking. It allows utilities to cover their historical, average costs of production so that when current costs are falling, utilities will earn excess profits, and when current costs are rising, utilities will incur losses. Unless costs, technologies, and electric demands are constant from period to period, rate-of-return regulation will not lead to competitive profit levels.

2

COMPETITION IN THE PRODUCTION OF ELECTRICITY

Asghar Zardkoohi

INTRODUCTION

The electric power industry is often characterized as a natural mono-poly. While some competition exists already, a major current policy concern is whether restructuring the industry could enhance competition and so improve economic efficiency. This chapter examines whether the need for competition among generating plants precludes the efficiency attributed to power pooling, coordination, and inter-connection among vertically integrated utilities. Pooling is generally defined as the common facility planning, construction and use by several independent companies. Two major benefits are: (1) pools substantially improve reliability at considerably reduced cost; and (2) pooling can result in substantial cost savings in power-generating and transmitting.[1]

Existing research has used the economies-of-scale framework to examine the feasibility of competition in the electric power industry. A finding of constant returns to scale or decreasing returns to scale

---

1. For an evaluation of power pooling, see: Federal Energy Regulatory Commission, Office of Electric Power Regulation, *Power Pooling in the South Central Region; Power Pooling in the Northeast Region; Power Pooling in the North Central Region; Power Pooling in the Western Region; Power Pooling in the Southeast Region.* (Washington D.C.: U.S. Government Printing Office, 1980–1981).

has often prompted researchers to propose restructuring the industry to improve competition. This chapter examines the literature on economies of scale as applied to the electric power industry. A major conclusion is that much of the literature is tainted by a serious misinterpretation of the observed data. Theorists have often assumed that the data reflects the behavior of independent or wholly separate utilities; in fact, most electricity is generated, transmitted, and distributed by closely planned, coordinated, and interconnected utilities. Since the results of past research utilized data of pooled, coordinated, or interconnected utilities yet treated the data as if it represented the behavior of fully isolated utilities, many policy implications derived from such studies lack support.

This chapter first describes the structure of the industry. This is pertinent to a study on the feasibility of competition because it sheds light on the conflict between competition, on the one hand, and the properties of pooling, coordination, and interconnection, on the other. Second, the chapter reviews and critiques the literature on economies of scale in the industry. Third, it discusses transmission and distribution and examines the question of whether the need for enhancing competition in the production and distribution of electricity precludes the gains from coordination among utilities. Fourth, it reviews various policy proposals regarding the desirability and feasibility of competition among firms in the industry. Finally, the chapter evaluates the effects of such competition.

THE STRUCTURE OF THE ELECTRIC POWER INDUSTRY: AN OVERVIEW

This section is divided into two parts. The first examines the technical structure of the industry; the second discusses the market structure.

Technical Structure

The electric power industry is conventionally divided into three functions: generation, transmission, and distribution. In the past transmission was not an important component because power was produced by relatively small utilities and sent directly to consumers over low-voltage distribution lines. Competition in the wholesale market was effectively precluded because high transmission costs associated with low-voltage transmission lines kept distant generating plants out of the local markets. Recently, however, transmission has changed, so that large blocks of power can be transported over long distances with improved reliability and lower costs. Traditionally, transmission lines had a voltage capacity of less than 200 kilovolts and could transport power only over relatively short distances.[2] Today, however, high-capacity transmission lines and grids of near 1,000 kilovolt capacity can transport power long distances.[3]

A primary difference between low- and high-voltage transmission lines is that low-voltage lines lose power. The higher the voltage, the lower the power loss. Furthermore capital and operating costs of transmission facilities increase in roughly direct proportion to the voltage, whereas transmission capacity increases as the square of voltage, meaning that the larger the transmission lines, the cheaper the transmission costs are per unit.[4]

The new transmission technology has facilitated power pooling, coordination, and interconnection among independent utilities, resulting in many advantages. Through interconnection and coordination, utilities can avail themselves of the following services:[5] (1) economy interchange or central economic dispatch, whereby loads are allocated to the utility with the lowest operating costs; (2) maintenance coordination, whereby staggered shutdowns of generating units are scheduled for periodic maintenance, reducing the need for extra capacity to prevent interruptions during maintenance; (3) reserve sharing, whereby interconnected utilities share reserve in the event of equipment failure (thus transmission facilities substitute for extra generating equipment to maintain reliability); (4) diversity exchange, which allows interconnected utilities to benefit from divergent peak-load patterns, reducing capacity requirements; and (5) joint planning, whereby utilities coordinate future investment to reduce generating costs (individual utilities, given their loads, may not realize full economies of generating units but together would have sufficient load to justify investment in large units).

Other benefits of the new transmission technology include greater

---

2. See *Hearings on S. 3136 Before the Senate Committee on Commerce,* 89th Cong., 2d sess., ser. 89–71 (1966).

3. See Federal Power Commission, *1970 Federal Power Commission Report 19–20* (Washington D.C.: U.S. Government Printing Office, 1971). Also see Robert Miller, *Power System Operation* 2d ed. (New York: McGraw-Hill, 1983), p. 143.

4. See Charles Scherer, *Estimating Electric Power System Marginal Costs* (Amsterdam: North-Holland, 1977), pp. 81–84 and 207–12.

5. Based on Joe Pace and John Landon, "Introducing Competition into the Electric Utility Industry: An Economic Appraisal," *Energy Law Journal* 3 (1982): 8.

flexibility in plant location. For example, high-voltage transmission lines can render alternative plant sites more economical in situations where restrictions on land use or environmental pollution pose legal problems or high generating costs. Furthermore transmission lines allow spatially dispersed load centers to be served at lower costs by a relatively small number of large generating plants instead of many small and isolated plants.

Market Structure

The electric power industry was organized in a holding-company structure in the 1920s and early 1930s. Concentration peaked in 1932 when sixteen electric power holding companies owned 75 percent of the power produced in the United States.[6] This high concentration gradually ended after passage of the Public Utility Holding Company Act of 1935.[7]

The present structure of the industry is characterized by diverse ownership modes, power pooling, coordination, and interconnection. About 3,500 electric utilities in the United States engage in the generation, transmission, and distribution of electric power.[8] These include private investor-owned utility systems, rural cooperative systems, municipal and state systems, and federal power systems. The utilities vary substantially in size, type, and mix of generating units, function, regulation, and so on. For example, there are utilities with 30,000-megawatt (mw) capacity, constituting about 5 percent of the U.S. capacity, and utilities that function only as distributors. Approximately 237 private utilities accounted for the bulk of the generating capacity, some 78 percent in 1980. The federal systems were next, accounting for 9.6 percent of the capacity. Municipal utilities, state systems, and rural cooperatives accounted respectively for 5.6, 4.5, and 2.5 percent of the generating capacity in the United States.

The private systems are highly diverse. Many have no generating capacity, relying on other utilities, public or private, for the power they purchase wholesale and distribute to their customers. Private utilities that generate power can also buy power from or sell power to

---

6. Terry Ferrar, Frank Clemente, and Robert Uhler, *Electric Energy Policy Issues* (Ann Arbor, Mich.: Ann Arbor Science, 1970), p. 2.

7. *Public Utility Holding Company Act of 1935*, 15 U.S.C. 79 *et seq.* 1935.

8. The statistics in the next three paragraphs are based on Paul Joskow and Richard Schmalensee, *Markets for Power: An Analysis of Electric Utility Deregulation* (Cambridge: MIT Press, 1983), chap. 2, pp. 11–23. The original source is U.S. Department of Energy, *Electric Power Annual*, DOE/EIA-0345 (Washington D.C.: U.S. Government Printing Office, 1982).

other private or public utilities with or without generating capacity. Most private utilities, however, have franchised monopoly rights in well-defined service territories. A limited number of utilities have overlapping service areas in several states.[9]

One factor characterizing private utilities is that most are vertically integrated: They generate, transmit, and distribute electricity. Furthermore most utilities are interconnected, and a majority are coordinated or belong to a power pool. As of 1979 about 60 percent of the generating capacity belonged to utilities that had formed "formal pools."[10] Informal pools and other types of pools characterize most of the remaining utilities.[11]

The Department of Energy classifies pooling in three categories: informal agreements, bilateral or multilateral agreements, and formal pooling. Formal agreements specify members' operational and investment responsibilities, covering a relatively wide range of activities. Formal agreements are subject to the Federal Energy Regulatory Commission (FERC) approval. Informal pooling agreements aid coordination of activities but have no legal force and do not require regulatory approval. Bilateral or multilateral agreements include contracts between two or more utilities regarding exchanges of power and transmission services.

Pooling arrangements yield many benefits. Pooling can facilitate investment coordination and construction of large generating units and transmission lines, leading to economies of scale in generation and transmission. Furthermore pool members with diverse loads can interchange power to reduce capital and operating costs. They can also effect cost reductions by sharing reserve capacity and transmission facilities. Finally pooling can facilitate emergency assistance and scheduled outage assistance, reducing capital and operating costs.[12]

9. See Walter J. Primeaux, Jr., "A Reexamination of the Monopoly Market Structure for Electric Utility," in A. Phillips, ed., *Promoting Competition in Regulated Markets* (Washington D.C.: Brookings Institution, 1975), chap. 6, pp. 175–200. Primeaux examined competition at the distribution level in markets with more than one utility and concluded that the natural-monopoly argument loses force when utility firms face competition. Primeaux's methodology and interpretation have been criticized; see, for example, Joskow and Schmalensee, *Markets for Power*, pp. 61–62; also Pace and Landon, "Introducing Competition," pp. 47–50.

10. For more details, see U.S. Department of Energy, *Power Pooling: Issues and Approaches DOE/ERA/6385-1* (Washington D.C.: U.S. Government Printing Office, 1981).

11. U.S. Dept. of Energy, *Power Pooling*.

12. For example, see Federal Energy Regulatory Commission, *Power Pooling in the Western Region, FERC-0054* (Washington D.C.: U.S. Government Printing Office, 1981), pp. 1–2, and reference in note 10 for a discussion of the gains from power pooling.

Power pooling, coordination, and interconnection can, however, limit market competition among utilities. The hard policy question is whether the economic gains attributed to these arrangements are worth the costs of limiting competition. Should public policy promote rivalry even though such policy may jeopardize the economic efficiency attributed to interconnection and coordination among utilities? Do schemes exist that would preserve the gains from pooling, coordination, and interconnection without precluding competition?

ECONOMIES OF SCALE IN THE ELECTRIC POWER INDUSTRY

This section is divided into two parts. The first discusses the theoretical aspects of economies of scale; the second reviews and critically examines existing empirical work on economies of scale.

Theory

Economists often try to justify regulation by pointing to certain categories of alleged market failures. Externalities—uncompensated benefits (or costs) that spill over from one decision maker to another—constitute one such category. For electric utilities economists have claimed that the markets fail because of the existence of a natural monopoly: when the range of demand for electricity does not extend beyond the area of decreasing long-run average costs. In these instances the market is able to support only one utility. The traditional claim is that natural monopolies induce wasteful competition because monopoly profits invite duplicate investments. According to this argument, regulation becomes a means of eliminating monopoly profits, thereby discouraging wasteful duplication and competition.

As the prime rationale for regulation, natural monopoly has been the focus of numerous empirical investigations. An important feature of the empirical results has been the conclusion that scale economies exist in electric generation over the entire range of demand at the plant level. Recently, however, a few empirical studies indicate diseconomies of scale and/or constant returns to scale beyond a given level of output. A major policy implication of the recent results has been that a small number of large utilities is no longer required for efficient production and that the market is capable of supporting a large number of competitors.

This policy implication may not necessarily follow, however. The existence of decreasing or constant returns to scale beyond a given level of output does not necessarily imply that the market can support a large number of firms or that competition is viable in the market. Put differently natural monopoly may exist even if all scale economies are exhausted at the firm's chosen level of output. This result may stem from any of the following three conditions. First, when diseconomies of scale exhibit over a relatively small range of output, average cost may be greater for two firms than for one. Consider, for example, Figure 2–1 in which the long-run average cost curve reaches its minimum at the output level Q_1, and the firm is regulated to produce at Q_2. The firm operates in the range of decreasing returns to scale, yet average cost, AQ_3, when two firms share the market equally, exceeds average cost, BQ_2, when there is only one firm.

Second, the existence of economies of vertical integration in conjunction with economies of scale at one hierarchical level of operation

Figure 2–1.   Economies and Diseconomies of Scale.

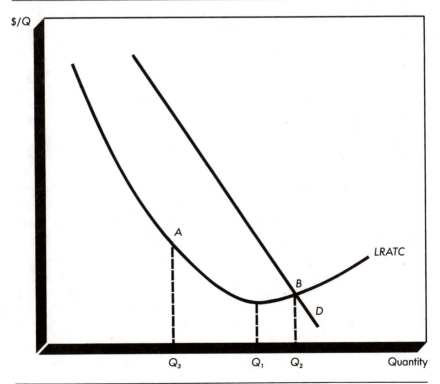

(say, at the distribution level) may result in economies of scale in the entire operation even though production does not exhibit economies of scale. Put differently a vertically integrated firm could be a natural monopoly in its entire operation even though the production process of the product may not enjoy economies of scale. Consider, for example, a multilevel production and distribution firm where the production stage, P, is vertically tied to the distribution stage, D. Assume that the distribution component enjoys economies of scale, so one firm is more efficient than two. Also assume, however, that the production component experiences diseconomies of scale over a wide range of output. Finally assume that the operations linking the production stage, P, to the distribution stage, D, are complex and less costly if controlled internally by one firm than if consummated externally across two or more firms.

It is now simple to see that if the gains from economies of vertical integration outweigh the added costs due to the diseconomies of scale at the production stage, the entire operation as a unit would be a natural monopoly. It is true that nonintegration would render production less costly because competition, by assumption, is viable at this stage. The cost at the delivery point to consumers, however, would be greater under nonintegration than under integration. Related to the electric industry, an empirical result that shows diseconomies in generation does not necessarily imply the economic superiority of vertical nonintegration unless it is shown that the gains from competition at the generation level exceeds the loss of economies of vertical integration.

Third, a multiproduct firm could be a natural monopoly in product A even though product A's production process suffers from diseconomies of scale. This result could exist when the firm produces more than one product and enjoys "economies of scope."[13] Economies of scope occur when the total cost to a single firm for producing a bundle of goods is less than the cost when each product is produced by different firms; that is, the benefits from joint production outweigh adverse scale effects.

The electric industry can be characterized as a multiproduct operation. For example, the production process for peak loads is dif-

13. This discussion is based on William Baumol, John Panzar, and Robert Willig, *Contestable Markets and the Theory of Industry Structure* (New York: Harcourt Brace Jovanovich, 1982).

ferent from that for basic or intermediate loads.[14] Peak loads are met using relatively inexpensive generating units (e.g., gas or oil turbines) that require relatively expensive fuels; whereas basic and intermediate loads are met using relatively expensive equipment (e.g., steam or hydro generating units) that use relatively inexpensive fuel, that is, coal and water. Furthermore, peak-load equipment is specially designed to be switched on almost instantaneously to meet unexpected and transitory loads. Basic-load equipment, though, may require hours of preparation before it can be switched on. Another example of product variation is that different customer groups use electricity at different voltage levels. Industrial customers often draw electricity from high-voltage transmission lines; whereas residential and commercial customers receive electricity from distribution substations at low-voltage levels.

The characterization of the electric industry as representing a multiproduct operation may have implications for the emergence of large-system power pools. Large systems operate much like single firms and produce more than one "product." If product variety increases with the size of a system, then the economies of scope associated with power pooling may outweigh adverse scale effects in any given product, leading to multiproduct natural-monopoly conditions.[15]

In sum an empirical result showing that electric generation characterizes constant returns to scale or decreasing returns to scale does not necessarily imply that either vertical nonintegration or horizontal nonintegration is a more economical alternative than the present integrated structure. Careful accounting of the benefits of the vertical and horizontal properties of the industry structure is needed before any restructuring proposal can be implemented.

Empirical Work

An often-cited example of past research is Komiya, who examined a steam-electric production function using data for 235 new plants constructed from 1938 to 1956. The purpose of the study was "to analyze technological progress in steam-power production . . . and to find out how much, if any, of the decline in the input requirements is

14. For a discussion on the type and features of generating units, see W. D. Marsh, *Economics of Electric Utility Power Generation* (Oxford: Clarendon Press, 1980), pp. 98–115.
15. This assumption is plausible because the larger a system is, the greater the variation across customer groups and thus the greater the product variety.

attributable to . . . (1) economies of scale; (2) factor substitution; and (3) the shift in the production function."[16] Komiya concluded that "the scale effect[s] . . . are very important in the steam power generation."[17]

Three problems overshadow Komiya's results. First, the sample used for the analysis was biased toward small units. Of the 235 plants, "only fifteen plants were larger than 400 mw, and no units were larger than 210 mw.[18] This is serious bias since more recent empirical research indicates that diseconomies of scale begin to appear with units exceeding the 300–400 mw range. Second, Komiya used plant rather than firm data. The latter is preferable because (a) investment and other decisions are made at the firm level, and (b) firms not plants are regulated.[19] Third, and most important, the results were interpreted as if they represented the behavior of single-product plants that operated in isolation. In fact the data represented multiproduct operations and diverse product mixes across interconnected and vertically integrate plants.

Galatin evaluated the effects of scale economies and technical change in a model that took into account important characteristics of steam-generating electric units. For example, the study explicitly recognized differences between various unit types according to vintage, size, and fuel type. The model assumed, however, that fuel was the only variable input.[20] Galatin used a sample of 158 electric plants installed between 1938 and 1953 in the United States and divided them into six vintage classes.[21] The results for each vintage class indicated that "the fuel input per unit of output decreases the larger is the machine, but this fuel saving diminishes as machines of successively larger scale

16. R. Komiya, "Technical Progress and the Production Function in the United States Steam Power Industry," *Review of Economics and Statistics* 44 (1962): 156.
17. Komiya, "Technical Progress," p. 156.
18. David Huettner, "Scale, Costs and Environmental Pressures," in B. Gold, ed., *Technical Change: Economics, Management and Environment* (Oxford: Pergamon Press, 1975), chap. 3, p. 74. This provides details of the data Komiya and a few other researchers have used.
19. See Marc Nerlove, "Returns to Scale in Electricity Supply," in C. Christ, ed., *Measurement in Economics* (Stanford: Stanford University Press, 1963), chap. 7, pp. 167–98. He presents the problems of using plant-level instead of firm-level data to evaluate economies of scale.
20. The model specified a technology in which inputs were not substitutable.
21. The vintage classes were: 1920–24, 1925–29, 1930–39, 1940–44, 1945–50, 1951–53.

are compared."[22] The scale effects were not highly satisfactory with respect to capital and labor inputs.

Galatin's results suffer from the same problems as Komiya's. For example, the sample was seriously biased toward small-size units: The sample included 158 plants of which only two were larger than 300 mw and the largest generating unit was 152.5 mw.[23] Also, plant rather than firm data were used; in addition, the effects of vertical integration or economies of scope were not taken into account.

Barzel examined the production and technological characteristics of 200 steam-electric generation plants. The sample was biased in favor of small units because it included only 2 units larger than 200 mw and 19 plants larger than 400 mw.[24] The estimation results indicated important economies of scale with respect to fuel, labor, and capital.[25]

Dhrymes and Kurz investigated the question of returns to scale in the steam-power industry in the United States.[26] Their sample was biased toward small-size units because, of the 362 plant observations, only 2 were larger than 200 mw, and 19 plants larger than 400 mw.[27] The model allowed substitution possibilities only between fuel and capital; and it assumed cost-minimizing behavior on the part of the plant. The results indicated that "increasing returns to scale is the prevailing phenomenon in (steam) electric generation."[28] Furthermore the results showed a general tendency for the degree of returns to scale to decline with size.

Nerlove used a cost function to examine the characteristics of production technology in electric supply. Unlike the previous studies cited, this sample used firm-level data including a cross section of 145 steam-electric firms. Nerlove concluded: "There is evidence of a marked

22. Malcolm Galatin, *Economies of Scale and Technological Change in Thermal Power Generation* (Amsterdam: North-Holland, 1968), p. 120.

23. Galatin, *Economies of Scale,* p. 120; see also Appendix A, pp. 153–76 for details of the data.

24. Yoram Barzel, "Productivity in the Electric Power Industry, 1929–1955," *Review of Economics and Statistics* 45 (1964): 74, Table 1.

25. The coefficients indicating scale economies were .896, .626, and .815 for fuel, labor, and capital, respectively. The capital input function included 178 plants.

26. The authors also estimated measures of technological change and evaluated the degree of input substitution.

27. Huettner, "Scale, Costs and Pressures," p. 74.

28. Phoebus Dhrymes and Mordecai Kurz, *Econometrica* 32 (1964): 308.

degree of increasing returns to scale at the firm level; but the degree of returns to scale varies inversely with output and is considerably less, especially for large firms, than that previously estimated for individual plants."[29] A major criticism of Nerlove's results is that he used kwh as the measure of output without explicitly considering the firm's generating capacity, size, or scale of operation.[30] To the extent that capacity utilization systematically varies with size, Nerlove's results overestimate returns to scale.[31]

In contrast to these early studies, recent research shows constant returns to scale or decreasing returns to scale in the electric power industry. A much-cited study reflecting this is by Christensen and Greene, who used a 1970 sample of 114 firms and holding companies. They employed a translog cost function to investigate the nature of scale economies in the electric industry. The empirical results indicated that "by 1970 . . . the bulk of U.S. electricity generation was by firms operating in the essentially flat area of the average cost curve."[32] Thus they concluded that "a small number of extremely large firms are not required for efficient production and that policies designed to promote competition in electric power generation cannot be faulted in terms of sacrificing economies of scale."[33]

Another often-cited recent work is by Huettner and Landon, who estimated a cost function using 1971 data for 74 electric firms. The empirical results identified a U-shaped cost curve that reached its minimum at a firm size of 1,600 mw, "well within the range of observation."[34] One major criticism of this study is that the results are based on operating costs only; capital costs were excluded from the cost data. Given the capital intensity of electric generation and the variation of unit size and type across the firms, capital cost exclusion may have biased the results seriously.

29. Nerlove, "Returns to Scale," p. 186.
30. For other criticisms, see Thomas Cowing and Kerry Smith, "The Estimation of Production Technology: A Survey of Econometric Analysis of Steam-Electric Generation," *Land Economics* 54 (1978): 156–86.
31. There is an indication that this is the case. See John Stewart, "Plant Size, Plant Factor, and the Shape of the Average Cost Function in Electric Power Generation: A Nonhomogeneous Capital Approach," *Bell Journal of Economics* 10 (1979): 562–63 and Tables 5 and 6.
32. Laurits Christensen and William Greene, "Economies of Scale in U.S. Electric Power Generation," *Journal of Political Economy* 84 (1976): 655.
33. Christensen and Greene, "Economies of Scale," p. 655.
34. David Huettner and John Landon, "Electric Utilities: Scale Economies and Diseconomies," *Southern Economic Journal* 44 (1978): 892.

Stewart modeled an empirical analysis that included the effect of plant size, unit fuel efficiency, and nature of output on average cost of electric power generation. Stewart considered output to be two dimensional: (1) the instantaneous rate of output or kilowatt power; and (2) the volume measure of output or kwh.[35] The author maintained that "though rate and volume are related, failure to recognize their potentially differential effect on costs can create problems."[36] For example, "It is possible to observe plants with the same maximum instantaneous rate of output producing different cumulative levels of output or to observe plants with the same cumulative level of output producing different maximum instantaneous rates of output."[37] Utilities are expected to consider both dimensions of output in making investment decisions. Incorporating one dimension only, Stewart stressed, may lead to dubious empirical results.

Using a sample of 58 newly constructed fossil-fuel plants that went into service in 1970 and 1971, Stewart ran a translog regression to estimate the average kw cost of generating units. The cost function included the effects of two fuel efficiency factors—kw capacity of the unit and number of units in the plant—and three dummy variables specifying different regions of the country. The results indicated that the average cost declined at a decreasing rate as fuel efficiency increased.[38] Moreover generating unit size

[had] a relatively small impact on the cost of equipment. For gas turbine units, plant cost decline[d] with unit size over only part of the range of unit sizes. At the mean heat rate of the gas turbines in the sample . . . plant cost decline[d] with unit size only for units smaller than 70 mw. For steam plants, per kw plant cost decline[d] with unit size only for very small units of relatively low fuel efficiency, and plant cost increase[d] with unit size over most of the reasonable range of unit sizes and fuel efficiency, though at a relatively modest rate.[39]

In sum past research on scale economies share fundamental problems. First, the studies have treated diverse power systems as single-product firms or plants. This could have created estimation problems because the cost of a power system crucially depends on the mix of

35. Stewart, "Plant Size, Plant Factor," pp. 562–63.
36. Ibid.
37. Ibid., p. 551.
38. Ibid., p. 557.
39. Ibid., p. 559.

products it produces, which in turn determines optimal investment patterns. In this regard Joskow and Schmalensee contend that

> No power systems produce the same mix of products, and product mix differences affect the magnitude and form of optimal investments in transmission and distribution . . . . Moreover accounting cost data for actual utilities reflect arbitrary accounting conventions (particularly those applying to depreciation) and firms' histories (especially the scale and construction dates of their existing plants), as well as the long-run forces that are of primary interest. Given the complexity of real power systems, their multiproduct character, and the importance that history derives from asset longevity, *it is not clear that any economic meaning can be attached to the Christensen-Greene estimates or to any others that might be obtained using standard econometric techniques with available data.* (Emphasis added.)[40]

Second, the research has generally been based on data for vertically integrated utilities that generated, transmitted, and distributed electricity. The results, however, have been construed as reflecting cost patterns of nonintegrated generating concerns. So long as vertical integration affects investment decisions and operating costs, policy implications drawn from empirical results are doubtful and suspicious. Joskow and Schmalensee contend that "we cannot look to econometric studies for information about firm-level economies of scale for nonintegrated generating firms since available data are made up almost entirely of integrated firms that perform other closely related functions as well."[41]

Finally research has used data for interconnected, coordinated, and pooled utilities. Results based on such data cannot be construed to reflect self-contained or isolated utilities. The evidence needed to test hypotheses about economies of scale at the firm or plant level must represent self-contained firms or plants, but the available data come mostly from interconnected and pooled utilities. Furthermore the data represent considerable variation in how much the utilities participate in interconnection, coordination, or pooling arrangements. A major problem with such data could be that the estimated coefficients bias the scale at which average cost reaches its minimum downward.[42] The

---

40. Joskow and Schmalensee, *Markets for Power,* p. 55.
41. Ibid.
42. Laurits Christensen and William Greene, "An Econometric Assessment of Cost Savings from Coordination in U.S. Electric Power Generation," *Land Economics* 54 (1978): 139–55. This has shown that pooling does not render any significant benefits because observed

reason is that while pooling extends the scale of operation and is effectively analogous to horizontal merger, the results are nevertheless construed as reflecting the scale of self-contained utilities. Obviously these utilities have smaller scales than do the pools or systems they join.

In summary policy implications based on questionable data are similarly questionable. This does not mean, though, that the present structure is optimal. Regulatory constraints have probably affected the industry structure and investment decisions for the worse.[43] Nevertheless implementing proposals based on dubious empirical work can produce parallel inefficiencies. Researchers need to do careful empirical investigations, which would incorporate the effects on investment decisions and operating costs of vertical integration, coordination, interconnection, and pooling, in order to form a basis for policy recommendations.

The following questions might help form a basic framework for such future empirical research:

1. What effect does vertical integration have on investment decisions and operating costs in the generation, transmission, and distribution components?
2. What effect does vertical integration have on facilitating interconnection, coordination and pooling across utilities? Put differently, would a nonintegrated electric industry require more costly arrangements to interconnect, coordinate, or pool than would an integrated one?
3. If vertical nonintegration renders interconnection, coordination, and pooling more costly, what would be the costs of less pooling? How much more reserve capacity would each self-contained util-

---

costs of self-contained utilities and those that join pools are not significantly different. Joskow and Schmalensee, (*Markets for Power,* p. 230), however, have criticized this result. First, they contend that the data only included formal power pools. Other types were excluded. Second, the results are based on some questionable observations. Joskow and Schmalensee maintain that the authors relied "on the 1970 *National Power Survey,* which apparently describes the New England Power Pool and the New York Power Pool as centrally dispatched. But the New England agreement was not signed until 1971, and the New York pool did not actually go to full central dispatch until 1977."

43. See, for example, Harvey Averch and Leland Johnson, "Behavior of the Firm under Regulatory Constraint," *American Economic Review* 52 (1962): 1052–69. Also see Alfred Kahn, *The Economics of Regulation: Principles and Institutions,* vols. 1 and 2 (New York: John Wiley & Sons, 1970), vol. 1, pp. 147–48 and vol. 2, pp. 101–2, 106–7, and 267–68.

ity have to maintain? What would be the effect of this on service reliability? What would be the cost of maintaining the same reliability standard as under integration?

4. What would be the nature of contracts between the generation, transmission, and distribution utilities under vertical nonintegration? How risky would the contracts be? Could the contractual arrangements resolve the associated externality problems inherent in the physical connections between components? How likely would opportunistic behavior be in each component?

5. If vertical nonintegration renders pooling more costly and thus results in fewer and less extensive pools, what would be the effect of central economy dispatch arrangements among competing utilities? Would competing utilities be likely to reveal their true marginal cost? How sympathetic would utilities be to meeting the emergency problems of competing utilities? What would be the costs of maintaining extra spinning reserve units to safeguard against emergency situations?

These questions need to be reckoned with in evaluating proposals designed to restructure the industry.

TRANSMISSION AND DISTRIBUTION OF ELECTRICITY

Transmission is strategically important in an electric power system. Often transmission and generation decisions are tightly interrelated and cannot effectively be separated. Location, type, and size of generating plants are factors decided in conjunction with the configuration of transmission lines. Recent technological developments in transmission, as discussed above, have allowed transportation of large blocks of power over long distances with high levels of reliability and minimum power loss. Furthermore coordination and pooling are made possible by this new transmission technology.

Despite its importance transmission accounts for only 15 percent of total utility capital costs, compared to 53 percent for generation and 32 percent for distribution. Operating and maintenance costs of transmission are only 2 percent of the total operating and maintenance costs for the entire system.[44] Detailed transmission cost data are not,

---

44. Joskow and Schmalensee, *Markets for Power,* pp. 62–63.

however, published. Scherer collected such data for the New York State Electric and Gas system, NYSEG, to arrive at that system's estimated transmission costs. See Table 2–1 for a summary of the data for new transmission lines and Figure 2–2 for the associated graph. The stepwise total cost function, approximated as the *RR* line, indicates the existence of scale economies. This is true because average cost, represented by the slope of the rays from the origin to various points on the *RR* line, decreases with the transmission-line capacity.

Huettner and Landon attempted to estimate the shape of transmission average cost curve for a sample of seventy-four utilities. To do this, they regressed short-run average variable transmission costs on the natural log of total capacity and its square, utilization rate and its square, and other variables.[45] The empirical results showed a statistically insignificant relationship between long-run average variable transmission costs and the scale variables. The coefficient signs indicated that the cost curve is shaped like an inverted U, "with the maximum point of this curve occurring at a capacity of 4,000 trillion mw."[46] The authors also observed that average transmission costs "increased steadily with increased firm size, but the estimated magnitude of the increase was only 0.1 mill/kwh as firm size increased

Table 2–1. Single Circuit Transmission Line Capital for the NYSEG System.

Voltage (kv)	115	230	345
Capacity (mva)[a]	220	440	1,320
Cost ($/mile)			
New	70,000	76,000	126,000
Existing	57,000	63,000	111,000

SOURCE: Charles R. Scherer, *Estimating Electric Power System Marginal Costs* (Amsterdam: North-Holland, 1977), Table 6–21, p. 208.

[a]Installation of a line on an existing corridor is cheaper than clearing an entire new corridor; hence the lower cost. An mva is approximately equal to an mw.

45. The other variables included utilization of total capacity and its square, three regional dummy variables, wage cost, average underground circuit-miles per customer, average structure-miles per customer, commercial and industrial consumption and sales to municipal utilities (as percentages of total consumption), and finally three dummy variables indicating holding company status.

46. Huettner and Landon, "Electric Utilities," pp. 894–95.

Figure 2–2.   New Corridor Transmission Cost Function.

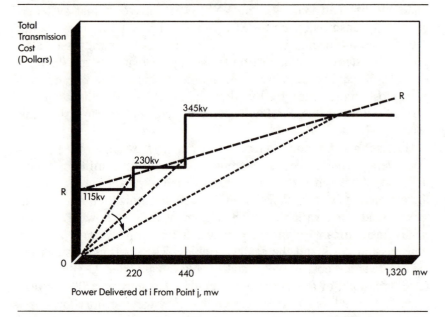

Power Delivered at i From Point j, mw

SOURCE: Charles R. Scherer, *Estimating Electric Power System Marginal Costs* (Amsterdam: North-Holland, 1977), p. 82.

---

from 100 mw to 9,000 mw."[47] These results suffer from two major shortcomings. First, the model failed to account for the effects of capital costs, although transmission is highly capital intensive. Moreover, it disregarded the effects of vertical integration, interconnection, and pooling on transmission costs. The available cost data does not separate out such effects.

Huettner's and Landon's results notwithstanding, two main factors affect transmission costs. First, as mentioned, transmission costs increase in approximately direct proportion to the voltage, but transmission capacity increases as the square of voltage; that is, the larger the transmission line justified by the load, the cheaper the transmission cost per unit of capacity. Second, the relative loss of power is reduced as the voltage increases. Consequently the cheapest way to transmit a given volume of electricity between two points is to deliver the entire amount on one line.

---

47. Huettner and Landon, "Electric Utilities," p. 895.

Distribution

Distribution is the delivery of low-voltage electric power from load center substations to residential, commercial, and industrial users—in short, the selling of electric power to end users. Distribution includes activities such as load dispatching, customer installations, equipment maintenance, meter reading, billing, demonstrating, and advertising.

Much of the literature on the economics of distribution presumes the existence of economies of scale. For example, Cohen asserted, "Given the natural monopoly character of local distribution, most states impose territorial restrictions that prevent direct competition between two or more retailers in the same community."[48] Similarly Meeks argued that "in economic terms, the distribution plant presents a near perfect example of a local natural monopoly."[49] Scherer contended that "distribution costs generally manifest significant scale economies: Two wires can be run overhead or placed in a ditch almost as cheaply as one. Average capital costs for distribution (the prime component of distribution costs) therefore fall as load density in the distribution area increases."[50] However, "If 'urban sprawl' continues and population density decreases faster than per capita usage increases, the decreasing costs once associated with distribution of electric power might disappear."[51]

Recent empirical research challenges the natural-monopoly status of distribution, however. For example, Weiss concludes in a much-cited work that "there would . . . seem to be no technical barrier to the existence of many geographically small distribution systems in an area. Some direct competition at the retail level may be possible (if not prevented by state territorial assignments or antipirating laws) for larger industrial loads that are close enough to service area boundaries to make the extension of transmission lines across such boundaries

48. Matthew Cohen, "Efficiency and Competition in the Electric-Power Industry," *The Yale Law Journal* 88 (1979): 1521.

49. James Meeks, "Concentration in the Electric Power Industry: The Impact of Antitrust Policy," *Columbia Law Review* 72 (1972): 74.

50. Scherer, *Estimating Electric Power*, p. 305.

51. Ibid.

feasible or where open land between distribution utilities is being developed."[52]

Weiss's conclusion was based on an analysis that included thirty privately owned utilities. The sum of average distribution and sales costs was regressed on load density, kwh consumption per customer, and number of customers served. The results indicated a statistically significant inverse relationship between the average cost variable and load density, but they showed no significant relationship between the average cost variable and the number of customers. The load-density relationship was to be expected because an increase in consumption should decrease average distribution and sales costs, given the installed capital facilities. The statistically insignificant relationship between the average cost and number of customers is especially important because it challenges the conventional natural-monopoly concept for distribution; that is, changes in the scale of operation do not affect average distribution and sales costs.

Neuberg modeled a distribution cost function that included the number of customers as its primary measure of output. Neuberg criticized Weiss's results on four counts. First, Weiss's model indicated an apparent multicollinearity between the load density variable and number of customers. Second, a log-linear relationship—instead of the linear-additive form—might have produced a significant relationship between cost and number of customers. Third, Weiss's conclusion that competition is feasible among many geographically small distribution units may not be appropriate because the model did not account for the effect of customers' geographical dispersion. Finally Weiss's conclusion that no "technical" barrier to competition existed is not robust because "the question of whether or not average cost is related to a variable 'absolute size' (= of output) appears to have little in common with the usual formulation of the returns to scale question."[53]

The model Neuberg used took into account the effect on total distribution costs of overhead distribution line length, size of service territory, price of capital, price of labor, and mode of ownership. He

52. Leonard Weiss, "Antitrust in the Electric Power Industry," in A. Phillips, ed., *Promoting Competition in Regulated Markets* (Washington D.C.: Brookings Institution, 1975), chap. 5, p. 146.

53. Leland Neuberg, "Two Issues in the Municipal Ownership of Electric Power Distribution System," *Bell Journal of Economics* 8 (1977): 305.

used two samples to obtain two sets of results. One sample included 185 privately owned and 189 government firms. The other sample included 90 privately owned and 75 government firms. The author concluded that the long-run average distribution cost "appears to be U-shaped rather than L-shaped with significance probability ≤0.015."[54] More important, the cost curve reached its minimum at the first 10 percent of the output range (i.e., the number of customers) in the sample. Beyond this limited range, diseconomies of scale characterized distribution. This suggests that large markets could probably accommodate more than one small distribution firm.

Huettner and Landon also supported the finding that long-run average distribution cost is U-shaped. Unlike the Weiss and Neuberg studies, Huettner and Landon used megawatt capacity of the utilities as the measure of output.[55] The authors analyzed the effects on average distribution costs of many variables including the use rate of total capacity, regional dummy variables, wage rate, consumption by various customer groups, and a variable indicating whether the utilities were holding companies. Their empirical results suggested the existence of scale economies in distribution within approximately the first 30 percent of the capacity range included in the sample. Diseconomies of scale characterized the remaining 70 percent, supporting the conclusion from other studies that large markets could possibly accommodate more than one distribution firm.

PROMOTING COMPETITION IN THE ELECTRIC POWER INDUSTRY

In the early days of the electric power industry, public policy was procompetitive, and nonexclusive competitive franchises were freely granted. Hardly a city did not grant several overlapping franchise rights. Wilcox observed that "competition was so thoroughly recognized at the beginning of the industry as proper and possible that in some cases general franchises were granted to all companies desiring to supply electric lights and power."[56] For example, in Chicago, at least forty-seven electric franchises were granted, of which twenty-seven "were granted by the city itself, though only a few of them covered the entire

54. Neuberg, "Two Issues in Municipal Ownership," p. 310.
55. Huettner and Landon, "Electric Utilities," pp. 895–97.
56. Delos Wilcox, *Municipal Franchises,* vol. I (New York: Gervaise Press, 1910), p. 142.

city."[57] In Buffalo, New York, the mayor vetoed a resolution granting an exclusive franchise to the Brush Electric Light Company in 1891. The mayor wanted the resolution to allow franchise rights to other companies that might thereafter apply for the same privilege. Noting that the modification "is desirable in order that there may be competition in the business, and, further, that the streets may not be overburdened with poles, since an arrangement can doubtless be made by which the various companies will use one set of poles."[58]

The procompetitive policy was not always successful. Consolidation and price fixing followed franchise proliferation. For example, in Chicago, consolidation resulted in one utility to supply the entire market by 1897.[59] In Buffalo the Brush Electric Light Company consolidated with the Thomson-Houston Electric Light and Power Company. In central New York the electric rates dropped 60 percent when a hydroelectric company was established to compete with established companies. The rate returned to its original level, however, when the companies reached an agreement to fix their prices.[60]

Reliance on market competition was abandoned in favor of regulated monopolies in the early 1900s. For example, in 1907, the National Civic Federation Commission reported:

> the public utilities studied are so constituted that it is impossible for them to be regulated by [market] competition. Therefore, they must be controlled and regulated by government . . . or they must be operated by the public. . . . None of us is in favor of leaving them to their own will, and the question is whether it is better to regulate or to operate. . . . Public utilities . . . are best conducted under a system of legalized and regulated monopoly.[61]

Regulation received more support than public ownership, and in the few years after Wisconsin and New York first adopted regulation in 1907, two-thirds of the states established commissions with regulatory powers. The new state commissions began by establishing policies against market competition.[62] For example, the New York Public Ser-

57. Wilcox, *Municipal Franchises,* p. 143.
58. Ibid.
59. Meeks, "Concentration in the Electric Power Industry," p. 200–01.
60. Ibid., pp. 184–88.
61. National Civic Federation Commission on Public Ownership and Operation, *Report on Municipal and Private Operation of Public Utilities* (New York: The Federation, 1907), vol. 1, p. 23.
62. Delos Wilcox, "Effects of State Regulation Upon the Municipal Ownership Movement," *American Academy Annals* (1914): 71.

vice Commission favored a merger between two otherwise competing electric utilities against strong objections of the state and city. The Commission stated:

A business which supplies . . . a public utility like . . . electric . . . power, is one in which free and full competition between two companies . . . cannot be expected to prevail permanently. It can doubtless be demonstrated . . . that better service and fair prices . . . be given by one corporation than by several.[63]

Politicians voiced similar feelings against competition in the industry. In a campaign speech at Portland, Oregon, in 1932, Franklin D. Roosevelt maintained:

We assume the soundness of the economic proposition that the lighting business is essentially noncompetitive in its nature. . . . Competitive public utilities of the same nature inevitably result in burdening the service and its customers with duplicate plants, the fixed charges of which more than offset such reductions in the rates as may result from competition.[64]

Recent concern about the electric power industry has emphasized interconnection, coordination, and pooling among self-contained power systems.[65] This policy grew in the 1960s as a result of a continuing and substantial increase in the demand required of isolated systems. Reliability became an important component of the policy because power failure in isolated systems could not at the time be met by drawing power from other systems. A Federal Power Commission (FPC) survey stressed that the benefits from interconnection and coordination "point up to the Nation's interest in encouraging every power generating system to look far beyond its own service areas in its planning of new capacity and of interconnections for capacity savings. . . . The nation can afford no less."[66] The survey, however, acknowledged the difficulties of achieving full coordination because competition "between segments of the industry [have] frequently resulted [in] . . . boundaries for utility system planning and operation."[67]

To achieve greater reliability and economy, Congress enacted the Federal Power Act of 1976, which directed the FPC to "promote and

63. Neuberg, "Two Issues," p. 23.
64. Richard Hellman, *Government Competition in the Electric Utility Industry: A Theoretical and Empirical Study* (New York: Praeger, 1972), p. 14.
65. See, for example, Federal Power Commission, *National Power Survey* (Washington, D.C.: U.S. Government Printing Office, 1964).
66. Ibid., p. 8.
67. Ibid., p. 5.

encourage . . . interconnection and coordination" on a voluntary basis.[68] The 1978 act, however, authorized the FPC to order interconnection and wheeling, a transmission service rendered by a utility to a former (or potential) customer for the power purchased by the customer from the utility's competitor. But the FPC's authority was severely limited because the act required that no mandatory wheeling disturb "existing competitive relationships."[69]

Proposals to Promote Competition

The literature on electric power is replete with proposals for regulatory reform. Some proposals call for substantial restructuring of the industry, while others suggest modest modifications. This section discusses both.

Complete restructuring of the industry was the focus of a study by Berlin et al., who contended that "it is particularly important that interutility competition for customer loads be promoted. . . . The desire to achieve efficient allocation of resources and to stimulate technological innovation demands no less."[70] They propose ending vertical integration by separating generation and transmission from distribution. Furthermore, they advocate adopting a regional-commission system of regulation to guarantee adequate electrical supplies. In the absence of such regional safeguards, the authors stress that state and federal regulation may not be adequate to inhibit "undue concentration and control" in the electric power industry.[71]

Weiss concludes in his work that vertical integration and combination utilities are two major barriers to competition in the electric industry. He suggests two alternative classes of modifications. The first class is to induce "maximum competition," but it would require a complete restructuring of the industry as follows:

(1) the separation of generation-transmission companies from distribution companies; (2) the dissolution of combination utilities; (3) the elimination of public and private territorial restrictions on sales to distributors or large industrial customers; (4) a general requirement of interconnection and

68. *Federal Power Act*, 16 U.S.C. §824a (Supp. IV 1980).

69. *Federal Power Act*, 16 U.S.C. §824j(c)(a) (Supp. IV 1980).

70. Edward Berlin, Charles Cicchetti, and William Gillen, "Restructuring the Electric Power Industry," in W. Shaker and S. Wilbert, eds., *Electric Power Reform: The Alternatives for Michigan* (Ann Arbor, Mich.: University of Michigan Press, 1976), p. 232.

71. Berlin, Cicchetti, Gillen, "Restructuring the Electric Power Industry," p. 233.

wheeling at reasonable charges; (5) the elimination of preferential access to federal power and preferential tax and capital-cost treatment for municipals and cooperatives; (6) the elimination of legal restrictions on entry into bulk power; and (7) the limitation of horizontal mergers among generation-transmission companies to cases where the partners are too small to negotiate effectively with other bulk-power producers of a region.[72]

Weiss believes such a thorough restructuring is probably neither practical nor politically possible in the foreseeable future. He offers a more modest set of modifications, which "may be more nearly attainable" to induce "modified competition."[73] This calls for

(1) the elimination of private and public territorial restrictions on sales for resale, and possibly private restrictions on sales to large industrial customers, as well; (2) a general requirement of interconnection and wheeling; (3) control of horizontal and vertical mergers; and (4) at least some divestiture of gas properties in connection with further mergers.[74]

A by-product would be "a further reduction in vertical integration because of the increased access of municipals and cooperatives to power at competitive prices and the increased competitive pressure on small utilities that are presently integrated."[75]

Both plans would still leave some room for regulation. For example, the supply of wheeling and wheeling charges would remain regulated. Weiss stressed that such regulation would be essential, although difficult administratively, because "the decreasing costs of transmission result in marginal costs that are below average costs. How effective regulation of these charges would be is not certain."[76]

These proposals do not adequately address the costs associated with: (a) wheeling requirements, (b) the limitations on vertical integration, and (c) the consequent reductions in the extent of interconnections and pooling arrangements. A requirement to wheel, for example, could affect the market position of some pool members: Cooperative members could become rivals, resulting in a breakdown of the existing pools and probably discouraging the formation of new pools. The dilemma is whether the gains from the new rivalry are worth the costs

72. Weiss, "Antitrust in the Electric Power Industry," pp. 169–170.
73. Ibid., p. 170.
74. Ibid.
75. Ibid.
76. Ibid., p. 172.

associated with breaking down the existing pools and inhibiting the formation of new ones.

Cohen addressed this dilemma explicitly:

> By coordinating the operation of two or more generating plants . . . utilities can produce power more efficiently than if each plant operates in isolation. The hard question is whether the need for coordination among generating plants precludes competition among utilities in the production and distribution of electricity.[77]

His solution was to organize regional bulk-power dispatching corporations, or RDCs. Each RDC would be directed "to acquire all of the high-voltage transmission capacity within its region, to lease generating plants from producers, and to dispatch electricity for resale to independent distribution companies."[78] Under this approach the RDCs would have the exclusive right to "dispatch bulk-power facilities, to transmit electricity at high voltage, and to sell bulk power at wholesale."[79]

This plan would leave the structure of distribution unchanged, and utilities at this stage would still be subject to rate regulation. Transmission would also be subject to rate regulation because each RDC would have a monopoly over the transmission network in its region. Presumably the scheme would improve efficiency because it would not only preserve the benefits of interconnection, coordination, and scale in generation but would also introduce competition at the generation level. Furthermore the vertical integration structure would be left intact to a large extent. The RDCs would control generation and transmission. The only component not subject to integration would be distribution.[80]

Meeks contends that "a moderate degree of competition is possible in the wholesale market."[81] He stresses though that achieving market

77. Joskow and Schmalensee, *Markets for Power*, p. 1513.
78. Ibid., p. 1539.
79. Ibid.
80. Notice, however, that Cohen's scheme (Cohen, "Efficiency and Competition") has drawbacks. First, the fact that it could take over a decade to construct generating units requires the RDCs to bid for generating capacity a decade or more before the new capacity is built. The unpredictability of production costs and the uncertainty of environmental regulation makes investment in the plants a high-risk undertaking. Furthermore no provision in the proposed plan would induce the RDCs to act efficiently. In fact the RDCs could have incentives to overinvest in transmission because capital costs would be included in the rate base. See Cohen (p. 1547) for a discussion of some problems with the scheme.
81. Meeks, "Concentration in the Electric Power Industry," p. 76.

competition could be at odds with realizing the benefits of large plant size. Meeks found the balance in (1) a careful application of the antitrust laws and (2) a provision that would treat "transmission facilities as common carriers . . . at least so long as there is unused capacity, to all potential 'shippers'."[82] Specifically,

> antitrust policy should be used as a guide in framing legal prohibitions of conducts and structures that result in a decrease in competitive possibilities or in an extension of monopoly power unless the conduct or structures are essential to achieve real economies of scale. Underlying this proposal is the view that regulatory and antitrust policies are not necessarily inconsistent, but may be used complementarily in order to eliminate the inadequacies of each.[83]

The common carrier scheme has its drawbacks. First, the unused transmission capacity can become highly indeterminate to wholesale customers. Abrupt changes in the load at various points could unpredictably change the unused capacity. Moreover the unused capacity may be planned for use as demand increases over time. Such capacity would not sustain continued reliance, therefore.

Finally Joskow and Schmalensee evaluated the cost effectiveness of four scenarios in a vertically integrated utility. The utility was assumed to be a member of a tight pool, interconnected with several utilities operating in three separate adjacent power pools. The first scenario calls for eliminating all price and entry regulations at all levels of the industry.[84] The market would determine the internal organization of the firms, the structure of the industry, and the level and structure of prices. The utility would be free to wheel power, join in power pools, or enter into various joint ventures; but it would remain subject to antitrust scrutiny.

The second scenario calls for deregulation of wholesale transactions "between utilities in areas where the federal government certifies that access to transmission, coordination, and power pooling is open to all . . . and that the wholesale market is workably competitive."[85] Regulation would continue in other areas. For example, retail rates would be regulated at the state level, and power pooling and

---

82. Meeks, "Concentration in the Electric Power Industry," p. 87.
83. Ibid., p. 76.
84. Joskow and Schmalensee, *Markets for Power*, p. 97.
85. Ibid., p. 98.

wheeling arrangements would remain subject to federal regulation. The only major change would be that the utility would be able to buy and sell wholesale power freely without regulation once the federal commission certified the region to be workably competitive.[86]

The authors expect no substantial changes in the structure of the industry as a result of the above two plans.[87] They anticipate that integrated utilities would continue to produce a significant amount of electric power. The major difference would be that the terms of contract for wholesale power supplies would be determined by negotiation rather than imposed by regulatory authorities.

The third scenario proposes a separation of distribution from generation and transmission components and, as in plan 2, calls for deregulation of wholesale power transactions. The distribution companies would be operated either as independent companies, with monopoly franchises subject to price regulation, or as municipal utilities. The generation and transmission components would be integrated under generation-transmission entities that would compete with other such entities to sell power to independent distribution systems.[88] Wholesale transactions would be determined through market negotiations, although charges for transmission and other coordination services would be regulated. Wheeling and interconnection would be subject to regulation and antitrust laws.

Finally the fourth scenario calls for complete vertical nonintegration of the utilities and, as in plans 2 and 3, proposes deregulation of wholesale power transactions. Each sector would be owned and operated by different entities. The ownership and operation of all transmission capacity would be transferred to "a regional power pooling and transmission entity, which could be a public corporation or a regulated private corporation."[89] The ownership of generating capacity would be reorganized to achieve all significant scale economies and market competition for bulk power supply. Transactions between independent distribution companies and independent generating entities would be free of regulation. The same would hold true for transactions between transmission-pooling entities and independent generating companies. Transactions between distribution companies and

---

86. Joskow and Schmalensee, *Markets for Power*, p. 100.
87. Ibid., p. 149.
88. Ibid., pp. 100–03.
89. Ibid., p. 104.

transmission-pooling entities, however, would be governed by regulation. Retail services would be provided by franchised monopolies, and retail rates would be subject to state regulation.[90]

The authors conclude that if deregulation of some type is to take place, it should adopt "a detailed long-run plan providing for a transition from scenario 2 to scenario 3 and ultimately to scenario 4."[91] A fundamental component of the scheme should be some pooling and coordination entity that would serve as an intermediary between generating companies and distributing companies. While the exact characteristics of such an entity could vary, they maintain that

> its existence is critical for achieving the efficiencies associated with economic dispatch, monitoring power flows over the transmission system, eliminating potential externality problems associated with system expansion, aggregating demand profiles of individual utilities, and other systemwide functions. Such a pooling organization could conceivably be largely a clearinghouse for consummating short-run and long-run contractual relationships, much like a stock or commodity exchange.[92]

Joskow's and Schmalensee's transmission-pooling entity appears to function much like Cohen's RDCs. Both schemes seem to preserve scale and coordination properties while enhancing competition in the wholesale market. The pooling entity would have incentives to make arrangements with the generating companies to obtain scale economies. Furthermore having control over transmission facilities, the pooling entity would have incentives to allocate load to the utilities with the lowest operating and capital costs.

EFFECTS OF INTERFIRM COMPETITION

Any systematic and accurate evaluation of the effects of interfirm competition on economic efficiency in the industry is difficult. By their nature, such evaluations have to be speculative because the available data only reflect the effects of the existing regulatory framework. Data from nonregulated utilities is necessary for an accurate examination of the effects of deregulation.

The effects of interfirm competition, however, is expected to depend on the specific characteristics of the proposed deregulation plan.

90. Joskow and Schmalensee, *Markets for Power*, pp. 104–5.
91. Ibid., p. 208.
92. Ibid., p. 114.

Thus different plans would probably result in different competitive effects. This section uses Joskow's and Schmalensee's deregulation scenarios and attempts to speculate as to their economic effects. This is a useful approach because their four scenarios generally incorporate the plans of other commentators as well.

Recall that scenario 1 proposes complete deregulation of the industry. All price and entry regulations would be eliminated at all levels, whereas at present regulators attempt to reach the average-cost-pricing outcome, where price equals average cost, and profits are normal. Would competition prevail under such altered conditions? Presently integrated utilities have monopoly control in retail markets. For competition to prevail in the short run would require de novo entry at the retail level as well as access to transmission facilities and generation capacity.

Competitive entry, of course, would be a long-run phenomenon. First, the established firms would have no incentive to allow competitors access to transmission facilities. Second, the lead time required to construct generation and transmission facilities would be too long to be conducive to competition in the short run. Furthermore multiple transmission grids and distribution capacity would likely lead to costly duplication.

In the long run, however, potentials for competition look more promising. First, established utilities may become takeover targets because past investment patterns induced by regulation would signal inefficiency to outside inventors. Relatedly the inefficiency may also signal opportunities for profitable entry. The experience of the airline industry under deregulation could indicate possible developments. Furthermore established utilities might resort to the entry limit pricing strategy to deter entry. While prices under such a regime might not reflect marginal cost, they would be closer to marginal cost than monopoly prices would. Additionally scenario 1 is expected to enhance intermodal competition. For example, gas appliances would become more popular, coal burners would become more appealing, and so on. Finally alternative sources of energy, such as solar and wind power, would receive investment boosts.

Scenario 2 allows competition in the wholesale market in areas where competition is considered feasible by the Federal Energy Regulatory Commission, the FERC. Scenario 2 promises a few efficiency gains. First, market prices, rather than regulated prices, would direct production in the wholesale market. Relatedly market prices would control power transfers between utilities. Furthermore market prices would be expected to induce efficient investment patterns in generation and transmission.

Scenario 3 is the same as scenario 2 except for proposing the separation of the distribution component from fully integrated utilities. The generating and transmitting components would remain integrated and subject to federal jurisdiction. The independent distributing companies would be regulated by state commissions or else be publicly owned. Wheeling, pooling, and other transmission activities would be regulated by the FERC. Transmission and pooling facilities would by requirement be made available to all buyers and sellers of power. Furthermore wholesale power transactions would be deregulated only in areas where the FERC considers competition to be feasible.

The benefits attributed to scenario 3 are similar to those of scenario 2. Being regulated, however, the distributing companies would lack incentive to shop for the cheapest source of power. This factor could mitigate the overall competitive effects of deregulation in the wholesale market.

Scenario 4 calls for a complete vertical disintegration of the industry and deregulation of wholesale power transactions. A regulated transmission-pooling firm in each area would own and operate transmission facilities. The transmission-pooling firm would purchase power from the generating plants and resell it to the distributing companies, or the firm would sell transmission, pooling, and coordinating services.

This scenario has a few advantages. First, it would avoid conflicts between pooling and competition, as in Cohen's RDCs. Generating companies would compete to sell power to the transmission-pooling company, which in turn could design its purchasing pattern to minimize production and thus purchasing costs. Second, the transmission-pooling company could compete with selected generating plants to sell power—received from other generating plants—to the distributing companies.

Scenario 4 is not, however, without problems. First, the fact that it calls for regulation of the transmission-pooling company presumes that the free market would not find a way to retain the gains from pooling through contractual arrangements. This presumption could be baseless. Second, as a regulated entity, the transmission-pooling company could overinvest or underinvest in transmission facilities, depending on the allowed rate of return. Third, the transmission-pooling company would obtain "tremendous market power vis-à-vis both generating entities and distribution entities," which could lead to opportunistic behavior.[93] To avoid such behavior, the FERC would probably have to make and enforce detailed and complex long-term contracts. Fourth, investment plans for the generation, transmission, and distribution components would have to be closely coordinated years in advance. Fifth, since profitability of each component would depend on the behavior of the other two components, investment risks would be higher than those under full integration. Finally the problems at the distribution level would be similar to those under scenario 3. Weighing the benefits and costs should allow economists to determine the cost effectiveness of this scenario.

SUMMARY

This chapter addressed two fundamental issues regarding competition in the electric power industry. The first is the conventional understanding that finding constant returns to scale or decreasing returns to scale in generation implies the viability of competition in the industry. The assumptions this conclusion has been based on generally refer to conditions atypical of the electric power industry in the United States. For example, past research has often assumed self-contained utilities that produced a single product. Accordingly the conclusion that restructuring would effect efficiency and competition has been drawn without considering the effects of economies of scope or the attributes of vertical integration. The analysis in this chapter questions the general applicability of such conclusions.

Relatedly another major shortcoming of past research has been the general inadequacy of the data and misinterpretation of the empirical results. The available data represent vertically integrated and horizontally coordinated utilities. Such data, however, has been used as if it reflected the behavior of self-contained and vertically disintegrated utilities. Further research must evaluate the effects of vertical integration, coordination, and power pooling on the efficiency and cost of generation, transmission, and distribution.

It is important to note that the industry faces potentially conflicting goals. The gains from vertical integration, coordination, and pooling

---

93. Joskow and Schmalensee, *Markets for Power*, p. 174.

may have to be sacrificed in order to enhance competition. More crucial, however, is the fact that the present regulatory framework is inefficient as it has lessened competition and led to poor resource allocation. Future research needs to seriously consider competitive entry as a long-run phenomenon. The work by Cohen and that by Joskow and Schmalensee are promising and deserve careful attention.

3

TAX POLICY AND PUBLIC UTILITY REGULATION

*Milton Z. Kafoglis**

Public utilities make substantial tax payments to all levels of government. They are assessed the entire array of taxes that apply to business in general, pay special taxes because they are unique enterprises, and are collection agents for a variety of consumer excise taxes levied once more by all levels of government. Utility taxation is also an instrument for implementing local industrial development policies, environmental programs, and national energy and investment policies.

Because public utilities are regulated monopolies, more or less insulated from direct competition, the incidence and economic effects of utility taxes have not received serious attention. Instead attention in this area has been focused on the details of tax administration—especially the complexities of property-tax administration—and revenue yields. In short economists view utility taxation as a special problem in state and local finance. The major concern regarding the impact taxation has on efficient resource use has been the distortion created by the favored tax status of publicly owned utilities as a part of the larger private-public power controversy.

Interest in the economic effects of utility taxation has heightened in recent years with the introduction of tax incentives—accelerated

*The author wishes to thank Richard F. Muth for useful insights and Phyllis Chaney for handling the manuscript.

depreciation and investment tax credits—in the structure of the corporate income tax. Since these tax incentives were designed to stimulate investment (by increasing the return to capital assets), a conflict has developed between federal tax policy and state regulatory policy, which seeks to implement its statutory and court-directed mandate to maintain profits at a level appropriate for attracting the capital needed to serve the public. The energy crisis, federal regulation of oil and gas prices, and the imposition of federal taxes on the end use of fuels have added still another national policy dimension that must be implemented through independent state regulatory commissions. These changes in federal tax policy have aggravated the already existing conflict between federal and state regulatory policies involving jurisdictional questions about interstate commerce and the allocation of regulatory functions between state and federal agencies.

This chapter attempts to assess utility taxation within this complex and changing policy environment. The emphasis is on utility taxation as it affects the efficiency and equity of utility rate structures, the level and mix of consumption and investment, and intergovernmental tax and regulatory relationships.

THE LEVEL OF TAXES IN THE UTILITY SECTOR

Direct tax payments by business corporations account for about 30 percent of total tax revenues of all levels of government in the United States. In 1980 these business tax payments amounted to $268 billion with the public-utility sector—transportation, communications, electricity and gas—remitting $35 billion or about 13 percent of all direct business tax payments. (See Tables 3–1 and 3–2.) In addition utility

Table 3–1. Direct Tax Payments by the Corporate Sector, 1960–1980 (dollars in millions).

Year	Corporate Sector	Public Utility Sector	Transport	Communications	Electricity
1960	$ 42,996	$ 7,841	$ 2,226	$2,372	$ 3,243
1970	82,816	13,207	3,430	4,457	5,320
1980	268,145	34,893	10,084	9,821	14,988

SOURCE: Internal Revenue Service, *Statistics of Income: Corporate Income Tax Payments,* 1960, 1970, and 1980.

Table 3–2.   Percent of Corporate Sector Taxes Paid.

Year	Public Utility Sector	Percent of Sector Total			
		Total	Transport	Communications	Electricity
1960	18.2	100.0	28.4	30.3	41.3
1970	15.9	100.0	26.0	33.7	40.3
1980	13.0	100.0	28.9	28.1	43.0

SOURCE: Internal Revenue Service, *Statistics of Income: Corporate Income Tax Payments,* 1960, 1970, and 1980.

firms collected about $10 billion in consumer excise taxes levied on utility bills.[1] These figures do not include taxes paid by the unincorporated utility sector or the profits of municipally owned utilities, which frequently substitute for property taxes. A conservative estimate of tax revenues raised annually through the utility sector would be in the neighborhood of $55 billion. (This estimate does not include special taxes on fuel uses and a variety of miscellaneous taxes not separately classified in Census and Internal Revenue Service publications.)

In 1980 direct business taxes absorbed 6.6 percent of utility sector operating revenues (14 percent of electric utility revenue) compared to 4.2 percent for the entire corporate sector, a comparison frequently made by the industry to support its view that utilities are overtaxed (Table 3–3). The current level of utility taxation, however, is modest by historical standards. In 1946, for example, taxes accounted for over 20 percent of electric operating revenues.[2] Table 3–2 also shows that the share of total business taxes paid by the utility sector has declined from 18.2 percent in 1960 to 13.0 percent in 1980 despite the fact that the utility sector has grown at virtually the same rate as the economy as a whole.

The electric utility share of total direct business tax payments has declined from 7.5 percent in 1960 to 5.6 percent in 1980; there has been no significant shift in tax shares within the public utility sector. The decline in the relative levels of utility sector taxation is due almost entirely to federal corporate income tax incentives, which pro-

1. U.S. Bureau of the Census, Governments Division, *Governmental Finances in 1980–81,* series GF (Washington, D.C., April 1983).

2. Edison Electric Institute, *Statistical Bulletin* (July 1947): 35.

Table 3–3. Direct Taxes Paid by Corporate Sector, 1960–1980 (dollars in billions).

	1960		1970		1980	
	All Industries	Public Utility Sector	All Industries	Public Utility Sector	All Industries	Public Utility Sector
Taxes paid	$ 43.0	$ 7.8	$ 82.8	$ 13.2	$ 268.1	$ 34.9
Gross revenue	849.1	65.9	1,750.8	135.5	6,361.3	523.8
Gross national product	506.5	45.8	992.7	85.6	2,631.7	233.9
Taxes paid as percent of gross revenues	5.1%	11.8%	4.7%	9.7%	4.2%	6.6%
Percent of GNP	8.5%	17.0%	8.3%	15.4%	10.2%	14.9%

SOURCE: Internal Revenue Service, *Statistics of Income: Corporate Tax Returns*, 1960, 1970, and 1980.

100

vide differential tax advantages to capital-intensive industries. Indeed federal tax incentives have led to vastly increased reserves that seem to exceed the investment requirements of many utilities.[3]

Notwithstanding the recent decline in relative tax burden, conventional (and crude) measures of relative tax burden can support the view that the public utility sector is overtaxed. The differential impact of taxation is sometimes evaluated in terms of value added or contribution to gross national product. The comparisons in Table 3–3 reveal that by this measure the differential tax treatment of utilities has been reduced but not eliminated.

The aggregate interindustry tax differentials shown in Table 3–3 reflect the combined influence of many factors—the mix of taxes and tax rates, differences in capital-labor ratios, regional differences, and many others. Though these traditional measures of interindustry tax differentials do not necessarily imply tax-induced inefficiency or lack of neutrality, they certainly prompt more inquiry than they have so far received.

Key tax trends from 1972 to 1981 in the electric utility industry are shown in Table 3–4. State and local taxes account for about four-fifths of the taxes paid by electric utilities and have grown more rapidly than corporate income taxes. Inclusion of consumer excise taxes (Table 3–4 includes only direct business tax payments) would increase the state and local proportion. Though the property tax utilities pay continues to weigh heavily in the state and local tax picture, it now ranks behind gross receipts, sales, and other state and local levies on utility revenues.[4]

In addition to the property tax and a wondrous variety of sales taxes, utilities pay state and local franchise taxes, stock and bond taxes, pole taxes, and mileage taxes. State and local governments have a disproportionate fondness for the utility revenue base, and their coffers have been major beneficiaries of the escalating utility bills that followed the energy crisis.[5] The use of ad valorem rather than unit

---

3. The proposed "Phantom Tax Reform and Least-Cost Electric Energy Planning Act" (HR 4923) would give state commissions the discretion to convert these reserves into lower utility rates provided the state commission has established a "least-cost" investment strategy.

4. Donald J. Reeb, Howard Shapiro, and Louis R. Tomson, "State and Local Taxes and Electric Utilities," *Public Utilities Fortnightly* 17 (August 1982): 29–37.

5. In New York State, revenues derived from sales and consumer excise taxation of utility services increased at twice the rate of total state and local revenue during the period 1972–1980. Reeb, Shapiro, and Tomson, "State and Local Taxes," p. 31.

Table 3–4.   Taxes Paid by Electric Utilities, 1972–1981 (dollars in millions).

					Percent	
Year	Total	Federal Income Tax	State and Local[a]	Total	Federal Income Tax	State and Local
1972	$4,172.3	$ 974.3	$3,198.0	100.0	23.9	76.1
1973	4,257.1	884.1	3,373.0	100.0	20.8	79.2
1974	4,340.2	554.0	3,786.2	100.0	12.8	87.2
1975	5,140.1	810.1	4,330.0	100.0	15.8	84.2
1976	5,469.9	628.7	4,841.2	100.0	11.5	88.5
1977	6,174.7	789.6	5,385.1	100.0	12.8	87.2
1978	6,844.7	1044.3	5,800.4	100.0	15.3	84.7
1979	6,864.8	743.5	6,121.3	100.0	10.8	89.2
1980	8,039.9	1214.1	6,825.8	100.0	15.1	84.9
1981	9,455.4	1737.8	7,717.6	100.0	18.4	81.6

SOURCE: Federal Energy Regulatory Commission, *Statistics of Privately Owned Electric Utilities, 1981*, Table 3.

[a]Includes payroll and state income taxes; does not include consumer excise taxes.

taxes (as in gasoline and cigarettes) has provided a tax windfall that merits the attention of those who believe that equity requires utility-rate relief for small users, the poor, and the elderly.[6] There are, however, wide state and local variations. The state and local governments of New York, for example, garner 15.2 percent of utility operating revenues, followed closely by other states in the Northeast. In addition to the local property tax, state and local governments in New York each impose their own gross receipts and sales taxes—all in all four separate taxes based on revenues. California, on the other hand, collects only 3 percent of electric utility operating revenues.[7]

The issues raised by this brief description of utility taxation relate to (a) the rationale for utility taxation, (b) the economic effects of such taxation, and (c) the distributive justice of employing the utility-rate structure as a means of raising revenue.

6. Public utility excise taxes are regressive to income. Studies of taxation in Ohio revealed that only cigarette taxes are more regressive to income than public utility excises. See John H. Bowman, "Changes in Sales Tax Regressivity Over Time," *Revenue Administration*, 1979 (Washington, D.C.: Federation of Tax Administrators, undated), p. 234.

7. Reeb, Shapiro, and Tomson, "State and Local Taxes," p. 34.

THE RATIONALE FOR UTILITY TAXATION

Utilities are a highly visible focal point representing vast revenues and tangible wealth. Taxes at low rates can yield large and stable flows of revenue at almost no administrative and enforcement costs. The imperatives of raising revenue, therefore, are the dominant explanation for the layer of special taxes levied by state and local governments. This has not always been the case, however.

Current policies for utility taxation contrast sharply with those that prevailed during the period immediately before and after the Civil War. The eagerness of the public to obtain utility services then led to grants and subsidies that were frequently more generous than wise, first to the transportation industries and later to the electric utilities. Traditionalist economic historians frequently credit these subsidies with "opening up the West" and providing a take off for a new era of prosperity, an interpretation that has been questioned in recent years and that was in fact controversial at the time.[8]

Taxation of utilities followed the failure of municipal regulation and the agrarian discontent during the latter part of the nineteenth century as a policy of neutrality in taxation gradually evolved. During the thirties, however, neutral tax treatment gave way to special taxation, a policy that remains in place and reached a peak during World War II. Writing in 1950, Eli Clemens noted that the discovery of the utility as a tax collector was an accident, but the revenue potential assured that utilities would continue as tax collectors for a "good long time."[9] Notwithstanding the fact that utilities are frequently (and realistically) viewed as tax-collecting agencies, from time-to-time, economic analysis has been brought to bear on this subject.

Tax Exemption

One can make a persuasive economic argument for exempting the regulated natural-monopoly sector from taxation. Taxation of industries characterized by declining average costs restricts consumption, inhibits assimilation of the available economies of scale, and en-

---

8. Stanley Engerman, "Some Economic Issues Relating to Railroad Subsidies and Evaluation of Land Grants," *Journal of Economic History* 52, no. 2 (June 1972): 102–16.

9. Eli W. Clemens, *Economics and Public Utilities* (New York: Appleton-Century, 1950), pp. 526–27.

courages excess capacity in both the short and long run. Since economic efficiency in decreasing cost situations requires marginal cost prices (coupled, perhaps, with public subsidy), taxation of public utilities at either the firm or the consumer level would seem to be an inefficient policy prescription. As a matter of fact inframarginal or nonlinear pricing developed by the utilities themselves has helped to overcome the economic inefficiency inherent in the taxation of industries that have strong economies of scale.

The incidence of taxes imposed on a utility-rate structure (even one that conforms to the inverse-elasticity rule) has no clear relationship to tax efficiency criteria for financing public goods, and it violates widely accepted notions of tax justice. Moreover since such taxes are included in the utility-rate structure, their incidence will vary with the design of that structure, which is, in the main, a managerial prerogative constrained only by rate-of-return regulation. The level of the tax may not be hidden, but its distribution among taxpayers is anybody's guess.

One can also reason that tax exemption will not generate excessive distortion in the allocation of resources. Since the cross-elasticities between the regulated and nonregulated sectors are probably low and since the demands for regulated services are less elastic, one would not anticipate significant resource misallocations. The main effects of tax exemption would be income effects that might be desirable from a distributional point of view.

Finally tax policy in regulated industries may conflict with regulatory policies implemented by independent commissions. Shifting taxes in the regulatory process may not be consistent with tax shifting in the unregulated sector, where market forces determine prices, and firms react to unrestrained profits. A related argument sometimes made for tax exemption, especially in the electric utility field, is that taxation of investor-owned utilities aggravates the distortions that might be created by the tax-exempt status of publicly owned utilities.

Uniform Taxation

The conventional criterion for interindustry taxation is neutrality in the sense that tax-induced distortions are minimized. However, taxation that attempts to recognize the "special" circumstances that characterize each industry (which would be needed to minimize economic distortion) would put tax policy out to sea without a rudder. In practice the neutrality criterion translates into uniform taxation. Implementation of uniform taxation would remove the overlay of special taxes that apply to utilities (as well as to a number of other industries) and impose in-lieu taxes on the publicly owned utility sector.

A committee of the National Taxation Association reviewed these issues many years ago, concluding that, though the weight of the theoretical arguments inclined toward tax concessions, the "counsel of wisdom" is to adopt a policy of equality.[10] This continues to be the policy stance of utility economists and tax analysts who maintain that utilities should be treated as if they were competitive. The energy crisis encouraged a break with the uniform taxation tradition, however, and recent special federal tax incentives suggest a return to special treatment. The separate or independent treatment of tax and regulatory policies seems increasingly strained and inappropriate.

Taxation as Regulation

We can look at taxation as an alternative to regulation. Indeed the failure of municipal regulation in the late 1800s was a major reason for instituting utility taxation. Since utilities have monopoly power that may be ineffectively controlled, special-purpose utility taxation can be justified as a recapture of monopoly profits. Crudely put, if the consumer is to pay a monopoly price in any case, steep taxation—especially corporate income taxation—would provide a means for recapturing the monopoly profits.

Economic theorists have considered the possibility of substituting taxation for regulation. A theoretical but impractical version of this recapture approach was informally set forth by E. A. G. Robinson.[11] This required the lump-sum taxation of utility profits coupled with a per-unit output subsidy equal to the difference between average and marginal cost at the competitive output to encourage optimal output expansion. This model does not come to terms with the problems of inefficient production or waste that might reduce lump-sum tax or profits to a level insufficient to finance the optimal subsidy. Though

---

10. Clemens, *Economics and Public Utilities,* p. 544.

11. The scheme was later described by Joan Robinson, *Economics of Imperfect Competition* (London: Macmillan & Co., 1961), pp. 163–65. A more recent treatment is in William J. Baumol, *Welfare Economics and the Theory of the State* (Cambridge: Harvard University Press, 1965) pp. 108–11. Baumol describes other plans for controlling monopoly, but these do not involve taxation.

it would provide an incentive to expand production beyond the monopoly level, it does not insure that costs will be minimized.

Another version suggested by Williamson's expense-preference model assumes that profits are effectively controlled by the regulatory commission, but that costs escape scrutiny. In this case management has an incentive to wastefully expand staff, emoluments, and fringes and to generate X-inefficiencies.[12] Firms then become ordinary profit (or revenue) maximizers with a great deal of slack at their disposal, while price and output remain at the monopoly level. If wasteful costs absorb the full amount of slack, additional taxation at that level of cost and output would require the management to reduce waste. Imposition of the tax would presumably convert managerial waste into more productive tax revenues. This would not eliminate the deadweight loss or reduce prices, but it would provide tax revenue while generating real resource savings. Under such extreme assumptions, one can make a similar argument for deregulation, a policy that would convert the waste generated in the existing regulatory system into profits that might be channeled into more efficient uses in other sectors of the economy.

Recent theoretical treatments of rate-base regulation have demonstrated that managerial waste reduces the rate base by which allowable profits are measured and that such waste would not characterize a constrained profit-maximizing firm.[13] The firm can more profitably use resources devoted to waste, gold-plating or rate-base padding to expand output and capital usage. The price of attaining managerial efficiency is to permit a return that exceeds the cost of capital in order to provide a profit incentive.

Utility taxation has also been related to regulatory lag. Continuous or automatic regulatory response to rising costs removes a major managerial incentive to keep costs down, and it also reduces tendencies toward the use of redundant capital and distorted capital-labor ratios. On the other hand excessive regulatory lag leads to rates that are increasingly inappropriate to current costs. During inflationary periods regulatory lag leads to erosion of earnings and deterioration in the

12. Oliver Williamson, *The Economics of Discretionary Behavior,* (Englewood Cliffs, N.J.: Prentice-Hall, 1964).

13. Elizabeth E. Bailey, *Economic Theory of Regulatory Constraint* (Lexington, Mass.: Lexington Books, 1973), pp. 23–39.

quality of service. But then, if real costs are falling, regulatory lag may prevent rate reductions and perpetuate excessive earnings.

During the 1930s, when consumers were denied prompt rate relief, the government used taxation to counteract excessive regulatory lag. During World War II, the failure of the Michigan State Commission to order rate reductions prompted the city of Detroit to levy a 20 percent gross-receipts tax on the city's public utility. The commission responded to the tax pressure by ordering rate reductions.[14] A number of state legislators sought to tax the "excess" profits adduced to lethargic regulation by instituting special utility taxes during this period, many of which remain in force today. In Hawaii, for example, counties impose a local gross-receipts tax that is triggered when utility earnings climb above a certain level. Thus the counties share in excessive earnings. This provides a type of local tax regulation that establishes limits within which conventional rate regulation can function.[15]

Energy and Taxes

The energy crisis of the seventies, which brought higher utility rates and tax revenues (on a growing gross-revenue base), has dampened any state and local government tendencies to raise tax rates or impose new utility taxes. On the other hand it has focused attention on the relationship between tax policy and the efficient use of energy resources. The National Energy Policy Act sought to conserve energy, keep utility bills low, and, at the same time, reallocate scarce fuel supplies to their most efficient uses via nonprice devices. To keep gasoline "cheap" at the pump, policy imposed end-use taxes on oil and gas used by electric utilities in order to encourage a shift to lower-cost coal. The Public Utility Regulatory Policies Act was passed to encourage energy savings through the redesign of what can only be described as output-maximizing rate structures. Thus a new layer of federal taxes, rationalized on energy efficiency grounds, was grafted onto the state and local system of sales, gross receipts, and excise taxes.

14. Clemens, *Economics and Public Utilities,* p. 540.

15. John H. Bowman and Michael Pratt, "Selective Excise Taxation as a Means of Local Revenue Diversification" (Paper Presented at the Sixteenth Annual Conference of the National Tax Association, Washington, D.C., October 1983), p. 10.

The effort to encourage a shift from oil to coal created a direct conflict between energy and environmental policy. To the extent that this effort succeeded, however, the increase in demand for coal opened the door for increased railroad rates on coal and increased state severance taxation leading to an expanded conflict involving, among others, the Department of Energy, the Environmental Protection Agency, the Interstate Commerce Commission, the Internal Revenue Service, and state regulatory commissions.

Whether efficient or not, the federal taxation of specific fuel inputs had little effect. Rapidly rising fuel costs led to the widespread adoption of fuel adjustment clauses that permitted the prompt pass through of rising energy costs. A major incentive to shift to more economical fuels in response to end-use taxes was thus dampened because the regulatory lag penalty was removed. More important, perhaps, was the geometric increase in policy and intergovernmental conflicts.

Models of Utility Taxation

Taxation in the public utility sector has become much more complex. The analytical techniques for assessing the impact of this complex tax structure on the efficiency of resource allocation and distribution are poorly developed and often predict outcomes inconsistent with the facts. Our approach, therefore, is eclectic, emphasizing the interaction between tax theory, the regulatory process, and the behavior of the constrained natural monopoly. A loose interpretation of the regulatory process suggests that commissions seek to mimic as-if competitive outcomes. Though highly developed, the theory of competitive tax shifting is only of limited use because the regulated firm is in fact monopolistic and can design rate structures that take into account the spread between price and marginal revenue. But then the pure theory of natural monopoly, which does take these rate-making possibilities into account, is also limited because tax shifting under monopoly occurs through the impact of taxes on profits. Yet profits are regulated. Only in the presence of regulatory lag do the standard predictions of economic theory have much to offer.

Economists use two special-purpose models—the Averch-Johnson (A-J) model of the profit-maximizing regulated firm and the more practical revenue-requirements model—to predict outcomes under utility taxation. These models do not yield consistent conclusions, and this discussion makes an effort to reconcile these differences.

TAXES IN THE AVERCH-JOHNSON MODEL

Economists frequently examine the behavior of the regulated firm in terms of the A-J model.[16] This section briefly summarizes the essential features of the model and then examines the impact various taxes have on output level and production efficiency. The model assumes that the firm sells its output to a single class of consumers and maximizes profits subject to a rate-of-return profit ceiling, established by the regulatory commission. The allowable rate of return is assumed to exceed the market cost of capital providing a premium to capital. The profit function is:

$\Pi = P(Q)Q - wL - rK$, where

$P(Q)$ is the demand function

K and L are factors of production with respective factor

prices r and w

The profit function is maximized subject to the constraints:

$$P(Q)Q - wL/K' < s; \qquad s > r$$

where s, the allowable rate of return, exceeds the cost of capital, r. For our purposes it is convenient to specify the constraint in terms of the relationship between the cost of capital and the allowable rate of return. Multiplying both sides of the profit constraint by K and deducting the total cost of capital, rK, from both sides yields:

$$P(Q) - wL - rK' < (s - r)K$$

This formulation emphasizes that, for given demand and cost conditions, the equilibrium of the firm under regulatory constraint is determined by the difference between the allowable rate of return and the cost of capital $(s - r)$. This means that the cost of capital by itself does not determine the level of output, capital usage, or factor combinations. When the constraint is tightened by reducing the allowable rate of return, $(s - r)$ decreases. This reduction in the premium to capital leads to more, not less, capital usage and output. If the allowable return is reduced or if cost of capital rises, one would expect

16. Harvey Averch and Leland Johnson, "Behavior of the Firm Under Regulatory Constraint," *American Economic Review* 52 (December 1962): 1053–69.

less capital usage. This would only reduce total profits, $(s - r)K$, however. When the constraint is tightened, profits, capital usage, and output can be increased by using more capital to expand output and substitute for labor. The reverse, of course, occurs when the restraint is loosened.

Other key characteristics of the A-J equilibrium are:[17]

1. The firm hires noncapital factors, L (labor, fuel, and so on) up to the point that their marginal revenue products equal their prices.
2. The firm uses capital beyond the point where its marginal revenue product is equal to the cost of capital. The firm, therefore, employs an excess of capital relative to labor at any given level of output.
3. Since the marginal revenue product of capital is less than the cost of capital, output necessarily is expanded to a point that marginal cost of output exceeds marginal revenue ($MC > MR$).
4. Marginal revenue must be positive. The firm, therefore, must operate in the elastic portion of its demand curve where $MR > 0$.

In essence the firm maximizes profits in the presence of the regulatory constraint by (a) expanding output beyond the monopoly level and (b) inefficiently substituting capital for labor at the selected level of output.

The Corporation Income Tax

The corporate income tax does not affect either the cost of capital or the allowable rate of return. Imposition of an income tax merely reduces the firm's profit function by a fixed percentage. This is illustrated in Figure 3–1 where profits before tax are shown as Π, and after tax profits, as $(1 - t)\Pi$, where t is a flat tax rate on net income. The constraint, $(s - r)K$ is not affected. Before the tax is imposed, the firm uses K capital along with the associated labor and output.

The immediate effect of the tax is to reduce profits to level T, leading the firm to reduce capital usage to K_t with a consequent re-

---

17. For a detailed treatment of these conditions, see Bailey, *Economic Theory*, pp. 65–86.

Figure 3–1.   Corporation Income Tax.

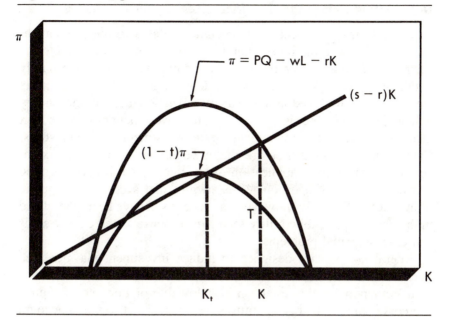

duction in output and a higher price. Since the A-J model specifies that the firm must operate in the elastic portion of its demand curve, total revenue declines. The reduced level of output continues to be produced with an excessive amount of capital relative to labor.[18] In the case of a competitive industry, a similar adjustment would be made via exit of marginal firms until the after-tax return to capital was again equated to the cost of capital. Since the regulated firm does not produce its output at least cost, and since it earns a premium on capital, the output response is theoretically smaller than in the case of a competitive industry. On the other hand it would be greater than the response of a profit-maximizing monopolist.[19] The major issues surrounding the corporate income tax center on the accounting treatment of depreciation and corporate income tax incentives.

18. Figures 3–1 and 3–2 are from Bailey, *Economic Theory*.
19. For a detailed analysis of the regulated firm's factor demand elasticities, see Robert M. Spann, "Taxation and Electric Utility Regulation and the Efficient Allocation of Resources," in C. J. Cicchetti and J. L. Jurewitz, eds., *Studies in Electric Utility Regulation* (Cambridge, Mass.: Ballinger Publishing Company, 1978), pp. 171–213.

Depreciation Policy and Tax Incentives

Historically the treatment of depreciation related to the problem of matching depreciation to the economic life of capital assets and to the adequacy of reserves to replace existing equipment. These are purely regulatory issues. When accelerated depreciation and investment tax credits were introduced as instruments of national fiscal and energy policies, tax policy became an issue. The government has applied tax incentives designed to induce aggregate investment to all industries. Capital-intensive industries are major beneficiaries of these tax incentives, and uniform application of tax rates and rules seem biased in view of the disproportionate tax savings that accrue to the public utility sector. Recently, however, tax incentives have been liberalized in the case of the public utility sector in response to the energy crisis and environmental problems.

Federal tax policies designed to induce investment via increased rates of return to capital can and frequently do conflict with state regulatory policies that establish an allowable or fair rate of return. Moreover, the regulatory commission presumably takes into account the investment and capacity requirements of regulated firms. Since national and state perceptions of investment needs may diverge, theorists pay considerable attention to ways of coordinating policy and to evaluations of the actual impact of federal tax incentives on investment decisions. Such evaluations are complicated by the fact that tax incentives operate differently in the regulated industries because the regulated firm reacts to the spread between the allowable rate of return and the cost of capital rather than to the gross return to capital.

In the absence of taxation, alternative depreciation policies do not affect the rate of return or discounted cash flow of unregulated firms.[20] For regulated firms, however, depreciation affects the rate base used to measure allowable profits. Rapid depreciation for the regulated firm means that the premium to capital ($s - r$) is earned for a shorter number of years. Alternatively the increased current cash flow due to more rapid depreciation can earn only r for stockholders in the nonregulated sector, whereas it earns s in the rate base. The regulated firm shuns reductions in book values. Thus utilities have been reluc-

---

20. Ezra Solomon, "Alternative Rate of Return Concepts and Their Implications for Utility Regulation," *Bell Journal of Economics and Management Science* 1, no. 11 (Spring 1970): 70–71.

tant to employ rapid depreciation even in the presence of substantial tax incentives.[21]

The conventional view then is that utilities have no reason to prefer accelerated depreciation even for tax purposes. Spann, however, argues that the lower price made possible by taking the tax savings stimulates output, which increases capital usage and the rate base. Since the A-J model requires that demand be elastic, price reductions must lead to an increase in both output and total revenue. The conventional view does not consider this response, supposing that tax savings will not influence anything other than consumers' tax bills. Predictions about the impact of tax incentives are very sensitive to assumptions about the elasticity of demand. Regardless of the output response, however, both the utility and its customers are better off (and the U.S. Treasury worse off) if tax incentives are used. The practical problem confronting regulatory commissions is one of developing a sharing scheme that does not violate the fair-return criterion.

Regulatory commissions have used two methods for distributing the tax savings due to accelerated depreciation for tax purposes. Under flow-through, the utility's reduced income tax bill is passed directly on to consumers via reductions in the rate level, but the utility is required to use straight-line depreciation for rate-making purposes. This prevents rapid depreciation of the utility's rate base, but it does not improve cash flow and provides no reserve for the payment of higher future taxes. Thus one can argue that future consumers will subsidize current consumption. The gain to the firm, if any, must come through the net output effects of lower prices today coupled with higher prices tomorrow. In present-value terms, these output effects are positive. The position of the utilities, however, is to oppose the flow-through of tax savings to consumers, suggesting that the output effects are not positive enough to overcome the immediate cash-flow disadvantages.

An alternative accounting treatment, normalization, requires that the value of the tax reduction be placed in reserve for deferred taxes and passed on to consumers gradually over the life of the asset. The reserve for deferred taxes is deducted from the rate base so that the utility does not earn a return on what amounts to an interest-free loan

21. Ben W. Lewis, "The Duty of a Public Utility to Reduce its Income Tax Liability by Using Accelerated Depreciation," *Land Economics* 35, no. 2 (May 1959).

from the U.S. Treasury. In the meantime the utility has use of the funds while consumers have higher current rates (and lower future rates) than under the flow-through technique.

Regulatory commissions and consumer groups have favored the flow-through approach; utilities and federal tax authorities have favored normalization. One view is that flow-through frustrates congressional intent by preventing tax benefits from accruing directly to the firm and its stockholders, thus creating stimulative effects akin to those in the nonregulated sectors. The opposing view is that regulators, not Congress or the tax authorities, are best equipped to evaluate utility investment decisions as well as to distribute the tax saving. Thus the availability of federal tax savings has led commissions to pressure utilities to accept tax concessions in order to keep utility rates low. The commissions, in turn, have been pressed by the utilities and federal tax authorities to honor the investment incentive features of the tax law and to preserve the increased cash flow in the form of a deferred tax reserve available for financing increased investment. Current federal law, therefore, mandates normalization as a condition for receiving the tax benefits of accelerated depreciation.

The Investment Tax Credit

The Investment Tax Credit (ITC), designed as an additional incentive to stimulate capital formation, poses similar problems. Prior to 1975, the investment tax credit was 4 percent for public utilities and 7 percent for other industries. This differential recognized the fact that investment tax credits at uniform rates would favor capital-intensive industries. Following the energy crisis and the development of a more aggressive environmental program that imposed additional capital burdens on utilities, the Tax Reduction Act of 1975 increased the ITC to 10 percent and eliminated the lower public utility differential.

Unlike accelerated depreciation, the investment tax credit is a tax subsidy that reduces the acquisition cost of capital assets. There is no future tax obligation requiring the establishment of a deferred tax reserve. In the unregulated sector, the ITC temporarily increases the rate of return to capital, stimulating capital formation, expanded output, and reduced prices. Whether the tax savings are flowed through to current profits or amortized over the life of the investment is essentially a matter of accounting convention with no implication to the rate of return on investment. In the regulated sector, however, the effect of the credit is to immediately raise the firm's after-tax return, violating the regulatory profit constraint. Since the regulatory response to excess returns is to order rate reductions, the utilities maintain that the firm and its stockholders are deprived of the rewards and incentives that accrue in the unregulated sector. Congress, impressed by the as-if competitive rationale, has established guidelines and tax accounting options designed to ensure that investors and rate payers "share" the tax benefits.

Most utilities have selected cost-of-service normalization, one of the options permitted by the tax code. Under this option the ITC tax credit is placed in a deferred account and passed on to consumers in increments that can be rated over the life of the asset. In the meantime the firm has use of the funds. Moreover the asset is placed in the rate base at its original cost. The utility, therefore, earns the allowable rate of return on an increment of capital provided at zero cost to the firm and its stockholders. Economic normalization would require that the ITC be deducted from the rate base (or treated as zero-cost capital) and that the tax savings be passed on to consumers over the life of the asset. The rate-making procedure currently required for accelerated depreciation is consistent with economic normalization; the treatment of the investment tax credit is not. The federal tax code builds a federally mandated distortion into the rate-making process because regulatory agencies are required—as a condition of receiving the tax savings—to provide a higher rate of return to stockholders than they deem appropriate. This has created an unresolved conflict between state and federal concepts of the allowable rate of return and investment requirements. Changes in the tax code that require uniform accounting treatment of tax incentives would eliminate some, but not all, of the controversy that centers on the efficiency and distributional implications of federal tax incentives.

"Phantom Taxes"

The concern that the traditional flow-through regulatory treatment of tax incentives prevents attaining national investment policy may be misplaced. If these tax savings lead to output expansions and increased capital usage, the objectives of federal tax policy can be achieved. Since utility factor demands have some elasticity and are (under A-J assumptions) even more elastic than factor demands in the nonregulated sector, the regulated firms' investment response to tax incentives—which are flowed through directly to consumers—might actually exceed the response of firms in the unregulated sector.[22] The mechanism through which responses are transmitted is, however, very different. In the nonregulated sector these incentives increase the return to capital assets and stimulate investment and output expansion via the market mechanism. In the regulated sector this process is short-circuited by the regulatory commission that orders direct price reductions.

Most accountants and some economists have criticized flow-through regulatory treatment because it does not conform to as-if competitive standards and ordinary accounting procedures.[23] This reasoning emphasizes form in place of substance. The competitive market forces that transfer tax benefits to consumers in the nonregulated economy are deliberately muted by the regulatory process. Efforts to force regulators to mimic marketlike adjustments through the utilities investment function contradict the fundamental rationale of rate-of-return regulation.

Robert Spann, who has carefully examined the issues in the framework of the A-J model, concludes that under either method of accounting accelerated depreciation increases the profits of the firm. Between the two accounting methods, firms should favor flow-through, and consumers should prefer normalization. These conclusions are, of course, conditioned by the rather stringent assumptions made by the A-J model and are the opposite of those expressed by the contending interests.[24] We can explain such inconsistencies in terms of the different discount rates that might apply to consumers and to utilities, to uncertainties about the permanence of the tax savings—a bird in hand being worth two in the bush—and to the possibility that theorizing on the basis of the A-J model may overestimate the elasticity of factor demands, as noted later.

Federally mandated rules requiring normalization of the tax savings

22. Empirical estimates developed by Spann indicate that the responses of regulated firms exceed those of unregulated firms. Spann's analysis, however, hinges on crucial assumptions about demand elasticities. See "Taxation and Electric Utility Regulation," pp. 180–85.

23. Donald W. Kiefer, "The Effects of Alternative Regulatory Treatments of the Investment Tax Credit in the Public Utility Industry," *Journal of Business* 54 (June 1981): 549–76. The accounting profession, emphasizing the problem of "matching" costs and revenues over time, has also recommended normalization.

24. However, predictions made on the basis of the A-J model are supported by simulation analyses made by Donald W. Kiefer who employs the more practical revenue-requirements model.

provide increased cash flow to utilities at a time when interest rates are high and amidst claims that utility investment is not keeping pace with needs. On the other hand, normalization creates huge tax reserves that, in a growing economy, continue to grow. Consumer groups view the deferred tax reserves—now $34 billion or $400 per household—as taxes that have been paid by consumers but are sequestered by the utilities.[25] In 1983 consumers' bills included $7 billion in corporate income taxes; $2 billion of this was actually remitted to the Treasury, with $5 billion channeled into deferred tax accounts. Assuming continued growth of the utility sector, these reserves will continue to grow, possibly at a more rapid rate than the growth of total assets.

The utilities point to severe capacity and investment requirements, implying that state regulatory commissions react excessively to consumer pressures for lower current rates by sacrificing efficient operations and the maintenance of future quality service. No doubt many utilities are under severe financial pressures, but many others have excessive reserve capacity, and their recent rates of increase in demand have been below the levels predicted only a few years ago when the tax incentives were liberalized. The reserves of some utilities have reached unrealistic levels, and a few could even be described as "cash cows." Investment analysts have recommended some utility common stocks on the basis of potential diversification and expansion into unregulated markets.[26] Recently utilities have sought modifications of the Public Utility Company Holding Act of 1935 that would remove some of the statutory barriers to diversification. Though this effort is consistent with the present deregulatory thrust of public policy, it also creates the possibility of cross-subsidized competitive entry.

More important, perhaps, is the fact that current tax incentives favor the selection of capital-intensive technologies rather than small-scale alternatives like cogeneration, improved transmission and interconnection, and so on. Pressures from consumers and the state regulatory commissions have led to the introduction of HR 4927, the Phantom Tax Reform and Least Cost Energy Planning Act. This bill would give state regulatory commissions the option of using either flow-through or normalization techniques, provided the commissions

25. U.S. Department of Energy, *Statistics of Privately Owned Electric Utilities, 1982* (Washington, D.C.: Energy Information Administration, 1982).

26. *Value Line* (September 1984), p. 1720.

establish a "least-cost" investment strategy. In essence the bill would require the state commissions to develop the staff and techniques to monitor and even develop cost-efficient utility investment programs. Historically utilities have received virtually automatic approval of their investment programs, and they resent intrusion into what has been a managerial prerogative. Yet it seems inappropriate to provide federal tax incentives with no strings attached, especially to an industry whose profits hinge on rate-base maximization and which demonstrably favors high-cost, long-term investment projects. Testimony on HR 4923 (June 1984) presented before the House Subcommittee on Energy Conservation and Power revealed numerous instances of projects alleged to excessively favor capital-intensive technologies and inefficiently large centralized plants. Testimony also alleged a lack of enthusiasm for small-scale labor-intensive alternatives.

Though increased federal involvement in the taxing, rate-making, and investment policies of the utility sector has created new conflicts, it has also addressed important shortcomings in the performance of state regulatory commissions and public utilities. If federal tax incentives to the utility sector accomplish nothing more than a distributional tug-of-war, it may be best either to eliminate them altogether or to tie them directly to projects that have environmental and energy components or externalities of a purely national concern.

Property Taxation

Property taxes utilities pay are a major source of local revenue. In general, the state tax assessor assesses utility property on a unit-rule basis. This aggregate value is then allocated among local governments, which apply local tax rates to their individual allocations. The tax base used for property tax purposes—usually capitalization of earnings—is typically different than the rate base used for rate-making purposes, a situation that sometimes leads to legalistic confrontations between the taxing and the regulatory authorities. Since property taxes are shifted through the systemwide utility-rate structure, local governments seek more than their fair share of the property assessment, creating interlocal (or even interstate) cross-subsidies. For example, a generating plant located in one county but distributing power throughout the state may become a tax bonanza for the local community. The complexities of property tax administration have received a great deal of attention, but the situation today is not much different than it was many years ago when Clemens wrote: "The tax commission, after judiciously scrutinizing its records which it can comprehend but dimly and believe not at all, will don an owlish expression and arrive at a value 'by guess and by God,' modified to a certain extent by a consideration of the squawking of the goose."[27]

Evaluating the effects of the property tax within the A-J framework is relatively straightforward. The effect of the tax is to shrink the profit hill (Figure 3–2) by an amount gK where g is the property tax rate; the profit hill shrinks by a larger amount for large values of K than for small values of K. The effect is a reduction of output, capital usage, and profit. Though the property tax does increase the cost of capital, suggesting a decreased capital-labor ratio, it also tightens the restraint $(s - r)$, which leads to a higher capital-labor ratio. The increased user cost of capital will not ameliorate the A-J bias, a point previously made relative to the corporate income tax.

An increase in the local property tax rate amounts to a tightening of the constraint established by the state regulatory commission, but the impact is on statewide operations. As noted, taxation can act as

Figure 3–2.   Property Tax.

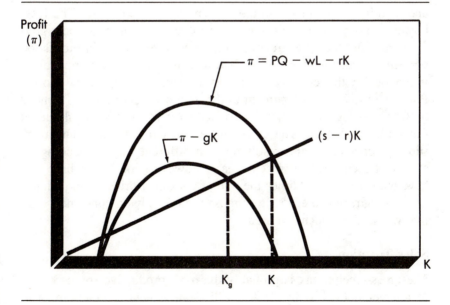

---

27. Clemens, *Economics and Public Utilities*, p. 547.

a substitute for regulation. Local taxing authorities that view utility earnings as excessive can try to impose their own regulation through differential taxation.

Lump Sum and Franchise Taxes

Both state and local governments impose permits and license fees levied independently of input or output levels. In the case of an unregulated monopoly firm, the full impact of such taxes would be on profits, with both price and output remaining unchanged. In the A-J model, however, these taxes reduce the profit function (Figure 3–2) by a fixed amount, leading to a lower level of output, capital, and profits and to higher prices. The adjustment would be almost identical to that of a lump-sum tax imposed on a fully competitive industry. Equal-yield corporate income, property, and lump-sum taxes will have identical effects on output and price.

In most states local governments are permitted to levy franchise fees that are usually measured by gross revenues derived within the jurisdiction of the local government. Legally such taxes are justified in terms of right-of-way use, use of local roads, and streets, and so on. Most regulatory commissions view such charges as cost of service and permit their inclusion in the systemwide rate structure. The fees, however, seem to have little relation to costs imposed on local governments, and localities treat them as general revenues. In Florida 60 percent of franchise fees are shifted to consumers who do not reside in the locality that collects the fee. In the region served by the Florida Power Corporation, 5.5 percent of the municipal budgets are financed by franchise fees; one municipality had 67 percent of its local budget funded by such fees. The courts have debated this particular cross-subsidy for many years, resolving it in different ways depending on state and local law. In recent years, however, local franchise fees have increased at four times the rate of consumer prices, and officials are making renewed efforts to impose the tax only on consumers who live within the franchised area.[28]

Sales Taxation

The gross-receipts tax is probably the most productive source of tax revenue embodied in the electric utility-rate structure. In a number of

---

28. Jerome S. Oosteryoung, "Franchise Fees Reexamined," *Public Utilities Fortnightly* 12 (24 November 1977): 29–31.

states it is substituted for the property tax, which merits examination. Moreover the preference for ad valorem taxes rather than unit taxes warrants consideration.

Tax shifting of ad valorem and unit taxes under competitive conditions depends on the slopes of industry demand and supply functions; the outcome is the same under either tax levy. Unit and ad valorem tax shifting is less under monopoly than under competition because the slope of the monopolist's marginal revenue curve is steeper than the demand curve. The effect of the regulatory profit ceiling restraint in the A-J model is to produce a price-output outcome somewhere between the competitive and monopolistic outcomes. If the restraint is very tight, taxes will be shifted forward as in a competitive industry.

The effects of ad valorem and unit taxes appear in the A-J model as reductions in marginal revenue or as increases in marginal cost. Since the wage rate and cost of capital are not affected, the A-J firm reduces output and raises price until the marginal revenue product of labor is again equated to the wage rate. The degree to which the price rises will vary depending on the slopes of demand and cost functions, and regulatory constraint.

On grounds of general economic efficiency, the tax that generates the same yield with a lesser price increase is preferable. Musgrave and others have analyzed these complex tax-shifting relationships in detail with the following conclusions.[29]

1. Under competition, unit and ad valorem taxes that provide the same revenue yield result in the same price; the choice of unit or ad valorem taxes is a matter of indifference.
2. Under unregulated monopoly, equal revenue yields require higher prices (less output and greater profits) under the unit tax than under the ad valorem tax. The unregulated monopolist would prefer the unit tax; the taxing authority would prefer the ad valorem tax. The regulated firm whose allowable profits are a function of output (rate base) would prefer the ad valorem tax.
3. For the case of unregulated monopoly, the yield from any given unit tax is always smaller (and profits larger) than the yield from an ad valorem tax that results in the same final price and output. On this criterion both regulated and unregulated monopolists will

---

29. Richard A. Musgrave, *The Theory of Public Finance* (New York: McGraw-Hill, 1959), pp. 304–11.

prefer the unit tax because, at any equilibrium, it yields less tax revenue than an ad valorem tax. The relative advantage of the unit tax decreases, however, as elasticity of demand increases. The fact that the regulated monopolist is already restrained means, in general, that elasticity of demand at the regulated output will be greater than that of an unregulated monopolist and that the preference for a unit tax under these assumptions may not be very strong.

These comparisons suggest that regulated monopolists would prefer an ad valorem tax if the two taxes are to have equal yields but a unit tax if tax rates are equivalent at the final level of output. Anything approaching an effective profit constraint may eliminate any conflict between the regulatory agency, the firm, and the taxing authority (which, according to standard treatments, should prefer the ad valorem tax in the presence of monopoly).[30]

These generalizations from standard tax theory are appropriate, given the single-price assumptions of the A-J model. Taken together, they suggest that utility firms as well as tax authorities would prefer ad valorem taxes. Gross-receipts taxes in the utility sector, however, are not levied in a single-price setting but rather on total revenues raised through a declining block rate structure. Nonlinear pricing means that an ad valorem tax always leads to a lower marginal tax rate than an equal-yield unit tax. Under unit taxation, average tax is equal to marginal tax. Under nonlinear pricing, average revenue, and therefore average tax, always exceeds marginal revenue, and marginal tax. In view of these tax-rate relationships, we can understand the preference utility firms have for gross-receipts taxation. They can raise tax revenues with a minimum impact on marginal rates and output.

A number of states have substituted the gross-receipts tax for the property tax. Given equal-yield taxes and a single-price utility-rate structure, the effect of the substitution is neutral on both price and output. (Recall that taxation of capital affects the level of output of the A-J firm but not the factor combination used to produce that output.) Given nonlinear pricing, however, the property tax would probably be treated as a lump-sum tax to be distributed through inframarginal alterations in the rate structure. But then the gross-receipts tax does have an effect on marginal revenues. This suggests

30. Musgrave, *Theory of Public Finance*, p. 10.

that the impact of the gross-receipts tax on output might be somewhat greater and that the firm might prefer the property tax since it provides greater leeway in rate design. Given the problems of property tax administration described earlier, though, substituting the gross-receipts tax for the property tax probably contributes to lower costs of administration and less intergovernmental conflict. The gross-receipts tax places responsibility for both taxation and regulation at the same governmental level, reducing the number of taxing units and the possibility of interregional cross-subsidy.

Consumer Excise Taxes

All levels of government have found consumer excise taxes a reliable source of revenue involving almost no collection costs. These excise taxes are of the ad valorem variety levied on the total utility bill of consumers. They are remitted directly to the government that imposes the tax. Their incidence and equity are governed by the design of the utility rate structure, which they mirror.

Economists have, for years, been concerned about the distributional and efficiency aspects of consumer excise taxation. Utility excise taxation can only add to this concern. The federal government has used utility excise taxes from time to time as budget-balancing devices. In virtually every instance such taxes have been "temporary," but in times of fiscal stringency these excises are either extended or rediscovered. At the state and local level, utility excise taxes are a permanent part of the tax system, accounting for about three-fourths of local revenues derived from excise taxes. The annual growth rate of local utility excise tax revenues over the period 1971–1980 has been 14.9 percent, much larger than the 9.3 percent growth rate of own-source general revenues in local governments.[31] The growth of these revenues during the past decade is in large measure due to the increased revenue base created by higher utility rates following the energy crisis.

Some of the implications of utility excise taxation are shown in Figures 3–3 and 3–4. In Figure 3–3, which assumes a single-price structure, the "net" demand available for taxation is D_T, the vertical subtraction of price from the market demand curve. A unit tax rate b imposed at the output level, Q, is equivalent in terms of yield (bQ)

---

31. Bowman and Pratt, "Selective Excise Taxation," p. 10.

Figure 3–3.   Unit and Ad Valorem Tax Rates.

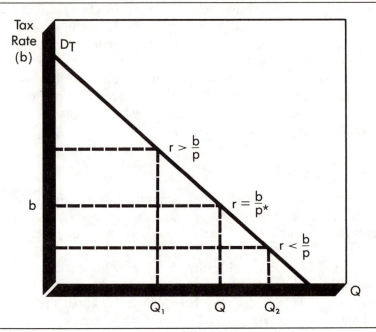

to an excise or sales tax rate, $r = b/p$, imposed at the same output level. Since all consumers pay the same price, tax bills under either the unit tax or the ad valorem tax will vary among consumers directly with consumption. Moreover marginal and average tax rates are equal and apply uniformly to all consumers. This simply restates the equivalence of unit and ad valorem taxes when imposed in a competitive market. The straight line $Qb = rPQ$ in Figure 3–4 depicts the consumer's tax bill at different levels of consumption under either unit or ad valorem taxation.

If the firm practices some form of nonlinear pricing, with all consumers paying the same marginal price (but different average prices), the total level of consumption, Q, in Figure 3–3 will not be altered. However, the effective excise tax rates will differ by consumer, depending on the amount consumed. If Q_1 is consumed, the effective ad valorem rate is higher than if Q_2 is consumed (Figure 4–3).

We can calculate an equal-yield ad valorem tax for this system at output Q and can insert this tax function in Figure 3–4. For a consumer who purchases Q, the two systems are equivalent. The equiv-

Figure 3–4.   Tax Bills.

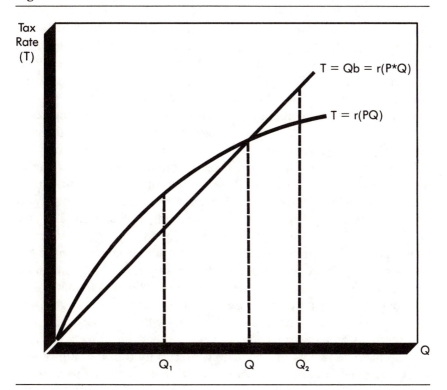

alence between ad valorem and unit taxes indicated by the intersection of Q_b and $r(PQ)$ no longer holds for all consumers, however. For consumers buying less than Q, tax rates will be higher; for consumers buying more than Q, tax rates will be lower. Moreover average and marginal tax rates will diverge and be different for each customer class. Thus even if utility rates reflect reasonably efficient nonlinear pricing (by making marginal rates equal for all consumers), excise taxation at uniform "nominal" rates will undermine efficiency. As a practical matter, utilities do not make marginal prices equal for all consumers missing this efficiency objective by a very wide margin. The excise tax system aggravates this inefficiency.

Aside from its lucrative and stable yield, many local governments justify the utility excise tax as a means of taxing renters who do not pay property taxes, people who reside outside the city, transients in motels and hotels, and in some cases they use it as a means of shifting some of their tax responsibility to other jurisdictions served by the utility. One of the major appeals of the utility excise tax is that, unlike sales, gasoline, or other excise taxes, it does not create serious border problems or intercity tax competition. Local sales, gasoline, and cigarette taxes can be avoided by simply driving across the border where tax rates are lower. The utility excise tax is not great enough to encourage taxpayers to shift to residences across the border.

In most states municipal governments have delegated taxing powers and may impose excise taxes whose legal incidence is on the utility rather than the consumer. In such cases a municipality may be able to export locally legislated taxes to other cities. For example, the Washington Commission refused to permit the flow-through of excise taxes levied by the city of Seattle and ordered the utility to return the tax revenue to the consumers who had paid them. The city in turn sued the commission for unlawfully exercising a municipal taxing power. The state supreme court, in this instance, upheld the commission; yet tax exporting, in one form or another, remains a serious problem even in the case of obviously direct taxation.[32]

Though utility excise taxes seem least burdensome to large users (whose effective marginal tax rates decline with use), they can have severe effects on industrial and commercial users when utility services are intermediate factors of production. Electricity (or other utility services) are a large component of the cost of production in many industries. In these cases demands are more elastic, and utility rates (and effective excise tax rates) are lower. Yet even at these lower effective rates, excise taxation of industry may conflict with local policy on industrial development. The local response to this problem takes varied forms. In many states the nominal excise tax rate is reduced for certain industrial and commercial users, usually through introducing a special "classification," which often applies to a single customer. For example, the city of Gainesville, Florida, provided a special rate for a veterans' hospital it sought to attract; the rate did not apply to other hospitals in the area. In some instances the tax is only applied to residential users.

Utility excise taxes are not neutral with respect to interutility competition. The customers of municipally owned utilities may be tax exempt from certain excises because of the legal status of their supplier. Seattle imposed excise taxes on the consumers of Puget Sound

---

32. Clemens, *Economics and Public Utilities*, p. 539.

Power and Light Company but not on the consumers of an adjacent municipal utility with which PSP&L competed. The tax was sustained by the supreme court.[33] We could cite many other examples, some bizarre indeed, of manipulating utility excise taxes to achieve a variety of objectives. Few seem fair; most are inefficient.[34]

Utilities, of course, must adjust their own systemwide rate structures to local taxation because of their impact on demand. If a utility seeks to adjust its statewide rate in order to reflect the demand effects of local excise taxation, it may be guilty of price discrimination. Utilities appear not to have challenged many of the local practices that seem questionable, except where interutility competition is involved.

UTILITY TAXATION AND THE REGULATORY PROCESS

The preceding discussion tries to shed light on the response the regulated firm has to taxes. If the firm purchases its factors in competitive markets, special utility taxes cannot be shifted backward, and it is doubtful that they will affect factor combinations. The A-J factor bias can be eliminated or reduced only by tax policies that increase the effective rate of return. The regulatory agency can, however, react by taking measures to offset such intrusions by the tax authority. Though taxes cannot affect the level of investment through their direct impact on profits, the effects on investment through tax-induced price changes could be strong. The short-circuiting of the traditional investment mechanism does not mean that the taxpaying utility is simply a passive conduit for flowing taxes through to consumers—an assumption frequently made by regulators, legislators, and many economists. On the other hand the A-J model, at least in its simpler form, fails to capture the essence of utility rate-making, which involves inframarginal rate adjustments not permitted by the single-market assumption made in the A-J model.

The orginal Averch-Johnson paper had two parts. The first part related to biased factor combinations at any given level of output; the second, to excessive levels of output and to the possibility of sales below marginal costs. For twenty years economists have belabored part one, the input side, while almost completely neglecting the mo-

33. Clemens, *Economics and Public Utilities*, p. 540.
34. Bowman and Pratt, "Selective Excise Taxation," p. 4.

nopoly power that can be exerted on the demand side through the design of multipart rate structures.[35]

Since the utility firm is a monopoly that can (within the broad parameters of allowable level of revenue) design the rate structure, the firm can control output effects to a much greater extent than suggested by the formal A-J model. The firm will adjust its rate structure so as to minimize the impact of taxes on the level of output and capital usage. This, the demand side of the A-J model, helps to explain the ease with which the revenue-requirements or zero-elasticity model has been accepted by regulators, legislators, and practical people. According to this model the full amount of taxes can be flowed through without affecting output. In short taxes affect consumers' utility bills but nothing more; tax issues become purely distributional.

The propriety of flow-through continues to be a major source of controversy, especially with respect to the flow-through of tax incentives. The legal controversy was settled in the Galveston case in 1922. In that decision Justice Brandeis said: "in calculating . . . a proper return, it is necessary to deduct from gross revenue the expenses and charges, and all taxes which would be payable if a fair return were earned. There is no difference in this respect between state and federal taxes, or between income taxes and others."[36] The Galveston decision sanctions a revenue-requirements interpretation of the regulatory process. Though most economic models treat the fair return as the relevant regulatory constraint, the revenue-requirements model implies that total allowable revenue is the relevant constraint. If the firm can design alternative rate structures yielding different outputs and total revenues, any one of which can yield a fair return on the investment, the output level is not constrained by rate-of-return regulation alone as the A-J model suggests. Rather it is determined by the ability to raise money. The A-J premium to capital, $(s - r)$, is a major determinant of factor combinations but may have no significance as a determinant of output and investment levels.

Rate proceedings are triggered by a decline in the fair rate of return, and they result in a revised revenue requirement or rate level.

---

35. These deficiencies in the A-J model have been analyzed by Charles Needy, *Regulation Induced Distortions* (Lexington, Mass.: Lexington Books, D.C. Heath, 1975); and Roger Sherman and Michael Visscher, "Rate of Return Regulation and Price Structure" in M. Crew, *Problems in Public Utility Economics* (Lexington, Mass.: Lexington Books, D.C. Heath, 1979), pp. 119–32.

36. *Galveston Electric Co.* v. *Galveston*, 258 U.S. 388, 399, 1922.

Commission approval of specific rate tariffs is, for the most part, automatic—especially in the absence of intervenors. The conventional interpretation of this process is that the revenue requirement is the sum of all costs, taxes, and fair return at a given or test-year level of output. The firm then raises rates in order to increase total revenues at that given level of output. This procedure is not consistent with the theoretical proposition that the regulated monopolist—or any monopolist for that matter—will always operate in ranges where demand is elastic. Increased allowable revenues cannot be attained along with increased prices in the elastic portion of the demand curve. According to Spann, the revenue-requirement's model assumes "zero elasticity of demand," implying that the traditional approach is flawed in this respect. But then the A-J model assumes a single linear price to predict outcomes in an area where linear pricing does not exist and probably should not be used.

Consider Figure 3–5 where *TC* is total cost including a fair return,

Figure 3–5. Revenue Requirements.

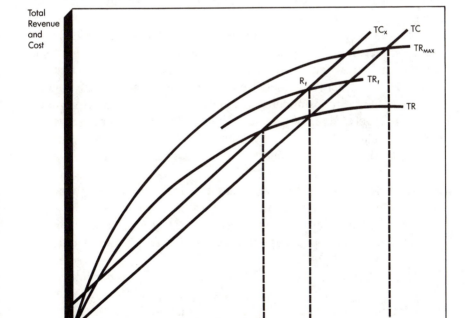

and *TR* is the total revenue schedule drawn on the assumption that the firm sells its output at a uniform price to a single class of consumers, as specified in the original A-J model. As shown regulation is "ideal" at output Q^* where $P = MC$. Moreover marginal revenue is positive, and the firm breaks even at the Q^* level of output. (If the A-J factor bias is introduced, *TC* will be higher, depending on the degree to which capital has been inefficiently substituted for labor.) Outputs either to the right or left of Q^* violate the regulatory rate-of-return constraint.

Suppose now that someone imposes a lump-sum tax, shifting *TC* to TC_x so that profits are reduced at the existing level of output, Q^*. Standard flow-through regulation would increase allowable revenues to level R_f. But R_f cannot be achieved given that the static revenue schedule, *TR*, is price elastic. The new $P = MC$ equilibrium at Q requires a lower revenue requirement. If demand is elastic in the relevant range, as posited by the A-J model, tax increases should lead to lower output, revenue, and profits coupled with higher prices—an outcome inconsistent with the revenue-requirements model, which predicts higher total revenue and higher prices following a rate hearing prompted by tax increases. Nor is the A-J prediction consistent with experience. Utility rate increases are not associated with lower total revenue, though they could be associated with lower total output. An outcome consistent with the A-J model is the railroad experience of the 1920s, when rate increases brought about decreases in total revenue—the railroads apparently believed they were operating in an inelastic range of demand. We can explain these apparent contradictions in a number of ways, each having different implications about the effects of cost and tax increases on price and output.

1. The revenue and cost functions in the A-J model are static, whereas the regulatory process operates in an environment of changing, usually increasing, demand so that R_f is attainable at a higher level of prices. In short increases in demand between rate adjustments can explain the contradiction.

2. Under regulation the firm operates in an inelastic portion of demand that will permit both increased prices and total revenues as experience and the revenue-requirements model suggest. That is, regulation is so effective that the firm is forced to operate in a range where marginal revenues are negative. This explanation is inconsistent with most of the theoretical literature on the behavior

of the profit-maximizing regulated firm. It is entirely consistent, however, with output maximization and with various bureaucratic theories of the firm. Profit maximization is, after all, an assumption. The argument that firms will be taken over unless they maximize profits might not have much force in the protected utility sector. Survival is not inexorably tied to profit maximization when regulatory protection is the rule.

3. The firm can attain R_f through an improvement in its rate structure—increased price discrimination, nonlinear pricing, two-part tariffs, and so on. A monopolist can be very skillful in raising money. [37] If circumstances recognize the full revenue-raising potential of the monopolist, the total revenue schedule becomes TR_{MAX}, well within the revenue requirement, R_f. One can interpret TR_{MAX} as the maximum revenue obtainable by a perfectly discriminating monopolist.

Between TR and TR_{MAX} many total revenue curves exist, one of which is TR_f. TR_f is attainable by redesigning the rate structure so that Q^* can be sold for a larger total revenue. If the firm is able to implement TR_{MAX}, it can satisfy a rate-of-return constraint at Q_{MAX}, where output and rate base are maximized. Moreover, utilities can sell $Q^* - Q_{MAX}$ output at prices below marginal cost and yet retain profitability. This type of behavior has not received the attention it merits. [38] Since the equilibrium of any constrained monopolist is characterized by $MC > MR = P(1 + 1/E)$, it follows that some prices might fall below marginal cost provided that (a) demand in some markets is sufficiently elastic and (b) that prices in other markets are sufficiently above average cost to recover the "loss" imposed by selling some output at a price below marginal cost.

Where inframarginal and discriminatory adjustments in the rate structure are available, all taxes can be passed through without reductions in output and, theoretically, without any changes in marginal rates. Under these circumstances taxes will be shifted in a way that will minimize output reduction, an objective not much different than that posited by theoretical models. The difference is that if taxes are "loaded" inframarginally, no reduction in output or revenue will oc-

---

37. Sherman and Visscher, "Rate of Return Regulation," p. 1.

38. It has not remained unnoticed, however. Sherman and especially Needy have emphasized such output effects (see note 35).

cur. These considerations point to the possibility of socially excessive output and to the distribution of taxes through a rate structure that bears almost no relation to conventional notions of tax justice. Tax rates under such structures would be regressive to the tax base and probably regressive to income as well.

CONCLUSION

Theorists have criticized the revenue-requirements model for assuming zero elasticities of demand and invariant factor combinations. The impression the model leaves is that resource allocation in the regulated sector is either unresponsive to tax policy or, as Spann emphasizes, that the regulatory agency has complete control over the firm's behavior. An alternative interpretation is that the revenue-requirements model recognizes that total revenue—not fair return—determines the level of output and investment, and that regulatory agencies have little control over the behavior of the firm beyond profit control at a level of resource use selected by the firm. Rate-of-return regulation, by itself, does not constrain the level of output.

The average revenue schedule of the regulated firm that practices nonlinear pricing lies above and is more elastic than its demand curve. Revenues that are marginal to this operational average revenue curve will be positive, but the firm could operate in an inelastic portion of the conventional demand curve.

To the extent that rate adjustments are inframarginal, the firm can behave asymmetrically in response to tax changes. The firm can pass on increases in taxes through inframarginal rate adjustments, minimizing output contractions; it can place reductions in taxes in the marginal components of the rate structure, leading to output expansions. In this case output expansions will be greater and contractions smaller than those predicted by the A-J model. Thus restrictive tax policies may be blunted, while expansionary tax policies may be strengthened. When government imposes taxes, average rates rise while marginal rates can change very little. When governments reduce taxes, both average and marginal rates decline.

The response to increases in unit taxation will be symmetrical because they impinge uniformly at the margin. As a positive instrument of tax policy, unit taxes are superior. On the other hand gross-receipts, sales, and excise taxes are likely to have a relatively "neutral" allocative outcome but significant distributional effects.

Tax incentives—accelerated depreciation and investment tax credits—can aggravate the tendency toward excess investment inherent in firms whose profits depend on rate-base expansion and whose total revenues are open-ended. Moreover the cost of tax incentives to the U.S. Treasury is significant, whereas the benefits are not obvious. Given existing regulatory institutions and competing needs for tax revenues, we should consider eliminating all such tax incentives.

Institutional choices involve (1) more intensive regulation of rate structures with particular emphasis on below-marginal-cost prices and investment decisions coupled with (2) the erosion of monopoly power on the demand side by exposing protected utility rate structures to whatever competition can be mustered by innovative deregulatory policies.

4

INFLATION, REGULATION, AND FINANCIAL ADEQUACY

Robert E. McCormick*

INTRODUCTION

In 1956 the electric utility industry in the United States paid an average 25.4¢ per million Btu's for fuels consumed in generation. By 1982 this cost had risen to $2.34 per million Btu's, an increase of 821 percent. By comparison, over the same period the consumer price index increased by 247 percent. At the same time, the average revenue the industry received increased from 1.64¢ to 5.79¢ per kwh, an increase of 253 percent. In an unregulated, competitive economy these facts would be cause for little concern. Input price increases would lead to higher output prices through natural market forces. Typically higher input prices lead to higher marginal and average costs for industry firms. These higher costs cause prices to increase in the short run, and lead ultimately to the exit of some firms. (Whether input price changes lead to increases or decreases in marginal cost and exit of firms depends upon the factor of production and the technical production process.)[1]

*Thanks go to Michael Maloney, John Moorhouse, and Jerry Zimmerman for their help. The usual caveat applies.

1. For a detailed discussion, see Richard D. Portes, "Long-Run Scale Adjustments of a Perfectly Competitive Firm and Industry: An Alternative Approach," *American Economic Review* 61 (1971): 430–34.

The U.S. electric power industry does not, however, suffer the constraints of competition. Entry and exit are controlled by state utility commissions. Moreover price is determined in the political arena rather than the free marketplace. This raises several important questions. Do input price increases adversely affect the electric power industry? Does the regulatory decision-making process create a lag between input price increases and output price changes? Have the large price increases of fuels in the 1970s impaired the electric power industry's ability to survive financially and provide electricity in the future? This chapter attempts to answer some of these questions.

The chapter is divided into five sections including this introduction. The following section examines a selection of the literature on electric utility regulation. The third section provides summary statistics on important aspects of the electric utility industry. The fourth section critically analyzes these data and assesses their impact on the industry. The last section is a summary and conclusion.

SURVEY OF ELECTRIC UTILITY REGULATION

Few topics in the economics literature have received as much attention as the subject of utility regulation. This section, of necessity, provides only a brief overview of the literature. Other chapters offer further coverage, and the bibliography lists additional references. Two basic theories of regulation exist: the public-interest theory and the economic theory. The public-interest theory is traceable to the work of A. C. Pigou, among others, and the economic theory is primarily due to the work of George Stigler.

The public-interest theory is primarily normative. In the context of public utilities, it holds that electricity is produced under conditions of decreasing cost. This leads to a natural monopoly, and for this reason the forces of competition are short circuited. According to this theory, the remedy to the problem of ruinous competition is for government to regulate entry of firms and to assign territorial rights. It follows logically that price must be regulated as well. The primary conclusion of this theory is that regulation leads to lower prices than would prevail under competition.

Dissatisfaction with much of the public-interest theory—especially its limitation in explaining many aspects of regulation in actual practice—led to the development of the economic theory of regulation.[2] This theory posits that regulation is designed and implemented to serve the interests of the regulated. The strong arm of the law is used to prevent competition by limiting entry, and the effect is reduced output and higher price. In other words, regulation creates rather than prevents monopoly. The public-interest theory and the economic theory stand in direct contrast to each other. Public-interest theory predicts that regulation lowers price, while economic theory predicts that regulation raises the price.

In the case of electricity the evidence is mixed. Stigler and Friedland report that regulation has no impact on price.[3] Jarrell finds that in its early days, regulation first came in those jurisdictions with the lowest prices, not the highest.[4] He also finds that price increased after the onset of regulation. Meyer and Leland also discuss the effectiveness of price regulation.[5]

Since the act of price setting by regulatory commissions takes time, there is a natural tendency to believe that a lag occurs between input and output price changes. This lag can work in two directions. When prices are rising, output price increases will lag input price increases. In a period of stable prices, output price decreases will lag technological advances that lower cost. It is an empirical issue whether regulators rationally anticipate these changes and program them into rate structures in advance.

2. For a sampling of the literature, see George J. Stigler, "The Theory of Economic Regulation," *Bell Journal of Economics and Management Science* 2 (1971): 3–21; Sam Peltzman, "Toward a More General Theory of Regulation," *Journal of Law and Economics* 19 (1976): 211–40; and Richard A. Posner, "Taxation by Regulation," *Bell Journal of Economics and Management Science* 2 (1971): 22–50. For a recent survey of the literature, see Robert E. McCormick, "The Strategic Use of Regulation: A Review of the Literature," in R. Rogowsky, ed., *The Political Economy of Regulation* (Washington, D.C.: Federal Trade Commission, 1984). For direct application to electric utility regulation, see W. Mark Crain and Robert E. McCormick, "Regulators as an Interest Group," in J. Buchanan and R. Tollison, eds., *The Theory of Public Choice II* (Ann Arbor: University of Michigan Press, 1984); and Michael Maloney, Robert McCormick, and Robert Tollison, "Economic Regulation, Competitive Governments, and Specialized Resources," *Journal of Law and Economics* 27 (1984): 329–38.

3. George J. Stigler and Claire Friedland, "What Can Regulators Regulate? The Case of Electricity," *Journal of Law and Economics* 5 (1962): 1–16.

4. Gregg A. Jarrell, "The Demand for State Regulation of the Electric Utility Industry," *Journal of Law and Economics* 21 (1978): 269–98.

5. Robert A. Meyer and Hayne E. Leland, "The Effectiveness of Price Regulation," *Review of Economics and Statistics* 62 (1980): 555–64.

Spann models the lagged regulatory decision-making process, contending that regulators systematically underestimate the impact of cost increases.[6] This means that in periods of rising costs, utilities are in a never-ending battle to catch up for past cost increases. Or in periods of relatively stable prices, technological progress reduces costs, and so output price-declines lag cost reductions. In the first case wealth transfers from producers to consumers. In the second case the transfer is reversed. Spann estimated that this lagged process transferred large sums. In the relatively price-stable period around 1960, he estimates that the lagged price-setting process transferred about $18 billion (in present-value terms) to producers. In the rising-price period around 1973, he estimated the transfer to consumers to be more than $50 billion in present-value terms.

It is important to note that these estimates of wealth transfer are based on the idea that regulators set the price for the next period to equal the average cost in the current period. This means they are crude estimates, as Spann offers no evidence that regulators actually behave this way. What is really at issue and what has not been adequately addressed is whether regulators use a lagged price-setting process or instead formed rational forecasts about future costs. That is, do they set prices based on expectations of cost next period? In a period of rapidly rising input prices, the financial success and even survival of regulated electric utilities depends on the answer to this question.

Fuel adjustment clauses are one method regulators have used to mitigate the lagged adjustment problem. Kendrick offers a theoretical analysis of automatic revenue adjustment clauses.[7] Later in this chapter I examine the time series of electricity prices to see if a lagged adjustment process shows up even with adjustment clauses.

DESCRIPTIVE STATISTICS

Table 4–1 reports summary statistics for several variables important to the electric utility industry for the period 1960 through 1982. All figures are average annual percentage changes for the whole period.

6. Robert M. Spann, "The Regulatory Cobweb: Inflation, Deflation, Regulatory Lags and the Effect of Alternative Administrative Rules in Public Utilities," *Southern Economic Journal* 43 (July 1976): 827–39.

7. John W. Kendrick, "Efficiency, Incentives and Cost Factors in Public Utility Automatic Revenue Adjustment Clauses," *Bell Journal of Economics* 6 (Spring 1975): 299–313.

Table 4–1.   Average Annual Changes in Variables Affecting the Electric Utility Industry.

Variable	Mean 1960–1982
Return to common stock	11.208%
Inflation	5.409%
Market return	16.759%
Long-term debt	7.958%
Fuel cost	9.536%
Price of electricity	5.345%
Output	5.244%

Figures 4–1 through 4–7 chart these percentage changes as they vary over this period. Annual return to common stock is the equally weighted average return to 103 electric utility common stocks listed on the New York Stock Exchange (NYSE), and it includes dividends and other disbursements. These companies are listed in an appendix to this chapter. Inflation is the annual percentage change in the consumer price index. Market return is the dividend-adjusted, equally weighted

Figure 4–1.   Annual Inflation.

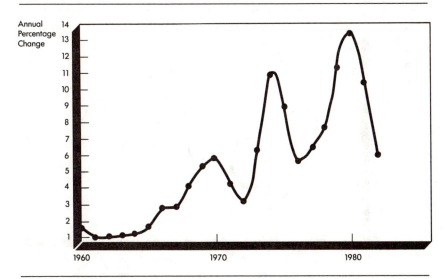

Source: *Statistical Abstract of the United States* (Washington, D.C.: U.S. Bureau of the Census, various issues).

Figure 4–2.   Total Long-Term Debt, Investor-Owned Utilities.

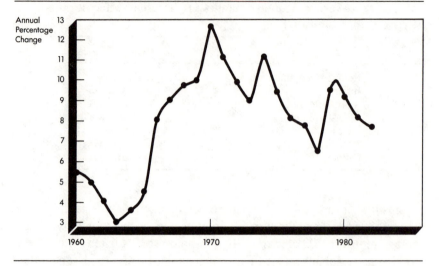

SOURCE: *Statistical Yearbook of the Electric Utility Industry* (Washington, D.C.: Edison Electric Institute, 1960–1982).

Figure 4–3.   Average Revenue per KWH.

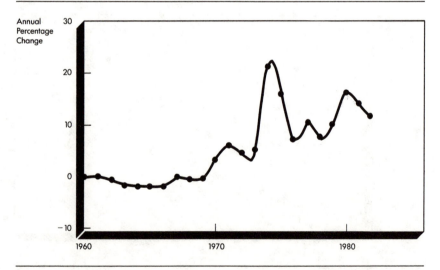

SOURCE: *Statistical Yearbook of the Electric Utility Industry* (Washington, D.C.: Edison Electric Institute, 1960–1982).

Figure 4–4.   KWH Sold.

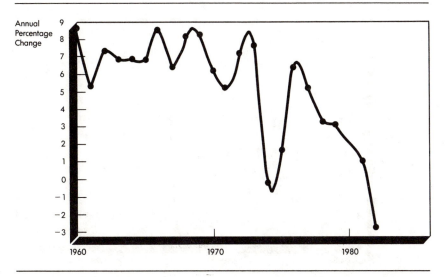

SOURCE: *Statistical Yearbook of the Electric Utility Industry* (Washington, D.C.: Edison Electric Institute, 1960–1982).

Figure 4–5.   Fuel Cost per KWH.

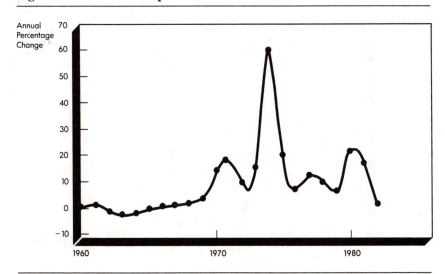

SOURCE: *Statistical Yearbook of the Electric Utility Industry* (Washington, D.C.: Edison Electric Institute, 1960–1982).

Figure 4–6.   Return to Common Stock, 103 Electric Utility Companies on NYSE.

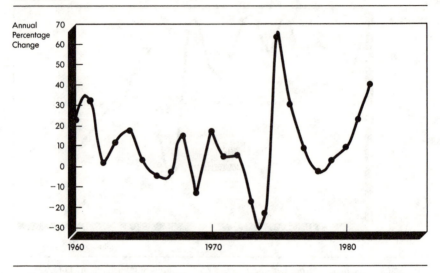

SOURCE: Monthly Stock Returns File, Center for Research in Securities Prices (Chicago: University of Chicago, Graduate School of Business, 1984).

Figure 4–7.   Return to all NYSE Stocks.

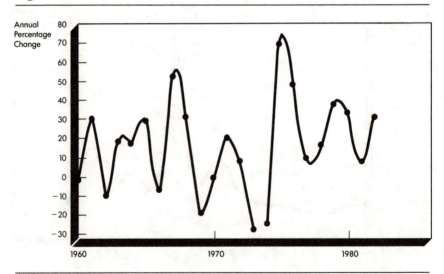

SOURCE: Monthly Stock Returns File, Center for Research in Securities Prices (Chicago: University of Chicago, Graduate School of Business, 1984).

return to all stocks listed on the NYSE. Long-term debt is only for investor-owned electric utilities. It excludes municipal electric companies, the Tennessee Valley Authority (TVA), rural electric cooperatives, and state-operated power authorities. Fuel cost is the average price per million Btu's consumed. Electricity price is the average revenue per kwh received by the total electric industry from all sources: commercial, industrial, residential, and governmental. Output is total kwh sold to these same sources by the total industry. All numbers are U.S. averages.

From the figures we see that the growth rate of debt peaked in 1970 and is currently running about 8 percent per year. Average revenue declined in the early 1960s, but it has increased considerably since then. The largest annual increase was 21 percent in 1974. The growth rate of output is positive, but it shows a small and steady decline over the two decades. In fact output actually declined in 1982. Fuel cost has grown slowly except in the 1973–75 and 1979–80 periods. The return to equity shows the random walk expected of stock prices in a capital market.

Figure 4–8 combines the annual inflation rate with the annual percentage change in the price of electricity. The picture does not suggest a lagged relationship between inflation and price. But 1970 appears to be a pivotal year. Prior to 1970 electricity price increases were several percentage points less than inflation. After 1970 electricity price increases generally exceeded inflation. The post-1973 period is probably due to the large increases in fuel cost, but the 1970–1973 period cannot be explained so easily.

A preliminary look at fuel cost and electricity prices casts some doubt on the seriousness of the lagged adjustment problem. Table 4–2 reports the fuel expenditures per net kwh produced by the total

Table 4–2. Changes in Fuel Cost 1956–1982.

Year	Cost of Fuel per Net kwh Produced	Average Revenue per kwh	Ratio	Difference
1956	0.29¢	1.64¢	.177	1.35¢
1960	0.28¢	1.69¢	.166	1.41¢
1979	1.62¢	3.82¢	.424	2.20¢
1982	2.46¢	5.79¢	.425	3.33¢

Figure 4–8.   Inflation and Electricity Prices.

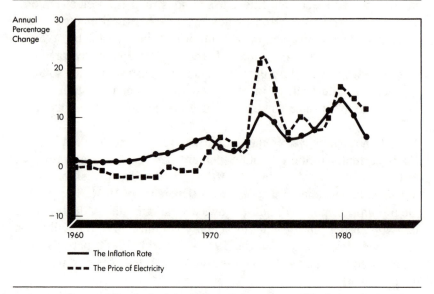

SOURCE: *Statistical Yearbook of the Electric Utility Industry* (Washington, D.C.: Edison Electric Institute, 1960–1982); and *Statistical Abstract of the United States* (Washington, D.C.: U.S. Bureau of the Census, various issues).

electricity industry and the average revenue for the whole industry for several years. The ratio of fuel cost to average revenue has increased from 0.177 in 1956 to 0.425 in 1982. That is, 42.5 percent of every revenue dollar went to purchase fuel in 1982. If we subtract fuel cost per kwh from average revenue, we see that the difference has increased from 1.41¢ per kwh in 1960 to 3.33¢ per kwh in 1982. Over this same time period the compounded annual increase in inflation is 246.9 percent. If we multiply the inflation factor, 2.469, times the difference between fuel cost and average revenue in 1960, we get 3.48¢, which is almost the same as the actual difference.

The difference between average revenue and fuel cost allows the electric company to pay its employees, service its debt, pay taxes, advertise, lobby, compensate its owners, and otherwise manage its affairs. We see that for the 1960–1982 period at least, the industry's ability to pay these bills has kept pace with inflation almost exactly. Again this suggests that inflation has not been a serious problem to the extent anyway that it can be measured using this approach. Put another way, these numbers suggest that inflation is no more a problem for electric utilities in 1982 than it was in 1960.

Another way to investigate the impact of inflation on the financial security of electric utilities is to examine the time series of debt. Among U.S. corporations, electric utilities are uncommonly leveraged. For example, using accounting numbers, long-term debt accounted for 49.3 percent of the value of all investor-owned electric utility companies in 1982.[8] As Figure 4–9 demonstrates, the annual change in debt runs hand-in-hand with changes in the cost of fuel.

Consider the following simple model of debt accumulation:

$$PCTDDEBT = \beta_0 + \beta_1 PCTDAR + \beta_2 PCTDFC + \beta_3 INFLATION$$
$$+ \beta_4 DEBTLAG1$$

where *PCTDDEBT* = annual percentage change in long-term debt
             of investor-owned utilities,
       PCTDAR = annual percentage change in average revenue,
       PCTDFC = annual percentage change in cost of fuel per
             million Btu's,

Figure 4–9.   Long-Term Debt and Fuel Prices.

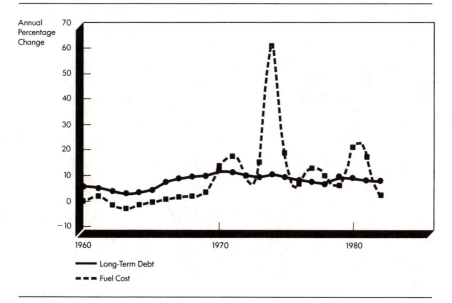

SOURCE: *Statistical Yearbook of the Electric Utility Industry* (Washington, D.C.: Edison Electric Institute, 1960–1982).

8. See *Statistical Yearbook of the Electric Utility Industry* (Washington, D.C.: Edison Electric Institute, 1982), p. 82.

> *INFLATION* = the inflation rate as measured by changes in the CPI, and
>
> *DEBTLAG1* = last year's annual change in long-term debt.

All data were corrected for inflation by the CPI. The coefficients, β_i, were estimated using ordinary-least-squares, and the results are reported in Table 4–3.[9]

The results are interesting. A 10-percent increase in inflation is associated with a 3.8-percent increase in real debt. A 10-percent increase in real average revenue is associated with a 2.8-percent decline in real debt. A 10-percent increase in fuel cost is linked with a 0.7-percent increase in debt. Debt changes in any one year spill over to the next year. A 10-percent change in debt one year leads to a 7.1-percent change the subsequent year. All coefficients are statistically significant at the 5-percent level.

These data lead to several conclusions. First, electricity debt follows a rational path. Price decreases or cost increases are, in part, financed through the sale of debt. Second, shocks that change the level of debt are distributed intertemporally. That is, an increase in debt in one period induces the industry to sell more debt the subsequent period. The effect is dampened over time, however. In fact estimates of the model including a two-year lagged value of debt show that no statistically reliable association exists between debt in the current year and debt two years before. Inflation and cost increases raise the debt of electric utilities in the current year and the subsequent

---

Table 4–3.   Regression Coefficients—Debt Equation.

Variable	Coefficient	t-ratio	Probability
Intercept	0.797	0.891	0.38
Average revenue	−0.279	−2.85	0.01
Fuel cost	0.075	2.27	0.03
Debt lag 1	0.711	6.50	0.01
Inflation	0.380	2.82	0.01
F-ratio = 18.55	R^2 = .788		D-W statistic = 1.96

---

9. The coefficients were also estimated using a one- and two-year autoregressive lag structure in the errors. The autoregressive parameters were nor significant, nor did their inclusion affect the other estimates.

year, but the effect does not persist. In addition revenue changes have the opposite effect, and they do not persist either.

Using a similar methodology, we can directly investigate whether a regulatory lag exists by looking at the time-series of electricity prices and costs of production. Consider the following reduced-form model of electricity prices:

$$P = \alpha_O + \alpha_1 CAP + \alpha_2 INF + \alpha_3 Q + \alpha_4 FC + \alpha_5 FCLAG_1$$
$$+ \alpha_6 FCLAG_2 + \alpha_7 FCLAG_3 + \alpha_8 Y + \alpha_9 PGAS$$

where P = annual percentage change in average revenue for the total electric power industry,

CAP = annual percentage change in total generating capacity,

Q = annual percentage change in output,

FC = annual percentage change in fuel cost,

$FCLAG_i$ = ith lag of fuel cost,

Y = annual percentage change in disposable personal income, and

$PGAS$ = annual percentage change in the price of natural gas.

Previous studies on electricity supply and demand suggest the following signs on the coefficients: α_2, α_4, α_8, $\alpha_9 > 0$ and α_1, $\alpha_3 < 0$.[10] Higher inflation increases costs; higher fuel prices raise costs. To the extent that electricity is a normal good, higher income raises demand, and presumably electricity and natural gas are gross substitutes. On the other hand increased capacity and higher output imply lower cost to the extent that there are economies of scale in production and transmission and to the extent that they imply higher use rates of existing capital. The question of regulatory lag is addressed by the signs on α_5, α_6, and α_7. If there is no lag, then each of these coefficients will be zero. If there is a lag, one or more of them will be positive. The model used annual data from 1960 to 1982 for estimates. The results of estimating the model by ordinary-least-squares (OLS) are reported in Table 4–4. This table also shows estimates of the model assuming there is a two-year lag autoregressive structure in the errors.

These results do not support the regulatory-lag hypothesis. Fuel cost increases in the current year have a positive and significant im-

---

10. See, for example, Lester Taylor, "The Demand for Electricity: A Survey," *Bell Journal of Economics* 6 (1975): 74–110; Jarrell, "Demand for State Regulation," pp. 269–98; and Maloney, McCormick, and Tollison, "Economic Regulation."

Table 4–4.   Regression Coefficients—Electricity Price Equation.

Variable	Using Ordinary Least Squares		Using an Autoregressive Structure	
	Coefficient	t-ratio	Coefficient	t-ratio
Intercept	2.62	1.75	2.81	2.29
Capacity	−0.05	−0.31	−0.11	−1.22
Inflation	0.43	2.35	0.44	2.89
Output	−0.58	−4.35	−0.54	−4.34
Fuel cost	0.16	5.92	0.18	9.37
Fuel cost lag 1	0.03	0.78	0.04	1.11
Fuel cost lag 2	−0.01	−0.22	−0.02	−0.89
Fuel cost lag 3	0.03	0.98	0.03	1.08
Income per capita	−0.04	−0.18	−0.06	−0.39
Customers	0.001	1.07	0.003	1.88
Gas price	0.21	1.61	0.21	2.06
Error lag 1			−0.37	−2.00
Error lag 2			0.48	2.62
F-ratio	133.92			
R^2	0.9911		0.9954	
Joint F-test on lagged fuel cost	0.07			

pact on electricity prices. The elasticity estimate is 0.179. A 10-percent increase in fuel cost is associated with a 1.79-percent increase in the price of electricity. Fuel cost increases in previous years, however, do not have a significant impact on price this year, but the point estimate is positive.[11] The joint F-statistic on the three lags is 0.07, which is not significant.

Perhaps the failure to find a lagged fuel-cost effect is due to the fuel adjustment clauses implemented by most regulatory commissions in the 1970s. I reestimated the model using only the 1960–75 period, and the results are the same as those reported in Table 4–4. No significant relationship shows up between price and lagged fuel cost, but again the point estimate is positive. It is arguable that costs other than fuel are the ones that lag. The model was also estimated using lagged

11. The results are not sensitive to specification. Specifying the model in real terms does not affect the results. Deleting inflation has no effect. Including lagged values of electricity, price only serves to increase the Durbin-Watson statistic toward 2.0. Using only one lag of fuel cost has no impact either.

values of inflation instead of lagged values of fuel cost. The lagged values of inflation are not significant.

These results suggest that regulatory lag is not a serious economic problem. If there is a lag, it is less than one year in duration. The only other obvious explanation is that the lag is infinite; that is, electric utilities never recover input price increases.

ACCOUNTING RULES

States vary in their regulation of electric utility production. For example, some regulators are elected, and others are appointed by state officials. Table 4–5 lists the state utility commissions, the method of selecting regulators, the allowed rates of return, and the appropriate accounting standards for the investment tax credit and for evaluating the rate base, all for 1967 and 1980.[12]

In 1967 nineteen states used original-cost accounting to calculate the rate base. Nine states used the fair-market value approach, while the rest used some other method. By 1980, however, almost all states had switched to original-cost accounting. It is interesting to note that the chi-square test of independence between the method of commission selection and the accounting practice used for evaluating the rate base in 1967 is 5.90 with 4 degrees of freedom. This suggests that the method of selecting the regulators is associated with the way they regulate. Moreover allowed rates of return are marginally different across the two types of commissions. The mean allowed rate of return for elected states in 1967 was 5.99 percent, while the average allowed rate of return was 6.22 percent in states with appointed commissioners. This difference is statistically different at the 10-percent level using a one-tailed t-test. The allowed rates of return in 1980 are 13.89 percent and 14.38 percent for elected and appointed commissions respectively. This difference is also statistically significant at the 10-percent level.[13]

In 1967 the elected commissions showed a relative propensity to use fair-market value as opposed to original-cost accounting. In a pe-

12. See Chapter 10 by Peter Navarro in this volume; R. Blaine Roberts, G. S. Maddala, and Gregory Enholm, "Determinants of the Requested Rate of Return and the Rate of Return Granted in a Formal Regulatory Process," *Bell Journal of Economics* 9 (1978): 611–21; and Crain and McCormick, "Regulators as an Interest Group," for analysis of the impact of commission structure.

13. See Crain and McCormick, "Regulators as an Interest Group."

Table 4–5.   Electric Utility Accounting Rules.

State	Return 1967	Return 1980	Rate Base 1967	Rate Base 1980	ITC 1967	ITC 1980	Commission
Alabama		12.5	fair	orig		norm	elected
Alaska	7.00		fair				appoint
Arizona	6.50	15.0	fair	fair		norm	elected
Arkansas		13.8	orig	orig	comb	norm	appoint
California	6.26	15.0	orig	orig	flow	flow	appoint
Colorado	6.35	15.5	orig	orig		norm	appoint
Connecticut	6.00	15.1	orig	orig	flow	flow	appoint
Delaware	6.50	15.0	fair	orig	comb	norm	appoint
Florida[1]		14.5	orig	orig	norm	norm	elected
Georgia[2]	6.00	14.4	orig	orig	norm	norm	elected
Hawaii	6.50	14.8	orig	orig	comb	norm	appoint
Idaho	6.10	14.9		orig	norm	norm	appoint
Illinois	5.85	14.3	fair	orig	norm	norm	appoint
Indiana		13.8	fair	fair	norm	norm	appoint
Iowa		12.5		orig		norm	
Kansas		13.9	orig	orig	norm	norm	appoint
Kentucky		13.9		orig	norm	norm	elected
Louisiana	6.00	14.0	orig	orig	flow	norm	elected
Maine		13.8	orig	orig	flow	norm	appoint
Maryland	6.25	14.0	fair	orig	other	norm	appoint
Massachusetts		14.2		orig	norm	norm	appoint
Michigan	6.42	13.5	orig	orig	norm	norm	appoint
Minnesota		13.5	other	orig	norm	norm	elected
Mississippi		14.0	fair	orig	norm	norm	elected
Missouri		13.8	fair	orig	comb	norm	appoint
Montana	5.30	13.5	fair	orig	comb	norm	elected
Nevada	6.85	15.0	orig	orig	flow	norm	appoint
New Hampshire	6.50	15.9	orig	orig	comb	norm	appoint
New Jersey		13.8	fair	orig	comb	norm	appoint
New Mexico		15.5	fair	orig	norm	norm	elected
New York		14.1	orig	orig	flow	norm	appoint
North Carolina		14.2	fair	orig	norm	norm	appoint
North Dakota		13.3	prudent	orig	comb	norm	elected
Ohio	5.75	14.6	repro	orig	comb	norm	appoint
Oklahoma[2]	6.13	15.3	orig	orig	norm	norm	elected
Oregon		15.2	orig	orig	flow	norm	appoint
Pennsylvania	5.90	15.8	fair	orig	norm		appoint
Rhode Island	6.00	13.8	orig	orig	comb	norm	appoint
South Carolina		12.5	other	orig	comb	norm	appoint
South Dakota		13.0	other		norm	norm	elected
Tennessee	6.00		orig		norm		elected
Texas		15.5	prudent	orig	flow	norm	elected
Utah	6.15	16.8	orig	orig	comb	norm	appoint
Vermont	6.11	14.5	orig	orig	flow	norm	appoint
Virginia	6.38	13.5	orig	orig	flow	norm	appoint
Washington	6.10	15.3	orig	orig	comb		appoint
West Virginia	6.25	14.5	orig	orig	other	norm	appoint
Wisconsin	6.00	13.3	prudent	orig	flow	norm	appoint
Wyoming	5.60	13.0	orig	orig	norm	norm	appoint

1. Switched from elected to appointed in January 1979.
2. Also used fair-market criterion in some cases in 1967.

riod of rising prices, original-cost accounting methods understate the true value of the rate base, while fair-market value has at least the potential for accurately describing the opportunity cost of the invested capital. In other words, in 1967, electric utilities in states with elected regulators stood to fare better under inflation than their counterparts in states with appointed commissioners, other things being the same. All this is fine, except that when inflation really became a serious problem in the 1970s, most elected commissions switched to original-cost accounting. Moreover states with the lowest allowed rates of return were the ones most likely to switch to original-cost accounting, just the opposite of what is required to offset the effects of inflation.

Between 1967 and 1980 nine states changed their method of accounting for the rate base. A dummy variable indicating whether a state changed its rate-base accounting method (1 = yes, 0 = no) was regressed on the allowed rate of return in 1967. The coefficient is −3.20 and the chi-square statistic is 3.40, which is significant at the 10-percent level. States with low allowed rates of return are more likely to have switched to original-cost accounting during a period of significant inflation.

In the context of the economic theory of regulation, regulation appears to have shifted in the direction of being proconsumer. This does not mean that regulation now benefits consumers, but rather that regulation in the 1980s is more sensitive to consumer pressure than it was in the 1960s. Given the increase in the proportion of the consumer's budget spent on electricity, this is not surprising. As consumers spend a larger proportion of their income on electricity, they find it in their interest to spend more time lobbying and voting to fight off the monopoly effects of regulation.[14]

Examining accounting rules also shows that in 1967 eleven states required that the investment tax credit be flowed through—deducted from taxes for purposes of rate-making—in the year of the credit. Twenty states required electric utilities to defer or extend over the depreciable life of the asset the credit against taxes for purposes of rate-making. Thirteen states used a combination of the two techniques, and the rest used some other method.

Which accounting method is best for the electric utility depends

---

14. See Peltzman, "Toward a More General Theory," pp. 211–40. In terms of this model, as the proportion of income spent on electricity increases, voters become more sensitive to price regulation, and regulators set prices closer to the competitive level. That is, the price falls.

upon the investment in question, its depreciable life, and the discount rate. Consider the following example. Utility A uses the flow-through method of accounting for the investment tax credit. Utility B uses the deferred method. Both companies make a $100,000 investment, which has a depreciable life of ten years. The investment tax credit is 10 percent. Both companies have annual earnings of $100,000, and the income tax rate is 50 percent. Both companies have tax liability in 1970 of $(0.5)(\$100,000) - (0.1)(\$100,000) = \$40,000$. Actual taxes are $40,000 for both A and B. For purposes of rate-making, however, the two companies are different. In the first year company A is allowed to recover its taxes, $40,000, plus operating expenses, depreciation, and rate of return on its capital base. B is the same except its taxes appear higher by the deferred method of accounting. B's taxes are made to appear as $(0.5)(\$100,000) - (0.1)(0.1)(\$100,000) = \$49,000$. So in the first year company B gets to recover $9,000 more than A because of the accounting method. In subsequent years, assuming the same income and tax rates and no further investment, A recovers all of its tax liabilities, $50,000, but B has to credit $1,000 against taxes so it gets to recover only $49,000 over the depreciable life of the original investment. In general terms the present value of the income taxes that can be recovered under flow-through accounting is:

$$PV_F = T - C + \sum_{i=1}^{D} T/(1 + r)^i$$

where $T =$ the actual tax liability before the investment tax credit,
   $C =$ the investment tax credit,
   $D =$ the number of years over which the asset is depreciated, and
   $r =$ the interest rate.

The present value of income taxes that can be recovered with the deferral method is

$$PV_D = T - C/D + \sum_{i=1}^{D} (T - C/D)/(1 + r)^i.$$

PV_F is greater than or less then PV_D as

$$\sum_{i=1}^{D} 1/(1 + r)^i \gtreqless D - 1$$

In the example just given the present value of income for *A* (ignoring operating expenses, depreciation, and rate of return) is $327,951, assuming a discount rate of 10 percent. For *B* the present value is $331,192 so the company prefers deferred accounting.

In general for a discount rate of 10 percent, $PV_F > PV_D$ only if the life of the asset is less than five years. At a discount rate of 20 percent, $PV_F > PV_D$ only if the depreciation life of the asset is less than four years. Given the long life of most electric utility investments, the deferred method of accounting will generally result in higher incomes. We can note that on two separate occasions the Accounting Practices Board has faced heavy lobbying pressure from the Arthur Andersen Company to require that firms use the deferred method. (Arthur Andersen represents a large proportion of the electric utilities in the United States). In 1971, however, Congress decreed that either method is permissible. By 1980 all except two state utility commissions, California and Connecticut, had chosen the deferral method of accounting. This stands in contrast to the unregulated business community. In 1981 88 percent of U.S. companies used the flow-through method.[15]

FINANCIAL MARKET ANALYSIS

The modern theory of finance holds that capital markets are efficient in processing information. At any point in time the price of a security incorporates the present discounted value of all information generally available to the market about future cash flows. Hence an asset such as common stock acts as a barometer of future events and can be used to assay the future effects of current events. The empirical evidence in support of this proposition is overwhelming. For just a small sample of the literature with specific application to regulation, see Schwert.[16]

It is commonly held that inflation has a negative impact on the stock market, which a number of authors have claimed is due to accounting practices. For example, depreciation is based on book value or historical costs, not replacement value. Hence, in a period of general inflation, real depreciation expense is understated, thereby raising

15. See Donald E. Kieso and Jerry J. Weygandt, *Intermediate Accounting*, 4th ed. (New York: John Wiley & Sons, 1983), p. 542.

16. G. William Schwert, "Using Financial Data to Measure Effects of Regulation," *Journal of Law and Economics* 24 (April 1981): 121–58.

the actual tax burden of the firm.[17] Others claim that inflation is just a harbinger of overall bad times. Thus inflation is a signal that the economy is sick, which coincidentally causes the stock market to decline. French, Ruback, and Schwert examine what they call the nominal-contracting explanation for the negative association between inflation and stock prices, but they find little empirical support for the proposition.[18] Contracts written at fixed prices will cause wealth transfers if there are subsequent unexpected changes in prices. A company that has sold debt will receive a wealth transfer from the debt holder if inflation rises more than anticipated at the time the debt was sold. Given the large amount of debt held by electric utility companies, we might expect that unanticipated price increases or decreases would cause their stock prices to be especially vulnerable to these shocks. But if there is regulatory lag, unanticipated price increases will cause costs to rise more than revenues. This will transfer wealth from stockholders to consumers or the reverse when there are unanticipated price declines. Wealth transfers will have an effect on stock price of the opposite sign. Thus we have the basis for a test. If unanticipated inflation causes electric utility stock prices to rise, we conclude that there is a wealth transfer from bondholders to stockholders. If unanticipated inflation causes stock prices to fall, we conclude that a regulatory lag exists and there is a wealth transfer from stockholders to the consumers of electricity.

Consider the market model:

$$r_{it} = \alpha + \beta r_{mt} + \gamma U_t + e_t$$

where r_{it} = return to security i at time t,

r_{mt} = return to the market at time t,

17. For examples, see the work of John B. Shoven and Jeremy I. Bulow, "Inflation Accounting and Nonfinancial Corporate Profits: Physical Assets," *Brookings Papers on Economic Activity* 3 (1975): 557–98; Martin Feldstein and Lawrence Summers, "Inflation and the Taxation of Capital Income in the Corporate Sector," *National Tax Journal* 32 (December 1979): 445–70; Robert N. Freeman, "On the Association Between Net Monetary Position and Equity Security Prices," *Journal of Accounting Research* 16 (1978 supplement): 111–45; Nicholas J. Gonedes, "Evidence on the 'Tax Effects' of Inflation Under Historical Cost Accounting Methods," *Journal of Business* 54 (April 1981): 227–70; and Douglas H. Joines, "Estimates of Effective Marginal Tax Rates on Factor Incomes," *Journal of Business* 54 (April 1981): 191–226.

18. Kenneth R. French, Richard S. Ruback, and G. William Schwert, "Effects of Nominal Contracting on Stock Returns," *Journal of Political Economy* 91 (February 1983): 70–96.

U_t = unanticipated inflation at time t, and
e_t = random deviation at time t.

The return to the market, r_{mt}, will capture the overall effects of inflation, which—for whatever reasons—are negative. γ measures the effect of unanticipated inflation on the specific asset r_{it} above and beyond the market effect.

To examine the effect of inflation on electric companies, we formed a portfolio of 103 common stocks. (The companies and the states in which they operate are listed in the chapter appendix.) The rate of return to each stock is calculated as the percentage change in price from the end of one month to the end of the next month plus any disbursements. That is:

$$r_{it} = (P_{it} - P_{i,t-1} + D_{it})/P_{i,t-1}$$

where P_{it} = the price of the ith stock at time t and
D_{it} = any disbursement received at time t.

The portfolio return is simply the equally weighted average return to these 103 stocks. The market return is the equally weighted return to all stocks listed on the NYSE.

Unexpected inflation at time t, U_t, is estimated using the French, Ruback, Schwert model. They suggest the following model of inflation:

$$I_t = \mu_0 + \mu_1 I_{t-1} + \mu_2 I_{t-2} + \mu_3 TB_t + \mu_4 IP_{t-1}$$
$$+ \mu_5 IP_{t-2} + \mu_6 M_{t-1} + \mu_7 M_{t-2} + U_t$$

where I_t = inflation at time t as measured by the consumer price index,
T_t = yield to maturity on three-month Treasury bills at time t,
IP_t = growth rate of industrial production on nondurable consumer goods at time t, and
M_t = growth rate of the monetary base at time t.

The inflation model was estimated using monthly data from January 1960 through June 1979, taken from the Citibank database. Table 4–6 reports the coefficient estimates.

Unexpected inflation, U_t, is calculated by using the residuals from

Table 4–6. Regression Coefficients—Inflation Model.

Variable	Coefficient	t-ratio	Probability
Intercept	−0.002	−3.81	0.01
Inflation lag 1	0.125	1.85	0.06
Inflation lag 2	0.173	2.65	0.81
Inflation lag 3	0.017	0.24	0.81
T-bill	0.001	6.23	0.01
IP lag 1	−0.011	−0.54	0.59
IP lag 2	−0.013	−0.64	0.53
Base lag 1	−0.001	−0.44	0.66
Base lag 2	−0.0003	−0.14	0.89
F-ratio = 39.86	R^2 = 0.577		D-W statistic = 1.967

the inflation equation. The predicted value of inflation is calculated using the estimated model and is then subtracted from the actual value, leaving the residual, U_t, which is the estimate of unanticipated inflation. The value of U_t as an estimate of the actual amount of unanticipated inflation depends upon the accuracy of the prediction equation. Examining the residuals suggests that the model performs fairly well. At least it satisfies rational-expectations criteria. The autocorrelation of U_t with twelve lags of itself shows no significant correlations. The residuals were regressed on twelve lags of actual inflation. Only one coefficient had a t-ratio greater than 1.0, and the regression was not significant. Both of these tests suggest that U_t is white noise. Thus we have confidence that U_t is a reliable estimate of unanticipated inflation.

This allows us to estimate the market model including U_t. The results are provided in Table 4–7 for the period 1960–1979. The estimate of β is 0.55, which is consistent with other estimates of the covariance of utility stocks with the market. Unexpected inflation has

Table 4–7. Regression Coefficients—Market Model 1960–1979.

Variable	Coefficient	t-ratio	Probability
Intercept	0.0007	0.37	0.71
Market return	0.551	15.46	0.01
Unexpected Inflation	1.003	1.02	0.31
F-ratio = 122.13			R^2 = 0.519

a positive but insignificant impact on electricity stock prices, other things being equal. Keep in mind that a negative relationship exists between unexpected inflation and the market, so unexpected inflation has two effects on electricity stock prices. The first works indirectly through the market, which in turn affects utility stock performance, and the second works separately and directly on the utility stocks themselves. The positive coefficient γ means that compared to the market, electric utilities perform better than average under unexpected inflation.

We can also assess the total impact of inflation on the electricity portfolio: R_{mt} was regressed on U_t. The coefficient estimate is -5.801. The t-ratio is -3.25. The intercept is 0.01. Substituting these estimates into the market model for r_{mt}, we get $r_{it} = 0.01 - 2.196 U_t$. I also estimated this equation directly, with almost identical results. The coefficient on U_t has an 89 percent chance of being different from zero. This is interpreted to mean that the total effect of unexpected inflation on stock prices is negative, but the basic result remains. Other things being the same, unexpected inflation has a positive but statistically insignificant impact on electricity stock prices.

This is further evidence against the regulatory-lag hypothesis. Electric utilities do no worse than unregulated companies when unexpected inflation occurs. In fact they do slightly better, but that estimate has a low statistical reliability.

Two other statistical tests were performed using the market model. The 103 companies were partitioned based on whether they operated in a state with appointed or elected commissioners. The market model was reestimated separately for each group, and the coefficients compared. No evidence was found that the coefficients are unequal. Electricity stock performance is not a function of the type of regulatory commission.

The time period was divided into five-year intervals, and the market model was reestimated for each period. The coefficient estimates are provided in Table 4–8. Again the results support the view that unexpected inflation does not have a negative impact on stock prices. In sum these numbers cast doubt on the seriousness of the regulatory-lag problem, at least to the extent that it can be measured this way.

This methodology does not exhaust the possible explanations for the positive association between unanticipated inflation and electricity stock performance. A regulatory-lag problem could exist but be swamped by a wealth redistribution from bondholders to stockhold-

Table 4–8. Regression Coefficients—Market Model, Five Year Subsamples.

Variable	1960–64 coefficient	t-ratio	1965–1969 coefficient	t-ratio	1975–1979 coefficient	t-ratio
Intercept	.007	2.50	−.005	−.95	.001	.224
Market return	.69	10.83	.387	3.53	.589	8.59
Unexpected inflation	2.54	1.61	.300	0.10	.533	.24
F-ratio	58.94		6.73		38.28	
R^2	.69		.23		.64	

ers. To satisfactorily resolve the issue, it would be necessary to measure the impact of unanticipated inflation on electric utility bond prices. The sum of the two impacts, value weighted, would measure the extent of any regulatory lag more precisely. Bond price data availability make this project untenable at the present. For the moment the best we can say is that there is no evidence of a regulatory lag, but the issue remains quite open.

CONCLUSION

Electricity prices are set by fiat and not through the daily interaction of market demand and supply. This fact has caused some people to worry about the ability of electric companies to survive in a period of rising prices. Although the issue is far from decided, the preliminary evidence presented here suggests that regulatory lag is not a serious economic problem. Specifically electricity prices are not a function of lagged input price increases. Although long-term debt of electric utilities does respond positively to input price increases, it also responds negatively to revenue increases. Moreover no dramatic or secular increase in debt occurred in the inflationary period of the 1970s.

Perhaps most important the financial community does not appear to worry very much about the impact of inflation on the industry. In fact, although the estimate has weak statistical reliability, the best guess at this point is that inflation makes electric utility companies richer.

Finally some evidence shows that regulation has shifted in a pro-consumer direction. Accounting standards seem to have adjusted in a way that, at the margin, benefit consumers. This is probably due to increased political pressure from consumers, whose expenditures on electricity have increased as a proportion of their total income.

APPENDIX

Company	Operating States
Allegheny Pwr. Sys. Inc.	PA WV MD
American Elec. Pwr. Inc.	MI IN OH WV VA
Arizona Pub. Svc. Co.	AZ
Atlantic City Elec. Co.	NJ
Baltimore Gas & Elec. Co.	MD
Black Hills Pwr. & Lt. Co.	SD WY
Boston Edison Co.	MA
Brooklyn Edison Inc.	
C.P. Natl. Corp.	CA NV OR
Carolina Pwr. & Lt. Co.	NC
Centel Corp.	CO KS
Central & South West Corp.	TX OK LA AR
Central Hudson Gas & Elec.	NY
Central Ill. Lt. Con.	IL
Central Ill. Pub. Svc. Co.	IL
Central Louisiana Elec. Inc.	LA
Central Maine Pwr. Co.	ME
Central Vermont Pub. Svc. Corp.	VT
Cincinnati Gas & Elec. Co.	OH
Cleveland Elec. Illum. Co.	OH
Columbus & Southern Ohio Elec.	OH
Commonwealth Edison Co.	IL IN
Commonwealth Energy System	MA
Consolidated Edison Co. N.Y.	NY
Consumers Pwr. Co.	MI
Dayton Pwr. & Lt. Co.	OH
Delmarva Pwr. & Lt. Co.	DE MD
Detroit Edison Co.	MI
Duke Pwr. Co.	NC SC
Duquesne Lt. Co.	PA
Eastern Utils. Assoc.	MA
Empire Dist. Elec. Co.	KS MO
Florida Pwr. & Lt. Co.	FL
Florida Progress Corp.	FL
General Pub. Utils. Corp.	NJ PA
Green Mountain Pwr. Corp.	VT
Gulf States Utils. Co.	TX LA
Hawaiian Elec. Inc.	HI
Houston Industries Inc.	TX
Idaho Pwr. Co.	ID OR
Illinois Pwr. Co.	IL

Appendix (Continued)

Company	Operating States
Indianapolis Pwr. & Lt. Co.	IN
Interstate Pwr. Co.	IA MN
Iowa Elec. Lt. & Pwr. Co.	IA
Iowa Ill. Gas & Elec. Co.	IA IL
Iowa Pub. Svc. Co.	IA
Kansas City Pwr. & Lt. Co.	KS MO
Kansas Gas & Elec. Co.	KS
Kansas Pwr. & Lt. Co.	KS
Kentucky Utils. Co.	KY VA
Long Island Ltg. Co.	NY
Louisville Gas & Elec. Co.	KY
Manila Elec. Corp.	AR MO MS LA
Minnesota Pwr. & Lt. Co.	MN
Missouri Pub. Svc. Co.	MO KS
Montana Dakota Utils. Co.	MT ND SD
Montana Pwr. Co.	MT
Nevada Pwr. Co.	NV
New England Elec. Sys.	MA RI NH
New York State Elec. & Gas Corp.	NY
Niagara Mohawk Pwr. Corp.	NY
Northern Ind. Pub. Svc. Co.	IN
Northern States Pwr. Co. Minn.	MN ND SD
Ohio Edison Co.	OH
Oklahoma Gas & Elec. Co.	OK AR
Orange & Rockland Utils. Inc.	NJ NY
Pacific Gas & Elec. Co.	CA
Pacific Pwr. & Lt. Co.	WA ID CA WY MT
Pennsylvania Pwr. & Lt. Co.	PA
Philadelphia Elec. Co.	PA
Portland Gen. Elec. Co.	OR
Potomac Elec. Pwr. Co.	MD
Public Svc. Co. Colo.	CO
Public Svc. Co. Ind. Inc.	IN
Public Svc. Co. N.H.	NH VT
Public Svc. Co. N. Mex.	NM
Public Svc. Elec. & Gas Co.	NJ
Puget Sound Pwr. & Lt. Co.	WA
Rochester Gas & Elec. Corp.	NY
St. Joseph Lt. & Pwr. Co.	MO
San Diego Gas & Elec. Co.	CA
Savannah Elec. & Pwr. Co.	GA
Sierra Pac. Pwr. Co.	NV CA
South Carolina Elec. & Gas	SC
Southern Calif. Edison Co.	CA
Southern Ind. Gas & Elec. Co.	IN
Southwestern Pub. Svc. Co.	TX OK

Appendix (Continued)

Company	Operating States
Teco Energy Inc.	FL
Texas New Mex. Pwr. Co.	TX NM
Texas Utils. Co.	TX
Toledo Edison Co.	OH
Tucson Elec. Pwr. Co.	AZ
U.G.I. Corp.	PA
Union Elec. Co.	MO IL IA
United Illum. Co.	CT
Utah Pwr. & Lt. Co.	UT ID WY
Virginia Elec. & Pwr. Co.	VA WV NC
West Penn. Co.	PA
Wisconsin Elec. Pwr. Co.	WI MI
Wisconsin Pwr. & Lt. Co.	WI IL
Wisconsin Pub. Svc. Corp.	WI MI

SELECTED BIBLIOGRAPHY
PART I

Acton, Jan Paul. "An Evaluation of Economists' Influence on Electric Utility Rate Reform." *American Economic Review* 72 (1982):114–19.

Alm, Alvin L., and Daniel A. Dreyfus. *Utilities in Crisis: A Problem of Governance*. New York: Aspen Institute for Humanistic Studies, 1982.

"Are Utilities Obsolete?" *Business Week* (21 May 1984):116–29.

Averch, Harvey, and Leland L. Johnson. "Behavior of the Firm Under Regulatory Constraint." *American Economic Review* 52 (December 1962):1052–69.

Bailey, Elizabeth E. "Peak Load Pricing Under Regulatory Constraints." *Journal of Political Economy* 80 (1972):662–79.

———. *Economic Theory of Regulatory Constraint*. Lexington, Mass.: Lexington Books, 1973.

———. "Contestability and Design of Regulatory and Antitrust Policy." *American Economic Review* 71 (1981):178–83.

Bailey, Elizabeth E., and Ann F. Friedlander. "Market Structure and Multiproduct Industries." *Journal of Economic Literature* 20 (1982):1024–48.

Bailey, Elizabeth E., and John C. Panzar. "The Contestability of Airline Markets during Transition to Deregulation." *Journal of Law and Contemporary Problems* 44 (1981):125–45.

Baron, David P., and Robert A. Taggart, Jr. "A Model of Regulation Under Uncertainty and a Test of Regulatory Bias." *Bell Journal of Economics* 8 (1977):151–67.

Barro, Robert T. "The Control of Politicians: An Economic Model." *Public Choice* 14 (Spring 1973):19–42.

Barzel, Yoram. "Productivity in the Electric Power Industry, 1929–1955." *Review of Economics and Statistics* 45 (1963): 395–408.

Baumol, William J. *Welfare Economics and the Theory of the State.* Cambridge: Harvard University Press, 1965.

————. "On the Proper Cost Test for Natural Monopoly in a Multiproduct Industry." *American Economic Review* 67 (1977):809–22.

Baumol, William J.; Elizabeth E. Bailey; and Robert D. Willig. "Weak Invisible Hand Theorems on the Sustainability of Prices in a Multiproduct Monopoly." *American Economic Review* 67 (1977):350–65.

Baumol, William J., and David F. Bradford. "Optimal Departures from Marginal Cost Pricing." *American Economic Review* 60 (June 1970):265–83.

Baumol, William J., and Alvin K. Klevorick. "Input Choices and Rate-of-Return Regulation: An Overview of the Discussion." *Bell Journal of Economics and Management Science* 1 (1970):162–90.

Baumol, William J.; John C. Panzar; and Robert D. Willig. *Contestable Markets and the Theory of Industry Structure.* New York: Harcourt Brace Jovanovich, 1982.

Baumol, William J., and Robert D. Willig. "Fixed Cost, Sunk Cost, Entry Barriers and Sustainability of Monopoly." *Quarterly Journal of Economics* 96 (1981):405–32.

Becker, Gary S. "A Theory of Competition Among Pressure Groups for Political Influence." *Quarterly Journal of Economics* 98 (August 1983): 371–400.

Becker, Gary S., and George J. Stigler. "Law Enforcement, Malfeasance, and Compensation of Enforcers." *Journal of Legal Studies* 3 (January 1974):1–18.

Berg, Sanford, ed. *Innovative Electric Rates.* Lexington, Mass.: Lexington Books, 1983.

Berlin, Edward; Charles J. Cicchetti; and William J. Gillen. *Perspective on Power: A Study of the Regulation and Pricing of Electricity.* Cambridge, Mass.: Ballinger Publishing Co., 1974.

————. "Restructuring the Electric Power Industry." In W. Shaker and W. Steffy, eds., *Electric Power Reform: The Alternatives for Michigan.* Ann Arbor: University of Michigan, 1976.

Berry, William W. "The Case for Competition in the Electric Utility Industry." *Public Utilities Fortnightly* 110 (16 September 1982):13–20.

Boyes, William J. "An Empirical Examination of the Averch-Johnson Effect." *Economic Inquiry* 14 (1976):25–35.

Breen, William J., and Eugene M. Lerner. "On the Use of β in Regulatory Proceedings." *Bell Journal of Economics and Management Science* 3 (1972):612–21.

Breyer, Stephen. *Regulation and Its Reform*. Cambridge: Harvard University Press, 1982.

Breyer, Stephen, and Paul W. MacAvoy. *Energy Regulation by the Federal Power Commission*. Washington, D.C.: Brookings Institution, 1974.

Buchanan, James M. "Theory of Monopolistic Quantity Discounts." *Review of Economics and Statistics* 20 (1953):199–208.

Capron, William M., ed. *Technological Change in Regulated Industries*. Washington, D.C.: Brookings Institution, 1971.

Carron, Andrew S., and Paul W. MacAvoy. *The Decline of Service in Regulated Industries*. Washington, D.C.: American Enterprise Institute, 1981.

Christensen, Laurits R., and William H. Greene. "An Econometric Assessment of Cost Savings from Coordination in U.S. Electric Power Generation." *Land Economics* 54 (1978):139–55.

———. "Economies of Scale in U.S. Electric Power Generation." *Journal of Political Economy* 84 (1976):655–76.

Cicchetti, Charles J.; William J. Gillen; and P. Smolensky. *The Marginal Cost and Pricing of Electricity: An Applied Approach*. Cambridge, Mass.: Ballinger Publishing Co., 1977.

Cicchetti, Charles J., and John L. Jurewitz, eds. *Studies in Electric Utility Regulation*. Cambridge, Mass.: Ballinger Publishing Co., 1975.

Clemens, Eli W. *Economics and Public Utilities*. New York: Appleton-Century, 1950.

Coase, Ronald H. "The Theory of Public Utility Regulation." In *The Economics of the Regulation of Public Utilities*. Evanston, Ill.: Northwestern University, 1966.

Cohen, Matthew. "Efficiency and Competition in the Electric-Power Industry." *Yale Law Journal* 88 (1979):1511–49.

Cohon, Robert L., and S. Robert Lichter. "Nuclear Power: The Decision Makers Speak." *Regulation* (March/April 1983):32–37.

Colberg, Marshall R. "Utility Profits: A Substitute for Property Taxes." *National Tax Journal* 8 (1955):382–87.

Comanor, William S. "Should Natural Monopolies Be Regulated?" *Stanford Law Review* 22 (1970):510–18.

Corio, Marie R. "Why Is the Performance of Electric Generating Units Declining?" *Public Utilities Fortnightly* (29 April 1982):3–8.

Council of Economic Advisers. *The Economic Report of the President*. Washington, D.C.: U.S. Government Printing Office, 1984.

Coursey, Don R.; R. Mark Isaac; and Vernon L. Smith. "Natural Monopoly and Contested Markets: Some Experimental Results." *Journal of Law and Economics* 27 (1984):91–113.

Courville, Léon. "Regulation and Efficiency in the Electric Utility Industry." *Bell Journal of Economics and Management Science* 5 (1974):53–74.

Cowing, Thomas G., and V. Kerry Smith. "The Estimation of a Production

Technology: A Survey of Econometric Analyses of Steam Electric Generation." *Land Economics* 54 (1978):156–86.

Crain, W. Mark, and Robert B. Ekelund. "Chadwick and Demsetz on Competition and Regulation." *Journal of Law and Economics* 19 (1976):149–62.

Crain, W. Mark, and Robert E. McCormick. "Regulators as an Interest Group." In J. Buchanan and R. Tollison, eds., *The Theory of Public Choice II*. Ann Arbor: University of Michigan Press, 1984.

Crew, Michael A. "Managerial Discretion and Public Utility Regulation." *Southern Economic Journal* 46 (January 1979):696–709.

———. *Problems in Public Utility Economics and Regulation*. Lexington, Mass.: Lexington Books, 1979.

———. *Issues in Public-Utility Pricing and Regulation*. Lexington, Mass.: Lexington Books, 1980.

———, ed. *Regulatory Reform and Public Utilities*. Lexington, Mass.: Lexington Books, 1982.

Crew, Michael A., and Paul R. Kleindorfer. "Reliability and Public Utility Pricing." *American Economic Review* 68 (1978):31–40.

———. *Public Utility Economics*. New York: St. Martin's Press, 1979.

Danielson, Albert A., and David R. Kamerschen, eds. *Current Issues in Public Utility Economics*. Lexington, Mass.: Lexington Books, 1983.

DeAlessi, Louis. "An Economic Analysis of Government Ownership and Regulation: Theory and Evidence from the Electric Power Industry." *Public Choice* 19 (1974):1–42.

———. "Some Effects of Ownership on Wholesale Prices of Electric Power." *Economic Inquiry* 13 (1975):526–38.

Delaney, James B., and T. Crawford Honeycutt. "Determinants of Research and Development Activity by Electric Utilities: Comment." *Bell Journal of Economics* 7 (1976):722–25.

Demsetz, Harold. "Why Regulate Utilities?" *Journal of Law and Economics* 11 (1968):55–65.

Dhrymes, Phoebus J., and Mordecai Kurz. "Technology and Scale in Electricity Generation." *Econometrica* 32 (July 1964):287–315.

Eckert, Roger D. "On the Incentives of Regulators: The Case of Taxicabs." *Public Choice* 14 (Spring 1973):83–99.

Edison Electric Institute. *Deregulation of Electric Utilities: A Survey of Major Concepts and Issues*. Washington, D.C.: Edison Electric Institute, 1981.

———. *Alternative Models of Electric Power Deregulation*. Washington, D.C.: Edison Electric Institute, 1982.

———. *Statistical Yearbook of the Electric Utility Industry/1982*. Washington, D.C.: Edison Electric Institute, 1983.

Evans, David S., and James J. Heckman. "A Test for Subadditivity of the

Cost Function With an Application to the Bell System." *American Economic Review* 74 (1984):615–23.

Fairman, James F., and John C. Scott. "Transmission, Power Pools, and Competition in the Electric Utility Industry." *Hastings Law Journal* 28 (1977):1159–207.

Fama, Eugene F. "Efficient Capital Markets: A Review of Theory and Empirical Work." *Journal of Finance* 25 (1970):383–417.

———. "Stock Returns, Real Activity, Inflation, and Money." *American Economic Review* 71 (September 1981):545–65.

Fanara, Philip, Jr.; James E. Suelflow; and Roman A. Draba. "Energy and Competition: The Saga of Electric Power." *Antitrust Bulletin* 25 (Spring 1980):125–42.

Faulhaber, Gerald R. "Cross-Subsidization: Pricing in Public Enterprise." *American Economic Review* 65 (1975):966–77.

Faulhaber, Gerald R., and Stephen B. Levinson. "Subsidy-Free Prices and Anonymous Equity." *American Economic Review* 71 (1981):1083–91.

Federal Energy Regulatory Commission (FERC). *Power Pooling in the United States*. FERC-0049. Washington, D.C.: FERC, 1981.

———. *Bulk Power Market Experiments at the Federal Energy Regulatory Commission*. Washington, D.C.: FERC, 1982.

Feldstein, Martin. "Inflation and the Stock Market." *American Economic Review* 70 (December 1980):839–47.

Feldstein, Martin, and Lawrence Summers. "Inflation and the Taxation of Capital Income in the Corporate Sector." *National Tax Journal* 32 (December 1979):445–70.

Ferrar, Terry A.; Frank Clemente; and Robert G. Uhler. *Electric Energy Policy Issues*. Ann Arbor, Mich.: Ann Arbor Science, 1979.

Foster, J. Rhoads; George R. Hall; Stevan R. Holmberg; Charles F. Phillip, Jr.; and Richard L. Wallace, eds. *Boundaries Between Competition and Economic Regulation*. Washington, D.C.: Institute for Study of Regulation, 1983.

Freeman, Robert N. "On the Association Between Net Monetary Position and Equity Security Prices." *Journal of Accounting Research* (supplement) 16 (1978):111–45.

French, Kenneth R.; Richard S. Ruback; and G. William Schwert. "Effects of Nominal Contracting on Stock Returns." *Journal of Political Economy* 91 (February 1983):70–96.

French, Richard X., and Suheil Z. Haddad. "The Economics of Reliability and Scale in Generating Unit Size Selection." *Public Utilities Fortnightly* 109 (23 April 1981):33–38.

Galatin, Malcolm. *Economies of Scale and Technological Change in Thermal Power Generation*. Amsterdam: North-Holland, 1968.

"Generators of Bankruptcy." *Time* (23 July 1984), p. 81.

Givens, David. "Last of Duke's N-Plants Nears Completion." *Winston-Salem Journal,* 22 July 1984, p. G1.

Goldberg, Victor P. "Regulation and Administered Contracts." *Bell Journal of Economics* (1976):426–48.

Gollop, Frank H., and Stephen H. Karlson. "The Impact of Fuel Adjustment Mechanisms on Economic Efficiency." *Review of Economics and Statistics* 60 (November 1978):574–84.

Gonedes, Nicholas J. "Evidence on the 'Tax Effects' of Inflation Under Historical Cost Accounting Methods." *Journal of Business* 54 (April 1981):227–70.

Gordon, Myron J., and John S. McCallum. "Valuation and the Cost of Capital for Regulated Industries: Comment." *Journal of Finance* 27 (1972): 1141–46.

Gordon, Richard L. *Reforming the Regulation of Electric Utilities: Priorities for the 1980s.* Lexington, Mass.: Lexington Books, 1982.

———. "Hobbling Coal—How to Serve Two Masters Poorly." *Regulation* (July/August 1978):36–45.

Graham, David, and Daniel P. Kaplan. "Airline Deregulation IS Working." *Regulation* (May/June 1982):26–32.

Hagerman, Robert L., and Brian T. Ratchford. "Some Determinants of Allowed Rates of Return on Equity to Electric Utilities." *Bell Journal of Economics* 9 (1978):46–55.

Hayashi, Paul M., and John M. Trapani. "Rate of Return Regulation and the Firm's Equilibrium Capital-Labor Ratio: Further Empirical Evidence on the Averch-Johnson Hypothesis." *Southern Economic Journal* 42 (1976):384–98.

Hellman, Richard. *Government Competition in the Electric Utility Industry: A Theoretical and Empirical Study.* New York: Praeger Publishers, 1972.

Heuttner, David A. "Scale, Costs and Environmental Pressures." In B. Gold, ed., *Technological Change: Economics, Management and Environment,* pp. 65–106. Oxford: Pergamon Press, 1975.

Heuttner, David A., and John H. Landon. "Electric Utilities: Scale Economies and Diseconomies." *Southern Economic Journal* 44 (1978):883–912.

Isaac, R. Mark. "Fuel Adjustment Mechanisms and the Regulated Utility Facing Uncertain Fuel Prices." *Bell Journal of Economics* 13 (1982):158–69.

Jackson, Raymond. "Regulation and Electric Utility Rate Levels." *Land Economics* 45 (1969):372–76.

Jaffee, Bruce L. "Depreciation in a Simple Regulatory Model." *Bell Journal of Economics and Management Science* 4 (1973):338–42.

Jarrell, Gregg A. "The Demand for State Regulation of the Electric Utility Industry." *Journal of Law and Economics* 21 (October 1978):269–98.

Joines, Douglas H. "Estimates of Effective Marginal Tax Rates on Factor Incomes." *Journal of Business* 54 (April 1981):191–226.

Joskow, Paul L. "The Determination of Allowed Rate of Return in a Formal Regulatory Hearing." *Bell Journal of Economics and Management Science* 3 (1972):632–44.

————. "Pricing Decisions of Regulated Firms: A Behavioral Approach." *Bell Journal of Economics and Management Science* 4 (1973):118–40.

————. "Inflation and Environmental Concern: Structural Change in the Process of Public Utility Price Regulation." *Journal of Law and Economics* 17 (1974):291–328.

————. "Contributions to the Theory of Marginal Cost Pricing." *Bell Journal of Economics* 7 (1976):197–206.

————. "Electric Utility Rate Structure in the United States: Some Recent Developments." In W. Sichel, ed., *Public Utility Ratemaking in an Energy Conscious Environment*, pp. 1–22. Boulder, Colo.: Westview Press, 1979.

————. "Problems and Prospects for Nuclear Energy in the U.S." In G. Daneke, ed., *Energy, Economics, and the Environment: Toward a Comprehensive Perspective.* pp. 231–54. Lexington, Mass.: Lexington Books, 1982.

Joskow, Paul L., and Martin L. Baughman. "The Future of the U.S. Nuclear Energy Industry." *Bell Journal of Economics* 7 (1976):3–32.

Joskow, Paul L., and Paul W. MacAvoy. "Regulation and the Financial Condition of the Electric Power Companies in the 1970s." *American Economic Review* 65 (May 1975):295–301.

Joskow, Paul L., and Roger G. Noll. "Regulation in Theory and Practice: An Overview." In G. Fromm, ed., *Studies in Public Regulation*, pp. 1–65. Cambridge: MIT Press, 1981.

Joskow, Paul L., and Richard Schmalensee. *Markets for Power: An Analysis of Electric Utility Deregulation.* Cambridge: MIT Press, 1983.

Kahn, Alfred E. *The Economics of Regulation: Principles and Institutions.* Vols. 1 and 2. New York: John Wiley & Sons, 1970.

Kalt, Joseph P., and Peter Navarro. "The Energy Crisis—Moral Equivalent to Civil War." *Regulation* (January/February 1980):41–43.

Kendrick, John W. "Efficiency Incentives and Cost Factors in Public Utility Automatic Revenue Adjustment Clauses." *Bell Journal of Economics* 6 (Spring 1975):299–313.

Keran, Michael W. "Inflation, Regulation, and Utility Stock Prices." *Bell Journal of Economics* 7 (1976):268–80.

Kiefer, Donald W. "The Effects of Alternative Regulatory Treatments of the Investment Tax Credit in the Public Utility Industry." *Journal of Business* 54 (June 1981):549–76.

Kieso, Donald E., and Jerry J. Weygandt. *Intermediate Accounting,* 4th ed. New York: John Wiley & Sons, 1983.

Killian, Linda R., and Robert R. Trout. "Alternatives for Electric Utility Deregulation." *Public Utilities Fortnightly* (16 September 1982):34–39.

Komiya, Ryutaro. "Technical Progress and the Production Function in the United States Steam Power Industry." *Review of Economics and Statistics* 44 (1962):156–66.

Latimer, H. A. "The Cost and Efficiency of Revenue Adjustment Clause." *Public Utilities Fortnightly* (15 August 1974):19–24.

Leibenstein, Harvey. "Allocative vs. X-Efficiency." *American Economic Review* 56 (June 1966):392–415.

Leland, Hayne E. "Regulation of Natural Monopolies and the Fair Rate of Return." *Bell Journal of Economics and Management Science* 5 (1974):3–15.

Leland, Hayne E., and Robert A. Meyer. "Monopoly Pricing Structures With Imperfect Discrimination." *Bell Journal of Economics* 7 (1976):449–62.

Lewis, Ben W. "The Duty of a Public Utility Is to Reduce Its Income Tax Liability by Using Accelerated Depreciation." *Land Economics* 35 (May 1959):104–14.

Lewis, W. Arthur. "The Two Part Tariff." *Economica* 8 (August 1941):249–76.

Lipsey, Richard G., and Kelvin Lancaster. "The General Theory of Second Best." *Review of Economic Studies* 24 (1956):11–32.

Loose, Verne W., and Teresa Flaim. "Economies of Scale and Reliability: The Economics of Large versus Small Generating Units." *Energy Systems and Policy* 4 (1980):37–56.

Lowry, Edward D. "Justification for Regulation: The Case for Natural Monopoly." *Public Utilities Fortnightly* 92 (1973):1–7.

MacAvoy, Paul W., ed. *The Crisis of the Regulatory Commissions*. New York: W. W. Norton, 1970.

Magat, Wesley A. "Regulation and the Rate and Direction of Induced Technological Change." *Bell Journal of Economics* 7 (1976):478–96.

Maloney, Michael T.; Robert E. McCormick; and Robert D. Tollison. "Economic Regulation, Competitive Governments, and Specialized Resources." *Journal of Law and Economics* 27 (October 1984):329–38.

Marsh, W. D. *Economics of Electric Utility Power Generation*. Oxford: Clarendon Press, 1980.

Mayo, John W. "Technological Determinants of the U.S. Energy Industry Structure." *Review of Economics and Statistics* 66 (1984):51–58.

———. "Multiproduct Monopoly, Regulation, and Firm Costs." *Southern Economic Journal* 51 (1984):208–18.

McCormick, Robert E. "The Strategic Use of Regulation: A Review of the Literature." In R. Rogowsky, ed., *The Political Economy of Regulation*. Washington, D.C.: Federal Trade Commission, 1984.

McGraw, Thomas K. "Regulation in America: A Review Article." *Business History Review* 49 (Summer 1975):159–83.

McKie, James W. "Regulation and the Free Market: The Problem of Boundaries." *Bell Journal of Economics and Management Science* 1 (1970):6–26.

Meeks, James E. "Concentration in the Electric Power Industry: The Impact of Antitrust Policy." *Columbia Law Review* 72 (1972):64–130.

Meyer, Robert A., and Hayne E. Leland. "The Effectiveness of Price Regulation." *Review of Economics and Statistics* 62 (1980):555–64.

Miller, Robert H. *Power System Operation*. 2d ed. New York: McGraw-Hill, 1983.

Mitchell, Bridger M., and Paul R. Kleindorfer, eds. *Regulated Industries and Public Enterprise*. Lexington, Mass.: Lexington Books, 1979.

Mitchell, Edward John. *Toward Economy in Electric Power*. Washington, D.C.: American Enterprise Institute, 1975.

Moore, Thomas G. "The Effectiveness of Regulation of Electric Utility Prices." *Southern Economic Journal* 36 (1971):365–75.

Mueller, Dennis C. "Public Choice: A Survey." *Journal of Economic Literature* 14 (June 1976):395–433.

Musgrave, Richard A. *The Theory of Public Finance*. New York: McGraw-Hill, 1959.

Myers, Stewart C. "On the Use of β in Regulatory Proceedings: A Comment." *Bell Journal of Economics and Management Science* 3 (1972):622–27.

———. "The Application of Finance Theory to Public Utility Rate Cases." *Bell Journal of Economics and Management Science* 3 (1972):58–97.

Navarro, Peter. "The Politics of Air Pollution." *Public Interest* 59 (1980):36–44.

———. "Electric Utility Regulation and National Energy Policy." *Regulation* 5 (January/February 1981):20–27.

———. "Save Now, Freeze Later." *Regulation* 7 (September/October 1983):31–36.

Needy, Charles W. *Regulation-Induced Distortions*. Lexington, Mass.: Lexington Books, 1975.

Nelson, Randy A. "Regulation, Capital Vintage and Technological Change." *Review of Economics and Statistics* 66 (1984):59–69.

Nerlove, Marc. "Returns to Scale in Electricity Supply." In C. Christ, et al., eds., *Measurement in Economics: Studies in Mathematical Economics and Econometrics in Memory of Yehuda Grunfeld*, pp. 167–98. Stanford: Stanford University Press, 1963.

Netzer, Dick. *Economics of the Property Tax*. Washington, D.C.: Brookings Institution, 1966.

Neuberg, Leland G. "Two Issues in the Municipal Ownership of Electric

Power Distribution Systems." *Bell Journal of Economics* 8 (1977):303–23.

Niskanen, William A., Jr. *Bureaucracy and Representative Government*. Chicago: Aldine-Atherton, 1971.

Owen, Bruce M., and Ronald Braeutigam. *The Regulation Game: Strategic Use of the Administrative Process*. Cambridge, Mass.: Ballinger Publishing Co., 1978.

Pace, Joe D., and John H. Landon. "Introducing Competition Into the Electric Utility Industry: An Economic Appraisal." *Energy Law Journal* 3 (1982):1–65.

Panzar, John C., and Robert D. Willig. "Economies of Scale in Multi-Output Production." *Quarterly Journal of Economics* 91 (1977):481–94.

———. "Free Entry and the Sustainability of Natural Monopoly." *Bell Journal of Economics* 8 (1977):1–22.

———. "Economies of Scope." *American Economic Review* 71 (1981):268–72.

Peltzman, Sam. "Pricing in Public and Private Enterprises: Electric Utilities in the United States." *Journal of Law and Economics* 14 (1971): 109–48.

———. "Toward a More General Theory of Regulation." *Journal of Law and Economics* 19 (August 1976):211–40.

Penn, D. W.; James B. Delaney; and T. Crawford Honeycutt. *Coordination, Competition and Regulation in the Electric Utility Industry*. Washington, D.C.: U.S. Nuclear Regulatory Commission, 1975.

Peterson, H. Craig. "An Empirical Test of Regulatory Effects." *Bell Journal of Economics* 6 (1975):111–26.

Pettway, Richard H. "On the Use of β in Regulatory Hearings." *Bell Journal of Economics* 9 (1978):239–48.

Pfannenstiel, Jackalyne. "Implementing Marginal Cost Pricing in the Electric Utilities Industry." In W. Sichel and T. Gies, eds., *Applications of Economic Principles in Public Utility Industries*, pp. 53–72. Ann Arbor: University of Michigan, 1981.

Phillips, Almarin, ed. *Promoting Competition in Regulated Markets*. Washington, D.C.: Brookings Institution, 1975.

Pigou, Arthur C. *The Economics of Welfare*. London: Macmillan, 1932.

Portes, Richard D. "Long-Run Scale Adjustments of a Perfectly Competitive Firm and Industry: An Alternative Approach." *American Economic Review* 61 (June 1971):430–34.

Posner, Richard A. "Natural Monopoly and Its Regulation." *Stanford Law Review* 21 (1969):548–643.

———. "Taxation by Regulation." *Bell Journal of Economics and Management Science* 2 (Spring 1971):22–50.

———. "Theories of Economic Regulation." *Bell Journal of Economics and Management Science* 5 (Autumn 1974):335–58.

————. "The Social Costs of Monopoly and Regulation." *Journal of Political Economy* 83 (1975):807–27.

Primeaux, Walter J., Jr. "A Reexamination of the Monopoly Market Structure for Electric Utilities." In A. Phillips, ed., *Promoting Competition in Regulated Markets*, pp. 175–200. Washington, D.C.: Brookings Institution, 1975.

————. "The Decline in Electric Utility Competition." *Land Economics* 51 (1975):144–48.

————. "Some Problems With Natural Monopoly." *Antitrust Bulletin* 24 (1979):63–85.

Ramsey, Frank. "A Contribution to the Theory of Taxation." *Economic Journal* 37 (1927):47–61.

Reeb, Donald J.; Howard Shapiro; and Louis R. Tomson. "State and Local Taxes and Electric Utilities." *Public Utilities Fortnightly* 17 (August 1982):29–37.

Roberts, R. Blaine; G. S. Maddala; and Gregory Enholm. "Determinants of the Requested Rate of Return and the Rate of Return Granted in a Formal Regulatory Process." *Bell Journal of Economics* 9 (1978):611–21.

Robinson, Joan. *Economics of Imperfect Competition*. London: Macmillan, 1961.

Russell, Milton, and Robert B. Shelton. "A Model of Regulatory Agency Behavior." *Public Choice* 20 (1974):47–62.

Scherer, Charles R. *Estimating Electric Power System Marginal Costs*. Amsterdam: North-Holland, 1977.

Scherer, Frederic M. *Industrial Market Structure and Economic Performance*. 2d ed. Chicago: Rand-McNally, 1980.

Schiffel, D. "Electric Utility Regulation: An Overview of Fuel Adjustment Clauses." *Public Utilities Fortnightly* (19 June 1975):23–31.

Schmalensee, Richard. "Estimating the Costs and Benefits of Utility Regulation." *Quarterly Review of Economics and Business* 14 (1974):51–64.

————. "A Note on Economies of Scale and Natural Monopoly in the Distribution of Public Utility Services." *Bell Journal of Economics* 9 (1978):270–76.

————. *The Control of Natural Monopoly*. Lexington, Mass.: Lexington Books, 1979.

————. "Economies of Scale and Barriers to Entry." *Journal of Political Economy* 89 (1981):1228–38.

Schwert, G. William. "Using Financial Data to Measure Effects of Regulation." *Journal of Law and Economics* 24 (April 1981):121–58.

Shaker, William H., and Wilbert Steffy, eds. *Electric Power Reform: The Alternatives for Michigan*. Ann Arbor: University of Michigan, 1976.

Sharkey, William W. *The Theory of Natural Monopoly*. New York: Cambridge University Press, 1982.

Shepherd, William G. "Entry as a Substitute for Regulation." *American Economic Review* 63 (1973):98–105.

————. "Contestability vs. Competition." *American Economic Review* 74 (1984):572–87.

Shepherd, William G., and Thomas G. Gies, eds. *Utility Regulation: New Directions in Theory and Policy.* New York: Random House, 1966.

Shepherd, William G., and Clair Wilcox. *Public Policies Toward Business.* 6th ed. Homewood, Ill.: Irwin, 1979.

Sherman, Roger E. "Electric Utility Regulation and Performance After Diversification." Paper for Southern Economic Association Meetings. Washington, D.C., November 1982.

Sherman, Roger E., and Michael L. Visscher. "Rate-of-Return Regulation and Price Structure." In M. Crew, ed., *Problems in Public Utility Economics and Regulation,* pp. 119–32. Lexington, Mass.: Lexington Books, 1979.

Shoven, John B. "Inflation Accounting and Nonfinancial Corporate Profits: Physical Assets and Liabilities." *Brookings Papers on Economic Activity,* no. 1 (1976):15–57.

Shoven, John B., and Jeremy I. Bulow. "Inflation Accounting and Nonfinancial Corporate Profits: Physical Assets." *Brookings Papers on Economic Activity,* no. 3 (1975):557–98.

Sichel, Werner, and Thomas G. Gies. *Applications of Economic Principles in Public Utility Industries.* Ann Arbor: University of Michigan, 1981.

Singer, S. Fred, ed. *Free Market Energy.* New York: Universe, 1984.

Smith, V. Kerry. "The Implications of Regulation for Induced Technological Change." *Bell Journal of Economics and Management Science* 5 (1974):623–32.

Smithson, Charles W. "The Degree of Regulation and the Monopoly Firm: Further Empirical Evidence." *Southern Economic Journal* 44 (1978):568–80.

Solomon, Ezra. "Alternative Rate-of-Return Concepts and Their Implications for Utility Regulation." *Bell Journal of Economics and Management Science* 1 (1970):65–81.

Spann, Robert M. "Rate of Return Regulation and Efficiency in Production: An Empirical Test of the Averch-Johnson Thesis." *Bell Journal of Economics and Management Science* 5 (1974):38–52.

————. "The Regulatory Cobweb: Inflation, Deflation, Regulatory Lags and the Effect of Alternative Administrative Rules in Public Utilities." *Southern Economic Journal* 43 (July 1976):827–39.

————. "Taxation and Electric Utility Regulation." In C. Cicchetti and J. Jurewitz, eds., *Studies in Electric Utility Regulation,* pp. 171–211. Cambridge, Mass.: Ballinger Publishing Co., 1978.

Spence, A. Michael. "Monopoly, Quality, and Regulation." *Bell Journal of Economics* 6 (1975):417–29.

Spiro, Peter S. "Alternative Methods of Inflation Adjustment in Utility Ratemaking." *Public Utilities Fortnightly* 101 (1978):30–31.

Steiner, Peter O. "Peak Loads and Efficient Pricing." *Quarterly Journal of Economics* 71 (1957):587–610.

Stelzer, Irwin M. "Electric Utilities—The Next Stop for Deregulators?" *Regulation* 6 (July/August 1982):29–35.

Stewart, John F. "Plant Size, Plant Factor, and the Shape of the Average Cost Function in Electric Power Generation: A Nonhomogeneous Capital Approach." *Bell Journal of Economics* 10 (1979):549–65.

Stigler, George J. "The Theory of Economic Regulation." *Bell Journal of Economics and Management Science* 2 (Spring 1971):3–21.

Stigler, George J., and Claire Friedland. "What Can Regulators Regulate? The Case of Electricity." *Journal of Law and Economics* 5 (October 1962):1–16.

Taylor, Lester D. "The Demand for Electricity: A Survey." *Bell Journal of Economics* 6 (1975):74–110.

Telson, Michael L. "The Economies of Alternative Levels of Reliability for Electric Power Generation Systems." *Bell Journal of Economics* 6 (1975):679–94.

Trebing, Harry M. *Essays on Public Utility Pricing and Regulation.* East Lansing, Mich.: Institute of Public Utilities, Michigan State University, 1971.

———. "Realism and Relevance in Public Utility Regulation." *Journal of Economic Issues* 8 (1974):209–33.

———. "Equity, Efficiency, and the Viability of Public Utility Regulation." In W. Sichel and T. Gies, eds., *Applications of Economic Principles in Public Utility Industries,* pp. 17–52. Ann Arbor: University of Michigan, 1981.

Trebing, Harry M., and R. Hayden Howard, eds. *Rate of Return Under Regulation.* East Lansing, Mich.: Institute of Public Utilities, Michigan State University, 1969.

Tullock, Gordon. *Politics of Bureaucracy.* Washington, D.C.: Public Affairs Press, 1965.

Turvey, Ralph. *Optimal Pricing and Investment in Electricity Supply.* Cambridge: MIT Press, 1968.

U.S. Department of Agriculture. *1982 Statistical Report, Rural Electric Borrowers.* REA Bulletin 1-1. Washington, D.C.: U.S. Department of Agriculture, 1983.

U.S. Department of Energy. *Statistics of Privately Owned Electric Utilities in the United States, 1981 Annual.* DOE/EIA-044 (81). Washington, D.C.: U.S. Department of Energy, Energy Information Administration, 1983.

———. *Statistics of Publicly Owned Electric Utilities, 1981 Annual.* DOE/EIA-0172 (81). Washington, D.C.: U.S. Department of Energy, Energy Information Administration, 1983.

Watts, Ross L., and Jerold L. Zimmerman. "Towards a Positive Theory of Accounting Standards." *Accounting Review* 53 (January 1978): 112–34.

———. "The Demand for and Supply of Accounting Theories: The Market for Excuses." *Accounting Review* 54 (1979):273–305.

———. "Auditors and the Determination of Accounting Standards." (Unpublished manuscript, 1981.)

Weidenbaum, Murray L. *The Future of the Electric Utilities.* Washington, D.C.: American Enterprise Institute, 1975.

Weiss, Leonard W. "Antitrust in the Electric Power Industry." In A. Phillips, ed., *Promoting Competition in Regulation Markets,* pp. 135–73. Washington, D.C.: Brookings Institution, 1975.

———. *Case Studies in American Industry.* 3d ed. New York: John Wiley & Sons, 1980.

Wenders, John T. "Peak Load Pricing in the Electricity Industry." *Bell Journal of Economics* 7 (1976):232–41.

Westfield, Fred M. "Innovation and Monopoly Regulation." In W. Capron, ed., *Technological Change in Regulated Industries,* pp. 13–43. Washington, D.C.: Brookings Institution, 1971.

Wilcox, Clair, and William G. Shepherd. *Public Policies Toward Business.* Homewood, Ill.: Irwin, 1975.

Wilcox, Delos F. *Municipal Franchises.* Vol. 1. Rochester, N.Y.: Gervaise Press, 1910.

———. "Effects of State Regulation Upon the Municipal Ownership Movement." *Annals of the American Academy* 53 (May 1914):71–84.

Wilder, Ronald P., and Stanley R. Stansell. "Determinants of Research and Development Activity by Electric Utilities." *Bell Journal of Economics and Management Science* 5 (1974):646–50.

Williamson, Oliver E. *The Economics of Discretionary Behavior: Managerial Objectives in a Theory of the Firm.* Englewood Cliffs, N.J.: Prentice-Hall, 1964.

———. *Markets and Hierarchies: Analysis and Antitrust Implications, A Study of the Economics of Internal Organization.* New York: Free Press, 1975.

———. "Franchise Bidding for Natural Monopolies—In General and With Respect to CATV." *Bell Journal of Economics* 7 (1976):73–104.

———. "Transaction-Cost Economics: The Governance of Contractual Relations." *Journal of Law and Economics* 72 (1979):233–62.

Willig, Robert D. "Pareto-Superior Non-Linear Outlay Schedules." *Bell Journal of Economics* 9 (1978):56–69.

———. "Multi-Product Technology and Market Structure." *American Economic Review* 69 (1979):346–51.

Zajac, Edward. *Fairness or Efficiency: An Introduction to Public Utility*

Pricing. Cambridge, Mass.: Ballinger Publishing Co., 1978.

Zimmerman, Martin B., and Randall P. Ellis. "What Happened to Nuclear Power: A Discrete Choice Model of Technology Adoption." *Review of Economics and Statistics* 65 (1983):234–42.

ENVIRONMENTAL, FUEL, AND SOCIAL REGULATION OF UTILITIES

PART II: ENVIRONMENTAL, FUEL, AND SOCIAL REGULATION OF UTILITIES

John C. Moorhouse

Part II considers three additional regulatory constraints on electric utilities. They are environmental regulation, fuel-use standards, and policies designed to redistribute income among user classes via rate-structure regulation. These constraints originated recently, and they represent an attempt to employ utility regulation to further a set of additional social goals. The way these regulations are imposed and the way they interact with traditional rate regulation generates consumption and production inefficiencies and economic uncertainty.

Contemporary environmental regulation of electric utilities covers plant siting and construction, air and water emissions, and waste disposal. In Chapter 5 Ringleb outlines the applicable environmental legislation and then details compliance costs. The capital costs alone are staggering. Electric utilities made fully 30 percent of total industrial expenditures on pollution control during the 1970s. In addition environmental regulation increases operating costs and can generate costly delays in bringing new capacity on stream. Ringleb argues that the approach to environmental regulation taken in the 1970s—"command and control," new-source performance standards, the treatment of low-sulphur coal, "prevention of significant deterioration" rulings (particularly as they applied to areas with little or no air pollution), and the regulation of nuclear power plants—unnecessarily raised the cost of achieving sensible environmental goals. Ringleb's brief is not a condemnation of concern for the environment; rather he maintains that the form and administration of the regulation, as they apply to electric utilities, is grossly inefficient and environmentally unsound.

In recent years the choice of fuel and the design of future generating capacity by electric utilities has had to conform with highly complex and often contradictory government policies. Chapter 6 reviews the myriad regulatory policies governing fuel use by electric utilities. These include price controls, environmental standards, fuel-use standards, and automatic fuel adjustment clauses. Conflicting policies abound. For example, Grennes shows how the provisions of the Power Plant and Industrial Fuel Use Act (1978) directly conflict with environmental protection regulations. Regulatory discrimination against the use of low-sulphur western coal, price controls, and automatic fuel adjustment clauses distort relative fuel costs and lead to using inefficient combinations of productive resources. More important, Grennes's analysis highlights the interdependence of markets for electricity, oil, natural gas, and coal and goes on to forge the link between domestic and world energy markets. These interdependencies involve both production and consumption. He argues that we cannot analyze the impact of regulation on markets for electricity meaningfully without recognizing these interdependencies. Indeed Grennes shows that regulation of related energy sources impinges on the efficiency of electric utilities.

In Chapter 7 Bolton and Meiners detail the politicization of electric utility regulation. Political pressure has led the government to sell federally produced electricity at heavily subsidized rates to preferred consumers. The growth of the consumer movement has put added political pressure on state utility commissions. Typically consumer groups have fought for and obtained lower rates for residential users and direct subsidies for low-income consumers. The implied departure from marginal-cost pricing not only means a redistribution of income toward favored groups, it also entails intergenerational transfers, and additional production and consumption inefficiencies. Bolton and Meiners offer a fascinating account of how these subsidies are masked to avoid public scrutiny.

5

ENVIRONMENTAL REGULATION OF ELECTRIC UTILITIES

Al H. Ringleb

INTRODUCTION

The past fifteen years have witnessed an explosion in the public's concern with the environmental effects of economic growth and technological change.[1] In partial response to that concern, the United States Congress enacted several dozen major pieces of environmental legislation during that same period, providing a legal basis for the protection of the environment.[2] Coupled with implementing regulations

1. Consider the following quote from an article published in 1970:

Coupled with a growing energy crisis is a growing environmental crisis. Public apprehension over environmental degradation of all sorts has risen sharply in the last year. Increasing public demand for environmental controls is reflected in new and proposed legislation, and in the proliferation of recent court actions. Protection of our environment has almost overnight become a matter of urgent national priority.

Our need for more electricity conflicts directly with our desire for a cleaner environment. Each method of power generation has its own specific type of impact on the environment. . . .

Electric utilities are thus caught between two crushing and inexorable imperatives.

Turner T. Smith, Jr., "Electricity and the Environment—The Generating Plant Siting Problem," *The Business Lawyer* 26 (1970): 169–97.

2. According to Professors Bonine and McGarity:

While environmental concerns have been the subject of some laws, lawsuits, and government action for decades . . . , the "modern era" of environmental law can be said to have had its genesis in the 1960s and to have firmly begun with the signing by the President, on January 1, 1970, of the National Environmental Policy Act of 1969 (NEPA).

and executive action, that legislation created a federal environmental structure that in turn stimulated the creation of parallel state environmental structures.[3] A large number of citizens' groups inspired subsequent legal developments. These groups ranged from long-established institutions, such as the Sierra Club, to ad-hoc community groups organized in response to particular projects.[4]

From the beginning of this environmental movement, the energy industries—and in particular the electric utility industry—were earmarked as major sources of environmental pollution.[5] Due to the growth in state and federal environmental structures during that time period, the electric utility industry effectively lost its ability to make free decisions with regard to utility location, design, construction, and equipment because their choices became increasingly constrained by a growing maze of environmental regulation.[6] In contrast to more eco-

---

Environmental concerns had been building throughout the 1960s. Public attention focused on all three branches of state and national government: new bills were introduced in Congress and state legislatures; executive agencies were petitioned to change their old policies; and private citizens began using the courts in new ways. . . . The Wilderness Act of 1964 was passed after decades of effort. The first version of the Endangered Species Act went on the books in 1966. . . . The Wild and Scenic Rivers Act became law in 1968. Federal and state air and water pollution laws were changed and then changed again. Finally, in 1970, Congress radically rewrote the Clean Air Act. Then it did the same one and one-half years later to the federal water pollution law and the federal pesticide law. All these were "regulatory" laws in which private activities affecting the environment were the main targets, and federal agencies were given new duties to control private activities.

John E. Bonine and Thomas O. McGarity, *The Law of Environmental Protection* (St. Paul, Minn.: West Publishing Co., 1984), pp. 2–3.

3. See, for example, David P. Currie, "State Pollution Statutes," *University of Chicago Law Review* 48 (1981): 27–81.

4. See, for example, *Scenic Hudson Preservation Conference* v. *Federal Power Commission*, 354 F.2d 608 (2d Cir. 1965) cert. denied, 384 U.S. 941, 86 S.Ct. 1462 (1966); *Citizens Committee for the Hudson Valley* v. *Volpe*, 425 F.2d 97 (2d Cir. 1970).

5. See, generally, William Ramsay, *Coal and Nuclear: Health and Environmental Costs* (Washington, D.C.: Resources for the Future, 1978); Cyril L. Comar and Leonard A. Sagan, "Health Effects of Energy Production and Conversion," *Annual Review of Energy* 1 (1976): 581–600.

6. According to Dennis P. Ward, head of the Environmental Division of Sargent & Lundy:

Because of today's government regulations, many of the design features of a power plant are not based solely on engineering considerations. . . . [T]he presumption that the latest design incorporates the latest engineering concepts is invalid. . . . Statutes, regulations, and court decisions altered engineering design rules by imposing legal rules. . . . Today, before design can begin, engineers, environmental specialists, and attorneys must review the proposed project, the environment of the site, and the applicable regulations.

Dennis P. Ward, "The Rules of the Game: Regulations and the Power Plant Design Process," *Public Utilities Fortnightly* 107 (1981): 28–29.

nomically efficient means of regulating environmental quality, the command-and-control means of regulation Congress chose resulted in pollution abatement requirements that were either often technologically infeasible or inefficient and expensive when feasible.[7] Engineering advances in virtually all phases of the industry were often delayed or abandoned as decision makers found that the environmental review costs associated with the introduction of those advances exceeded the potential benefits.[8] Thus although utility capital expenditures alone amounted to nearly $3.2 billion in 1981, roughly one-third of total capital expenditures by all businesses that year, that expenditure represents only a portion of the costs environmental regulation imposed on utilities and society.[9]

The following section gives a general overview of the impact state and federal environmental regulation has had on the electric utility industry. Then it discusses the major environmental enactments affecting electric utilities, with particular emphasis on state site-approval legislation, the Clean Air Act, the Clean Water Act, and environmental enactments and litigation affecting the use of nuclear power. Next the chapter examines the utility costs of complying with environment regulations, including costs associated with investment in administration, equipment, and delay. The chapter concludes with some remarks about the impact of environmental regulation and a comment on the prospects for change.

THE EXTENT OF ENVIRONMENTAL REGULATION OF UTILITIES: AN OVERVIEW

In the 1965 to 1980 period electric utilities were forced to respond both to a new and significant body of state and federal environmental law and to the litigation growing out of implementing that law. Prior to this body of legal directives, decisions governing the type, capacity, location, and environmental impact of new power-generating facilities had largely been made by the utility companies themselves.

7. See, generally, Richard D. Cudahy and J. Robert Malko, "Electric Peak-Load Pricing: Madison Gas and Beyond," *Wisconsin Law Review* (1976).

8. See, generally, Alfred C. Aman, Jr., and Glen S. Howard, "Natural Gas and Electric Utility Reform: Taxation Through Ratemaking?" *Hastings Law Journal* (1977); and Cudahy and Malko, "Electric Peak-Load Pricing."

9. Environmental Protection Agency, *The Macroeconomic Impact of Federal Pollution Control Programs: 1981 Assessment*, EPA-230 (Washington, D.C.: Government Printing Office, 1981), p.17, Table 2 (prepared by Data Resources, Inc.).

After the enactment and implementation of environmental laws, however, many of those decisions became seriously constrained by requirements that they not be undertaken without prior state or federal approval. With regard to location and land use decisions, the approval of the state's utility commission or some other agency is required for the construction and operation of a new transmission line or a generating unit. Prior to this period, the construction and operation of all hydroelectric and nuclear power plants had certainly required licensing, respectively, by the Federal Power Commission and the Nuclear Regulatory Commission. In this period, however, those licensing proceedings became forums for broad and detailed inquiries into the environmental impacts associated with hydroelectric and nuclear power. Although no specific federal legislation requiring the licensing of fossil-fueled generating plants exists, if a federal decision were required (say for federal water rights or the use of federal lands), the appropriate agency would be required to prepare and circulate an environmental impact statement (EIS) in that regard, in keeping with the provisions of the National Environmental Policy Act (NEPA) of 1969.[10] In addition many states required parallel statements when a state action was involved.[11] Given the readiness of the federal (and state) courts to hold up projects when draft statements were challenged by environmental groups, utilities had to put substantial time and effort into adequately preparing those statements.[12]

With the enactment of the Clean Air Amendments of 1970, existing power plants were required to reduce air pollution, often through the application of expensive and inefficient technology.[13] New power plants became governed by strict national new-source performance standards (NSPS) after the 1977 amendments.[14] These new standards require

10. *The National Environmental Policy Act,* Pub. L. No. 91-180, 83 Stat. 852, codified at 42 U.S.C. §4331 et seq. (Supp. IV 1980).

11. As of January 1, 1976, environmental-impact-statement requirements had been adopted by thirty states. See William H. Rodgers, Jr., *Environmental Law* (St. Paul, Minn.: West Publishing Co., 1977), pp. 809–22.

12. See, generally, Roger C. Crompton and Richard K. Berg, "On Leading a Horse to Water: NEPA and the Federal Bureaucracy," *Michigan Law Review* 71 (1973): 511, 529; Arthur W. Murphy, "The National Environmental Policy Act and the Licensing Process: Environmentalist Magna Carta or Agency Coup de Grace," *Columbia Law Review* 72 (1972): 963.

13. *Clean Air Act Amendments of 1970,* Pub. L. No. 91-604, 84 Stat. 1676, codified at 42 U.S.C. §1857 et seq. (1976).

14. *Clean Air Act Amendments of 1977,* Pub. L. No. 95-95, 91 Stat. 685, codified at 42 U.S.C. §7401 et seq. (Supp. IV 1980).

the use of continuous control technology—that is, scrubbers or pre-combustion processing—on all new coal-fired generating plants.[15] Many critics believed the use of low-sulfur coal alone as an environmental safeguard was sufficient in many areas of the country. In addition the amendments require utilities wanting to build new generating plants in areas not in compliance with federal ambient standards to meet specific preconstruction review requirements that included arranging for some existing source(s) to reduce pollution by as much as or more than the emissions of the new power plant.[16] In clean-air areas the owners or operators of a prospective new power plant may be required to monitor air quality for a year prior to beginning even the preconstruction review process.[17]

With regard to water pollution, the Clean Water Act of 1972 and its 1977 amendments require national emissions standards for each class of facilities.[18] Although current regulations do not pose the burden that the air pollution regulations do, regulations for the control of thermal pollution could hurt the industry.[19] The thermal pollution-control problem is particularly acute and expensive in nuclear power plants.

In addition many other federal agencies get involved in utility decision making on specific issues. If an environmental impact statement is circulated, diverse agencies and private groups can offer comments or criticisms. If federal water rights are being used, for example, this requires the approval of the Department of the Interior. At the same time many state agencies require their approval before the project can begin or operation commence. A large project, all told, can easily involve a utility company with dozens of state and

15. *Clean Air Act* (CAA) §111(a)(1); 42 U.S.C. §7411(a)(1) (Supp. IV 1980). See, generally, Bruce A. Ackerman and William T. Hassler, "Beyond the New Deal: Coal and the Clean Air Act," *Yale Law Journal* 89 (1980): 1466–571; Elizabeth H. Haskell, *The Politics of Clean Air: EPA Standards for Coal-Burning Power Plants* (New York: Praeger Publishers, 1982).

16. CAA §§171–178; 42 U.S.C. §§7501–7508 Supp. IV 1980) (Part D—Plan Requirements for Nonattainment Areas).

17. CAA §§160–169A; 42 U.S.C. §§7470–7479, 7491 (Supp. IV 1980) (Part C—Prevention of Significant Deterioration of Air Quality).

18. *Water Pollution Prevention and Control Act*, 33 U.S.C. §1251 et seq. (Supp. IV 1980).

19. John R. Quarles, Jr., *Federal Regulation of New Industrial Plants* (Washington, D.C.: John R. Quarles, Jr., 1979), pp. 95 (as a general rule, the Clean Water Act does not represent the same degree of regulatory complexity or potential barriers to the construction of new plants as do corresponding provisions of the Clean Air Act).

federal agencies and authorities in its effort to obtain the required approvals, permits, and licenses.

Nuclear energy has become the most controversial of all environmental issues related to generating electricity. Although nuclear energy represented both a significant potential energy source and a long-term solution to the energy crisis, the public's concern with its potential environmental impacts has brought the nuclear energy industry to a virtual halt.[20] In addition the Supreme Court dealt the industry a serious blow in ruling that states may ban the construction of future nuclear power plants until the federal government creates permanent disposal sites for high-level nuclear wastes.[21]

MAJOR ENVIRONMENTAL ENACTMENTS AFFECTING UTILITIES

A variety of state and federal environmental laws and regulations impact both directly and indirectly on the electric utility industry. As Table 5–1 indicates, Congress enacted over forty environmental statutes in the 1969 to 1981 period. The federal enactment most significantly affecting the industry was (and is) the Clear Air Act, although other enactments have had more serious effects on specific projects.[22]

Of the state environmental enactments, site-approval legislation has had an increasing impact on the electric utility industry. As early as 1920 many states had adopted legislation empowering commissions to regulate electric utilities.[23] Today every state has a regulatory body with the authority "for assuring adequate electric service at reasonable

20. "A Blow to Nuclear Power," *Newsweek*, 2 May 1983, pp. 67–68.

21. *Pacific Gas and Electric Company* v. *State Energy Resources Conservation and Development Commission*, 103 S.Ct. 1713 (1983): ruling that a California statute imposing a moratorium on the certification of new nuclear plants until the federal government "has approved and there exists a demonstrated technology or means for the disposal of high-level nuclear waste" was not preempted by federal law.

22. A well-known example is the impact of the Endangered Species Act, 16 U.S.C. §1531 et seq. (Supp. IV 1980), on TVA's Tellico Dam and Reservoir Project. See *Tennessee Valley Authority* v. *Hill*, 437 U.S. 153, 98 S.Ct. 2279, 1978. See also, John H. Sheridan and John L. Mullally, 'Energy vs. Environment: What Gives?," *Industry Week* 193 (1977): 45–54 (a $600 million hydroelectric project held up by the discovery of the Furbish lousewort; $2 billion Seabrook nuclear power plant held up by the EPA because the cooling water system may pose a hazard to clam larvae and other forms of marine life).

23. William K. Jones, "Origins of the Certificate of Public Convenience and Necessity: Developments in the States, 1870–1920," *Columbia Law Review* 79 (1979): 426–516.

Table 5–1.   Major Federal Environmental Protection Statutes, 1969–1980.

Year	Public Law Number	Title
1969	91-190	National Environmental Policy Act
1970	91-224	Water and Environmental Quality Act
	91-512	Resource Recovery Act
	91-596	Occupational Safety and Health Act
	91-604	Clean Air Act Amendments
1972	92-500	Federal Water and Pollution Control Act (Clean Water Act)
	92-522	Marine Mammal Protection Act
	92-532	Marine Protection, Research, and Sanctuaries Act
	92-574	Noise Control Act of 1972
	92-583	Coastal Zone Management Act
1973	93-205	Endangered Species Act
1974	93-254	Marine Pollution Act
	93-378	Forest and Range Land Renewable Resources Planning Act
	93-523	Safe Drinking Water Act
	93-627	Deep Water Ports Act
	93-633	Transportation Safety Act
1976	94-370	Coastal Zone Management Act Amendments
	94-377	Federal Coal Leasing Amendments Act of 1975
	94-469	Toxic Substances Control Act
	94-477	Natural Gas Pipeline Safety Amendments
	94-532	Whale Conservation and Protection Study Act
	94-579	Federal Land Policy and Management Act
	94-580	Resource Conservation and Recovery Act
	94-588	National Forest Management Act
1977	95-87	Surface Mining Control and Reclamation Act
	95-95	Clean Air Act Amendments
	95-190	Safe Drinking Water Act Amendments
	95-217	Clean Water Act Amendments
1978	95-273	National Ocean Pollution Research and Development and Monitoring Planning Act of 1978
	95-372	Outer Continental Shelf Lands Act Amendments
	95-514	Public Range Lands Improvement Act
	95-604	Uranium Mill Tailings Radiation Control Act
	95-632	Endangered Species Act Amendments
1979	95-95	Archaeological Resources Protection Act
	96-129	Pipeline Safety Act

Table 5–1.   (continued)

Year	Public Law Number	Title
1980	96-332	Marine Protection, Research, and Sanctuaries Act
	96-366	Fish and Wildlife Conservation Act of 1980
	96-464	Coastal Zone Management Improvement Act
	96-478	Act to Prevent Pollution from Ships
	96-482	Solid Waste Disposal Act Amendments
	96-501	Pacific Northwest Electric Power Planning and Conservation Act
	96-502	Safe Drinking Water Act Amendments
	96-510	Comprehensive Environmental Responses Compensation and Liability Act
	96-515	National Historic Preservation Act Amendments of 1980
	96-573	Low-Level Radioactive Waste Policy Act
1981	97-304	Endangered Species Act Amendments
	97-425	National Nuclear Waste Policy Act

rates."[24] The nature of the government utility regulation is such that a regulatory body can frequently require a utility to obtain approval for practices a business regulated in less detail would be free to institute without prior governmental approval.[25] The authority of many utility commissions was expanded through the 1970s, as many states enacted power-plant siting laws, further constraining utility decision making processes.[26]

Site Approval Legislation

Power-plant siting laws often make issuing construction permits conditional on a state agency's assessment of how compatible the proposed site is with surrounding land uses as well as on the physical, technical, and economic suitability of the site.[27] In 1970 only four states had enacted power-plant siting laws; however, by 1976 the

24. Congressional Research Services, *Report on the Electric Utility Sector: Concepts, Practices, and Problems* (Washington, D.C.: U.S. Government Printing Office, 1977) p. 12.

25. *Jackson* v. *Metropolitan Edison Co.*, 419 U.S. 345, at 347, 95 S.Ct. 449, at 456 (1974).

26. See, generally, Harold W. Young, "Power Plant Siting and the Environment," *Oklahoma Law Review* 26 (1973): 193–238.

27. Michael S. Hamilton, "Power Plant Siting: A Literature Review," *Natural Resources Journal* 19 (1979): 75–79.

number of states possessing such statutes had increased to twenty-seven.[28] Geographically states enacting such legislation were generally located in the West and Northeast, while relatively few states in the South and Southwest enacted such legislation.

The most significant effect of these power-plant siting laws was to directly involve numerous state regulatory agencies in the utility's site-selection process.[29] In general each such agency was responsible for very narrow and independent review activities. As the site-selection review process expanded through the 1970s, the utility industry was overwhelmed with the increasing complexity of and lead times required for the necessary hearings and procedures.[30] In many cases environmentalists were successful in pushing for a comprehensive review of proposed sitings that was broad both in scope and in detail. Already plagued by labor problems, material delays, supply shortages, and increasing energy costs, the utility industry was forced to contend with increased regulatory lag or delay due to lengthy environmental proceedings and inquiries. Each independent regulatory agency involved with the siting, construction, or initial operation of a facility, whether at the local, state, or federal level, now had the jurisdiction to fully impede a new project.[31] According to A. Joseph Dowd of the Edison Electric Institute:

> The construction and operation of major energy facilities located entirely within the confines of a single state require approximately 40 to 50 li-

---

28. John V. Winter and David A. Conner, *Power Plant Siting* (New York: Van Nostrand, 1978), pp. 23–24; Mason Willrich, "The Energy-Environmental Conflict: Siting Electric Power Facilities," *Virginia Law Review* 58 (1972): 257–336; Rodgers, Jr., *Environmental Law*, pp. 186–207.

29. For example, thirteen West Virginia state permits were required for a coal liquefaction facility in Morgantown, a project not subject to the Public Utility Commission; nor were any local permits required. U.S. Department of Energy (DOE), *Solvent Refined Coal–II, Demonstration Project, Final Environmental Impact Statement* (Washington, D.C.: U.S. Government Printing Office, 1981).

30. According to Ted Agres:

> Industry experts point to the following as major areas blocking adequate growth of electric utilities: [1.] Regulatory and legislative constraints. Over-regulation and redundant regulation by federal and state governments provides numerous opportunities for licensing delays. The result is that construction lead times for new fossil-fuel plants have been extended from six to ten years and for nuclear plants from twelve to fourteen years.

Ted Agres, "Utilities Future: Dim and Getting Dimmer," *Industrial Research/Development* 21 (1979): 48.

31. A. Joseph Dowd, "Environmental Considerations in Energy Production," *Public Utilities Fortnightly* 106 (1980): 89.

censes, permits, or other forms of public approval from a multiplicity of federal, state, and local agencies—the issuance of any one of which may be the subject of judicial review and the failure to obtain any one of which could block a project. This provides the opponents of such projects with an almost unlimited number of forums within which to delay or kill a project. Where more than one state is involved, these "opportunities" are multiplied. Thus, to secure approval of a California-to-Texas pipeline, the Sohio Company spent five years acquiring 700 separate permits. Sohio finally gave up on this badly needed energy project because it faced seemingly endless legal challenges.

A basic unfairness lies in the fact that the energy developer must win every battle, whereas his opponent need win only once.

Despite their good intentions, evidence indicates that those evaluative procedures were not as meaningful as they appeared.[32]

As Table 5–2 indicates, states have enacted a variety of power-plant siting laws with varying degrees of impact on utility companies.[33] The type and extent of power-plant siting legislation enacted depended on the amount of power generated in the jurisdictional area and its anticipated growth trends. Those states with significant industrial development, extensive existing power generation, and corresponding high-load growth patterns generally enacted detailed and comprehensive site-approval legislation. In those states the public perceived the environmental impacts associated with new power-generating plants combined with existing industrial pollution as aggravating otherwise acceptable impacts in developed or developing areas. The state's siting agency thus evolved as a method of insuring total review of the proposed facility and its associated impacts.

By comparison states with more moderate levels of industrial development, extensive amounts of "undisturbed" acreage, and moderate needs for power chose to control environmental effects by other means than power-plant siting legislation. As an alternative many of these states established mechanisms to investigate and analyze power-plant siting environmental impacts and the possibilities for their con-

32. See, for example, Paul L. Joskow, "Approving Nuclear Reactors: Cost-Benefit Analysis or Administrative Charade?" *Bell Journal of Economics and Management Science* 5 (1974): 327–33.

33. For a discussion of the factors influencing some pollution control agencies to set and enforce more stringent standards than others, see Marc J. Roberts and Jeremy S. Bluhm, *The Choices of Power: Utilities Face the Environmental Challenge* (Cambridge, Mass.: Harvard University Press, 1981), pp. 327–37.

Table 5–2.   State Power-Plant Siting Legislation.

States Having Minimal Power-Plant Siting Legislation

Alabama	Michigan	South Dakota
Alaska	Mississippi	Tennessee
Colorado	Missouri	Texas
Delaware	North Carolina	Utah
Hawaii	Oklahoma	Virginia
Indiana	Pennsylvania	West Virginia
Lousiana	Rhode Island	

States Having Moderate Power-Plant Siting Legislation

Arkansas	Kansas	New Jersey
Georgia	Kentucky	New Mexico
Idaho	Maine	North Dakota
Illinois	Nebraska	South Carolina
Iowa	Nevada	Vermont

States Having Extensive Power-Plant Siting Legislation

Arizona	Massachusetts	Ohio
California	Minnesota	Oregon
Connecticut	Montana	Washington
Florida	New Hampshire	Wisconsin
Maryland	New York	Wyoming

SOURCE: John V. Winter and David A. Conner, *Power Plant Siting* (New York: Von Nostrand Reinhold Co., 1978) p. 26.

trol. For example, Alabama established an Energy Advisory Council; Louisiana, a Nuclear Energy Advisory Committee; Texas, a Governor's Advisory Committee on Power-Plant Siting; and Pennsylvania, an Environmental Quality Board.[34]

A number of states chose to regulate power-plant siting through their public service commissions. In those jurisdictions the commission determines the public convenience, necessity, and environmental compatibility of the proposed facility. Other states assign site-approval responsibility to a specific environmental agency in the state government. That is, the state places control of the review process within an agency such as the Department of Natural Resources and Conservation, the State Health Department, or the Environmental Protection Office. In addition many states are affected by coastal-zone

34. Winter and Conner, *Power Plant Siting*, p. 27.

management legislation.[35] Such states are concerned that new industrial developments not deteriorate the state's coastal region. Although such laws were enacted to control all development and land use in the coastal area, energy facilities quickly became the major jurisdictional targets. The necessity for large amounts of water for cooling, the physical location of fuel deposits, and the separation factor for nuclear plants prompted the use of coastal regions for power-plant siting.

There is little question that power-plant siting laws have required economic and technical choices to be made that are different from those that would have been preferred by utility industry decision makers operating in an unregulated market.[36] Perhaps more important the review process imposed significant delays in utility construction and operation.[37] Although delays were not always adverse, extensive delays in approving such an energy project often escalated final costs. Both delay costs and the additional costs associated with the forced use of alternative technologies ultimately become reflected in increased consumer energy costs. In extreme cases, and in particular those involving nuclear power plants, numerous utility projects for

35. *Coastal Zone Management Act of 1972*, Pub. L. No. 92-583, 86 Stat. 1280, 16 U.S.C. §§1451–68, as amended Pub. L. No. 94-370, 90 Stat. 1013 (1976). The act encourages the development of programs preserving environmental values along the nation's coasts. Federal grants are authorized to allow states to develop and administer coastal protection programs. See, for example, *American Petroleum Institute* v. *Knecht,* 609 F.2d 1306 (9th Cir. 1979) (federal approval of California coastal zone program).

36. See Ward, "The Rules of the Game," p. 28 and Hamilton, "Power Plant Citing", p. 77.

37. According to the Department of Energy, prolonged procedures for obtaining necessary licenses or certificates from government agencies and legal challenges were the cause of delay in over 18 percent of coal-fired power plants and in nearly 40 percent of nuclear power plants. U.S. Department of Energy, Energy Information Administration, *Inventory of Power Plants in the United States* (Washington, D.C.: U.S. Government Printing Office, 1979), Table 3. To illustrate consider the following examples:

Three particularly extreme cases illustrate how problems can mount. In November 1966, Pacific Gas and Electric ordered the first unit of its Diablo Canyon plant. While other plants ordered at the same time were completed between 1972 and 1974, Diablo Canyon was only near completion in 1981 (and design flaws were discovered shortly before operations were supposed to start). Similarly, Long Island Lighting's Shoreham plant was ordered in February 1967; several other plants ordered at about the same time were completed by 1973; Shoreham is scheduled for 1983 completion. Northern Indiana Public Service's effort to build a nuclear unit at its Bailly site started in 1967. However, opposition was so intense that by 1981 delay had caused the construction license to lapse with only 1 percent of the work complete. The plans were canceled in 1981.

Richard L. Gordon, *Reforming the Regulation of Electric Utilities* (Lexington, Mass.: D. C. Heath, 1982), pp. 181–82.

expanding capacity were postponed or abandoned.[38] In addition the combined exclusionary implications of some state power-plant siting laws and the increased reliance on domestic energy resources forced many utility companies to locate in areas outside the one they served. This pattern of development, most pronounced in Western states, has generated legal concerns about regional exploitation and states' rights.[39]

The Clean Air Act

Although the federal government passed significant legislation to control air pollution during the 1960s, the basic statutory framework now in effect was established by the Clean Air Act Amendments of 1970.[40] The act was further amended in 1974 to deal with energy-related questions,[41] and again in 1977, the latter amendments being particularly important to the approval of new power plants.[42] The keystone of the act is the concept of setting and achieving national ambient air-quality standards (NAAQS).[43] For each pollutant controlled, the EPA was to develop a primary national ambient air-quality standard (NAAQS) based on public health effects and a secondary national ambient air-quality standard based on public welfare effects.[44] In 1971 the EPA initially developed primary and secondary standards for six pollutants including: particulates, sulfur dioxide, ozone, hydrocarbons, carbon monoxide, and nitrogen oxides. The EPA later promulgated standards for lead emissions. Table 5–3 presents the applicable standards for those pollutants.

Following the EPA's establishment of air-quality standards, the act directed state agencies to develop state implementation plans (SIPs), setting forth the specific control efforts necessary to achieve compli-

---

38. Over sixty nuclear projects have been canceled or postponed since 1975, and no new plants have been ordered since 1978. For an insight into sitting problems associated with nuclear power plants, see Joel Yellin and Paul L. Joskow, "Siting Nuclear Power Plants," *Virginia Journal of Natural Resources Law* 1 (1980): 1–67.

39. See R. D. Lamm, "States Rights vs. National Energy Needs," *Natural Resources Lawyer* 9 (1976): 41–48; J. L. Plummer, "The Federal Role in Rocky Mountain Energy Development," *Natural Resources Lawyer* 17 (1977): 247–55.

40. Refer to note 13.

41. *The Energy Reorganization Act of 1974*, Pub. L. No. 93-438, 88 Stat. 1237, codified at 42 U.S.C. §§5801–91 (Supp. IV 1980).

42. Refer to note 14.

43. CAA §109; 42 U.S.C. §7409 (Supp. IV 1980).

44. CAA §109(b); 42 U.S.C. §7409(b) (Supp. IV 1980).

Table 5–3.   National Ambient Air-Quality Standards.

Pollutant	Averaging Time	Primary Standard Levels	Secondary Standard Levels
Particulate matter	Annual (geometric mean)	$75\mu g/m^3$	$60\ \mu g/m^{3a}$
	24 hours[b]	$260\ \mu g/m^3$	$150\ \mu g/m^3$
Sulphur oxides	Annual (arithmetic mean)	$80\ \mu g/m^3$ (0.03 ppm)	———
	24 hours[b]	$365\ g/m^3$ (0.14 ppm)	———
	3 hours[b]	———	$1300\ \mu g/m^3$ (0.5 ppm)
Carbon monoxide	8 hours	$10\ mg/m^3$ (9 ppm)	Same as primary
	1 hour[b]	$40\ mg/m^3$ (35 ppm)[c]	Same as primary
Nitrogen dioxide	Annual (arithmetic mean)	$100\ \mu g/m^3$ (0.05 ppm)	Same as primary
Ozone	1 hour[b]	$240\ \mu g/m^3$ (0.12 ppm)	Same as primary
Hydrocarbons (nonmethane)[d]	3 hours (6 to 9 A.M.)	$160\ \mu g/m^3$ (0.24 ppm)	Same as primary
Lead and its compounds	3 months (arithmetic mean)	$1.5\ \mu g/m^3$	Same as primary

SOURCE: Council on Environmental Quality, *Environmental Quality—1980*, December 1980, p. 172.

Note: Measurements are shown in micrograms per cubic meter of air ($\mu g/m^3$), milligrams per cubic meter of air (mg/m^3), and in parts per million (ppm)

a. This secondary nonhealth-related "standard" is a guide to aid in achieving the 24-hour standard.

b. Not to be exceeded more than once a year.

c. EPA has proposed amending this standard to read: $29\ \mu g/m^3$ (25 ppm).

d. A nonhealth-related standard used as a guide for ozone control.

ance with the NAAQS.[45] The act required that the plans assure achieving the primary NAAQS within three years, subject to a two-year extension under certain conditions, thereby establishing an ultimate statutory deadline of July 31, 1977. The 1977 Amendments post-

45. CAA §110; 42 U.S.C. §7410 (Supp. IV 1980).

poned that deadline until December 31, 1982, and created two additional complex regulatory frameworks that impose preconstruction permit requirements on new (or modified) plants. Those permit requirements vary if the plant is to be located in a prevention-of-significant-deterioration (PSD) area, where the air quality is cleaner than that prescribed by the national standards, or in a nonattainment area, where the air quality violates the national standards.

Nonattainment Provisions. Owners or operators of new (or modified) "major emitting facilities" in any nonattainment area must obtain a permit for its construction and operation.[46] The principal conditions for such a permit are:[47]

1. a net reduction in total emissions (termed an offset);
2. the application of the "lowest achievable emission rate technology" to the new (or modified) plant;[48]
3. a demonstration that the owner's or operator's other plants in the area comply with the applicable SIP requirements; and,
4. that the applicable SIP is being carried out by the state.

The net intended effect of operating a new or modified plant under the nonattainment provisions (referred to as the offset policy) was to decrease pollution and therefore improve the area's air quality. That is, the quantity of offsets the owners or operators of the new plant obtained must match emissions from their new plant on a "more than

46. The act defines a major emitting facility as "any stationary . . . source of air pollutants which . . . has the potential to emit . . . one hundred tons per year or more of any air pollutant. . . ." CAA §302(j); 42 U.S.C. §7602(j) (Supp. IV 1980). See *Alabama Power Company* v. *Costle*, 636 F.2d 323 (D.C. Cir. 1979). When determining a facility's potential to emit air pollutants, the EPA must look to the facility's "design capacity," a concept that takes into account the anticipated functioning of the air-pollution-control equipment designed into the facility.

47. CAA §173; 42 U.S.C. §7503 (Supp. IV 1980).

48. According to the act, the term "lowest achievable emission rate" means:

. . . for any source, that rate of emissions which reflects—

(A) the most stringent emission limitation which is contained in the implementation plan of any State for such class or category of source, . . . or

(B) the most stringent emission limitation which is achieved in practice by such class or category of source, whichever is more stringent.

In no event shall the application of this term permit a proposed new or modified source to emit any pollutant in excess of the amount allowable under applicable new source standards of performance.

CAA §171(3); 42 U.S.C. §7501(3) (Supp. IV 1980).

one-for-one" basis. Thus in addition to their pollution control expenditures for the new plant, the owners or operators must purchase control devices for its existing plants or the plants of others in the area. Clearly the nonattainment provisions will impose a substantial cost on utility companies intending to locate in such areas.

The PSD Provisions.   Although many areas exceeded the national ambient air-quality standards, other areas had pollution levels lower than those the national standards prescribed. The EPA saw no requirement under the 1970 Clean Air Act to control sources of pollution in such clean-air areas. EPA reasoned that if a new plant would not cause air pollution levels to exceed the national ambient air-quality standards, the plant would not require environmental protection measures. In 1972, however, the Sierra Club sued EPA, arguing that the Clean Air Act required EPA to prevent the "significant deterioration" of air quality in clean-air areas. The Supreme Court's decision in the case required the EPA to establish regulations to prevent significant deterioration of the air quality in clean-air areas.[49] In response EPA developed the Prevention of Significant Deterioration (PSD) Regulations.[50] Under those regulations, clean-air areas became either Class I, Class II, or Class III areas. Class I areas were the most pristine and included wilderness areas and national parks. Class II and III areas were progressively less pure and included rural areas and small communities. Increases in air pollution by new plants were allowed in each class but were limited by regulations to a "maximum allowable increase." Because it would take relatively more additional pollution to cause significant deterioration of the air quality, the maximum allowable increase grew in size from Class I to Class III areas. Once that allowable increase in additional air pollution in an area was used up, the regulations allowed for no further new plant construction. PSD regulations are implemented by preconstruction review and are limited in application to two air pollutants: sulfur dioxide and particulate matter.

The PSD provisions Congress enacted in its 1977 amendments closely

49. *Sierra Club* v. *Ruckelhaus,* 344 F. Supp. 253 (D.D.C. 1972) aff'd per curiam, 4 Env't Rep. Cas. 1205 (BNA), aff'd sub nom. by an equally divided court, *Fri* v. *Sierra Club,* 412 U.S. 541, 93 S.Ct. 2770 (1973).

50. 39 Fed. Reg. 42510 (1974). Those regulations were challenged unsuccessfully by the Sierra Club, industrial firms, and the State of New Mexico. *Sierra Club* v. *Environmental Protection Agency,* 540 F.2d 1114 (D.C. Cir. 1976).

parallel the EPA's basic regulatory approach.[51] Like the regulations, the provisions rely on the three-class system and a maximum allowable increase that varies according to the area's class designation. Congress specifically defined many areas in the provisions as mandatory Class I areas, however.[52] This made it much harder for states to redesignate Class II areas as Class III areas.[53] Further Congress made a further requirement for major emitting facilities.[54] They must now apply the best available control technology (BACT).[55] It also expanded the number of plants subject to the PSD preconstruction review and required prospective owners or operators to do more monitoring.[56] Finally it expanded the regulation's procedures for government review and public scrutiny of PSD applications.

In a significant addition, the provisions apply special rules to any PSD applicant impairing visibility in federal lands within a mandatory Class I area.[57] In these cases the preconstruction permit approval can

51. Refer to note 17.
52. CAA §162(a); 42 U.S.C. §7472(a) (Supp. IV 1980).
53. CAA §164; 42 U.S.C. §7474 (Supp. IV 1980).
54. The definition of major emitting facility is much more specific under the Clean Air Act's PSD provisions. According to section 169 of the act:

> The term "major emitting facility" means any of the following stationary sources of air pollutants which emit, or have the potential to emit, one hundred tons per year or more of any air pollutant . . . : fossil-fuel fired steam electric plants of more than two hundred and fifty million British thermal units per hour heat input. . . . Such term also includes any other source with the potential to emit two hundred and fifty tons per year of any air pollutant.

CAA §169(1); 42 U.S.C. §7479(1) (Supp. IV 1980).
55. New major emitting facilities are required to obtain a permit. CAA §165(a); 42 U.S.C. §7475(a) (Supp. IV 1980). As a requirement for the issuance of such a permit, the proposed facility must be subject to the "best available control technology." CAA §165(a)(4); 42 U.S.C. §7475(a)(4) (Supp. IV 1980). The act defines best available control technology as:

> . . . an emission limitation . . . which the permitting authority, on a case-by-case basis, taking into account energy, environmental, and economic impacts and other costs, determines is achievable for such facility through application of production processes and available methods, systems, and techniques, including fuel cleaning or treatment or innovative fuel combustion techniques for control of each . . . pollutant.

CAA §169(3); 42 U.S.C. §7479(3) (Supp. IV 1980).
56. According to the act:

> The [preconstruction] review shall be preceded by an analysis . . . by the State . . . or by the major emitting facility applying for such permit, of the ambient air quality at the proposed site. . . . Such data shall be gathered over a period of one calendar year preceding the date of application for a permit.

CAA §165(e); 42 U.S.C. §7475(e) (Supp. IV 1980).
57. The Bureau of National Affairs, Inc., *Environment Reporter* 7 (1977): 1778.

turn on the effect of the new plant's emissions upon "air quality-related values (including visibility)" of such lands.[58] In a case where emissions from the source would not exceed the applicable Class I increment, the permit can still be denied if the federal land manager determines that such air quality-related values would suffer an adverse impact.[59] The visibility impacts present an especially vexing problem for coal-fire generating plants intending to locate in Western states, as emphasis has shifted toward the use of domestic energy resources. In addition pressure from the National Commission on Air Quality urges including surface coal mining as a source subject to regulation in order to protect visibility.

The combined effect of all these changes and additions converted the PSD review into a formidable regulatory obstacle confronting new electricity-generating plants. Economists have estimated that the PSD provisions of the 1977 amendments could cost energy consumers $4.65 billion by 1990.[60] The PSD review requirements are a focal point of current debates in Congress over the Clean Air Act.

It should be noted that both the act's PSD and nonattainment provisions are applied on the basis of individual pollutants. Thus a new power plant could seek location in an area that is nonattainment for one or more of the plant's pollutants but is an attainment area for others. In such instances the power plant must satisfy both the procedural and the substantive requirements of both programs, thereby increasing costs associated with administration and delay significantly.

New-Source Performance Standards.   Through the Clean Air Act, Congress first authorized the federal government to set performance standards limiting emissions from large new stationary sources of air pollution in 1970.[61] In response to the act's directive, the EPA issued a new-source performance standard (NSPS) for large fossil-fueled steam generators operated by utilities in December 1971.[62] The first NSPS applied to units capable of firing more than 250 million Btu's per hour, and it limited sulfur dioxide emissions to 1.2 pounds per million Btu's and particulate matter emissions to 0.10 pounds per million

58. CAA §169A; 42 U.S.C. §7491 (Supp. IV 1980).
59. CAA §§165(a)(5) & (d); 42 U.S.C. §§7475(a)(5) & (d) (Supp. IV 1980).
60. CAA §165(d)(2)(C)(ii); 42 U.S.C. §7475(d)(2)(C)(ii) (Supp. IV 1980).
61. CAA §111; 42 U.S.C. §7411 (Supp. IV 1980).
62. 36 Fed. Reg. 24 (1971), codified at 40 C.F.R. §60.40 (1977).

Btu's. Under this standard new generating facilities could satisfy the emission limitations required by simply burning low-sulfur coal.[63] If a new power plant intended to burn high-sulfur coal, the 1971 NSPS required flue-gas desulfurization systems—scrubbers—to remove sulfur dioxide from the flue gases. Although western low-sulfur coal was more expensive than eastern high-sulfur coal, many utilities located in the East found it was less expensive to transport and use western low-sulfur coal than to buy scrubbers.[64] As a result the established coal regions of the East began to lose some of their market to low-sulfur coal suppliers from Montana, Wyoming, and Colorado.[65]

Two significant changes, however, were made to section 111 in the 1977 amendments.[66] The first change added a "percentage reduction" requirement to NSPS for power plants.[67] This encouraged the use of scrubbers rather than low-sulfur coal to meet emission standards.[68] The second change called for the use of "continuous" emission controls and was intended to prevent the use of less expensive, but noncontinuous, dispersion techniques.[69] To pass this later requirement, eastern coal producers—who wanted to keep a market for their high-sulfur coal—joined forces with western environmentalists—who wanted to prevent deterioration of air quality in the West by ensuring that western power-plants burning low-sulfur coal still used scrubbers.[70] These changes have been heavily criticized by the electric utility industry. According to Ackerman and Hassler:

> Rather than encouraging policymakers to define each plant's cleanup obligations in light of local environmental conditions, the Act's provisions for new-source performance standards require all plants of the same type, regardless of their location, to meet the same emission ceiling for each type of pollutant. . . . By lifting the NSPS process out of the general effort to tailor cutback requirements for existing plants to local environ-

63. Daniel B. Badger, Jr., "New Source Standard for Power Plants I: Consider the Costs," *Harvard Environmental Law Review* 3 (1979): 48, 50.

64. Haskell, *Politics of Clean Air*, p. 10.

65. Badger, "New Source Standard," p. 50.

66. See generally Haskell, *Politics of Clean Air*, pp. 12–18; David W. Hercher, "New Source Performance Standards for Coal-Fired Electric Power Plants," *Ecology Law Quarterly* 8 (1980):748–51.

67. CAA §111(a)(1)(A)(ii); 42 U.S.C. §7411 (a)(1)(A)(ii) (Supp. IV 1980).

68. *Clean Air Act Amendments of 1977, Conference Report*, H.R. Rep. No. 95–564, 95th Cong., 1st Sess. (1977), p. 130.

69. CAA §111 (a)(1)(c); 42 U.S.C. §7411(a)(1)(c) (Supp. IV 1980).

70. See Peter Navarro, "The Politics of Air Pollution," *Public Interest* 59 (1980):36–44.

mental goals, the Act makes it easier for policymakers to push NSPS beyond the point of justification. From the vantage point of the environment, it makes no difference . . . whether the sulfur is removed by a primitive hosing or by the most advanced gismo ever conceived by the mind of man. What matters is the impact of the sulfur dioxide on the world outside the power plant. And this depends not only on emissions but on a host of other factors—the height of the stack, the direction of the wind, and the plant's proximity to population centers. [Footnotes omitted][71]

The EPA promulgated the corresponding new NSPS for power plants in 1979.[72] The new standards increased pollution control requirements for new coal-fired electric power plants by tightening restrictions on emissions of sulfur dioxide and particulate matter. When high-sulfur coal is being burned and sulfur dioxide emissions to the atmosphere are more than 0.60 pounds per million Btu's, they limit sulfur dioxide emissions to a maximum of 1.2 pounds per million Btu's and require a 90-percent reduction in potential uncontrolled sulfur dioxide emissions.[73] When low-sulfur coal is burned and sulfur dioxide emissions are less than 0.60 pounds per million Btu's, the utility must reduce the potential uncontrolled sulfur dioxide emissions by no less than 70 percent.[74] Thus the new NSPS provide a sliding-scale requirement for the control of sulfur dioxide. In addition they limit emissions of particulate matter to 0.03 pounds per million Btu's.[75]

The EPA predicted that by 1995 the new standards would reduce national sulfur dioxide emissions from new plants by 50 percent and national particulate matter emissions by 70 percent. The new standards necessitated the use of some form of flue-gas desulfurization technology, however, and these new standards are expected to cost electric utilities tens of billions of dollars, worsen the environment in some areas, and encourage electric utilities to run their older plants

---

71. Ackerman and Hassler, "Beyond the New Deal," pp. 1477–79.

72. Environmental Protection Agency, "New Stationary Sources Performance Standards: Electric Utility Steam Generating Units," Fed. Reg. 44 (1979), codified at 40 C.F.R. §§60.40a–60.49a (1979). EPA's regulations were upheld against challenges by both environmentalists and the industry. *Sierra Club* v. *Costle,* 657 F.2d 298 (D.C. Cir. 1981). It is conservatively estimated that it cost $3.2 million for EPA to set the NSPS for fossil-fuel fired utility boilers. Haskell, *Politics of Clean Air,* p. 118 (Table 8.1).

73. 40 C.F.R. §60.43(a)(1).

74. 40 C.F.R. §60.43(a)(2).

75. 40 C.F.R. §60.43(a)(3).

longer.[76] According to A. Joseph Dowd of the Edison Electric Institute, the sulfur dioxide percentage-reduction requirement will require increased expenditures for pollution control of $1,700 per ton by 1990 or nearly twelve times the required expenditures under the NSPS without the percentage-reduction requirement.[77]

The Clean Water Act

The Federal Water Pollution Control Act Amendments of 1972 and 1977 (Clean Water Act) established the framework for controlling water pollution.[78] The central mechanism of the act was to prohibit any discharge of pollutants into any public waterway unless authorized by a permit.[79] The act required that EPA develop and impose technology-based standards for the control of water pollution, and established that those standards be met in two phases. Phase I, to be met by 1977, required every discharger to install the "best practicable control technology" (BPT).[80] The second phase, to be met by 1984, required that

---

76. According to Ackerman and Hassler:

A careful analysis of the EPA's decision will reveal the way our institutions are resolving a critical environmental trade-off generated by the energy crisis. We have concluded that Congress' well-intentioned effort in 1970 to improve environmental quality through an improved administrative process has led, in 1979, to an extraordinary agency decision that will cost the public tens of billions of dollars to achieve environmental goals that could be reached more cheaply, more quickly, and more surely by other means. Indeed, the agency action is so inept that some of the nation's most populous areas will enjoy a *worse* environment than would have resulted if the new policy had never been put into effect. . . . Worse yet, by adding up to 15 percent to the cost of new construction, forced scrubbing will give utilities an economic incentive to run their old plants longer than they otherwise would. Because old plants are often permitted to emit four or five pounds of SO2 per MBtu, one old plant produces as much SO2 as three or four new ones subject to a 1.2 ceiling. Thus, even if a relatively small fraction of old plants are induced to stay on line for an extended period, the overall impact could be quite serious. Indeed, in the industrial Midwest, the old-plant effect swamps the extra reductions achieved by forcing all new plants to scrub—causing the Midwest to impose 170,000 *more* tons on the Northeast in 1995 than it would have under the old 1.2 NSPS.

Ackerman and Hassler, "Beyond the New Deal," pp. 1460, 1524.

77. American Enterprise Institute for Public Policy Research, Legislative Analysis, *The Clean Air Act: Proposals for Revisions* (Washington, D.C.: American Enterprise Institute, 1981), p. 30.

78. *The Federal Water Pollution Control Act,* Pub. L. No. 92-500, 86 Stat. 816, as amended Pub. L. No. 95-217, 91 Stat. 1566, 3 U.S.C. 466 et seq. (Supp. IV 1980).

79. According to the act, unless a "point source" has an authorizing permit, "the discharge of any pollutant by any person shall be unlawful." CWA §301(a); 33 U.S.C. §1311(a) (Supp. IV 1980).

80. CWA §301(b)(1)(A); 33 U.S.C. §1311(b)(1)(A) (Supp. IV 1980).

the technology to be used depended on the pollution the source discharged: a best-conventional-technology limitation applied to the discharge of certain conventional pollutants;[81] a best-available-technology economically achievable standard, to the discharge of toxic pollutants;[82] and a best-available-technology economically achievable limitation subject to possible compliance extension to 1987 applied to the discharge of certain other (so-called nonconventional) pollutants.[83] In addition to its technology standards, the 1972 act required each discharger to comply with applicable state water-quality standards by the 1977 BPT deadline.[84] Those state standards often imposed a requirement for controls stricter than the EPA's BPT standards in localities where receiving waters were severely polluted. In addition those standards often covered more pollutants than the federal requirements, and they are currently a source of some thermal pollution regulation.

In a steam electric power plant, the most significant water pollutants are those associated with the plant's cooling water in the form of thermal pollution (discharges of heated water) and chemical pollution. Cooling water is used to absorb the heat that is freed from the steam when it is condensed to water for return to the boiler. Two basic types of cooling-water technologies are currently used: once-through cooling water and recirculating cooling water systems.[85] In a once-through system, the cooling water is withdrawn from the water source, passed through the system, and returned directly to the water source. The most significant environmental concern with once-through cooling water systems is its thermal impact on that receiving water source. Approximately 65 percent of existing steam electric power plants use this technology.[86]

---

81. CWA §301(b)(2)(E); 33 U.S.C. §1311(b)(2)(E) (Supp. IV 1980). The act defines conventional pollutants to include "pollutants classified as biological oxygen demanding, suspended solids, fecal coliform, and pH." CWA §304(a)(4); 33 U.S.C. §1314(a)(4) (Supp. IV 1980).

82. CWA §§301(b)(2)(A), (C) & (D); 33 U.S.C. §1311(b)(2)(A), (C), & (D) (Supp. IV 1980).

83. CWA §§301(b)(2)(A) & (F); 33 U.S.C. §1311(b)(2)(A) & (F) (Supp. IV 1980).

84. CWA §§301(b)(1)(C) & 303; 33 U.S.C. §§1311(b)(1)(C) & 1313 (Supp. IV 1980).

85. U.S. Environmental Protection Agency, *Development Document for Effluent Limitations Guidelines and Standards for the Steam Electric Point Source Category*, EPA-440/1-80/029-6 (Washington, D.C.: U.S. Government Printing Office, 1980), pp. 59–116.

86. EPA, *Development Document for Effluent Limitations*, p. 59.

In a recirculating cooling water system, the cooling water is withdrawn from the water source and passed through the system several times. The heat absorbed by the cooling water is removed either through the use of cooling ponds or cooling towers. Cooling ponds are generally more appropriate in arid climates (roughly 75 percent of existing ponds are in the South and Midwest) and in locations where large land areas are available, as a large plant will have a cooling pond with a surface area of 1,200 or more acres. The most significant water pollutants from discharges in recirculating systems are dissolved solids and chemical additives. The water that evaporates from the system increases the dissolved-solids content of the water remaining in the system.[87] If allowed to build up, the dissolved-solid concentration will cause scale deposits. Utilities control the deposits either through cooling tower blowdown, a process that periodically discharges some of the cooling water or through chemical additives (usually chlorine) in the recirculating water.

In addition to wastewaters from the cooling system, coal-fired steam electric plants also generate wastewaters from air-pollution control equipment and rainfall runoff from coal storage piles. Recall that the NSPS under the Clean Air Act require new coal-fired generating plants to use scrubbers.[88] In an average day such an air-pollution-control system will remove nearly 200 tons of sulfur dioxide from the exhaust

---

87. In the Southwest at average annual climatic conditions, over 7,000 gallons of water are evaporated each minute in generating 1,000 megawatts of electricity. David Abbey, "Energy Production and Water Resources in the Colorado River Basin," *Natural Resources Journal* 19 (1979): 280.

Water consumption is a significant concern in the arid Southwest. Thus since evaporation from cooling ponds is considerably less than from cooling towers, ponds are favored in the Southwest. According to Governor Briscoe of Texas (as quoted by the Fourth Circuit Court of Appeals):

> The level of consumptive use of water that would be necessitated by [requiring cooling towers instead of allowing cooling ponds] is not merely unacceptable; Texas simply does not have the water resources to comply.

Appalachian Power Company v. *Train,* 545 F.2d 1351 (4th Cir. 1976).

88. Refer to notes 72–77 and the accompanying text. Scrubbers or flue gas desulfurization systems depend on a large-scale chemical reaction. As exhaust gases flow up the power plant smokestack, they are exposed to a lime or limestone solution sprayed in their path. Sulfur dioxide in the gas reacts with the spray and goes into solution. It is then removed from the solution, dewatered, and disposed of in the form of sludge. U.S. Environmental Protection Agency, *Flue Gas Desulfurization System Capabilities for Coal-Fired Steam Generators,* EPA-600/7-78-032b, vol. 2 (Washington, D.C.: U.S. Government Printing Office, 1978), pp. 3–2 to 3–8.

gases of a typical generating plant while consuming over 400 tons of limestone and thousands of gallons of water.[89]

In 1974 the EPA promulgated water-pollution-control standards for the steam electric point source category—which includes both fossil- and nuclear-fueled generating plants—as required by the Clean Water Act.[90] Effluent limitations were imposed on new and existing steam electric power plants for the discharge of thermal pollution, chemical pollution (particularly chlorine, suspended solids, and other cooling- or boiler-system maintenance chemicals), and coal-pile runoff. The regulations required the implementation of closed-cycle cooling systems on new and existing steam electric power plants by July 1, 1981, thereby establishing that no thermal pollution could be legally discharged into navigable waterways beyond that date. Economists estimate that by 1981 the required thermal pollution controls would have necessitated capital expenditures of over $5 billion by the electric industry.[91]

In 1976, however, the U.S. Court of Appeals for the Fourth Circuit, in *Appalachian Power*, remanded EPA's thermal and coal-pile runoff limitations.[92] This remand of the thermal limitations was due to EPA's inability to show any net benefits associated with the zero-discharge standard it had chosen to impose on the industry or that the application of such a standard would result in "reasonable further progress" toward the act's goals.[93] Interestingly the EPA has not reissued limitations on thermal discharges; nor has it issued limitations on flue-gas desulfurization wastewaters. The EPA's current regulatory scheme, however, does place effluent limitations on chemical additives and coal-pile runoff.[94] Economists estimate that the industry will incur $120 million in capital expenditures between 1985 and 1995

89. U.S. Environmental Protection Agency, *Proceedings: Symposium on Flue Gas Desulfurization*, EPA-600/7-78-058a, vol. 1 (Washington, D.C.: U.S. Government Printing Office, 1978), pp. 118, 121, 134.

90. U.S. Environmental Protection Agency, "Steam Electric Power Generating Point Source Category; Effluent Limitation Guidelines, Pretreatment Standards and New Source Performance Standards," Fed. Reg. 39 (1974): 36186–36199.

91. *Appalachian Power* v. *Train*, p. 1365.

92. *Appalachian Power* v. *Train*, p. 1365.

93. *Appalachian Power* v. *Train*, pp. 1363–65.

94. U.S. Environmental Protection Agency, "Steam Electric Power Generating Point Source Category; Effluent Limitations Guidelines, Pretreatment Standards and New Source Performance Standards," *Federal Register* 47 (1982): 52289–52302, codified at 423 C.F.R. §519 (1983).

in meeting those limitations.[95] While those estimates are insignificant compared to the industry's expected outlays for air-pollution controls, further regulations on thermal pollution and flue-gas desulfurization wastewaters could substantially increase future outlays for water pollution control expenditures.

REGULATING NUCLEAR ENERGY

In response to the oil embargo and the consequential crude oil price escalation brought about by the Organization of Petroleum Exporting Countries (OPEC), the Western industrial countries made a strong commitment to nuclear power. In the early 1970s President Nixon announced Project Independence, which called for nuclear energy to provide nearly 40 percent of U.S. electrical needs by late 1980s.[96] This federal commitment to nuclear power was reflected in Congress's extension of the Price-Anderson Act's coverage (limiting private liability in the event of a nuclear accident) until 1987.[97] It was also expressed in their clear preclusion of natural gas and oil as primary energy sources in new power plants.[98] Other Western leaders expressed similar views on nuclear power as a long-term solution to the energy crisis.[99]

Nuclear power has not, however, been without serious controversy. No other energy source has elicited as much praise and condemnation. Supporters point to a safety record far surpassing that of the coal industry and to the prospects of nuclear energy providing a long-term solution to the energy crisis. Its opponents cite the dangers of radiation, waste disposal problems, terrorist threats, and cost overruns that have become strongly associated with the use of nuclear power.

As of 1981 seventy-two licensed nuclear power plants were operating in the U.S., accounting for about 12 to 13 percent of the

95. EPA, "Steam Electric Power Generating Standards," p. 52298 (derivation from expected yearly outlays, in 1982 dollars).

96. See U.S. Federal Energy Administration, *Project Independence Report* (Washington, D.C.: U.S. Government Printing Office, 1974).

97. *The Price-Anderson Act Amendments*, Pub. L. No. 94-197, §2–14, 89 Stat. 1111, 42 U.S.C. §§8301(b)(3), 8311, 8312(a) (Supp. IV 1980).

98. *The Power Plant and Industrial Fuel Use Act of 1978*, Pub. L. No. 95-620, 92 Stat. 3291, 42 U.S.C. §§8301(b)(3), 8311, 8312(a) (Supp. IV 1980).

99. See, for example, remarks of French Premier Jacques Chirac, *First Conference of the European Nuclear Society*, Paris, 1975, as reported in Robert Stobaugh and Daniel Yergin, *Energy Future: Report of the Energy Project at the Harvard Business School* (New York: Random House, 1979), p. 108.

electricity generation. Some states—Connecticut, Illinois, Maine, Maryland, and Wisconsin—rely on nuclear power for more than 25 percent and as much as 50 percent of their electrical needs. Due to the growing controversy about nuclear energy's environmental effects, however, over sixty projects have been canceled or deferred since 1975, and no new plants have been ordered since 1978. After the Three Mile Island incident in 1979, the nuclear power industry has been brought to a virtual halt.[100] Environmental concerns have effectively imposed a de facto moratorium on any further nuclear energy development.

An Overview of the Nuclear Waste Dilemma

A nuclear reactor must periodically be refueled and the "spent fuel" removed. This spent fuel—consisting of isotopes of uranium, plutonium, radium, strontium, cesium, and other elements—is intensely radioactive and must be carefully stored. The general practice at present is to store the fuel at the reactor site in a water-filled pool.[101] For many years, planners assumed this fuel would eventually be reprocessed; accordingly, the storage pools were designed as short-term holding facilities with limited storage capacities.[102] By 1982, however, no commercial reprocessing plants were operating in the United States. As a consequence the spent fuel has accumulated in the storage pools, creating the risk that nuclear reactors may eventually have to be shut down. A shutdown would become necessary if insufficient room remained in a pool to store spent fuel and also if insufficient space remained to hold the entire fuel core if certain inspections or emergencies required unloading the reactor. Some 8,000 metric tons of spent nuclear fuel have already accumulated, and it is projected by the year 2000 that this will grow to 72,000 metric tons.[103] Government studies indicate that a number of reactors may be forced to shut down in the early 1990s due to their inability to store any more spent fuel.[104]

100. See, for example, *Report of the President's Commission on the Accident at Three Mile Island* (Washington, D.C.: U.S. Government Printing Office, 1979).

101. Stobaugh and Yergin, *Energy Future*, p. 128.

102. Report to the Congress by the Comptroller General, *Federal Facilities for Storing Spent Nuclear Fuel—Are They Needed?* (Washington, D.C.: U.S. Government Printing Office, 1979), p. 1.

103. Office of Technology Assessment, *Managing Commercial High-Level Waste* (Washington, D.C.: U.S. Government Printing Office, 1982), p. 9.

104. Office of Technology Assessment, *Managing Commercial High-Level Waste*, p. 27.

Moreover even assuming sufficient pools in which to safely store all the spent fuel produced during the working lifetime of the reactor, permanent disposal is still needed because the spent fuel will remain radioactive for thousands of years under current technology.[105] Although scientists have extensively examined a number of long-term nuclear waste-management strategies, most attention has focused on placing the wastes in subsurface geologic repositories such as salt deposits.[106] The lack of an adequate long-term disposal option increases the risk that the limitations of current storage space will lead to reactor shutdowns, rendering nuclear energy an unpredictable and uneconomical adventure.

In response to this concern, Congress enacted the Nuclear Waste Policy Act of 1982.[107] The act authorizes repositories for disposal of high-level radioactive waste and spent nuclear fuel, provides for licensing and expansion of interim storage, authorizes research and development, and provides a scheme for financing. More specifically the act provides a strict timetable for the Department of Energy to select sites for two underground repositories, the first of which must be in operation by 1998. States most likely to be considered for the first site include Louisiana, Mississippi, Nevada, Texas, Utah, and Washington.

The Regulation of the Nuclear Industry

The Atomic Energy Act of 1954 established the basic scheme of the federal regulation for the commercial use of nuclear energy.[108] The act ended the government's monopoly over nuclear energy and promoted the participation of the private sector in the development and use of nuclear power. The House and Senate reports confirm that it was "a major policy goal of the United States" that the involvement of private industry would speed the further development of the peaceful uses of nuclear energy.[109] That same purpose was manifest later

---

105. See *Vermont Yankee Nuclear Power Corporation* v. *Natural Resources Defense Council,* 435 U.S. 519, 528 n. 6, 98 S.Ct. 1197, 1204 n. 6 (1978).

106. *Report to the President by the Interagency Review Group on Nuclear Waste Management* (Washington, D.C.: U.S. Government Printing Office, 1979), pp. 37, 47, 61.

107. *Nuclear Waste Disposal Act of 1982,* Pub. L. No. 97-425, 96 Stat. 2201 (1982).

108. *The Atomic Energy Act of 1954,* chap. 1073, 68 Stat. 919, as amended 42 U.S.C. §§2011–2296 (1970).

109. *Amending the Atomic Energy Act,* H.R. Rep. No. 2181, 83rd Cong., 2d Sess., 9 (1954); *Amending the Atomic Energy Act,* S. Rep. No. 1699, 83d Cong., 2d Sess. 9 (1954).

in the passage of the Price-Anderson Act, amending the Atomic Energy Act to limit private liability from a nuclear accident.[110]

The act authorized the Atomic Energy Commission (AEC), later succeeded by the Nuclear Regulatory Commission (NRC), to issue licenses for commercial utilization facilities.[111] The commission exercises a comprehensive licensing program regulating the design, construction, and operation of nuclear power plants. The act provided that the electric energy produced in such facilities and transmitted in interstate commerce was subject to the regulatory provisions of the Federal Power Act, but the authority of the appropriate local, state, or federal agency to regulate the generation, sale, or transmission of electric power was left intact. Thus, according to the Supreme Court, "The Commission's prime area of concern in the licensing context ... is national security, public health, and safety."[112]

During the first decade after the 1954 acts, most nuclear licensing activities drew only limited public attention. From 1962 through 1966 only three of twenty-six applications for construction permits were contested. In the next four years, however, twenty-four of seventy-four applications, nearly one-third, were contested; in the 1970s it was the exceptional license that was not contested. For a variety of reasons ranging from environmental worries to health and safety concerns to antimilitary sentiment, nuclear power became intensely controversial. The NRC's licensing proceedings became a focal point for discontent with nuclear power in general and specific nuclear power projects in particular. As a consequence the lead time required before a nuclear power plant could be operational increased from four to six years, to ten to fourteen years, rendering many such projects impractical.

State Regulation of Nuclear Power

In other energy fields health and safety concerns are the primary responsibility of state and local governments. In contrast the Atomic

---

110. *The Price-Anderson Act*, Pub. L. No. 85-256, §4, 71 Stat. 576, as amended 42 U.S.C. §2021 (1970). See *Duke Power Company* v. *Carolina Environmental Study Group, Inc.*, 438 U.S. 59, 63–67, 98 S.Ct. 2620, 2625–2627 (1978).

111. *The Energy Reorganization Act of 1974*, §§104(a)–(b), & 201(f); 42 U.S.C. §§5814(a)–(b) and 5841 (Supp. IV 1980). "Commission" is used in this section to refer to both agencies.

112. *Vermont Yankee Nuclear Power Corporation* v. *National Resources Defense Council*, 435 U.S., p. 550, 98 S.Ct., p. 1215.

Energy Act gave the federal government primacy over the regulation of nuclear power, particularly with regard to national security and public health and safety. In 1959, however, Congress handed some responsibility for nuclear matters over to the states.[113] The statute authorized the NRC to enter into an agreement with the governor of any state to discontinue its regulatory authority over by-product materials, source materials, and special nuclear materials in quantities insufficient to form a critical mass. The statute specifically excludes the imposition of state standards more restrictive than those promulgated by the NRC, however. Approximately one-half of the states have entered into such agreements with the NRC.

In recent years conflict has erupted as states and localities have tried to ban nuclear power uses or tighten controls on nuclear power within their jurisdictions.[114] Individual controversies have involved the shipment of nuclear waste through populated areas; the short-term or long-term storage of nuclear waste; radiation release from nuclear operations; and the siting, construction, and operation of nuclear electric generating plants. Those state or local restrictions imposed for safety reasons have not withstood judicial review due to their preemption by federal law.[115]

In 1983, however, the Supreme Court upheld a California statute imposing a moratorium on the certification of new nuclear power plants until the federal government creates permanent disposal sites for high-level nuclear wastes.[116] While conceding that the federal government maintains complete control over the safety aspects of nuclear energy generation, the Court agreed with the California State Energy Resources Conservation and Development Commission that the Cali-

113. *Act of September 23, 1959*, Pub. L. No. 86-373, 73 Stat. 688, as amended by 1970 Reorganization Plan No. 3, §§2(a)(7), 6(2), 84 Stat. 2086, 5 U.S.C. App. (1970) (abolition of the Federal Radiation Council created by §274[h] and transfer of its functions), 42 U.S.C. §2021 (1970).

114. See Arthur W. Murphy and D. Bruce La Pierre, "Nuclear 'Moratorium' Legislation in the States and the Supremacy Clause: A Case of Express Preemption," *Columbia Law Review* 76 (1976): 392–456; and Daryl H. Owen, "Waste Not, Want Not: The Role of the State in Nuclear Waste Facility Siting," *Louisiana Law Review* 41 (1981): 1227–55.

115. See, for example, *Washington State Building and Construction Trades* v. *Spellman*, 684 F.2d 627 (9th Cir. 1982) (Washington state statute prohibiting transportation and storage within state of radioactive wastes produced outside state held an unconstitutional violation of supremacy and commerce clauses) and *People of State of Illinois* v. *General Electric Company*, 683 F.2d 206 (7th Cir. 1982) (Illinois statute prohibiting shipment of spent nuclear fuel into the state for storage violates commerce clause).

116. *Pacific Gas and Electric Company* v. *State Energy Resources Commission*.

fornia statute was aimed at economic, not safety, concerns. The California Commission had argued that without a permanent means of disposal, the nuclear waste problem could become critical, leading to unpredictably high costs to contain the problem, or worse, to reactor shutdowns.[117] Thus the Court reasoned the California statute lies outside the occupied field of nuclear safety regulation.[118]

The immediate impact of the Court's decision will be slight since it only deals with nuclear plants not yet built, and no new plants are currently planned. Without a federal waste disposal site, however, the decision strikes a significant blow to nuclear power as a potential energy source. Reflective of the decision's strength, seven states have now enacted moratorium legislation patterned after California's. Clearly the future of the nuclear power industry depends on establishing a permanent disposal site.

THE IMPACTS OF ENVIRONMENTAL REGULATION IN THE 1970s

Beginning in the 1960s, and continuing through the 1970s, environmentalists took three basic approaches in their attacks on electric utilities. The first was an unprecedented involvement in the legislative process at both the state and federal levels. In response to the political pressures they were able to bring to bear, Congress enacted several laws that firmly established the federal presence in environmental matters. Principally through the efforts of environmentalists, those laws contained rigid deadlines, strict quality standards, and provisions allowing citizen groups to bring court actions to either force the administrator of the EPA to act or require a source to comply.[119] Similar political pressures proved fruitful for environmentalists at the state level.

With state and federal laws and implementing agencies established, the second approach was to challenge siting and operating licenses for power-generating and transmission facilities. Since decisions in that regard required approval at many levels, challenges to a particular

117. *Pacific Gas and Electric Company* v. *State Energy Resources Commission*, p. 1727.

118. *Pacific Gas and Electric Company* v. *State Energy Resources Commission*, pp. 1727–28.

119. In response to environmentalist demands, Congress has acted repeatedly to give citizens an enforcement role under the environmental laws. See, for example, CAA §304; 42 U.S.C. §7604 (Supp. IV 1980) and CWA §505; 33 U.S.C. §1365 (Supp. IV 1980).

project were commonly ongoing in local, state, and federal regulatory agencies and then later in the judicial system as those decisions were brought to the courts for review. Although both Congress and the judicial system attempted to overcome the delays and other difficulties associated with this process, the impact was to extend construction time considerably beyond what was usual in those time periods prior to the environmental era of the 1970s. Through the use of the National Environmental Policy Act (NEPA) at the federal level, and NEPA-like statutes at the state level, environmentalists successfully forced federal and state agencies to consider and reconsider the environmental impacts of their approval decisions. Although implemented with good intentions, evidence indicates that some of the evaluate procedures employed by those agencies to meet the mandate of NEPA and NEPA-like statutes were not as meaningful as they appeared.[120]

Third, environmentalists successfully challenged the design or structure of public utility rates before state utility commissions.[121] Of the many types of challenges environmentalists presented, this was probably the most surprising. They argued that utility commissions had the responsibility to carefully regulate the structure of utility rates as well as to determine a fair rate of return. Further they contended that the existing declining block-rate structure encouraged the uneconomical expansion of consumption, leading to unnecessary capacity expansion and overconsumption. Along with economists, these groups advocated a rate design or structure that more closely approximated marginal-cost pricing (e.g., flat rates, invented block rates, and so

---

120. Refer to note 32 and accompanying text.
121. According to Cudahy and Malko:

The design of electric rates has recently emerged from the closet of regulatory neglect to a new prominence. Traditionally, state public service commissions have concerned themselves primarily with aggregate utility revenue requirements . . . and have left rate design . . . to the utilities.

This newly found concern for rate structure is associated with strong . . . claims for the significance of rate design for the energy economy and the environment. A few years ago, environmentalists and others having a strong interest in influencing electric demand, usage, and production became concerned about what they denominated "promotional" rate structures. Technically, these included rate designs which recovered less than long-run marginal cost from some categories of use and some categories of users and which thereby induced "wasteful" usage and perpetuated and exacerbated an uneconomic rate of growth in electric usage. "Wasteful" use and uneconomic growth, in turn, stimulated the construction of allegedly unneeded (and environmentally burdensome) power plants and a potential thicket of transmission lines.

Cudahy and Malko, "Electric Peak-Load Pricing," p. 47.

Table 5–4.   **Estimated Incremental Investment for Pollution Control, 1970–**

	1970	1971	1972	1973	1974	1975	1976
All Industries	2,872	3,807	5,480	5,665	5,422	6,054	5,779
Manufacturing Industries	1,694	2,256	3,272	3,385	3,613	4,290	3,733
Primary Metals	314	422	650	686	772	1,042	880
Electric Machinery	16	26	41	42	40	27	29
Nonelectric Machinery	12	22	41	43	46	35	40
Transportation Equipment	69	88	120	124	110	63	65
Stone, Clay, Glass	89	118	183	195	249	183	88
Other Durables	55	84	139	146	190	152	106
Food including Beverages	137	174	230	234	206	162	196
Textiles	19	25	32	32	30	42	50
Paper	243	310	416	424	569	668	419
Chemicals	293	372	485	491	626	857	990
Petroleum	436	598	903	935	720	1,010	820
Rubber	2	6	13	14	32	18	21
Other nondurables	11	13	19	20	26	30	28
Nonmanufacturing	1,178	1,551	2,207	2,280	1,809	1,764	2,046
Mining	69	88	115	115	28	74	83
Public utilities	876	1,167	1,687	1,743	1,634	1,516	1,790
Commercial	234	296	407	422	147	175	172

SOURCE: Environmental Protection Agency (EPA), *The Macroeconomic Impacts of Federal Pollution* p. 17 (prepared by Data Resources, Inc.).

on) albeit for different reasons.[122] Economists favored marginal-cost pricing on grounds of economic efficiency, whereas environmentalists viewed it as a way of reducing consumption and, therefore, the necessity for constructing new power plants that would add to existing pollution levels.

The Costs of Environmental Compliance

Table 5–4 gives an estimate of the incremental investment for pollution control in the 1970 to 1987 period. As the table shows, expenditures on pollution control by the utility industry averaged $2 billion a year in the 1970 to 1980 period, and they are expected to average nearly twice that in years beyond 1980. The fact that the utility industry made expenditures averaging nearly 30 percent of all industry expenditures through the 1970s, and these expenditures are expected to exceed 35 percent through the 1980s, indicates the rel-

122. See, generally, Aman, Jr., and Howard, "Natural Gas and Electric Utility Rate Reform;" and Cudahy and Malko, "Electric Peak-Load Pricing."

1987: Industry Sources. (in millions of 1979 dollars)

1977	1978	1979	1980	1981	1982	1983	1984	1985	1986	1987
5,574	6,760	7,019	7,573	9,454	9,898	11,109	11,861	11,855	11,858	11,577
3,521	3,951	3,977	4,541	5,797	5,960	6,810	7,332	7,390	7,352	7,119
840	752	811	1,010	1,131	1,110	1,235	1,168	1,108	1,066	1,010
26	130	114	126	177	194	240	285	328	354	309
36	111	88	97	114	100	125	161	145	140	142
62	224	261	350	455	546	644	734	728	728	760
82	164	145	176	245	327	369	442	470	499	459
96	181	166	199	235	281	317	355	338	336	343
188	172	148	150	188	209	251	321	323	375	386
48	29	31	36	51	81	84	112	113	108	105
396	239	297	300	300	397	394	393	390	388	305
945	565	440	476	1,281	1,284	1,732	2,066	2,196	2,162	2,274
757	1,294	1,385	1,536	1,521	1,293	1,267	1,134	1,110	1,081	921
20	58	62	53	68	78	88	96	76	56	55
27	32	29	27	31	60	64	65	65	59	50
2,053	2,809	3,042	3,032	3,657	3,938	4,299	4,529	4,465	4,506	4,468
57	152	167	171	186	194	203	215	224	220	216
1,833	2,472	2,715	2,658	3,151	3,426	3,776	3,994	3,921	3,964	3,920
164	185	160	203	320	318	320	320	320	322	322

Control Programs: 1981 Assessment, EPA-230 (Washington D.C.: Government Printing Office, 1981),

ative impact environmental regulation has had on the industry. During a time period of rapidly rising costs due to escalating energy expenses and inflationary pressures, the amounts for investment in pollution control increased from insignificant levels prior to the 1970s to a level representing a sizable portion of total utility costs from the 1970s on.

Although the utility industry's direct expenditures on pollution control were substantial through the 1970 to 1980 period, those expenditures could represent just a portion of the costs actually associated with environmental compliance. In addition to investment expenditures, many utility companies spent substantial amounts to engage in the required administrative and agency hearings. Then in many instances those hearings resulted in litigation requiring more outlay. Those costs became compounded as many projects were delayed, and then they were impacted by growing interest and construction costs as inflation rapidly increased material, labor, and capital costs. For the most part, such elevated costs were eventually reflected in higher utility bills.

In addition to these administrative and delay costs, however, important intertemporal costs were not reflected in utility bills. Environmental opposition, reinforced by a strict legal structure, was successful in stopping completion of numerous coal-fired and nuclear power plant projects through the 1970s and early 1980s. Given the lead time necessary for building such plants—now more than ten years—future utility users will bear the social costs of those decisions in the form of power shortages; increased dependence on increasingly expensive oil and gas, much of which is likely to come from foreign sources; increased construction costs; and, in some areas, construction moratoriums on certain industrial-development projects. As industry relocates to more power-surplus or power-growth areas, jurisdictions imposing high entrance barriers in the form of environmental control requirements will experience declines in business and industrial activity and, consequently, in employment and their tax base.

Alternatives to Command and Control Regulation: An Overview

Virtually all the environmental laws either the federal or state governments have enacted over the past fifteen years undertake a command-and-control approach to environmental regulation. Congress or the state legislature would proscribe particular business conduct and then back up its commands with strict legal sanctions.[123] The EPA has tried to give sources greater flexibility so they could adopt less expensive and more innovative technological controls.[124] Nonetheless, the command-and-control approach—relative to more market-oriented approaches to environmental regulation—has proven costly and inefficient, with some exceptions.[125]

---

123. See, generally, Allen V. Kneese and Charles V. Schultze, *Pollution, Prices, and Public Policy* (Washington, D.C.: Brookings Institute, 1975).

124. An example is EPA's "bubble concept." For regulatory purposes, this concept treats all buildings and facilities of a firm's industrial complex as a single pollution source. Pollutants within the industrial complex are examined in aggregate, as if the firm's complex were under a bubble with a single stack emitting pollutants from which all emissions are measured. Thus owners may install or modify equipment within the complex without meeting the Clean Air Act's permit conditions if the alteration will not increase the aggregate emissions from the complex. The concept gives the plant manager the flexibility to find the places and processes within a complex that control emissions most cheaply. See *Chevron, U.S.A., Inc.* v. *Natural Resources Defense Council*, 104 S.Ct. 2778 (1984) (upholding EPA's bubble concept).

125. Consider, for example, the following discussion by Paul R. Portney, senior fellow at Resources for the Future:

In amending the Clean Air Act, Congress specified that the emissions limits on new facilities were to be achieved through "technological" means and that the percentage re-

At the center of these federal and state enactments is the requirement that discharge limitations or technological requirements be set for individual sources. Due in large part to the many and diverse sources and source locations in the United States, this approach does not lead to cost-effectiveness. Most significantly, it is nearly impossible for an agency to acquire the information needed to determine where environmental pollution can most cheaply be reduced. This is particularly the case when that information is not well known or understood by the industry or else changes over time. In addition the procedural costs involved in gathering and assimilating the pollution-control information, along with the associated uncertainty and delay costs, are by themselves substantial.

A much more cost-effective approach to pollution control would involve using market incentives such as effluent charges or pollution permits.[126] Such approaches would require considerably less centralized information collection; it would minimize waste by allowing a continuous balancing of costs and benefits and would send proper signals to the industry and its consumers about the costs of environmental resources.[127] Each source would decide on the basis of its own control costs how much of its pollution to control. Sources with high control costs would choose to control less pollution and pay more in fees or charges; sources with low control costs would find it advantageous to remove a larger percentage of its pollutants. The net result is that the average cost of control per unit of pollutant would be lower than under the command-and-control approach, which does not allow this type of private decision making.

---

ductions were to be "continuous." Translated, that told EPA to stop allowing new power plants to meet air quality goals through fuel substitution and start requiring scrubbers and other control equipment. . . . In 1979 EPA's implementing regulations made the message explicit: henceforth all coal burned in new power plants was to be scrubbed. . . . Scrubbers are very expensive: a new 1,000-megawatt power plant might cost $1 billion, $200 million of which would be spent on scrubbers. Generally, the same reduction in emissions could be had much more cheaply by burning low-sulfur coal and taking various other steps.

Paul R. Portney, "How *Not* to Create a Job," *Regulation* (November/December 1982): 36. See also, Richard B. Stewart and James E. Krier, *Environmental Law and Policy*, 2d. ed. (Charlottesville, Va.: Bobbs-Merrill Company, 1978), pp. 556–57.

126. See, generally, F. R. Anderson et al., *Environmental Improvement Through Economic Incentives* (Baltimore: The Johns Hopkins University Press, 1977).

127. Stephen Breyer, "Analyzing Regulatory Failure: Mismatches, Less Restrictive Alternatives, and Reform," *Harvard Law Review* 92 (1979): 552–53.

SUMMARY

Environmental regulation has significantly impacted the electric utility industry. The imposition of state and federal environment regulations through the 1970s severely constrained electric utility decision-making processes in the areas of location, design, fuel use, construction, and operation. In regulating environmental quality, the command-and-control approach that all governmental levels imposed has proven much less cost-effective than would an approach based on economic incentives such as pollution charges or fees. As a consequence, pollution control outlays will average nearly $4 billion a year through the 1980s under the current approach, despite the availability of less expensive alternatives.

Environmentalists were most effective in impacting the nuclear power segment of the industry. They were able to severely thwart the industry's attempt to provide a long-term solution to the energy crisis by bringing about a moratorium on the use of nuclear power. Further, under a recent Supreme Court ruling, states may now ban new nuclear power plants until the federal government develops a permanent waste disposal site.

With oil scarce, nuclear power risky, solar embryonic, and hydro-electric limited, the electric utility industry started looking at coal-fired generating plants as an energy source for the future. The relative abundance of cheap domestic coal supplies makes coal an attractive alternative. Environmental regulations have substantially increased the costs of coal use, however, by requiring that scrubbers be used to control air pollution. Further concern is growing about the potential for expensive and inefficient "acid rain" regulation in the not-too-distant future.[128] Clearly environmental regulation will continue to take up a significant portion of electric utility costs and will impose a significant burden on the industry in its attempts to meet future energy needs.

---

128. See, for example, the proposed "National Acid Deposition Control Act of 1983," H.R. 3400, 98th Cong., 2d. Sess. (1984).

6

ELECTRIC UTILITY REGULATION IN AN OPEN ECONOMY

Thomas J. Grennes

INTRODUCTION

Accumulating evidence indicates that government regulation of the electric power industry in the United States has been ineffective.[1] The common criticisms of regulation are: the scope of regulation is too broad, and certain components of regulation conflict with other components of energy policy. It follows from this that a less intrusive and better coordinated national energy policy would improve the performance of the electric power industry. In formulating an effective energy policy, it is important to consider the interdependence of energy markets. One cannot study electrical power without considering its relationship with oil, natural gas, coal, and other energy forms. Similarly one cannot understand domestic energy issues in the United States without considering the link between domestic and world markets. This chapter examines the implications of interdependence for regulation of the electric power industry in the United States.

1. Richard L. Gordon, *Reforming the Regulation of Electric Utilities* (Lexington, Mass.: Lexington Books, 1982); Paul MacAvoy, *Energy Policy: An Economic Analysis* (New York: Norton, 1983); Michael A. Crew, ed., *Issues in Public Utility Pricing and Regulation* (Lexington, Mass.: Lexington Books, 1980); Michael A. Crew, ed., *Regulatory Reform and Public Utilities* (Lexington, Mass.: Lexington Books, 1982); Joseph P. Kalt, *The Economics and Politics of Oil Price Regulation* (Cambridge, Mass.: MIT Press, 1981); Paul Joskow and Richard Schmalensee, *Markets for Power* (Cambridge, Mass.: MIT Press, 1983).

Ironically energy protectionism is becoming more fashionable just as deregulation of the electric power industry is gaining greater support.[2] But a policy aimed at actively managing the level of energy imports to offset some alleged private failure—that is, energy protectionism—requires government agencies to possess information, motivation, and coordination that they have not had in the history of electric power regulation to date. This chapter claims that the electric power industry will be better served by a policy of free trade in energy. Free trade means neither subsidizing energy imports, as United States policy did in the 1970s, nor taxing them. A free-trade policy would result in lower cost fuel and a more reliable supply of fuel for electricity generation. An unrestricted energy import policy would complement deregulation of electric power.

Recent support for energy protectionism is based on two arguments. First, supporters claim that the free-trade policies of oil-importing countries contributed to the high oil prices OPEC achieved. The actual U.S. policy of the 1970s, which indirectly subsidized oil imports, did contribute to the success of OPEC, but this should not be confused with free trade. Since decontrol of U.S. oil prices began in 1980, U.S. oil imports declined, to be replaced by a worldwide oil glut. The substitution of freer trade for subsidized imports weakened the market position of OPEC.

The second argument favoring energy protectionism is that the unreliability of oil imports constitutes a cost that private agents will not take into account in choosing the volume of imports. The effectiveness of this argument, however, depends on the suggestion that government administrators possess superior information about supply interruption.[3] The validity of this point is questionable as the information will be public and private agents with the same information will reduce imports and diversify among import suppliers. Data on the sources of U.S. oil imports already show considerable diversification (see Table 6–1), and the two largest U.S. suppliers—Canada and Mexico—are not members of OPEC. A related point is that total oil imports may be stable even if imports from individual suppliers are unstable. Stability of total imports will occur so long as distur-

2. MacAvoy, *Energy Policy: An Economic Analysis;* Morris A. Adelman, "Coping with Supply Insecurity," *Energy Journal* 3 (April 1982):1–17; William Nordhaus, "The Energy Crisis and Macroeconomic Policy," *Energy Journal* 1 (January 1980):11–20; James L. Plummer, "Policy Implications of Energy Vulnerability," *Energy Journal* 2 (April 1981):25–36.

3. George S. Tolley and John D. Wilman, "The Foreign Dependence Question," *Journal of Political Economy* 85, no. 2 (April 1977): 323–47.

Table 6–1. Sources of United States Imports of Crude Oil and Products (thousand barrels per day).

OPEC	1973	Percent of Oil Imports	1983	Percent of Oil Imports
Algeria	136	2	235	5
Libya	164	3	0	0
Saudi Arabia	486	8	336	7
United Arab Emirates	71	1	29	1
Indonesia	213	3	335	7
Iran	223	4	48	1
Nigeria	459	7	294	6
Venezuela	1,135	18	414	8
Other OPEC	106	2	140	3
Total OPEC	2,993	48	1,832	37
Total Arab OPEC	915	15	625	13
Non-OPEC				
Bahamas	174	3	122	2
Canada	1,325	21	542	11
Mexico	16	0	822	16
Netherlands Antilles	585	9	187	4
Trinidad and Tobago	255	4	96	2
United Kingdom	15	0	381	8
Puerto Rico	99	2	40	1
Virgin Islands	329	5	283	6
Other non-OPEC	465	7	684	4
Total non-OPEC	3,263	52	3,156	63
Total Imports	6,256		4,988	

SOURCE: *Monthly Energy Review*, February 1984.

bances that alter individual country supplies are not perfectly correlated. For example, a supply decrease by Saudi Arabia could be offset by a supply increase from the United Kingdom, making total imports stable. Because of such offsetting balances, the actual instability of total import supply has been exaggerated. Indeed the instability of domestic oil supply associated with changes in tax laws, environmental policy, and price controls could exceed the instability of total oil imports. Thus a free-trade policy in oil may serve as a cushion against domestic disturbances.

Interdependence of Energy Markets

Markets for various forms of energy are highly interdependent; consequently, disturbances in one market are quickly transmitted to the others. Electricity competes directly with oil and natural gas as a source of heat. In addition we can use several alternative fuels to generate electricity. Coal, petroleum, and natural gas are fossil fuels that compete with hydroelectric and nuclear-generated electricity. Table 6–2 shows U.S. energy consumption by source. In 1982 petroleum provided 43 percent of all energy, followed by natural gas with 26 percent and coal with 22 percent. Prices of these fossil fuels tend to move in the same direction, but their imperfect substitutability permits relative prices to change. Table 6–3 shows the prices of fossil fuels paid

Table 6–2.   United States Consumption by Source.

	1973 Quadrillion Btu 10^{15}	1973 Percent	1982 Quadrillion Btu 10^{15}	1982 Percent
Coal	13.300	18	15.412	22
Petroleum	34.840	47	30.416	43
Natural gas dry	22.512	30	18.489	26
Hydroelectric	3.010	4	3.571	5
Nuclear electric	0.910	1	3.084	4
Total	74.572		70.972	

SOURCE: *Monthly Energy Review*, December 1983, p.4.

Table 6–3.   Cost of Fossil Fuels Delivered to Steam Electric Utility Plants (cents per million Btu).

	Coal	Residual Oil	Oil Relative to Coal	Gas	All Fossil Fuels
1973	40.5	78.8	1.95	33.8	47.5
1974	71.0	191.0	2.69	48.1	90.9
1975	81.4	201.4	2.47	75.4	103.0
1976	84.8	195.9	2.31	103.4	110.4
1977	94.7	220.4	2.33	130.0	127.7
1978	111.6	212.3	1.90	143.8	139.3
1979	122.4	299.7	2.45	175.4	162.1
1980	135.1	427.9	3.17	221.4	190.4
1981	153.2	529.4	3.46	282.5	222.5
1982	164.7	475.5	2.89	340.6	222.5
1983*	163.3	473.4	2.90	340.7	215.5

SOURCE: *Monthly Energy Review*, March 1984, p. 98.

*November

by electric utility plants over the decade 1973–1982. Column 4 shows that the ratio of oil prices to coal prices ranged from 1.9 to 3.5 during the period. Absent other restrictions, that amount of price variation should provide an incentive to substitute cheaper forms of fuel. A complicating factor is that price control held the price of domestic crude oil below the world price for most of the period. Table 6–4 shows that the domestic price of crude oil was approximately 70 percent of the world price in the five years preceding 1981.

OPPORTUNITIES FOR FUEL SUBSTITUTION

The choice of fuel for electrical generation depends on technological considerations as well as relative price. Although technology permits fuel substitution, the amount possible is much greater at the design stage of a plant than after it has been built. Table 6–5 shows the relative importance of various fuel sources from 1946 to 1980. Coal has been the source of approximately 50 percent of the electricity generated, and its importance shows little variation over this period. There has been a long-term decline in the importance of hydroelectric power with the diminishing availability of new sites. Its share declined from 35 percent in 1946 to 12 percent in 1980. Nuclear power increased from 1 percent in 1970 to 11 percent in 1980, but this expansion reflects investment decisions made much earlier. No new nuclear plants have been ordered since 1978, and recent plant cancelations indicate that nuclear power will not grow rapidly in the near future. Oil and gas increased in importance until the mid-1970s and declined since. Oil increased from 6.3 percent in 1946 to 15.1 percent in 1975

Table 6–4. Refiner Acquisition Cost of Crude Oil.

Year	Price of Domestic	Price of Imported	Domestic Relative to Imported
1976	$ 8.84	$13.48	66
1977	9.55	14.53	66
1978	10.61	14.57	73
1979	14.27	21.67	66
1980	24.23	33.89	71
1981	34.33	37.05	93
1982	31.22	33.55	93
1983	28.87	29.30	99

SOURCE: *Monthly Energy Review*, March 1984, p. 88.

Table 6–5.   Alternative Sources of Electric Generation
(percent of total).

	Hydroelectric	Coal	Petroleum	Gas	Nuclear
1946	35.1	50.0	6.3	8.4	0.0
1950	29.2	46.7	10.3	13.5	0.0
1955	20.7	55.1	6.8	17.4	0.0
1960	19.3	53.5	6.1	20.0	0.1
1965	18.4	54.1	6.1	21.0	0.4
1970	16.2	46.1	11.9	24.4	1.4
1975	15.7	44.5	15.1	15.6	9.0
1980	12.1	50.9	10.7	15.2	11.0

SOURCE: Richard L. Gordon, *Reforming the Regulation of Electric Utilities*, pp. 114–15.

before declining to 10.7 percent in 1980. Natural gas rose from 8.4 percent in 1946 to 24.4 percent in 1970 before declining to 15.2 percent in 1980.

The elasticity of demand for electricity reflects the options available to users. Table 6–6 shows the major categories of electricity users in the years 1961 and 1979. Industrial buyers remain the major source of electricity demand, but their share declined from 40 percent in 1961 to 34 percent in 1979. The commercial and residential shares both increased by three percentage points during this period.

Electricity producers are regulated utilities whose rates are reviewed by state commissions. Most state laws promise shareholders a fair rate of return on their investment. In addition to state rules power companies must comply with various federal and local regulations involving the environment and fuel use. The fragmented nature of this regulation creates an obstacle to establishing a coherent natural-energy policy. For example, certain regulations encourage power

Table 6–6.   Electricity Use (percent).

	1961	1979
Residential	24	27
Commercial	18	21
Industrial	40	34
Other	18	18

SOURCE: Richard L. Gordon, *Reforming the Regulation of Electric Utilities*. p. 228.

companies to use more coal while at the same time other regulations discourage coal use.

The traditional justification for public utility regulation is that electrical power is a natural monopoly. This stems from the idea that if average cost declines with output over the relevant range, total cost will be less when one large firm serves the entire market than when several smaller firms do so. It is in the interest of the monopolist, however, to appropriate the benefit from such lower costs by charging a price above cost. Hence the purpose of a regulatory commission is to appropriate the benefits of large-scale production for consumers. Increasingly observers of the industry have questioned the assumption of natural monopoly for the generation of electricity. If average costs increase with output, total cost is smaller with several firms producing, and competition is viable. The possibility of viable competition appears greatest for electrical generation, whereas the biggest problem of sustaining competition lies in the distribution of electrical power. Hence several reform proposals call for deregulation of electrical generation.[4]

INTERDEPENDENCE BETWEEN UNITED STATES AND FOREIGN ENERGY MARKETS

International trade provides a direct link between energy markets in the United States and abroad. Since trade tends to equalize product prices, a disturbance in one country moves quickly to another country. This possibility—the international transmission of disturbances—has led to concern about excessive dependence on imports. Conversely events that disturb energy production in the United States can be offset by varying the quantity of energy imports. Hence the opportunity to import energy could constitute a source of security for the American economy rather than a source of disruption. Crude oil and oil products are the major energy import for the United States. They are in fact the largest import category of any kind. Table 6–7 shows that oil imports increased from 7 percent of total imports in 1970 to 32 percent in 1980. Following decontrol of domestic prices, the share declined to 21 percent in 1983. Import volume increased from 3.75 million barrels per day in 1970 to a peak level of 9.30 in

---

4. Gordon, *Reforming the Regulation of Electric Utilities;* Irwin M. Stelzer, "Electric Utilities: Next Stop for Deregulation?" *Regulation* 6 (July / August 1982):29–35.

Table 6–7. United States Petroleum Imports.

Year	Price in Current Dollars	Price in Constant 1967 Dollars	Import Volume (in million barrels per day)	Value of Imports (in billions of dollars per year)	Oil Imports as Percent of Total Imports
1970	2.16	1.86	3.75	$ 2.9	7
1971	2.43	2.00	4.14	3.6	8
1972	2.57	2.05	5.00	4.6	8
1973	3.33	2.50	6.83	8.4	12
1974	10.98	7.43	6.61	26.6	26
1975	11.45	7.10	6.50	27.0	28
1976	12.14	7.12	7.81	34.6	28
1977	13.29	7.23	9.30	45.0	30
1978	13.28	6.80	8.74	42.3	24
1979	18.67	8.59	8.81	60.0	28
1980	30.46	12.35	7.09	78.9	32
1981	34.02	12.49	6.25	77.6	29
1982	31.26	10.81	5.36	61.2	25
1983	28.40	9.52	5.20	53.8	21

SOURCE: *Federal Reserve Bulletin*, April 1981 and April 1984.

1977. Import volume declined to the neighborhood of 5 million barrels per day in 1982 and 1983.

In addition to importing crude oil and petroleum products, the United States imports natural gas and a small quantity of electricity from Canada. Table 6–8 shows the relative importance of imported energy by source. In 1982 imports of oil and oil products equaled 49 percent of U.S. production. The United States imports natural gas by pipeline from Canada and Mexico and liquified natural gas from Algeria. Natural gas imports equaled 4 percent of domestic production in 1982.[5] The United States is a major world exporter of coal, exporting 15 percent of domestic coal production in 1982. When expressed in Btu equivalents, coal exports in 1982 equaled 40 percent of crude oil imports. Thus the domestic energy sector is linked with the world energy market through imports of oil and natural gas and exports of coal.

5. However, the Federal Energy Regulatory Commission might have contributed to the low volume of natural gas imports by denying certain import licenses and discouraging others. James L. Plummer, ed., *Energy Vulnerability* (Cambridge, Mass.: Ballinger Publishing Company, 1982), p. 33.

Table 6–8.   Net United States Imports of Energy by Source.

Energy	1973 Imports Quadrillion Btu 10^{15}	1973 Imports as of Production	1982 Imports Quadrillion Btu 10^{15}	1982 Imports as of Production
Crude Oil				
and Products	12.980	67	9.031	49
Crude Oil	6.883	——	6.907	——
Products	6.097	——	2.124	——
Natural gas dry	0.981	4	0.892	4
Electricity	0.148	——	0.326	——
Coal	−1.443	10	−2.763	15

SOURCE: *Monthly Energy Review,* December 1983.

Because trade provides a connection between domestic and foreign markets, domestic and foreign energy policies are inseparable. In the case of oil the formal link consists of the import demand and supply equations. Import demand is the difference between total domestic demand for oil and the domestic production. Imports can be reduced directly by imposing a tariff or quota on imported oil. Alternatively imports can be reduced indirectly by instituting domestic policies that reduce oil demand or enhance domestic supply. In general a tariff is equivalent to a consumption tax plus a production subsidy on the importable product. The gradual removal of oil price controls that held domestic prices below world prices reduced the demand for imports. The price controls themselves acted as a de facto subsidy to oil imports. Similarly a collection of policies that discouraged the use of domestic oil substitutes (coal, natural gas, nuclear power) added to the demand for imported oil. Because of energy interdependence, one must simultaneously consider both domestic and foreign components to formulate a coherent energy policy.

The supply of imported oil to the United States is the difference between oil demand and oil supply in the rest of the world. Import supply depends not only on new discoveries and production rates from existing wells but also on worldwide consumption policies. Total import supply is the sum of individual supplies from many oil-producing countries. Because certain disturbances to particular supplying countries will be offset by disturbances to other countries, total import supply to the United States will be more stable than the sum of disturbances to all import suppliers. For example, the supply of oil available to the United States will be completely stable if a K-percent reduction in Iranian supply is offset by a K-percent increase in Nigerian supply during the same period. Hence it is misleading to conclude that imports for the United States are an unstable source merely because the supply in Iran is unstable. Of course no offsetting would happen if all foreign suppliers created an embargo. Such a collusive action has never occurred, however, and it seems extremely unlikely that it could in the future. Popular discussions of oil embargoes overlook the fact that U.S. oil imports are heavily diversified by source (see Table 6–1). In 1983 the majority of U.S. imports (63 percent) came from non-OPEC sources, the most important being Mexico, Canada, and the United Kingdom. Even within the OPEC category, most of the imported oil came from non-Arab members, the largest being Venezuela, Indonesia, and Nigeria.

Free trade connects national oil markets by equalizing foreign and domestic prices. Thus trade also works to transmit disturbances between countries. One nation can insulate its market from foreign disturbances by restricting trade; however, several disadvantages accompany such national insulation. First, higher-cost domestic production is substituted for imports. Second, the opportunity to vary imports to offset unstable domestic supply is relinquished. Even if home production is more stable than imports, a policy of insulation merely shifts instability to the rest of the world, which encourages other countries to retaliate, expanding rather than neutralizing instability.

Domestic Price Regulation of Alternative Fuels

Regulation of Domestic Oil Prices.   The federal government can encourage or discourage imports by lowering or raising the price of domestic oil relative to the foreign price. The federal government did not intervene actively in the domestic crude-oil market until the Eisenhower administration imposed a voluntary import quota in 1957, followed by a mandatory quota in 1959.[6] Previously state governments in producing areas had restricted output through prorationing policies. The Texas Railroad Commission was the most prominent agency using prorationing. In the early days of prorationing, imports were not competitive with domestic oil. The development of Middle

6. Douglas R. Bohi and Milton Russell, *Limiting Oil Imports: An Economic History and Analysis* (Baltimore: Johns Hopkins University Press, 1978).

Eastern supplies in the 1950s, however, threatened domestic producers and stimulated requests for an import quota. The result of the import quota was to keep the domestic price of crude oil more than a dollar above the world price in the 1960s. Residual oil, imported to the East Coast from the Caribbean, was exempt from the quota.

The 1970 Cabinet Task Force on Oil Import Control recommended a lower level of protection for oil and substituting a tariff for a quota. President Nixon replaced the quota with a fee system, which lasted until 1974. By that time foreign oil had become so expensive that it was no longer a threat to high-priced domestic oil. The Arab oil embargo of the United States and the Netherlands, which formally lasted from October 1973 to March 1974, stimulated concern about the reliability of foreign oil supply.

Oil was subject to the general price controls imposed by the Nixon administration in August 1971.[7] The 1973 Emergency Petroleum Allocation Act, extended controls and also gave the government authority to allocate petroleum products. By the mid-1970s the entitlements program was developed, and it granted certain refiners the right to buy domestic crude oil at artificially low prices. Some legislation in 1978 was designed to reduce dependence on imported crude oil by requiring that certain electrical power companies substitute coal for oil in generating electricity. World oil prices rose again in 1979, following the turmoil associated with the overthrow of the Shah of Iran. In 1980 Congress passed the Crude Oil Windfall Profits Tax, which contained a schedule for decontrolling prices of domestic crude oil. It also included a sales tax based on the difference between the controlled domestic price of crude oil and the higher world price. The price-control program that prevailed from 1971–1980 increased oil imports, whereas the earlier import quota that began in 1959 decreased imports.

REGULATION OF NATURAL GAS

The Federal Power Commission began to regulate the interstate price of natural gas in 1954, following a Supreme court decision. In *Phillips Petroleum Co. v. Wisconsin,* the Court held that the Natural Gas Act of 1938 made the commission responsible for regulating both the

7. Kalt, *Economics and Politics of Oil;* MacAvoy, *Energy Policy: An Economic Analysis;* Gordon, *Reforming the Regulation of Electric Utilities.*

wellhead prices of natural gas and the rates charged by interstate pipe-lines.[8] In the 1960s shortages developed in the interstate market where prices were kept artificially low. At the same time, prices were higher in the unregulated intrastate market. The Natural Gas Policy Act of 1980 included a complex schedule for price deregulation based on the age of wells and their depth. The price of gas from new wells deeper than 5,000 feet would be deregulated January 1, 1985. New gas from shallower wells would be deregulated January 1, 1987, and controls were extended to the intrastate market. By 1982 the excess demand for natural gas had disappeared. Demand for natural gas was curtailed by the Fuel Use Act of 1979 and the Energy Supply Act of 1975, which encouraged power companies to substitute coal for natural gas. By reducing the profitability of domestic production, the natural gas price-control program added to the demand for imported oil.

Electric Utility Regulation of Fuel Use

Distortion of Relative Fuel Prices.   Government regulation indi-rectly influences the fuel used by power companies via its effect on relative prices. The previous section discussed ways in which the gov-ernment has altered relative fuel prices through domestic price con-trols and import policy. In addition to U.S. government policy, external forces that raised the world price of crude oil in 1973–74 and 1979–80 motivated utilities to substitute cheaper fuel for oil. An unregu-lated firm has an incentive to use the least-cost combination of fuel and other inputs. A regulated utility, however, might not convert to a cheaper fuel unless a regulatory commission permits the conversion cost to be included in its rate base. Conversion also depends on state and local government approval.

DIRECT CONTROL OF FUEL USE

In addition to indirect effects via relative prices, the federal govern-ment has directly controlled the fuel choice of power companies. En-vironmental policy discouraged coal use because of potential air pollution. As oil became more expensive in the 1970s, however, firms developed an incentive to substitute coal for more expensive oil. The profitability of conversion depends partly on technical considerations

8. MacAvoy, *Energy Policy: An Economic Analysis,* p. 81.

such as the age of the plant and the size of its boiler. It also depends on the sulfur content of the coal and whether regulatory commissions permit conversion costs to be included in the firm's rate base. A 1977 amendment discouraged the use of low-sulfur western coal by requiring that antipollution controls utilize the "best available control technology."[9] The net effect was to require eastern plants to use eastern coal. Requiring the use of the "best available control technology" involved removing pollutants from coal by scrubbing. By encouraging the use of an inefficient combination of eastern and western coal, the law increased the total cost of a given amount of coal. State regulatory commissions also used their rate policies to discourage conversion from oil to coal. In 1978 the Public Utility Regulatory Policies Act (PURPA) and the Power Plant and Industrial Fuel Use Act (PIFUA) changed the direction of policy by requiring the substitution of coal for petroleum in electricity generation. New plants were forbidden to use petroleum or natural gas. Old plants were also expected to convert to coal, but the act permitted a complex set of exemptions based on cost. The policy dilemma is that greater national energy independence calls for using domestic coal in place of imported oil, but environmental policy calls for the opposite. The use of nuclear power was curtailed by environmental restrictions, particularly after the accident at the Three Mile Island plant in Pennsylvania in 1979. There has been a high rate of delay and cancelation of new nuclear plants. The incentive power companies have to protect against discharge of radiation has been distorted by the Price-Anderson Act that limits liability to $560 million. Risk from accidents has been shifted from the stockholders to consumers, or the public. Suggestions for reform include abandoning the liability limit and deregulating electricity rates.

ENVIRONMENTAL CONTROLS

The first environmental legislation was enacted in 1955.[10] The basic problems environmental legislation deals with are air pollution, water quality, solid waste disposal, and land use. The possibility of radiation discharge is a special problem for nuclear power. The 1969 National Environmental Policy Act (NEPA) required an environmental impact statement for each major federal action. The basic criticism

9. Gordon, *Reforming the Regulation of Electric Utilities.*
10. Ibid.

of regulation is that regulators get involved in details of the production process about which they know very little. A second problem is that federal, state, and local controls are not well coordinated, a fundamental characteristic of a decentralized political system. In addition the regulated parties influence the regulatory process in ways that promote their private interest at the expense of the national or public interest. An example is the 1977 legislation requiring the use of "best available control technology," which promoted eastern mining interests at a high cost to the society as a whole.

FUEL CONVERSION AND THE RATE BASE

Power companies are regulated as public utilities, and regulatory legislation promises investors a fair rate of return on their investment. Consequently the link between management decisions and the welfare of shareholders is more remote than in competitive industries. Management mistakes may be passed on to consumers if regulatory commissions permit unwarranted additional costs to be included in the rate base. Federal regulation might, for example, require conversion from oil to coal, but the profitability of conversion depends on whether state or local rate commissions permit the cost of conversion to enter the rate base. Poor coordination between federal and state regulators has caused problems for power companies. Due to environmental consequences, local governments have also gained some authority over fuel-conversion decisions. The regulatory process can contain incentives that lead a utility company to choose one fuel over another cheaper fuel. In a deregulated situation, the relevant base for determining the rates of a firm would be competition with other generating companies.

AUTOMATIC FUEL ADJUSTMENT CLAUSES

The objective of rate-of-return regulation is to set rates that insure the survival of the firm without permitting excess profits. A fundamental weakness is that regulation can provide perverse incentives for the regulated firm. Rigid adherence to a rate-of-return rule could lead to (1) rewards for increases in inefficiency and (2) punishments for efficient decisions. During periods of small and infrequent changes in cost and demand, regulatory lag has reduced this problem of adverse incentives. The large and frequent economic changes during the 1970s, however, increased the lag between rate-change requests and commission decisions to the point that the survival of some firms was threatened. General inflation and sweeping changes in relative energy prices were the main causes of disturbances. In an attempt to reduce the lag, most state regulatory commissions adopted automatic fuel adjustment clauses. The practice dates back to World War I, but the widespread use of such clauses for residential customers began in the 1970s. In 1970 only 35 percent of the states had these clauses, but by 1973 65 percent used them. By 1979 all except five states employed automatic fuel adjustment clauses.[11] According to a 1974 study, two-thirds of all electric power rate increases resulted from automatic adjustment clauses rather than explicit decisions by commissioners. This development led critics to charge that commissions were losing their authorized review power. A more damaging criticism is that while the clauses might reduce excessive regulatory lag, they could also lead to greater inefficiency.

The purpose of an automatic fuel adjustment clause (FAC) is to automatically adjust the product price by an amount equal to the change in average cost attributable to the change in fuel cost. Thus profit would be invariant to changes in the fuel price, and investors would earn a fair rate of return without frequent formal rate reviews. This administrative advantage would be important in periods of large and frequent fuel-cost changes. If profitability is invariant to the fuel price, however, the firm has little incentive to conserve fuel. The FAC may distort choices between fuel and nonfuel inputs and among alternative forms of fuel. It could also encourage the adoption of more fuel-intensive technology than firms would choose in the absence of such a clause. The problem is similar to the widely discussed Averch-Johnson effect. If permissible rates are based on the value of the capital the firm uses, managers have an incentive to choose a greater capital intensity than they would select under an alternative rule. Although regulatory rules can induce or retard factor substitution, substitution potential is limited in the short run. Potential substitution is much greater at the design stage than after capital is in place. In the case of firms subject to FAC, managers have an incentive to select greater fuel intensity than they would otherwise choose. Critics have suggested that these adverse incentives could be reduced by only permitting rates to increase a fraction of the fuel-cost increases and by permitting the rate to lag behind fuel-cost increases. This factor dis-

---

11. David P. Baron and Raymond R. DeBondt, "Fuel Adjustment Mechanisms and Economic Efficiency," *Journal of Industrial Economics* 27 (March 1979):243–61.

tortion could be avoided by extending the automatic clause to include all cost increases rather than treating fuel cost as a special case. A comprehensive cost adjustment clause would retain administrative convenience and avoid wasteful substitution of fuel for nonfuel inputs. Making profit invariant to cost, however, weakens the incentive of managers to restrain costs.

In addition to the theoretical reasons for expecting fuel adjustment clauses to induce greater fuel intensity, some empirical evidence supports this hypothesis.[12] In addition to the effect on fuel intensity, Scott presented evidence from the period 1970–75 showing that utilities subject to fuel adjustment clauses experienced smaller profit variance than comparable firms without these clauses. If financial markets discount variable earnings streams, fuel adjustment clauses enhance the market value of the firm. Thus the FAC lowers administrative costs and stabilizes profits, but it also induces uneconomic fuel substitution. Due to these offsetting effects of FACs, it is not clear that production would be more efficient under administrative review. The problem of whether to shift fuel cost increases to consumers would not disappear in an unregulated market, but the decision would be made by the automatic and impersonal forces of supply and demand.

Optimal Fuel Choice in an Open Economy

Deregulation of Electric Power and Trade Policy. Trade policy affects the electrical power sector through its influence on the price of fuel, particularly crude oil. Thus trade policy influences the average price of electricity and its variability. At the same time, the domestic regulation of energy has heavily influenced trade policy for oil. Domestic policies that increased the cost of domestic energy production and depressed domestic prices indirectly added to the demand for imported oil. Domestic energy regulation and international trade policy are inseparable. Thus we should consider deregulation of the domestic electrical power industry simultaneously with free trade in oil and natural gas.

In the decade of the 1970s the energy sector was shaken by many

---

12. Frank H. Gollop and Stephen H. Karlson, "The Impact of the Fuel Adjustment Mechanisms on Economic Efficiency," *Review of Economics and Statistics* 60 (November 1978):574–84; Daniel Violette and Michael D. Yokell, "Fuel Cost Adjustment Clause Incentives: An Analysis with References to California," *Public Utilities Fortnightly* (June 10, 1982):33–39.

foreign and domestic disturbances.[13] The development of OPEC, political and military disputes in the Middle East, and the adoption of floating exchange rates all affected our energy industry. Important domestic disturbances included changes in tax laws, environmental restrictions, price and quantity controls. The future is inherently uncertain, but it does seem unlikely that the energy sector will be free from major disturbances. For this reason, it is important to design an energy policy that is capable of responding to economic disturbances. An appropriate trade policy can reinforce deregulation of domestic energy in achieving a system that is more responsive to economic change. Thus a coherent energy policy can only be achieved when domestic and foreign components are compatible. Deregulation of the electric power industry combined with free trade in energy would make it easier to achieve a coherent energy policy. Free trade in energy can contribute to cheaper electric power and greater stability of the electrical industry.

HISTORY OF UNITED STATES OIL TRADE POLICY

Whether or not to protect our oil industry from imports was not a serious policy issue until the 1950s. American oil producers had a comparative advantage from the time that oil was discovered in Titusville, Pennsylvania, in 1859. From that time until the 1950s, most of the world's oil was produced in the United States. The U.S. share of world oil production totaled 63 percent in 1940 and 51 percent in 1950.[14] The earliest formal expression of concern about oil availability was President Taft's decision in 1909 to set aside 3 million acres of public land that became the Naval Petroleum Reserve.[15] The first U.S. oil tariff, described in the Internal Revenue Act as an import fee, was imposed in 1932. The United States ceased being a net exporter of oil in 1948, and its domination of the world oil market was then challenged by the development of Middle Eastern oil in the 1950s. As oil from other countries became generally available, the U.S. share of world production continued its decline: 34 percent in 1960, 24 percent in 1970, 14 percent in 1980. The attempt by state government agencies, such as the Texas Railroad Commission, to raise the do-

13. Albert L. Danielsen, *The Evolution of OPEC* (New York: Harcourt Brace Jovanovich, 1982).
14. Danielsen, *The Evolution of OPEC*, p. 129.
15. Bohi and Russell, *Limiting Oil Imports*, p. 20.

mestic price by restricting production (prorationing) was negated by the increase in oil imports.

A voluntary import quota applied by the federal government in 1957 was not effective, and then President Eisenhower imposed a mandatory import quota by executive order in 1959. The quota was expressed as a percentage (12 percent) of U.S. oil production. In 1970 the Cabinet Task Force on Oil Import Control recommended the substitution of a tariff for the quota at a lower level of protection. A tariff would transfer revenue from holders of import licenses to the government, and it would permit the volume of imports to respond to changes in demand and supply.

President Nixon imposed an import fee, but it was abandoned in 1973 as oil became more scarce on the world market. Beginning in 1971, domestic price controls encouraged oil imports, and this held U.S. oil prices below the level of world prices. By discouraging domestic production and exploration and encouraging domestic consumption, the price-control program acted as an implicit import subsidy. In its zeal to do something about the energy problem, Congress also banned exports of Alaskan oil.[16] President Carter attempted to impose a tariff on oil in 1980, but a court determined that he lacked constitutional authority. Decontrol of domestic oil prices began in 1980 in conjunction with the Windfall Profit Tax Act. The tax was effectively a sales tax based on the difference between the price of oil with and without controls. Decontrol was completed in 1982 during the Reagan administration. In recent years an oil tariff has been proposed by certain political leaders (ex-President Carter and Senator Gary Hart) as well as a number of economists.[17]

Successful collusion by oil exporting countries motivated oil importers to cooperate. The integrated nature of the world oil market suggests that a disruption affecting the supply to one country will spread to all other importing countries. The possibility of transshipping and rerouting oil makes it impossible for exporters to deny oil to a group of importers without denying it to all importing countries. The experience with the 1973–74 oil embargo directed at the United

---

16. Political support for the ban came from the domestic shipping industry and maritime labor unions. The Jones Act of 1920 requires that U.S. ships be used for all domestic trade, including Alaska.

17. Adelman, "Coping with Supply Insecurity"; MacAvoy, *Energy Policy: An Economic Analysis;* Nordhaus, "The Energy Crisis and Macroeconomic Policy"; Plummer, "Policy Implications of Energy Vulnerability."

States and the Netherlands provided support for this proposition. Oil imports to these two countries were not reduced by more than to other importing countries.[18] World oil prices increased because of a reduction in total exports and world production, not because of shortages in the United States and the Netherlands. Because of this market interdependence, the import policy of each country affects all other importing countries. An incentive exists for importing countries to act together in determining policy toward oil imports and inventories.

Following the oil embargo of 1973–74 by the Organization of Arab Oil Exporting Countries, Secretary of State Kissinger proposed formal cooperation. In November, 1974, the International Energy Agency (IEA) was established as an independent organization within the Organization for Economic Cooperation and Development (OECD). Two of the stated goals of the IEA are (1) reducing dependence on imported oil by member countries and (2) sharing limited oil in the case of an emergency. To accomplish these goals, the IEA has encouraged members to develop stockpile policies and to follow pricing policies that encourage conservation and domestic production. United States pricing policy for oil and natural gas has usually not conformed with this prescription. Thus the IEA has not been effective in bringing about a unified import policy for member countries.

As with most international agencies, the IEA has no actual authority to enforce its proposals. IEA members all confront a free-rider problem since each individual country benefits from letting others add to inventories or reduce imports. The IEA did not act during the 1979–1980 shortage. Certain importing countries have appeared reluctant to pursue policies—such as stockpiling—that the OPEC governments might view as hostile acts.

In response to the 1973–74 embargo, the United States initiated a Strategic Petroleum Reserve in 1977. A stockpile of oil is accumulating in underground salt caverns, located primarily in Louisiana. By July, 1984, a reserve of 415 million barrels of oil had accumulated, which equalled 90 days of U.S. imports at that time. The Department of Energy manages the reserve, but it has never been clear under what circumstances it would be used. Government managers were criticized for failing to install pumps in time to use the reserve during the Iranian Crisis of 1979–80.

---

18. Danielsen, *The Evolution of OPEC*, pp. 190–93.

NEW OIL PROTECTIONISM

The debate about whether free trade in oil by the United States would result in excessive dependence on imports has continued since 1957. The success of OPEC since 1973 has stimulated a kind of new protectionist literature.[19] It is ironic that government management of oil imports is sometimes advocated by some of the same people who concluded that domestic-energy regulation has been inefficient. The new protectionist literature uses the concept of an "oil import premium" in an attempt to rationalize trade barriers. The concept is a vague one, but in general it refers to the excess of social over private cost in importing oil. As an example of the concept's lack of precision, Bohi and Montgomery cite sixteen estimates of the premium done in 1980–81 that range from near zero to $100 per barrel.[20] Nordhaus reports a narrower range of $13 to $46 per barrel.[21] Included in the premium are three kinds of effects. First is the terms-of-trade effect that appears in the international trade literature as the national optimum tariff argument. Second is the potential cost of an oil import supply disruption. If there are short-run economic costs of adjusting to a disruption that private agents do not take into account, the volume of imports that would occur under free trade may be excessive. A third broad category includes indirect macroeconomic effects such as inflation, unemployment, and balance of payments problems. Since these problems depend on labor market response to macroeconomic disturbances, they are best corrected at the source rather than with a tariff. In addition the effect of an oil price change depends on the level of oil consumption, not the volume of imports.[22] Hence a tariff is an inappropriate remedy. The next two sections consider the first two components of the oil premium.

IMPORTS AND THE AVERAGE PRICE OF OIL

Any policy that reduces the import volume of a large country also reduces the price paid to foreign suppliers. In general any buyer pos-

---

19. Adelman, "Coping with Supply Insecurity"; MacAvoy, *Energy Policy: An Economic Analysis;* Nordhaus, "The Energy Crisis and Macroeconomic Policy"; Plummer, "Policy Implications of Energy Vulnerability."

20. Douglas R. Bohi and W. D. Montgomery, *Oil Prices, Energy Security, and Import Policy* (Baltimore: Johns Hopkins University Press, 1982), p. 3.

21. Nordhaus, "The Energy Crisis and Macroeconomic Policy," p. 16.

22. Bohi and Montgomery, *Oil Prices, Energy Security,* chap. 3.

sessing monopsony power can obtain a more favorable price by reducing the quantity purchased. For each $1 of benefit appropriated by the monopsonist, however, other groups suffer losses of more than $1. Thus there exists a tariff level for a large country that will simultaneously increase national income and decrease world income. The concept of a nationally optimal tariff has been clear since the early discussion by Bickerdike and Edgeworth. The chief danger in levying an optimal tariff on one product is the possibility that other countries will impose their own optimal tariffs against one's exports. If the United States imposed an optimal tariff on a major import, this would conflict with the entire pattern of multilateral tariff reduction accomplished in the postwar period under the auspices of the General Agreement on Tariffs and Trade. Many U.S. products would become vulnerable to foreign tariffs, particularly agricultural exports. Another problem with an optimal tariff on oil is that oil exporting countries may retaliate. A more serious problem is that the application of an optimal tariff by the world's largest trading nation would lead other large countries to pursue similar nationalistic policies for other products. The resulting trade warfare could lead to lower national incomes for all countries. The imposition of an oil tariff by all oil importing countries would depress the world price of oil by more than a unilateral optimum tariff by the U.S. Such a collusive effort would, however, also invite trade warfare.

According to the traditional argument, the purpose of an optimum tariff is to depress the product price below the level that would prevail in a competitive market. Since the success of OPEC in the 1970s, the world oil price has been far above the competition level. Some economists argue that a tariff or import quota on oil could be used to force OPEC sellers to transform prices from monopolistic to competitive levels. The object of such a policy would be to improve the terms of trade for the United States, but the initial position would be a monopoly import price. This goal has the virtue of increasing world income. Fortunately it can be achieved without departing from free trade in oil.

In interpreting trade policy of the 1970s, it is important to recognize that the United States did not practice free trade in energy. On the contrary the net effect of various features of domestic energy policy was a subsidy to oil imports, that is, a negative tariff. Even though no explicit subsidy to oil importers existed, domestic price controls on crude oil and natural gas had the same impact on domestic consumption, production, and the volume of imports as an explicit import subsidy would have. Because imports were in effect subsidized by the largest oil-importing nation, the world price was higher than it would have been under competition and free trade. Thus U.S. energy policy contributed to a deterioration in the national terms of trade, and the presence of an unconscious ally made it easier for the members of OPEC to enforce a monopoly price for oil.

The United States can make a major contribution to the promotion of competition in the world oil market without imposing a tariff on oil. Abolishing remaining price controls and making a commitment to refrain from future energy price controls would contribute to lower oil prices worldwide. Members of the International Energy Agency have explicitly advocated pricing policies that encourage conservation and greater domestic production, although the United States has violated those principles for an extended period. Since decontrol of oil prices began in the United States in 1980, the volume of imports and the world price of oil have decreased. Table 6–9 shows that the volume of petroleum imports has been declining; in 1983 imports were the lowest in ten years. Table 6–9 also shows that the relative importance of oil imports declined from 46.5 percent of domestic supply in 1977 to 28 percent in 1983. The price of imported oil (see Table 6–7) also declined from a peak of $34.02 in 1981 to $28.40 in 1983. The United States has improved its terms of trade and become more

Table 6–9.   United States Dependence on Petroleum Net Imports (thousand barrels per day annual rate).

	Net Imports of Petroleum	Domestic Petroleum Products Supplied	Percent Imports Relative to Domestic Supply
1973	6,025	17,308	34.8
1974	5,891	16,653	35.4
1975	5,847	16,322	35.8
1976	7,090	17,461	40.6
1977	8,564	18,431	46.5
1978	8,001	18,847	42.5
1979	7,985	18,513	43.1
1980	6,365	17,056	37.3
1981	5,401	16,058	33.6
1982	4,298	15,296	28.1
1983	4,249	15,184	28.0

SOURCE: *Monthly Energy Review*, March 1984, p. 19.

self-sufficient in oil without resorting to a tariff. Abandoning the negative tariff implicit in price controls was sufficient. The optimal trade
policy for the United States is to avoid both positive and negative
tariffs on oil. In formulating energy policy, it is important, as stated
earlier, to recognize that domestic and trade policy are inseparable.
In particular the benefits from decontrolling the domestic electric power
industry would be enhanced by a policy of free trade in oil.

TRADE POLICY AND THE STABILITY OF FUEL SUPPLY

Trade policy can affect the stability of fuel supply to the electric power
industry as well as the average price. Trade-policy literature since
1973 has emphasized the role of tariffs as a means of protecting against
an unreliable supply of imported oil. Unlike the optimum tariff situation, the problem of uncertain supply does not depend on monopsony power of the importing country. The literature was inspired
by the Arab oil embargo in 1973–74, the Iranian Revolution of 1979–
80, and the Iran-Iraq War, which has threatened to disrupt Persian
Gulf oil supplies since 1980. In order to justify a tariff based on uncertainty, one must show that (1) the government has an advantage
over private agents in forecasting and protecting against a supply interruption and (2) a tariff is superior to alternative policies such as
inventories.

   Theoretical papers by Bhagwati and Srinivasan and Mayer conclude that a tariff is the optimal policy when a country faces an embargo threat. Both papers assume that authorities in the importing
countries know the probability and expected duration of an embargo,
but that private agents in that country would ignore the embargo threat.
Since uncertain import supply is the source of difficulty in this formulation of the problem, the optimal solution is a tariff that restricts
import supply. This solution represents an application of the principle
that distortions should be corrected at the source. This solution depends, however, on asymmetric information between policymakers
and private agents. If private consumers and producers possess the
same information as the government about the embargo, they will
respond in the socially optimal way. Tolley and Wilman show that
when faced by an embargo threat, households have an incentive to
reduce consumption, and firms have an incentive to increase production. Demand and supply respond to the expected price of the im-

ported product rather than to the current price. In the absence of external effects, the socially optimal level of imports will occur without the need for a tariff or any other government intervention. Thus the theoretical justification for a tariff to counteract an embargo threat is based on the assumption of unequal information. Even if the home government had access to superior information about the likely trade policy of foreign governments, it could avoid the need for an optimal tariff by sharing that information with the public. When private agents possess the relevant information, they will automatically curtail imports from unsafe sources during the nonembargo period. If safe sources of imports are also available, private agents will diversify imports to favor safe sources.

There is also reason to doubt that the president, executive agencies, and Congress actually possess greater information about the world oil market than interested oil companies. Most of the data available to the government represents public information, and much of the classified information comes from private corporations. Congress, which has the authority to set tariffs, deliberates in public. Similarly no one in government possesses a model of the world oil market superior to those available to private analysts. In fact government agencies usually rely on private consultants for their most reliable analyses.

Government energy agencies have also shown that they have no superior forecasting ability. For example, George Daly has pointed out serious forecasting errors in the 1974 Project Independence Report and the 1977 National Energy Plan.[23] The former substantially underestimated the price of oil and overestimated the contribution of nuclear power. The Project Independence Report forecasts steady growth in oil imports that would lie within the range of 12 to 16 million barrels per day in 1985. In fact 1983 imports were less than 5 million barrels per day, down from the peak of 9 million barrels per day in 1977. Any investment decisions based on either report would have resulted in costly errors. Even the Federal Reserve, which should have access to inside information, has suffered losses from its foreign-exchange-market intervention in recent years.[24] Placing an economic value on risk is a traditional function of private markets, and agents who

23. George Daly, "Recall the Attempts at a Mini-Industrial Policy," *Wall Street Journal* (16 March 1984), p. 26.

24. Dean Taylor, "Official Intervention in the Foreign Exchange Market, or Bet Against the Central Bank," *Journal of Political Economy* 90 (April 1982):356–68.

are excessively either optimistic or pessimistic will not survive in a competitive market. For example, in the summer of 1984 when both Iran and Iraq were attacking commercial ships in the Persian Gulf, marine insurance companies had a strong proprietary interest in assessing the true risk, and because of this, they adjusted insurance premiums continuously in response to new information. It is doubtful whether Congress, the Department of Energy, or any other government agency possessed a superior index of the relevant commercial risk at that time.

In addition to their lack of superior information, government agencies also lack the motivation to impose a nationally optimal tariff. Empirical studies on the political economy of tariffs indicate that the president, cabinet agencies, and the Congress respond to the lobbying efforts of interested parties rather than to the general notion of social welfare.[25] Evidence from U.S. tariff history does not support the proposition that Congress is motivated to select tariff levels that internalize the expected cost of supply interruption. Thus a tariff generated by the political process that includes domestic oil producers could be higher than the hypothetical social optimum. Even in absence of retaliation, a sufficiently high tariff will produce a lower national income than free trade. For example, the political process that produced "voluntary" import quotas on automobiles, steel, and textiles has imposed losses on consumers that exceed the benefits to domestic producers and owners of industry-specific capital. What would motivate the same government institutions to produce a different result in the case of an oil tariff?

A more fundamental problem is that the government is not a single, homogeneous institution with clear economic goals. At any point in time it is a set of many heterogeneous institutions with overlapping jurisdictions. Each agency may respond to different lobbying groups so that one agency might support domestic oil price controls at the same time other agencies call for greater energy independence. In a decentralized system it is difficult to achieve a coherent policy for any product. In addition changes in presidents, Congress, and cabinet agencies make it difficult to produce consistent policies over time. Foreign diplomats are perplexed by the drastic changes in U.S. foreign policy over recent years. Our electoral process also creates an

---

25. Edward J. Ray, "The Determinants of Tariff and Non-Tariff Trade Restrictions in the United States," *Journal of Political Economy* 89 (February 1981):105–21.

extremely short time-horizon for government planners. The democratic political process offers few rewards for government agents who produce nationally optimal tariffs.

In addition to possible information differences between government and the private sector, any appropriate tariff would depend on the relative importance of foreign and domestic disturbances. The development of OPEC and the Iranian revolution have been widely cited as foreign disturbances to import supply. Much of the discussion of trade policy has been aimed at protecting against such disturbances. We must also consider two other offsetting kinds of disturbances. First, certain foreign fluctuations that increase import supply will offset those that reduce supply. The relevant import supply to the United States is the supply from all over the world, not just the supply from Iran or OPEC. In a given year an embargo by certain suppliers may be offset by a new discovery or another country's expansionary-export policy. So long as all supply disturbances are not perfectly correlated, the rest of the world can remain stable trading partners, when taken as a unit, even though the supplies of individual countries could be volatile.[26] The variability of total import supply depends both on the variance of individual suppliers and the covariance of those suppliers. The situation is analogous to a risk-averse investor who seeks minimum earnings variance for given mean earnings. The total variance of the portfolio depends on individual variances and the covariance among assets. Assets with high variance may reduce total portfolio variance if their covariance with other assets is sufficiently low. Since the United States imports oil from such diverse sources as Canada, Mexico, the United Kingdom, Saudi Arabia, and Nigeria, there is reason to believe that the covariance of disturbances in those countries would not be high. In that case foreign suppliers of oil taken as a group would be a stable source of supply. A policy of free trade would provide oil at the lowest cost, and it would also stabilize the domestic price. Conversely if imports were an unstable source of supply, import barriers would stabilize the price, but the average cost of oil would be greater than under free trade. The world oil market con-

---

26. Gale D. Johnson, "Increased Stability of Grain Supplies in Developing Countries: Optimal Carryovers and Insurance" in J. Bhagwati, ed., *The New International Economic Order: The North-South Debate* (Cambridge: MIT Press, 1977), pp. 257–72.

tains a large number of exporting countries, many of whom do not belong to OPEC. In addition the costly war between Iran and Iraq is evidence that the political goals of OPEC countries sometimes conflict.

Just as it is possible to rely too heavily on uncertain imports, it is also possible to rely too heavily on uncertain domestic supplies. Domestic supplies of oil, natural gas, coal, and electrical power have been subject to many economic fluctuations over the last decade, with regulatory change the source of most disturbances. Although not the intention of regulators, disturbance of domestic supply was the indirect effect. Examples of supply disturbances are price controls, changes in tax laws, and environmental controls. These altered the supply of domestic fuel that was available to the electric power industry, and the availability of imported oil served as an offset to these domestic shocks. To the extent that foreign supplies taken as a group are more stable than domestic supply, foreign trade is a stabilizing force for the U.S. electric power industry. A tariff or quota that would reduce the availability of imported fuel would thus destabilize electrical utilities. It follows that a policy of free trade in energy would provide cheaper fuel and a more reliable supply of fuel than an alternative protectionist policy.

Evidence since 1973 indicates that U.S. buyers have diversified their imports without using tariffs or quotas. Table 6–1 shows the source of U.S. oil imports by country for 1973 and 1983. Total imports declined from 6,256 thousand barrels per day in 1973 to 4,988 thousand barrels per day in 1983. The percent of oil imported from OPEC countries declined from 48 percent in 1973 to 37 percent in 1983. The percent coming from Arab OPEC members declined from 15 to 13 percent. Imports from particularly volatile countries also declined: Iran, from 3 to 1 percent and Libya, from 3 to zero. In 1983 there were seven non-OPEC countries that supplied at least 2 percent of U.S. oil imports. In addition five OPEC members supplied at least 2 percent of U.S. imports. Those five are characterized by extreme geographical separation: North Africa (Algeria), West Africa (Nigeria), Persian Gulf (Saudi Arabia), South America (Venezuela), and Southeast Asia (Indonesia). Wars—for example the one between Iran and Iraq that threatened Persian Gulf shipping—and political events that affect one supplier are unlikely to affect all suppliers in the same way. Thus total import supply may be stable even if individual country supplies are not.

INVENTORIES AND SUPPLY INTERRUPTION

Uncertainty of import supply is a legitimate economic problem, but recent studies indicate that inventories are a lower cost solution than a tariff.[27] Although he advocates a tariff to improve the terms of trade, Adelman states unequivocally that "the only defense or mitigation of a supply crisis lies in stockpiling."[28] The optimal national inventory of oil depends on the probability, size, and duration of the supply interruption, the value of the damage done by the disturbance, and the cost of holding reserves. Some recent estimates of optimal inventories have produced a range of from 750 million barrels to 2,000 million barrels.[29] The 750-million-barrel figure coincides with the authorized capacity of the U.S. Strategic Petroleum Reserve, which had accumulated 415 million barrels by July 1984. Optimal inventories include both private and public inventories, but there is reason to believe that public holding substitute for private holdings. The profitability of private inventory holding depends on prices rising during a supply interruption.

The history of price controls during crisis periods, however, has severely reduced the incentive to hold private stockpiles. In the words of Adelman, "the almost unquestioned major premise among governments that in an emergency there has got to be a fair allocation at reasonable prices is possibly the greatest single aggravating force in making disruptions worse than they need to be."[30] Since the expectation of price controls reduces private inventories, each barrel in the Strategic Petroleum Reserve may not be a net addition to national reserves. If Congress had the will and capacity to convince private agents that they would abstain from price control forever, a government stockpile would be unnecessary. Since every law is subject to repeal, though, the credibility of any such promise would be limited. Congress could, however, alter private incentives by including in any current reserve legislation a promise to compensate private inventory

---

27. Bohi and Montgomery, *Oil Prices, Energy Security;* D. A. Deese and J. S. Nye, *Energy and Security* (Cambridge, Mass.: Ballinger Publishing Company, 1981).

28. Adelman, "Coping with Supply Insecurity," p. 10.

29. Adelman, "Coping with Supply Insecurity"; H. S. Rowen and J. P. Weyant, "Reducing the Economic Impacts of Oil Supply Interruptions: An International Perspective," *Energy Journal* 3 (January 1982):1–34; Plummer, "Policy Implications of Energy Vulnerability."

30. Adelman, "Coping with Supply Insecurity," p. 8.

holders in the event of future price controls.[31] A second-best policy would be free trade combined with a strategic stockpile.

SUMMARY

Successful regulatory reform must consider the context in which the electric power industry operates. A coherent regulatory policy must take into account the interdependence of various forms of energy and the link between foreign and domestic markets. Energy-import policy affects the average price of fuel and its variance for the electric power industry. Domestic price controls of the 1970s made the United States excessively dependent on imported oil. The trade distortion caused by that policy has, however, been eliminated by decontrolling domestic crude oil prices. The volume of U.S. imports and the world price of oil have declined substantially since decontrol began.

An additional tariff or import quota on oil would result in more costs then benefits. Just as price controls made oil artificially cheap in the 1970s, imposing oil import barriers would make oil artificially expensive in the future. As a result electricity would not be generated using the minimum-cost combination of fuels. Rather the cost of electricity would be inflated by excessive use of high-cost domestic oil and oil substitutes. The possibility of an interruption of import supply is a legitimate concern, but oil protectionism is not the least-cost solution. Diversification of imports and inventory accumulation are more direct solutions. When we take the large number of diverse oil-import sources into account, the total supply of imported oil may be more stable than the supply of domestic oil. A policy of free trade could provide fuel for electrical generation that is both cheaper and more reliable than a policy of oil protectionism.

31. Plummer, "Policy Implications of Energy Vulnerability."

7

THE POLITICIZATION OF THE ELECTRIC UTILITY INDUSTRY

Craig J. Bolton and Roger E. Meiners

INTRODUCTION

The electric utility industry in the United States is a complex collection of investor-owned utilities (IOUs), electric cooperatives, and municipal and federal projects. Some companies or agencies specialize in the production of power, some in its wholesale distribution, and others in retail sales to residential and commercial consumers. State rate boards or commissions regulate rates at the retail level, and the Federal Energy Regulatory Commission regulates wholesale distribution rates.

Despite the variety of firms and regulatory bodies participating in the production and distribution of electricity, we can discern a few industrywide patterns. Virtually all electricity firms at the generation, wholesale distribution, and retail levels have suffered from a decade-long decline in the rate of demand increases for their output. From 1945 to 1970, electric power usage grew at an annual compound average rate of 7.8 percent, and peakloads grew at 8.1 percent. Since the oil embargo of 1973, however, power usage growth has dropped to an annual rate of 2.8 percent and peak-load growth to 3.5 percent.[1]

---

1. Scott A. Fenn, *America's Electric Utilities* (Washington, D.C.: Investor Responsibility Research Center, 1983), pp. 6–7.

Industry forecasters failed to predict this declining rate in demand for electricity, and the industry has been slow to adjust to the new trend. As a result, excess generation capacity in the industry increased from 21 percent in 1973 to 39 percent in 1982, the latter being the highest level of excess capacity since the depth of the 1930s depression.[2]

The growth in excess capacity has led utilities that sell directly to consumers to adopt a variety of demand expansion rate policies, such as the lifeline rates described below. In addition many retail utilities have sought unprecedented rate increases from their rate-makers, usually justifying such requests as adjustments to inflationary pressures on operating costs during the past decade.[3] Some utilities have also repudiated their traditional preference for a fair-return-on value-invested standard of rate setting. Since value invested is usually based on historical costs, and since the prospects for replacing old capacity with new are limited in an environment of a flat demand and high interest rates, the value-invested standard generates lower profits than it had in years past.[4]

Although federal generation and distribution systems have experienced many of the same difficulties as IOUs, their proportionately greater concentration in hydroelectric and coal-fired facilities has generally resulted in lower fuel-cost increases. And, unlike the IOUs, they have not had to meet a market test for profitability of ownership shares. Although difficult to estimate with precision, the public subsidy to users of federal power has probably increased in real terms during the last decade. For example, as we discuss below, electric cooperatives receiving Rural Electrification Administration loans have experienced an enormous and unambiguous windfall increase in interest subsidies during that period.

This increase in the real subsidy to federal power users is due in part to a phenomena analogous to the regulatory lag experienced by IOUs. With both federal power agencies and IOUs, decision makers (agency heads or regulators, respectively) have been hesitant to grant rapid or large rate increases, anticipating adverse political reaction. As a result, IOUs have experienced lower profit rates, whereas federal facilities have simply decreased paybacks to the Treasury or increased appropriations subsidies from Congress.

2. Fenn, *America's Electric Utilities*, p. 7.
3. Ibid., pp. 40, 53.
4. Bridger M. Mitchell, Willard G. Manning, Jr., and Jan P. Acton, *Peak-Load Pricing* (Cambridge, Mass.: Ballinger Publishing Co. for Rand Corp., 1978), pp. 46–47.

In the following sections we consider how the traditional pricing policies of electric utilities in the United States have differed from what would be expected under competition. Then we examine some of the income redistribution policies various utilities have adopted and discuss the role the federal government plays in subsidizing the power system and using it as a mechanism for distributing benefits to favored groups. We conclude with some remarks about the impact politicization has had on the electric industry and society as a whole and comment on the likelihood of change.

SUBSIDIES IN ELECTRICITY PRICING

The production, transmission, and distribution of electric power usually occurs in a monopolized environment, though the presumed natural-monopoly character of the electric industry no longer applies to power generation or transmission.[5] This makes speculation on the details of what a competitive rate structure could be uncertain, but we can discern the broader features of such a system and look at how it differs from what now exists.

The present rate structure is bifurcated between commerical and residential users, with commercial users generally receiving lower rates than residential users. Residental users pay a monthly service fee and/ or a minimum monthly rate charge, plus a declining-block rate for power usage beyond the initial minimum block. Many utilities have a four-block rate schedule; some have as few as two blocks.[6] While many utilities have experimented with peak-load pricing, inverted-block schedules, or flat rates, the so-called lifeline rate programs, described below, are the only innovation in retail pricing widely adopted and used as a "permanent" rate device.

Commercial and industrial users usually pay some form of the Hopkinson tariff. This rate schedule combines a discount proportioned directly to the business's maximum demand, or highest rate of usage during a given period, with a declining block schedule for total energy usage during a billing period.[7]

There is an explanation for the absence of peak-load premiums or other pricing policies that would act to reduce excess capacity requirements in regulated electric utilities. The management in these

5. See Philip Fanara, Jr., James E. Suelflow, and Roman A. Draba, "Energy and Competition: The Saga of Electric Power," *Antitrust Bulletin* 25 (1980): 134–37.

6. Mitchell, Manning, and Acton, *Peak-Load Pricing* pp. 10–12.

7. Ibid., pp. 13–14.

utilities faced incentives to overinvest in capital under a fair-return-on-value-invested standard. These managers find a positive relationship between the size of the plants they manage and their ability to hide fringe benefits. Such benefits—thicker carpeting, fancier offices, conferences in nice resorts, and other "perks"—are hidden in the firm's rate base. Firm stockholders suffer little due to this managerial rent seeking because the regulated structure of the industry prevented lower cost-competitive firms from entering the market, and the rate of return allowed is based on total costs. Although consumers pay more as a result of these rate-making policies, some consumers actually pay lower rates than they would under peak-load pricing. Firms constrained by the demand characteristics of their markets from economizing on peak-load usage of electricity, such as shopping centers, benefit from the absence of peak-load premiums. Even firms that would adopt revised production schedules to economize on peak-usage electricity charges must benefit in lower direct costs under the traditional system, or there would be no incentive to undertake load conservation measures under peak-load pricing. The political result of this is that a typical regulator is faced with a variety of business interests opposed to peak-load pricing, including the utility being regulated. Meanwhile the average electricity consumers—who would benefit from peak-load premiums through somewhat lower rates—have little incentive either to educate themselves on the issues or to petition the regulators for a policy change.

Certain changes in the utility operating environment have made peak-load rates somewhat more acceptable to some utility managers. These changes include an unplanned growth in excess generation capacity due to reduced demand growth rate, a corresponding decline in utility profits, and the more activist protests of consumers regarding the large rate increase requests made by many utilities. In this environment the need to limit costs and expand profits had become more urgent than management's interest in the magnificence of their offices.

Prevailing residential and commercial rate structures are, however, still largely different from what might be expected if rates were subject to a competitive environment. All electrical generation systems experience peak–off-peak cycles on a daily and/or yearly basis. Such cycles are costly for continuous, or "firm," power supply because they require the utility to always have enough capacity available to meet peak-level demand. The fuel requirements of the quick start-up/shut-down gasoline-fired supplemental generators that utilities call into service during peak periods make them high-cost producers of electricity. These high operating or variable costs or peak-period generators add to the financial burden, or fixed costs, of maintaining and storing the generators as excess capacity during off-peak periods.[8] Since plant and equipment costs account for the greatest percentage of operating costs, any saving in this peak-load generator capacity would lower total costs for the utility.

Competitive pricing policies would include peak-load surcharges for daily and seasonal peak usage. Such rates would not fully eliminate peaks and troughs in usage since some customers place a higher value on electricity use in peak periods than the producer's marginal cost of maintaining and operating the facilities required to produce this peak power. A competitive pricing structure could, however, be expected to flatten the demand for electricity on an hourly or seasonal basis, lower the average generating capacity needed by power producers, and place the marginal cost of peak loads on those receiving the benefits of peak-period production. The exact nature of the peak-usage charges would depend on demand characteristics and the type of generating plant used. As noted in Table 7–1, hydroelectric system peaks are seasonal, whereas thermal system peaks (oil, coal, or nuclear) are time-of-day.

One alternative to peak–off-peak pricing in a competitive environment would be the system, adopted by a few utilities, of "interrupt" service. Under this plan, customers who agree to bear the inconvenience of service interruption during peak periods are charged lower rates than those who require continuous, or firm, service. The utility then

Table 7–1.   Pattern of Marginal Generating Costs by Type of Generating System.

Marginal Generating Cost Characteristics	Type of System		
	All Thermal	*Thermal-Hydro*	*All Hydro*
Daily variation	Extreme	Moderate	None
Seasonal variation	Generally small	Moderate	Pronounced
Period of peak	A few hours daily	A long daily period	All hours of the dry season or dry years

SOURCE: Mitchell, Manning, and Acton, *Peak-Load Pricing,* p. 33.

8. Mitchell, Manning, and Acton, *Peak-Load Pricing,* pp. 24–25, 30–33.

can turn off the power to the interrupt customers when the system nears its peak, resulting in a capacity savings similar to peak-load pricing.[9]

Under competition, charges for service could be on a flat-rate basis rather than the traditional declining block system. The flat-rate schedule would be modified by peak-load premiums to reduce auxilliary generator capacity. It would probably also include some form of the monthly connection charges as well as the difference in rates between industrial and residential users found in current pricing systems. Monthly service fees are economically sensible because of the costs of replacing and maintaining line connections and meters for all users. Lower rates for industrial users are justified insofar as these customers use the higher voltages generated or purchased by the retail power company. Most residential and commercial users require lower voltages that are obtained only by building and maintaining expensive "step-down" equipment.[10]

INCOME REDISTRIBUTION SCHEMES

The market and political constraints facing electric utilities in recent years have led to a variety of rate-modification proposals. In this section we examine two of the most popular and widely accepted: lifeline rates and energy audits. Our thesis is that these innovations in utility services and pricing serve to redistribute income between a utility's customers and provide the utility a politically secure source of revenues. The reader should keep in mind that we can judge political policies by their actual effects as well as by their proponents' intentions.

Lifeline Rates

One of the most widely adopted innovations in electric rate-making policies are lifeline rate programs.[11] Such programs usually involve a two-step increasing rate schedule, with qualified low-income consumers paying below the standard residential rate for an initial block

9. Mitchell, Manning, and Acton, *Peak-Load Pricing*, pp. 58–59.

10. Mitchell, Manning, and Acton, *Peak-Load Pricing*, p. 36.

11. An excellent introduction to lifeline rate programs is found in Frank A. Scott, Jr., "Estimating Recipient Benefits and Waste from Lifeline Electricity Rates," *Land Economics* 57 (1981): 536–43.

of power service and then the standard rate, including standard declining blocks, for service above that lifeline amount. Lifeline rates usually abolish the monthly minimum service fee assessed on qualified accounts and provide for a utility's recovery of losses and costs attributed to the program in higher overall residential rates.

Despite the fact that a lifeline rate program "to provide low-priced power to low income households" was promoted by the Federal Energy Administration as early as 1975—and was a much touted plank in President Carter's Public Utilities Regulatory Policies Act of 1978—it is unclear whether such programs in fact provide a significant subsidy to low-income consumers. For instance, a 1981 study of a 50-percent lifeline rate reduction for the first 300 kwhs of monthly power used by qualified households estimated an income-equivalent savings to the lowest income households of only $42.57 per year.[12]

Part of the reason for this rather small impact on real consumer income is explained by a well-established theorem of welfare economics, which states that consumers will be made less well off by a policy that devotes resources to reducing the price of one good they consume than one that devotes the same resources to direct income grants paid to these consumers. This theorem is collaborated by the commonsense observation that needful consumers prefer to spread extra income among expenditures on food, clothing, shelter, and other goods rather than devote all added income to higher consumption of only one item such as electric power.[13] Several empirical studies have confirmed this theorem in the case of lifeline-rate programs. One study concluded that only consumers in the highest income group of lifeline-rate beneficiaries receive the full value of the rate reduction as the equivalent of an income subsidy. That is, only those consumers who would have bought more than the maximum subsidized electricity block, regardless of the availability of lifeline rates, enjoy the full benefits of the program as a pure income windfall.[14]

12. Scott, "Estimating Recipient Benefits," p. 543.

13. Scott, "Estimating Recipient Benefits," p. 543, and, for a more general treatment, Roger L. Miller, *Intermediate Microeconomics*, rev. ed. (New York: McGraw-Hill, 1982), pp. 55–57.

14. See Scott, "Estimating Recipient Benefits," p. 543; Dionissis Dimopoulos, "Pricing Schemes for Regulated Enterprises and Their Welfare Implications in the Case of Electricity," *Bell Journal of Economics* 12 (1981): 185–200, especially p. 199; and Giles Burgess and Morton Paglin, "Lifeline Electricity Rates as an Income Transfer Device," *Land Economics* 57 (1981): 41–47, especially pp. 45–46.

If lifeline-rate programs are not efficient forms of public welfare, why have so many electric utilities supported these programs? As mentioned above, lifeline programs usually abolish the standard minimum service fee and allow the utility to recover the "losses" of charging less than the standard rate for covered units of service, as well as all other "costs" of the program, by charging higher rates to nonlifeline users of electricity. Since utilities face frequent political challenges by regulatory bodies to their requested rate increases, provisions to recover the "expenses" of what is billed as a charitable program for the necessities of life creates a uniquely protected revenue source. Further, while political support for the utility and its regulators is enhanced by the gratitude of program recipients, the subsidy costs are spread to a large number of other users, who have little or no idea of the subsidies they provide via their electric bills.

Energy Audits

Another income transfer that has been misunderstood is the electric utility's provision of "energy audits" for customers who request them.[15] Energy audits were promoted as a part of President Carter's "energy crisis" legislative program and were formalized in the Energy Conservation and Policy Act of 1978. An energy audit is an assessment by a certified energy auditor, usually an architect or engineer in the case of commercial audits, of improvements in insulation or other energy-saving measures that audited customers can use to reduce energy consumption. Although mandated a direct fee for the audit of $15 for a home or $35 for an office or apartment, the utility's reported cost of the audit is $111–260 for homes and $186–500 for apartments or offices.[16] The utility recovers the differences between the fees the customers pay and the costs of audits from ratepayers in general.

Public response to the energy-audit program has been less than enthusiastic. As might be expected, typical respondents have been upper-income households, and the net result of the audits in energy saved has been small. Lone Star Gas and Electric, a major Texas utility, found a 2 percent reduction in power consumed by audited customers.

Given that utilities have no incentive to estimate the true cost of

15. For a general description of energy audits, see Milton R. Copulos, "H.R. 3966: Reconsidering Energy Audits," (Heritage Foundation Issue Bulletin, 1984). (Mimeo.)

16. Copulos, "H.R. 3966," pp. 4–5.

running energy audits given the resulting small reduction in demand, and given that any actual reduction will be in the consumer's last and the utility's least profitable block of service, the energy audit program looks suspiciously similar to the lifeline programs: It is a secure justification for increasing the utility's rate base. The persistent efforts of the federal Residential Conservation Service to target low-income consumers for energy audits reinforces this suspicion.[17] So does the special leeway given utilities to provide free (i.e., entirely ratepayer financed) audits for many such consumers.[18] Such policies are designed to expand the demand for energy audits by adding subsidies beyond those inherent in the below-cost rates mandated for the audits. As with the lifeline-rate programs, the energy-audit programs provide a politically popular way to expand utility activities and rate bases, which allow a subsidy to some consumers at a small and probably unidentifiable cost imposed on all utility users.

While the alleged motives for such programs may be laudable, the notion that electricity consumers do not have the common sense or motivation to take economically justifiable steps to lower their own energy consumption and electric bills is economic nonsense. The purpose of economic analysis is to study the results of a policy, rather than assume that the political rhetoric is indicative of what is actually occurring.

INTERGENERATIONAL TRANSFERS

Subsidized financing of electric generating and transmitting facilities creates intergenerational transfers of income or wealth through the governmental electric power system. People often misunderstand the direction of such transfers, with a subsidy to future electricity consumers being misinterpreted as a "burden" passed on by the present generation to future generations.

Intergenerational transfers often occur in the following way: A municipal utility, or federally funded cooperative, receives subsidized financing through a loan in which a government—usually the federal

17. The Residential Conservation Service is a federal agency created by the Energy Security Act of 1980 to promote residential energy audits and other residential energy conservation measures.

18. Some audit programs extend the subsidy to cover capital expenditures by consumers to reduce electricity consumption. For example, Florida Power and Light pays up to one-half the cost of insulating attics and up to $600 for installing "energy-efficient" air conditioners.

government—acts as the lender, or through the sale of tax exempt and/or government-guaranteed bonds. With a direct loan from a governmental lender, the interest rate is usually substantially below the current market rate, repayment is over an extended period, often up to fifty years, and collection in cases of default are irregular or non-existent. Current taxpayers bear the cost of subsidizing the project, the difference between the market cost of financing and the actual cost to the utility. The same pattern holds, in probabilistic terms, when utilities use government-guaranteed loans to construct power facilities. The rate the utility borrower pays is below the market rate, and the government bears the full cost of the risk of default.

The most difficult case to assess arises when a utility or power project is authorized to issue tax-exempt bonds. If this leads to more borrowing than would have otherwise occurred—which should be the case since the utility's cost of borrowing has been substantially reduced—the market rate of interest to borrowers competing for the funds lent to such utilities will be somewhat higher, and tax revenues will be lower. It is impossible to determine the magnitude of these effects without detailed case-by-case information, however.

Intergenerational subsidies arising from below-market interest rates thus take the form of below-market electric rates for future power customers—those buying electric services after the investment in plant and equipment has been sunk. Merely receiving subsidized financing does not, of course, guarantee that the utility will pass on its savings to future customers in lower rates, especially as most utilities face no direct competition in their services. The utility could simply capitalize the savings in higher equity values or higher profit rates. However, certain government owned and operated facilities were originally intended to supply power at below market rates, and they have consistently done so. It is no coincidence that Bonneville Power customers have enjoyed the lowest electric rates in the country and the Tennessee Valley Authority's customers the second lowest rates. Thus consumers of federal utilities, and of the retail municipal and cooperative utilities supplied by federal projects, benefit from subsidized rates that do not reflect the cost of the equipment used in generating or transmitting the electricity they consume. Most federal government power projects must now pay back the federal investment in the project to the Treasury over a forty or fifty year period. As the subsequent discussion of TVA, the PMAs, and REAs demonstrates, however, the percentage of investment paid back declines rather than rises as the agency develops.

A different situation prevails with the investor-owned utilities (IOUs). A line of economists, beginning with Averch and Johnson, developed evidence indicating that prior to the early 1970s the typical IOU would have realized above-competitive levels of profit if it had not operated under regulatory constraints on profits.[19] The effect of imposing regulatory constraints was not, however, to lower the rates charged utility consumers. Rather the utilities engaged in "gold plating," that is, they overinvested in plants and equipment as a way of artificially expanding costs and decreasing realized profits.

Due to a combination of factors, IOUs currently face almost the opposite situation. Since the inflation of the last two decades and the energy crisis of the early 1970s, regulators have been simultaneously barraged with utility rate increase requests and increased political pressures to reduce, delay, or deny these requests. The resulting fall in real rates of return on capital invested in the electric industry, combined with higher market loan rates on the funds the IOUs borrow to finance new construction, is causing most utilities to follow a policy of "capital minimization," as evidenced by the drastic downward revisions in new construction schedules.[20] A study by Peter Navarro concludes that the recent period of "rate suppression" will lead either to much higher rates in the future or much less reliable power service.[21]

Thus we may be seeing a curious pattern of current taxpayers subsidizing future ratepayers within the governmental power sector while future ratepayers are subsidizing current ratepayers in the IOU power sector. The expected outcome of this scenerio—should it reach its logical extreme—is that the government will be "compelled" to take over more of the power system from a "failing" private sector or else provide more subsidies to the industry.

FEDERAL POWER: SUBSIDIES TO PREFERENCE CUSTOMERS

One feature of the federal electricity structure that distinguishes it from municipal, cooperative, or IOU producers and distributors is its policy of favoring and promoting certain interest groups and bestow-

---

19. For a thorough presentation of the Averch-Johnson thesis and a survey of recent related topics, see Frederick H. Murphy and Allen L. Soyster, *Economic Behavior of Electric Utilities* (Englewood Cliffs, N.J.: Prentice-Hall, 1983).

20. Fenn, *America's Electric Utilities*, p. 7.

21. Peter Navarro, "Save Now, Freeze Later," *Regulation* 7 (1983): 31–36.

ing "priority" (first-in-line) status on certain power users. For instance, the Rural Electrification Administration (REA) makes loans exclusively to power cooperatives and municipal utilities. The first major REA policy decision rejected a plan for financing IOU expansion into rural areas as an alternative to the de novo establishment of REA-sponsored cooperatives there.[22]

The five federal Power Marketing Associations (PMAs) are required to sell the power the Army Corp of Engineers hydroelectric projects generate to "preference customers." The PMAs have sometimes chosen to allow excess capacity (water flow) to dissipate rather than to sell it on the open market. PMA preference customers include municipal utilities, REA cooperatives, and other federal power users.[23]

For some decades, a running war existed between the Tennessee Valley Authority (TVA) and IOU power distributors and producers. Although the TVA retails power directly to only a few large industrial users, it always sought to replace the IOUs in its local geographic areas with municipal or cooperative retailers. Congressional action, resulting in the 1959 TVA Revenue Act's restriction on the boundaries of the TVA, finally ended the friction between the TVA and the IOUs.[24] This action ended the threat to IOUs that had not yet been incorporated into the TVA's previously expanding service area.

Lastly, the Federal Energy Regulatory Commission (FERC) has seriously impeded IOUs from wholesale power marketing. FERC is charged with establishing "just and reasonable rates for the transmission and sale for resale of electric power by public utilities in interstate commerce," and it has zealously sought to carry out this directive. In 1981 of the rate requests for increases totaling $750 million, $600 million were suspended, subject to refund, and set for hearings. In 1982 of the $730 million in requested increases, $650 million were suspended, subject to refund, and set for hearings. Although it also scrutinizes the PMAs, the FERC's charge in these cases is to "assure that the rates charged by PMAs conform to statutory requirements."

22. John D. Garwood and W.C. Tuttle, *The Rural Electrification Administration* (Washington, D.C.: American Enterprise Institute, 1963), pp. 5–6.

23. See Subcommittee on Appropriations, House of Representatives, 98th Congress, *Energy and Water Development Appropriations for 1985*, p. 5 (Washington, D.C.: U.S. Government Printing Office, 1984). p. 391. Hereinafter, PMA Hearings.

24. See Marc J. Roberts and Jeremy S. Bluhm, *The Choices of Power* (Cambridge, Mass.: Harvard University Press, 1981), p. 71.

Judgments regarding the reasonableness of PMA rates are not relevant considerations.[25]

Tennessee Valley Authority

The Tennessee Valley Authority is the largest federal public utility in the United States. As the TVA history in this chapter's appendix explains, the TVA has evolved over time to its present status as a multipurpose agency providing general taxpayer subsidies to the electricity users in its service area.

Despite nationwide declining growth in electricity demand, current demand for TVA power is probably artificially high. The TVA's dominant program objective has always been to supply electricity at the lowest possible rates, with capital costs largely discounted away. In 1983 TVA customers paid lower rates than customers of all other power systems except for the federal Bonneville Power Authority. Residential and industrial rates were, respectively, about 70 and 80 percent of the national average.[26] The TVA's unusually low rate structure results from its methods of financing power facilities. Congressional appropriations up to 1959 financed construction. Since that time, power construction has been "self-financed" through the sale of revenue bonds. As of 1984 the TVA had borrowed $16 billion and is authorized to borrow another $14.5 billion. By comparison total capitalization of the five regional federal PMAs, including Bonneville, is $14 billion.

The TVA has several features that enhance its ability to offer "low" rates. It pays no taxes to the states or municipalities in which it operates, and it is exempt from their regulatory control. As an independent federal agency, it is not bound by the procedures or monitoring of GSA or GAO, nor are its 6,100 employees a part of the federal civil service system. Congress oversees TVA operations only in the broadest terms and has seldom questioned the details of its various projects. Congressional appropriations presently account for less than 3 percent of the TVA's annual budget. The TVA is thus blessed with a substantial capital plant, obtained at little or no cost from its per-

25. Subcommittee on Appropriations, House of Representatives, 98th Congress, *Energy and Water Development Appropriations for 1985*, p. 4 (Washington, DC.: U.S. Government Printing Office, 1984), p. 1913. Hereinafter, FERC Hearings.

26. Tennessee Valley Authority, *1983 TVA Annual Report* (Knoxville, Tenn.: Tennessee Valley Authority, 1983), p. 11.

spective, that generated about $4.7 billion in revenues in 1984, supplemented by nearly $1 billion more in borrowing and Congressional appropriations.[27]

Table 7–2 showing some TVA projects in progress and those planned for the future gives a sample of the TVA's character. It has become little less than a regional planning board, unconstrained by many of the institutional checks other government agencies face.[28]

The TVA has developed a permanent political constituency: those subsidized by its low rates, the beneficiaries of its nonpower production programs, and, of course, its employees. Potential opposition within its operating region has long since been defused. The TVA Revenue Act of 1959 set permanent boundaries on TVA territory, silencing the IOUs that bordered on the TVA's previously expanding territory and thus eliminating the main organized opposition to the TVA's existence. The notion that the TVA only costs taxpayers a minimal amount—about $120 million a year in Congressional appropriations—which is amply repaid in low power rates and other "public benefits" has become a broadly accepted popular myth. This belief ignores the issue of whether the enormous capital and land resources of the TVA might be more efficiently used.

Table 7–2.   Selected TVA Nonpower Production Projects.

Administration of $40 million jobs-bill fund.
Production of ammonia from coal.
Production of ethyl alcohol from hardwoods.
Soil erosion control for agricultural lands.
Home garden demonstration program.
Forest resource development program.
"Townlift"—technical assistance to revitalize downtown business districts of
    small and medium-sized "rural communities."
Tourism development program.
Hazardous waste management program.
Coordination of municipal zoning as a means of floodplain damage control.

SOURCE: TVA Hearings

---

27. Subcommittee on Appropriations, House of Representatives, 98th Congress, *Energy and Water Development Appropriations for 1985*, p. 3 (Washington, D.C.: U.S. Government Printing Office, 1984), p. 772. Hereinafter, TVA Hearings.

28. TVA is routinely referring to itself as a "regional development agency" in its press releases. See, for example, *The Atlanta Constitution*, 8 August 1984, p. 3.

The TVA is now an institution that any politician can endorse without fear of offending any organized group of voters. It provides substantial subsidies to various groups, the costs of which are spread among unknowing taxpayers. Given its lack of political enemies and its large resource base, the TVA has become a self-perpetuating fiefdom with an internal diffusion of authority, costs, and responsibility typical of well-established bureaucratic structures.

The three-member TVA board of directors seems mainly concerned with deciding among alternative new projects and keeping peace among internal divisions. While decision making within TVA is decentralized, a strong tendency, if not an explicit policy, exists of promoting from within. Turnover among TVA nontechnical employees is small, though engineers, technicians, and scientists have recently been discovering higher wages elsewhere. Managers tend to view TVA as a lifetime job, and seldom are any of the TVA directors appointed from outside. The board has, in fact, vigorously opposed a recent proposal to expand its number to include representatives from each state in its service area.

Power Marketing Associations

The federal Power Marketing Associations (PMAs) are a major component—with the REA, TVA, and the Army Corp of Engineers power-generation projects—of the federal electricity system.[29] Four of the five PMAs, Alaska, Southeastern, Southwestern, and Western, deal almost exclusively with maintaining and operating systems for the transmission, distribution, storage, and interconnection of electricity generated by Corp of Engineers hydroelectric projects. The activities of the fifth PMA, Bonneville, also concern power marketing. Bonneville, however, also a major power producer, is becoming the TVA of the Northwest through its programs to coordinate regional economic planning and development.

All PMAs are purportedly managed in accordance with currently popular political doctrines regarding the power industry. That means promoting hydroelectric power generation over other forms and, recently, coal-fired over nuclear, oil, and gas plants. In addition the PMAs coordinate their activities with federal agencies responsible for

---

29. The history of the PMAs is briefly reviewed in the Appendix to this chapter.

flood control, irrigation, international and Indian treaty commitments, recreational water use, and environmental objectives.[30]

PMAs were supposed to repay their investments within fifty years of start-up. In fact the oldest of these projects, Bonneville, was only 8 percent repaid after forty-eight years of operation. As Table 7–3 shows, the percent of investment repaid seems to fall rather than rise with project age. This result may reflect that an agency assumes increasing functions, powers, and financial responsibilities the longer it is in existence.

As economists would predict, the level of satisfaction or dissatisfaction with PMA policies is not a function of largess received compared to the full cost of service. It is, rather, a function of what is perceived as the normal and expected subsidy as established in previous periods. When there is danger of a decrease in some group's subsidy, the legislature is always responsive. For instance, in 1984, Congress provided approximately $5 billion to repair and expand Hoover Dam so that its customers will continue to enjoy below-market power bills.[31]

The Rural Electrification Administration

The Rural Electrification Administration (REA) was created by Presidential Order in 1935.[32] As conceived, it was a labor-relief program

Table 7–3.   Repayment Status of PMAs (through fiscal year 1983).

Year Founded	Power Association	Percent Repaid
1936	Bonneville	8
1944	Southwestern	5
1950	Southeastern	27
1967	Alaskan	12
1977	Western Area	36

SOURCE: PMA Hearings, p. 929.

30. FERC Hearings, pp. 1691–92.
31. *Wall Street Journal*, 2 August 1984, p. 5.
32. This historical sketch of the REA is drawn largely from the official summary history of the REA contained in Subcommittee on Appropriations, House of Representatives, 98th Congress, *Agriculture, Rural Development and Related Agencies, Appropriations for 1985*, p. 8 (Washington, D.C.: U.S. Government Printing Office, 1984), pp. 57–61 Hereinafter,

under the Department of Agriculture.[33] Originally funded at $50 million, the program was to employ unskilled laborers to construct power transmission lines to farm households. It soon became apparent that the skill level required for such work was higher than originally estimated, so later in 1935, the government removed the relief-work features of the program and reconstituted the REA as a loan-assistance program to promote the electrification of America's farms.

Despite the decline in the number of farm households, REA loans have increased substantially. In 1963 REA electrification loans totaled $5.02 billion. By 1983 the total had risen to $17.2 billion. Telephone loans in 1963 stood at $.99 billion, and by 1983 they had risen to $4.5 billion. Loans from the Rural Telephone Bank, established in 1971 to supplement direct REA telephone loans, now total about $2 billion. In addition REA loan guarantees on electrical and telephone service, authorized by a 1973 amendment to the REA Act, are $33.7 billion.

Interest paid by direct borrowers from the REA for electrical or telephone purposes has fluctuated from a weighted average of 2 percent, over the years 1945–1972, to 4.9 percent in 1983. The rate paid on new loans was 2 percent until 1973 and either 2 or 5 percent from 1973 to the present. Qualifications for borrowing at the 2 percent rate were tightened in 1981, reducing the proportion of loans granted at that level.

By comparison the annual interest rate paid on marketable Treasury securities with a life of ten years or more has exceeded the average rate REA borrowers have paid since 1951. In 1981 REA borrowers paid an average rate of 4.8 percent and a marginal rate of 2 or 5 percent. Treasury securities in 1981 paid 12.4 percent on average. Hence the interest cost to the federal government was 7.4 to 10.4 percent on every dollar lent to REA borrowers.

Loans arranged through REA's loan-guarantee programs from non-REA financial institutions bear higher rates, although interest costs are below private market rates because of the REA's financial status as a federal agency. In addition the REA provides a variety of no-

---

REA Hearings, and in the excellent, if somewhat dated, survey and history contained in Garwood and Tuttle, *Rural Electrification Administration*. More of the REA history is developed in the Appendix to this chapter.

33. Executive Order No. 7037 promulgated under the authority of the Emergency Relief Appropriations Act of 1935 (49 Stat. 115).

cost services to its borrowers—including management assistance and counseling in a wide range of areas and several conferences each year for the managers and directors of its utility-customers.

As might be expected, the REA is at times a vehicle for congressional special interests that have only the most tangential connection with its primary purposes. One small but amusing example is drawn from the REA House Appropriations Hearings. The current REA director was given a repeated tongue-lashing by the chairman of the appropriations subcommittee for his failure to translate REA bulletins into Arabic. The translations were purportedly needed for an international marketing campaign to sell pine logs as telephone poles. The rebuke was administered by Jamie Whitten of Mississippi, a leading state in telephone-pole production. Chairman Whitten justified his concern by reference to the unfavorable balance of trade the United States has and the urgency of the need to increase our competitive advantage against Scandinavia in the world telephone-pole market.

SOCIAL POLICY AND UTILITY REGULATION

The professed objectives of utility regulation traditionally include establishing fair and reasonable rates for service and assuring dependable and reliable service while providing regulated firms with a fair return for invested capital. The consensus was originally that utilities were inherently monopolistic. Theorists touted regulation as the way to protect consumers from the abuses of private monopoly while securing the cost savings that arise from economies of large-scale production.

As demonstrated in other contributions to this volume, recent economic research on the theory and record of utility regulation has arrived at conclusions that differ from the traditional view. According to updated theory, established firms in an industry may demand regulation as a way of keeping new competitors from entering the market and establishing and enforcing cartel arrangements that cut industry output and increase prices. In addition the traditional regulatory rate-setting policy—allowing a fair rate of return on invested capital—increases the proportion of a firm's expenditure devoted to plant, equipment, and managerial perquisites beyond the level of a competitive optimum, according to recent evidence. Regulated firms have less efficient structures than they would have otherwise because of protection from competition and increased managerial leeway in promoting their own interests rather than stockholder profits.[34]

While this view of the regulatory process is more realistic than the traditional model of agencies that act purely in the public interest, it is perhaps too narrowly focused. One shortcoming of the theory that regulated firms capture their regulators is that it postulates only one effective interest group: firms within the regulated industry or the suppliers. Consumers are merely an amorphous and uncoordinated group that purchases whatever output is provided. In fact regulators face pressures from groups outside the industry they regulate—for example, municipal officials seeking to expand their tax base and local business interests wanting to expand their markets. The rubric for the demands of these groups is "regional economic development." Yet their favored policies are simply to use political control to shift capital from one locale to another.

New organized interests under the label of environmental concerns also exemplify using regulatory controls to promote special interests. National legislation—enforced by the Environmental Protection Agency and supplemented by federally required state clean air and water standards and by various state and federal conservation acts—has forced utilities to spend vast sums modifying existing or planned facilities. Yet substantial evidence indicates that the underlying goals of these programs often are other than environmental. And even when they are environmental, they constitute a form of income redistribution via the regulatory process. The TVA and a California utility provide contrasting examples.

The TVA's record of responsiveness to environmental concerns was—until the recent downturn in electric demand—one of the worst in the electric production industry. The TVA's attitude toward environmentalism was characterized by encouragements to strip mining and an almost total disregard of standards on the smokestack emission of sulfuric acid. On the other hand the privately owned and publicly regulated California firm of Pacific Gas and Electric (PG&E) has been a model of environmental concern. It operates under the scrutiny of several of the most vigilant regulatory commissions in the United States, including the Bay Area and Monterey-Santa Cruz pollution control

34. Louis De Alessi, "The Economics of Property Rights: A Review of the Evidence," *Research in Law and Economics* 2 (1980): 1–47.

districts, the California Public Utility Commission, and the California Energy Resources Conservation and Development Commission. California is also home base for the Sierra Club and other groups active in lobbying for environmental controls.

Technically the TVA and PG&E have many similarities. Both originally produced power primarily by hydroelectric facilities, and in recent decades both have moved to greater reliance on fossil fuel and atomic generators. Both primarily produce and transmit electric power, selling output to a variety of smaller municipal or IOU distributing companies that service consumers. Why then the differences in concern about the environment?

Fundamental differences exist in the institutional settings of the two utilities, producing incentives that help to explain their divergent behavior. The TVA is an autonomous federal agency, independent of state or federal regulation in electricity pricing. Due to the support historically provided to the TVA for capital expenditures and its freedom in pricing and composition of service, TVA is largely free to maximize whatever its managers and directors believe to be in its best interests. PG&E, however, is subject to numerous regulations, including a fair-rate-of-return-on-capital-invested criterion for rate setting.

TVA's activities appear to be a response to the interests in its region, carefully tailored to keep its political support high. Since coal production is important to local interests, the TVA used coal as a fuel, national environmental objections to the contrary. Undoubtedly the citizens of the TVA's service area like clean air, but the income generated by the coal industry and its political clout dominate such concerns. Similarly the TVA has catered to local interests by continued expenditures in power generation and nonpower projects that increase land values and—according to the saviors of the snail darter—damage the natural environment. Now that the TVA has entered a period of stable electricity demand, it has developed a sudden concern for environmental issues and other matters of social welfare, as illustrated by the testimony of its officials before Congressional appropriations committees and its budget requests to these committees. By expressing concern for environmental causes, and devoting some budget to activities that are supported by various environmental special interest groups, the TVA is expanding its political constituency to strengthen its base of support for obtaining funding from Congress.

On the other hand PG&E operates in an area that relies upon hydroelectric or imported fuel to generate electricity, so few interests are accommodated by favoring local fuel producers. PG&E's lack of political incentive for selecting one production method over another has allowed groups favoring environmental quality—apparently made up of individuals with higher-than-average incomes—to press the utility to spend resources on measures that provide them with benefits they value. Due to flat electricity demand and regulatory controls, PG&E has lacked the ability to expand its production capacity and rate base by expanding nuclear facilities. As a substitute, the utility has spent substantial amounts on measures that please environmental interest groups, regulators, and, simultaneously, achieve the desired expansion of costs and attendant authorized profits.[35]

The lesson here is not that TVA or PG&E officials have different attitudes towards the environment, local employment and development, or any other such concerns. Rather, because they are in politicized industries, they respond to whatever concerns dominate their areas. Like other utilities, they serve as income redistributors regardless of the product they provide. They spend money on projects that might not exist if they functioned in a world of customer service and profit maximization unconstrained by political interests.

CONCLUSION

> While concerned laymen who observe people with shabby housing want to provide them with decent housing . . . economists instinctively want to provide them with more cash income. Then they can buy the housing and food if they want to, and, if they choose not to, the presumption is that they have a better use for the money.[36]
>
> James Tobin

The previous sections have traced various direct and indirect subsidies in the federal power system and in some utility pricing schemes. Economists have long decried such subsidies as poor substitutes for direct-income grants to promote the well-being of intended beneficiaries. A dollar's worth of "free electricity" is not worth as much as a dollar in hand to some consumers, especially low-income consumers. Electricity may be something we all want, but it does not

---

35. In one instance, PG&E was willing to write off a $10 million investment in a generating plant cooling system that was not satisfactory to the thermal pollution standards of the Bay Area Air Pollution Control District. (Roberts and Bluhm, *The Choices of Power*, p. 150.)

36. Quoted in Donald McCloskey's *The Applied Theory of Price* (New York: Macmillan, 1982) p. 102.

follow that, dollar for dollar, we prefer more electricity to more of the other things in life.

While this point is well established in economic theory—as well as appealing to common sense—political realities produce other results. First, in-kind payoffs to groups of voters or financial supporters are often more attractive to politicians than cash subsidies. Politicians must maximize the odds of being elected or reelected. In the case of electricity that often means advocating policies characterized as "economic or industrial development" or "providing for basic human needs." Once such subsidies are in place, beneficiaries will fight their removal or reduction. Also, only rarely is much pressure exerted to terminate subsidies: The benefits are usually concentrated, and understood, while the costs are dispersed and often not recognized.

Another point has to do with the nature of bureaucracies. The older a government program, the more likely it is to have developed an agenda that has diverged from its original purpose, one that provides a justification for maintaining or increasing the agency's staff and budget. The TVA, the REA, and Bonneville are all good examples of agencies that have expanded into areas thinly or not at all justified by their original mandates. The TVA has an administrative structure staffed mostly by lifetime employees; at the upper levels, these managers devote considerable energy to developing new programs to justify the continued expansion of an agency that met its original purpose years ago.

Federal intervention in the electric utility industry was justified in the 1930s as necessary to assure the expansion of service to all households. Despite the achievement of that goal, no one would predict that Congress will reduce federal intervention in the industry. Similarly, at the state and local levels, politicians have incentives to continue to use the industry as a means for providing benefits to certain interest groups. These benefits are paid for not only through the rate structure—a tax imposed on unsuspecting users—but also by the less efficient structure of an industry denied the chance to develop into a competitive market.

APPENDIX: THE DEVELOPMENT OF THE TVA, PMAs, AND THE REA

The Tennessee Valley Authority

The roots of the TVA are found in the Wilson Administration's decision to establish nitrate manufacturing plants on the Tennessee River at Muscle Shoals, Alabama, as a way of reducing United States dependence on German and Chilean supplies of nitrates. Nitrates are used in the production of gunpowder. Although the nitrate plants remained unfinished at the end of World War I, the government financed an associated hydroelectric plant and dam (Wilson Dam) to completion by 1925. Despite repeated attempts by various interests to have the Muscle Shoals project expanded, Congress did not increase the federal investment beyond the initial $100 million until the Great Depression. Then Congress enacted legislation in 1933 to extend the Muscle Shoals development to the entire Tennessee River Valley.[37] Subsequently the boundaries of what became the Tennessee Valley Authority, or TVA, expanded to include almost all of Tennessee, over one-half of Mississippi, about one-fourth of Kentucky and Alabama, and some counties in Georgia, Missouri, and North Carolina.

The TVA Act of 1933 was intended to promote development of hydroelectric facilities along the Tennessee River as a part of the make-work programs of the Roosevelt Administration. Despite F.D.R.'s often lavish rhetoric regarding planning in speeches advocating the TVA, his enthusiasm for the less-than-pragmatic parts of the program cooled soon after its adoption. A reading of the TVA Act of 1933 discloses that its language is indicative of a straightforward intent to provide low-cost power, flood control, and jobs. Only two brief and vague sections of the Act, §§22 and 23, make any direct reference to planning.

The first TVA Chairman, Arthur E. Morgan, attempted to broaden the scope of the TVA, but these were crushed, apparently with Roosevelt's blessing.[38] Eventually, however, the dynamics of bureaucratic growth accomplished what Morgan had sought, and the TVA became the region's monopoly wholesaler of power and evolved into the multifaceted planning and development agency it is today.

In its first burst of growth, the TVA constructed and acquired dams throughout the Tennessee and Cumberland valley regions. By 1959 the TVA had built twenty-one major dams and had obtained another eleven dams that had been investor owned, often by using techniques that in private settings would have been characterized as cutthroat competition.[39]

---

37. 48 Stat. 58 (1933). Codified as 16 U.S.C. §12A (1982).
38. Roberts and Bluhm, *The Choices of Power*, p. 67.
39. Curiously, TVA has recently sought congressional appropriations to repair twenty-one

The TVA expanded its original "power mission" in new directions during World War II by moving into the construction and operation of fossil-fuel (that is, coal-fired) generating stations, proportedly to supply the power needs of the Oak Ridge experimental laboratories and the neighboring aluminum refining operations. By 1962 75 percent of the power produced by the TVA was from coal-fired plants. Later attempts to expand the TVA's power production by building nuclear plants have been only modestly successful. Three nuclear plants are in operation, and plans exist to complete another four plants between 1985 and 1991. Four planned plants have been canceled, however, and another four plants have been "deferred" indefinitely.

The decline in the growth rate of new generator capacity is due to increasing expected costs of nuclear plant construction and operation and to lower than expected demand for TVA electricity. TVA administrators recently estimated a $2^{1}/_{2}$–3 percent growth in electricity demand for the next decade, with no additional generating plants needed until the end of that period. The TVA's 1983 annual report noted that electricity sales to industrial customers were at a twenty-year low; sales to residential customers and federal agencies had fallen substantially; and sales to municipal and cooperative distributors had increased only marginally.

The seriousness with which TVA views its surplus production capacity is illustrated by its refusal to modify a $1.23 billion power sales contract it has with the Department of Energy (DOE). Although the DOE subsequently determined that it has no use for the electricity, the TVA has refused either to rescind the contract or to allow the DOE to resell the power. Instead the TVA has allowed the 1,400 megawatt facility it constructed to generate the DOE power to remain idle, billing the DOE for electricity not, in fact, being generated.[40]

Until recently the TVA used these revenues to justify a program of continued intensive and extensive expansion of its power facilities. However, the 1959 TVA Revenue Act resulted in some increases in the relative cost of pursuing power generation programs compared to nonpower programs and limited the geographic boundaries of TVA,

---

of its thirty-two dams that failed to meet federal design safety standards; see TVA Hearings, pp. 876–78. We were unable to discover which of these twenty-one dams were among the twenty-one constructed by TVA.

40. "DOE, TVA, and the Sale of Power," *Public Utilities Fortnightly*, 16 February 1984, pp. 39, 48.

preventing further expansion into new service areas. The relatively flat demand for electricity in the last decade has reduced the ability to justify capacity increases within the TVA system. As might be expected, the TVA has turned increasingly to environmental concerns and a variety of regional development and assistance programs.

The TVA Act of 1933 was intended to promote electric power production through the construction of hydroelectric facilities and to be a Depression era jobs program for the Tennessee region. Buried in sections 22 and 23 of the 1933 act, however, was authorization to "foster an orderly and proper physical, economic and social development" of the TVA's area of operations, through cooperative development with the states in the areas of "surveys . . . plans . . . studies, experiments or demonstrations as may be necessary and suitable" to promote development. These sections of the act were complemented by a similarly phrased Presidential Executive Order (No. 6161) of 1933. From the mid-1930s through the early 1960s, the TVA focused most of its attention on expanding its power network and generating capacity. In its new operating environment, however, the incentives the TVA faces are leading it to seek a wider range of concerns. Its managers have been developing extensive, broadly defined programs in pursuing a vague goal of "promoting regional economic development." In the words of its current Chairman:

> Our monitoring and analysis of the region's economy has pinpointed five problem areas in the Valley: job creation, job skill deficits, resource waste and abuse, rural viability, and developing institutions for regional leadership and initiatives. To help solve these problems, TVA's economic development strategy for the next five years is to concentrate on eight primary thrusts:
>
> (a) Exemplary operation of our power system, reservoirs, and national fertilizer research activities.
>
> (b) Utilizing the region's forest resources for jobs and economic development while protecting their environmental and ecological integrity.
>
> (c) Utilizing the region's coal resources for jobs and energy by finding ways to efficiently and effectively minimize the environmental costs of using those resources.
>
> (d) Emphasizing the use of the region's university and scientific resources to further economic development.
>
> (e) Protecting the region's water resource advantage.
>
> (f) Utilizing the region's agricultural resources for jobs and economic development while protecting the quality of life and environmental amenities of rural areas.

(g) Helping to solve the region's industrial/hazardous waste problems.

(h) Encouraging improved education and training for the region's people.[41]

The Power Marketing Associations

The governing concept in PMA marketing is that of satisfying all "preference customers" before extending service to other customers or selling any excess power in the market. In some cases this mandate has meant excess power is dissipated rather than being sold to private firms. According to the Reclamation Projects Act of 1939, which—along with the Flood Control Act of 1944—governs federal power marketing: "Preference shall be given to municipalities and other public corporations and agencies; and also to cooperative and other non-profit organizations financed in whole or in part by loans made pursuant to the Rural Electrification Act of 1936 and any amendments thereof." The PMA system thus provides an additional subsidy to customers served by non-IOU utilities, and this is probably in part responsible for the lower rates its customers pay. Despite subsidized rates, several PMAs have recently experienced a flood of litigation, including cases attempting to block rate increases for certain types of service and claims of discriminatory treatment by certain preference customers. The 1985 Appropriation Hearings note forty-three outstanding cases filed against Bonneville, for example.[42]

The Rural Electrification Administration

The REA initially approached existing IOUs requesting their estimates on the cost of extending their service to targeted rural households. Despite the utilities' rapid compliance, the REA Commissioner—perhaps inspired by the TVA philosophy of subsidized power—had already concluded that IOU expansion was less desirable than creating a network of REA-financed rural cooperatives and municipally owned enterprises.[43]

By the Rural Electrification (Norris-Rayburn) Act of 1936, the REA became an independent agency.[44] The REA was funded at $50 million

---

41. TVA Hearings, p. 783.
42. FERC Hearings, pp. 1635–48.
43. Garwood and Tuttle, *The Rural Electrification Administration*, pp. 5–6.
44. Codified as 7 USC §901 (1980).

for its first year of operations and $40 million per annum thereafter. Funding of the REA was raised to $100 million per year three years later in 1939. The REA initially functioned as a secured lender for government-guaranteed loans. Loans made to preference borrowers, cooperatives, and municipalities financed the construction of generating plants and electric transmission lines and systems.

At the behest of rural political interests, and to stimulate demand for electrical and other services, the REA was also authorized to grant "loans for the purpose of financing the wiring of premises or persons in rural areas and the acquisition and installation of electrical and plumbing appliances and equipment."[45] These loans were channeled to farm beneficiaries either through their cooperative or municipal utility or through the local equipment supplier or installer. This expanded and reinforced the base of political support for the REA. The REA originally charged borrowers a rate on loans equal to the average rate of interest payable by the United States on its obligations having a maturity of ten years or more, the so-called cost of borrowing to the Treasury. Note terms were initially twenty-five years.

Fifty percent of REA loans were to be appropriated among the states according to the national proportion of farms not receiving electricity within each state. This was based on the original REA emphasis, providing electrical services to farm families. Loans were restricted to providing service to rural areas.[46] By 1944, the power loan program had increased the proportion of farms receiving electrical services from 11.6 percent to 42.2 percent.

REA support also increased as the number of program beneficiaries grew. By the Agricultural Organic (Pace) Act of 1944, the interest charged both previous and new REA borrowers on electric and household improvement loans was reduced to 2 percent, creating a substantial subsidy to those borrowers. The act also extended the loan repayment period to thirty-five years, and new borrowers were granted a five-year interest-free grace period before beginning repayment. The REA Act was further amended in 1944 to grant priority assistance to cooperatives in discharging or refinancing their obligations to the TVA.[47]

---

45. 7 USCA §905 (1980).

46. A rural area is defined as any area outside of the political boundaries of a city, village, or borough with a population in excess of 1,500 inhabitants; 7 USCA §924(b) (1980).

47. 7 USCA §904, Historical Notes (1980).

Four years later the REA was instructed to provide the same assistance to municipally owned utilities in refinancing their TVA debt.

By 1949 78.2 percent of all farms had electrical service, and the REA faced diminution or extinction due to succeeding in its mission. Not only were the remaining unserved farms in low-density, high-cost service areas, they were also of marginal political significance. Congressional response to the prospect of a federal agency either losing its reason for existence or devoting its efforts to a trivial number of beneficiaries was predictable. Congress broadened the REA's scope of activities to new areas: It was authorized to finance the "improvement and expansion of existing [rural] telephone facilities and the construction and operation of such additional facilities as are required to assure the availability of adequate telephone service to the widest practical number of rural users of such service."[48] Loans for these purposes were to be granted on a preference basis to cooperatives.

The telephone program, which initially gave the REA a new base of support and justified its continued existence, suffered the same success as the electrification program. By 1983 the proportion of U.S. farms receiving electrical service was 98.8 percent. Since the remaining farms without service represent less than one-third of the number of Amish and Mennonite households in the United States, it may be that the lack of service to 1.2 percent of total farm households is due to a lack of interest.

The same story characterizes REA financing of rural telephone service. In 1949 36 percent of all farms had telephone service; by 1983 96 percent had obtained service.[49] The main improvement in farm telephone service from 1972–1982 was in the proportion of customers receiving single-party service. In 1972 49.6 percent of U.S. farms had multiparty lines. By 1982 only 15.8 percent of farm households had multiparty lines. The director of the REA noted in testimony before a House Appropriations Subcommittee in 1984 that the Bureau of the Census had ceased compiling statistics on rural households involuntarily without telephone service "more than 20 years ago, because the number of persons . . . was statistically insignificant."[50]

The population shift from farms to cities and the subsequent reapportionment of Congress threatened to reduce the REA's base of

48. 7 USCA §921 (1980).
49. REA Hearings, p. 63.
50. REA Hearings, p. 15.

political support. That has not happened because Congress has continued to expand the scope of the REA's activities. Partly in response to the increasing saturation of the rural telephone market, Congress acted in 1962 to broaden the definition of telephone service to "any communication service for the transmission of voice, sounds, signals, pictures, writings, or signs of all kinds through the use of electricity" excluding only telegram and community antenna services.[51] In 1972 the restriction against REA loan support to community antennas was removed as part of congressional approval of a Rural Community Development Fund within the REA.[52]

The percentage of farm households served by the REA has not changed for two decades. The number of ultimate customers served by REA utilities has doubled, however, from 5 million in 1962 to 10 million in 1982.[53] This increase took place at the same time that the farm population has dropped substantially and the explanation is that the REA is serving more nonrural areas, despite prohibitions against such service in its enabling legislation. By 1979 there were 125 REA borrower-utilities serving areas that were more than half urban.[54] The most densely populated REA service area has a population over seven times as dense as the standard for a rural area.[55]

The urbanization of REA service has been a point of contention between the House and the Senate. A majority in the House wants to preserve and promote REA activities in the more urban areas, while the Senate has been less sympathetic to such efforts. Nevertheless Congress continues to support the REA, as evidenced by the $200 million voted to support the REA revolving loan fund in 1984, the amount of the deficit in that program.[56]

51. 7 USCA §924 (1980).
52. REA Hearings, p. 117.
53. REA Hearings, p. 67.
54. REA Hearings, pp. 20 ff.
55. REA Hearings, p. 21.
56. REA Hearings, p. 6; SB 1400.

SELECTED BIBLIOGRAPHY
PART II

Abbey, David. "Energy Production and Water Resources in the Colorado River Basin." *Natural Resources Journal* 19 (1979): 280.

Ackerman, Bruce A., and William T. Hassler. "Beyond the New Deal: Coal and the Clean Air Act." *Yale Law Journal* 89 (1980): 1466–1571.

Adelman, Morris A. *The World Petroleum Market.* Baltimore: Johns Hopkins University Press, 1972.

———. "Coping With Insecurity." *Energy Journal* 3 (April 1982): 1–18.

American Enterprise Institute for Public Policy Research. *The Clean Air Act: Proposals for Revisions.* Washington, D.C.: American Enterprise Institute, 1981.

———. *Reauthorization of the Clean Water Act.* Washington, D.C.: American Enterprise Institute, 1983.

Anderson, Frederick R.; Allen V. Kneese; D. D. Reed; S. Taylor; and R. B. Stevenson. *Environmental Improvement Through Economic Incentives.* Baltimore: Johns Hopkins University Press, 1977.

Badger, Daniel B., Jr. "New Source Standard for Power Plants I: Consider the Costs." *Harvard Environmental Law Review* 3 (1979): 48.

Baron, David P., and Raymond R. DeBondt. "Fuel Adjustment Mechanisms and Economic Efficiency." *Journal of Industrial Economics* 27 (March 1979): 243–61.

Baumol, William J. "Productivity Incentive Clauses and Rate Adjustment for Inflation." *Public Utilities Fortnightly* (22 July 1982): 11–18.

279

Bhagwati, Jagdish N., and T. N. Srinivasan. "Optimal Trade Policy and Compensation Under Endogenous Uncertainty." *Journal of International Economics* 6 (November 1976): 317–36.

Bickerdike, C. F. "The Theory of Incipient Taxes." *Economic Journal* 16 (December 1906): 529–35.

Bohi, Douglas R., and Milton Russell. *Limiting Oil Imports: An Economic History and Analysis*. Baltimore: Johns Hopkins University Press, 1978.

Bohi, Douglas R., and W. David Montgomery. *Oil Prices, Energy Security, and Import Policy*. Baltimore: Johns Hopkins University Press, 1982.

Bonine, John E., and Thomas D. McGarity. *The Law of Environmental Protection*. St. Paul, Minn.: West Publishing Co., 1984.

Breyer, Stephen. "Analyzing Regulatory Failure: Mismatches, Less Restrictive Alternatives, and Reform." *Harvard Law Review* 92 (1979): 552.

Burgess, Giles, and Morton Paglin. "Lifeline Electricity Rates as an Income Transfer Device." *Land Economics* 57 (1981): 41–47.

Cabinet Task Force on Oil Import Control. *The Oil Import Question: A Report on the Relationship of Oil Imports to the National Security*. Washington, D.C.: Government Printing Office, 1970.

Copulos, Milton R. "H.R. 3966: Reconsidering Energy Audits." Washington, D.C.: Heritage Foundation. Issue Bulletin, 1984. (Mimeo.)

Cox, James C., and Arthur W. Wright. "A Tariff Policy for Independence from Oil Embargoes." *National Tax Journal* 28 (March 1975): 29–42.

Crew, Michael A., ed. *Regulatory Reform and Public Utilities*. Lexington, Mass.: Lexington Books, 1982.

Crompton, Roger C., and Richard K. Berg. "On Leading a Horse to Water: NEPA and the Federal Bureaucracy." *Michigan Law Review* 71 (1973): 511.

Daly, George. "Recall the Attempts at a Mini-Industrial Policy." *Wall Street Journal*, 16 March 1984.

Danielson, Albert L. *The Evolution of OPEC*. New York: Harcourt Brace Jovanovich, 1982.

Deese, David A., and Joseph S. Nye, eds. *Energy and Security*. Cambridge, Mass.: Ballinger Publishing Co., 1981.

Dimopoulos, Dionissis. "Pricing Schemes for Regulated Enterprises and Their Welfare Implication in the Case of Electricity." *Bell Journal of Economics* 12 (1981): 185–200.

Edgeworth, Francis Y. "Mr. Bickerdike's Theory of Incipient Taxes and Customs Duties." In *Papers Relating to Political Economy*. Vol. 1. London: Macmillan, 1925.

Environmental Policy Institute. *Centralized Power*. Washington, D.C.: Environmental Policy Institute, 1979.

Environmental Protection Agency (EPA). *The Macroeconomic Impact of Federal Pollution Control Programs: 1981 Assessment*, EPA-230. Washington, D.C.: Government Printing Office, 1975.

Erickson, Edward W., and Leonard Waverman. *The Energy Question: An International Failure of Policy.* 2 vols. Toronto: University of Toronto Press, 1974.

Fanara, Philip, Jr.; James E. Suelflow; and Roman A. Draba. "Energy and Competition: The Saga of Electric Power." *Antitrust Bulletin* 25 (Spring 1980): 125–42.

Fenn, Scott A. *America's Electric Utilities.* Washington, D.C.: Investor Responsibility Research Center, 1983.

Garwood, John D., and William C. Tuthill. *The Rural Electrification Administration.* Washington, D.C.: American Enterprise Institute, 1963.

Gollop, Frank H., and Stephen H. Karlson. "The Impact of the Fuel Adjustment Mechanisms on Economic Efficiency." *Review of Economics and Statistics* 60 (November 1978): 574–84.

Gordon, Richard L. *An Economic Analysis of World Energy Problems.* Cambridge: MIT Press, 1981.

———. *Reforming the Regulation of Electric Utillities: Priorities for the 1980s.* Lexington, Mass.: Lexington Books, 1982.

Grennes, Thomas, and Herbert S. Winokur, Jr. "Oil and the U.S. Balance of Payments." In E. Erickson and L. Waverman, eds., *The Energy Question: An International Failure of Policy.* Vol. 1. Toronto: University of Toronto Press, 1974.

Hall, Robert E., and Robert S. Pindyck. "The Conflicting Goals of National Energy Policy." *Public Interest* 47 (Spring 1977): 3–15.

Hamilton, Michael S. "Power Plant Siting and the Environment." *Oklahoma Law Review* 26 (1973): 193–238.

Hargrove, Erwin C., and Paul K. Conkin, eds. *TVA: Fifty Years of Grass-Roots Bureaucracy.* Urbana: University of Illinois Press, 1983.

Haskell, Elizabeth H. *The Politics of Clean Air: EPA Standards for Coal-Burning Power Plants.* New York: Praeger Publishers, 1982.

Jevons, William Stanley. *The Coal Question: An Inquiry Concerning the Progress of the Nation and the Probable Exhaustion of Our Coal Mines.* 1906. Reprint. New York: A. M. Kelley, 1965.

Johnson, D. Gale. "Increased Stability of Grain Supplies in Developing Countries: Optimal Carryovers and Insurance." In J. Bhagwati, ed., *The New International Economic Order: The North-South Debate.* Cambridge: MIT Press, 1977.

Joskow, Paul L. "Approving Nuclear Reactors: Cost-Benefit Analysis or Administrative Charade?" *Bell Journal of Economics and Management Science* 5 (1974): 327–33.

Joskow, Paul L., and Paul W. MacAvoy. "Regulation and the Financial Condition of the Electric Power Companies in the 1970s." *American Economic Review* 65 (May 1975): 295–301.

Joskow, Paul L., and Richard Schmalensee. *Markets for Power: An Analysis of Electric Utility Deregulation.* Cambridge: MIT Press, 1983.

Kalt, Joseph P. *The Economics and Politics of Oil Price Regulation*. Cambridge: MIT Press, 1981.

Kline, David M., and John P. Weyant. "Comment on International Energy Agency's World." *Energy Journal* 4 (October 1983): 91–94.

Kneese, Allen V., and Charles V. Schultze. *Pollution, Prices and Public Policy*. Washington, D.C.: Brookings Institution, 1975.

MacAvoy, Paul. *Crude Oil Prices: As Determined by OPEC and Market Fundamentals*. Cambridge, Mass.: Ballinger Publishing Co., 1982.

Mayer, Wolfgang. "The National Defense Tariff Argument Reconsidered." *Journal of International Economics* 7 (November 1977): 363–77.

Mitchell, Bridger M.; Willard G. Manning, Jr.; and Jan Paul Acton. *Peak Load Pricing*. Cambridge, Mass.: Ballinger Publishing Co., for Rand Corporation, 1978.

Murphy, Arthur W. "The National Environmental Policy Act and the Licensing Process: Environmentalist Magna Carta or Agency Coup de Grace." *Columbia Law Review* 72 (1972): 963.

Murphy, Arthur W., and D. Bruce La Pierre. "Nuclear 'Moratorium' Legislation in the States and the Supremacy Clause: A Case of Express Preemption." *Columbia Law Review* 76 (1976): 392–456.

Murphy, Frederick, and Allen L. Soyster. *Economic Behavior of Electric Utilities*. Englewood Cliffs, N.J.: Prentice-Hall, 1983.

"New Source Performance Standards for Coal-Fired Electric Power Plants." *Ecology Law Quarterly* 8 (1980): 748.

Nordhaus, William. "The Energy Crisis and Macroeconomic Policy." *Energy Journal* 1 (January 1980): 11–20.

Plummer, James L. "Methods for Measuring the Oil Import Reduction Premium and the Oil Stockpile Premium." *Energy Journal* 2 (1981): 1–18.

———. "Policy Implications of Energy Vulnerability." *Energy Journal* 2 (April 1981): 25–36.

———, ed. *Energy Vulnerability*. Cambridge, Mass.: Ballinger Publishing Co., 1982.

Quarles, John R., Jr. *Federal Regulation of New Industrial Plants*. Washington, D.C.: John R. Quarles, Jr., 1979.

Ray, Edward J. "The Determinants of Tariff and Non-Tariff Trade Restrictions in the United States." *Journal of Political Economy* 89 (February 1981): 105–21.

Roberts, Marc J., and Jeremy S. Bluhm. *The Choices of Power*. Cambridge: Harvard University Press, 1981.

Rodgers, William H., Jr. *Environmental Law*. St. Paul, Minn.: West Publishing Co., 1977.

Rowen, Henry S., and John P. Weyant. "Reducing the Economic Impacts of Oil Supply in the United States." *Energy Journal* 3 (January 1982): 1–34.

Sargent, D. Alec. "The Role in the International Thermal Coal Market." *Energy Journal* 4 (January 1983): 79–98.

Scott, Frank A., Jr. "Fuel Adjustment Clauses and Profit Risk." In M. Crew, ed., *Issues in Public Utility Pricing and Regulation*. Lexington, Mass.: D. C. Heath, 1980.

———. "Estimating Recipient Benefits and Waste From Lifeline Electricity Rates." *Land Economics* 57 (1981): 536–43.

Smith, Turner T., Jr. "Electricity and the Environment—The Generating Plant Siting Problem." *The Business Lawyer* 26 (1970): 169–97.

Stelzer, Irwin M. "Electric Utilities: Next Stop for Deregulation?" *Regulation* 6 (July/August 1982): 29–35.

Steward, Richard B., and James K. Krier. *Environmental Law and Policy*. 2d ed. Charlottesville, Va.: Bobbs-Merrill Company, 1978.

Stobaugh, Robert, and Daniel Yergin, eds. *Energy Future: Report of the Energy Project at the Harvard Business School*. New York: Random House, 1979.

Subcommittee on Appropriations, House of Representatives, 98th Congress. *Agriculture, Rural Development and Related Agencies, Appropriations for 1985*, part 8. Washington, D.C.: Government Printing Office, 1984.

———. *Energy and Water Development Appropriations for 1985*, parts 3, 4, and 5. Washington, D.C.: Government Printing Office, 1984.

Taylor, Dean. "Official Intervention in the Foreign Exchange Market, or Bet Against the Central Bank." *Journal of Political Economy* 90 (April 1982): 356–68.

Tolley, George S., and John D. Wilman. "The Foreign Dependence Question." *Journal of Political Economy* 85 (April 1977): 323–47.

U.S. Department of Energy. *Monthly Energy Review*. Washington, D.C.: Government Printing Office, various issues.

Verleger, Philip K. "The U.S. Petroleum Crisis of 1979." *Brookings Papers on Economic Activity*, no. 2 (1979): 463–70.

Violette, Daniel, and Michael D. Yokell. "Fuel Cost Adjustment Clause Incentives: An Analysis With References to California." *Public Utilities Fortnightly* 109 (10 June 1982): 33–39.

Ward, Dennis P. "The Rules of the Game: Regulations and the Power Plant Design Process." *Public Utilities Fortnightly* 107 (26 March 1981): 28–29.

Weyant, John P. "The Energy Crisis Is Over Again." *Challenge* 26 (September/October 1983): 12–17.

Willrich, Mason. "The Energy-Environment Conflict: Siting Electric Power Facilities." *Virginia Law Review* 58 (1972): 257–336.

Winter, John V., and David A. Conner. *Power Plant Siting*. New York: Van Nostrand, 1978.

THE BEHAVIOR OF UTILITY COMMISSIONS

PART III: THE BEHAVIOR OF UTILITY COMMISSIONS

John C. Moorhouse

Part III focuses on an explanation of state utility commission behavior and an evaluation of their performance. Chapter 8 places the evolution of utility regulation in historical perspective. Then it goes on to analyze commission behavior in a demand for and supply of regulation framework. Special-interest groups are the demanders and state governments are the suppliers. In order to evaluate the impact of electric utility regulation, Jarrell goes back to a period, 1912–1920, when not all states regulated electric utilities. Thus he can compare the performance of utilities under state regulation with those that were not. The evidence suggests that commissions were quite sensitive to pressures from the utility companies. Consumer prices and utility profits were higher in states with regulation. Though the pattern of favoritism is quite different today, Jarrell's study is significant precisely because it documents the importance of political pressure in shaping utility regulation.

If Chapter 8 explains the demand for electric utility regulation, Chapter 9 goes further as it seeks to explain the form and content of current regulation. In essence Wenders asks the question: If present regulation is not working well, why do we have the kind of regulation we do? He finds the answer in the politics of the regulatory process. The actors in the story are the regulators, the electric utility companies, and various classes of consumers. Wenders rejects the simple capture theory of regulation whereby the regulated firms eventually influence the content and effects of regulation in a way favorable to themselves. No evidence shows electric utilities as the major beneficiaries of current regulation; the evidence is quite to the contrary in fact. Moreover, Wenders finds no reason or evidence to support the thesis that in recent years large industrial consumers have gained by influencing the rate structure. A careful analysis of the underlying political and economic factors involved in the regulatory process and a review of the data suggests to Wenders that politically sensitive regulators are most responsive to the block of residential consumers. This bias became particularly acute during the period of high inflation in the late 1970s. Wenders concludes by offering a case study in the regulatory failure surrounding the Washington Public Power Supply System fiasco.

In Chapter 10 Navarro provides an up-to-date evaluation of state utility commissions. Regulatory commissions are ranked according to six criteria: (1) allowed rate of return, (2) regulatory lag, (3) if construction-in-progress is counted in the rate base, (4) whether historical or future test year cost data are used, (5) tax treatment of depreciation, and (6) whether an AFA clause is in effect. He sees the regulatory climate as influencing the cost of capital. Navarro finds evidence that many commissions have been engaging in rate suppression in recent years. This tilt toward current consumers is not only reflected in lower ratings for utility bonds and stock prices below book value, but it also reduces capital investment and threatens our having adequate, reliable, and affordable electric power in the future.

Chapter 11 moves beyond the distorting effects of political pressure on the regulatory process to examine a more fundamental issue: the quality of information available to regulators and utility managers. Pasour shows how traditional regulation destroys meaningful information about relative values. Since, for example, electricity prices are set politically, utility managers have no firm market information about user class demand conditions with which to base future investment plans. Moreover asset valuation has no meaning in a regime where rates of return on the rate base, however defined, are guaranteed. Regulation eliminates the entrepreneurial function and stifles the discovery process. In short, though regulators may know in the abstract how to achieve static competitive conditions in the electric power industry, they possess neither the information nor the incentive to employ that information, if available, to mimic the competitive market.

Pasour argues that the "real problem" solved by the market process is not some constrainted maximization problem based on marginal revenue–marginal cost equalities, but the problem of coordinating information about relative (subjective) values. Indeed regulation precludes the generation of such information. Pasour concludes that efforts to reform or fine tune regulation are doomed to failure and that policymakers should rely on interproduct competition and free entry for superior long-run, dynamic performance.

8

THE DEMAND FOR ELECTRIC UTILITY REGULATION

Gregg A. Jarrell

THE EVOLUTION OF UTILITY REGULATION

The electric utility industry has been regulated since its founding in 1879. Electric utilities were incorporated under general state law, like all corporations. But in addition electric utilities required special franchises allowing them to use public streets for retail distribution.[1] The use of public streets is controlled by state legislation, according to American law. But by 1880 most states had constitutional provisions or laws forbidding the state from granting special franchises without the consent of the affected municipality.[2] In practice most municipalities exercised considerable control over special franchises to public utilities.[3]

The era of municipal regulation via special franchises spans 1880 to 1907, which is when powerful state commissions were first established by New York and Wisconsin. Although practice varied across

---

1. Delos F. Wilcox, *Municipal Franchises*. 2 vols. (Chicago: University of Chicago Press, 1910), p. 10.

2. Martin G. Glaeser, *Outlines of Public Utility Economics* (New York: Macmillan Company, 1931), p. 202.

3. Wilcox, *Municipal Franchises*, pp. 16–19. The state routinely granted franchises to public utilities for incorporation, while cities granted special franchises regulating the use of city streets.

cities, the consensus at the time was that municipal regulators fostered very competitive conditions with their profligate franchise granting.[4] Burton Behling wrote that the era of municipal regulation was:

> one of full and free competition. The issuance of franchises was usually the prerogative of the municipal governments, and the latter were generally of the opinion that their only protection lay in granting competing franchises . . . The common policy was to grant franchises to all who applied.[5]

Most major municipalities issued many blatantly overlapping franchises. Chicago granted forty-five franchises for electricity between 1882 and 1905. Only one was exclusive, covering a small area. Sixteen were duplicative in that they granted rights to a territory already served by another electric utility. Three franchises covered the entire city.[6]

Despite the municipal authorities' early policy of granting duplicative franchises, electric utilities became increasingly consolidated. By 1905 the merged entity of Chicago Edison and Commonwealth Electric constituted a Chicago monopoly in the electric lighting and power business. Wilcox wrote that in 1887 a single resolution granted competitive franchises to six different electric companies in New York City.[7] Nevertheless by 1907 the electric lighting business in old New York was entirely dominated by the Consolidated Gas Company, and the major gas and electric companies in Greater New York were owned by Standard Oil interests.[8]

Some municipalities explicitly sanctioned these consolidations by municipal ordinance or by offering valuable new franchises to replace previously issued, overlapping ones.[9] Examples of municipal antagonism toward consolidations, however, are easy to find.[10] In some cases the municipal authorities granted (or threatened to grant) com-

---

4. Burton Behling, *Competition and Monopoly in Public Utility Industries* (Urbana, Ill.: University of Illinois Press, 1938), pp. 18–22.

5. Behling, *Competition and Monopoly*, p. 23.

6. National Civic Federation, *Municipal and Private Operation of Public Utilities*, 3 vols. (New York: National Civic Federation, 1907), p. 719.

7. Wilcox, *Municipal Franchises*, p. 147.

8. Ibid., pp. 140, 209–10.

9. Ibid., pp. 157, 186.

10. Ibid., pp. 184–85; National Civic Federation, *Municipal and Private Operations*, pp. 676–77.

peting franchises if existing utilities merged or otherwise proved insubordinate to the authorities.

Therefore the era of competitive municipal franchises offers many examples of heavy-handed regulation. Although technical restrictions were absent from many special franchises—or shoddy records and confusingly overlapping franchises rendered existing provisions useless—the municipalities' control of entry apparently constituted considerable power to regulate public utilities.

The historical record contains examples where towns used municipal regulation primarily to benefit producers as well as to protect consumers from exploitation by entrenched utilities. Indeed some municipalities followed both policies, but at different periods in their histories.[11] Widespread criticism of municipal regulation blamed the system for both types of excess.

Experts generally agreed that the competition fostered by early municipal regulation was bad policy.[12] The policy was futile since competition gave way to consolidation anyway, it was argued. Furthermore the short-term competition from duplicative franchises was chaotic and destructive.

> Competition which was relied upon to insure for the public reasonable rates and satisfactory service proved to be elusive and non-enduring . . . It continually was disappearing as a result of bankruptcies, consolidations, and formal or informal agreements, leaving in its wake torn-up streets, 'dead' wires and useless poles and pipes, enormous overcapitalization, and paralyzed service.[13]

Some also criticized municipal regulation for fostering too little competition on occasion. New York City's experience with corrupt municipal regulation that benefited monopolistic electric utilities was the subject of a vigorous investigation by Charles Hughes. His campaign resulted in the passage of a state commission law in the face of vigorous opposition by hostile utilities and despite a state legislature "controlled as it had been for decades by the utility interests."[14]

In sum detractors of municipal regulation charged that it was rarely done well. Local regulators caused destructive competition by granting duplicative franchises, or they were captured by consolidating util-

---

11. Wilcox, *Municipal Franchises*, pp. 152–61.
12. Behling, *Competition and Monopoly*, p. 54.
13. Ibid., p. 20.
14. William E. Mosher and Finla G. Crawford, *Public Utility Regulation* 24 (1933):25.

ity interests in the corrupt environment of local politics. Municipal regulation's failure was not consistently manifested in proutility or proconsumer regulatory policies, according to these critics. Local regulators simply were not up to the task. Their peculiar character flaws and underfinanced, ill-conceived regulatory machinery resulted in merely "inappropriate" regulation. The competition duplicative franchises induced was wasteful and counterproductive. The consolidation some municipalities sanctioned brought monopoly prices. This was the conventional criticism:

> Local regulation was rarely done well. It often became entangled in the confusion of local politics; the regulatory machinery was poorly adapted to the rapidly changing technical conditions; such matters as accounting and financial regulation commonly were neglected; and, worst of all, untrained men struggled to fix rates and service standards—or were bribed.[15]

State commission regulation offered a solution by remedying a major underlying flaw of municipal regulation—the regulators. Competent, central administrative authority would replace unsystematic, misguided local regulation. State regulators would be at a distance from the urban political jungles; they would be highly paid, well-educated men with exceptional "social consciences" that put them above petty politics. Scientific valuations and fair rate-of-return rules would replace sordid "regulation-for-pay" principles that held sway in local government.

This was the message the proponents of state electric utility regulation broadcast. The argument rested heavily on claims that local regulation had failed to serve the public interest. Supporters further argued that enlightened state commissions would abandon attempts to discipline utilities with the threat of competition. Instead state regulators would sanction wholesale consolidation and encourage local monopolization to provide for maximum efficiency of production. In addition they would effectively regulate prices to avoid price gouging, relying instead on modern accounting principles of valuation. The triumph of the economic theory that natural monopolies are immune from the discipline of free entry lent scientific support to the cry for state commissions.

In the decade following 1907—the year New York and Wisconsin enacted state commission laws—a wave of states passed similar laws

---

15. Emery Troxel, *Economics of Public Utilities* (New York: Rinehart & Company, 1947), p. 49.

embracing the policy of regulation by state commissions. Whereas before 1907 only Massachusetts had a (rather weak) state commission to regulate electric utilities, between 1907 and 1914 twenty-seven states enacted public utility laws. Most modeled their laws after the New York and Wisconsin versions. The remaining states eventually passed state commission laws at a much slower rate compared with the wave of legislation between 1907 and 1914.

The Wisconsin statute, a landmark of American law, served as a model for much legislation after 1907. The Wisconsin law (1) converted all existing utility franchises to "indeterminate franchises"; (2) required a certificate of convenience and necessity for new public utilities; (3) authorized the state commission to establish service standards, to fix rates in accordance with accepted valuation principles, and to investigate rates upon complaint and on its own initiative; and (4) empowered the commission to control the capitalization and issuance of securities by public utilities.[16]

The indeterminate (or terminable) franchise sets no limit on the life of the utility's franchise but provides that municipalities can terminate the utility's franchise by purchasing its plant and equipment at a price set by the state commission.[17] Thus an indeterminate franchise is perpetual unless terminated by municipal takeover, and the state commission controls the terms of the takeover.

New utilities require certificates of convenience and necessity, whether they are owned by investors or municipalities; the same holds for existing utilities wishing to expand operations. This administrative device gives the state commission tight control over entry into the state electric utility industry.

Finally the Wisconsin law gives the state commission authority to establish the prices of electricity sold to all ultimate consumers and to other utilities for resale. Local ordinances, municipal commissions, and franchise provisions that previously set electricity prices were set aside by the state commission law, except in the few home-rule states.

There were some important transitional difficulties.[18] Nonetheless

16. Truman C. Bigham, and Eliot Jones, *Principles of Public Utilities* (New York: Macmillan Company, 1937), pp. 184–88.

17. Blythe E. Stason, "The Indeterminate Permit for Public Utilities," *Michigan Law Review* 25 (1927):34.

18. The presence of rate contracts between utilities and municipalities caused jurisdictional difficulties upon enactment of state commission laws. For more on this issue, see Victor Abramson and Leverett S. Lyon, *Government and Economic Life.* (Washington, D.C.: Brookings Institution, 1940), p. 640.

legislation establishing a state commission effectively shifted regulatory powers over prices, entry, and service in the electric utility industry from the numerous municipal governments to a single state commission.

The Public-Interest Theory

The public-interest theory of regulation posits that the state regulates to maximize social welfare. Thus the government intervenes, it is said, where the market fails in some important respect. The electric utility industry possesses the characteristics of a natural monopoly. This classic case of market failure arises when production is subject to continuous economies of scale, or decreasing average cost of production.[19] If average cost declines over the entire extent of market demand, then a single firm can always produce the market output more efficiently than can multiple firms. Therefore the theory predicts that cutthroat competition or consolidations will eventually result in a natural monopoly in this marketplace. But this result is not optimal since theorists posit that the sole surviving producer will exploit its monopoly status by charging supracompetitive prices and restricting output.[20]

It is almost universally concluded that the private market will fail to produce desirable results when such conditions of natural monopoly exist. The usual normative prescription is for the government to bar unnecessary entry and establish regional monopolies (to minimize production costs), set price equal to marginal cost at the socially optimal rate of output, and subsidize producers' losses from the treasury.[21] This solution avoids wasteful competition and duplication by establishing state-sanctioned monopolies; yet it prevents monopolistic exploitation by regulating prices.[22] In this way regulation would serve

---

19. Arthur C. Pigou, *Wealth and Welfare* (London: Macmillan & Co., 1912), p. 100.

20. For a cogent discussion, see Armen A. Alchian and William R. Allen, *University Economics* (Belmont, Calif.: Wadsworth Publishing Co., 1964), p. 412.

21. Glaeser, *Outlines of Public Utility Economics,* pp. 634–36.

22. In practice, the rule of rate-making as applied to public utilities was announced by the United States Supreme Court in the leading case of *Smyth* v. *Ames,* 169 U.S. 466, 527 (1898). This rule stated that "reasonable rates" must yield a "fair return" on the "fair value" of the property used by the utility. The implementation of this rule by state commissions is generally not equivalent to the theoretical solution that calls for a price equal to marginal cost. The degree of divergence between rate-making in practice and the theoretical ideal is a subject of much contention in the economics literature.

society as a superior substitute for private enterprise in naturally monopolistic industries.

This theory of natural monopoly rose to prominence simultaneously with the movement to establish state commission regulation over public utilities. Electric utilities were subject to extensive economics of scale in production, and rapidly evolving technological advances heightened the advantage of large-scale electricity generation. Although the theory of natural monopoly did not indicate whether municipal or state regulation would be best, proponents of state regulation argued that ample experience with municipal regulation had proved inadequate. The inexorable consolidation by electric utilities validated the theory of natural monopoly, and the local regulators' reliance on competition and duplicative franchises showed their ignorance of the theory's normative prescription. Proponents of state regulation argued that a new system of public utility regulation could be implemented, with state commissions being guided by the welfare theoretic solution to the natural monopoly problem. The practical problems state commissions faced, such as measuring costs and demand, could be alleviated by access to reliable information that the increasingly scientific accounting of the industry's operations would produce.

The central implication of the public-interest theory in effect is that state regulation would reduce prices and profits and increase output as natural monopolies became subject to the more effective control of state commissions. Furthermore the public-interest theory implies that the demand for state commissions was highest where municipal regulation was least effective. Therefore state commissions should have first been established in states containing the most monopolistic producers, as evidenced by relatively high prices (given costs) and profits.

The theory of natural monopoly has recently been subjected to critical reappraisal.[23] Harold Demsetz challenges the theory's basic conclusion that the natural monopolist will be able to set a monopoly price. He agrees that sufficiently extensive economies of scale will result in one producer in equilibrium, but if no legal barriers to entry exist, and there are only trivial costs of forming contracts with pro-

---

23. Harold Demsetz, "Why Regulate Utilities?" *Journal of Law and Economics* 11, no. 55 (1968):52–63.

spective customers, then competition from "potential" rivals (or bidders) will force the single successful producer to charge a competitive price. He argues that economies of scale in production determine the number of ultimate producers, but they do not determine, and need not be related to, the number of rival bidders or potential competitors. Therefore if many bidders have access to the necessary inputs of production at market prices, and if the costs of collusion among the (numerous) bidders are high, competition will prevail regardless of the degree of scale economies, and the actual producer is expected to earn only competitive or normal returns.

The winning bid would not entail any deadweight losses since a rival could propose a different pricing scheme to eliminate the deadweight loss and thereby become the winning bidder. If the established producer attempts to earn above-normal returns by raising the price, a potential rival would materialize, especially if the entrant can easily negotiate long-term contracts with the demanders at lower rates. If the established firm maintained the above-competitive price, customers would quickly sign the rival's contracts. Even if the established firm's assets were specialized, the asset's highest valued use would be to sell them to the entrant. There is no reason to expect any duplicative investment from this competitive process; only one firm will produce the output in equilibrium.[24]

The Demsetz critique raises the possibility that the method of regulation many municipalities once used might have been effective. The policy of granting (or threatening to grant) duplicative franchises could have afforded local regulators powerful leverage over public utilities. The availability of efficient potential producers who would utilize new franchises would have made this type of municipal regulation effective, according to the Demsetz view of potential competition. Municipal regulation could achieve a competitive electric utility industry even with consolidated producers through this policy of retaining the right to grant competitive franchises. The municipal regulators could also achieve supracompetitive prices and reduced output by withdrawing the threat to issue competitive franchises.

Therefore this method of regulation could, in theory, have allowed

24. There has been some debate over the social efficiency of the competitive process envisioned by Demsetz in "naturally monopolistic" industries. See Lester Telser, "On the Regulation of Industry: A Note," *Journal of Political Economy* 77 (1969):937, and Harold Demsetz, "On the Regulation of Industry: A Reply," *Journal of Political Economy* 79 (1971):356.

municipal authorities to have effective and flexible control over the electric utilities despite the problem of natural monopoly. In short, there may have been a method to their madness.[25]

The Positive Theory of Regulation

The positive theory of regulation rejects the assumption that regulation exists principally to correct private market failures. Rather the positive theory maintains that economic regulation serves the private interests of politically effective interest groups.[26] The focus here is on regulation as a tool used to redistribute wealth between identifiable groups, with the regulators' goal being to maximize political support. According to the positive theory, the systematic tendency of regulation to selectively help and harm various interest groups and to engage in cross-subsidization between interest groups is integral to the regulatory process.

We will sketch the principal components of a positive theory of regulation in order to learn the theory's implications about the demand for and the effects of state commission regulation. For convenience we assume that two interest groups exist in any state's marketplace for electricity—producers and consumers. The interests of each group are identified with their respective stakes—profits for producers and consumer surplus for consumers. Let an index S_i measure the political support from interest group i, and S_i depends directly on the incremental wealth received due to the regulator's redistributive policies.

$$(1) \quad S_p = f_p (X_r - X_u)$$

$$= \text{political support from the producer group,}$$

$$(2) \quad S_c = f_c (W_r - W_u)$$

$$= \text{political support from the consumer group,}$$

where X_r = profit under state regulation,

---

25. The history of the electric utility industry contains accounts of new franchise holders competing with established utilities by negotiating long-term contracts. See Wilcox, *Municipal Franchises*, pp. 184–85, and National Civic Federation, *Municipal and Private Operation*, pp. 676–77.

26. See George J. Stigler, "The Theory of Economic Regulation," *Bell Journal of Economics and Management Science* 2 (1971):3; Sam Peltzman, "Toward a More General Theory of Regulation," *Journal of Law and Economics* 19 (1976):211; and Richard A. Posner, "Taxation by Regulation," *Bell Journal of Economics and Management Science* 2 (1971):22.

X_u = profit without state regulation,
W_r = consumer surplus under state regulation,
W_u = consumer surplus without state regulation,
f_i = transformation function governing the production of political support (S_i) from regulatory wealth redistribution.

The model assumes that regulatory benefits to either group yield positive, but decreasing, returns; that is, $f_i' > 0$, $f_i'' < 0$. Ineffective regulation occurs if the regulator sets $X_r = X_u$ (or, equivalently, $W_r = W_u$), and this generates neither support nor opposition in this simple world ($f_i(0) = 0$). If the regulator sets X_r greater than X_u, causing positive support from producers ($S_p > 0$), then W_r is less than W_u, causing opposition from consumers ($S_c < 0$).

Equations (1) and (2) gloss over several interesting questions concerning what determines an interest group's political effectiveness. Although the theory of cartels suggests some variables that affect a group's costs of influencing regulators, economists remain ignorant of the effects a host of variables have upon a group's ability to cartelize or secure advantageous legislation.[27] I will not fill in this gap in the theory, but the issue does deserve some attention.

If it is difficult (that is, costly) to exclude nonpaying members of an interest group as recipients of a prospective regulatory benefit, members have an incentive to share the benefits without sharing the costs of acquiring them. The expense of overcoming this "free-rider" problem (monitoring and enforcement costs) is expected to rise rapidly as the interest group's size increases.[28] Hence on this score large groups are at a disadvantage in securing regulatory benefits. This argument somewhat rationalizes the pervasive assumption that the generally smaller industry groups are more politically effective than the large, diverse consumer groups. Consistent with this, the model assumes producers are politically more effective than consumers ($f_p' > f_c'$). In this way the model recognizes differences in the political effectiveness of the interest groups without specifying what determines political effectiveness.

---

27. For the classic treatment on the economics of collusion, see George J. Stigler, "A Theory of Oligopoly," *Journal of Political Economy* 72 (1964):72.

28. His lack of participation will reduce both the probability of receiving the regulatory benefit and the size of the benefit. Therefore, his ride is "cheap" but not "free." See George J. Stigler, "Free Riders and Collective Action: An Appendix to Theories of Economic Regulation," *Bell Journal of Economics and Management Science* 5 (1974):359.

In addition to assumptions about the marginal political effectiveness of the producers and consumers, the model requires an assumption about the organization of the electric utility industry absent state regulation. This is because political support depends on the incremental wealth generated by state regulators. For example, the political support of consumers resulting from state regulators enforcing a competitive market solution is strongest where the alternative of no regulation would lead to monopoly. If the unregulated solution would be perfectly competitive, then state regulation that merely mimics this outcome will generate zero support from consumers. In essence state regulation must change things in order to generate support or opposition.

Applying this to the case of electric utilities, history provides evidence that (1) municipal regulation was an important factor in determining the organization of electric utilities before state regulation; and (2) the degree of competition municipal regulators fostered in the early 1900s varied across cities (and states). Since the economics of organizing groups for political influence generally favors small groups with large per-capita stakes, we would expect electricity producers to be more politically effective than consumers with their state commissions.

Together these conditions imply that state regulation will maximize net political support by increasing prices and profits towards monopolistic levels. Furthermore the political demand for state commissions is highest in states characterized by more competitive markets for electricity. Electricity producers in states where municipal franchise regulation fostered competitive conditions were the primary demanders of state regulation. Therefore states that established commissions to regulate utilities relatively early (before 1922) should have had more competitive electricity markets under municipal regulation than did states that established commissions later (after 1922).

The implications of the positive theory about the demand for and effects of state regulation are diametrically opposed to those of the public-interest theory. The public-interest theory predicts that state commissions would be established first where natural monopolies were most prominent and that state regulators would lower prices and profits. The positive (or producer-interest) theory predicts that state commissions would be established first where municipal franchise regulation fostered competitive conditions and that state regulators would increase prices and profits.

The Empirical Evidence

These conflicting theoretical implications have recently been tested in fact using aggregate state data on electricity prices, costs, and profits.[29] The tests consist primarily of reduced-form price, output, and profit regressions fitted with cross-sectional data from the years 1912, 1917, and 1922. The states are divided into two groups. The early-regulated group includes the twenty-five states that established regulatory commissions between 1912 and 1917. The later-regulated group includes those remaining states that established commissions after 1917. (Most of these came well after 1917.) The price, profit, and output regressions account for differences in demand and cost variables across states. The regressions include dummy variables that distinguish between early-regulated and later-regulated states. This technique shows net differences in prices, profits, and output between these two types of states, having taken into account the influences of the demand and cost variables.

These regressions show that in 1912, before the advent of state commissions in these states, the early-regulated states had 45 percent lower prices on average than did later-regulated states. The early-regulated states also exhibit about 30 percent lower profits, and 25 percent higher per-capita output in 1912 compared with later-regulated states. Since the regressions account for important differences in demand and cost variables, this large price difference is attributed to the effect of municipal regulation on market structure. Further these differences show up in 1907 and 1902, with the early-regulated states showing substantially lower prices and profits compared with later-regulated states.

This evidence contradicts the hypothesis that state commissions were first established in states with naturally monopolistic electric utilities. The low prices and profits indicate that early-regulated states were characterized by relatively competitive electric utilities. These data also suggest that municipal franchise regulation may have had profound effects on the degree of competition among public utilities.

To gauge the effects of substituting state commissions for municipal regulation on the electricity markets, the regressions are fitted

29. Gregg A. Jarrell, "The Demand for State Regulation of the Electric Utility Industry," *Journal of Law and Economics* 21 (October 1978):269.

with data from 1917 and 1922. By this time state commissions were firmly established in the twenty-five early-regulated states. The regressions show that the dramatic differences in prices, profits, and output that had existed from 1902 to 1912 had largely disappeared by 1917. This means that the imposition of state commissions in these states is associated with a 25-percent increase in average price and a 40-percent increase in average profit. Tracing the data to 1937 further supports the interpretation that state commissions allowed large increases in electricity prices and producer profits in these twenty-five states, compared with the later-regulated states.

These results support the producer-interest hypothesis. Although state commissions were not perfect agents for the producers, they apparently allowed electric utilities large price increases during the first five years or so after their establishment in these twenty-five states. This evidence of large producer benefits largely contradicts the public-interest theory, which implies that state commissions should have reduced prices and profits from their naturally monopolistic levels under municipal regulation. Instead state regulators relieved electricity producers from the disciplinary effects of municipal franchise competition by encouraging consolidation, barring municipalities from granting franchises, and instituting supracompetitive electricity rates.

The evidence raises a puzzling question concerning how the regulatory process resulted in these large transfers of wealth from electricity consumers to producers. The state commissions all used rate-of-return regulation to set electricity rates. Such a base would seem to preclude utilities from earning supracompetitive returns. If it was illegal for state regulators to allow electric utilities to earn greater than the fair rate of return allowed by law, how did utilities and regulators get away with the large price and profit increases measured between 1912 and 1917? I have found no evidence that rates of return on capital were sufficiently low before state regulation to explain the marked increase under state regulation. The answer, according to recent research, is that the reported value of assets comprising the rate base was increased significantly by including franchises with inflated values.[30] This allowed a supracompetitive return on the (competitive value of) capital to be earned without exceeding the fair rate-of-return constraint.

---

30. Gregg A. Jarrell, "Pro-Producer Regulation and Accounting for Assets: The Case of Electric Utilities," *Journal of Accounting and Economics* 1 (1979):93.

Regulation by state commissions ushered in a new system of accounting-based procedures for setting prices, profits, and output. This system transformed the mechanics of accounting into an instrument of regulatory control. The most important element of this system is determining the rate base (or invested capital) since allowed net revenues are a proportion of the rate-base fair value. The Supreme Court suggested that among "the matters for consideration in determining fair value" should be the "original cost" (defined as the first among expended) and "the amount expended in permanent improvements."

The enumeration of types of assets and charges to be excluded from the rate base also received considerable attention. Intangible assets, such as municipal franchises, presented a very difficult problem. Regulators realized that including franchises at values based on prospective supracompetitive earnings would inflate the rate base and provide excess profits due to the mechanics of rate-of-return regulation. The policy was to exclude from the rate base amounts representing the capitalized value of future returns in excess of reasonable amounts.

As a practical matter, however, the typical electric utility during this time was the product of many mergers and consolidations of physical plant and franchises. These franchise values were inflated because the state commission regulation converted them into permanent, exclusive franchises and because their acquisition value reflected the capacity of the utility to earn excess returns under the regulatory system. There was also an absence of arm's-length bargaining in many instances where the acquisition was from an affiliated owner.

Even though state regulators increased the value of existing franchises, it may have been difficult for utilities to revalue these franchises upward on their books without some transaction. However, the consolidation movement, which new state regulators actively and sometimes quite aggressively encouraged, caused countless utilities to change ownership, often several times. This offered ample opportunities for sellers to realize the new higher value of these franchises and for purchasers to increase their asset bases by recording the franchises and other properties at acquisition cost.

These may have been mostly "arms-length" transactions with the acquisition price of the franchise representing an accurate estimate of the prospective earnings expected to accrue to its holder under the new environment of state regulation. It is also likely, however, that some acquisitions were rigged between affiliated companies so franchises and other assets could "legitimately" be revalued upward and included in the rate base. Either way the effect was the same—the rate base was inflated so that monopoly earnings could be charged while not violating the maximum-allowable-accounting-return constraint.

There seems to be little doubt that in fact these franchise assets were often included in the utilities' asset accounts. In describing the "value of plant and equipment" account in the 1917 Census of Electrical Industries, it is explained:

> it should be noted that some companies include many intangible items in the valuation in addition to the actual physical property used. Good-will franchises of different sorts, prospective earnings, and other items frequently find their way into the book value of the plant.[31]

Empirical evidence shows that the asset accounts of electric utilities in the twenty-five states regulated between 1912 and 1917 increased dramatically during this period. Specifically cross-sectional regressions that measure the effect of state regulation on asset-to-output and asset-to-capacity ratios shows that both ratios increased substantially—after accounting for other important factors—for utilities in these twenty-five states. Although these data do not distinguish between tangible and intangible assets, the overall results support the view that state commissions allowed inflated franchise values to enter the rate base. In this way, the state commissions provided large price and profit increases through the use of fair rate-of-return regulation.

---

31. U.S. Bureau of Census. *Census of Electrical Industries 1907* (Washington, D.C.: U.S. Government Printing Office, 1920), p. 34.

9

EFFICIENCY, SUBSIDY, AND CROSS-SUBSIDY IN ELECTRIC UTILITY PRICING

John T. Wenders

Electric power is one of the most heavily regulated industries in the United States. With only a few exceptions some regulatory authority sets the prices of electricity in one way or another. State regulatory commissions, in particular, typically have the authority to review and determine retail electricity prices. The purpose of this essay is to investigate how these state regulatory commissions have dealt with electric power prices.

The perspective used here is the standard of economic efficiency as it would exist under competition. Using this standard, I investigate electric power pricing by asking two essential questions: How has the electric power regulatory process—necessarily part of our larger political process—altered the distribution of income both between producers and consumers and among the various classes of electricity customers? This is the distribution question. The second question is, How has the regulatory process altered the economic efficiency of the electric power industry? This is the efficiency question.

Since state regulatory bodies are a part of the political process, we must investigate the theory of economic regulation as applied to electric rate-making to understand their behavior.

THEORIES OF REGULATION

Historically three theories of regulation have been developed to explain the regulation of industries. The first of these, sometimes called the public-interest theory, argues that the reason for regulation is to avoid the market failures of monopoly when an industry is naturally monopolistic.[1] This theory presumes that the regulatory goal is to produce the equivalent of a competitive outcome in an industry where this is impossible because of continually declining costs. I think it is accurate to say that few economists now believe that the regulatory process works very much in this way. Good intentions are not enough when a regulatory agency is given real economic power and turned loose in the political marketplace.

The second theory was popularized by Stigler and Peltzman.[2] This is the theory of economic regulation, with the central outcome that the dominant group in the regulatory game is likely to be a small one that has a relatively large per-capita stake. This leads to the conclusion that "producer interest tends to prevail over the consumer interest."[3] This conclusion has also been reached by Becker who proposes that "Politically successful groups tend to be small relative to the size of the groups taxed to pay their subsidies."[4]

While economists have used the theory of economic regulation primarily to explain how regulation has altered the distribution of gains between an industry's producers and its customers, it can also address the internal or cross-subsidy question. In this instance the capture conclusion suggests that the regulatory process would underprice services to the few at the expense of the many. For the electric power industry this means that the regulatory mechanism would subsidize the industrial and commercial classes at the expense of the residential class.[5]

1. James C. Bonbright, *Principles of Public Utility Rates* (New York: Columbia University Press, 1961), chap. 8.

2. George J. Stigler, "The Theory of Economic Regulation," *Bell Journal of Economics and Management Science* 1 (1971):3–21; and Sam Peltzman, "Toward a More General Theory of Regulation," *Journal of Law and Economics* 19 (1976):211–40.

3. Peltzman, "Toward a More General Theory," p. 212.

4. Gary S. Becker, "A Theory of Competition Among Pressure Groups for Political Influence," *Quarterly Journal of Economics*, 97 (1983):385.

5. It is useful to illustrate the usage distribution among customer classes. In 1978 Baltimore Gas and Electric had 441 large industrial customers with an average annual consumption of 13,329,000 kwh, 4,687 large general service customers who had average annual consumption of 658,000 kwh, 69,108 small general service customers with an average annual consumption of 20,645, and 734,186 residential customers with average annual consumption of 7,465 kwh. Put another way, 36.4 percent of the kwh usage was concentrated in the top 592 (.075 percent) customers, and 55.4 percent of the kwh usage was concentrated in the top 5,167 (.65 percent) customers. Such a usage distribution is typical for the industry.

Finally there is the public finance or taxation-by-regulation approach Posner emphasized. He argues that regulators use the regulatory process similar to the taxing and spending function of all governments to subsidize one part of the electorate at the expense of another in order to maximize the political capital of the regulators.[6]

As we shall see, the existing special interest and capture conclusions that flow from the theory of economic regulation do not adequately explain the way in which state regulatory authorities have dealt with either the distribution or efficiency questions in the electric power industry. I suggest that the public finance or taxation-by-regulation approach works better to describe what has happened in the electric power industry.

THE THEORY OF ECONOMIC REGULATION AND PUBLIC UTILITY PRICING

Since electricity prices are the result of political decision making, I begin with some public choice and economic regulation theory. In their economics text, Gwartney and Stroup discuss the special-interest problem of the political process:

> A special interest issue is one that generates substantial personal benefits for a small number of constituents while imposing a small individual cost on a large number of other voters. A few gain a great deal individually, while a large number lose a little as individuals.[7]

This special-interest theory is really a generalization of the theory of economic regulation. The essence of this theory has been summarized by Peltzman:

> The size of the dominant group is limited in the first instance by the absence of something like ordinary-market-dollar voting in politics. Voting is infrequent and concerned with a package of issues. In the case of a particular issue, the voter must spend resources to inform himself about its implications for his wealth and which politician is likely to stand on which side of the issue. That information cost will have to offset the prospective gains, and a voter with a small per capita stake will not, therefore, incur it. In the consequence the numerically large, diffuse in-

---

6. Richard A. Posner, "Taxation by Regulation," *Bell Journal of Economics and Management Science* 1 (1971):22–50.

7. James D. Gwartney and Richard Stroup, *Economics: Private and Public Choice*, 3d ed. (New York: Academic Press, 1982), p. 76.

terest group is unlikely to be an effective bidder, and a policy inimical to the interest of a numerical majority will not be automatically rejected. A second major limit on effective group size arises from the cost of organization. It is not enough for the successful group to recognize its interests; it must organize to translate this interest into support for the politician who will implement it. . . . While there may be some economies of scale in this organization of support and neutralization of opposition, these must be limited. The larger the group that seeks the transfer, the narrower the base of the opposition and the greater the per-capita stakes that determine the strength of the opposition, so lobbying and campaigning costs will rise faster than group size. The cost of overcoming "free riders" will also rise faster than group size. This diseconomy of scale in providing resources then acts as another limit to the size of the group that will ultimately dominate the political process.[8]

The capture conclusion suggests that the regulatory process would underprice services to the few industrial customers at the expense of the many residential customers. One contention of this chapter is that this application of the theory of economic regulation yields results that are inconsistent with what has in fact happened in the electric power industry.

Finally I shall also argue that the capture-theory conclusion, that it will be the producers who dominate the regulatory process, is wrong. This conclusion is inconsistent with the observation that the regulatory process in the electric power industry has resulted in the appropriation of at least some of the intramarginal rents—which under competition would have accrued to electricity producers—and redistributed at least part of these rents to electricity customers. For these reasons, I investigate the implications of this theory in more detail.

AN ALTERNATIVE RESULT

Public choice and economic regulation theory says that individuals— whether politicians, regulators, or voters—will make political decisions based on their own self-interest; and because it is votes not dollars that count in the political process, this fact often produces outcomes damaging to general economic welfare. One reason for this perverse outcome is that the voter simply finds it costly to determine the relative costs and benefits of alternative courses of political action and to make one's political power felt. Thus the cost of acquiring infor-

---

8. Peltzman, "Toward a More General Theory," p. 213.

mation regarding alternatives and then acting on this information plays a large role in political behavior.

In my view, public utilities are unique among our regulated industries in the sense that all consumer-voters have very good information about the effect of these industries on their well-being. Consumers are very aware of their utility bills, since they receive an explicit itemized bill for services every month, and they are very aware of the fact that some regulatory agency determines utility prices.

The same is not true of other regulated industries, such as railroads, trucking, and airlines, because the average consumer seldom comes in frequent direct contact with these industries. When food prices go up as a result of an increase in truck rates, the average consumer has no way of knowing the cause, and might not even realize that such rates are regulated.

Thus, consumers are not only fairly well informed about how public utilities affect their well-being, but they also have a well-defined and in-place political mechanism for complaint.

A second, and possibly more potent, reason why consumers are sensitive to electricity prices is the difficulty and cost of substituting for electricity in the short run. All electricity is consumed via complementary appliances. When, say, the price of electricity rises, we can see the consumer's response in short- and long-run effects. In the short run, consumers are stuck with their existing stock of complementary appliances, so all they can do is reduce appliance usage. This tends to produce very low short-run elasticities of demand. Of course, as demand studies show, as the stock of appliances wears out, and they can be replaced with appliances that consume less electricity, a greater opportunity exists for the consumer to substitute for electricity. But, in the jargon of the economist, an increase in electricity prices in the short run has a large, utility-reducing income effect. Thus dollar for dollar such an increase in electricity prices has a greater effect on the consumer's welfare than an increase in the prices of other goods and services for which there is the possibility of a greater short-run substitution effect.[9]

Finally little organizational effort is needed for electricity customers to affect the direct election process. All voters are electric power customers and are relatively well-informed on a monthly basis

9. Lester D. Taylor, "The Demand for Electricity: A Survey," *Bell Journal of Economics* 6 (1975):74–110.

about the impact of electricity prices. Moreover state regulators are quite closely responsive to the direct election process. Many are elected, and the rest are appointed by elected state officials such as the governor. The upshot is that almost no expensive and time-consuming effort is needed to get the regulatory officials' attention.

The sensitivity of consumers to electricity prices, the close tie-in state regulators have to the electoral process, and the simple observation that most electricity customers are in the residential class means that we should expect that the regulatory authorities have been extremely reluctant to raise residential electricity tariffs. Simply put, that's where the votes are.

As noted above, this observation counters the usual interpretation about the special-interest outcome or capture theory of economic regulation, which concludes that the political process will tend to favor special interests that are few in number and individually have much to gain from a particular policy. This can happen, according to the theory, because the greater total costs are so thinly spread among the majority, each of whom only hurts a little and thus has little incentive to either find out the extent of the hurt or to do something about it. Meanwhile the smaller aggregate benefits concentrate on a few, each of whom benefits greatly and so has a strong incentive to fight for continued benefits through the political process. In short the special-interest or capture conclusion says that the many will be made to subsidize the few; whereas my observations indicate—and the record confirms —public utility regulation has produced just the opposite result.

In my view the reason for this apparent inconsistency is not because the general theory of economic regulation is wrong, but rather because theorists have presumed, based on this theory, that it will be so costly for the large group, each with a small per-capita stake, to determine its interest and make its political presence felt that the payoff will not be worth the cost. If, as I have suggested, it is cheap and easy for members of a large group to know the impact of electricity prices on their well-being, and if the threat of the ballot box—either directly or indirectly—easily gets the attention of the regulators, then the outcome of the more general theory of regulation will be that the largest group will dominate the regulatory process. If a policy clearly and immediately benefits a lot of voters, even if only marginally, and they all clearly know it, and if the regulatory process is sensitive to the election process, then the minority who will be hurt by the policy will be dominated by the majority. This is especially true if, as in the electric power industry, the good that is underpriced has few short-run substitutes.

As Gary Becker has observed, the essence of an economic approach to regulation is that there be a balance at the margin.

> Although the "capture" theory is something attributed to Stigler, and he has made a few of these studies and encouraged others, he has also argued that rigid adherence to a "capture" theory is not consistent with the spirit of the economic approach. Analytically, economics is a theory of balance, not of all-or-nothing, as implied by the "capture" of legislation. Empirically even small but vocal minorities have to be appeased: minority opposition is not automatically muted simply because the majority has 51 or 75 percent of the vote. In other words, the concept of a "minimum winning coalition" . . . conflicts with the economist's view of balance at the margin.[10]

Thus a balance at the margin can indeed be struck where the minority few with a large per-capita stake are the net beneficiaries of regulation, but it can also be struck where they are not.

I illustrate these points, with appropriate qualifications, in the following discussion. For now, I only note that for the electric power industry, the capture and special-interest conclusions that emerge from the theory of economic regulation are incorrect. This is likely the case for other industries as well.[11] The conclusions are incorrect due to mistaken judgments about the cost of acquiring information and influencing the political process. There are certainly other instances in which capture does correctly emerge from the general theory of economic regulation, but the electric power industry is not one of them.

ELECTRICITY PRICES AND MARGINAL COSTS

Competitive theory holds that prices should gravitate to marginal costs in the long run. It is useful therefore to begin our investigation by comparing marginal prices and marginal costs for several electric utilities. Table 9–1 does this. These data show the synthesized marginal cost of a kilowatt hour (kwh) of electric power and the marginal price

10. Gary Becker, "Comment," *Journal of Law and Economics,* 19 (1976):245.
11. John T. Wenders, "An Economic History of the US Telecommunications Industry to 1995: A Public Choice Perspective," *New Directions: State Regulation of Telecommunications* (Seattle: Washington State Legislature Joint Select Committee on Telecommunications, 1984).

Table 9–1. Comparison of Marginal Prices and Marginal Costs for Selected Electric Utilities (cents/kwh).

Utility (year)	Summer		Winter	
	Peak	Off-Peak	Peak	Off-Peak
Delmarva[1] (1978)				
Residential				
Marginal cost	15.93	2.28	7.71	2.80
Marginal price	4.63	4.63	3.95	3.95
Commercial				
Marginal cost	9.63	2.28	6.84	2.80
Marginal price	7.15	7.15	6.99	6.99
Industrial				
Marginal cost	9.20	2.10	5.58	2.59
Marginal price	3.80	3.80	3.63	3.63
Baltimore Gas and Electric[2] (1978)				
Residential				
Marginal cost	14.95	2.30	5.13	2.64
Marginal price	4.56	4.56	4.33	4.33
Commercial				
Marginal cost	11.95	2.30	4.71	2.64
Marginal price	5.41	5.41	5.25	5.25
Industrial				
Marginal cost	9.09	2.15	4.18	2.48
Marginal price	3.23	3.23	3.16	3.16
PEPCO[3] (1980)				
Residential				
Marginal cost	25.71	3.08	8.63	3.73
Marginal price	5.39	5.39	5.25	5.25
Commercial				
Marginal cost	25.2	3.08	8.86	3.73
Marginal price	6.12	6.12	5.44	5.44
Industrial				
Marginal cost	15.97	2.65	6.90	3.32
Marginal price	4.74	4.74	3.90	3.90
Public Service Company of New Mexico[4] (1979)				
Residential				
Marginal cost	17.53	3.34	9.86	3.45
Marginal price	6.27	6.27	6.27	6.27
Small Commercial				
Marginal cost	17.88	3.34	9.86	3.45
Marginal price	7.57	7.57	7.57	7.57
Large Commercial				
Marginal cost	19.08	3.34	9.09	3.45
Marginal price	5.73	5.73	5.72	5.72

Table 9–1.   (continued)

Utility (year)	Summer		Winter	
	Peak	*Off-Peak*	*Peak*	*Off-Peak*
Industrial				
Marginal cost	15.51	3.09	8.72	3.22
Marginal price	5.31	5.31	5.31	5.31
Illinois Power[5] (1979)				
Residential				
Marginal cost	22.00	1.61	3.35	1.61
Marginal price	4.66	4.66	2.52	2.52
Commercial				
Marginal cost	17.59	1.61	3.14	1.61
Marginal price	5.65	5.65	3.01	3.01
Industrial				
Marginal cost	15.02	1.58	2.62	1.58
Marginal price	2.75	2.75	2.75	2.75
Special Industrial				
Marginal cost	12.92	1.55	2.57	1.55
Marginal price	2.03	2.03	2.03	2.03

1. Maryland Public Service Commission, Case No. 7174 (Delmarva Power and Light Company of Maryland), 1980.
2. Maryland Public Service Commission, Case No. 7159 (Baltimore Gas and Electric Company), 1980.
3. Maryland Public Service Commission, Case No. 7441 (Potomac Electric Power Company), 1981.
4. New Mexico Public Service Commission, Case No. 1554 (Public Service Company of New Mexico), 1980.
5. Illinois Commerce Commission, Docket No. 80-0544 (Illinois Power Company), 1981.

the average consumer faces in the three broad customer classes of each utility.[12]

It is useful to discuss these data in detail. These data were obtained from marginal-cost studies conducted either by the author or the utilities in question using a methodology developed by National Economic Research Associates, Inc., for the Electric Power Research

12. Synthesized marginal costs are long-run marginal costs that have two components: capacity costs, which are primarily caused by the use of kilowatts of capacity during the peak hour, and short-run operating, or energy, costs, measured in kilowatt hours. The kilowatt costs are synthesized by dividing them by the kilowatt hours consumed during the period in question.

Institute.[13] This technique asks the question, In the long run, what additional costs are imposed on the utility if electricity load increases during various seasonal-time-of-day periods? The marginal costs obtained using this technique are static equilibrium marginal costs in the sense that it ignores the discrete nature of utility investments, and assumes that the utility has optimally adjusted its mix of alternative generating equipment. The data show long-run marginal cost in the sense that marginal capacity costs (generation, transmission, and distribution) are included.[14] Summer peak-period prices are significantly higher due to the proper attribution of most capacity costs to this period. The costs of the residential and commercial classes during the peak periods are significantly higher because these classes take fewer kilowatt hours relative to their kilowatts demanded during these periods. It should be noted that these data show the relevant prices and marginal costs for electricity usage only. Customer costs are excluded. In all cases where data is available, the monthly nonusage-sensitive costs of hooking a customer to the electric system significantly exceed the fixed monthly charge—the first part of the multipart tariff under which virtually all electricity is sold.

The Cross-Subsidy Question

One purpose of this paper is to investigate the alteration of income distribution among the various customer classes. Table 9–1 focuses some light on this question. Even ignoring for a moment the failure of electricity prices to follow the seasonal-time-of-day (STD) pattern of marginal costs, it is difficult to say which class has been favored the most by electricity usage prices.

A naive approach would be to look at the cross-subsidy question by simply comparing the marginal prices the various customer classes paid. Table 9–2 shows the simple marginal price each class faced, averaged without weights across the four time periods. These data show that in all instances the industrial class has significantly lower average marginal prices (3.55 cents/kwh) than either the residential

13. National Economic Research Associates, Inc., *A Framework for Marginal Cost Based Time-Differentiated Pricing in The United States* (Palo Alto, Calif.: Electric Power Research Institute, Electric Utility Rate Design Study, Report No. 15, 1977).

14. For a further discussion of the various methodologies for marginal costing, see *Comments on 'An Evaluation of Four Marginal Costing Methodologies'* (Palo Alto, Calif.: Electric Power Research Institute, Electric Utility Rate Design Study, Report No. 67, June 12, 1980).

Table 9–2. Comparison of Average Marginal Prices for Selected Electric Utilities (cents/kwh).

Utility	Residential	Commercial	Industrial
Delmarva	4.29	7.07	3.72
Baltimore Gas and Electric	4.45	5.33	3.20
PEPCO	5.32	5.78	4.32
Public Service Company of New Mexico	6.27	7.57–5.73	5.31
Illinois Power	3.59	4.33	2.75–2.03
Average	4.78	5.97	3.55

SOURCE: Calculated by the author from Table 9–1.

(4.78) or commercial (5.97) classes. This evidence alone would lead one to conclude that the industrial class was receiving preferential treatment over the other two classes.[15] Since industrial customers, and their direct constituents, are typically outnumbered by residential and commercial customers, this observation by itself would seem to indicate that the capture conclusion does explain the cross-subsidy issue.

Table 9–1 shows that marginal costs vary considerably across the various customer classes, so the cross-subsidy issue cannot be settled solely by looking at prices. It is possible that the price variations in Table 9–2 merely reflect variations in marginal cost. Comparing prices with marginal costs yields a somewhat different story. Consider Table 9–3, which shows the ratio of the sum of prices to the sum of marginal costs across time periods for each class for each of the utilities in Table 9–1. On this score, we see that the residential and industrial classes have the lowest price to marginal cost ratio (.612 and .623 respectively) and the commercial class has the highest (.853).[16] This yields the conclusion that the residential and industrial classes are favored equally over the commercial class.

Neither of these tests for cross-subsidy is satisfactory, however. The primary reason is that all of the prices and marginal costs given

15. Since residential and commercial users consume a higher proportion of their electricity during peak periods, when prices are sometimes higher, weighting the marginal prices by kwh in each time period in Table 9–1 would strengthen this conclusion.

16. Since weights across time periods would be the same for both prices and marginal costs, weighting by kwh in each time period would not alter these results.

Table 9–3.   Comparison of Price/Marginal Cost Ratios for Selected Electric Utilities.

Utility	Residential	Commercial	Industrial
Delmarva	.597	1.312	.763
Baltimore Gas and Electric	.711	.987	.714
PEPCO	.517	.566	.599
Public Service Company of New Mexico	.734	.877–.655	.695
Illinois Power	.503	.723	.529–.437
Average	.612	.853	.623

SOURCE: Calculated by the author from Table 9–1.

in Table 9–1 ignore the nonmarginal, customer-specific costs of a hook-up to the electric system, and these costs are proportionately smaller for high usage customers such as large commercial customers and industrial class customers. Thus it is possible for all customer classes to have the same price to marginal cost ratios for electricity usage, apparently indicating no traditional price discrimination. Customer classes still pay a varying share of their customer-specific costs, however, indicating that some classes were favored over others by the regulation process. As we will see, this is indeed what happened. Thus, the real test of cross-subsidy is how the total revenues of the utility are divided up among the various customer classes relative to what they would be in a competitive, marginal-cost-pricing environment where all prices, including the fixed monthly charge, are set equal to marginal cost. If one customer class is paying a higher proportion of these revenues than some other class, then we can say that the former is subsidizing the latter.

One of the problems with this approach is that the total revenues that would be collected by strict marginal cost pricing usually far exceed the revenues that the regulators have allowed the companies to collect. A variety of reasons explain this, and I will discuss them below. The essence of my reasoning is that the regulatory process has appropriated some of the intramarginal rents and quasi-rents, which under competition would have accrued to electricity producers, and has redistributed these rents to electricity customers.[17] For our present

---

17. This probably has the same general political appeal as price controls on old oil, and the taxing of windfall capital appreciation of old energy assets that occurred as energy prices increased in the last 15 years.

purposes all this means is that virtually all customer classes are paying less in total than they would pay if the electric utilities were charging competitive long run marginal costs. In a sense then all customer classes are being subsidized, and the question of cross-subsidy can only be answered by seeing whether one customer class is paying more or less than the fraction of total revenues that it would pay under full marginal cost pricing.[18]

Table 9–4 presents data relevant to this question. The table presents both actual class revenues under present prices and class revenues under strict marginal cost pricing as a percentage of total utility revenues allowed (revenue requirements) in each case. (Due to limitations in data, it was not possible to present comparable data for all the utilities used in the previous tables.) Column (1) shows the percentage of total revenues the company collected in each class. Column (2) shows what this percentage would have been if strict marginal cost pricing had been followed. For example, in the residential class for Illinois Power, actual class revenues allowed were 39.8 percent of the utility's total revenue requirements, while under marginal cost pricing this same class would have paid 44.6 percent of the utility's revenue requirements. Thus in this instance the residential class is paying only 89.2 percent of the revenues it would have to pay if it were paying the same proportion of revenues as it would under competitive marginal cost pricing.

The conclusions we can draw from Table 9–4 are that the residential class is paying less than its share of total costs, 82.8 percent on average for the sample in Table 9–4. The commercial and industrial classes are paying more than their share: 111.5 percent and 112.0 percent respectively.[19] This is the basis for my contention that a proper application of the general theory of economic regulation to the electric

18. For a more thorough discussion of this whole approach determining cross-subsidy, see John T. Wenders, "The Marginal Cost Pricing of Electricity and the Determination of Class Revenue Requirements," *Electric Ratemaking* 2 (1983):50–54.

19. In fact, the data presented in Table 9–4 probably underestimate the degree to which the residential class has been favored over the industrial class. The estimates of revenue that would be collected by strict marginal cost pricing presented in column (2) are simply a repricing of present quantities consumed at marginal cost. No allowance for price elasticity was made. If an allowance for elasticity were made, the proportion of revenues collected under marginal cost pricing would rise for the residential class and fall for the industrial class. A rise in prices would undoubtedly produce more of a reduction in electricity by the industrial class. This would happen for two reasons. First, proportionately more additional revenue would be raised from the residential class by raising the perfectly inelastic fixed monthly charge to its marginal cost. Second, generally speaking, the sensitivity of electricity usage is generally higher for the industrial class at least in the long run. See Taylor, "The Demand for Electricity."

Table 9–4.   Comparison of Actual Class Revenues with Revenues Under Marginal Cost Pricing.

			Percent of Total Revenues		
			(1)	*(2)*	*(3)*
				Marginal	*Actual*
			Actual	*Cost*	*Over*
Customer			*Class*	*Class*	*Marginal*
Class	*Utility*	*Year*	*Revenues*	*Revenues*	*Cost*
Residential	So. Cal. Ed.	1981	30.5	40.1	76.1
	So. Cal. Ed.	1983	29.9	40.2	74.4
	So. Cal. Ed.	1984	30.6	36.0	85.0
	P G & E	1982	30.8	34.5	87.0
	Cen. Il. PS	1981	38.8	45.6	85.1
	Ill. Power	1982	39.8	44.6	89.2
	B G & E	1978	42.1	49.4	85.2
Commercial	So. Cal. Ed.	1981	31.0	27.2	114.0
	So. Cal. Ed.	1983	31.4	26.7	117.6
	So. Cal. Ed.	1984	33.1	31.6	104.7
	P G & E	1982	10.0	8.9	112.4
	Cen. Il. PS	1981	17.4	16.1	108.1
	Ill. Power	1982	23.9	21.3	112.2
	B G & E	1978	35.3	29.0	122.0
Industrial	So. Cal. Ed.	1981	33.7	27.8	121.2
	So. Cal. Ed.	1983	33.8	28.3	119.4
	So. Cal. Ed.	1984	31.9	28.2	113.1
	P G & E	1982	23.3	24.8	94.0
	Cen. Il. PS	1981	42.4	36.1	117.5
	Ill. Power	1982	36.3	34.1	106.5
	B G & E	1978	22.6	21.6	104.3

SOURCES: For So. Cal. Ed. (1981 & 1983): California Public Utilities Commission, Application No. 61138.

For So. Cal. Ed. (1984): California Public Utilities Commission, Application No. 83-12-053.

For Pacific Gas and Electric: California Public Utilities Commission, Application No. 60153.
For Central Illinois Public Service: Illinois Commerce Commission, Docket No. 82-0039.
For Illinois Power Company: Illinois Commerce Commission, Docket No. 82-0152.
For Baltimore Gas & Electric: Maryland Public Service Commission, Case No. 7159.

power industry leads to the conclusion that the regulatory mechanism subsidizes the majority of customers at the expense of the minority. This is contrary to the special-interest or capture conclusions of the theory of economic regulation.

It is instructive to discuss why the conclusions drawn from Table 9–4 are different from those drawn from Table 9–3. Recall that the data in Table 9–3 relate only to the prices and costs of electricity used. Yet this classification of costs misses the nonusage-sensitive customer costs of connecting each subscriber to the electric system—costs that loom proportionately much larger for the smaller, residential, customers. Thus in Table 9–4, when the revenues that would be collected under strict marginal cost pricing are included in the analysis—including setting the fixed monthly charge equal to marginal customer costs—the residential class shows up paying less than its share.

The Subsidy Question

It is appropriate at this point to discuss the almost universal fact that in recent years regulators have allowed electric utilities to collect revenues that invariably fall far short of the revenues that would be raised by full marginal cost pricing. This, of course, is implicit in the data in Table 9–3.

For example, for Baltimore Gas and Electric in 1978, the marginal cost pricing of usage alone—ignoring marginal customer costs—would have overrecovered revenue requirements by 16.1 percent. When marginal cost prices for customer costs were added, revenues were overrecovered by 39.4 percent. For Delmarva Power and Light in 1978, the overrecovery would have been 17.7 percent in the former case and 39 percent in the latter. For Public Service Company of New Mexico in 1979, the overrecovery would have been 16.2 percent when all rate elements were priced at marginal cost.

The change in usage that would occur by adjusting prices to marginal cost would not change this conclusion. As Table 9–1 shows, present prices depart most from marginal cost in peak periods. Since the overall elasticity of demand for electricity is probably somewhat less than unity, and the reduction in usage would reduce total costs, if we take into account demand and cost changes, marginal cost pricing would probably increase revenues and reduce costs, thus increasing overrecovery of revenue requirements.

In my experience, these same general results—overrecovery of revenue requirements under strict marginal cost pricing—have prevailed for almost every utility in the United States for the past fifteen years.

In a sense we might say that marginal costs lie above average revenue requirements, where the latter term is the regulatory proxy for average costs. This, of course, suggests that the capture conclusion also fails to explain the distribution of intramarginal rents between producers and consumers.

Why is this true? There are both mechanical and substantive reasons. At first glance, this overrecovery of revenues due to marginal cost pricing would seem patently inconsistent with natural monopoly theory, which holds that marginal costs should lie below average costs. But this apparent inconsistency disappears when we remember that the total revenue requirements that emerge from the regulatory process are a far cry from the total-costs-of-price theory.

Specifically the regulatory process significantly understates the rate base and the marginal cost of capital that the electric utility is allowed to earn. In an inflationary period with little technological change, such as the past twenty years in this industry, the practice of using the book value of assets severely understates the actual value of such assets and the allowed revenues based on these asset valuations. In addition, in a period of rising interest rates, the practice of using the embedded cost of debt as the cost of debt capital severely understates the marginal cost of debt. The consequence of these practices is that the total revenues electric utilities are allowed to collect usually fall far short of the revenues that would be collected under long run marginal cost pricing since the latter use proper current or forward-looking costs as their basis and the former use embedded or book costs.

So much for the ways regulators have used to lower average revenue requirements below marginal cost. The real question is why regulators have been able to get away with "below cost" pricing without driving the industry out of existence. The reason is that the regulatory process has appropriated the intramarginal rents and quasi-rents of the electric power industry and redistributed these to the industry's most potent political constituency—its consumers. Note that, again, this flatly contradicts the conclusions of the special-interest or capture theory, under which we would expect both rents and some monopoly profits to accrue to the industry. And even though one might argue that the industry has succeeded in gold-plating its operations, this cannot explain why competitive revenues exceed allowed revenues.

It is clear then that the regulatory process has resulted in subsidizing electric power customers as a whole relative to what would happen in a competitive situation, and this subsidy has flowed disproportionately to the politically potent residential class.

The Efficiency Question

Economic efficiency focuses on whether or not the optimal amount of resources has been allocated to the electric power industry. The relevant test is whether or not prices and costs are equal at the margin. It is important to understand that the subsidy and efficiency questions are quite separate. Thus it would be quite possible to have electricity consumers subsidized, in the sense that total costs and rents were more than collected revenues, and still have prices equal to costs at the margin. In the electric power industry this would require that prices be set equal to costs on the margin, with intramarginal prices—including the fixed monthly connection charge—appropriately lowered to meet the lower revenue requirements determined by the regulatory process. This would have resulted in inverted or ascending block rate structures and very low, or negative, monthly fixed charges.

This, of course, is not what happened. Even casual inspection of the data presented above shows that, on the average, marginal prices were set well below marginal costs, especially during the peak periods. The primary reason for this is that no mechanism is operating, as in a competitive market, to equate prices and costs on the margin. The mechanism of regulation, being necessarily a politically driven one, is primarily concerned with effecting its taxation-by-regulation function, as Posner has put it; and the regulation of the industry is so tight that very little real competition exists.

The data in Table 9–1 show that the major distortion to economic efficiency occurs because prices have generally been much too low during the peak periods. This distortion is certainly greater than any additional distortion caused by setting off-peak prices above marginal cost. Defenders of industry pricing practices often point out that this failure to set time-of-day prices (TOD) is not necessarily inefficient since the additional metering necessary to record consumption by time of day might offset the distortions to efficiency eliminated by TOD pricing. Depending on the size of these relative costs and benefits of TOD pricing, this argument might be correct. It is possible to show, however, that in most instances it is not.[20]

20. John T. Wenders and R. Ashley Lyman, "An Analysis of the Benefits and Costs of Seasonal-Time-of-Day Electricity Rates," in M. A. Crew, ed., *Problems in Public Utility Economics Regulation* (Lexington, Mass.: D. C. Heath, 1979), chap. 5, pp. 73–91. John T.

Time-of-use pricing really has two aspects, of which time of day is only one. The other is seasonal pricing under which prices do not vary over the day but are set uniformly higher during peak, usually summer, seasons and lower during off-peak, winter, seasons. Seasonal pricing is necessarily a second-best proposition, but it has the virtue of being costless to implement because it does not require the additional metering costs necessary to effect TOD pricing. TOD and seasonal pricing are connected in the sense that economists cannot determine the additional benefits to TOD pricing—the additional distortions to efficiency eliminated by such pricing—until optimal seasonal prices have been set.

Thus assessing the desirability of TOD pricing on efficiency grounds involves a two-step procedure. First, regulators must set optimal seasonal prices. Such prices should be set to minimize the remaining distortions in the peak and off-peak TOD periods of each season. Any single price for the whole day will distort economic efficiency by failing to follow the TOD pattern of marginal costs. The goal of optimal season pricing is to set this single price so as to minimize the remaining distortions. After the optimal price is set in each season, then planners can weigh the additional gains from going to TOD prices against the additional metering costs of charging such prices. Here the additional gains to TOD pricing are the distortions remaining after the optimal seasonal prices have been set.

Two outcomes of this procedure are important for assessing whether or not the failure of present electricity prices to follow TOD costs is justified. First, even the most conservative efforts to quantify the benefits and costs of TOD pricing show that such pricing is of clear net benefit for the largest customers who are concentrated primarily in the industrial and larger commercial classes. Indeed, it is quite possible that TOD pricing is of net benefit for even the top 30–40 percent of the residential and small commercial classes.[21] In any event if TOD

Wenders and R. Ashley Lyman, "Determining the Optimal Penetration of Time-of-Day Electricity Tariffs," *Electric Ratemaking* 1 (1982):15–20. These references explain in detail the theory behind the assessment of the benefits and costs of seasonal-time-of-day pricing.

21. The most conservative assessment of the net benefits of time-of-day pricing for residential customers concludes that only the top few percent of customers in the residential class would pass a benefit-cost test. See Douglas W. Caves, Laurits R. Christensen, Wallace E. Hendricks, and Phillip E. Schoech, "Cost-Benefit Analysis of Residential Time of Use Rates: A Case Study for Four Illinois Utilities," *Electric Ratemaking* 1 (1982–1983):40–46. Because the authors excluded capital costs from their marginal cost calculations and used only a short-

pricing were instituted for only large customers whom it clearly benefits, the typical result would be TOD prices for less than 1 percent of the utilities' customers, who are, though, responsible for over 50 percent of the utility's load.

Second, optimal seasonal pricing is costless, and therefore no economic reason exists for failing to set such optimal seasonal prices. Yet seasonal differentials are absent in many utilities' tariff schedules, and those that do exist are far short of the optimal differential in seasonal prices. For example, for one utility the summer peak and off-peak marginal costs were 15.5 and 1.8 cents/kwh respectively, and 4.1 and 2.0 cents/kwh respectively in the winter. Estimated optimal season prices were 8.8 and 3.1 cents/kwh; far different from the 3.26 and 2.26 cents/kwh the utility charged.[22] The same kind of results prevail in every situation in which I have investigated the relative benefits and costs of TOD pricing.

Thus the failure of almost all utilities to use reasonable TOD tariffs cannot be due to a rational judgment of the benefits and costs of such a policy. Even if cost-to-benefit calculations led to a rejection of TOD prices on benefit-cost grounds, the same calculus would lead to implementing optimal seasonal prices. Since such seasonal prices are either absent or far from optimal in every utility I know of, we can only conclude that pricing policies are based on factors other than economic efficiency.

My earlier explanation of the observed subsidies and cross-subsidies cannot explain the absence of TOD pricing. After all, as I have shown, political pricing results in prices and revenues being too low for all electric power customers, and within these customer classes most benefits flow to the residential class. This outcome stems from the fact that regulators find it advantageous to redistribute income from the few to the many in the case of electric power. But an optimal implementation plan for TOD pricing would also involve instituting such pricing for the largest customers—industrial and commercial, the same ones who proved weakest in the taxation-by-regulation game.

The only other explanation for the failure to implement any kind

---

run elasticity of demand, I feel that their conclusion is unduly conservative. In any event, it does not change my conclusion that full time-of-day rates would be beneficial for all large commercial and industrial customers.

22. Wenders and Lyman, "An Analysis of the Benefits and Costs," p. 85.

of peak-load pricing consistent with the regulators' pro-residential customer bias is that peak-load pricing was perceived as being anti-residential, because the residential class consumes a higher proportion of electricity in the peak periods.

Peltzman's extension of Stigler's work on regulation provides one explanation of this phenomenon.[23] Consider a regulatory agency trying to increase prices to two groups of customers in such a way that opposition is minimized. Opposition from the two groups must be equated at the margin. This in turn means that the price increase must be shared in some way, even when normal competitive conditions would not require it, because only in this way can the opposition from the two groups continue to be equated at the margin. Thus a tendency exists for price structures to suppress cost differences and produce the kind of rate averaging so common in utility rate structures.

Whether or not Peltzman's explanation holds for the case of peak-off-peak pricing is open to question. After all peak and off-peak customers are typically not different customers. My explanation for the failure to implement time-differentiated pricing is much more straightforward and possibly consistent with the Peltzman result. Time-differentiated pricing has not been implemented simply because it serves no purpose in the subsidize and cross-subsidize game that drives electric utility pricing. One can envision a set of marginal conditions that determine the extent to which regulators can appropriate intramarginal rents and redistribute them to the electric utility's customers, and the extent to which they can spread cross-subsidies among the various customer classes. If these conditions can be satisfied with traditional, simple pricing arrangements, why go to the trouble of introducing complex time-differentiated tariffs that have no payoff in the real regulatory game of redistributing income?

It is often reasoned that the failure of the electric power industry to employ time-of-use pricing results from the desire of the utilities to expand their invested capital or to gold-plate their rate base. There are two problems with this explanation. First, why should regulators allow this if it is in their interest to keep electric prices as low as possible? Second, since flatter load curves require the construction of more capital-intensive base-load generating facilities, it may not be

23. Peltzman, "Toward a More General Theory," 1976.

true that more capacity automatically means more investment and a higher rate base. In fact the opposite may be true.[24]

A CASE IN POINT: THE PACIFIC NORTHWEST'S ELECTRIC POWER INDUSTRY

The fact that the electric power industry has been heavily regulated and insulated from most internal competitive forces has important implications for the way this industry has developed over the past few decades. Isolation from competition and a concern for politics implies not only economic inefficiency and a tendency toward income distribution, as I have discussed above, but it also weakens the ability of the industry to manage its affairs in a technically efficient manner. In a world of politics where the penalties for technical inefficiency are reduced, the ability to produce efficiently, forecast demand, and understand the subtleties of the marketplace begins to atrophy.

I will illustrate these points with a brief economic description of how the electric power industry developed in the Pacific Northwest over the past few decades. We shall see that the points made above have played a dominant role in producing the recent excess supply situation and financial debacles.

That the Northwest's electric power industry should have captured national attention for its inefficiency and mismanagement is ironic. The region is blessed with abundant natural hydroelectric resources that political influences have used to produce the lowest electricity prices in the nation. Yet the failure to realize that these abundant and cheap sources of electric power are no longer marginal, together with the politics of electricity pricing, have produced the local industry's present disarray. The Northwest's electric power industry ignored, and continues to ignore, several fundamental laws of economics. Its pervasive regulation and government ownership, in which politics dominate markets, allows this. Yet these laws of economics continue to surface as much as the industry would like to bury them.

Failure to Set Prices at the Margin

No more important proposition in economics exists than the one that, under competition, prices will tend to equal the cost of production at

---

24. See John T. Wenders, "Peak Load Pricing in the Electric Utility Industry," *Bell Journal of Economics* 7 (1976):232–41.

the margin. Further, economists can show that under this marginal-cost pricing rule, static economic efficiency is maximized. Under competition what is, is also what ought to be.

Electric power in the Northwest has been dominated for decades by the Bonneville Power Administration (BPA), a federal agency created in 1937 to market and transmit electric power from Bonneville Dam.[25] Over the years its authority has expanded to cover the transmission and marketing from all federal dams in the Northwest; as late as 1978 these dams had a capacity of 16,441 megawatts (mw) that produced about 54 percent of the region's kilowatt hours.

Until the 1960s the region was able to supply almost all of its power demands from these hydroelectric sources. But by then it was becoming obvious that opportunities for obtaining additional power from cheap hydro sources had been exhausted and that the margin of the system had moved to thermal-generated power. BPA and over a hundred other local public and private utilities entered into an agreement that BPA was to develop the remaining hydro-peaking potential from its dams, and the other utilities were to build the new thermal-power base-load generating plants needed to meet projected demand. BPA was to build the transmission capacity to meet these projected power demands. By 1978 approximately 21 percent of the region's capacity was thermal.[26]

BPA's charter from the federal government requires it to continue the long-standing regulatory tradition of setting prices equal to, but no higher than, embedded average costs. Because the embedded cost of hydro—when the margin of production has moved to thermal power—is far less than marginal cost, this policy resulted in severe underpricing of electric power in the Northwest. The residential-consumer dominance of this regulatory process is demonstrated by BPA's charge to set power rates sufficiently low "to encourage widespread use of electric energy and provide the lowest possible rates to consumers consistent with sound business principles."[27] Such is the regulatory mechanism for capturing the intramarginal rents that would

25. For a description of the Northwest's power industry and an analysis of the marginal versus average cost question, see Yvonne Levy, "Pricing Federal Power in the Pacific Northwest: An Efficiency Approach," *Federal Reserve Bank of San Francisco Economic Review* (1980):40–63.

26. Levy, "Pricing Federal Power," p. 44.

27. Quoted in Levy, "Pricing Federal Power," p. 49.

have accrued to the owners of hydroelectric sites in a competitive market.

The result was that in 1979 BPA was selling wholesale power— which makes up about one-half the cost of downstream retail power— for about .412 cents/kwh when the marginal cost of this power was about 3.13 cents/kwh.[28] In the Northwest the average retail price of electric power in 1960 was 58 percent of the national average. In 1970 it was 62 percent of the national average, and in 1980 it was 47 percent.[29] Table 9–5 compares the Northwest's residential electricity rates with those from other parts of the United States. No wonder the average residential electricity consumption in the Northwest is almost twice the national average.[30]

By the end of 1984, the BPA expects the long-run marginal cost of its electricity to be about 4.06 cents/kwh.[31] In 1983 utilities paid 1.8 cents/kwh for this wholesale power, and this is expected to rise to 2.28 cents/kwh by 1985.[32] Underpricing electric power continues in the Northwest.

Failure to Consider Demand Elasticity

Until the late 1960s the average real price of electricity fell steadily, and demand continued to grow at about 7 percent per year (see Figure 9–1). These were the halcyon days of the electric power industry nationally and in the Northwest. Coupling this economic environment with the general insulation from market forces that regulation and government ownership gave the electric power industry produced the widespread belief that the demand for electricity was very insensitive

---

28. Levy, "Pricing Federal Power," p. 48.

29. Pacific Northwest Utilities Conference Committee, *Participant Handbook, Model Input Workshop, October 17–18, 1983*, (Portland, Ore., 1983), p. 59.

30. For example, in 1979 the states with the three lowest average residential electricity prices were Washington (1.53 cents/kwh), Idaho (2.30 cents), and Oregon (2.47 cents). At the same time that the national average annual residential consumption was 8,833 kwh, these states had three of the four highest average annual residential consumptions in the nation (17,175 kwh, 15,035 kwh, and 14,182 kwh respectively). The fourth was Tennessee, where prices have been subsidized by the Tennessee Valley Authority. See Electricity Consumers Resource Council, *State Electricity Profiles* (Washington, D.C., 1981).

31. Calculated by the author from Bonneville Power Administration, *Time Differentiated Long Run Incremental Cost Analysis* (Portland, Ore.: BPA, WA-83-FS-BPA-06, 1983), p. 41.

32. Jim Camden, "BPA Chief about to Set New Regional Rates," *Spokesman Review*, Spokane, Wash., 25 Sept. 1983, p. B1.

Table 9–5.   Comparative Residential Electricity Rates (cents/kwh for 1,000 kwh, May 1982).

Utility	Residential Electricity Rate
Northwest	
Snohomish (WA) PUD	2.7 cents/kwh
Seattle City Light	1.5
Clark (WA) PUD	3.2
Washington Water Power	2.2
Portland General Electric	3.4
Pacific Power & Light (OR)	2.9
Montana Power	3.2
Idaho Power	3.1
Remainder of United States	
Los Angeles DWP	7.2
Public Service of Oklahoma	5.1
Houston Lighting	8.2
Tampa Electric	6.3
Georgia Power	5.2
Consolidated Edison	10.9
Boston Edison	10.5

SOURCE: Northwest Power Planning Council, *Northwest Energy News* 1, no. 8 (December 1982): 15.

to price. This meant that forecasts could be made independent of electricity prices. As I have observed, there is no question—due to the relative fixity of the complementary stock of appliances (including housing)—that the short-run price elasticity of demand for electricity is rather low, probably on the order of −.1 to −.2. But over the longer term, as the stock of electricity-using appliances turns over, and the energy-use character of buildings changes, the price sensitivity of electricity demand becomes much higher, probably on the order of −1.0.[33]

Failing to adequately consider the price sensitivity of electricity demand was not the only reason for the overly optimistic forecasts of electricity demand in the country, but it was probably the major cause. Nor was the demand overestimation confined to the Northwest. For the United States as a whole, in every year for at least the past decade, forecasts of demand exceeded realized demand.[34] Given this back-

33. Taylor, "Demand for Electricity."
34. Electric Power Research Institute, *Journal* (December 1982):11.

Figure 9–1.   BPA Power Rates, 1937–1983.

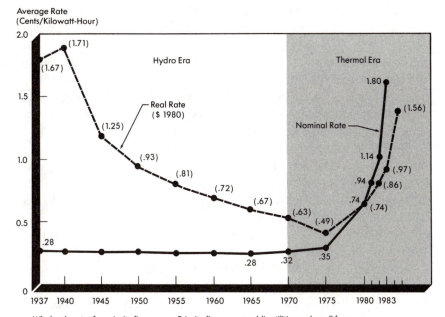

Wholesale rates for priority firm power. Priority firm serves public utilities and small farm and residential customers of private utilities.

"Real" dollars have been adjusted for inflation. All figures based on 1980 dollars. "Nominal" dollars have not been adjusted for inflation.

SOURCE: Northwest Power Planning Council, *Northwest Energy News* 1 (no. 9, January/ February 1983):29.

ground, it is easy to see how a commitment to building base-load units, which require a lead time of a decade or more, proved a disaster.

In the Northwest the Washington Public Power Supply System (WPPSS) was to be the major supplier of projected base-load thermal capacity. WPPSS was a cooperative venture of eighty-eight municipally owned and government-supported cooperative retail power companies. In essence, because of the below-cost electric power prices in the region and the failure to adequately consider the effect of price increases on forecasted demand, WPPSS was caught in the following trap: Price was set equal to the average embedded cost of electricity, rather than the higher marginal cost. Consumption was growing at the rate of 7 percent annually. The utilities could only meet rising consumption by building long lead-time thermal base-load units at higher than average cost and price. Then cost overruns and mismanagement raised the cost of the new thermal plants above earlier estimates. As the cost of the new thermal plants was averaged in with the cheaper hydro power, electricity prices rose. The run up in energy prices drove the cost of operating even older thermal-generating units up. Rising electricity prices did not affect demand forecasts that were motivating thermal-plant construction, but these higher prices did affect actual demand. A gap widened between forecasted capacity and consumption. The result? The so-called WPPSS (or whoops!) fiasco.

The broad outlines of what happened to WPPSS were headlines in the financial media for almost a year. Five nuclear power plants had been planned that would meet the region's power demand to the year 2000 at an estimated cost of $4 billion. At the present time WPPSS has defaulted on $2.25 billion in loans and presently owes $24 billion on the five plants, none of which were in operation by the middle of 1984 and two of which have been permanently abandoned.[35]

Other factors also contributed to the WPPSS problem, of course, but they were not the major cause of this debacle. The root cause was the Northwest power community's attempt to defy some basic laws of economics. Laws that operate regardless of any wishful-thinking attempt to repeal them.

Consumer Dominance

The previous sections have emphasized the residential-consumer dominance of traditional state regulation in the electric power industry. In the Northwest, where government-supported utilities—municipals and cooperatives—produce about three-fourths of the electric power, residential-consumer dominance is even more pronounced. These electric utilities are directly controlled by their consumers, most of whom are residential.

We can get the flavor of how residential-consumers dominate decision making in the Northwest's government-supported utilities by noting what happened when WPPSS's number 4 and number 5 nuclear plants were canceled, and the eighty-eight-member utilities were left to pay off the debt. That obligation amounted to about $24 per

35. *Idahonian/Palouse Empire News,* 9 March 1984, p. 8.

customer per month.[36] For most of the participating utilities, this amounted to far less than 1 cent per kwh. Of course no one would want to take on such an obligation voluntarily, but no question exists that the obligation could have been paid off with a minimum of hardship. Adding $24 to the monthly bills of local ratepayers would not even have brought their bills up to the national average.

Controlled by the residential consumers, the public utilities who made up WPPSS responded by simply refusing to pay their debt obligations. Instead they immediately went to the courts. The courts, in turn, revealed an unwillingness to raise electricity prices by invalidating the "take or pay" clauses that obligated the utilities for WPPSS's debts. As a backup position, these same utilities were prepared to file for bankruptcy, and one, Orcas, in fact did on the grounds that the elasticity of demand for power was so elastic that there was no way an additional $24 per month could be raised from consumers! Given the height of electricity bills current elsewhere in the United States, this argument is ludicrous. Even if the elasticity of demand for electricity usage were very high so that no additional revenue could be raised by increasing usage rates, this does not mean that such revenues could not be raised by increasing the flat monthly (or customer) charge, the price elasticity of which is virtually zero.[37]

The refusal of the WPPSS participating utilities to meet their debt obligations, and the legal support the region's courts gave this position is merely another example of the consumers' dominance in the regulatory and government-ownership framework of the United States electric power industry.

The Bonneville Power Administration is presently $687 million behind on its payments to the federal Treasury on its $7.3 billion debt. About two-thirds of this results from falling behind on repayment of debt incurred to finance hydroelectric projects; the remaining third is interest, operation, and maintenance costs that have not been covered by revenues. Clearly, the BPA not only has its rates set below marginal cost, but they are even below current short-run operating costs. Yet when the Reagan Administration proposed that BPA rates be raised sufficiently to cover the cost of operations plus debt repayment, the

36. Calculated by the author from *Clearing Up: A Weekly Report to Northwest Utilities*, 51, 6 May 1983, pp. 11–13.

37. See John T. Wenders, "Two-Part Tariffs and the 'Spiral of Impossibility' in the Market for Electricity," *Energy Journal* 5 (1984):177–79.

Northwest's political community went into apoplexy. All kinds of disastrous predictions were made for the region's economy, even though the proposal would have raised the electricity bill for an all-electric home by $24 per month, to about 57 percent of the national average.[38]

So long as this situation exists, electric power in the Northwest and elsewhere will continue to be priced far below marginal cost, producing a continuing massive misallocation of resources in one of the most important energy industries in our economy.

CONCLUSION

My general thesis in this chapter is that electric power has been priced below marginal cost and that this underpricing has been greatest for the residential class of customers. This result is contrary to the findings from the few other studies that have addressed these same issues. Jordan reviewed studies by Stigler and Friedland, Jackson, and Moore.[39] From these he concluded:

> Taken together, these three studies indicate that regulation has had a limited effect on lowering electric utility rates, and that most of its benefits have been enjoyed by commercial and industrial customers rather than the more numerous residential customers. . . . With regards to price levels, if regulation has had any effect on electric utilities, it has been limited, slow in developing, and mainly in favor of large consumers who already possess significant market power.[40]

Similarly, Primeaux and Nelson found that "price discrimination does exist in the rate structure of private electric utilities, and that this discrimination favors industrial customers relative to commercial and residential users; the latter two groups are treated equally."[41]

38. See Northwest Power Planning Council (NPPC), "B.P.A. Behind on Debt Payments," *Northwest Energy News* 5, no. 4 (April 1983), p. 4; Jim Camden, "N.W. Power Rate Shock Is Feared," *Spokesman Review*, Spokane, Wash., 16 Jan. 1985, p. 8; "Bonneville Power Debt," *Lewiston Tribune*, Lewiston, Idaho, 8 March 1985, p. 9B.

39. George J. Stigler and Claire Friedland, "What Can the Regulators Regulate? The Case of Electricity," *Journal of Law and Economics* 5 (1962):1; Raymond Jackson, "Regulation and Electric Utility Rate Levels," *Land Economics* 45 (1969):372; Thomas Gale Moore, "The Effectiveness of Regulation on Electric Utility Prices," *Southern Economic Journal* 36 (1970):365.

40. William A. Jordan, "Producer Protection, Prior Market Structure, and the Effects of Government Regulation," *Journal of Law and Economics* 15 (1972):156, 163.

41. Walter J. Primeaux, Jr., and Randy A. Nelson, "An Examination of Price Discrimination and Internal Subsidization by Electric Utilities," *Southern Economic Journal* 47 (July 1982):84–99.

Several reasons could account for these variant results. First of all the data used in the present analysis are concentrated in the late 1970s, when the industry was experiencing unprecedented general inflation, rapidly rising energy costs, and high marginal costs of capital. Thus the economic conditions differed significantly from those that prevailed over the much longer and earlier time periods analyzed in these other studies. It is possible that the conclusions I draw from my data merely show how the regulatory process has reacted to the somewhat unique conditions of the late 1970s. On the other hand I see no reason why the political process should suddenly begin behaving differently than it has in the past.

Second, except for Primeaux and Nelson, the conclusions these earlier studies reached came largely from looking only at the prices the various customer classes paid. It might be noted that the conclusions I drew about cross-subsidy from looking at marginal price data were consistent with the conclusions from these earlier studies. As I have indicated above, I do not think that we can learn much about the cross-subsidy issue just by looking at prices since such an approach implicitly presumes that the costs of production are the same for all customer classes. This is simply not true; for example, the residential class systematically concentrates its usage during peak periods when electricity is most costly to produce.[42]

Finally the cost data available to me are simply better suited to the questions asked. One result of the general inflation of the 1970s and the run-up in all energy prices was that electric utility regulators began to demand much more sophisticated cost support in rate cases. This in turn led to the development of sensible marginal costing methodologies that produced the kind of data employed in my analysis. If comparable data on costs and prices had been available for earlier periods analyzed by these other studies, I would expect that they would arrive at the same general conclusions about at least the cross-subsidy issue as presented in this chapter.

---

42. Primeaux and Nelson use the price-to-marginal-cost ratio as a measurement of subsidy to reach their conclusion that the industrial class has received favored treatment. As I have argued above, I do not think this is the appropriate measure of cross-subsidy. In addition Primeaux and Nelson allocated capacity costs to customer classes in proportion to their contribution to total kwh demand. A proper allocation of such costs would have done so based on contribution to peak demand, a procedure that would have properly attributed more costs to the residential and commercial classes and less to the industrial class, which would probably have reversed their conclusions.

The consumer-dominance conclusion would be much harder to test during these earlier periods since strict marginal cost pricing might very well have underrecovered revenue requirements for classic natural-monopoly reasons. Then at least some prices would have been above marginal cost even if only competitive rates of return were being allowed to the utilities. A consumer or producer dominance test would then have hinged on a determination of whether or not utilities earned monopoly or competitive rates of return. But such a task would face insuperable accounting and rate-base valuation questions. In the end, any dominance hypothesis about these earlier periods might be untestable with available data.

10

THE PERFORMANCE OF UTILITY COMMISSIONS

Peter Navarro

Before the Arab oil embargo in 1973, the public utility commissions that regulate virtually all U.S. investor-owned electric utility companies were sleepy backwaters where few toiled and few taxpayer dollars were spent. That peace was broken by a series of shocks, beginning in the late 1960s, that drastically changed the dynamics of the electric utility industry and its regulators. The first of these shocks is the precipitous rise in the rate of inflation brought about primarily by Lyndon B. Johnson's spending on social programs at the time that the nation carried the heavy financial burden of the Vietnam War. Combined with Treasury and Federal Reserve policies, this refusal to trade butter for guns sent the United States—and later the world—economy on a roller-coaster ride. Inflation hit the electric utility industry hard. Its capital costs ratcheted upward, and in the face of large government budget deficits, money grew hard to come by.[1]

The next shock was the rise of consciousness about the environment. Following the publication of Rachel Carson's *Silent Spring,* United States' citizens became much more aware of spreading environmental pollution. The then-considerable pollution coal- and oil-fired utility power plants emitted came under scrutiny, and in re-

---

1. Douglas Anderson, *Regulatory Policies and Electric Utilities* (Boston: Auburn House, 1981), pp. 48–51.

sponse to newly aroused public awareness, legislators enacted the Clean Air Act. That act and subsequent amendments, coupled with rules stipulated by the Environmental Protection Agency, required the utility industry to install sophisticated and expensive pollution-control technologies and in some cases forced utilities to burn cleaner—though more expensive—fuels. These regulations raised the cost of building and operating a power plant by as much as 25 percent.[2]

The magnitude of these first two shocks was dwarfed, however, by the third—the Arab oil embargo of 1973–74. A fourfold increase in petroleum prices hit all utilities, but petroleum-dependent electricity generators were devastated. Just a few years before many utility companies had converted their coal burners to oil in an effort to meet tighter emissions standards. Now their oil dependency made them particularly vulnerable to economic turmoil in the world oil market.

To escape the stranglehold of tough emissions standards and avoid the blows of OPEC price hikes, some utilities embarked on ambitious schemes to build nuclear power plants. Then came the fourth shock: greatly tightened nuclear power plant safety standards. This increased the cost of operating plants by setting higher safety standards and requiring substantial retrofitting of existing plants. Moreover the costs of plants under construction went through the roof. In 1972 building a nuclear plant cost $208 per kilowatt hour; by 1982 the cost had shot to $966 per kwh.[3] The demand for labor, materials, and equipment all soared, and so the costs of these inputs rose dramatically.

These shocks, combined with the fact that utilities had exhausted their economies of scale, meant that the economics of electricity generation had changed forever. The cost of producing electricity seemed to rise monthly.

As a result, public utility commissions were abruptly shaken and urged to respond to the changes around them. While before this period years might pass before a utility filed for a rate change—and at that, it might have filed for a decrease because costs had been steadily falling—now utility companies were coming to their PUCs often to file for rate hikes that never seemed to be enough to match rising costs. This has been the pattern of the past decade or so. Utilities' costs are outrunning their revenue, partly because of the failure

2. *Electric Utility Week,* 26 December 1983, p. 4.
3. Atomic Industrial Forum. Personal communication, September 1984.

of the regulatory commissions to adjust to the industry's changed circumstances.

RANKING THE REGULATORS

For a variety of political, institutional, and ideological reasons, PUCs have been "suppressing" rates. That is, despite their regulatory mandate to allow utilities in their jurisdictions to earn a fair and reasonable rate of return, they often deny utilities that opportunity. If we consider that the Supreme Court has interpreted "fair and reasonable" to mean that the utilities must be allowed the chance to earn their cost of capital on both existing and new investment, we can say that any PUC that does not allow utilities to earn their market cost of capital is practicing rate suppression.[4]

Since 1973 rate suppression has been more the rule than the exception. Economists Eugene Brigham and Dilip Shome have estimated that the utility industry as a whole should have been allowed to earn a return on equity of some 14 percent during the period 1973 to 1980; the actual average allowed return for that period, however, was only 13 percent.[5] Several causes result in rate suppression. The most obvious is when—for political or ideological reasons—PUC commissioners purposely set the allowed rate of return below the utility's market cost of capital. Some PUCs have done just that.

Other factors can cause a utility's earnings to fall short of its market cost of capital, even if the PUC does allow the company an opportunity to earn those costs. Chief among them is regulatory lag. The rate-making process is far from instantaneous. For a utility to raise its rates, it must first make a formal request, which is handled through courtlike proceedings. The time between filing for a rate hike and actually having it granted is the lag time. Rate-making formulas typically do not include a calculation to allow for inflation. When regulatory lag is long—as it is in many states—the utility loses out on the potential earnings during the rate-setting process, and then inflation erodes the real value of any eventual increase. Keep in mind that combined with an allowed rate of return already below the utility's market cost of capital, regulatory lag can lead to an actual return that

4. The relevant cases are *Bluefield Co.* v. *Public Service Commission,* 262 U.S. 679, 1922, and *Federal Power Commission* v. *Hope Natural Gas Co.,* 320 U.S. 59, 1944.

5. Eugene F. Brigham and Dilip F. Shome, "Equity Risk Premiums in the 1980s," (unpublished), and the Edison Electric Institute.

is far less than what the utility needs in order to be financially healthy.

On the surface rate suppression seems to benefit consumers, whose rates are being held down. As I will discuss later, however, no one benefits from rate suppression in the long run because it affects utility executives' decisions. Those decisions in turn affect the long-term reliability and cost of electricity. Any threat to what has so far been a reliable, affordable supply of electrical power should concern consumers and the nation as a whole.

Investors, and those who advise them, keep a watchful eye on the regulatory treatment utility companies receive; they of course want to invest only in those companies that promise a good return. Accordingly a number of Wall Street investment firms have formalized the way they evaluate the riskiness of investing in an electric utility company. To sort out utilities by degree of risk, investment firms such as Goldman Sachs, Duff & Phelps, and Valueline use the notion of regulatory climate to describe the overall regulatory treatment PUCs give the utility companies in their jurisdictions. Then they can recommend for or against investment in a utility company depending on its PUC's rating.

While minor differences show up among the twenty or so firms that rank the PUCs (some use a scale from A through E and some, from 1–3 to 1–5), each uses a similar method to identify the "very favorable," the "favorable," and the "unfavorable" commissions from the viewpoint of the investor. The rankings are based on six objective criteria: (1) the allowed rate of return on common stock, (2) the average regulatory lag, (3) whether a historical or future test year is used, (4) whether construction work-in-progress is allowed in the rate base or, alternatively, whether an allowance for funds used during construction is computed, (5) whether the tax benefits from accelerated depreciation and investment tax credits are "normalized" so that they produce some benefit to the firm or flowed through to the ratepayer, and (6) whether an automatic adjustment clause is in effect.

The logic of these criteria is perhaps transparent. In general the higher the rate of return a PUC allows on utility stock, the higher a utility's profit. A short lag time preserves the value of earnings by minimizing the erosive effect of inflation. Rate-making formulas that use a future rather than a historic test year also shield the utility's real earnings by recognizing and taking into account the effects of inflation. If regulatory lag is necessarily long, a PUC can help the utilities in its jurisdiction by giving them interim rate relief. That is, a PUC may stipulate that a utility company can temporarily raise its rate by a certain amount—say, a percentage of the rate hike sought—until the rate case can be formally assessed. At that point the PUC can make adjustments for rates that are too high or, as is more likely, too low.

The allowance of construction work in progress (CWIP) in the rate base affects the quality of earnings more than the level of earnings. Let's say a utility is building a plant for $5 million. Its PUC has the choice of: (1) allowing part of the construction costs into the rate base as the project progresses under CWIP or, (2) waiting until the facility is up and running before including it *and* an accrued allowance in rate calculations under the accounting convention called allowance for funds used during construction (AFUDC). While the earnings are said to be equal on a net present-value basis, in the latter case, cash payments are deferred. Investors typically prefer immediate cash returns to earnings that will be realized in the future and appear only on paper.

Investors view tax benefits similarly. They favor the PUCs that allow utilities to use accelerated depreciation and investment tax credits to boost cash flow in the early years over those that stipulate that tax benefits must be flowed through to ratepayers.

Automatic fuel adjustment clauses (FACs) and purchased power adjustment clauses (PACs) allow the utility to immediately adjust its rates to account for a sudden rise in its costs for fuel or purchased power. FACs and PACs are widely used, but some allow only partial recovery of rising costs. Also some PUCs require a hearing first. For obvious reasons investors like clauses that allow immediate and full-cost recovery. They also prefer a fair-value rate base to an original-cost base, again because the former lessens the damaging effects of inflation.

Based on these criteria, we can come up with a mix of policies that would command a "very favorable" rating from the Wall Street community. A PUC that investors find attractive would set a relatively high allowed rate of return and would use CWIP in the rate base. It would process rate cases speedily, provide for interim rate relief, use normalized accounting and a future test year, have automatic adjustment clauses, and use a fair-value rate base.

In an investor's nightmare, though, a PUC would have a low allowed rate of return to begin with. It would also let rate cases drag on for many months and deny the utility company any interim relief. It would look back in time for costs to include in the rate base rather

Table 10–1.   Regulatory Climate Rankings of State Public Utility Commissions.

Very Favorable	Favorable	Unfavorable
Arizona	Arkansas	Alabama
Florida	Colorado	California
Hawaii	District of Columbia	Connecticut
Indiana	Idaho	Georgia
New Mexico	Illinois	Iowa
North Carolina	Kansas	Louisiana
Texas	Maryland	Maine
Utah	Michigan	Massachusetts
Wisconsin	Minnesota	Mississippi
	Nevada	Missouri
	New Hampshire	Montana
	New Jersey	North Dakota
	New York	Rhode Island
	Ohio	South Dakota
	Oklahoma	West Virginia
	Oregon	
	Pennsylvania	
	South Carolina	
	Vermont	
	Virginia	
	Washington	
	Wyoming	

than using a future test year. This PUC would deter compensation for construction costs until the plant was up and running and would pass any tax benefits on directly to ratepayers. And if purchased power or fuel prices suddenly shot through the ceiling, the utility would have to patiently file a rate case and await a verdict, and then the rate base would be figured on an original-cost basis.

Table 10–1 shows a composite of the rankings of five investment firms for a representative year: Goldman Sachs, Salomon Brothers, Valueline, Merrill Lynch, and Duff & Phelps. We can view how the financial community ranks PUCs as a measure of both the regulatory risk a utility is exposed to in a given PUC jurisdiction and, collaterally, the return that that utility can be expected to earn.

REGULATORY CLIMATE AND THE COST OF CAPITAL

Research has confirmed what the financial community has long known: The more unfavorable the regulatory climate, the higher a utility's cost of both debt and equity capital. And regulatory climate affects the availability of both debt and equity capital. The link between regulatory climate and the cost of debt capital is direct. Electric utilities typically borrow debt capital in the long-term bond market, and the relative cost of that capital—manifested by interest rates—is determined by their bond ratings. Because roughly half of all new investment in the electric utility industry is financed through borrowed funds raised by selling bonds (the other half is financed primarily through equity funds, including both the issuance of new stock and the use of retained earnings), higher costs for borrowed money carry great ramifications.

Thus it is not surprising that the cost of debt capital is tied to regulatory climate. In general people and institutions allow others to use their money only if they believe such use will render them a profit. Although most investments involve some degree of risk, the degree varies. In order to attract capital, riskier ventures must offer the promise of earning a higher average rate of return. Therefore when a company that looks like a risky investment needs to borrow money, it must offer to pay a higher return on that money than would a company seen as a safer investment. In the case of borrowed funds, that higher return takes the form of higher interest rates.

To raise money utilities regularly sell bonds through Wall Street investment houses at interest rates that vary according to their bond ratings. Those ratings are set by Wall Street firms, of which Moody's and Standard and Poor's are the most influential bond raters. These ratings signal investors about a utility's capacity to pay its debt; ratings are based on factors including the utility's expected rate of return and its coverage ratio (the ratio of the company's earnings before interest and taxes to its interest charges for the period), factors that are heavily dependent on PUC regulatory treatment.

For example, the more a utility is expected to earn, the more funds it is likely to have to service its debt with and thus the less risky it will be to investors. Similarly a higher coverage ratio means that the utility has a larger cushion of earnings to pay its debt; again, that means less risk. The relation of these factors to rate suppression is clear: When a utility operates in a rate-suppressive regulatory environment, its expected return and its coverage ratio tend to be lower, which makes the utility a riskier investment.

Wall Street characterizes bond ratings as high quality, investment grade, substandard, or speculative. They range from the lowest risk, highest quality, investment-grade AAA category to the higher risk, substandard, or speculative categories of BBB and below. In 1970 Standard & Poor's rated 120 out of 130 utilities as A or above, which placed them at investment grade or better. After a decade of rate suppression, however, utility bond ratings have slumped. In every year except one since the Arab oil embargo, more utility bonds have been downgraded than have been upgraded. The mid-1970s and early 1980s, in particular, witnessed downgradings in unprecedented numbers. According to the consulting firm of Booz, Allen & Hamilton, Standard and Poor's made one hundred more downgradings of utility bonds between 1973 and 1981 than upgradings.

Not surprisingly most of these bond deratings occurred for utilities operating in states with the most rate-suppressive PUCs. In 1978 90 percent of the utilities with Standard and Poor's ratings of A to BBB were in jurisdictions with an "unfavorable" regulatory climate, while only 13 percent of the utilities with higher quality AAA or AA ratings were regulated by PUCs ranked "unfavorable."

Today only 80 utility companies hold a rating of A or better, while the number below A has more than quadrupled (from ten to forty-seven) in the past ten years. The median in 1972 was AA; in 1983, it was A. As of September 30, 1983, of the seventy-five largest investor-owned utilities, only one company—Texas Utilities—held a AAA rating, while seven companies—Long Island Lighting Company, Public Service of Indiana, Public Service of New Hampshire, Cincinnati Gas & Electric, Dayton Power & Light, United Illuminating, and Consumers Power—held BB ratings. (LILCO's infamous financial problems center primarily around its difficulties in getting its Shoreham nuclear plant into the rate base.) Although the trend has slowed somewhat, Wall Street investment companies continue to downgrade many utilities' bond ratings, and downgradings still outnumber upgradings.

The contribution of a bond derating to the cost of capital is significant when translated into dollars and cents. Analyzing the effect of regulatory climate on the cost of debt suggests that moving the otherwise average utility from a very favorable to an unfavorable regulatory climate results in a bond derating of several steps. We can calculate the numerical effect on the cost of debt capital by consulting the latest interest costs associated with each rating.[6]

To illustrate, let's assume that a utility's bond rating fell from AAA

6. See Jeffrey A. Dubin and Peter Navarro, "Regulatory Climate and the Cost of Capital," Harvard University Discussion Paper E-82-03, April 1982.

to BBB and that the company must issue $500 million in bonds for a new coal plant. Let's also assume that the interest rate on a BBB bond is two hundred basis points higher than on a AAA bond—say, 14 percent as opposed to 12 percent. This two-percentage-point gap, which approximates the average spread witnessed over the past five years, means that the BBB-rated utility has to pay $10 million more per year in interest charges than if it were rated AAA.

But higher interest charges are not the only fallout from rate suppression because debt capital availability is also affected. Rate-suppressed utilities typically have less debt capital on tap for them. This is because the largest groups of investors in utility bonds tend to be institutions, particularly pension funds, and the Employment Retirement Income and Securities Act prohibits such investors from purchasing low-rated bonds. Low-rated utilities therefore have a shrunken pool of potential investors in which to cast their lures.

The same problem of higher capital costs arises, albeit more indirectly, when a utility issues stock to raise investment funds. The price of a stock depends primarily on the return investors expect to earn; this return comes in the form of both dividends and capital gains, and it is based on the ratio of income realized by the stock to the stock's price. An unfavorable regulatory climate affects this relationship in several ways.

First, when a utility earns an actual return lower than the expected return, the price of its stock falls. The reason is that new investors will always expect a certain return, and if the utility cannot sustain that return, then what that return is being earned on (the stock price) must fall. For example, suppose investors expect a 10-percent return on a utility stock that sells for $100. Assuming that the stock has no appreciation and that all earnings are distributed as dividends, the utility must deliver $10 in dividends to realize this return. But if it only delivers $9, the stock price will fall to $90 so that new investors would continue to realize a 10-percent return.

Second, as rate suppression increases, so does the perceived risk of investing in the utility's stock. Investors are wary of a possible further drop in stock prices and the concomitant possible capital loss to existing shareholders. This perception of increased risk raises the return that investors expect; according to a number of studies, the resultant "risk premium" adds another 100 to 200 basis points to the expected return. This higher expected return puts more downward pressure on the stock.

When the utility's stock prices are down, it must sell more shares to raise the same amount of money. Doing so upsets existing shareholders because raising funds by selling new shares of stock is almost certain to devalue or dilute the value of their shares by driving down the stock price—and hence, any potential capital gains. Disgruntled shareholders who fear a devaluation of their holdings put pressure on—and sometimes sue—management to prevent it from selling any new stock. Accordingly not only does the cost of equity capital rise but its availability declines as well.

One way to measure a stock's desirability is to look at its market-to-book ratio (M/B). The M/B ratio quantifies the relationship between the price a utility company's common stock is able to command on the market and the book value of the assets. Utilities' M/B ratios have been falling steadily, beginning in the mid-1960s. Estimates show that the M/B ratio falls 8 points and the cost of equity capital increases 228 basis points for the otherwise average utility that moves from a more to a less favorable regulatory climate.[7]

In the decades when new technologies and economies of scale continually brought the cost of producing electricity down, the interests of ratepayers and shareholders did not conflict. Now, however, they most certainly do. The situation that has emerged is a distributional struggle between the value of stock (represented by M/B ratios) and the price of electricity to consumers. As the falling M/B ratios show, consumers have been the financial victors in the distributional struggle, which PUCs mediate. Electricity rates, while rising steadily in nominal terms, have not kept pace with the true costs of generating power. The financial loss to shareholders is now evident. The long-term consequences for everyone, though severe, are thus delayed.

INVESTMENT STRATEGY UNDER RATE SUPPRESSION

Common sense might indicate that utility executives unable to get capital or having to pay dearly for it are likely to use as little of it as possible. Indeed given the reality of expensive capital in short supply, many utility executives have adopted a capital-minimization strategy whereby they hold spending down as much as they possibly can. Under such a strategy, they are likely to make decisions based only

7. Dubin and Navarro, "Regulatory Climate."

on short-term financial considerations, sometimes at the long-term expense of ratepayers. Herein lies the electric utility executive's dilemma: Utility company managers have a responsibility to shareholders to maintain the financial integrity of their holdings and to avoid undue risk to those investments, but they must, according to regulatory mandate, provide reliable, affordable power to consumers.

The utility companies' ability to meet present demand is the result of earlier ambitious construction efforts. At that time the combined factors of low capital and energy costs and increasing economies of scale led to a boom in plant construction. In the 1960s the electric utility industry—the most capital-intensive sector in the United States—spent some $62 billion on construction. Today the industry accounts for one-fifth of the nation's total construction expenditures.

While some people argue that conservation will continue to hold back increases in electricity demand, most experts predict electricity demand will grow at a rate of about 3 percent. According to a Department of Energy study, assuming demand growth at that 3 percent rate, the electric utility industry would have to build roughly 438 gigawatts of new capacity by the year 2000 to meet that need and to replace or convert current uneconomical capacity.[8]

It seems then that for the industry to fulfill its regulatory mandate to provide power in whatever quantities consumers demand, it should construct new plants and convert inefficient ones. But with capital at such high cost and often unavailable, utility managers have simply been unable or unwilling to make even the most prudent capital investments.

One way to understand the links between utilities' rates of return and their operating and investment strategies is to look at what researchers who have studied the industry have found. In 1962 Averch and Johnson devised a model in which a utility could choose some proportion of labor and capital (from unlimited supplies of both) to produce a given output of electricity.[9] They concluded that when the allowed rate of return is above the market cost of capital, the utility company will use far more capital in proportion to labor than needed to minimize its costs. In other words when capital is readily available—as it is under rate regulation that allows the utility to earn a

---

8. *The Future of Electric Power in America* (Washington, D.C.: U.S. Department of Energy, June 1983).

9. Harvey Averch and Leland Johnson, "Behavior of the Firm Under Regulatory Constraint," *American Economic Review* 52, no. 5 (December 1962): 1052.

profit—the utility will increase its use of capital relative to other inputs. Because of this so-called A-J effect, a utility earning a profit builds more plant than it needs to provide least-cost service.

Averch and Johnson studied the effect of rates of return that were higher than the market cost of capital because this phenomenon was widespread at the time they conducted their research. In the 1960s utilities commonly earned such comfortable rates of return; at that time their investment strategies, in conformity with the predictions of Averch and Johnson, included ambitious schemes for power-plant construction. Some observers called the industry's tendency to overbuild—that is, to construct more plant than was actually needed—gold-plating.

In the 1960s no one bothered to consider what utility executives would do if they earned less than the market cost of capital. If they thought about it at all, most people assumed that in such circumstances the utility company would simply close up shop. That assumption, however, is faulty. Utility companies are required by law to provide service to customers, and the industry is also characterized by large, capital-intensive power plants that have few alternative uses. Therefore utilities do not leave the electricity market just because they cannot earn a fair rate of return. What they can do is decide not to make any further capital investments. And that is, in fact, what many financially crippled utilities have decided to do.

In today's financial circumstances, utility managers have chosen what seems the only viable option: to curb any further capital investment. Squeezed by rate-suppressive regulation, utility companies have minimized their capital expenditures. Recent research shows that just as rates of return above the cost of capital lead utilities to overinvest in plant, when a utility earns less than its market cost of capital, it tends to underinvest in new capacity and other economic investments. This relationship between rate suppression and capital minimization is called the reverse A-J effect.

The years after 1973 have furnished ample evidence of the verity of the reverse A-J effect. Utilities' capital minimization strategies are demonstrated particularly well by the frequency of plant cancellations.

Many utility executives who once proclaimed the need to plan and build for projected demand have been quietly and systematically delaying or canceling many of their own construction and conversion plans. The North American Electric Reliability Council (NERC) reports that in 1979 over half of the new coal and nuclear plant capacity scheduled for 1979 through 1988 was delayed an average of almost twenty months. In 1981 and 1982 U.S. utilities canceled forty-seven major power plant projects that would have boosted capacity by 50 million kilowatts, or 8 percent.[10] From 1977 to 1982 about 140 generating units representing some 150,000 megawatts of electricity were canceled or deferred indefinitely.[11] Further no new nuclear units have been ordered since 1978, and no new orders for any major generating projects were placed in 1982.[12]

Some top utility executives might try to justify their antiinvestment strategies on the grounds of consumers' conservation efforts, but others speak to a different rationale. Charles T. Dougherty, chief executive officer of Union Electric of St. Louis, spoke of his company's decision to cancel the second unit of its Calloway nuclear plant saying that inadequate regulation made funding the unit "very unattractive in spite of the overall economic advantage."[13] South Carolina's Duke Power Company indefinitely delayed completion of its Cherokee Nuclear Station. William H. Grigg, the company's legal and financial vice-president explained: "To willingly embark upon a plan to further dilute shareholders' equity by raising new equity through the sale of common stock at below book value would in our view be unconscionable."[14] And Lelan F. Sillin, Jr., chief executive officer of Northeast Utilities, has repeatedly announced that until his utility can earn a fair rate of return on new investment, he will not sell new stock to finance either the completion of Millstone III (a 1,200-megawatt nuclear unit) or a number of coal-conversion projects.

We witness the utility companies' adoption of a capital minimization strategy not only in the torrents of delays and cancelations, but also in their increased tendency to seek sources of additional power for which they do not have to bear the investment burden. Such third-party financing includes the purchase of power from Canada and Mexico

10. "The Vicious Circle That Utilities Can't Seem to Break," *Business Week,* 23 May 1983, p. 178.

11. Atomic Industrial Forum, "Historical Profile of U.S. Nuclear Power Development," 31 December 1980, updated through November 3, 1982.

12. Scott A. Fenn, *America's Electric Utilities* (Washington, D.C.:Investor Responsibility Research Center, 1983).

13. Statement to the press, 9 October 1981.

14. Testimony before the South Carolina Public Service Commission, docket no. 80-378-E, August 1981.

as well as the cogeneration of electricity with other industrial facilities. Utility companies see such arrangements as opportunities to fulfill their mandate while avoiding the adverse financial burden of undertaking investment on their own.

While these options may seem like simple, practical solutions to the utility industry's problems, they tend to mask the problems rather than solve them. Often a newly constructed plant would generate electricity at less expense than buying that same amount of power. And because of the way prices for cogenerated power are set, cogeneration can also be more expensive than if the utility company were to build a new facility of its own.

Moreover a financially strapped utility company tends to cut its budget for operating and maintenance expenses. Doing this means that the company might at first eliminate waste and inefficiency, but once it has trimmed its fat, inadequate funding can lead to poorly maintained plants. The possible results are reduced generating efficiency and, worse, total system failure. Such potential problems are especially frightening in the case of nuclear plants.

CONSUMER WELFARE AND RATE SUPPRESSION

Although electricity consumers ostensibly benefit from capital minimization, in truth they are likely to become the biggest losers. Consumers' losses will come in the form of higher rates for less reliable service. Higher rates will result from continuing to use more expensive fuel when utilities forego plant conversion (a "fuel penalty") and from the higher cost of capital rate-suppressed utilities must face (a "cost-of-capital penalty"). Less reliable service will result directly from cutbacks in spending on the maintenance and operation of existing plants (the "reliability penalty"). By and large consumers will only begin to bear these costs when it is too late to do anything to avoid the consequences. This is so because sound long-run investment is traded off for the short-run benefits of rate suppression.

In a study I conducted for the Department of Energy under the auspices of the Energy and Environmental Policy Center at Harvard University, I compared the costs and benefits of rate suppression.[15] The

15. Peter Navarro, "Long Term Consumer Impacts of Electricity Rate Regulatory Policies," prepared for the U.S. Department of Energy, Office of Policy, Planning, and Analysis, January 1983.

aim of that study was to forecast future electricity rates and system reliability under rate suppression. The results were clear: Under plausible assumptions about fuel prices and energy demand growth, both rates and reliability will suffer if rate suppression continues.

As we can infer from the discussion so far, utility executives base their investment and operating strategies not just on the outcome of their most recent rate case but also on the regulatory treatment they expect in the future. In general a utility granted only a modest rate hike does not invest wildly in the hope that its PUC will be generous the next time a rate case is filed.

We have also seen that in the presence of rate suppression, utility executives are likely to underinvest in long-term projects necessary to keep the lights on and electricity prices as low as possible. This underinvestment in turn creates fuel, cost-of-capital, and reliability penalties. The trade-off of rate suppression, then, is that in the short run rates are lower than they otherwise would be because the PUC fails to give the utility the opportunity to earn its market cost of capital and fully recover its expenses. In the longer run, however, even if the PUC continues to hold rates below the utility's market cost of capital, rates are higher than they would have been without rate suppression. This is so because the fuel and cost-of-capital penalties will drive the utility's expenses higher than they would otherwise be.

Thus electricity rates under rate suppression start out relatively low. At some point in the future, however, they become higher than rates would be if the utility had been allowed to earn its market cost of capital. Under rate suppression, rates start low but rise more steeply than they otherwise would.

Are consumers better off paying rates that follow the path of rate suppression or that of capital attraction? In other words is it to their benefit to pay lower rates now but higher rates later (rate suppression) or to pay slightly higher rates now so that rates will be lower in the future (capital attraction)?

Figure 10–1, which plots two sets of electricity prices, provides information we can use to answer the foregoing question. Area *A* represents the dollar value of the benefits of rate suppression, and area *B* represents the extra costs of rate suppression. By comparing these two areas, we can tell whether the costs of rate suppression outweigh the benefits or vice versa. Before drawing a comparison, though, we must first make adjustments to account for the time value of money. That is, we must take into account the fact that because

Figure 10–1. Typical Time Profile of Electricity Rates in Two Regulatory Regimes

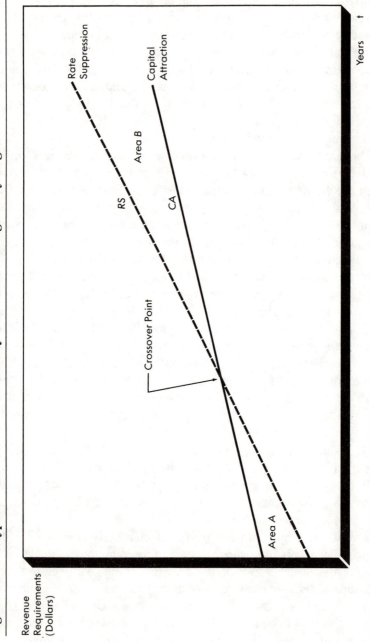

SOURCE: *Long Term Consumer Impacts of Electricity Rate Regulatory Policies*, prepared by Peter Navarro of the Harvard University Energy and Environmental Policy Center for the U.S. Department of Energy, January 1983.

of the opportunity to earn interest on one's money, one dollar today is worth more than one dollar a year from today. To convert the streams of numbers over time into two numbers representing values in terms of today's dollars, we will use net present value discounting.

To see how this tool works, suppose that the benefits of rate suppression will be $20 in the first year, $10 in the second year, and zero in the third year (the "crossover point"). At an interest rate of 10 percent per year, the net present value of these benefits will be roughly $26. On the other hand suppose the costs of rate suppression will be $10 per year in the fourth year, $20 in the fifth year, and $30 in the sixth year. At an interest rate of 10 percent, the net present value of these costs will be roughly $40. Thus in this case the dollar value of area *A* (the benefits) would be $14 less than the dollar value of area *B* (the costs), which means that consumers would be worse off in the long run.

Using this approach to the dynamics of rate suppression, I forecast future electricity rates and system reliabilities for a representative sample of the nation's utilities employing a rate-making model widely used by PUCs. I chose utilities with varied load growth, percent petroleum in the generation mix, and regional location—the three characteristics most important in determining the magnitude of the regulatory penalties. The more a utility's load is expected to grow, for instance, the more it will need additional sources of electricity. If the utility builds new plants to meet that growth, the cost-of-capital penalty will be more severe. If it, instead, purchases power at a cost above generating costs, the fuel penalty will rise. And if those additional sources of power are unavailable, the reliability penalty will increase. Similarly the greater a utility's dependence on petroleum, the greater potential it has for reducing expensive petroleum consumption. Thus the fuel penalty is higher for a utility that relies more heavily on petroleum power plants than on other fuel-fixed plants.

The six utilities are representative in that they reflect different combinations of conditions typical of the industry as a whole. They come from six regions of the country—New England, the Southeast, the Southwest, the Midwest, the Rocky Mountains, and the Pacific Coast. Their forecast load growths range from 1.5 percent to 4 percent a year, and their petroleum dependence ranges from zero to 60 percent. (Because of the political sensitivity of the rate-suppression issue with respect to ratepayers and PUCs, all the participating utilities requested anonymity.)

I asked each utility to forecast the investment program it would pursue in response to two different hypothetical regulatory climates. I described the rate-suppressive regime as a regulatory climate in which the utility could expect to earn a real (inflation-adjusted) return on common equity of 4 percent (three percentage points less than the 7-percent real return on equity utilities needed to meet their estimated market cost of capital in the last decade). The 4-percent rate of return approximates the real return the utility industry has obtained since the Arab oil embargo. I described the capital-attraction regime as a regulatory climate in which the utility would be allowed to earn a 7-percent return—its full market cost of capital.

In the rate-suppression regime each utility forecast it would continue its current strategy of holding capital expenditures as low as possible. But faced with the regulatory-reform or capital-attraction scenario, they all forecast robust programs of capital expansion.

In the capital-attraction scenario the *New England* utility, for instance, invested a total of $9.9 billion over the forecast period (to the year 2000). During the 1980s it converted over 800 megawatts of existing oil capacity to coal, and it finished on schedule the construction of a large nuclear plant. During the 1990s it also built four 600-megawatt coal plants (in which it retained two-thirds ownership) to meet projected load growth, and it retired aging plants on schedule. It used purchased power to meet a negligible portion of its peak demand.

In contrast under the rate-suppression scenario the New England utility spent only $4.1 billion. It converted less than 200 megawatts of oil capacity to coal and sold half of its share in the nuclear plant under construction in order to finance the plant's completion (rather than borrowing or issuing stock). To meet load during the 1980s, it cut back on electricity sales to outside customers. In fact by the end of the 1990s it was a net purchaser of electricity, buying power equivalent to roughly 175 megawatts of capacity, or 3 percent of its peak load. It retired none of its existing capacity.

Under the capital-attraction scenario the *Midwest* utility completed on schedule several large nuclear plants that were under construction in the 1980s. During the 1990s it built four additional coal units (totaling over 2,000 megawatts) and assumed a 75-percent share of two additional 1,100-megawatt nuclear units coming on line at the turn of the century. Finally it built an intermediate-load ("cycling") coal plant in the early 1990s. All plants were retired on schedule.

Under the rate-suppression scenario this utility delayed two-thirds of the new nuclear capacity four years so that the completion date of the last unit was pushed from 1986 to 1990. It undertook no further construction, nor was any existing plant retired, except for one small plant retired in both scenarios. To meet its load the utility more than doubled its purchased power and increased the use of its existing oil and natural gas capacity. It used more than twice as much oil and three times as much gas than in the capital-attraction scenario.

The *Southwest* utility steadily added over 5,000 megawatts of new coal capacity in 600-megawatt increments between 1982 and 1997 and added a similar amount between 1998 and 2009 in the capital-attraction scenario. It built each plant before it was needed to meet growth in demand, and the plants were used to displace natural gas consumption.

In the second scenario the utility built 2,000 megawatts less coal capacity in the time frame 1982–97, solely to meet load. At the same time it extended its existing oil and gas capacity well beyond the planned service life. By 1998 the utility was forced to undertake the construction of 6,000 megawatts of new coal capacity through the year 2009 to replace its aging plants. Between 1982 and 1990, however, its spare capacity fell dangerously low.

The pattern of investment for the *Pacific Coast, Rocky Mountain,* and *Southeast* utilities is similar. Each utility's choices of inputs differ widely for the alternative scenarios. Under the capital-attraction scenario, when the utility expects to earn its cost of capital, it chooses a considerably larger capital budget and a correspondingly smaller level of fuel and purchased power expenses than under the rate-suppression regime.

Consider, for example, the New England utility's choices. In the capital-attraction scenario it sets a $9.9 billion capital budget and spends $29.9 billion on fuel and purchased power. Under rate suppression it invests only $4.1 billion but spends more than $43.2 billion on fuel and purchased power. Similarly the Midwest utility chooses a $40.6 billion capital budget and spends $110.4 billion on fuel and purchased power in the capital-attraction scenario, but given rate suppression, it only invests $23.9 billion but then spends $139.4 billion on fuel and purchased power.

Only the Southwest utility invests more under rate suppression. The higher capital budget under rate suppression in large part reflects the higher (nominal) capital costs of the 6,000 megawatts it waits until

1998 to build. And because the utility foregoes economic gas displacement before 1998 under rate suppression, its fuel and purchased-power expenses are higher under rate suppression than under capital attraction ($201.0 billion compared with $152.1 billion).

The results of the DOE study substantiate the reverse A-J effect. Let's now see which set of investment strategies is better for consumers. To calculate the six utilities' annual electricity rates for the next two decades, I made separate sets of calculations for the two investment strategies. I utilized a rate-making model widely used among the PUCs (the regulatory-analysis model) and two different assumptions about fuel prices. The rising-fuel-price case assumed a 2-percent real annual increase in the prices of oil and natural gas and a 1-percent real annual increase in the price of coal. These assumptions are in line with forecasts from the Department of Energy, the Electric Power Research Institute, and other observers. The stable-fuel-price case assumed no increase in real fuel prices.

As expected, under rate suppression, rates were lower in the early years. Then as higher fuel costs and carrying charges accumulated, rates eventually "crossed over," typically during the mid-1980s. (This is true for both the rising and the stable-fuel-price cases.) From that point on electricity prices were consistently higher than in the capital-attraction scenario. The gap in electricity rates widened steadily so that by the year 2000 rates were much higher under rate suppression than under a capital-attraction regime. In the rising-fuel-price case electric bills to Pacific Coast utility customers were 11 percent higher; for Southeast utility ratepayers they were 33 percent higher. Note that despite these higher prices, the rate-suppressed utilities were still earning a lower return on investment.

I compared these two streams of future electricity prices by using net present value discounting. Table 10–2 shows the results. In all cases except one, consumers stand to lose money under rate suppression in the long run. In a scenario of moderately rising fuel prices, the benefits gained from capital attraction range from $242 million for the Midwest utility to $2.8 billion for the Southeast utility.

What happens to these whopping benefits when we assume fuel prices remain stable? In particular does the fuel penalty shrink to the point where rate suppression becomes worthwhile for consumers? The answer is a no. For four of the six utilities, ratepayer benefits under capital attraction still range from the hundreds of millions to billions of dollars. The New England utility, for example, saves its ratepayers

Table 10–2.   Costs to Ratepayers of Rate Suppression.

Representative Utility	Assuming Rising Fuel Costs	Assuming Stable Fuel Costs
	Net present value of benefits (millions)	Net present value of benefits (millions)
New England	$1,289	$513
Midwest	242	−279
Southwest	2,302	995
Southeast	2,840	1,555
Pacific Coast	1,530	3
Rocky Mountain	607	695

$513 million. The weakest case is the Midwest utility, which has the lowest rate of oil consumption and hence the smallest fuel penalty. With steady fuel prices its .atepayers actually lose $279 million (in a present-value sense) under an improved regulatory climate.

Besides the costs to ratepayers, I also wanted to explore the reliability of electrical power under both regulatory regimes. To assess reliability I calculated the percent of spare capacity above peak load, that is, the utilities' "reserve margins." I found dangerously low reserve margins for four of the six utilities, with the most perilous situation occurring in the Midwest. A rule of thumb in the industry is that a utility needs a 15 to 20 percent reserve margin to ensure uninterrupted service. Under rate suppression the Midwest utility's reserve margin plunged from 23 percent to a razor-thin 5 percent by the year 2000. Similarly the Southwest utility's reserve margin fell to 8 percent.

In sum, for all six utilities, lower rates for a few years in the 1980s result in dramatically higher rates over many years or far less reliable service or both. These results raise doubts about the wisdom of electricity rates that do not represent the true cost of generating power. Under rate suppression consumers lose out in terms of cost and reliability. They might also lose in other, more indirect, ways. With electricity supply uncertain manufacturers might postpone introducing productivity enhancing—but electricity-intensive—innovations. The United States as a whole could thereby miss out on the opportunity to boost its economy through increased productivity. Rate suppression also perpetuates heavy petroleum consumption, which goes against our national energy policy goal of reducing dependence on foreign—mostly Middle Eastern—oil. With continued dependence comes the prospect of increased military tension in the Middle East.

Clearly then we may all be losers when electricity rates are suppressed. Public utility commissions that lack the wherewithal (the staff, computers, and so on) to regulate more effectively or that fail to see the consequences of responding to only the immediate demands of ratepayers may be sabotaging their own efforts to ensure a reliable, affordable future of electrical power through realistic, responsive regulation of the electric utility industry. And consumers who press for rate relief without understanding the long-term implications may be setting themselves up to be unpleasantly surprised in years to come.

SUMMARY

The dynamics of electricity production have changed drastically in the past ten years or so. Yet those who regulate the electric utility industry will not or cannot adapt the way they perform their task of setting the rates of return their utilities are allowed to earn to meet the changed circumstances. For ideological, political, or institutional reasons, PUCs often practice rate suppression, which means the allowed rate of return is set below the utility's market cost of capital. An allowed rate of return that is too low, coupled with the erosive effects of inflation, can mean the actual return the utility earns will fall far short of the cost of capital.

Given this situation, utility executives are understandably reluctant to undertake even prudent investment for fear that they will never recoupe that money. They have adopted a strategy of capital minimization and so tend to forego investment in new plants and coal conversion projects and to cut back spending on maintenance.

The rate-suppression–capital-minimization syndrome in effect trades off the long-term welfare of consumers and the society as a whole for short-term rate relief. The consequences of this failure to plan for a future of reliable, affordable electrical power are severe, and we should turn our attention to reversing the current trend.

11

INFORMATION, INCENTIVES, AND REGULATION

E. C. Pasour, Jr.

"No reform can remove the bureaucratic features of the government's bureaus. . . . With regard to the performance of bureaus no method for establishing success or failure by calculation is available."[1]

Increasing evidence shows that utility regulation has reduced profitability in the electric power industry to a level below that required to sustain the quality and growth of service.[2] At the same time consumer groups and other critics contend that regulators protect poorly managed companies with cost-plus regulation that lacks efficiency incentives. Still another group of analysts, using the insights of von Mises and Hayek, stresses the implications of the information problems inherent in economic regulation. In this view even if regulators could overcome the perverse incentives inherent in bureaucratic agencies, they still could not obtain the information required to discharge their duties well. Thus no agreement exists at present on why utility regulation is failing to achieve its stated purpose.

1. Ludwig von Mises, *Bureaucracy* (New Rochelle, N.Y.: Arlington House, 1969), pp. 122–23.
2. Paul W. MacAvoy, *Regulated Industries and the Economy* (New York: W. W. Norton & Company, 1970). Paul W. MacAvoy, *Energy Policy: An Economic Analysis* (New York: W. W. Norton & Company, 1983). Peter Navarro, "Save Now, Freeze Later: The Real Price of Cheap Electricity," *Regulation* 7 (1983): 31–36. Irwin M. Stelzer, "Electric Utilities—Next Stop for Deregulators," *Regulation* 6 (1982): 29–35.

There is also disagreement about the potential for solving the political and economic problems associated with economic regulation. MacAvoy suggests that a critical step in improving performance of regulated industries is to "develop better administrative processes."[3] Economists believe current public utility regulatory practices—especially during periods of high inflation and low growth in demand—impose substantial costs on the economy due to the rigid nature of price controls, which leads to unreliable service.[4] Coase, who seems to agree with MacAvoy on improvability of utility regulation, attributes at least part of the regulatory lack of success to "economists' failures"—the inability of economists to solve economic problems involved in economic regulation.[5] Navarro, on the other hand, holds that current regulatory mechanisms "cannot function properly, given the political, institutional, and ideological environment in which public utility commissions . . . are forced to operate."[6]

This paper does not minimize the importance of leadership, ideological environment, or institutional factors in utility regulation. The focus of this analysis, however, is on implementation problems endemic in economic regulation. We have no known way to assure that regulators will attempt to develop and implement regulatory policies that benefit the public at large. Even without leadership problems and with better administrative processes, information problems are inherent in all bureaucratic regulation of economic activity. Consequently a major conclusion of this study is that even if an economic regulator were a selfless public servant dedicated to regulation to achieve the "public interest," information problems would preclude this result.

This chapter is organized into several sections. The first discusses incentive problems in economic regulation posed by the separation of authority and responsibility. Then I briefly describe the general theory of bureaucracy before relating the theory explicitly to public utility regulation. Second, the chapter analyzes information problems arising from the separation of power and knowledge and emphasizes the subjectivity of the cost and returns data that influence entrepreneurial choice. I contrast the entrepreneurial market process approach with

---

3. MacAvoy, *Regulated Industries and the Economy*, p. 122.
4. MacAvoy, *Energy Policy: An Economic Analysis*, p. 156.
5. R. H. Coase, "Comment," in P. W. MacAvoy, ed., *The Crisis of the Regulatory Commissions* (New York: W. W. Norton & Company, 1970), pp. 55–56.
6. Navarro, "Save Now, Freeze Later," p. 32.

that of conventional welfare economics in the analysis of monopoly power, economic efficiency, and use of knowledge in society. Finally, the chapter ends by relating implications of the incentive and information problems inherent in the use of marginal cost and other pricing rules to public utility regulation.

PUBLIC CHOICE CONSIDERATIONS IN REGULATORY COMMISSION BEHAVIOR

The idealistic or public-interest view of public regulation is deeply imbedded in economic thought.[7] This view holds that regulation is instituted to protect the "public interest." During the past twenty-five years, however, the development and use of public-choice theory has shown that in fact economic regulation often benefits small groups at the expense of the public at large. Moreover although the purported advantage of economic regulation is the ability to take a long-run view and to disregard prior commitments if too costly or nonproductive, the quest for public support often encourages political decision makers to take a short-run perspective.[8] At a time of rapidly increasing costs, for example, utility regulators can hold prices below the level necessary to sustain production, benefiting present consumers at the expense of future consumers.

In analyzing the behavior of regulatory agencies, the public-choice approach stresses that the appropriate unit of analysis is the individual decision maker. Thus the key decision maker in economic regulation is the professional public servant—the bureaucrat. In the idealistic view of economic regulation, an implicit assumption exists that the employees who staff the regulatory commissions and otherwise devise measures to correct for market failure are "economic eunuchs," who act solely to maximize social efficiency without regard to their own utility, power, prestige, income, or vote appeal.[9] Given, though, the immensity of the government sector and the fact that individuals often move from private firms to the public sector, there is little or no rea-

---

7. George J. Stigler, "The Theory of Economic Regulation," *Bell Journal of Economics and Management Science* 2 (1971): 17.

8. James R. Schlesinger, "Systems Analysis and the Political Process," *Journal of Law and Economics* 11 (1968): 281–98.

9. John Burton, "Externalities, Property Rights and Public Policy: Private Property Rights or the Spoilation of Nature." in S. N. S. Cheung, ed., *The Myth of Social Cost* (London: Institute of Economic Affairs, 1978), p. 81.

son to assume that government employees are significantly different from an average cross section of the population having the educational qualifications required for that work.[10] That is, they have similar personal motivations and goals.

Why do individuals pursue bureaucratic careers? At least three reasons explain an individual's personal career choices: risk aversion, power, and subsequent opportunities in politics or the private sector.[11] This suggests that the individual is likely to place more weight on the expected effect of any particular decision on the decision maker's career than on the nation as a whole.[12] In addition to salary and tenure in office, the bureaucrat is also concerned with such things as size of budget, amount of patronage, power, and perquisites of office.[13] Since these welfare components typically increase with bureau growth, regulators face strong incentives to continually expand the scope of their agency's activities.[14]

This paper recognizes that the individual regulator is not motivated solely by financial considerations. Thus there is no implication that public-choice models can fully describe regulatory activities or how individual bureaucrats will act.[15] Public-choice theory has proven to be quite useful, however, in explaining the general behavior of regulatory agencies.

In 1971 Stigler proposed a capture theory of economic regulation, suggesting that the industry being regulated typically seeks regulation as a means of decreasing competition.[16] The explanatory power of this theory in the case of electric utilities, however, does not hold up

10. M. C. O'Dowd, "The Problem of 'Government Failure' in Mixed Economies," *South African Journal of Economics* 46 (1978):364. Forte's view is slightly different. "Bureaucratic man has to be a formally obedient, precise man . . . sometimes he has to be a specialized man, though he need not be an enterprising-economizing man." Francesco Forte, "The Law of Selection in the Public Economy as Compared to the Market Economy," *Public Finance* 37 (1982):235.

11. Roger Noll, "The Political Foundations of Regulatory Policy," *Journal of Institutional and Theoretical Economics* 139 (1983):395.

12. Gordon Tullock, "Bureaucracy and the Growth of Government," in *The Taming of Government* (London: Institute of Economic Affairs, 1979), pp. 23–38.

13. William A. Niskanen, Jr., *Bureaucracy and Representative Government* (Chicago: Aldine-Atherton, 1971), p. 38.

14. John A. Baden and Richard L. Stroup, "The Environmental Costs of Government Action," *Policy Review* 4 (1978):26.

15. James M. Buchanan, "The Achievement and the Limits of Public Choice in Diagnosing Government Failure and in Offering Bases for Constructive Reform," July 1980. (Mimeo.)

16. Stigler, "The Theory of Economic Regulation."

during the recent era of rapidly increasing costs. Noll, for example, suggests that the capture theory is inconsistent with two important regulatory developments: (1) the rise of environmental, health, and safety regulation; and (2) the recent deregulation movement affecting transportation, communications, and so on.[17]

Since one goal of the bureaucrat is to give the appearance of serving the public, regulators have incentives to hold prices down. Moreover regulation in a period of rapidly rising costs can severely restrict the regulators' ability to confer benefits upon the regulated even if they are so inclined because irate consumers are far more likely to mobilize effectively against the interests of utility shareholders than in easier times.[18] Regulators might also view regulation as a way of redistributing income to consumers of conventionally regarded necessities, such as electricity, in an inflationary period.[19] In view of the inflationary pressures of the past decade, it is not surprising that regulation has reduced electric power industry profitability below the level necessary to sustain the quality and growth of service, as MacAvoy found. This development reflects the possibility that the explanation of regulation of public utilities could be quite different from that of other economic regulation. Since 1970, for example, Congress has enacted a series of statutes reducing or eliminating regulation in transportation, communications, financial institutions, and energy. During the same period, "the Congress enacted a series of ambitious, complicated, and perplexing health, safety, and environmental statutes."[20]

A major conclusion of public-choice theory is that market failure is not a sufficient condition for government intervention. All markets will "fail" when measured against the benchmark of perfect competition—which requires price-taking behavior and perfect markets. Similarly utility commissions and all other government regulatory agencies will "fail" when measured against a benchmark that assumes away incentive and information problems.[21]

17. Noll, "The Political Foundations of Regulatory Policy," p. 402.

18. Navarro, "Save Now, Freeze Later."

19. Alan Peacock, "On the Anatomy of Collective Failure," *Public Finance* 35 (1980):37.

20. Robert W. Crandall, "Deregulation: The U.S. Experience," *Journal of Institutional and Theoretical Economics* 139 (1983):419. No one has satisfactorily explained the growth of health-safety-environmental regulation at a time when a general consensus exists that economic regulation was counterproductive in many areas.

21. William C. Mitchell, "Efficiency, Responsibility, and Democratic Politics," in J. R. Pennock and J. W. Chapman, eds., *Liberal Democracy* (New York: New York University Press, 1983).

We may well ask what specific forms of bureaucratic failure are likely in the case of utility regulation? First, firms operating under rate of return or profit controls have incentives to use regulation to their own advantage. If the price charged is to be based on cost, for example, management is motivated to inflate costs by padding expense accounts and taking returns in the form of nonmonetary perquisites such as lavishly decorated offices. Rate-of-return regulation is often identified with the so-called Averch-Johnson effect. The alleged result is that regulated companies are biased toward capital-intensive technologies so that the capital-to-labor ratio is higher than that which minimizes cost for the same level of output.[22]

Second, it is very difficult to dismantle a regulatory commission established in government service. Economic regulators have incentives to seek out new areas to regulate even if their original purpose no longer exists. Since bureaucrats are legally unable to capture profits directly, they have incentives to expand agency size beyond meaningful efficiency limits. Thus a rachet effect tends to lead to pyramid building in regulatory agencies regardless of changes in economic conditions.[23] Regulators of public utilities, therefore, are unlikely to passively accept either deregulation or measures to increase competition.[24]

Third, it is likely that public utility commissions (like other bureaucrats) will operate to minimize bureaucratic risk in order to reduce the amount of outside criticism and bureaucratic strain. An incentive exists to institute policies yielding immediate benefits and to forego policies involving potentially higher returns involving more risk. Thus regulation not only results in the misallocation of resources in the short run, it is also likely to reduce the rate of progress and the ability of regulated firms to adapt to changes in economic conditions, which is an important consequence.[25]

In brief public-choice theory implies that economic regulation of

22. S. C. Littlechild, *Elements of Telecommunications Economics* (Stevenage, U.K.: Peter Peregrinus Ltd., 1979), p. 190.

23. O'Dowd, "The Problem of 'Government Failure.'"

24. In the case of electric utilities, Navarro contends that small budget and staff have caused public utility commissions to suppress rates. Peter Navarro, "Save Now, Freeze Later." It should be stressed, however, that regulators would be unable to solve the information problems identified in the following section regardless of staff size.

25. Burton H. Klein, *Dynamic Economics* (Cambridge, Mass.: Harvard University Press, 1977), p. 217.

the electric power (or any other) industry is quite different than it would be if regulators were to follow the dictates of welfare economics. The incentive structure of regulatory agencies is inconsistent with the achievement of this goal since regulators bear neither the costs nor benefits of their regulatory actions. Moreover no way we know exists to determine the most profitable output level where whatever is being produced is not subject to the "incorruptible judgment of that unbribable tribunal, the account of profit and loss."[26] No one denies that some regulators undoubtedly try to serve their perceptions of the public interest. Even regulators who are selfless public servants are not, however, omniscient. Consequently, as I will show in the following section, even if no incentive problems occurred, regulators would still be unable to acquire the information necessary to implement a marginal-cost pricing rule.

OPPORTUNITY COST, MONOPOLY POWER, AND ENTREPRENEURSHIP

The previous section emphasized that regulators are unlikely to try achieving the public interest because of the separation of authority and responsibility. This section, focusing on information problems inherent in the central direction of economic activity, demonstrates that regulators cannot regulate in the public interest because of problems posed by the separation of power and knowledge. There is at present no known way the regulator can obtain information on individual preferences and production opportunities to determine the public interest. Thus it is impossible for any one bureaucrat to act in a way that will benefit the public at large because of inherent limits on information and the conflicting interests of other decision makers.[27] Moreover since choice hinges on expected costs and returns of alternative courses of action, the ex ante planning process inevitably involves subjective entrepreneurial judgments about the future.

Opportunity Cost

Although a consensus in economics states that opportunity cost is the appropriate measure of cost, there is little recognition of the implications for economic regulation. By definition opportunity cost is the

26. Von Mises, *Bureaucracy*, p. 35.
27. Niskanen, Jr., *Bureaucracy and Representative Government*, p. 39.

expected value of the opportunities foregone. The cost of a vacation trip by Jones, for example, is the expected value of the refrigerator, automobile, or other alternative that must be sacrificed if the trip is taken. Thus opportunity cost is always associated with an action by a decision maker. Since the alternative foregone is not actually experienced, opportunity cost—the decision maker's assessment of the rejected course of action—hinges on expectations about the future. In the words of Hayek:

> In no sense can cost during any period be said to depend solely upon price during that period. . . . Whether to make major adjustments to a given change in demand or to carry on as well as possible with the existing organization . . . depends at least in part on the views held about the future.[28]

Even in the case of purchased inputs, subjectivity enters cost calculations since the price paid for materials does not necessarily reflect the opportunity cost of using these materials. Price paid ignores the expenses involved in reselling materials already purchased, and it does not recognize the value of the materials if used elsewhere.[29] Following the large oil-price increases in the early 1970s, for example, the opportunity cost of coal or oil public utilities used was quite often much higher than the price actually paid. In general market outlays are equal to opportunity costs only under highly restrictive equilibrium conditions.[30]

In the case of electric power and other products requiring large capital investments, overhead costs are an important part of total production outlays. The relevant costs as they affect managerial decisions are not the accounting costs but the opportunity costs. Subjectivity inevitably enters overhead cost calculations, though, since depreciation and interest costs hinge on expectations about future conditions. Since the value of a sacrificed alternative is necessarily subjective, no reason exists to expect that the cost estimates of regulatory agencies will correspond to the costs that influence entrepreneurial decisions.

28. F. A. Hayek, *Individualism and Economic Order* (Chicago: University of Chicago Press, 1948), p. 198.

29. R. H. Coase, "Business Organization and the Accountant," in J. M. Buchanan and G. F. Thirlby, eds., *L.S.E. Essays on Cost* (London: Weidenfeld and Nicolson, 1973), p. 113.

30. James M. Buchanan, *Cost and Choice* (Chicago: Markham Publishing Co., 1969), pp. 49, 75. Even in full-market equilibrium, resource prices reflect opportunity costs only if nonpecuniary advantages or disadvantages are absent from choices to resource-supplying agents. Buchanan, *Cost and Choice*, p. 86.

Consider, for example, the cost of generating electricity in a nuclear electric power plant. Cost hinges on the unknown, and unknowable, future. Delays in plant construction and the probability that the plant once built will be prematurely closed for safety or other reasons are examples of unknown but possible cost factors. Yet the managerial response to these and similar factors hinges on the decision maker's expectations. Thus entrepreneurial expectations are crucial in cost calculations and decisions involving depreciation, interest, and operating outlays.[31]

Monopoly Power and the Entrepreneurial Process

Utility regulation is rooted in the theory of monopoly power. Economists typically define monopoly power as a *situation* in conventional neoclassicial theory—a situation in which a firm faces a negatively sloping demand curve for its product.[32] If every firm facing a negatively sloping demand curve were considered to have monopoly power, though, many sellers operating under competitive conditions would be classified as monopolistic, including the ten-year-old operator of a lemonade stand. If one departs from this situational definition of monopoly power, however, we have no objective method to differentiate a "harmful monopolist" from other price searchers facing less than perfectly elastic demand conditions. The case is similar for natural-monopoly theory, which presupposes a problem by assuming there are no good substitutes for the product. Since there are substitutes for all goods and services, any classification of what constitutes a natural monopoly on the basis of closeness of substitutes must also be arbitrary. Thus, as Rothbard suggests, there is no defensible way to determine whether the price charged in a free market is a "monopoly price."[33]

In practice economists often use the long-run competitive-equilibrium framework as a benchmark in identifying monopoly power. Perfect competition assumes price-taking behavior and perfect markets.[34] In long-run competitive equilibrium, the market process has come to

31. G. L. S. Shackle, *Epistemics and Economics: A Critique of Economic Doctrines* (London: Cambridge University Press, 1972), p. 19. As shown below, similar problems also arise in estimating demand.

32. Milton Friedman, *Price Theory* (Chicago: Aldine Publishing Co., 1976), p. 126.

33. Murray N. Rothbard, *Power and Market: Government and the Economy* (Menlo Park, Calif.: Institute for Humane Studies, 1970), p. 619.

34. Jack Hirshleifer, *Price Theory and Applications,* 2d ed. (Englewood Cliffs, N.J.: Prentice-Hall, 1980), p. 232.

an end, and there is no scope for harmless (or beneficial) profits.[35] Consequently, when measured against the benchmark of perfect competition, all profits are considered due to monopoly, which implies a welfare loss. Since expected profits and losses are the signals that direct entrepreneurial activity, it is inappropriate to use the long-run equilibrium framework to analyze the effects of firm profits under actual conditions in which returns include short-run disequilibrium profits gained through entrepreneurial alertness.

The alternative to the long-run equilibrium approach is the market-process approach. This stresses the necessity of using a model that recognizes the importance of above-average rates of return due to entrepreneurship. Indeed every successful penetration of the unknown attributable to foresight, entrepreneurial calculation, or plain luck gives the decision maker an edge that can be classified as a monopoly return.[36] Consider the example of the decision maker facing a downward sloping demand for a product due to entrepreneurial foresight and ingenuity. Clearly it is inappropriate to depict the producer's actions as socially harmful since the productive allocation of resources under actual conditions of risk and uncertainty requires that resources be devoted to coping with and initiating changes in economic conditions.[37] The fact that entrepreneurs in a world of "perfect competition" would have negligible influence on their environment has tended to mask the importance of entrepreneurship. Consider now the implications of the market-process approach in using the marginal efficiency conditions as a touchstone for public policy.

Marginal Analysis and Economic Efficiency

Given an optimal income distribution and perfect knowledge, a perfectly competitive market system results in the "optimal" allocation of resources. These "perfectly competitive" conditions, however, are never met in the world of actual experience. Marginal efficiency rules are inadequate guides to public policy when the analyses intended to

---

35. C. S. W. Torr, "The Role of Information in Economic Analysis," *South African Journal of Economics* 40 (1980):129. Hayek makes the same point: "An equilibrium presupposes that the facts have already all been discovered and competition has therefore ceased." F. A. Hayek, *New Studies in Philosophy, Politics, Economics and the History of Ideas* (Chicago: University of Chicago Press, 1978), p. 184.

36. Dean A. Worcester, Jr., "Economics and Principles," *Eastern Economic Journal* 8 (1982):87.

37. Worcester, Jr., "Economics and Principles," p. 86.

guide policy overlook the functions and requirements of entrepreneurial decision making.[38] Using marginal-cost pricing or other efficiency conditions in assessing firm behavior typically fails to consider the information and uncertainty problems that characterize all entrepreneurial decisions. What then are the implications for economic analysis? Worcester describes the "forbidding task" of constructing an economic model that can properly be used as a basis for policy making. "Economic analysis suitable for policy must provide a negative answer to the first and a positive answer to the second of these questions: (1) Is any unavoidable task ignored or excluded by assumption? (2) Has an equally skeptical investigation been made of the viable alternatives?"[39] Knowing the economic "logic of choice" in which the marginal rates of substitution between any two factors or products is equalized can help the decision maker find better choices as evaluated by the chooser's own standards. If made aware of the principle, the potential choice maker will weigh alternatives more carefully, think in marginal terms, and search more diligently for preferred alternatives.[40]

A recommendation that a regulatory commission use marginal analysis has little content in public utility regulation, which is heavily involved with estimates of prices, costs, and profits. The costs and benefits of alternative courses of action must first be determined if the regulator is to do more than present a personal value ordering. Furthermore little or no relationship may exist between the costs and benefits economic regulators define objectively and the evaluation that individual entrepreneurs place on alternatives in actual choice situations where the cost and revenue estimates are bound up in the personal judgment of the individual making the estimates.[41] As shown in the following section, regulation is also likely to stifle the discovery process of the market.

Regulation and the Stifled Discovery Process

Economic adjustment under actual uncertainty about the future is necessitated by unforeseen change. Discovering preferred production alternatives also involves risky entrepreneurial behavior. Least-cost methods of production, for example, are not given but must be dis-

---

38. Worcester, Jr., "Economics and Principles," p. 85.

39. Ibid., p. 87.

40. James M. Buchanan, *What Should Economists Do?* (Indianapolis: Liberty Fund, Inc. 1979), p. 41.

41. Buchanan, *What Should Economists Do?* p. 61.

covered. Competition is a discovery process that engenders more knowledge than any individual market participant can possess.[42] The competitive process will be most effective in prompting discovery of new knowledge only if contenders are free to experiment with methods they think will be most successful.[43] Thus a strong a priori case exists for competition in decentralized markets as the best method of coping with unforeseeable economic change.

If regulators could simulate competitive market conditions, market prices would provide no additional information. As indicated above, however, there is no known way for regulators to obtain the costs and returns that influence entrepreneurial decisions or for them to simulate at all closely the discovery process of the unregulated market. Economic rivals might frustrate one another's plans, but they also provide information. When one producer outbids another for a particular resource, for example, the excluded buyer is induced to economize by using a different combination of resources.[44] No single rival—including members of regulatory agencies—can know what will be discovered through such market rivalry. Moreover nothing in the course of the regulatory process suggests a tendency to discover unperceived opportunities.[45] Further it is unlikely discoveries will erupt under an incentive system antithetical to risky behavior. In competitive markets where the decision maker reaps the rewards, or costs, of risky behavior, a significantly stronger incentive pushes the discovery of new opportunities. In summary market competition "minimizes the chance of a good idea being overlooked or suppressed, and at the same time it serves to protect consumers."[46]

Sowell stresses that rapid transmission of information is unlikely under central direction since demand and price changes are virtually instantaneous, whereas the statistics available to regulators or other outside observers inevitably lag behind. Consequently information transmitted through nonmarket channels is necessarily historical and not the kind of data to motivate individual behavior. Millions of users make judgments about incremental trade-offs when faced with

42. Hayek, *New Studies in Philosophy, Politics, Economics*, p. 179.
43. Don Lavoie, *Industrial Policy: Son of Central Planning* (Washington, D.C.: Heritage Foundation, 1983), p. 9.
44. Lavoie, *Industrial Policy*, p. 8.
45. Israel M. Kirzner, *The Perils of Regulation: A Market-Process Approach* (Coral Gables, Fla.: Law and Economics Center, 1978), p. 15.
46. Littlechild, *Elements of Telecommunications Economics*, p. 230.

higher utility rates, for example, but no third party can capture these changing trade-offs in a fixed definition articulated to producers in advance.[47] Sowell graphically describes the problems confronting regulators if they attempt to measure these trade-offs:

> The real problem is that the knowledge needed is a knowledge of *subjective patterns of trade-off that are nowhere articulated*, not even to the individual himself. I might *think* that, if faced with the stark prospect of bankruptcy, I would rather sell my automobile than my furniture . . . but unless and until such a moment comes, I will never know my own trade-offs, much less anybody else's.[48]

If trade-offs are unknowable in advance, one could argue that the decision maker in decentralized markets faces information problems no less formidable than those regulators encounter. The information problems of market participants are fundamentally different, however, from those of the regulator. The individual market participant acts on information coordinated and transmitted through market prices, personal preferences, and subjective assessments about future conditions. In contrast, the economic regulator, although presumably interested in data influencing managerial decisions, has access to little or none of the subjective data informing such individual choices.

IMPLICATIONS FOR REGULATION OF PUBLIC UTILITIES

There is a great deal of discussion about efficient resource use in decreasing-cost industries where economies of scale result in average costs decreasing throughout the relevant range of production (Figure 11–1). In this case, average cost pricing (P_r in Figure 1) is often said to result in less than the "ideally efficient output," Q_c, where price is equal to marginal cost.[49] Indeed marginal-cost pricing occupies a key position in the theory of utility pricing: "The central policy prescription of microeconomics is the equation of price and marginal cost. If economic theory is to have any relevance to public utility pricing, that is the point at which the inquiry must begin."[50] Despite

47. Thomas Sowell, *Knowledge and Decisions* (New York: Basic Books, 1980), p. 216.
48. Sowell, *Knowledge and Decisions*, p. 218.
49. Hirshleifer, *Price Theory and Applications*, pp. 348–50.
50. Alfred E. Kahn, *The Economics of Regulation: Principles and Institutions* (New York: John Wiley & Sons, 1970), p. 65.

Figure 11–1.   Regulation of the "Natural Monopoly."

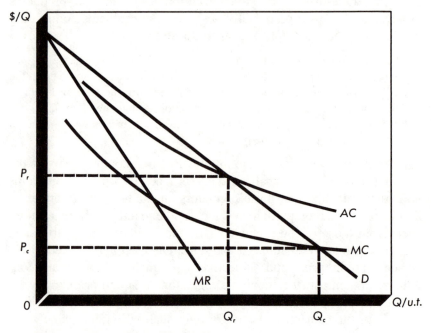

$/Q   = Price per unit of product
Q/u.t. = Quantity of product per unit of time
AC   = Average cost of production
MC   = Marginal cost of production
D   = Demand for product
MR   = Marginal revenue curve
Q_r = Quantity determined by average cost pricing
P_r = Price determined by average cost pricing
Q_c = Quantity determined by marginal cost pricing
P_c = Price determined by marginal cost pricing

this fact, government regulators seldom attempt to set price on the basis of marginal cost.[51] If price were set equal to marginal cost when average cost was decreasing, firm outlays would exceed receipts, and the firm would incur a loss. That is, at price P_c and output Q_c in

51. William H. Melody, "The Marginal Utility of Marginal Analysis in Public Policy Formation," in W. Samuels, ed., *The Methodology of Economic Thought* (New Brunswick, N.J.: Transactions Books, 1980), p. 369.

Figure 11–1, the firm does not cover costs. In such cases some economists have argued the merits of administered marginal-cost pricing coupled with a subsidy to prevent losses to the firm.[52] An alternative is to set price equal to average cost so that no subsidy is required.

Coase stresses that marginal-cost pricing in the public utility industry in which average cost is decreasing has "serious weaknesses" because it does not consider the importance of having a subsequent market test of whether consumers were willing to pay the total cost as a stimulus to correct forecasting; it ignores the likely effect on the administrative structure, with centralized operations superseding decentralized operations; it involves a redistribution of income in favor of consumers of products produced under conditions of decreasing costs; and it fails to consider misallocation of resources from additional taxation necessitated by the subsidy.[53]

The discussion of the relative merits of marginal versus average-cost pricing often proceeds as if data on costs and returns are given to the entrepreneur and to the regulator. Coase places the issue in perspective:

> As I see it, the argument for marginal cost pricing . . . is more concerned with diagrams on a blackboard than with the real effects of such policies on the working of the economic system. I have referred to this type of economics as 'blackboard economics' because, although factors are moved around and prices are changed, and some people are taxed and others subsidized, the whole process is one which takes place on the blackboard.[54]

This example—in which implementation problems associated with different pricing rules are implicitly assumed away—illustrates the distinction between the Robbinsian and Hayekian approaches to economic analysis. The widely accepted Robbins approach assumes that economics is concerned with the allocation of given means among given competing ends, and it largely assumes away the entrepreneurial element in economic activity.[55] If means and ends are given to the

---

52. Abba P. Lerner, "Conflicting Principles of Public Utility Regulation," in P. W. MacAvoy, ed., *The Crisis of the Regulatory Commissions* (New York: W. W. Norton & Company, 1970), pp. 25–26.

53. R. H. Coase, "The Theory of Public Utility Pricing and Its Application," *Bell Journal of Economics and Management Science* 1 (1970):113.

54. Coase, "Theory of Public Utility Pricing," p. 119.

55. Israel M. Kirzner, *Competition and Entrepreneurship* (Chicago: University of Chicago Press, 1973), pp. 32–33.

decision maker, no role for entrepreneurship exists, and profit maximization becomes wholly computational. Assessing profit opportunities in fact, though, is influenced not only by subjective judgments about the various outcomes possible but also by the decision maker's attitude toward risk.[56] Consequently "there is no one decision which can be considered to maximize profits independently of the attitude of risk taking of the businessman."[57] Yet the idea that information influencing entrepreneurial choice is given to or can be obtained by economic regulators occupies a key role in the discussion concerning the merits of marginal-cost pricing. In the words of Abba Lerner:

> It is not too difficult to get the capitalist to charge a price equal to marginal cost. . . . Where the marginal cost is below average cost, the right public utility price can be established only if the government steps in and . . . permits the price to be charged.[58]

The marginal-cost pricing rule Lerner advocates implicitly assumes that the regulator has or can obtain appropriate demand and cost data. It is not a matter of the public utility or the regulator discovering the demand or the cost curve however. The practical world never has an actual entity corresponding to the demand curve for electric power or any other product.[59] The amount of electricity users will purchase per unit of time at any price depends on a number of factors, including their income, the length of the adjustment period, expected prices of substitutes and complements, and expected product improvements. Moreover such conditions are not given to the firm but must be discovered by trial and error. Economist von Mises contends that no constants exist in economics and, consequently, we can discover no quantitative laws.[60] Results from a recent analysis on empirical estimates covering price elasticities of energy demand are consistent with the von Mises thesis:

56. Indeed, as Alchian has shown, the concept of profit maximization loses its precise meaning under natural conditions of uncertainty in which each action that may be chosen is identified with a distribution of outcomes, only one of which will materialize and where that one outcome cannot be foreseen. A. A. Alchian, *Economic Forces at Work* (Indianapolis: Liberty Press, 1977), p. 17.

57. Coase, "Business Organization and the Accountant," p. 104.

58. Lerner, "Conflicting Principles of Public Utility Rate Regulation," pp. 25–26.

59. Leland B. Yeager, "Methodenstreit Over Demand Curves," *Journal of Political Economy* 68 (1960):53–64.

60. Ludwig von Mises, *Human Action*, 3d ed. (Chicago: Henry Regnery Company, 1966), p. 55.

For any given energy product used by any consuming group, one can find a range of statistical results wide enough to support virtually any predisposition about the importance of the price effect.[61]

Likewise, the problem is not a question of discovering the cost curve. The amount of electric power a firm will produce at any given price depends on a number of factors affecting supply, including length of run, expected tax policies, and so on. This finding is consistent with the findings of a recent study by Littlechild:

> In practice . . . marginal cost depends on (i) the size of the marginal increment, (ii) the size of the output to which the marginal increment is added, (iii) the date at which the marginal increment is added, and (iv) the date at which the calculation is made. To each and every specification of these four 'parameters' corresponds a different marginal cost. Further, since cost refers in principle to foregone opportunities, it depends not on 'facts' about the past but on conjectures about the future—specifically, about revenues and money outlays associated with the proposed plan and with other, rejected, plans. Here, again, to each and every view about the future corresponds a different collection of marginal costs.[62]

Since such factors involve a substantial element of subjectivity, we have no reason to think that a regulator will assess these factors in the same way as the firm decision maker does. Thus the cost and revenue calculations for public utilities (and all other production processes) ultimately hinge on subjective opinion; in cases where a regulator is trying to regulate a firm, it is likely to be a matter of differences of opinion between the two.[63]

What are the implications of this information for utility regulation? Proposals to improve utility regulation often place little emphasis on information problems or on the effect such regulation has on competitive activity. MacAvoy identifies use of past-period cost estimates to establish future revenue as a major problem in utility regulation, for example, and recommends "profit constraints based on future costs of investments for providing service."[64] Although the criticism of the

61. Douglas R. Bohi, "Price Elasticities of Energy Demand: An Introduction," *Resources* 65 (1980):11.

62. Littlechild, *Elements of Telecommunications Economics*, pp. 226–27.

63. G. F. Thirlby, "Economists' Cost Rules and Equilibrium Theory," in J. M. Buchanan and G. F. Thirlby, eds., *L.S.E. Essays on Cost* (London: Weidenfeld and Nicolson, 1973), p. 281.

64. MacAvoy, ed., *Regulated Industries and the Economy*, p. 122.

use of past-period outlays by regulatory agencies is surely valid, the proposed solution does not fully reflect the importance incentive and information problems play in all regulatory attempts to measure choice-influencing costs.[65] As indicated above, implementation problems are endemic in the regulatory process. Thus there appears ample support for Thirlby's conclusion about regulatory agencies' cost forecasts:

> And when it is understood that any individual is uniquely situated in relation to past events on which such forecasts are based, it becomes clear that the result of the reckoning is dependent for what it is upon the unique knowledge and attitude (toward uncertainty and risk) of the unique and uniquely situated individual who calculates it, and the validity, correctness, or authoritativeness of an overriding calculation by someone else would often be dubious in the extreme.[66]

If it is accepted that we have no reason to expect regulators' cost and revenue estimates to correspond to those of the regulated firm, it follows that utility commissions cannot implement marginal-cost and other pricing rules, and that such rules "ought to fall away with the ground on which they are built . . . with the notion of perfect competition or competitive equilibrium."[67] Stated differently, since no objective way exists to implement a pricing rule, the regulatory agency cannot find the firm guilty of not following the rule; "all it can do is to disagree with the industry's view of the future or its choice of reasonable parameters."[68]

What implications does the preceding analysis have for assessing the viability of entrepreneurial decisions? For example, in recent years electric utilities have terminated nuclear plants under construction after large sums had already been invested. In other cases utility critics accuse them of paying too much for fuel following changes in relative prices of oil or coal. It is easy, in retrospect—on the basis of information not available to the decision maker at the moment of choice—to criticize these and other cases of "wasteful" expenditures. The fact that with passing time the result of a decision is different from what was anticipated, however, does not mean that the firm was inefficient in an economic planning or choice sense. All entrepreneurial deci-

65. E. C. Pasour, Jr., "Information: A Neglected Aspect of the Theory of Price Regulation," *Cato Journal* 3, no. 3 (Winter 1983–84):855–67.

66. Thirlby, "Economists' Cost Rules and Equilibrium Theory," p. 281.

67. Ibid., p. 275.

68. Littlechild, *Elements of Telecommunications Economics*, p. 227.

sions are made under uncertainty, and an action is only taken if the gains are expected to exceed the costs. The relevant costs and returns in a decision-making context are those based on the decision maker's expectation when the action was taken. Consequently we cannot determine a decision's correctness by subsequent events since an action's ultimate failure or success has no relevance to the preference at the moment of choice.[69] Therefore a utility commission can never establish that a utility firm's action is inefficient based on measuring the costs and returns that motivate the entrepreneurial choice.[70] Moreover so long as people fail to recognize the subjective nature of the costs and returns that influence entrepreneurial decisions, public policy is likely to demand of public utility commissions (and other regulators) something they cannot provide, namely, setting utility rates on the basis of costs.

Even though the correctness of decisions cannot be determined after the fact by subsequent events, in decentralized markets quite often profits provide a measure of how successful a firm has been in anticipating and accommodating consumer demand. Consequently survival is one criterion of firm success.[71] Survival as a measure of firm success, however, is largely negated under a regulatory regime where survival often hinges either on the firm's ability to obtain price increases or on subsidies to cover losses. Thus under economic regulation there can be no presumption that firm survival itself implies success in terms of meeting the market test.

CONCLUSIONS

Competition in the market process sense rests on freedom of entry. Government regulation, however, generally erects barriers to entry. And when competition is hampered, opportunities for discovery can be lost.[72] Regulation not only distorts the discovery process of the market, it also creates new profit opportunities for regulators as well as for regulated firms. Even if utility commissions could obtain the information needed to implement marginal-cost pricing or other ef-

---

69. Coase, "Business Organization and the Accountant," pp. 104–5.

70. E. C. Pasour, Jr., "Cost and Choice—Austrian vs. Conventional Views," *Journal of Libertarian Studies* 2 (1978):327–36.

71. Alchian, *Economic Forces at Work*, pp. 15–35.

72. Kirzner, *The Perils of Regulation*, p. 17.

ficiency rules, regulators have no incentives to use such information efficiently.

We can trace stress on the use of marginal-efficiency rules in utility regulation to the norm of "perfect competition." Perfect knowledge as a condition of the perfect market assumes away the central task of economic theory, which is to account "for the way information is brought to bear on the decisions of market participants and on the extent to which the market directs relevant information to those who can make the (socially) best use of it."[73] Decentralized competitive markets have a distinct advantage over economic regulation in making the best use of existing and as-yet undiscovered knowledge. The most serious negative impact of economic regulation might well be that it is likely to discourage, hamper, and even stifle the discovery process of the competitive market. Marginal-cost pricing or other rules do not meet the objective of fostering alertness to possible entrepreneurial opportunities. Instead, pricing rules merely,

> refer to a specified set of alternatives available; they do not prescribe how these alternatives are to be generated. In other words, the concept of entrepreneurial alertness to new opportunities is completely absent.[74]

The widespread assumption that regulation is required in the electric utility industry warrants more attention. Since competition can arise not only from producers of the same product but also from new products, abolishing the statutory monopoly enjoyed by electric utilities to permit freedom of entry may be more effective as a means of increasing competition than attempts to modify or fine tune utility regulation. That is, market competition may be more effective than regulation in honing in on those goods and services consumers prefer and in providing them most quickly at the lowest price.

What are the implications of the preceding analysis for economists making public policy recommendations? Deregulation of economic activity frequently means that prices rise—either for some groups in particular or in the short run relative to the long run. Consequently public policy recommendations—in public utility regulation as in all other areas—ultimately involve value judgments.[75] This emphasizes

---

73. Israel M. Kirzner, *Perception, Opportunity and Profit* (Chicago: University of Chicago Press, 1979), p. 32.

74. Littlechild, *Elements of Telecommunications Economics*, p. 229.

75. "Whenever we discuss distributional questions, we make our own estimates of the happiness afforded or the misery endured by different persons or groups of persons. But these

the importance of what Buchanan refers to as the "morally relevant" science of political economy.[76] In this approach the stress is on the institutional framework that provides the greatest opportunity for individuals to cooperate in pursuing their own ends through decentralized coordination of their activities.[77] Consequently the focus of economic analysis shifts from welfare maximization to the evaluation of institutional alternatives.

It is important to recognize and emphasize the shortcomings inherent in proposals to fine tune the current regulatory process. It might be possible to reduce the perverse incentive problems regulators face, but even so information problems would remain. That is, even if the problems of bureaucratic failure could be solved, there would be no known way for regulators to obtain the data needed to use a pricing rule. Consequently in evaluating the effects of deregulation, policy planners should compare market competition with economic regulation as each operates under actual conditions.[78] Given the inherent pitfalls of economic regulation—including the problems of monitoring the regulators—it may well be preferable not to regulate electric utilities and to suffer market failure rather than to suffer the inevitable political and economic imperfections associated with utility regulation.[79]

are our estimates. There is no objective measurement conceivable." Lionel Robbins, "Economics and Political Economy," *American Economic Review* 71 (1981):5.

76. James M. Buchanan, "The Related but Distinct 'Sciences' of Economics and of Political Economy," *British Journal of Social Psychology* 21 (1982):175–83.

77. Leland B. Yeager, "Economics and Principles," *Southern Economic Journal* 42 (1976):560.

78. Harold Demsetz, "Information and Efficiency: Another Viewpoint," *Journal of Law and Economics* 12 (1969):1–22.

79. Gary S. Becker, "Competition and Democracy," *Journal of Law and Economics* 1 (1958):105–9.

SELECTED BIBLIOGRAPHY
PART III

Abramson, Victor, and Leverett S. Lyon. *Government and Economic Life.* Washington, D.C.: Brookings Institution, 1940.

Alchian, Armen A. *Economic Forces at Work.* Indianapolis: Liberty Press, 1977.

Anderson, Douglas. *Regulatory Policies and Electric Utilities.* Boston: Auburn House, 1981.

Aranson, Peter H. *American Government: Strategy and Choice.* Cambridge, Mass.: Winthrop, 1981.

Armentano, Dominick. *Antitrust and Monopoly: Anatomy of a Policy Failure.* New York: John Wiley & Sons, 1982.

Armstrong, Donald. *Competition Versus Monopoly.* Vancouver, British Columbia: Fraser Institute, 1982.

Arzak, Enrique R., and Franklin R. Edwards. "Efficiency in Regulated and Unregulated Firms: An Iconoclastic View of the Averch-Johnson Thesis." In M. Crew, ed., *Problems in Public Utility Economics and Regulation,* pp. 41–54. Lexington, Mass.: D. C. Heath, 1979.

Averch, Harvey, and Leland Johnson. "Behavior of the Firm Under Regulatory Constraint." *American Economic Review* 52 (December 1962): 1052–69.

Baden, John A., and Richard L. Stroup. "The Environmental Costs of Government Action." *Policy Review* 4 (1978): 23–36.

Baumol, William J. "Entrepreneurship in Economic Theory." *American Economic Review* 58 (1968): 64–71.

Becker, Gary S. "Competition and Democracy." *Journal of Law and Economics* 1 (October 1958): 105–9.

――――. "Comment." *Journal of Law and Economics* 19 (1976): 245–48.

Behling, Burton. *Competition and Monopoly in Public Utility Industries.* Urbana: University of Illinois Press, 1938.

Bellamy, Jan. "Two Utilities Are Better Than One." *Reason* 13 (1981): 23–30.

Bigham, Truman C., and Eliot Jones. *Principles of Public Utilities.* New York: Macmillan, 1937.

Bohi, Douglas R. "Price Elasticities of Energy Demand: An Introduction." *Resources* 65 (1980): 11–12.

Bonbright, James C. *Principles of Public Utility Rates.* New York: Columbia University Press, 1961.

Bonbright & Company, Inc. *The Bonbright Survey of Electric Power and Light Companies of the U.S.* New York: McGraw-Hill, 1927.

Bonneville Power Administration. *Time Differentiated Long Run Incremental Cost Analysis.* WP-83-FS-BPA-06. Portland, Ore.: Bonneville Power Administration, 1983.

Buchanan, James M. "Positive Economics, Welfare Economics, and Political Economy." *Journal of Law and Economics* 2 (1959): 125–38.

――――. *Cost and Choice.* Chicago: Markham Publishing Co., 1969.

――――. *What Should Economists Do?* Indianapolis: Liberty Fund, Inc., 1979.

――――. "The Achievement and the Limits of Public Choice in Diagnosing Government Failure in Offering Bases for Constructive Reform." July 1980. (Mimeo.)

――――. "The Related but Distinct 'Sciences' of Economics and Political Economy." *British Journal of Social Psychology* 21 (1982): 175–83.

Buchanan, James M., and Alberto di Pierro. "Cognition, Choice, and Entrepreneurship." *Southern Economic Journal* 46 (1980): 693–701.

Buchanan, James M.; Robert D. Tollison; and Gordon Tullock, eds. *Toward a Theory of the Rent-Seeking Society.* College Station: Texas A & M University Press, 1980.

Burton, John. "Externalities, Property Rights and Public Policy: Private Property Rights or the Spoilation of Nature." In S. Cheung, ed., *The Myth of Social Cost,* Epilogue, pp. 69–91. London: Institute of Economic Affairs, 1978.

Caves, Douglas W.; Laurits R. Christensen; Wallace E. Hendricks; and Phillip E. Schoech. "Cost-Benefit Analysis of Residential Time of Use Rates: A Case Study for Four Illinois Utilities." *Electric Ratemaking* 1 (1982–1983): 40–46.

Coase, Ronald H. "Comment." In P. MacAvoy, ed., *The Crisis of the Regulatory Commissions,* pp. 53–56. New York: W. W. Norton, 1970.

————. "Business Organization and the Accountant." In J. Buchanan and G. Thirlby, eds., *L. S. E. Essays on Cost,* pp. 95–132. London: Weidenfeld and Nicolson, 1973.

————. "The Theory of Public Utility Pricing and Its Application." *Bell Journal of Economics and Management Science* 1 (1970): 113–28.

Crandall, Robert W. "Deregulation: The U.S. Experience." *Journal of Institutional and Theoretical Economics* 139 (1983): 419–34.

Crawford, Finla G., and William E. Mosher. *Public Utility Regulation.* New York: Harper and Brothers, 1933.

"Debate Heats Up on Merits of Deregulating Utilities." *Wall Street Journal,* 2 June 1981, p. 3.

Demsetz, Harold. "Why Regulate Utilities?" *Journal of Law and Economics* 11 (April 1968): 55–65.

————. "Information and Efficiency: Another Viewpoint." *Journal of Law and Economics* 12 (1969): 1–22.

Fenn, Scott A. *America's Electric Utilities.* Washington, D.C.: Investor Responsibility Research Center, 1983.

Forte, Francesco. "The Law of Selection in the Public Economy as Compared to the Market Economy." *Public Finance* 37 (1982): 224–45.

Friedman, Milton. *Price Theory.* Chicago: Aldine Publishing Co., 1976.

Glaeser, Martin G. *Outlines of Public Utility Economics.* New York: Macmillan, 1931.

Gray, Horace. "The Passing of the Public Utility Concept." In E. Hoover, ed., *Readings in the Social Control of Industry.* Philadelphia: Blakiston Company, 1942.

Greenfield, Robert L., and Joseph T. Salerno. "Another Defense of Methodological Apriorism." *Eastern Economic Journal* 9 (1983): 45–56.

Gwartney, James D., and Richard Stroup. *Economics: Private and Public Choice.* 3d ed. New York: Academic Press, 1982.

Hayek, Friedrich A. *Individualism and Economic Order.* Chicago: University of Chicago Press, 1948.

————. *New Studies in Philosophy, Politics, Economics and the History of Ideas.* Chicago: University of Chicago Press, 1978.

Heyne, Paul. *The Economic Way of Thinking.* 4th ed. Chicago: Science Research Associates, Inc., 1983.

Hilton, George W. "The Basic Behavior of Regulatory Commissions." *American Economic Review* 49 (May 1972): 47–54.

Hirshleifer, Jack. *Price Theory and Applications.* 2d ed. Englewood Cliffs, N.J.: Prentice-Hall, 1980.

Hunt, Edward Eyre, ed. *The Power Industry and the Public Interest.* New York: Twentieth Century Fund, 1944.

Hyman, Leonard S. *America's Electric Utilities: Past, Present, and Future.* Arlington, Va.: Public Utilities Reports, 1983.

Jackson, Raymond. "Regulation and Electric Utility Rate Levels." *Land Economics* 45 (1969): 372–76.

Jones, Stiles P. "State Versus Local Regulation." *Annals of the American Academy* 53 (May 1914): 94–107.

Jordan, William A. "Producer Protection, Prior Market Structure, and the Effects of Government Regulation." *Journal of Law and Economics* 15 (April 1972): 151–76.

Joskow, Paul L. "Inflation and Environmental Concern: Structural Change in the Process of Public Utility Price Regulation." *Journal of Law and Economics* 17 (October 1974): 291–328.

Kahn, Alfred E. *The Economics of Regulation: Principles and Institutions.* 2 vols. New York: John Wiley & Sons, 1970 and 1971.

Keeler, Theodore E. "Airline Regulation and Market Performance." *Bell Journal of Economics and Management Science* 3 (Autumn 1972): 399–424.

Kerr, William. "Qualifications Needed for Public Utility Commissions." In W. Kerr, ed., *State Regulation of Public Utilities.* Philadelphia: American Academy of Political Science, 1914.

King, Clyde London, ed. *The Regulation of Municipal Utilities.* New York: D. Appleton and Company, 1912.

Kirzner, Israel M. *Competition and Entrepreneurship.* Chicago: University of Chicago Press, 1973.

———. *The Perils of Regulation: A Market-Process Approach.* LEC Occasional Paper. Coral Gables, Fla.: Law and Economics Center, 1978.

———. *Perception, Opportunity and Profit.* Chicago: University of Chicago Press, 1979.

Klein, Burton H. *Dynamic Economics.* Cambridge: Harvard University Press, 1977.

Kneier, Charles Mayard. *State Regulation of Municipal Utilities.* New York: D. Appleton and Company, 1912.

Lavoie, Don. *Industrial Policy: Son of Central Planning.* Backgrounder No. 319. Washington, D.C.: Heritage Foundation, 1983.

Leftwich, Richard H., and Ross D. Eckert. *The Price System and Resource Allocation.* Chicago: Dryden Press, 1982.

Lerner, Abba P. "Conflicting Principles of Public Utility Rate Regulation." In P. MacAvoy, ed., *The Crisis of the Regulatory Commissions,* pp. 18–29. New York: W. W. Norton, 1970.

Levy, Yvonne. "Pricing Federal Power in the Pacific Northwest: An Efficiency Approach." *Federal Reserve Bank of San Francisco Economic Review* (Winter 1980): 40–63.

Ling, Suilin. *Economies of Scale in the Steam-Electric Power Generating Industry.* Amsterdam: North-Holland, 1964.

Littlechild, Stephen C. *Elements of Telecommunications Economics.* Stevenage, U.K.: Peter Peregrinus, Ltd., 1979.

————. "Misleading Calculation of the Social Costs of Monopoly Power." *Economic Journal* 91 (1981): 348–63.

————. *The Fallacy of the Mixed Economy*. London: Institute of Economic Affairs, 1978.

Loasby, Brian J. *Choice, Complexity, and Ignorance*. New York: Cambridge University Press, 1976.

Lomax, K. S. "Cost Curves for Electricity Generation." *Economica* 19 (May 1952): 193–97.

Lovins, Amory B. *Soft Energy Paths*. Cambridge, Mass.: Ballinger Publishing Co., 1977.

MacAvoy, Paul W., ed. *The Crisis of the Regulatory Commissions*. New York: W. W. Norton, 1970.

————. *The Regulated Industries and the Economy*. New York: W. W. Norton, 1979.

————. *Energy Policy: An Economic Analysis*. New York: W. W. Norton, 1983.

McKenzie, Richard B., and Hugh H. Macaulay. "A Bureaucratic Theory of Regulation." *Public Choice* 35 (1980): 297–313.

Melody, William H. "The Marginal Utility of Marginal Analysis in Public Policy Formation." In W. Samuels, ed., *The Methodology of Economic Thought*, pp. 366–79. New Brunswick, N.J.: Transactions Books, 1980.

Mitchell, Bridger M.; Willard G. Manning, Jr.; and Jan Paul Acton. *Peak-Load Pricing: European Lessons for U.S. Energy Policy*. Cambridge, Mass.: Ballinger Publishing Co., 1978.

Mitchell, William C. "Efficiency, Responsibility, and Democratic Politics." In J. Pennock and J. Chapman, eds., *Liberal Democracy*, pp. 343–73. New York: New York University Press, 1983.

————. "Fiscal Behavior of the Modern Democratic State: Public Choice Perspectives and Contributions." In L. Wade, ed., *Political Economy*, pp. 69–114. Boston: Klumer-Nijhoff, 1983.

Moore, Thomas Gale. "The Effectiveness of Regulation on Electric Utility Prices." *Southern Economic Journal* 36 (1970): 365–75.

National Civic Federation. *Municipal and Private Operation of Public Utilities*. 3 vols. New York: National Civic Federation, 1907.

National Economic Research Associates, Inc. *A Framework for Marginal Cost-Based Time-Differentiated Pricing in the United States*. Electric Utility Rate Design Study, Report No. 15. Palo Alto, Calif.: Electric Power Research Institute, 1977.

Navarro, Peter. "Electric Utility Regulation and National Energy Policy." *Regulation* 5 (January/February 1981): 20–27.

————. "The Soft, Hard, or Smart Path: Charting the Electric Utility Industry's Future." *Public Utilities Fortnightly* 107 (18 June 1981): 25–30.

————. "The Public May Be the Big Loser in Pilgrim Power-Plant Cancellation." *Boston Globe*, 18 July 1981.

———. "Generating Real GNP Growth." *Business Week*, 20 March 1982.

———. "Public Utility Regulation: Performance, Determinants, and Energy Policy Impacts." *Energy Law Journal* 3 (April 1982): 119–39.

———. "Our Stake in the Electric Utility's Dilemma." *Harvard Business Review* 60 (May/June 1982): 87–97.

———. "Save Now, Freeze Later: The Real Price of Cheap Electricity." *Regulation* 7 (September/October 1983): 31–36.

———. *The Policy Game.* New York: John Wiley & Sons, 1984.

———. *The Dimming of America.* Cambridge, Mass.: Ballinger Publishing Co., 1985.

Navarro, Peter, and Jeffrey A. Dubin. "Regulatory Climate and the Cost of Capital." In M. Crew, ed., *Regulatory Reform and Public Utilities*. Lexington, Mass.: Lexington Books, 1982.

Navarro, Peter, and Thomas R. Stauffer. "A Critique of Conventional Utility Ratemaking Methodologies." *Public Utilities Fortnightly* 107 (26 February 1981): 25–31.

Nerlove, Marc. "Returns to Scale in Electricity Supply." In A. Zellner, ed., *Readings in Economic Statistics and Econometrics*. Boston: Little, Brown and Company, 1968.

Niskanen, William A., Jr. *Bureaucracy and Representative Government.* Chicago: Aldine-Atherton, 1971.

Noll, Roger. "The Political Foundations of Regulatory Policy." *Journal of Institutional and Theoretical Economics* 139 (1983): 377–404.

O'Driscoll, Gerald P., Jr. "Monopoly in Theory and Practice." In I. Kirzner, ed., *Method, Process, and Austrian Economics: Essays in Honor of Ludwig von Mises*, pp. 189–213. Lexington, Mass.: D. C. Heath, 1982.

O'Dowd, M. C. "The Problem of 'Government Failure' in Mixed Economies." *South African Journal of Economics* 46 (1978): 360–70.

Olson, Mancur. *The Rise and Decline of Nations.* New Haven, Conn.: Yale University Press, 1982.

Pasour, Ernest C., Jr. "Cost and Choice—Austrian vs. Conventional Views." *Journal of Libertarian Studies* 2 (1978): 327–36.

———. "Economic Efficiency: Touchstone or Mirage?" *Intercollegiate Review* 17 (1981): 33–44.

———. "Economic Efficiency and Inefficient Economics: Another View." *Journal of Post-Keynesian Economics* 4 (1982): 454–59.

———. "Monopoly Theory and Practice—Some Subjectivist Implications: Comment on O'Driscoll." In I. Kirzner, ed., *Method, Process, and Austrian Economics: Essays in Honor of Ludwig von Mises*, pp. 215–23. Lexington, Mass.: D. C. Heath, 1982.

———. "Information: A Neglected Aspect of the Theory of Price Regulation." *Cato Journal* 3 (Winter 1983–84): 855–67.

Peacock, Alan. "On the Anatomy of Collective Failure." *Public Finance* 35 (1980): 33–43.

Peltzman, Sam. "Pricing in Public and Private Enterprises: Electric Utilities in the United States." *Journal of Law and Economics* 14 (April 1971): 109–48.

———. "Toward a More General Theory of Regulation." *Journal of Law and Economics* 19 (August 1976): 211–40.

Pigou, Arthur C. *Wealth and Welfare*. London: Macmillan, 1912.

Posner, Richard A. "Taxation by Regulation." *Bell Journal of Economics and Management Science* 2 (1971): 22–50.

———. "Theories of Economic Regulation." *Bell Journal of Economics and Management Science* 5 (Autumn 1974): 335–58.

———. "The Social Costs of Monopoly and Regulation." *Journal of Political Economy* 83 (1975): 807–27.

Robbins, Lionel. "Economics and Political Economy." *American Economic Review* 71 (May 1981): 1–10.

Rothbard, Murray N. *Power and Market: Government and the Economy*. Menlo Park, Calif.: Institute for Humane Studies, 1970.

———. *The Ethics of Liberty*. Atlantic Highlands, N.J.: Humanities Press, 1982.

Schlesinger, James R. "Systems Analysis and the Political Process." *Journal of Law and Economics* 11 (1968): 281–98.

Shackle, George L. S. *Decision, Order and Time in Human Affairs*. 2d ed. London: Cambridge University Press, 1969.

———. *Epistemics and Economics: A Critique of Economic Doctrines*. London: Cambridge University Press, 1972.

———. "Means and Meaning in Economic Theory." *Scottish Journal of Political Economy* 29 (1982): 223–34.

Smith, J. Allen. "Effect of State Regulation of Public Utilities Upon Home Rule. *Annals of the American Academy* 53 (May 1914): 85–93.

Sowell, Thomas. *Knowledge and Decisions*. New York: Basic Books, 1980.

Stelzer, Irwin M. "Electric Utilities—Next Stop for Deregulators?" *Regulation* 6 (July/August 1982): 29–35.

Stigler, George J. "The Theory of Economic Regulation." *Bell Journal of Economics and Management Science* 2 (Spring 1971): 3–21.

———. *The Citizen and the State*. Chicago: University of Chicago Press, 1975.

Stigler, George, and Claire Friedland. "What Can Regulators Regulate? The Case of Electricity." *Journal of Law and Economics* 5 (October 1962): 1–16.

Stobaugh, Robert, and Daniel Yergin, eds. *Energy Future: Report of the Energy Project at the Harvard Business School*. New York: Random House, 1979.

Taylor, Lester D. "The Demand for Electricity: A Survey." *Bell Journal of Economics* 6 (Spring 1975): 74–110.

Thirlby, G. F. "Economists' Cost Rules and Equilibrium Theory." In

J. Buchanan and G. Thirlby, eds., *L. S. E. Essays on Cost,* pp. 275–87. London: Weidenfeld and Nicolson, 1973.

Torr, C. S. W. "The Role of Information in Economic Analysis." *South African Journal of Economics* 40 (1980): 115–31.

Troxel, Emery. *Economics of Public Utilities.* New York: Rinehart & Company, 1947.

Tullock, Gordon. "Bureaucracy and the Growth of Government." In *The Taming of Government,* IEA Readings 21, pp. 23–38. London: Institute of Economic Affairs, 1979.

U.S. Department of Energy. Assistant Secretary for Environment, Safety, and Emergency Preparedness. *The National Electric Reliability Study: Final Report.* Washington, D.C.: Federal Energy Regulatory Commission, April 1981.

————. Energy Information Administration. *Nuclear Plant Cancellations: Causes, Costs, and Consequences.* Washington, D.C.: Energy Information Administration, April 1983.

————. "Delays and Cancellation of Coal-Fired Generating Capacity." Washington, D.C.: Energy Information Administration, July 1983.

————. Office of Policy, Planning, and Analysis. *The Future of Electric Power in America.* Washington, D.C.: Department of Energy, in-house publication, June 1983.

Von Mises, Ludwig. *Human Action.* 3d ed. Chicago: Henry Regnery Company, 1966.

————. *Bureaucracy.* New Rochelle, N.Y.: Arlington House, 1969.

Wenders, John T. "Peak Load Pricing in the Electric Utility Industry." *Bell Journal of Economics* 7 (1976): 232–41.

————. "Marginal Cost Pricing and the Determination of Class Revenue Requirements." *Electric Ratemaking* 2 (1983): 50–54.

————. "Two Part Tariffs and the 'Spiral of Impossibility' in the Market for Electricity." *Energy Journal* 5 (1984): 177–79.

————. "An Economic History of the U.S. Telecommunications Industry to 1995: A Public Choice Perspective." *New Directions: State Regulation of Telecommunications.* Seattle: Washington State Legislature Joint Select Committee on Telecommunications, 1984.

Wenders, John T., and R. Ashley Lyman. "An Analysis of the Benefits and Costs of Seasonal-Time-of-Day Electricity Rates." In M. Crew, ed., *Problems in Public Utility Economics and Regulation,* pp. 73–91. Lexington, Mass.: D. C. Heath, 1979.

————. "Determining the Optimal Penetration of Time-of-Day Electricity Tariffs." *Electric Ratemaking* 1 (1982): 15–20.

Wenders, John T., and Lester D. Taylor. "Experiments in Seasonal-Time-of-Day Pricing of Electricity to Residential Users." *Bell Journal of Economics* 7 (1976): 531–52.

Wilcox, Delos F. *Municipal Franchises*. 2 vols. Chicago: University of Chicago Press, 1910.

———. "Effects of State Regulation Upon the Municipal Ownership Movement." *Annals of the American Academy* 53 (May 1914): 71–84.

Wolf, Charles, Jr. "A Theory of Nonmarket Failure: Framework for Implementation Analysis." *Journal of Law and Economics* 22 (1979): 107–39.

Worcester, Dean A., Jr. "Economics and Principles." *Eastern Economic Journal* 8 (1982): 83–88.

Yeager, Leland B. "Methodenstreit Over Demand Curves." *Journal of Political Economy* 68 (1960): 53–64.

———. "Economics and Principles." *Southern Economic Journal* 42 (1976): 559–71.

PART IV

REGULATORY REFORM

Part IV: REGULATORY REFORM

John C. Moorhouse

Part IV reviews alternatives to contemporary utility regulation. In Chapter 12 Primeaux summarizes the results of over ten years of research on competition in the electric power industry. Using a variety of data bases in his research, Primeaux finds that where consumers can choose among electric utilities or where electric utilities face competition from alternative energy suppliers, electric companies are more efficient, excess capacity is not a problem, and consumers enjoy lower electric rates. This evidence suggesting the efficacy of competition leads Primeaux to advocate policies that eliminate regulatory barriers and strengthen competition in the electric power industry.

Chapter 13 explores the economics of establishing property rights in utility franchises. Building on the earlier work of Demsetz, Ekelund and Saba analyze the arguments for and against replacing traditional regulation with competitive franchise bidding. They correctly observe that what is at issue are intertemporal contracting problems associated with sunk costs, contract administration costs, and technological innovation. Ekelund and Saba argue that while regulation is one way of addressing these problems, other alternatives exist, including that of encouraging competition by reducing entry control.

In the capstone chapter of this volume, Gordon reviews various proposals to reform electric utility regulation. His purpose is to foster open-minded discussion and to overcome an unwillingness to experiment with radical reform of utility regulation. In a fascinating discussion of the strategy of reform, Gordon observes that relatively few scholars are willing to confront the implications of their analysis of utility regulation defects. Despite the fact that their research often offers compelling reasons and evidence supporting radical reform, scholars do not recommend it, and they do not draw strong conclusions. Gordon goes on to analyze the myriad regulations imposed on electric utilities and to offer his own reform proposals.

12

COMPETITION BETWEEN ELECTRIC UTILITIES

Walter J. Primeaux, Jr.

INTRODUCTION

For a number of years now public utility specialists have focused much concern on the present form of electric utility regulation.[1] Recently the popular press has reflected this concern, and wide discussion currently explores questions about regulatory effectiveness that were raised several years ago by utility specialists.[2] Such discussions—on the electric utility industry and regulatory reform—have been extensive and have covered a range of topics and problems. One recent publication indicates that the present long-standing system of pricing, supplying, financing, and regulating might be outmoded, suggesting that drastic changes are likely to result because of current problems.[3] This source indicates that the absence of incentives to reduce costs under the present regulatory arrangement is an important cause of problems within the industry.[4]

---

1. For example, Burton N. Behling, *Competition and Monopoly in Public Utility Industries* (Urbana: University of Illinois, 1938), p. 28; and Horace M. Gray, "The Passing of the Public Utility Concept," *Land Economics* 16 (1940):8.

2. For example, Tom Alexander, "The Surge to Deregulate Electricity," *Fortune* (1981):98–105; and "Are Utilities Obsolete? A Troubled System Faces Radical Change," *Business Week*, 21 May 1984, p. 116.

3. "Are Utilities Obsolete?" p. 116.

4. Ibid., p. 118.

Suggested substitutes and remedies for regulatory failure involve a wide variety of changes. Some proposals focus on changing the regulatory process and others on changing the structural features of the industry and the way firms conduct their operations.

At a conference in 1971 I suggested that direct electric utility competition would be an effective way of eliminating regulatory problems in the industry.[5] The purposes of this chapter are to examine the present state of affairs concerning direct electric utility competition and to discuss some of the research that evolved from my original conference paper. This aspect of the chapter will educate the uninitiated reader about how extensive direct electric utility competition once was in this country and the degree to which it still exists today. The chapter briefly describes the degree to which this actual competition generates favorable or unfavorable outcomes for the relevant utility companies engaged and its consumers. In addition to direct electric utility competition, this study also examines the wholesale market for electricity, interfuel competition, and the question of whether competition could be a viable alternative to commission regulation.

DIRECT ELECTRIC UTILITY COMPETITION

The natural-monopoly concept is a long-standing institution. J. M. Clark, a prominent economist, says that the first germ of the concept was expressed, in spirit, by Adam Smith.[6] In my research the first reference I found that actually used the words *natural monopoly* was dated 1820 and attributed to a professor of law at the University of Virginia.[7] An extensive discussion of the theory of natural monopoly is beyond the scope of this chapter. Because other authors in this volume have discussed this theory, I only make a few brief comments about the concept and its pronouncements concerning direct electric utility competition.

In a nutshell, proponents of utility regulation assert that direct competition should not be permitted within an industry characterized as

5. Walter J. Primeaux, Jr., "A Reexamination of the Monopoly Market Structure for Electric Utilities," in A. Phillips, ed., *Promoting Competition in Regulated Markets* (Washington, D.C.: Brookings Institution, 1975), chap. 6, pp. 198–200.

6. John M. Clark, *Competition as a Dynamic Process* (Washington, D.C.: Brookings Institution, 1961), p. 26. He cited Adam Smith, *An Inquiry Into the Nature and Causes of the Wealth of Nations* (New York: The Modern Library, 1937), p. 17.

7. Joseph Dorfman, *The Economic Mind in American Civilization,* vol. 1 (New York: Augustus M. Kelley, 1966), p. 394.

a natural monopoly. They believe that cost conditions as well as other environmental characteristics that exist in natural-monopoly industries would cause competition to ultimately fail. Consequently, only one firm would survive because the industry is naturally monopolistic. From the customers point of view, competition would lead to higher utility costs, higher prices, and generally poor firm performance.

Gray criticizes the natural-monopoly idea, explaining that policy-makers used the natural-monopoly concept as a rationalization to resolve the conflict in philosophies between the traditional free-enterprise system and the public utility firm. Gray says that the fiction of natural monopoly was invented to explain the anticompetitive behavior of public utility firms in the early days of the industry.[8] Under the natural-monopoly theory, according to Gray, the government is forced to accept the fact that it is powerless to resist the natural trend. This behavior is not difficult to reconcile with free-market ideals because these "new" monopolies were really different in that they were *natural*; in contrast, other monopolies are unnatural or artificial.

These brief comments on the theory of natural monopoly indicate that it has not been embraced by all public utility specialists. Gray was not the only one to criticize the theory, but his perspectives serve to illustrate the general criticisms. Yet critics of the natural-monopoly theory were and have been in the minority. The majority of specialists claim to have priority on the truth, that natural monopoly accurately characterizes public utilities.

The theory of natural monopoly developed over time without systematic evidence supporting its contention. By designing an empirical test of the theory of natural monopoly, my research sheds light on the validity of current regulatory policies and on the possibility of relying on competitive market forces to protect consumer interests. My research on direct electric utility competition involves an examination of several key propositions of the theory of natural monopoly, using statistical data for the investigations.

Existing Direct Electric Utility Competition

Direct electric utility competition has existed over a long period of time. Indeed in the early days of the industry several electric firms often operated within a single city. The point is that the electric utility

8. Gray, "Passing of the Public Utility Concept," p. 10.

industry did not begin as a natural monopoly. As Gray explains, the justification for allowing only monopolies in the industry as a matter of policy was a compromise policymakers made.[9]

Phillips points out that six electric companies were organized in New York City in 1885. Five electric companies served Duluth, Minnesota, prior to 1895. Four electric firms serviced Scranton, Pennsylvania, in 1906, and in 1907, forty-five firms were authorized to sell electricity in Chicago.[10] Natural-monopoly theory, however, had a significant effect on the emerging policy toward electric utility firms, gradually cities served by two or more electric utility firms dwindled in number. Today relatively few such cities remain. F. Stewart Brown, then chief of the Bureau of Power of the Federal Power Commission, stated in a letter to me dated July 29, 1969, that as of January 1, 1966, direct competition between two electric utility firms existed in forty-nine cities with a population of 2,500 or larger.[11] The attachment to Brown's letter, giving a tabulation of the cities with direct competition, is presented in Figure 12–1. The figure shows that the competition occurred in sixteen different states: Nine competitive situations existed in Texas, eight in Ohio, seven in Michigan, and five in Oregon. The remaining states had fewer cases of direct competition. The significant thing to note is that despite the theory of natural monopoly, direct electric utility competition does exist. Moreover it has existed in some cities for a long time. For example there has been direct electric utility competition in Sikeston, Missouri, for fifty years; in Poplar Bluff, Missouri, for over sixty years; in Lubbock, Texas, since 1916; in Portland, Oregon, since 1912; The Dalles, Oregon, since 1910; and Hagerstown, Maryland, since before 1910.[12] This list does not necessarily include the cities where direct competition has lasted the longest period of time. It merely lists years when competition began for firms where the dates are known. The significant point is that direct competition has endured over a long period of time in more than one isolated case. This suggests that the dire predictions

9. Gray, "Passing of the Public Utility Concept," p. 10.

10. Charles F. Phillips, Jr., *The Economics of Regulation: Theory and Practice in the Transportation and Public Utility Industries* (Homewood, Ill.: Irwin, 1969), p. 551.

11. F. Stewart Brown, then chief of the Bureau of Power, Federal Power Commission, correspondence to the author, 29 July 1969.

12. Competition was discontinued in Portland, Oregon; The Dalles, Oregon; Hagerstown, Maryland; and some other cities. This will be discussed later.

Figure 12–1. Communities in Which Utilities Directly Compete (as of January 1966).

Alabama	Ohio
Bessemer	Brooklyn
Tarrant City	Cleveland
Troy	Columbus
Alaska	East Cleveland
Anchorage	Hamilton
Spenard	Newton Falls
	Piqua
Illinois	Pomeroy
Bushnell	
Jacksonville	Oklahoma
	Duncan
Indiana	
Fort Wayne	Oregon
	Keizer
Iowa	Portland
Maquoketa	Salem
	Springfield
Kentucky	The Dalles
Paris	
	Pennsylvania
Maryland	East Stroudsburg
Hagerstown	Stroudsburg
Michigan	South Carolina
Allegan	Greer
Bay City	
Bessemer	South Dakota
Dowagiac	Sioux Falls
Ferrysburg	
Traverse City	Texas
Zeeland	Commerce
	Electra
Missouri	Floydada
Kennett	Garland
Poplar Bluff	Lubbock
Sikeston	Seymour
Trenton	Sonora
	Vernon
	Winters

SOURCE: Letter to the author (29 July 1969) from F. Stewart Brown, former chief of the Bureau of Power of the Federal Power Commission.

proponents of natural-monopoly theory make about the failure of direct competition have not been borne out in fact in these cities. Consequently these situations reflect evidence contrary to the natural-monopoly theory. If the theory says that competition cannot endure over time and it has in fact lasted, the theory is probably faulty. The discovery of these real competitive situations launched me into a research program designed to examine some of the key assumptions and propositions of the theory of natural monopoly. The following sections examine this research in some detail.

It is probably useful to discuss generally why competition emerged in cities where two electric firms came to exist. In some cases competition emerged because the monopoly was providing poor service to customers. In other cases the monopoly was charging prices consumers considered excessive, creating pressure to allow competition in to moderate the high price levels. In one case the electric railroad had excess generating capacity so it began selling the surplus, and thus began the competition with an existing monopoly. This discussion does not present all of the inducements to entry; it does show, however, that consumer satisfaction with the regulated monopoly arrangement is not assured. This dissatisfaction is discussed extensively in Behling, Gray, and other sources.[13]

The Federal Power Commission stopped keeping records of communities with two electric utility firms in 1966; consequently, two other economists and I undertook a mail survey to update this information. Figure 12–2 presents the results of the survey. We can make a number of interesting points by comparing Figure 12–1 with Figure 12–2. The first point is that since 1966 competition has ended in seventeen cities; for example, all of the firms in Oregon (five) and Alaska (two) have discontinued competition. Communications with the state regulatory commissions in both states reveal that they discontinued competition because the regulatory body viewed it as unfavorable. In many ways this is consistent with the attitude that has caused the prohibition of direct competition whenever anyone attempted to introduce it in some states. In this way natural-monopoly thinking has again affected direct electric utility competition. I present an extensive discussion of these situations in a recently completed book manuscript.[14] I will not discuss the remaining incidents where competition ceased to exist due to regulatory policy changes because they go beyond the scope of this chapter.

13. Behling, *Competition and Monopoly*, p. 28, and Gray, "Passing of the Public Utility Concept," pp. 8–20.
14. Walter J. Primeaux, Jr., *Direct Electric Utility Competition: The Natural Monopoly Myth*, (New York: Praeger Publishers, 1986).

Figure 12–2. Communities in Which Utilities Directly Compete (as of April 1981[a]).

Alabama
  Bessemer (1971)
  Tarrant City
  Troy[b]

Alaska
  Anchorage (1973)
  Spenard (1978)

Illinois
  Bushnell
  Jacksonville (1973)

Indiana
  Fort Wayne (1975)

Iowa
  Maquoketa

Kentucky
  Paris

Maryland
  Hagerstown (1970)

Michigan
  Allegan (1968)
  Bay City
  Bessemer (1978)
  Dowagiac
  Ferrysburg
  Traverse City
  Zeeland

Missouri
  Kennett
  Poplar Bluff
  Sikeston
  Trenton

Ohio
  Brooklyn[e]
  Cleveland
  Columbus
  East Cleveland[f]
  Hamilton
  Newton Falls
  Piqua[c]
  Pomeroy[d]

Oklahoma
  Duncan

Oregon
  Keizer (approximately 1967)
  Portland (after 1966, date unknown)
  Salem (approximately 1967)
  Springfield (1975)
  The Dalles (1976)

Pennsylvania
  East Stroudsburg
  Stroudsburg

South Carolina
  Greer

South Dakota
  Sioux Falls (1976)

Texas
  Commerce (1979)
  Electra
  Floydada (1973)
  Garland
  Lubbock
  Seymour
  Sonora
  Vernon
  Winter (1978)

a. An update of the 1966 data presented in Figure 12–1. Year competition discontinued is in parentheses.

b. Direct competition comes about whenever annexation takes place. The cooperative retains its customers unless consumers elect to receive electric energy from the city.

c. Direct competition exists in area contiguous to the city but not within the city limit.

d. Columbus and Southern Ohio Electric Co. has been serving a small number of customers in Pomeroy for many years. The company explains that shared areas more appropriately decribes the situation than competition. Since both firms in Pomeroy are now owned by the same company, studies are in process to determine if it is economically feasible to eliminate one of these firms in the market.

e. The City of Brooklyn, Ohio, reports that a monopoly firm served the city at August 14, 1981; whether competition even existed in 1966 is unclear.

f. The City of East Cleveland, Ohio, reports that a monopoly firm served the city at August 17, 1981; whether competition even existed in 1966 is unclear.

Daniel Hollas and Stan Herren greatly assisted in updating this table.

The Issue of Direct Competition

Why are most state regulatory commissions hostile toward direct electric utility competition? A recently completed study suggests that there are a number of reasons.[15] The first is that regulated electric utilities use discriminatory rate structures.[16] Entry control is necessary to perpetuate this discrimination; thus increased competition through entry access would reduce the extent of the discrimination because increased competition reduces the ability of a firm to profitably engage in price discrimination.[17]

A second reason explaining utility commissions' hostility toward the entry of competition into markets is the substantial monopoly power already held by utilities established in the state. Regulatory policy is certainly affected by the power or influence of electric producers; of course, the regulatory commission's policy and attitude toward competition also affects the power and wealth of electric utilities.[18]

A third reason for regulatory hostility toward direct competition in electric markets is the power of the natural gas producers within their state. The logic of this argument is as follows: Consumers of natural gas benefit from electric utility competition in two ways. First, competition in the electric utility industry lowers electric rates and increases competition between electric and gas utilities. This outcome, of course, is restricted to cases where electric and gas sales are from two competing firms and not from a combination firm selling both gas and electricity. The new competition between two electric companies will benefit gas consumers because of the lower prices. The second benefit to gas consumers from the direct electric utility competition stems from the fact that some gas users will switch to electricity because of its lower price, and this will tend to reduce prices even more for those who continue to use natural gas. Consequently natural gas producers and retailers would oppose a policy of direct

15. Walter J. Primeaux, Jr., et al., "Determinants of Regulatory Policies Toward Competition in the Electric Utility Industry," *Public Choice* 43 (1984):173–86.

16. These discriminatory rate structures are discussed in Walter J. Primeaux, Jr., and Randy A. Nelson, "An Examination of Price Discrimination and Internal Subsidization by Electric Utilities," *Southern Economic Journal* 47 (1980):84–99; and Daniel R. Hollas and Thomas S. Friedland, "Price Discrimination in the Municipal Electric Industry," *Research in Law and Economics* 2 (1980):181–98.

17. Primeaux, Jr., et al., "Determinants of Regulatory Policies."

18. Ibid.

competition in electricity. Thus commissions in states with relatively more powerful natural gas distributors will be less likely to encourage competition.[19]

There is at least one other reason why regulatory commissions could tend to oppose direct electric utility competition. Regulators often view their task as a substitute for the stifled competitive function, which means that the presence of any competition would reflect adversely on their effectiveness. In other words if regulators were effective and a reasonable outcome came from the regulatory process, pressures for new competition would not have emerged. Thus since regulatory commissions are a major force in deciding whether direct competition should be allowed, their self-interests tend to make them oppose new entry.

All the above forces work against competitive entry into the electric utility industry. It should be obvious that the same forces tend to oppose the continuation of any existent competition. Although beyond the scope of this study, it is probably safe to conclude that commission hostility played an important part in affecting the continuity of competition in places where it has ceased since 1966. This subject is fertile ground for future intensive study, but it is enough to point out here that powerful forces restrict entry as well as affect the continuity of competition that still exists so that it generally faces a hostile environment.

Cost Levels and Direct Competition

One of the key propositions of natural-monopoly theory states that these kind of firms are special in that the cost levels would be higher if competitive firms served a given market than if only a single firm served that area.[20] It is these cost conditions which, the theory claims, would allow one of the firms to begin a price-cutting strategy that would drive the other rival(s) out of business, leaving only the monopoly survivor. The importance of cost behavior in the electric utility business whenever competitive forces are present led me to select that subject as the first element of my research program in direct public utility competition. Although theoreticians have woven the natural-

19. Primeaux, Jr., et al., "Determinants of Regulatory Policies."

20. The research discussed in this section is presented in detail in Primeaux, Jr., "A Reexamination of the Monopoly Market."

monopoly theory through time without using empirical data to substantiate its propositions, such data for statistical examination does exist in those communities that have or have had competing electric utility firms.

I obtained data for all possible firms listed in Figure 12–1 from sources published by the Federal Power Commission and additional data from other published sources. This consisted of the operating information for the individual companies, which gave me the statistical data needed to develop the cost curves for the two groups of firms; one cost curve represents the monopoly firms, and the second cost curve, the competitive firms.

In all cases for firms in the sample, the two firms operating in a single city consisted of a privately owned firm (investor-owned utility) competing with a publicly owned firm (municipally owned utility). The research design was conceived to accommodate availability of data that is affected by the nature of the operations of firms, as mentioned below.

The privately owned firms all operate in more than a single city, but they face competition in only a single city. In contrast, the publicly owned firms operate in just one city, in a situation that constitutes a competitive environment. Although the Federal Power Commission (FPC) compiles individual statistical reports of privately owned firms in an annual report, the cost data, unfortunately, are not useful because the report does not require that costs be allocated to individual cities for firms operating in more than one city. This makes cost comparisons for privately owned firms within a single city impossible. The reports required of the public service commission in most states also do not allocate costs to individual cities. Another information problem comes from the fact that municipally owned firms are required by law to file cost and revenue information with the FPC, but many do not do so. Thus the FPC's annual statistical reports are incomplete.

Due to the nature of the reported data and other problems. I confined this study to municipally owned firms and gathered cost data from as many municipally owned firms facing competition as possible from FPC reports. Then I used this subset of firms to indicate cost levels in the competitive environment. For comparison purposes I also selected another subset of firms not facing competition from the same reports. In general a matched firm without competition was selected for every firm without competition. All of the available data are used to develop the statistical analyses. Table 12–1 shows cities with competition as well as the matched monopoly cities and their sizes measured by kilowatt-hour sales in 1968.

The procedure to select the matched pairs involved criteria that I established to minimize possible statistical difficulties which could affect the validity of the results.[21] I used a number of factors to construct the cost levels for the firms in the study and to control for those effects that could influence operating costs of electric utility firms. Those factors include: scale factors, levels of capacity utilization, steam-electric fuel costs, hydroelectric fuel costs, and internal combustion fuel costs. I also introduced additional factors to consider the nature of sales by customer mix. This group of variables considered the relative importance of residential sales compared with commercial and industrial sales. I included another variable to consider the importance of consumption per commercial and industrial customer and another for consumption per residential customer. Additional variables also accounted for the cost of purchased power, the density of consumers (number of customers per square mile), the cost effects of being located in different states, and whether the competition caused costs to be higher or lower. As mentioned above, the theory of natural monopoly forecasts that competition of the kind described above would cause higher costs than a monopoly.

I made the appropriate statistical tests to assure that the pooling procedure is acceptable (see footnote 21) and to assess the interaction effects between competition and the other cost factors used in the analysis. The test results revealed that the pooling procedure is acceptable.

The overall results show that competition causes the average cost curve to shift downward by approximately 1.5155 mills and at the same time causes the slope of the total cost curve to increase so that average costs increase by approximately .0068 mills for each increase of one million kilowatt hours of electricity sold. The interpretation of these results is rather straightforward. Competition causes electric firms to operate at lower average cost levels than they would otherwise; at the same time, competing firms experienced higher additions to costs

21. The statistical procedure involved a pooling of cross section and time series data to strengthen and give depth to the available statistics. Data for the five-year period 1964–1968 were used in most cases. Notes to Table 12–1 indicate the cities for which fewer years were used. The relative sizes of the firms in terms of kilowatt-hour sales are also shown.

Table 12–1.   Cities with Monopoly or Duopoly Municipally Owned Electric
Utilities (by thousands of kilowatt hours sold, fiscal year 1968[a]).

Cities With Competition	Kilowatt Hour Sales	Matched Cities Without Competition	Kilowatt Hour Sales
Bessemer, Alabama	108,838	Florence, Alabama	447,181
Tarrant City, Alabama	56,573	Scottsboro, Alabama	98,280
Anchorage, Alaska	189,357	————[b]	————
Fort Wayne, Indiana	330,383	Richmond, Indiana	390,824
Maquoketa, Iowa	17,528	Algona, Iowa	28,186
Hagerstown, Maryland	106,089	Bristol, Virginia[c]	211,763
Allegan, Michigan	15,775[d]	Niles, Michigan	56,974
Bay City, Michigan	95,484	Wyandotte, Michigan	126,265
Dowagiac, Michigan	21,090	Hillsdale, Michigan	64,971
Ferrysburg, Michigan[c]	128,774	Lansing, Michigan	1,300,318
Traverse City, Michigan	67,299	Sturgis, Michigan	73,527
Zeeland, Michigan	26,952	Petoskey, Michigan	30,612
————	————	Carthage, Missouri	55,181
Kennett, Missouri	34,915	Rolla, Missouri	52,427
Poplar Bluff, Missouri	67,197	Columbia, Missouri	189,737
Trenton, Missouri	25,451	Marshall, Missouri	36,730
Lincoln, Nebraska	124,026[f]	Omaha, Nebraska	2,343,826[f]
Cleveland, Ohio	546,707	Springfield, Illinois[c]	692,543
Columbus, Ohio	166,771	Anderson, Indiana[c]	318,606
Piqua, Ohio	119,715	Logansport, Indiana[c]	130,236
Springfield, Oregon	166,707	Eugene, Oregon	1,185,032
Greer, South Carolina	47,727	Greenwood, South Carolina	77,747
Sioux Falls, South Dakota	23,526	Watertown, South Dakota	57,659
————	————	Springfield, Missouri	585,954
Garland, Texas	337,562	San Antonio, Texas	3,325,771

SOURCES: Federal Power Commission, *Statistics of Publicly Owned Electric Utilities in the United States,* 1968 (1969), and 1965 (1967) and 1967 (1969) issues.

a. This table, which presents data for 1968 except where noted, shows the relative size of the firms used in the regression model discussed in this chapter. In the model I used data for the five-year period 1964–68 except in the cases of Maquoketa and Algona, Iowa, for which 1964 data were not available; Greer, South Carolina, for which 1964–65 data were not available; Allegan, Michigan, for which 1964–67 data were used as there was no competition in 1968; and Lincoln, Nebraska, which had competition in 1964 and 1965 only. The fiscal year varies among the firms, generally ending either June 30 or December 31.

b. No suitable matched city could be found in Alaska.

c. Matched cities could not be found within the competitive firm's state. Some cost adjustments were made to compensate for state differences.

d. 1967 data; competition did not exist in 1968.

e. This city is served by both the city of Grand Haven Board of Light and Power and the Consumers Power Company.

f. 1965 data; competition did not exist in 1966–68.

as output levels increased compared with monopoly firms. This implies that the total cost curve is steeper under competitive conditions. Using the numbers generated from the statistical calculations, one finds that competition causes the firms to have lower average costs than the monopoly firms until production reaches 222 million kilowatt hours of annual sales; after that, monopolists produce at lower costs.

The nature of the sample may be partially responsible for this result. Only three companies in the sample of firms facing competition had annual sales in excess of 222 million kwh. If larger competitive firms had existed, with larger sales levels, it is quite likely that the level of sales where competition was more cost efficient than monopoly would have exceeded the annual level of 222 million kwh. This observation, however, must remain conjecture because no sample of larger firms exists.

Why do costs of competitive electric utility firms tend to rise as output increases? There are at least two credible explanations. The first has to do with economies of scale; the technology of the industry is such that complex networks of transmission lines, distribution lines, transformers, power plants, and so forth are located to provide power to serve a particular area. The larger the area involved, the more complex the interaction within the networks must be, and competition compounds this complexity. Second, management in a competitive environment must plan, coordinate, and control firms that are operating in the face of more unknowns than monopoly firms, and these managerial problems increase in larger cities. This combination of managerial and technological problems could tend to cause average costs to eventually rise in a competitive environment even though they are initially lowered by the rivalry.

The explanation of why competition causes firms to operate at lower costs than if they operated in a monopoly market structure rests in the X-efficiency theory.[22] Economic theory traditionally assumes that firms seek maximum profits; thus they will produce at minimum costs. There is no reason, in this context, to expect competition to lower operating costs below the monopoly level. X-efficiency theory, however, is based on the fundamental premise that the profit maximization assumption of economic theory is unrealistic, and that actual firms are under strong pressure not to maximize profits. There are many

22. The theory was originally developed in Harvey Leibenstein, "Allocative Efficiency vs. 'X-Efficiency'," *American Economic Review* 56 (1966):408.

facets of X-efficiency theory; the one that applies here has to do with the effects of competition on a firm's operating efficiency. Leibenstein explains that when competitive pressures are few, managers trade the disutility of greater effort, search, and control of other firms' activities for the utility of less pressure and better interfirm relations. The costs of such trades become high where competitive pressures are great. By raising the implicit price of managerial slack, competition provides a strong incentive to become more efficient.

The cost reductions from competition discussed above are readily explained by X-efficiency theory; competitive pressures induce efforts toward cost reduction, and costs tend to rise in the absence of such pressures. The public policy implications of these findings lead to serious questions about the natural-monopoly theory and past public policy that has generally prohibited direct competition between two electric utility firms. The natural-monopoly theory would expect higher costs under competitive conditions; yet actual costs turned out to be lower with rivalry.

Competition and Excess Capacity

Another main objection to competition between utility firms the proponents of regulated monopoly bring up is that rivalry would lead to excessive capital requirements.[23] These excessive requirements, they argue, come from the fact that direct competition leads rival companies to build more capacity than if only a single monopoly firm existed. All in all the basic plant requirements plus this additional excess capacity would require a larger financial outlay than if only a single firm were to operate in a given market. Ultimately this excess capacity also provides the incentive to cut prices and engage in price wars, according to natural monopoly theory.

Since direct competition actually exists in some cities, further research can examine whether competition actually causes more excess capacity than monopoly in the electric utility industry. No one had yet explored this question using statistical data. Essentially I used the same sample firms listed in Table 12–1, with one adjustment to eliminate firms that did not generate their own power requirements. Be-

23. The research discussed in this section is reported in full in Walter J. Primeaux, Jr., "The Effect of Competition on Capacity Utilization in the Electric Utility Industry," *Economic Inquiry* 16 (1978):237–48.

cause these firms did not have generating facilities, their inclusion in the sample would add unnecessary complications and ambiguity.

The statistical approach I used here is very similar to that used in the cost level study. The factors included in this analysis are different however, because their effects on capacity utilization are different. In this study, I considered scale of operation, the extent to which firms in the sample rely upon purchased power, hydroelectric generation, different consumption characteristics among customer classes, geographical effects, peak-load requirements of the companies, and whether or not a firm in the sample faced competition to determine their effects on capacity utilization.

The statistical results show that the outcome predicted by critics of direct electric competition do not occur in fact. That is, competitive firms do not experience a lower level of capacity utilization than monopoly firms; consequently firms engaging in real competition do not build unnecessary excess capacity.[24] These results show that another concern expressed by opponents of direct competition who favor regulated monopoly for the electric utility industry is without firm foundation. There is no reason to believe that direct competition would generate any higher capital cost than would regulated monopoly.

Price Wars and Price Flexibility

The theory of natural monopoly also predicts price wars whenever direct competition exists between public utilities.[25] Using the same basic sample as in the previous research, and price data reflecting actual prices consumers paid for service, I observed price movements in the competitive markets between the years 1959 and 1970. My objective was to determine whether a tendency occurred for competitive firms to follow price increases and decreases and whether any evidence showed of pricing behavior that reflected price wars when competition exists in a natural-monopoly environment. The results here also fail to support the natural-monopoly theory. Price wars do

---

24. Of course firms in this industry must have enough capacity to take care of peak-load requirements of customers so their rates of capacity utilization do not approach those of industrial firms. As mentioned earlier, the peak requirements are considered in the statistical analyses.

25. The research in this section is discussed in Walter J. Primeaux, Jr., and Mark Bomball, "A Reexamination of the Kinky Oligopoly Demand Curve," *Journal of Political Economy* 82 (1974) 851–62.

not occur. Moreover a mail survey of electric utility firm managers failed to reveal that price wars have been a problem in cities with competing electric firms.[26] Consequently predictions that under competition one competitor would drive the other out of business seem to be unfounded. Of course these results are consistent with the previous results of no greater excess capacity in monopoly markets. Without the existence of excess capacity, a strong pressure to engage in price wars is absent.

Direct Competition and the Level of Consumer Prices

The previous section concerned price flexibility and price wars. This section discusses research that examines the effect of competition on the prices consumers pay for electricity.[27] The sample consisted of essentially the same firms indicated in Table 12–1. The statistical procedure is similar to the cost examination; one difference is that the examination looks only at data for the year 1968 because previous research indicates this year to be a good one for making comparisons; conditions were rather stable in that year. Unsettled conditions generated by the energy crisis render later data problematic.

The statistical procedure considered factors that would affect consumer price levels, including income per household, average price of natural gas (a substitute energy source), number of customers per square mile, a consumer mix variable, operating and maintenance expense, purchased power, climatic variables, and whether or not a firm in the sample faces competition.

I examined consumer prices for three different residential rate categories (using marginal prices) and defined the marginal price as the difference between the price paid by a customer if consumed in one block and the price in the next highest block. In addition, I also examined average prices for residential consumption. The results reveal rather consistent price benefits to consumers from electric utility competition. The lowest residential rate category showed downward price pressure but no significant price reductions from competition. The second residential rate category showed price reductions amounting

---

26. This survey is discussed in detail in Primeaux, Jr., *Direct Electric Utility Competition*.

27. The research in this section is presented in detail in Walter J. Primeaux, Jr., "Estimate of the Price Effect of Competition: The Case of Electricity," *Resources and Energy* 7 (1985):2–16.

to 16 percent. The third rate category was reduced by 19 percent, and the average residential rate was decreased by 33 percent.

These pricing results contradict the natural-monopoly theory. The theory predicts higher prices from direct electric utility competition; however, the opposite results occur. This outcome is consistent with the results of the cost research discussed above. When firms experience lower costs, they are able to charge lower prices. This price behavior is probably a reflection of the cost behavior. Yet there is more to the story than this because if firms incur lower costs in the monopoly market structure, they would not necessarily be inclined to lower consumer prices. It is the competitive pressure that ultimately induces a firm to lower the price of its outputs. This behavior is quite consistent with what one would expect of firms in any industry.

An important difference between these statistical results and those predicted in natural-monopoly theory is that the consumer actually fares better with competition than with monopoly. Consequently proponents of regulated monopoly who profess to be defending consumer interests on natural-monopoly grounds must change their focus of attention. Consumer interests would best be served by competition, not monopoly.

Generating Versus Distribution

As dissatisfaction with existing regulatory practices has grown, a suggested alternative for improving utility performance is to deregulate electricity generation, with distribution remaining under regulation.[28] It is interesting to note that in the early discussion of natural monopoly, it is economies of scale in generation that is emphasized as one of the main features or characteristics of a firm requiring special treatment. Yet as the electric utility industry began to be characterized by diseconomies of scale, proponents of regulated monopoly changed the emphasis of their arguments to stress economies of scale in distribution. They allege, without statistical evidence, that competition would cause higher costs than monopoly because firms would lose economies of scale in distribution.

Research on the effect of competition on cost levels, discussed ear-

---

28. The research in this section is described in detail in Walter J. Primeaux, Jr., "Deregulation of Electric Utility Firms: An Assessment of the Cost Effects of Complete Deregulation vs. Deregulation of Generation Only," (University of Illinois, 1970). (Mimeo.)

lier, considered all firm costs together; that is, I added distribution and generating costs together to establish cost levels for comparison purposes. The main objective of this additional study is to determine whether, using the data from cities with direct competition, economies of scale in distribution warrant a policy of stopping short of total deregulation in retail markets. The central question I examined is whether competitive electric utility firms, which only distribute electricity, incur higher costs than monopoly firms operating in the same manner.

The sample is quite similar to the one used in the cost analysis study. Because of the nature of the competing firms, and the way information is reported, the research design is also similar to that discussed in the cost-analysis section of this chapter. The sample consists of pooled cross-section data by individual firm for the period 1964–1968. More recent data are not used for two reasons. First, as mentioned earlier, the number of available firms declined in recent years. Thus the mid-1960s offers the largest sample of relevant data. Second, more recent data is affected to some extent by the change in energy supply characteristics that took place in the 1970s. By comparison the period 1964–1968 presents a relatively stable economic environment.

Factors held constant for the statistical analysis are: scale effects, rate of capacity utilization, steam, internal combustion, and hydroelectric fuel costs, customer mix and consumption characteristics, costs of purchased power, effects of market density (number of customers per square mile), and state differences. The research results show that firms which only distribute power do not have higher costs under competition than under monopoly; consequently the concern by those who advocate deregulation of the generation but not distribution function seems unfounded. Even though monopoly distribution firms might have the capability of operating at lower costs than competitive distribution firms, we do not see that result. In a monopoly market structure X-inefficiency offsets the technical losses caused by direct competition. I have already mentioned these benefits from competition here and in some of my previous research.[29] Furthermore these

29. Primeaux, Jr., "A Reexamination of the Monopoly Market," and Walter J. Primeaux, Jr., "An Assessment of X-Efficiency Gained Through Competition," *Review of Economics and Statistics* 59 (1977):107–8.

results are consistent with the research discussed above that examined distribution and generating costs together.

Since this analysis uses data from real markets, where competition already exists (or does not exist in the case of the monopolists in the sample), the findings are useful for public policy consideration. The results show that complete deregulation seems practical because firms only distributing power, in a competitive market structure, do not incur higher average costs than their monopoly counterparts.

The advantage of complete deregulation for firms that generate and distribute power is that they would achieve cost economies through X-efficiency. The advantage of deregulating firms that only distribute electricity is that they incur no higher costs than monopolists when they face competition. If both groups are completely deregulated, it would become possible to have price competition in residential, commercial, and industrial service without concern for the arbitrary regulatory process of rate-of-return regulation or rate-making. The market mechanism can automatically perform the regulatory function as it does for most other industries.

The expected outcome from direct competition is that the rivalry would force the firms to become more efficient and operate at lower costs; this fact, along with the price rivalry discussed earlier in this chapter, would provide customers with lower prices. The lower prices would result from eliminating inefficiency and any excessive profits that might exist under the present regulatory arrangement.

THE WHOLESALE MARKET FOR ELECTRICITY

As explained above, some electric utility firms in this country only distribute power. In some cases, these firms do not even own generating facilities. This condition is independent of the market structure in which they operate. That is, there are both monopoly and competitive firms in the industry that do not generate power; there are also monopoly and competitive firms that do generate power. The firms that do not generate power, along with those who do not generate sufficient amounts of power to totally satisfy the demands of their customers, create the buyers' side of the wholesale market for electricity. At the same time other firms with excess generating capacity, as well as some public power authorities, constitute the sellers' side of the wholesale market for electricity.

Firms that generate power or only distribute it can be subjected to direct competition without creating conditions that adversely effect their costs levels and with beneficial effects on consumer prices. Effective and efficient wholesale markets can facilitate direct competition, and they could also permit vigorous competition at the wholesale level. Indeed some other researchers believe this to be the key to obtaining viable competition in the electric utility industry.

Linda Cohen presents an extensive discussion of a system of interconnected utilities in Florida, which uses spot prices for electricity; the system is designed to introduce market forces into the wholesale market for electricity. This section briefly discusses the operation of this system of wholesaling electricity, drawing heavily on Cohen's work.[30]

The Florida Electric Coordinating Group, Inc., is an informal power pool of electric utilities. This group is referred to as the Florida Energy Broker, and it has operated since 1978 to handle energy exchanges between utilities in the state.[31] Participating utilities bid to buy or sell energy each hour; these offers to buy and sell are transmitted through a computer. The computer matches bids to buy or sell and calculates contract prices for the next hour. The individual utility firms must then decide to either agree to exchange the energy or withdraw from the deal. As of June 1981 fifteen utilities of different sizes were participating; both municipally owned firms and privately owned (investor-owned) firms can take part. In 1980 savings to the participating utilities amounted to roughly 2 percent of the total fuel bill. Although the process is not without flaws, both utility firms and Florida regulators praise its operation.[32] Despite being regulated, the Florida Energy Broker system does illustrate one way of introducing greater competition and efficiency into the wholesale sector of the electric utility industry.[33]

In this arrangement, each individual utility retains control over its generation decisions. There are efficiency gains, however, that accrue from the coordinating function; these gains occur whenever low-cost generation from one utility is substituted for high-cost generation from another. Cohen points out that the spot-market arrangement shows

---

30. Linda Cohen, "A Spot Market for Electricity: Preliminary Analysis of the Florida Energy Broker," (Rand Corp., 1982). (Mimeo.)

31. Ibid.

32. Ibid.

33. Ibid.

that the generation sector of the industry can accommodate numerous independent operations, each operating efficiently.[34]

The Florida arrangement allows for profit incentives; that is, sellers keep profits from sales so they have incentives to generate and sell low-cost power. Short-term savings to purchasers are passed through to customers, but the utilities buying the power are able to avoid losses from generating high-cost power, according to Cohen.[35]

The coordination of short-term operations is probably the most interesting aspect of the Florida Energy Broker; Cohen explains that special features of the electric utility industry make the short-term coordination vital to decentralization. She emphasizes the random nature of supply and demand and the impossibility of storing energy as those special features.[36] The broker arrangement addresses the problem of short-term coordination that Cohen claims has long been considered an impediment to greater decentralization. Although the Energy Broker presents an interesting attempt to introduce competition into the electricity industry, it is not without its difficulties, as discussed by Cohen.[37] Nevertheless spot pricing could eventually emerge as an important feature of the modified environment in which electric utility firms will exist in the future. Significant change in the operating and regulated environment is imminent in the electric utility industry. It is important to remember, however, that the competitive effect of the energy broker is at the wholesale level, not the retail segment of the business. My previous research examined only the retail end of the business.

INTERFUEL COMPETITION

Electricity and natural gas are competitors for a number of household and industrial applications. In residential situations clothes drying, space heating, air conditioning, cooking, and refrigeration could all use either electricity or natural gas. This does not mean that the degree of technical substitutability of one fuel for the other is identical in each application or that customers would not prefer one fuel over the other for a particular application. The point is that the fuels are competitive to some extent, and if conditions develop where prices

34. Cohen, "A Spot Market for Electricity."
35. Ibid.
36. Ibid.
37. Ibid.

of one fuel become relative high or service becomes poor, customers will tend to substitute one fuel for the other for certain uses.

In industrial applications fuel substitutability is even more likely. The business responses to alternative fuels is similar to the residential responses already mentioned. Moreover in addition to gas-electric fuel substitution, business is able to substitute coal and/or oil for many applications. Even so industrial loads are probably of less importance from the regulatory point of view because prices in that market are commonly set by negotiation even when direct competition does not exist. Of course the existence and availability of the substitute fuels increase the probability that the industrial firm will fare well in its negotiations with the utility; the key is the existence of a substitute fuel. Because of the nature of industrial markets, the following discussion is restricted to gas-electricity competition; I will not consider fuel oil and coal at this juncture.[38]

Given the substitutability of gas for electricity in a number of uses, the degree of monopoly power in a market would increase substantially if a given electric company sold natural gas as well. Such marketing firms do, indeed, exist, and they are referred to as combination companies. Alfred Kahn is among those who argue that a combination company has substantially more monopoly power in a market than a firm selling either gas or electricity alone. Indeed Kahn says that combination companies substitute monopoly for duopoly (two competing firms) in a market.[39]

Economists have undertaken research to determine the extent to which combination utilities adversely affect consumer welfare. Alfred Kahn and Leonard W. Weiss discuss this work extensively. To date this research has not generated a set of widely accepted conclusions.[40] Some research shows beneficial results from having separate companies, while other studies find the opposite. I will discuss some of these studies briefly below.

---

38. This focus seems reasonable. In 1968, 77 percent of all new homes were heated by gas, 16 percent were heated with electricity, and only 6 percent with oil. Moreover the competition for cooking and clothes drying is almost entirely between gas and electricity. This statement is from Alfred E. Kahn, *The Economics of Regulation: Principles and Institutions,* vol. 2 (New York: John Wiley & Sons, 1971), pp. 276–77.

39. Kahn, *Economics of Regulation,* p. 276.

40. Kahn, *Economics of Regulation,* pp. 276–80, and Leonard W. Weiss, "Antitrust in the Electric Power Industry," in A. Phillips, ed., *Promoting Competition in Regulated Markets* (Washington, D.C.: Brookings Institution, 1975), chap. 5, pp. 139–41.

Franklin H. Cook found that total operating and maintenance costs for a sample of forty-eight to fifty-one straight (electric only) utility companies during the period 1957–1961 averaged 0.76 cents per kilowatt hour; in contrast, he found that seventeen to twenty-one electric-gas combination companies experienced cost levels of 1.03 cents per kilowatt hour.[41] A later study of average revenue (price) differences found that straight companies charged 2.31 cents per kilowatt hour for residential sales compared with 2.58 cents for combinations.[42] Bruce M. Owen also developed results consistent with the earlier research. He found that combination is an important significant factor in producing higher consumer prices and lower sales levels.[43]

There have been no recent studies on the effects of combination utilities on consumer welfare. It seems from the studies discussed here, however, that combinations adversely affect consumer welfare because they tend to suppress competition between electricity and natural gas.

COMPETITION AS A REGULATOR

Dissatisfaction with electric utility regulation is not entirely recent; indeed it has existed for a long time. It may be, however, that the level of dissatisfaction and concern with the process has reached an all-time high recently. Thus commission regulation, as we have known it in the past, is under extreme pressure. Critics originate from the academic community, government, research and public policy institutes, the regulatory ranks and public utility firms, and other walks of life. The fact is that objective examiners of the process are not convinced that commission regulation does an effective job in inducing firms to perform efficiently. This dissatisfaction is expressed in academic journals, newspapers, and magazines.[44] The extreme upward pressure on prices in recent years and the adverse social impact

41. Franklin H. Cook, "Comparative Price Economies of Combination Utilities," *Public Utilities Fortnightly* 79 (1967):34–36; cited in Kahn, *Economics of Regulation*, p. 277.

42. *Combination Companies: A Comparative Study* (National Economic Research Associates, Inc. 1968); cited in Kahn, *Economics of Regulations*, p. 277.

43. Bruce M. Owen, "Monopoly Pricing in Combined Gas and Electric Utilities," *Antitrust Bulletin* 15 (1970):713–26.

44. An interesting critique of the existing regulatory arrangement and suggestions for changes are presented in William H. Shaker, ed., *Electric Power Reform: The Alternatives for Michigan* (Ann Arbor: University of Michigan, 1976). Some of the suggested changes constitute radical departures from the status quo.

of high utility rates both on consumer welfare and economic growth and industrial development probably triggered the current intense interest in regulatory reform.

This growing concern about regulation is partially reflected in the widespread interest in whether utilities achieve a better outcome when regulators are elected or appointed. Studies in this area have generated mixed results, but a recent project found no difference in consumer prices caused by method of regulator selection.[45]

Some Recent Studies of Regulatory Reform

Concerns about regulatory effectiveness have caused the State of Pennsylvania to seriously consider existing regulatory arrangements and to seek improvements in utility performance. The Governor's Energy Council, chaired by William W. Scranton III, lieutenant governor, is charged with the responsibility of formulating the state's first comprehensive energy policy. Scranton recently presented some key ideas that have been developed for regulatory reform in Pennsylvania; the following discussion draws heavily on that work.[46]

Scranton points out that electricity costs have been rising even as the cost of other fuels have fallen, and this situation has stimulated at least two national-level investigations for reforming the regulation of electric utilities and a number of state-level inquiries.[47] He explains that the way states respond to these pressures for regulatory reform could be crucial in determining their future rate of economic growth.

> Excessive regulation has been the root cause of enormous escalations of both oil and natural gas prices since 1974. Current methods of regulation might well be the root cause of problems with electricity.[48]

Indeed a report issued by the task force set up to examine regulation suggests that regulation itself is an important part of the electric utility problem in Pennsylvania. Scranton points out that the task force report is remarkable for at least two reasons.

First, it provides seven guiding principles for reforming electric utility

---

45. This result is presented in Walter J. Primeaux, Jr., and Patrick C. Mann, "Regulator Selection Methods and Electricity Prices," *Land Economics* 62, no. 1 (February 1986):1–13.

46. The Honorable William W. Scranton III, "Reforming and Improving Electric Utility Regulation," *Public Utilities Fortnightly* (1983):19–23.

47. Scranton, "Reforming and Improving," p. 19.

48. Ibid.

regulation away from the conventional rate base approach towards a performance oriented system and a competitive market. Most other proposals for reform involve more government regulation (certificate of need, etc.) not less. Second, it represents the actual consensus of knowledgeable people . . . who otherwise are adversaries in adjudicatory and legislative proceedings.[49]

The task force dismissed competition in generation only as a viable policy alternative because total and immediate divestiture could cause short-run inequities and dislocations.[50] One should not conclude that the task force judgment in the above instance reflects an anticompetitive stance. In fact this is not at all the case.

The task force sought to identify a set of structural changes in regulation that would subject utility behavior to competitive market forces. A second objective, pursued simultaneously, was to target changes in regulatory arrangements that would cause utilities to begin acting as if they existed in a competitive environment. "To assist the group, a number of prominent experts in the utility field were invited to present their suggestions."[51]

As Scranton stated, the task force proposed seven principles of regulatory reform. I will not present these principles in detail here but instead will refer to several aspects of these principles that deal with injecting more competition or efficiency into the regulatory process.

The task force put forth the idea that the Pennsylvania Public Utility Commission should induce electric utility firms to operate more efficiently by providing incentives. The suggestions for achieving this include allowing the utilities to share in above-normal returns on investment profits or losses realized from operations. Under this arrangement firms share the efficiency gains or the cost effects of inefficiency.[52]

The task force also said that well-designed experiments should be conducted to determine whether various forms of competition can increase electric utility efficiency. The task force correctly explained that the present system of utility regulation does not induce optimal use of resources by utilities. Thus one alternative for improvement the task force advocated is less regulation. One could test the validity

49. Scranton, "Reforming and Improving," pp. 19–20.
50. Ibid., p. 20.
51. Ibid., p. 20.
52. Ibid., p. 21.

of this change by undertaking experiments in which competitive pressure is applied to stimulate both productivity gains and technological innovation. Both could lower electricity costs.[53]

The task force also suggests two types of experiments to determine whether competition can improve efficiency. The first involves pricing experiments in which selected industrial and commercial customers would allow participating customers to buy power from other nonutility generators within the utility service area.[54] The second would permit two or more utilities to compete for the right to serve specific customer groups within their collective service territories.

From the above discussion it is obvious that the task force understands the value of injecting competition into the regulatory process. Yet it stops short of recommending complete deregulation and substituting competition as the regulator. I was one of five utility specialists who spoke to the task force as it was developing its position concerning competition. In a private conversation one task-force member explained that political reality precluded a drastic move toward competition although he thought such a change would be beneficial. The implication was that the movement toward competition would have to be evolutionary, not revolutionary. His prediction holds true to date; yet it seems that Pennsylvania has taken some important first steps, and this situation could become something of a model for future changes toward imparting competitive vigor to the utility industry across the country. In contrast a similar task force in Illinois reaffirmed the natural-monopoly doctrine, asserting that there is insufficient evidence to support near-term deregulation; in its recent report it took the traditional stance toward competition. The only bright spot in the report is that it does acknowledge that future developments could render the natural-monopoly concept obsolete so the existing Public Utilities Act must be able to accommodate the possible passing of natural monopolies in some sectors of the utility industry.[55] This may reflect how difficult it will actually be to achieve even evolutionary changes toward more competition in industries that have long been viewed as natural monopolies. There could in fact be serious

53. Scranton, "Reforming and Improving," p. 23.

54. Ibid., p. 23.

55. *Sunset Task Force on Utility Regulatory Reform: Final Report to the Governor* (Springfield: State of Illinois Printing Services Division, 1984), p. 5.

reluctance on the part of examining bodies to be creative and innovative in changing regulatory procedures and introducing more competition into the process.

Competition as a Regulator

It is common to think of regulation as a substitute for competition. When the natural-monopoly concept evolved in the early days of the electric utility business, and policymakers reached the conclusion that competition should not be allowed in the industry, they substituted regulation for rivalry. As Farris and Sampson explain, the objective of regulation is to simulate a competitive result to "make the utilities act like competitive firms would act if competition were possible."[56] The idea was that if utility firms acted as competitive firms, they would not engage in monopoly abuses. Buried within this proposition is the conviction that monopolists would act to harm consumer welfare; moreover it recognizes that consumers are usually protected by competition; since competition is not permitted in this business, regulation must be the protector. Farris and Sampson point out that competition is "one of the best protective devices available to consumers and that among the results of a competitive environment will be good service and the prevention of excessive prices, unusually high earnings, and discriminatory rates."[57] They also say that when "the goal of regulation is substitution for competition, consumer protection follows naturally."[58]

The positive effects of competition already discussed do not constitute a complete list of how competition benefits the economy. The competitive process also forces firms to operate more efficiently in allocating both physical and monetary resources. When these competitive effects are absent, there is a loss to the companies, customers, and economy as a whole. The dissatisfaction with the regulatory process reflects concern that traditional regulation has not achieved its major objectives. Informed parties argue for significant reform and, perhaps, complete deregulation of the industry.

56. Martin T. Farris and Roy J. Sampson, *Public Utilities: Regulation, Management, and Ownership* (Boston: Houghton Mifflin Company, 1973), p. 157.
57. Farris and Sampson, *Public Utilities*, p. 157.
58. Ibid.

COMPETITION RATHER THAN REGULATION

In view of the principal regulatory objectives, one must conclude that consumers are not protected under the present regulatory system. An important point is that the notion of natural monopoly is no longer accepted as "truth" by scholars, who have raised a number of serious questions about its validity. One study examines the attributes of natural monopoly and concludes that they do not apply to electric utility firms. The results find that neither the prerequisites of natural monopoly, which are dependent on economies of scale, nor those dependent upon other structural conditions were found to be characteristic of electric utilities. The conclusion is that the natural-monopoly designation for electric utilities constitutes a misapplication of economic analysis and that economists must reassess the natural-monopoly theory as it is applied to electric utilities.[59]

My own previous research also finds that competition causes firms to operate at lower costs, sell electricity at lower prices, operate without engaging in price wars, and avoid excess capacity. This evidence clearly contradicts the theory of natural monopoly. By contrast the evidence suggests that direct competition is feasible between utility firms. Although changes to more competition may be difficult to implement due to political pressures, the time for change is now.

Perhaps an effective approach would be to make institutional changes to make direct competition possible. Thus whenever conditions are right, competition could enter; competitive forces would then provide consumer benefits that the present system of regulated monopoly can never provide.

A more direct route to gaining competitive vigor in electric utility markets would be complete deregulation of electric utility firms, allowing competition to occur in the unregulated market. This approach is appealing because it would facilitate competitive entry and eliminate a regulatory system that is now severely criticized. One fault of the present regulatory arrangement, one that is rarely mentioned, is

59. This study is Walter J. Primeaux, Jr., "Some Problems with Natural Monopoly," *Antitrust Bulletin: The Journal of American and Foreign Antitrust and Trade Regulation* 24 (1979):63–85.

that it gives consumers the illusion that someone is looking after their interests. This actually gives the public a false sense of security because the effectiveness of the regulatory process remains in serious doubt.[60] Nothing important would be lost by deregulating electric utilities, and very much could be gained.

---

60. Several economists have questioned both the importance and effectiveness of electric utility regulation. See George J. Stigler and Claire Friedland, "What Can Regulators Regulate? The Case of Electricity," *Journal of Law and Economics* 5 (1962) 1–16; Thomas G. Moore, "The Effectiveness of Regulation of Electric Utility Prices," *Southern Economic Journal* 36 (1970):365–75; Randy A. Nelson and Walter J. Primeaux, Jr., "An Examination of the Relationship Between Technical Change and Regulatory Effectiveness," December 1983. (Unpublished.)

13

ESTABLISHING PROPERTY RIGHTS IN UTILITY FRANCHISES

Robert B. Ekelund, Jr. and Richard Saba

INTRODUCTION

The current system of utility regulation has its foundations in the theory of natural monopoly. The validity of this theory is, however, now questioned by authors such as Demsetz, who provides serious arguments about why the theory as generally stated would not necessarily lead to monopoly pricing.[1] If these assertions have any merit, we must reconsider the justification for the present system of public utility (cost-plus) regulation and its intended goals.

The purpose of this essay is to consider and evaluate the critique of natural monopoly. Specifically our goals are twofold:

1. To survey and assess the literature, supportive and critical, on the static franchise-bidding model as it is most often proposed, that is, as a logical rejection of the received model of natural monopoly and as a possible substitute for cost-plus regulation of the traditional form;
2. To argue that the static franchise-bidding proposal dissolves into intertemporal problems of contracting in administrative-compet-

1. Harold Demsetz, "Why Regulate Utilities?" *Journal of Law and Economics* 11 (1968): 55–56.

itive process mechanisms as mentioned by Victor Goldberg and others.[2] These mechanisms are noted in the work of J. A. Schumpeter.[3] Unlike other observers, however, we will argue that while cost-plus regulation may be the predictable response to problems of contracting—especially when political considerations are included—regulation is best characterized as a means of avoiding antitrust actions or, equivalently, as a method of profitably eliminating open and free competition over time.

The justification for legally imposed intertemporal restrictions on competition and open property rights has centered, moreover, on matters related to assumed fixed or sunk capital in the electric and other utilities. We will conclude our essay with a modern criticism of this capital-specificity justification for regulation.

The Natural-Monopoly Model

Conventional wisdom, previous to Demsetz's proposition, stated that large-scale production economies meant that a single surviving firm would set price and output at the monopoly level. Figure 13–1 represents this argument graphically. Given the demand for the product (DD), the average cost per unit (AC) decreases over the relevant range of output. Therefore the firm that enters the market first and expands the fastest can always sell at a lower price than any competitor producing at a lower level of output. Once the initial firm has driven all others out of the market, it can restrict output and capture monopoly profits. This market scenario achieves three undesirable effects with respect to economic efficiency—economic efficiency defined as the results if the industry were competitive. First, the price charged by the remaining firm will be greater than marginal cost and thus greater than the price that would obtain if the industry were competitive. Second, the monopolist would restrict output below the level that would have been produced by a competitive industry. Third, the competition for initial market control leads to wasted resources by those firms driven out of the market. The argument for regulation stems from the presumption that such inefficiencies are the natural result of compe-

2. Victor Goldberg, "Regulation and Administered Contracts," *Bell Journal of Economics* 7 (1976): 426–48.
3. Joseph Schumpeter, *Capitalism, Socialism and Democracy*, 3d ed. (New York: Harper and Row, 1950).

Figure 13–1. Decreasing Average Cost and Production Scale Economies.

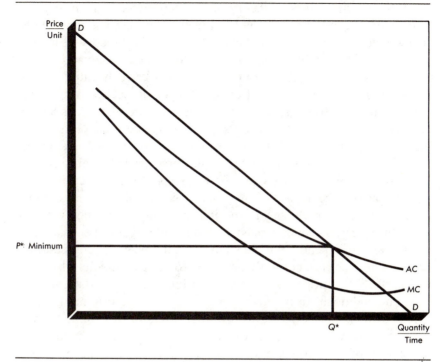

tition in this type of industry, and thus intervention into the market process via some regulatory authority is the only solution to this problem. Proponents of franchise bidding, however, argue that the problem is not in any inherent failure of the market process but rather in the lack of viable contracts between the producer and the consumers of the product. Moreover this lack of viable contracts is primarily due to restrictions imposed by regulatory systems now in common use.

The Franchise-Bidding Model

The franchise-bidding proposal as an alternative to government operation or regulation is an ancient idea best expressed in the writings of Jeremy Bentham and his policy-oriented secretary Sir Edwin Chadwick. Chadwick applied the concept to both natural monopoly and imperfectly competitive situations, including water and gas production and distribution, funeral parlors, beer and milk markets, and so on. This scheme, which involves radical alternatives in patterns of property-rights assignment in society, has overtones that are difficult to reconcile with orthodox theory of competitive capitalism.[4]

In his article "Why Regulate Utilities," Demsetz was one of the first contemporary writers to challenge the standard theory of natural monopoly and its implications for regulatory policy. Demsetz argues that "the asserted regulationship between market concentration and competition cannot be derived from existing theoretical considerations and that it is based on an incorrect understanding of the concept of competition or rivalry."[5] Demsetz poses two questions. First, why must rivals share the market, and second, why must unregulated market outcomes be monopoly price? In the first instance Demsetz sees no reason why rivals must share the market so long as there is competitive bidding.[6] The argument is that it is not the absolute number of firms actively producing in the industry that determines whether the industry can be characterized as competitive, but rather that competitive results depend upon the strength of the potential competition. Even if only one firm currently produces for a given market, that firm will be forced to price competitively so long as a potential exists of even one additional firm entering the industry if the original firm attempts to monopoly price. The firm that offers buyers the most reasonable terms will prevail, and therefore no reason can explain why the process of competitive bidding results in increases in per-unit production cost.

Second, Demsetz believes that "the competitiveness of the bidding process depends very much on such things as the number of bidders, but there is no clear or necessary reason for production scale economies to decrease the number of bidders."[7] Just because scale econ-

4. See Sir Edwin Chadwick, "Results of Different Principles of Legislation and Administration in Europe: of Competition for the Field, as Compared with Competition within the Field of Service," *Royal Statistical Society Journal* 22 (1859): 381. See also Mark Crain and Robert Ekelund, Jr., "Chadwick and Demsetz on Competition and Regulation," *Journal of Law and Economics* 19 (1976): 149–62. Contemporary speculation concerning the application of franchise bidding in Germany is reported in Walter Schulz, "Conditions for Effective Franchise Bidding in the West German Electricity Sector," in B. M. Mitchell and P. R. Kleindorfer, eds., *Regulated Industries and Public Enterprise*, (Lexington, Mass.: Lexington Books, 1979), chap. 4, pp. 57–69.

5. Demsetz, "Why Regulate Utilities," p. 55.

6. A similar concept of competition is espoused by William Baumol, John Panzar, and Robert Willig, *Contestable Markets and the Theory of Industry Structure* (New York: Harcourt Brace Jovanovich, 1982).

7. Demsetz, "Why Regulate Utilities," p. 57.

omies might lead to only one producer, that fact in no way limits the number of bidders. Buyers can call for bids, and as mentioned above the least cost bidder will prevail. Therefore Demsetz argues that "if the number of bidders is large or if, for other reasons, collusion among them is impractical, the contracted price can be very close to per-unit production cost."[8]

Assumptions of the Model

Demsetz claims that only two assumptions are necessary for competitive bidding to result in per-unit cost pricing. First, the resources used in the production process must be available to all bidders at prices determined in the open market. Second, the cost of collusion among bidders must be prohibitively high. Neither assumption seems overly optimistic. First, the fact that the initial capital investment in the utility industry is quite large relative to other industries in no way limits the availability of the resources at market price to potential bidders. Second, there seems to be no advantage concerning the cost of collusion in the utility industry compared to the cost of collusion in any other industry.

Demsetz, then, confronts two of the major reasons supporters offer for the necessity of regulation. They are the problem of duplication of resources and the desire to prevent the capture of windfall (monopoly) profits by utilities.

We can overcome the problem of resource duplication, Demsetz argues, by standard market instruments. If other industries can contract for the right to serve an individual, there is no reason why utilities cannot do this. Critics claim that the problem of duplication lies primarily in the means of transporting the product to the final consumer. In the case of the utility industry, this cost is exemplified by the extensive network of power lines running from the production source to the consumer. Demsetz argues that one of the reasons that such duplication would exist is that there is no market clearing price charged for the use of public right-of-ways. So long as no market clearing price exists, one would expect a misallocation of resources. This is not a problem specific to natural monopolies but one of externalities. The question then is how to internalize these external costs. Demsetz offers several suggestions, one of which is that the facility

---

8. Demsetz, "Why Regulate Utilities," p. 57.

be owned by the community and constructed and operated by competitive bidding.

The second problem, that of windfall profits, is indirectly related to the fixity of capital. Demsetz again argues that this is not specific to so-called natural monopolies. He claims that any industry operating in a world of uncertainty faces this problem. Once the investment is made and an opportunity cost is incurred to change investment plans, the possibility of windfall profits or losses exists. But, he argues, other markets also confront this problem and deal with it without resorting to regulation. He believes that contracts can be written to handle these problems and that regulation is a poor substitute for the market.

Contracting Costs

Implicit in Demsetz's proposal is the ability of the bidders to enter into incomplete contracts that provide for renegotiation. This implies that the cost of establishing and implementing such contracts would not be restrictive. Although Demsetz argues that such contracts are entered into daily by firms in other industries, it remains to be empirically demonstrated that the cost of contracting with the consumer in the utilities industry is no greater than the cost of contracting in other industries or, if higher, that the contracting cost is prohibitive. As we will show, establishing "optimal" contracts is the one issue that has not withstood the critics.

Posner's proposals are similar to those of Demsetz. Posner, however, suggested that one problem with the Demsetz proposal is the difficulty associated with the implementation of long-term contracts. He proposed that instead of long-term contracts with provisions for renegotiation, there should be a system of recurrent short-term contracts.

Where Demsetz was vague on the mechanism for establishing the initial contracts, Posner confronted the problem at a more specific level. Posner's proposal recommends there be an initial period before the franchise is awarded for all prospective bidders to solicit customers from within the local community. These contracts would contain specifications on the amount, quality, and price of the service. At the end of the period the:

> commitments received by the various applicants would be compared and the franchise awarded to the applicant whose guaranteed receipts, on the basis of subscriber commitments, were largest. In this fashion, the vote

of each subscriber would be weighted by his willingness to pay, and the winning applicant would be the one who, in free competitions with other applicants, was preferred by subscribers in the aggregate. To keep the solicitation process honest, each applicant would be required to contract in advance that, in the event he won, he would provide the level of service, and at the rate represented, in his solicitation drive.[9]

CRITICISMS OF FRANCHISE-BIDDING PROPOSALS

Oliver Williamson summarized and critiqued the major points critics of the franchise-bidding schemes put forth.[10] First, economists such as Telser argue that the franchise-bidding proposals give no assurance that output will be priced at marginal cost. Second, Williamson challenges both Posner and Demsetz on the grounds that both authors have assumed away the important question concerning the actual implementation of the franchise-bidding schemes. Williamson believes that the problem primarily lies in the inability of the franchise mechanism to efficiently generate plausible long-term contracts due to the existence of incumbent advantage, which eliminates the possibility of parity between the bids of the incumbent firm and the new competitors. Williamson's critique of the franchise-bidding schemes is to examine the three types of franchise contracts proposed by Demsetz, Posner, and Stigler.[11] These are incomplete long-term contracts, recurrent short-term contracts, and once-and-for-all contracts.

Contracting Problems

There are two types of once-and-for-all contracts, complete contingent claims, and incomplete contracts. Of the first, Williamson claims they are impossible to formulate for all practical purposes and, thus, he dismisses them as a possible policy. Incomplete contracts come in two forms. The first, espoused by Demsetz, is long-term contracts with provisions for negotiation. Williamson sees several problems with these. First, there is the problem of the initial award criterion, which

9. Richard A. Posner, "Natural Monopoly and Its Regulation," *Stanford Law Review* 21 (1969): 563.

10. Oliver Williamson, "Franchise Bidding for Natural Monopolies—In General and with Respect to CATV," *Bell Journal of Economics* 7 (1976): 73–104.

11. George Stigler, "The Theory of Economic Regulation," *Bell Journal of Economics* 2 (1976): 3–21.

he believes is "apt to be artificial or obscure." Some difficulties inherent in the initial award period are the determination of the quantity and quality of the product. Williamson sees this as a particular problem with highly technical products, such as electricity and broadcast signals. The average consumer is at a strong disadvantage to judge and monitor quality during the contract period. This leads directly to the second problem, that of execution, which Williamson feels is replete with problems of monitoring price-cost relations, other performance standards, and problems that arise from the political process.[12] Third, Williamson sees one major obstacle in the ability to reach parity at contract renewal between the incumbent and new rivals. This is also one of the major obstacles in recurrent short-term bidding, as proposed by Posner. Here Williamson argues that the efficacy of this type of bidding scheme depends totally on the assumption that "parity among bidders at the contract renewal interval is realized." He argues that the probability of bidding parity is ruled out because of specialized equipment and the nonfungibility of labor. These two problems will always move bidding advantages toward the incumbent firm.

Of the criticism mentioned above, Williamson believes that the lack of parity between the incumbent and the rival firms at contract renewal is the biggest hindrance to the franchise-bidding schemes. Peacock and Rowley raised this issue.[13] Later Williamson expanded on it, pointing to nonparity emerging at recontracting intervals due to the development of firm-specific, task-idiosyncratic labor supply. Williamson argues that: "under the assumption that competition at the contract renewal interval is efficacious, the hazards of contractual incompleteness which beset incomplete long-term contracts are avoided. . . . The efficacy of recurrent short-term contracting depends crucially . . . on the assumption the parity among bidders at the contract renewal interval is realized."[14]

12. Williamson's critique of the Demsetz-Posner model in "Franchise Bidding for Natural Monopolies," p. 83, is reminiscent of the so-called capture theories. However, Sam Peltzman in "Toward a More General Theory of Regulation," *Journal of Law and Economics* 19 (1976): 211–40 and Robert B. Ekelund and Richard Saba, "A Note on Franchise Bidding," *Public Choice* (1981): 203–8, contest this argument due to the distinctly local nature of franchise bidding.

13. Alan Peacock and Charles Rowley, "Welfare Economics and the Public Regulation of Natural Monopoly," *Journal of Public Economics* 1 (1972): 224–27.

14. Williamson, "Franchise Bidding for Natural Monopolies," p. 84.

Capital Fixities

Williamson and other critics believe that the difficulties involved in the transfer of human capital are major problems that proponents of franchise bidding have neglected. As Peacock and Rowley state, "the bidder who was initially successful, as a sitting tenant, would have substantial advantages, for example, with respect to market goodwill built up over the initial contract period, to market information and to its property rights in specialized factor input. Furthermore, the cost of transferring production rights to a new producer would also tell in favor of the existing producer."[15] Williamson proposes that an incumbent firm will have advantages over rivals because of certain firm-specific skills its employees will already have and because a risk premium would be required for incumbent employees to change jobs.

Briefly Williamson's arguments are as follows. Experienced workers of the incumbent firm acquire task idiosyncracies in a nontrivial degree that are firm specific. These idiosyncracies obtain because differences develop between experienced and inexperienced workers due to equipment idiosyncracies, processing economies, informal team accommodations, and communications idiosyncracies. Thus experienced workers would deal with the incumbent and rivals differently. Williamson also believes that another area of idiosyncracies develops from what is called "informal understandings" between the incumbent firm and its experienced labor. The incumbent and its employees reach informal agreements concerning job security, promotion, and internal due process. These task idiosyncracies and informal understandings make bargaining with outsiders over labor contracts more costly than bargaining with the incumbent firm because of transaction costs and the greater risk and uncertainty adhering to informal agreements with outsiders. Thus Williamson argues that experienced labor will command a premium to move to the rival firm. As Williamson explains:

> If original winners of the bidding competition realize nontrivial advantages in informational and informal organizational respects during contract execution, bidding parity at the contract renewal interval can no longer be presumed. Rather, what was once a large numbers bidding sit-

15. Peacock and Rowley, "Welfare Economics and Public Regulation," p. 245.
16. Williamson, "Franchise Bidding for Natural Monopolies," p. 89.

uation, at the time the original franchise was awarded, is converted into what is tantamount to a small numbers bargaining situation when the franchise comes up for renewal.[16]

A rather obvious point is that the advantages Williamson described would be fully anticipated in a competitive setting. Williamson concedes this when he states that the incumbent advantage would be anticipated and reflected in the bid at the outset, "in which event discounted certainty equivalent profits would be bid down to zero by large numbers competition for the original award."[17] Williamson does not think the argument satisfactory since he believes that a price less than cost for the initial contract will have to be adjusted upward to the level of alternative cost at contract renewal intervals, which easily results in resource utilization of an inferior kind. Can the argument be dismissed so readily, however?

For example, assume that all bidders are aware of possible cost advantages gained through production experience if they win the initial bid. As we point out elsewhere:

> Each bidder would form a probability distribution function upon which his estimate of the actual cost saving would be based. The risk of placing a bid to supply the product which might fall below actual cost could then be calculated. Assume, for simplicity, that all initial bidders form the same probability expectations. Under this assumption, the least risk adverse bidder would underbid all other bidders and receive the contract. If it happened that his bid were higher than the actual cost, the solution would still be optimal since the difference between the true cost and the bid would simply be compensation for the risk he incurred by taking on the contract.[18]

This type of risk is, again, not unique to franchise-bidding schemes but is confronted daily by firms operating under any system in this world of uncertainty.

Assuming that all such advantages are perfectly anticipated is, in a sense, begging the question. What if not all advantages were anticipated at the initial award but unexpectedly accrue during the initial production period? Will the incumbent be at an advantage? If we argue in the affirmative, then we are implicitly assuming that the owners of the firm have absolute power over the wage contract and are

17. Williamson, "Franchise Bidding for Natural Monopolies," p. 89.

18. Robert B. Ekelund, Jr., and Richard Saba, "Human Capital and Incumbent Advantages," *Southern Economic Journal* 47 (1980): 100–109.

able to capture all rents accruing to the increased productivity of labor in the firm or that labor is unaware of the increase in their marginal productivity over the initial contract period or that the increase in human capital must be of value only to the original owner. But this seems a rather unrealistic assumption. In Figure 13–2 the demand and marginal revenue curves are given for a typical firm. Suppose that the bid was won based on a price of P_i and quantity Q_i. Note that the price is lower and output greater than the conventional monopoly price of P_m and output of Q_m. The bid was made based on average cost curve AC_i, which does not anticipate the idiosyncratic advantages that will accrue to the firm over the contract period. If, as Williamson believes, idiosyncratic advantages are obtained over the contract interval, the incumbent will realize a fall in cost, from AC_i to AC_i' and

Figure 13–2. Human Capital Cost Internalization.

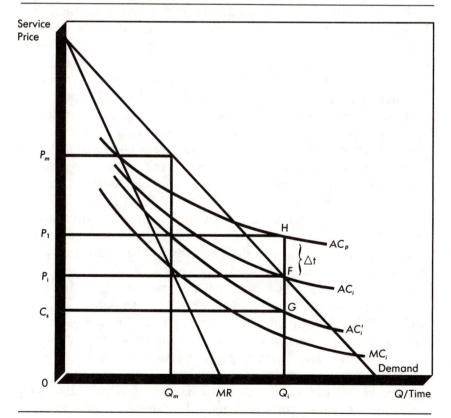

will be at a distinct advantage over rivals at contract renewal, being able to offer an output of Q_i for a price as low as C_s. This assumes, however, that labor is unaware, completely ignores, or is incapable of capitalizing on this increase in marginal product at the time of contract renewal. At contract renewal, the incumbent will be forced not only to negotiate contracts with the franchising agency but also with firm employees. If any task idiosyncracies have developed, labor will demand compensation for their increased contribution, and the firm will be forced to award such compensation or be confronted with the real possibility that these task idiosyncracies will be bid away by competing firms. These rents, P_iFGC_s, received by the incumbent during the initial contract period, are in the nature of Marshallian quasi-rents, and it is reasonable to assume that the rigor of successive competitive bidding at contract renewal will prevent the price from rising above P_i, given that quantity Q_i is produced and offered for sale under the initial contract.

A similar result occurs when dealing with transactions and uncertainty costs associated with job change. It is argued that labor would require a premium from outside bidders to compensate for the increased risk resulting from uncertainty relating to job advancement and tenure if management or ownership were changed. Assume the premium labor required is equal to Δt in Figure 13–2. The incumbent could then win the contract by offering a price equal to or below P_1 and earn a monopoly rent without eliciting competitive entry. However, we argue that these savings would be capitalized in the initial contract with labor because the firm must incur the costs of an initial training period and face possible loss due to being unable to replace tenured labor with more productive labor available in the labor market. Even if one ignores this argument, the incumbent is still restricted in the amount he or she can raise the price, given that the contract output remains at Q_1. In short these benefits will be internalized within well-known and predictable market processes.

While firm-specific human capital may not present problems for the franchise-bidding proposal as elaborated by Demsetz, Williamson and others have identified other problems related to long-term contracting. Transactions and enforcement costs of developing and enforcing the franchised contract, political considerations in auctioning the contract (to be considered in detail below), and cost and demand changes are all part of the costs associated with adjudicating long-term contract. These costs have moved a number of economists to conclude that regulation is a less costly method than other market or legal mechanisms for dealing with the problems and costs of long-term contracting. The primary reason for advocating the regulatory alternative relates to the alleged nontransferability of fixed capital. In some classifications the presence of fixed capital, along with the necessity of the service rendered, defines a public utility.

FIXED CAPITAL AND "OPTIMAL" INTERTEMPORAL CONTRACTS

For some the trump card in attacking alternatives to cost-plus regulation is the assumption of high fixed-capital requirements within public utilities. (For the moment, we equate fixed capital with "sunk" capital.) The implication is that such capital, with low or zero opportunity cost, would not be implaced or optimally implaced without some guarantee of at least market investment returns. This argument was a popular economic justification for the initial establishment of cost-plus regulation in the United States. The problem of capital fixity and transactions costs also underlies Victor Goldberg's modern argument.

Goldberg highlights "the fundamental similarity between regulation and a private contract for the right to serve," arguing that contractual complication and not declining average cost provides the rationale for monopoly.[19] Though Goldberg's analysis is principally concerned with regulation of natural monopolies, he clearly implies that his considerations are important for regulation of other industries as well.[20]

Goldberg recognizes the similarity between long-term relational contracts giving producers a right to serve and consumers a right to be served, and the process of regulation. Owing to uncertainty and other problems, both parties to the contract limit future options in order to achieve optimal positions over time.[21] In Goldberg's view contracts, or regulation, provide procedural mechanisms for adjudi-

19. Goldberg, "Regulation and Administered Contracts," p. 431.

20. Goldberg intends a wide application for this analysis. Consider his statement that "natural monopoly industries will be characterized in this paper not by their alleged decreasing average costs, but by the features which make long-term relationships between consumers and producers desirable and which further make it extremely difficult to determine at the outset the specific terms of that relationship," ("Regulation and Administered Contracts," p. 431). Features making long-term contracts desirable are characterized by numerous forms of economic organization.

21. The usual rules for optimally in static equilibrium do not apply or make much sense in an intertemporal context. Comparisons of utility functions over time and across or within individuals are strictly inadmissible. Though continuing the fiction (as many others do in dealing with intertemporal economic issues), we understand the limitations.

cating future contingencies. Increasing the producers' right to serve makes the contract more attractive to producers while simultaneously making the contract less attractive to consumers. The opposite is true of the consumers' interest in the right to be served. In Goldberg's words:

> Consumers want to maintain freedom to terminate the agreement so that they can take advantage of lower prices and/or superior technologies as they appear. The only variable under the agent's control is the level of protection of the right to serve. The optimal protection will be that at which the expected marginal benefits to the consumers of increased durability and decreased producer risk (lower prices) are just offset by the expected marginal costs of decreased flexibility.[22]

Thus Goldberg's justification for regulation is that long-term contracts are difficult to define and enforce because it is costly to delimit their many provisions ex ante. The regulatory body is an ongoing monitoring agent that continuously defines the relation between consumers and producers in much the same way that common-law courts continually interpret rights and duties of citizens vis-à-vis other citizens and the state.[23] Furthermore Goldberg is pessimistic about the efficacy of private contracting under the jurisdiction of the public law of contract.[24] But the case for regulation is not necessarily proved by this allegation. No market failure is cited, but Goldberg speculates that contracting costs might serve to justify some government intervention. Goldberg, of course, claims only to have a "case against the case against regulation" and not necessarily a case for regulation. Let us consider this claim in greater specificity, however.

AN INTERTEMPORAL ECONOMIC THEORY OF REGULATION

Goldberg's view features the high transactions costs of administering contracts as a possible raison d'être for regulation. We focus, how-

---

22. Goldberg, "Regulation and Administered Contracts," p. 433.

23. Goldberg, in "Regulation and Administered Contracts," employs a simplifying assumption that the agent (regulator) is a faithful representative of the principals' (consumers') interests, but Bruce Owen and Ronald Braeutigan (*The Regulatory Game: Strategic Use of the Administrative Process*, Cambridge, Mass.: Ballinger Publishing Company, 1976), pp. 16–17) argue that Goldberg's formulation seems inconsistent with the theory of administrative law wherein the public interest includes the interests of the regulated firm in addition to those of consumers.

24. Goldberg, "Regulation and Administered Contracts," pp. 444–45, fn. 68.

ever, on one possible theoretical scenario featuring the costs and un-certainties surrounding anticipated dislocations prompted by techno-logical change.[25] In this view present supplies are affected by poten-tial future technological innovations, a view well worn in the history of economic theory. Goldberg, for example, argues that "some tech-nological suppression will likely be desirable from the consumers' viewpoint regardless of the institutionally determined identity of the agent (i.e., private or public regulators)."[26] Such critics as Marx, Ve-blen, and Polanyi have all espoused the view that the market process generates too much change and thus contains the seeds of its own restrictions, if not its destruction. Schumpeter cites "the perennial gale of creative destruction" but is more ambivalent about its social value and hints that market forces are adequate to check undue change.[27]

Some of these critical observations about market processes are cor-rect. Changes in underlying market conditions create profit opportu-nities. These changes lead some resource owners to alter allocations of their resources, thereby imposing costs on owners of competing resources and consumers. Moreover standard economic theory typi-cally ignores the role of adjustment costs in the determination of ini-tial market equilibrium and, most particularly, neglects the role those who lose from change play in the political system where they attempt to attenuate the effects of such change.

At the microeconomic level capital gains are realized in some parts of the system and capital losses in others. The key to modeling actual microeconomic change is to recognize that market participants are not oblivious to the vicissitudes of the market and that no participants in the market system will make commitments that entail possible future losses without being compensated. In short current behavior (and spe-cifically investment behavior) is affected by anticipated future loss contingencies.

A Simple Model of the Intertemporal Competitive Process

We can treat these ideas more formally in a simple supply and demand framework. To do this we must invoke some minimal assumptions in

25. The simple model we draw from here is developed in detail in Robert B. Ekelund, Jr., and Richard Higgins, "Capital Fixity, Innovations, and Long-Term Contracting: An In-tertemporal Economics Theory of Regulation," *American Economic Review* 72 (1982): 32–46.
26. Goldberg, "Regulation and Administered Contracts," p. 435.
27. Schumpeter, *Capitalism, Socialism and Democracy*, pp. 81–105.

order to describe different possible outcomes under steady-state conditions:

1. We assume that the timing of the innovation follows a discrete-time analog of a Poisson process. This means that in a period analysis, an investment is made at the beginning of the period, and then it is revealed whether the innovation occurs. The probability that the innovation occurs in the first period is π. In any future period the probability that an innovation will occur in the period is π, unless an innovation has actually occurred in some earlier period, in which case $\pi = 0$ for all future periods.
2. We assume that capital investment is permanent and that there are no alternative uses for the capital once it is in place. This means that costs are fixed and sunk, that is, zero opportunity cost.
3. The parameters of supply and demand are assumed to be stationary over time.
4. The innovation occurs to an outsider who cannot be identified beforehand.
5. A perfect patent enforcement system confers a perpetual right to exclusive use of the new process on the innovator. Alternatively competitive entry could be allowed with the innovation and similar results obtained if the costs of capacity adjustment were taken into account.
6. No short-run variable costs of production occur; costs are variable ex ante and fixed ex post.

Leaving aside the technical solution to the model, we may summarize three possibilities with the help of Figure 13–3. We term these three possible solutions the bribe, no-bribe, and regulatory or long-term contracting solutions.

With respect to Figure 13–3, the initial price charged for the utility service is P_1 with costs of C_1, selling a quantity Q_1 of the service. Note that under competition, P_1 must initially be greater than C_1 to compensate competitors for the risk of (π) of an innovation. If the innovation occurs, however, and there is no more risk, incumbents would charge a price equal to C_1, increasing quantity sold. Thus the demand curve facing an innovator is BCD (with marginal revenue represented by $BCEF$). A cost-lowering innovation represented by cost curve C_2 would reduce price to P_2, creating profits to the in-

Figure 13–3.   Bribe, No-Bribe, and Regulatory of Long-Term Contracting Solutions.

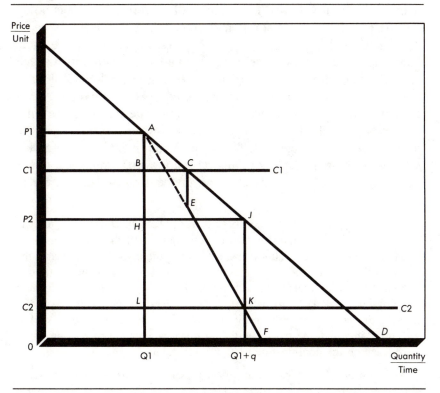

novator of *HJKL* and (approximate) capital losses to the incumbents of P_1AHP_2. Given these possibilities, what will happen? More specifically how will the market react today to the future possibilities?

First, consider the bribe solution. If there are low transactions costs among incumbent producers and if no antitrust enforcement exists, someone will bribe the innovator if the value of the innovation is less than the loss on the incumbent's fixed capital. If transactions costs are high, if antitrust enforcement is effective, or if the value of the innovation is greater than the capital loss of incumbents, the *no-bribe* solution will obtain. Under no bribe, consumers will pay an average of P_1 and P_2 in Figure 13–3.

In a regulatory or long-term contracting solution, entry is determined by an administrative tribunal (e.g., a traditional regulatory agency such as the CAB, the ICC, or the FPC) who utilize a cost-benefit test.

Assume one form of the cost-benefit test: If the value of the innovation is greater than the capital loss of incumbents, entry is allowed; if the innovation value is less, entry will be refused and technology will be repressed. Innovations and entry will be allowed as capital depreciates and the incumbent's loss is reduced to the value of the innovation. Our analysis also suggests that small inventions will tend to be disallowed while large improvements in technology will be admitted more rapidly. *The regulatory solution is totally analogous to the bribe solution,* but producers will prefer the former since under regulation no bribe is paid and profits are higher.

What factors will determine the outcome and, more important, which solution is optimal in an intertemporal framework with respect to public utilities? Goldberg hints at some of the factors determining the outcome:

> Other things equal, the firmer that assurance (of subsequent rewards), the more attractive the investment. So, for example, if the utility customers agree to give it the exclusive right to serve them for twenty years, then the utility would find construction of a long-lived plant more attractive than if it did not have such assurance. Of course, if a new superior technology were likely to appear within three years, the customers would not want the long-lived plant built. Nevertheless, there will be lots of instances in which the parties will find it efficacious to protect one party's reliance on the continuation of the relationship.[28]

The degree of risk aversion among utility consumers and the probability of an innovation-created capital loss are the two major factors determining the outcome of the intertemporal process. Subjecting the possibilities to consumer surplus analysis, we obtain the following results. When consumers of utility services are averse to risk, they will prefer some regulatory or long-term contracting solution to the no-bribe case, which is in turn preferred to the bribe solution. But when consumers are neutral to risk, they prefer the no-bribe solution to the regulatory or long-term contracting solution. They prefer the bribe solution least in this case also.

Goldberg's intertemporal analysis of regulation offers a number of insights, but our view differs. In our conception regulation is not devised to administer relational contracts between otherwise competitive

28. Victor Goldberg, "Relational Exchange: Economics and Complex Contracts," *American Behavioral Scientist* 23 (1980): 337–52.

firms and risk-averse consumers under conditions of capital fixity and prospective competing innovation. In short regulation is not in the consumer's interests. Instead regulation is a method of foreclosing markets to future competition—a method of circumventing antitrust laws. It is clearly in the interest of incumbents—who, by assumption, do not expect to be innovators—and some risk-averse consumers to have the market permanently foreclosed. This solution would make any future competition a tort. Politicians receive opportunities for present and/or future employment, and producers get market foreclosure under some circumstances. Risk-neutral consumers lose. The independent judiciary provides the guarantee that predictable entry criteria will be applied, raising the value of regulatory legislation to producers.

Fixed Costs Versus Sunk Costs

We have assumed in the above discussion that fixed costs were also "sunk"; that is, that capital installed by utilities has low or zero opportunity costs—a traditional justification for the necessity of regulation and inextricable part of the definition of natural monopoly. In addition to the fact that no well-executed empirical study has shown the existence of declining average costs in the long run, Baumol et al. have dealt a logical blow to the theory of natural monopoly and, with it, regulation in a recent work on contestable markets.[29]

The degree of contestability is directly related to the cost characteristics of firms. Specifically, as Baumol et al. argue, entry barriers relate to sunk as opposed to fixed costs. Economies of scale may relate to both fixed and sunk costs, but only sunk costs constitute an entry or exit barrier that affects contestability. These authors contrast the two types of costs:

> Long-run fixed costs are those costs that are not reduced, even in the long run, by decreases in output so long as production is not discontinued altogether. But they can be eliminated in the long run by total cessation of production . . . Sunk costs, on the other hand, are costs that (in some short or intermediate run) cannot be eliminated, even by total cessation of production. As such, once committed, sunk costs are no longer a portion of the opportunity cost of production.[30]

Economies of scale in production, in the presence of even enormous

29. Baumol et al., *Contestable Markets*.
30. Ibid., p. 280.

fixed costs, have nothing to do with market contestability as long as such investments have an opportunity cost. Sunk costs, once incurred, have zero opportunity cost so that potential entrants are not at parity with incumbents. Such markets will be imperfectly contestable or noncontestable.

High fixed costs—and Elizabeth Bailey's study of the airline industry is an illustration—do not constitute an entry barrier and do not prevent optimal welfare performance.[31] (Boeing 747s and other used "fixed" capital equipment are bought and sold every day.) A natural monopoly, for example, may exhibit "competitive" behavior if the market is fully contestable although it remains the only firm in the industry. With full contestability the firm may preclude entry with sustainable prices, but it must offer the same welfare benefits that the competition offers. As Baumol et al. conclude:

> with entry barriers, supernormal profits, inefficiencies, cross subsidies, and nonoptimal prices all become possible. But in a contestable market, which is perfectly consistent with the presence of fixed costs that are not sunk, matters change drastically, and government intervention can contribute far less, if anything, to the general welfare.[32]

It is clear that contestability theory has profound implications for public policy. These writers argue, correctly we believe, that most market failure is the result of policies that prevent contestability— that is, entry and exit regulation and regulation of incumbents' ability to respond to actual and potential entry. The invisible hand and free market forces are, potentially at least, far more powerful guardians of the general welfare than traditional theory would have us believe.

CONCLUSION: POLITICS AND UTILITY FRANCHISES

Franchising has been suggested as an alternative to forms of cost-plus regulation, as explained in the first part of this essay. Critics have argued that the problems of establishing property rights in franchises are akin to adjudicating long-term contracts. In this view regulation is a less costly method of policing and enforcing the complex provisions of long-term contracts. We have argued that restrictive

---

31. Elizabeth Bailey, "Contestability and the Design of Regulatory and Anti-Trust Policy," *American Economic Review* 71 (1981): 178–83.

32. Baumol et al., *Contestable Markets*, pp. 292–93.

property rights are assigned through the collective action of incumbents to forestall or postpone the introduction of new and loss-creating technologies. Regulation is not a preferred solution when consumers are risk neutral. The desire to forestall technology through a "legal bribe" is a motive for establishing restrictive property rights, but there is an additional explanation for such restrictions—politics.

The capture theory of regulation, proffered by George Stigler and generalized by Peltzman, is based on a competitive supply of and demand for regulation by coalitions of producers, consumers, and politicians. In Stigler's specification agencies are founded by the politicians' rent-creating supply of regulation in return for political favors (votes, money, influence, and so on) on the part of the demanding firms. Peltzman's generalization of the model emphasized the supply-side phenomena of agencies and politicians in examining vote margins through use of the regulatory process to effect redistributions. In the Stigler-Peltzman hypothesis effective coalitions of producers and politician-regulators are the principal beneficiaries of regulation (Peltzman does not exclude effective coalitions of consumer-voters); regulation redistributes wealth from some consumers to effective coalitions. Stigler and Peltzman thus do not consider the effect of potential innovations on present competitive market behavior. When we include this factor and we analyze long-run behavior, regulators, not firms, become rent recipients. Our analysis relating to technological innovation does not preclude short-run transitional gains to producers, but politician-regulators and some consumers are the only possible gainers in the long run.

If politics explains the existence of welfare and technology-reducing regulation, it would take a full overhaul of the political system to eliminate rent-seeking and cartel behavior among market and political participants. In the sentiments of George Stigler, one might as well—under present political conditions—chastise the Great Atlantic and Pacific Tea Company for selling groceries.

If sunk, as contrasted to fixed, costs are part of the explanation for technology and welfare-reducing forms of regulation, we agree with Baumol that energies could be directed toward making markets more, not less, contestable. In sum examining the property right aspects of the franchise bidding proposal leads to an examination of the whole intertemporal process of regulation. This quasi-Austrian perspective yields insight into the political and economic process that creates and perpetuates forms of entry control and cost-plus regulation.

14

PERSPECTIVES ON REFORMING ELECTRIC UTILITY REGULATION

*Richard L. Gordon**

Since the middle 1970s informed observers of the electric utility industry have considered it imperiled. The basic problem is the failure of traditional public utility regulation to respond to the radically changed state of the industry. The industry now faces problems of expensive energy, the resulting reduction of demand growth, and more stringent environmental regulations, particularly those affecting nuclear power.

Reform is clearly needed, and it should probably be more radical than most advocates of change have so far dared suggest. Only the staunchest supporters of government intervention contend that the problems are due entirely to transitory developments.[1] Others argue that the transition to slow growth in electricity consumption during a period of high inflation merely exposed defects inherent in the regulatory process.

*This article, an extension of my book, *Reforming the Regulation of Electric Utilities: Priorities for the 1980s* (Lexington, Mass.: Lexington Books, 1982), makes a particular effort to examine subsequent key works. Professor Roger Bohn and Professor John Moorhouse made invaluable comments on a draft of this chapter.

1. Alex Radin of the American Public Power Association is a vigorous advocate of this view. His "Don't Deregulate Power Production" appears in J. Plummer, T. Ferrar, and W. Hughes, eds., *Electric Power Strategic Issues* (Arlington, Va.: Public Utilities Reports, and Palo Alto, Calif.: QED Research, 1983), pp. 39–43. Similar views are summarized in the Edison Electric Institute, *Deregulation in the Electric Power Industry, Conference Proceedings* (Washington, D.C.: Edison Electric Institute, 1983), pp. 73–76.

Another crucial problem with the debate over utility regulation is that few can break the habit of compartmentalizing issues. Participants tend to talk as if we could consider public utility regulation separately from the other government policies that affect electric power. Industry problems often arise from the combined effects of different governmental actions. Thus solutions confined to one policy area can be thwarted by inaction or even perverse action from another realm.

Therefore the minimum acceptable reform would be deregulation of electricity generation, and total deregulation of electric utilities might be preferable. This deregulation of electricity generation should be supplemented by drastic changes in how the federal government conducts nuclear power and air pollution regulation and by elimination of state electricity planning programs. Public power should either be turned over to the private sector or required to borrow in the capital market without guarantees from general government revenues.

Warnings on the need for radical reforms made in 1982 were confirmed by the nuclear cancelations occurring in 1984.[2] A dominant problem was the inability to secure rate relief for plants that had faced severe difficulties in the nuclear regulatory process (see below).

More generally it has become routine for opponents of government decisions to use every possible forum. Environmentalists have led this process by using legal forums to object to nonenvironmental aspects of an issue. Conversely examples also exist of other interest groups intervening in environmental proceedings to attain nonenvironmental goals. A much-cited example occurred in 1977 when various eastern industrial interests, particularly the mine workers, joined with environmentalists to impose changes in air-pollution laws that tightened controls in ways that protected various eastern economic interests.[3] Less familiar is the fashion in which western ranchers and farmers cooperate with environmentalists to oppose mining—and then resist environmentalist attacks on ranching and farming.

Widespread concern about the utility industry has inspired much debate on how to remedy the situation. As is all too usual, the consensus—that drastic change is essential—gets submerged in squabbles over details. Most commentators recognize the deep, complex regulatory malaise afflicting electric power and realize major reforms

---

2. This was the theme of Gordon, *Reforming the Regulation of Electric Utilities*.
3. See Bruce A. Ackerman and William T. Hassler, *Clean Coal/Dirty Air* (New Haven: Yale University Press, 1981), for an extensive discussion of this point.

are needed. Uncertainties abound, however, about the wisdom and political feasibility of any specific proposed options. One can always find drawbacks to any possible change.

The useful contribution is to inspire action. The key need is to develop both short-term policies that can lead us in a clearly desirable direction and ways to better evaluate the various reform alternatives.

This review encourages opened-minded discussion among policymakers and informed observers. My hope is to stimulate a radical departure from the prevailing unwillingness to experiment more broadly with regulatory reform. The fears of and barriers to change are so great that years are required to implement even modest reform experiments.

This chapter reviews the pros and cons of the proposed cures in the public utility regulatory realm. I make an attempt to indicate which of the many suggestions on ways out of the muddle are the most attractive. Since other chapters deal with the background in which reform must operate, I limit review of specific policies. I do argue, however, the need for broad reform and make specific proposals.

I also made an effort to maintain the most radical possible approach to considering concepts for reform but to temper the argument with appropriate skepticism about the efficacy of all alternatives. As already suggested—and discussed more fully below—no perfect cure stands out. Our need for rapid action conflicts with our present inability to decide what will work. This situation is much different from those energy problems such as oil and gas price control in which the difficulty is getting support for easy-to-develop reform proposals.

Both the urgency of the problems and the widespread resistance to change necessitate that we not overdo caution. Too much handwringing and little, if any, action has occurred. It is particularly critical to ignore political feasibility. Not only is this a subject on which I am unqualified to judge, but it appears that no one can be sure what is possible before trying. This discussion therefore deliberately ignores the concern of a 1982 Edison Electric Institute (EEI) sponsored symposium about the lack of a constituency for reform. My objective here is to build a case and start a debate.

The idea of sticking to incremental reforms involves dangers of acting to thwart, rather than to initiate, a continued evolutionary process. Observers of natural gas regulatory reform worry about its implications for comparable partial-reform efforts in electric power. Some raised concerns that, given the difficulties of effecting partial deregulation, Congress has been reluctant to move further. Others fear that this could happen with incremental reform of electric power.[4]

This could overstate the case. The nature of electricity regulation could allow experiments to be on a sufficiently small, decentralized scale so that fewer frustrations would arise. Different states could serve as test areas for alternative approaches, and other states could learn from these experiences and adopt appropriate reforms. Few, if any, areas would then have expended all their energies on the first step.

The drawbacks to such a strategy of gradual reform are that it is difficult to envision who has the daring to lead and questionable whether the action would be fast enough. Moreover, as discussed more fully below, under existing laws, the most frequently proposed reforms usually transfer responsibility to the federal level and thus centralize regulatory decision making.

Incremental reform strategies, in short, fail to deal with the central problem: the reluctance of governmental organizations to change. We must pay more attention to the growing complaints about the intrinsic shortcomings of government intervention, yet few observers of regulation are willing to confront the broader implications of their own research.

These analysts almost invariably add ammunition to the overall antiregulation case, but many cannot shake the habit of balanced, restrained, cautious appraisals. They do not recognize that sound, careful analysis can lead to strong conclusions. In particular they are unwilling to admit how their work has supported a broad, libertarian antigovernment ideology. Their concern over the intemperance of libertarian rhetoric has prevented adequate consideration of its substance. Behind the philippics is a valid warning that we have unwisely allowed skepticism about government intervention to diminish.

Historically such skepticism has been a critical influence on economists and has never fully disappeared. We can view the substance of the libertarian agenda as synthesizing the results of contemporary applied economic research. It seems time to stop presenting only— and often valid—complaints about tone of the discussion and admit how much we accept the specific proposals.

---

4. The Edison Electric Institute (EEI) *Deregulation Conference Proceedings*, pp. 45–47, deal with the gas analogy; the problem of political feasibility is discussed at several points starting with John O'Leary's keynote speech, p. 4.

It is desirable to reaffirm the role economists play in showing the long-run benefit to every member of society of policies stressing economic efficiency. This, of course, implies leading the fight against the predations of well-intended but shortsighted interest groups. We should place particular stress on warning about the self-defeating nature of seeking government protection. This route includes dangers of an increasing spiral of interference that makes everyone worse off and a failure of the government aid to produce benefits even to those expecting gains.

ELECTRIC UTILITIES IN THE 1980s

Numerous problems plague the electric power industry. One widely recognized basic difficulty is that prevailing regulations make it extremely difficult to restructure the industry. We must overcome numerous institutional barriers to effect much of the improvement necessary in electric power.

It is often suggested that the dead hands of those who shaped the Public Utility Holding Company Act of 1935 have essentially immobilized the industry's structure; it remains in the form created when the act was implemented. This effort, which attempted to eliminate allegedly unwise linking of the ownership by the same parent company of many separate utilities, is currently an obstacle to any type of structural reform.

Changes—particularly consolidations—are difficult to effect under the act. It was designed to break up large concentrations of ownership unless clear, in-place offsetting efficiencies were gained through coordinated operation. Thus a bias arose against encouraging the creation of new combinations to increase efficiency.

The literature on the subject is surprisingly thin, and the underlying economics apparently have yet to be examined. The holding companies were clearly an effort to facilitate creating more optimally sized utilities. The competitive process of acquisition produced a tendency to make the holdings inadequately systematic in terms of proximity to each other and confinement to a specific industry. One doubts whether the Holding Company Act was superior to allowing further natural evolution to occur; problems of inappropriate organization generally get settled by further private transactions.

In any case the act reflects the policy influence of those who prefer to create more competitive market structures rather than rely on a planned (i.e., regulated) economy. Dispute between these views has long existed and was particularly intense in the thirties. Obviously my view is that both positions call for more government intervention than is desirable. Electric power, moreover, has the dubious distinction of being hamstrung by misuse of both the planning and restructuring approach.[5]

The act reenforces state public utility commission resistance to organizational changes. In addition control resides in an agency, the Securities and Exchange Commission, which lacks expertise in encouraging competition or with electric utilities. Criticism of this legacy is widespread. (Actually the law did not prevent a tidying-up process in which very small utilities merged or were acquired by larger ones. It is the bigger reorganizations that became difficult.)

Many of the problems this situation produced have since been alleviated by joint ventures created to permit construction of more optimally sized plants. Thus observation suggests that too many companies operate in New England, Iowa, Kansas, Wisconsin, and possibly New York. Joint construction ventures are, however, common in all these states.

We consider this situation undesirable because further reorganizations could still be needed. It might, for example, be appropriate to restructure formally as the still-extant advocates of creating fewer, larger utilities would argue. Believers in the superior efficiency of larger utilities vertically integrated into generation, transmission, and distribution would also like to see more ease of merger.

More critically the act might be a barrier to other types of reorganization, particularly the regulatory reforms considered here. Those seeking to increase decentralization can be concerned that the law also hinders breakup of existing companies. Certainly the act represents a solution to a problem that—if it ever existed—no longer does. In short repeal seems desirable.

However, many other institutional barriers remain to be overcome to bring about much of the improvement necessary in electric power. For example, Leonard Hyman of Merrill Lynch warns that restrictions on corporate action embedded in existing financial obligations are also

---

5. Most discussions of the act and the broader planning and restructuring debate are in history books. *Moody's Public Utilities* gives basic information about the components of the holding companies.

a barrier to reorganization.[6] As with all frictions, though, we can overcome the difficulties, at a cost.

Another critical problem is the existence of two or even three tiers of regulators that, in the name of preventing natural monopoly, have sweeping powers over the rates, construction, purchasing decisions, and other activities of privately owned utilities. The predominant influences are federal and state.

The Federal Energy Regulatory Commission (FERC), the successor to the Federal Power Commission, and state commissions are the principal actors. A few municipal regulatory agencies still exist as well. Basically the FERC regulates all wholesale transactions among companies in interstate commerce, and the state agencies regulate retail sales.

It is the involvement of the company in interstate commerce and not whether the electricity moves interstate that determines FERC involvement. The FERC thus controls sales within Massachusetts between the generation and transmission and the retail-distribution subsidiaries of holding companies in the state. It would not cover interstate but intracompany transfers such as from Texas to Louisiana within Gulf States Utilities.

Many complications exist. When a company has subsidiaries instead of being a legally unified entity—like Gulf States—intersubsidiary dealing is controlled by the FERC. Those utilities in Texas with no interstate operations insist on avoiding any dealings with other utilities that would subject their wholesale operations to FERC jurisdiction.[7]

The result provides a vivid illustration of the peculiarities electric utility structures endure under the holding company act. Most of Texas is in the Electric Reliability Council of Texas (ERCOT). Interstate companies such as Gulf States Utilities, however, are in other pools. Most are in the Southwestern pool, but El Paso Electric, which also operates in New Mexico, is in the Western Council.

The holding company Central and Southwest has both all-Texas

---

6. Hyman writes extensively on these matters and was a participant in the EEI deregulation conference (see EEI *Deregulation Conference Proceedings*, pp. 68–73). A fuller view by Leonard Hyman and Bennett W. Golub, "Financial Problems in the Transition to Deregulation" appears in Plummer et al., *Electric Power Strategic Issues*, pp. 93–115.

7. This discussion draws on reports from leading electric utilities and periodic discussions with executives of such companies.

and interstate subsidiaries. It placed its all-Texas subsidiaries in the ERCOT and the others in the Southwestern Pool. This conflicts with the Holding Company Act requirement that systems be integrated. The SEC has, however, waived other provisions of the act when enforcement was impractical; several electric utility holding companies have gas operations despite the prohibition in the act of multiindustry holding companies. Protests about the Central and Southwest situation, though, created regulatory pressures for change. Therefore Central and Southwest has been working on devising a means to interconnect its ERCOT and non-ERCOT units without subjecting the rest of the ERCOT to the FERC.

As already noted current regulation is widely criticized as being overly rigid and complex. Critics often consider state regulators grossly unqualified for their tasks, and outside of the largest states, the supporting staffs are often too small to handle the responsibilities.[8]

Many states have added further regulation in the form of some sort of energy office. The pattern varies considerably with California the extreme case to date. Its Energy Commission has total responsibility for both a master plan for capacity expansion and for approving specific projects that actually implement the plan. A similar situation prevails in New York, and a regional council operates in the Pacific Northwest.

The Pacific Council was created by a provision of a law trying to settle the problems of who should benefit from the existence of waterpower capacity far cheaper than new plants and the tendency of the Bonneville Power Agency to accumulate losses. Indiana created an ad hoc body to appraise the wisdom of continued construction of two nuclear-powered units.[9]

Creating such additional reviews greatly aggravates the intrinsic problem of multiple barriers to capacity addition. The desirability issue is artificially divided into an initial review by the energy commission of the need for a plant and an explicit financial appraisal by the public utility commission. Properly conducted, these proceedings duplicate one another. The only meaningful test of need is that the

---

8. For extensive data on the powers, staffing, and other aspects of the regulatory process, see National Association of Regulatory Utility Commissioners, *Annual Report on Utility and Carrier Regulation* (Washington, D.C.).

9. Edison Electric Institute, *Regional Regulation of the Electric Power Industry: Major Concepts and Issues* (Washington, D.C.: EEI, 1983), pp. 73–79, summarizes this type of regional regulation.

plant can be operated profitably. Further barriers relate to the possibility that the public utility commission will renege on providing rates sufficient to repay the investment.

Finally policymakers have created an overly complex system to control the known, suspected, and imagined side effects of electricity production. The Nuclear Regulatory Commission (NRC) seems the worst example. It remains a victim of its inherent defects and the widespread failure to understand the implications of the Three-Mile-Island accident and the investigations it inspired.

Regular calls for reform go unheeded. Change has never been a high priority item for the executive branch, and members of Congress opposed to nuclear power have gained powerful enough positions on critical subcommittees to thwart reform. (In 1984 the chairman of the NRC was criticized for urging that his staff consider the importance of not unduly delaying decision making.)

NRC procedures have become increasingly restrictive, and the tendency to add numerous rules has spread to deciding only after a plant is completed that it was improperly built. While this might be true of Cincinnati Gas and Electric's first unit, it seemed highly implausible for Commonwealth Edison's tenth.

In retrospect nuclear regulation appears more complex and unforgiving than desirable. Problems are inevitable in the construction of any complex industrial facilities. For example, coal-fired electric-power plants have had difficulties in meeting design objectives, and disagreement continues about how large a coal-fired plant can be before maintenance problems offset construction cost savings. Utilities, though, can resolve such problems quietly.

Defects—and possibly only the suspicion of defects—in nuclear construction inspire protracted NRC reviews. What may be unreasonable is not the imperfection of utility procedures, but rather the inability of the NRC to respond sensibly to unavoidable errors.

Air-pollution regulation remains likewise frozen. In its current status neither the call for removal of irrelevant 1977 overly protectionist provisions nor the campaign to tighten regulations to cure acid rain has succeeded.

The nuclear paralysis interacting with public utility regulatory difficulties and intervention by other state-level agencies became particularly critical in 1984. The fate of several regulation-plagued nuclear plants is at best in doubt due to state-level agencies' unwillingness to allow rates to reflect the cost increases caused by regulatory (or other forms of) delay. This reluctance is independent of the initial cause of problems—intervention by opponents of nuclear power such as at Shoreham on Long Island or Seabrook in New Hampshire, NCR-ordered suspensions of construction such as at Marble Hill in Indiana, or a utility go-slow attitude such as at Nine Mile Point in New York.

In the nuclear realm the interaction of policies has been particularly disastrous. The case for a broad-based assault on regulatory problems remains as great (and as widely unrecognized) as ever. The appropriate remedies outside public utility regulations are easy to state, at least in broad terms. The changes involve replacing the present cumbersome, excessively detailed regulations with streamlined programs that better use the profit motive by relying on financial pressures to motivate improved behavior (see below). Less clear-cut conclusions, as noted, are possible in the public utility arena.

AN OVERVIEW OF REFORM PROPOSALS

Ongoing concern over electric utility regulation has produced numerous reform proposals. In general the literature seems to stress ways to remove regulatory burdens, but some critiques consider various types of improved regulation. Even the hearty perennial of seeking to rationalize the ossified structure of the industry has been studied. (The 1982 EEI conference interpreted the draft version of the Joskow-Schmalensee study as an argument for bigger firms.[10] Creating such entities, while an incidental concern of the Joskow-Schmalensee study, ends up joining limited deregulation of wholesaling and reforming rate structures on the short list of options considered worth trying.)

Most attention in the regulatory realm is primarily directed at alternative ways to deregulate various portions of electricity generation. Suggestions differ, however, about the extent to which generation would be deregulated as well as what organizational structure would be developed under deregulation.

The basic ideas range from simply deregulating wholesale transactions to total deregulation. Further differences exist in the way various observers would implement any particular option. For example, observers have proposed several concepts about the exact form to adopt

10. The EEI discussion appears in EEI *Deregulation Conference Proceedings*, p. 45; see Paul L. Joskow and Richard Schmalensee, *Markets for Power: An Analysis of Electric Utility Deregulation* (Cambridge, Mass., MIT Press, 1983), conclusion chapter, pp. 211–21. This presents their views, which are not materially different from those in the draft.

in implementing the much discussed idea of creating independent generating companies.

Experiments in Deregulated Wholesaling

Work is already proceeding to experiment with modest deregulation of wholesaling. The FERC is allowing utilities in Arizona, New Mexico, and west Texas greater flexibility in wholesale pricing. (The Texas participants, Southwestern Public Service and El Paso Electric, are interstate companies operating in other councils instead of the isolated Texas pool mentioned previously). This effort represents a test of how far utilities could move toward decontrol.

FERC statements on the program, however, clearly suggest that the effort is extremely modest. One participant in the 1982 EEI conference correctly noted that the concern in this instance was more with encouraging greater interchange than with relief from critical regulatory problems.[11]

Thus one could accuse the FERC of using new slogans to promote an old goal rather than truly contributing to rate reform. We should not consider the FERC experiment a bold effort to test the prospects for total deregulation of wholesaling. It is, rather, unfortunate evidence that deregulating wholesale operations will be as hard to implement as any other reform. Worse, this experiment creates concerns about how many other reforms could be effected since they too will require FERC approval (see below).

Reform by Restructuring

The next type of widely discussed change is some separation of generation from transmission and distribution. Critics of regulation have considered this idea for a long time. Leonard Weiss's much-cited paper was published in 1975 but was originally presented in 1971. Berlin, Cicchetti, and Gillen endorsed the suggestion in their 1974 review of electric power and its regulation.[12]

---

11. The FERC viewpoint was expressed by Michael Rosenzweig in the EEI *Deregulation Conference Proceedings*, pp. 35–38, and by David Hughes, "The Potential Federal Role in Deregulation," in Plummer et al., *Electric Power Strategic Issues*, pp. 119–26. Robert McDiarmid emphasized the limited scope of the FERC initiative in the EEI *Deregulation Conference Proceedings*, pp. 39–42.

12. Leonard W. Weiss, "Antitrust in the Electric Power Industry," in A. Phillips, ed., *Promoting Competition in Regulated Industries* (Washington, D.C.: Brookings Institution,

Weiss advocated separating generation and transmission from distribution (and several other reforms, such as eliminating territorial restrictions on sales, removing barriers to entry, and severing gas utilities from electric companies). Berlin, Cicchetti, and Gillen went a bit further on restructuring by calling for independent transmission entities required to operate on a common-carrier basis. Most 1980s discussions of extensive restructuring have presumed a necessity for the dispatching organization to build, own, and operate the transmission system.

The restructuring concept, moreover, encompasses numerous variants. Some are considered first steps in a cautious move toward the Weiss vision; others are alternatives. Plummer suggests that reform could begin by extending the long-extant practice of maintaining separate generation subsidiaries.[13] The three oldest holding companies in New England—New England Electric, Commonwealth Energy (the former New England Gas and Electric Association), and Eastern Utilities—have long had the bulk of their generation from a separate generating subsidiary.

Several other companies have more recently established generating subsidiaries for new plants. Some joint ventures to build plants such as the Yankee Atomic plants in New England and three plants built in the Midwest to supply U.S. Atomic Energy Commission facilities have been separate corporations; others involved joint tenancy.

In examining the 10K reports for 1983 of other electric-utility holding companies, we find that most have established a generating unit of some sort.[14] In some cases, such as Texas Utilities, the subsidiary has responsibility for building and operating all generating plants. Others, such as American Electric Power and Middle South, are initially using the company to build a particular plant. Northeast Utilities and General Public Utilities have nuclear companies.

Those seeking to move even more slowly have suggested limiting

---

1975), pp. 135–73, and Edward Berlin, Charles J. Cicchetti, and William J. Gillen, *Perspectives on Power: A Study of the Regulation and Pricing of Electric Power* (Cambridge, Mass.: Ballinger Publishing Company, 1974). Cicchetti and Berlin were then highly proregulation—a position they abandoned.

13. See James L. Plummer, "A Different Approach to Electricity Regulation," in Plummer et al., *Electric Power Strategic Issues*, pp. 45–57.

14. The Securities and Exchange Commission long has required that publicly traded companies prepare a report called a 10K that provides data not always presented in regular annual reports. Companies now freely circulate these reports to interested parties.

separation to new plants. Others have moved in another direction, suggesting that sales to large industrial customers be deregulated as well.

Mason Willrich and Kermit Kubitz of Pacific Gas and Electric propose an alternative in which separate generating companies would be established as regionwide joint ventures to insure the financial strength needed for successful complete construction.[15] As Willrich and Kubitz note, their proposal would implement on a wide scale an aborted plan to form a generating company for New York state. The original suggestion failed because New York regulators resisted the loss of control and changes in growth prospects that radically reduced the need for new capacity. The extension of regional generating companies is related more to the older concept of seeking economies of scale than to the newer emphasis on decentralization. As the prior review of regulatory practices implied, the sole direct regulatory impact of creating generating companies would be the transfer of control to the FERC.

The next level of separating generation would be the creation of truly independent, preferably numerous, entities. A further step would be to the Weiss concept of thoroughly separating generation and other phases of operations and establishing regional coordinating bodies to secure power from the independent generating companies and transfer it to distribution companies that would then keep their historic role of final-user suppliers.

Problems of Restructuring

Critics have raised numerous real and imagined problems about restructuring. Many are related to concerns that I raised in 1982 over whether restructuring would really lead to deregulation, whether coordination would be inferior without integration, and whether high transaction costs impede change. (Those familiar with transaction-cost economics will note an oddity here; the concept is usually used to oppose regulation rather than to defend its preservation.)

The fear that deregulation will not occur is often expressed obliquely. Opponents of restructuring identify problems that can only occur if regulation continues. Yet those raising the issue often seem to miss

---

15. See Mason Willrich and Kermit Kubitz, "Regional Electric Power Supplies," in Plummer et al. *Electric Power Strategic Issues*, pp. 183–204.

its link to continuing regulation. Before discussing the general aspects of this, I want to examine a particular institutional problem—the critical role of the FERC.

All reorganization proposals implicitly or explicitly link any changes to relying on the FERC to exercise strong leadership. As the prior review of what determines FERC jurisdiction should have made clear, the creation of any separately incorporated generating entity, however owned, would automatically transfer regulation to the FERC, which is perceived as a more reasonable regulator. Then, the thinking goes, the FERC could work toward reducing controls. The key problems with this view are the timidity, noted above, of the FERC and the lack of assurance that the FERC is and will remain a good regulator.

This exposes a major much neglected transitional problem with any effort to separate generation from other aspects of electricity supply. All such changes lead to reliance on the FERC and thus to a centralization of decision making. This is perilous. It poses particular problems for advocates of gradualism. Piecemeal efforts are even less likely to succeed if the same agency must handle each experiment.

A further question is whether the faith in the FERC is justified. The timidity of the FERC approach so far, its preoccupation with natural gas, and the certainty of repressive congressional pressures if the FERC attempted daring action all lead to doubts about how effective the FERC can be.

More generally industry restructuring might not produce the improvements that its proponents expect. Seeing how electric utility regulators often challenge prices on both wholesale purchases and fuel procurement suggests that regulation could simply take a new form. Until the 1980s, however, regulation of natural gas transmission and distribution involved automatic pass through of payment for gas at the wellhead. Only as contracts unsuited to actual conditions began to emerge did challenges arise. This suggests that well-functioning arrangements between generators and distributors might alleviate my first concern.

When William W. Berry, president of what was then Virginia Electric and Power and is now Dominion Resources, presented his deregulation model at the 1982 EEI conference, participants raised doubts about the feasibility of prompt accords to build facilities given the complexities of siting regulations.[16] These doubts are less a criticism

_____

16. Berry's remarks are summarized in EEI *Deregulation Conference Proceedings*, pp. 11–26; much of pp. 16–33 deals with his views, with pp. 26–27 concentrating on financing

of restructuring, however, than they are an implicit recognition that limited changes in regulatory form do not insure substantive reform. They are also evidence of unconscious fears that regulation will not really vanish.

Concern over relations between generating companies and their wholesale customers leads immediately to consideration of a problem that does need fuller review—the appropriate way separate generating companies would deal with distribution and transmission entities under deregulation. In particular planners have raised considerable debate about the choice between contracts and open-market sales.

Some, such as Berry, argue that long-term contracts are necessary to insure that plants will be built. Others believe that emerging electronic technology makes feasible reliance on rapidly changing spot prices to allocate electricity output. Another group originally all at MIT, developed this general point particularly well. The group included Schweppe, Tabors, Caramanis, Bohn, and Golub.[17] Although they presented concepts designed for improving the operation of the industry as presently structured, the group eventually extended their analysis to discuss the role of spot pricing in deregulation.

Among the critical points they make is that the uncertainties attached to construction could disappear with deregulation. Other industries have problems similar to electric power—high levels of investment relative to both industry sales and total investment in the economy and demand uncertainty. When unregulated, these other industries have no difficulty raising capital without relying on contracts or vertical integration.

In examining these arguments, we should pay close attention to the skepticism in the Joskow-Schmalensee study since it reflects the care-

problems. Also see William W. Berry, "The Deregulated Electric Utility Industry," in Plummer et al., *Electric Power Strategic Issues*, pp. 3–25.

17. This group in various combinations have been producing a stream of articles, preprints, and working papers since the late 1970s. The most accessible include two chapters in Plummer et al., *Electric Power Strategic Issues* and a 1984 article in the *Energy Journal*. The two chapters are Roger E. Bohn, Fred C. Schweppe, and Richard D. Tabors, "Using Spot Prices to Coordinate Utilities, Customers, and Generators," pp. 265–82, and Bennett W. Golub, Richard D. Tabors, Roger E. Bohn, and Fred C. Schweppe, "An Approach for Deregulating the Generation of Electricity, pp. 59–92. The article is Roger E. Bohn, Bennett W. Golub, Richard D. Tabors, and Fred C. Schweppe, "Deregulating the Generation of Electricity Through the Creation of Spot Markets for Bulk Power," *Energy Journal* 5, no. 2 (April 1984): 71–91. Bohn, Schweppe, and M. C. Caramanis have worked extensively on the theory of spot pricing notably in their 1981 MIT Energy Laboratory Working Paper "Optimal Spot Pricing of Electricity: Theory."

ful analysis of two highly talented, experienced observers of the issues. Their argument seems, however, to start from a theoretical base intrinsically unsympathetic to spot pricing and to proceed by almost invariably adapting that framework to deregulation in a fashion that stresses its drawbacks.

Joskow and Schmalensee rely on concepts of transaction-cost economics Coase developed. These were then elaborated by various others such as Hayek, Stigler, and Williamson.[18] Coase pointed out that use of the market imposes transaction costs saved by vertical integration. The latter, however, can produce diseconomies of scale. Therefore firms seek an optimal procurement pattern following the basic marginality principle of economics—extend an activity until its marginal cost equals its marginal benefit. Coase recognized that contracting could be a way to ease transaction problems.

Coase has long been a leading exponent of the importance of transaction costs and a critic of the tendency to rush into regulation. He is well aware that high transaction costs can justify certain types of government intervention in supplying services to the public as a whole due to problems of individual transactions with each beneficiary.

Those concerned about transaction costs, however, are generally hostile to regulation. Hayek's writings on public policies stress that the combination of our ignorance about the consequences of regulation and the tendency for regulation to be dominated by special-interest groups make laissez-faire preferable even if competition is imperfect in some sectors. This argument emerges from a vision of the price system as a way to create a division of labor in everything including information. Hayek thus stresses that markets optimize the allocation of resources in a fashion that encompasses transaction as well as direct costs.

In any case, evidence on possible transactions methods is provided by viewing the fuel procurement side of electric utility activities. In my research on the area, the evidence makes clear that many arrange-

18. See Ronald H. Coase, "The Nature of the Firm," *Economica* NS4(1937): 386–405; George J. Stigler, "The Division of Labor is Limited by the Extent of the Market," in *The Organization of Industry* (Homewood, Ill.: Irwin, 1968), pp. 129–41; Friedrich A. Hayek, *The Constitution of Liberty* (Chicago: University of Chicago Press, 1960); Friedrich A. Hayek, *Law, Legislation and Liberty,* 3 vols. (Chicago: University of Chicago Press: 1973, 1976, and 1979); and Oliver G. Williamson, *Markets and Hierarchies, Analysis and Antitrust Implications, A Study of the Economics of Internal Organization* (New York: The Free Press, 1975). Stigler's book collects his articles; the cited item is from 1951.

ments can work. What is most relevant here is that when many suppliers are available, extensive spot buying can be satisfactorily employed.[19]

Williamson's extension of Coase concentrates on the problems of dealing with outsiders—particularly on a contractual basis. The result is a discussion that emphasizes the disadvantages of using markets. Joskow and Schmalensee rely heavily on the Williamson view, possibly overemphasizing the concerns about using markets.

They thus neglect an important alternative view—that of George Stigler—who pointed out that vertical integration becomes less essential as the market enlarges. He also anticipated many of the Williamson arguments about when integration was preferable.[20] Clearly Stigler's view forms the basis of a call for less vertical integration in the electric utility industry. The choice of Williamson over alternative discussions leads Joskow and Schmalensee to a heavy, probably excessive, bias against considering radical changes.

Most of the specific transactions problems raised by Joskow and Schmalensee are similar to those I considered. They add a further, particularly pessimistic, concern over the problems of reliance on contracting. They doubt both the feasibility of spot pricing and the ability to design adequate contracts.

Joskow and Schmalensee stress that the coordination needs of the electric power system require that reforms—particularly the most elaborate ones—solve the transaction-cost problem by heavy use of contracts and creation of a centralized power pool to purchase electricity and transfer it to distribution companies. The need for contracts is reenforced by the alleged problems of securing financing without the guarantees that such contracts provide.

Joskow and Schmalensee suggest that relying on contracts tends to establish relations so similar to existing ones that little real change occurs. They anticipate further problems in the inefficiencies of the contracting process. It would be, they feel, difficult to develop either proper incentives for efficiency or a pricing system that linked payments to industrywide marginal costs of production. Given the evi-

---

19. My most recent publication on this is "Resource Procurement: A Case Study of U.S. Electric Utilities," in D. W. Pearce, H. Siebert, and I. Walter, eds., *Risk and the Political Economy of Resource Development* (London: Macmillan & Co., 1984), pp. 319–37. An earlier study was "Optimization of Input Supply Patterns in the Case of Fuels for Electric Power Generation," *Journal of Industrial Economics* 23, no. 1 (September 1974):19–37.

20. See Stigler, "The Division of Labor," and Williamson, *Markets and Hierarchies*.

dence noted above, their analysis seems to excessively underrate the ability to design and implement reasonably efficient contractual arrangements.

If adopted, spot prices would be based on marginal costs as they actually occurred and not on some imperfect forecast built into the contract. The attractiveness of the spot-pricing option is that it avoids all the difficulties of contracting including the necessity Joskow and Schmalensee envision for tight pooling.

The fundamental problem is whether a spot-pricing system is workable as a coordinating tool. The difficulties appear overestimated. The information requirements do not seem all that different from those required for present optimized dispatch—namely information about power flows relative to plant availabilities, operation, and costs.

Joskow and Schmalensee recognize these advantages of spot prices but seem to feel that they are outweighed by the problems. Thus they see contracting and a tight pool as the more likely arrangement. (They reach this conclusion despite citing the interesting analysis by their colleague, Weitzman, on the difficulties of deciding whether price or quantity data are better guides to decision making, not to mention the general tradition in economics that prices are a particularly convenient way to convey information.[21])

Observation of trends in mineral marketing suggest that the difficulties of spot pricing are often exaggerated. Copper producers have abandoned efforts to price somewhat independently from the London Metal Exchange; a similar development is occurring in aluminum and even crude oil. Electric utilities are beginning to back off from heavy reliance on contracts for fuel.

Similarly utilities have found that while vertical integration into western coal mining has largely been a profitable venture, the same is not true for eastern coal or uranium. Spin-offs have been widespread. Substantial further divestiture has occurred, including the sale of a large part of the American Electric Power coal mines, the largest eastern utility coal-mining venture.[22] Thus we can go beyond the con-

21. See Martin L. Weitzman, "Prices vs. Quantities," *Review of Economic Studies* 41 (October 1974):477–91. Hayek's writings vigorously emphasize the advantages of allocation by price.

22. See Gordon, "A Resource Procurement," pp. 319–37, and Gordon, "Optimization of Input Supply Patterns," pp. 19–37; the material was updated from corporate reports and the trade press.

cern that dismissal of spot pricing is premature to conclude that the drawbacks were overstated.

Moreover even if contracting were used, a tight pool might not be needed to undertake the contracts. Berry's suggestion of relying on a more passive broker and contracting by distributors would alleviate the exercise of monopoly buying power by the coordinating body. The pool could be a passive organization that simply expedited the exchange of information. Contracting is often used effectively, including in electric utility fuel buying, and it has been designed to reflect current marginal costs. Therefore anxiety over contracting might also be excessive.

As the argument by the MIT advocates of spot pricing makes apparent, the financing problem seems essentially transitional. Successful deregulation would establish the wisdom of investing in new power plants for spot-market selling. The difficulties of making the transition are, however, formidable given the present uncertainties. Currently utilities must forecast both the most profitable future mix of plants and whether regulators will allow investments to proceed in a way that brings adequate profits. Deregulation would replace the latter risk with the more rational guide of the market test of profitability.

To be sure questions arise about whether this system (or any other) would work. The Joskow-Schmalensee analysis warns about the possible drawbacks of adopting the suggested reorganizations—and properly so. The problem is in concluding at so early a stage that only the institutional arrangements least conducive to vigorous competition will work.

Similarly it is not obvious that—as others fear—relying on decentralized decisions to build plants for a large grid is markedly more risky than trying to run the current gauntlet of regulatory restraints. Utilities are quickly learning that it no longer pays to be cautious enough to err toward assured supply. On the contrary many now seriously challenge the economic desirability of plants costing several billion dollars. Problems of securing rate relief are enough to create a poor investment climate. Other barriers, such as the requirements to prove a physical as well as a financial need for new facilities, aggravate the tendency to restrict building. Decentralized decision making under a system of less time-consuming licensing might be far preferable.

Another less convincing criticism of independent generation made at the 1982 EEI conference was that suboptimally sized plants are more likely to be built with decentralization than with integrated utilities.[23] The alleged problem is that utilities would reduce the risk of depending on any one supplier by making smaller purchases from several suppliers. It is not clear why this need be the case, particularly if deregulation is accompanied by improved ties among utilities. The dependability–economies-of-scale trade-off already exists within the industry. Deregulation with greater coordination could reduce the risks of large plants because the larger network could better absorb capacity loss and support more suppliers. Any suboptimal sizing due to regulation would disappear when the regulation was completely removed.

Some of Joskow and Schmalensee's worst fears about reorganization are, at most, loosely related to transaction costs. Two critical areas are that reorganization allegedly creates monopolies and that the reforms do nothing to alleviate inefficiencies in the electricity price to final users.

Joskow and Schmalensee identify two monopoly problems. The first is that noted above, the power that tight pools would possess. The other is the difficulty of establishing and maintaining a competitive market in generation. Obviously the problem would be most serious for the incremental reform of deregulating only new plants. This would become increasingly problematic if growth and hence capacity expansion remained at low rates. Joskow and Schmalensee are concerned, however, on the basis of estimates about what the actual market structure would be and about the ability to attain vigorous competition with even full deregulation. Again, we can question their tendency to err toward pessimism. (It should be noted that in fact—as Stigler and Williamson indicated—avoiding monopoly by integration is a form of saving on transaction costs.)

Two types of concerns arise about retail rates. The first is that if there is heavy reliance on contracts that poorly ape competitive market behavior, the cost of purchased power, which ultimately determines retail rates, will not properly reflect the true social cost of generation. Second, the reforms fail to eliminate the defects of present retail rates. These include failures either to vary charges to customers on the basis of the true difference in the cost of service or to change optimal prices as demand-supply relationships shift. It seems inappropriate to fault restructuring for not dealing with retail rates, however. Advocates of reorganization are certainly aware that it will not

23. EEI *Deregulation Conference Proceedings*, p. 25.

cure defective customer charges. More critically neither will doing nothing.

From all this I conclude that while one cannot be perfectly confident that restructuring and deregulating wholesale operations will work, it is a promising alternative. The defects have been exaggerated.

Full Deregulation

To date I apparently have been the only one suggesting we give serious consideration to total deregulation. (Primeaux argues for deregulating and creating rival distribution companies, which his econometric analysis indicates would be efficient.[24]) My basic case is that the competitive pressures on distribution companies could be so much stronger than conventionally recognized and regulation so bad that its removal would be an improvement. Retail rates, for example, would be designed much more efficiently.

An additional unquestioned benefit of total deregulation is that it avoids all reorganization costs. The discussion above indicated that such costs could be far smaller than Joskow and Schmalensee argue or I previously feared. Nevertheless some costs must inevitably arise. A partial reorganization process would involve significant outlays to transform extant companies into a new form.

In short, given the failings of regulation, the fact that the presumption of monopoly power rests on difficult-to-test instincts, and the costs of restructuring, it is folly to cling to the habit of dismissing total deregulation. We cannot say a priori that total deregulation is clearly inferior to the status quo or alternative reforms. Assuming that all reforms are flawed, the germane but much neglected question is, Which is least flawed.

Joskow and Schmalensee dismiss the total-deregulation alternative as inapplicable. Their concern seems mainly over political feasibility. They note that deregulation is inferior to perfectly administered controls. They recognize, however, that evidence is lacking on the comparative efficiency of deregulation and actual controls. They also fail to point out that the comparison between actual controls and their

24. Walter J. Primeaux, Jr., "A Reexamination of the Monopoly Market Structure for Electric Utilities" in A. Phillips, ed., *Promoting Competition in Regulated Markets*, (Washington: Brookings Institution, 1975), pp. 175–200.

absence is the critical one for policy appraisal. Thus they dismiss the option with only a cursory discussion.[25]

Since Joskow and Schmalensee are even more worried about the cost of reorganization and the need for better retail rates than I am, they should have been more sympathetic to total deregulation. Indeed they make an effective case for finding alternatives to restructuring. Joskow and Schmalensee are greatly concerned about both the limited improvements in regulation and the expensive disruption of industry organization associated with separating out and deregulating generation.

Given the scarcity of satisfactory alternatives, as noted, it is premature to close any options. The problem in electric utilities is primarily due to fear of radical changes. While one can always make a case for acting cautiously, nothing requires all of us to think unimaginatively.

I would further argue that the economic case against full deregulation is far weaker than generally recognized. In particular, competition in residential and commercial markets may be far greater than proponents of regulation believe. Interfuel competition is vigorous in space conditioning. This competition should limit the ability to exploit monopoly power in lighting and other electricity-specific demands. Rates on all uses would probably have to be lowered to undercut competition in space conditioning. It would be difficult to set separate charges for different uses, and such efforts could be considered violations of antitrust laws.

The principal barrier to competition is the existence of combination electric and gas utilities. Examination of the data makes clear that important cases of heavy involvement in both areas occur. In terms of size of each operation compared to the other and to other companies in their sector, the most important relevant companies by far are Pacific Gas and Electric in California and Public Service Electric and Gas in New Jersey. Other important entities prevail elsewhere—notably in New York, Illinois, Iowa, Kansas, and Colorado. Spinoff of gas ventures should therefore be made a condition of total deregulation.[26]

25. Joskow and Schmalensee, *Markets for Power*, pp. 154–56.

26. This overview came from first viewing U.S. government data on privately owned electric companies and then generating more satisfactory data from my files of "Uniform Statistical Reports" from individual utilities. The reports are prepared on a form jointly designed by the Edison Electric Institute and the American Gas Association. The primary advantage is that federal reports do not consolidate subsidiaries and the Uniform Statistical Reports are available on a consolidated (and also unconsolidated) basis.

Industrial customers have several options such as self-generation, actual or threatened plants' relocation or shift of work among plants, and in a few cases access to more than one supplier to increase competition. Deregulation could increase access to other companies.

Thus we should not summarily deny that unleashing prevailing competitive forces will produce a more efficient electric power industry than regulation as it is practiced. We are comparing two inadequate tools and again cannot determine which is better. In 1982 I was only prepared to propose consideration of total deregulation. The failure to secure progress for any sort of moderate change stimulates the feeling that some radical action is needed.

I now would argue that both carefully designed restructuring and total deregulation have considerable potential. Given the hopelessness of getting to regulators, I still tend toward total deregulation as a better option. This leaves the task of getting to our equally intractable legislators. With luck, though, this could mean replacing incessant struggles with a single decisive battle.

Notes on Better Regulation

The concept of better regulation is unappealing both analytically and factually. The analysis consists of simply noting all the errors made and calling for repentence. The key empirical point is that if observers of the subject thought that the prospects for more efficient regulation were great, they would not be bothering to propose moves to deregulation. Regulators continue to indicate that they are irredeemable.

It should be noted, however, that various observers—notably Berlin et al.—have suggested that regional cooperation could improve regulation. This argument stems from a recognition that operations are often interstate. Not only do individual corporations often operate in more than one state, but all the intercompany cooperative arrangements—except for the special Texas case noted above—cover several states.

A 1983 EEI report surveyed implementing multistate regulatory ventures.[27] It distinguished informal ties, formal accords among the extant state agencies, state-initiated regional agencies, and federally initiated regional agencies. The overall impression once more is of equal establishment difficulties but less gains than with more radical

27. Edison Electric Institute, *Regional Regulation of the Electric Power Industry* (Washington, D.C.: EEI, 1983).

changes. For example, anything short of a regional agency might be ineffective, and tricky constitutional questions arise from instituting such bodies. While the states might lack the power to act in this arena, they resent federal pressures.

Reforming Other Policies

As indicated, other elements of public policy bar the efficient operation of electric utilities. Whatever is done to public utility regulation should be accompanied by reforms of other regulations. I already advocated one such reform, the repeal of the Public Utility Holding Company Act. Other needs include radical changes in air-pollution and nuclear regulation and terminating state energy-planning and siting programs.

The prior discussion indicates that these planning boards duplicate existing public utility supervision. Worse they involve intense meddling in the areas where government is least competent to operate— that is, in estimating long-term trends. At best such intervention would be hard to carry out. As is all too usual, practice turns out worse than one could have anticipated when dealing only with theory.

California, with its unrelenting commitment to biennial reviews, provides the most striking bad examples. The basic reports are full of intellectual gymnastics used to support efforts at reducing the direct cost of energy to California consumers. There are predictable biases toward low forecasts, optimism about nonfossil-fueled, nonnuclear alternatives, and pessimism about nuclear and coal. There are various efforts to increase access to cheaply priced electricity such as that produced by federal hydroelectric projects. California is urged not only to take advantage of every available federal subsidy and tax break to alter energy-use patterns, but also to create similar policies of its own.[28]

Such survey reports are backed up by even less edifying efforts to support the projections more fully. Each electric utility in the state must submit detailed forecasts, and the commission staff then tries to judge whether an estimate is valid. This fascination with requiring

---

28. California Energy Commission, *1979 Biennial Report* (Sacramento, Calif., 1979); California Energy Commission, *Energy Tomorrow: Challenges and Opportunities for California, 1981 Biennial Report to the Governor and to the Legislature* (Sacramento, Calif., 1981); and California Energy Commission, *Securing California's Energy Future, 1983 Biennial Report to the Governor and to the Legislature* (Sacramento, Calif., 1983).

and evaluating elaborate forecasts has become widespread. Even where energy boards do not exist, someone such as the public utility commission will be demanding predictions.[29]

To be sure, as with every interest group, the commission will endorse those economically sound policies that advance its goals. Thus California correctly anticipated that it would be uneconomic to force electric utilities to eliminate burning gas as required by a 1978 federal law. Similarly the California Energy Commission's 1981 and 1983 reports chastized the demand-stimulating effects of the low electricity rates allowed.

On balance the energy-planning process does little good; it should be terminated. In particular the deregulated generator of electricity should be entrusted to decide what future construction will be needed and to suffer the boons or curses of those decisions. The siting process should be turned over to local governments, and various federal and state restrictions on land use should probably be repealed as well so that local government can decide what to allow or ban.

Experience suggests that localities are at least as anxious as state and federal governments to limit industrial land use. The proposal for decentralization, thus, is not a cry for abandoning the—probably excessive—prevailing concerns over protecting amenities from the encroachment of business activity. It is merely a way to simplify the process by reducing the number of actors and possibly allowing localities that believe they can tolerate a power plant to do so without interference.

As unfortunately is true of many government agencies, the NRC receives far less challenge than the evidence justifies. In practice, it has performed badly. Moreover, examination of the economic principles of intervention that might apply suggests no justification exists for the NRC. Economic theory indicates an NRC would be necessary with the existence of "publicness"—roughly the situation in which the result of a positive or negative act is made available indiscriminantly to everyone in society. Classic examples are how everyone benefits from defense and suffers from pollution. Government is needed because of the difficulties of transaction with all those affected.

Nuclear power is, however, a problem that private means can deal

---

29. Given a long-standing interest in forecasting, I made an effort during visits in 1980–81 to various electric utilities to learn about their practices. Universally, they were seeking to develop more elaborate models.

with effectively. Looking at the various criticisms of nuclear power suggests that the most critical area is creating liability for massive releases of radiation, which are most likely to occur by an accident at a power plant. Private damage suits can be a sufficient threat to obviate the need for government control so long as efforts to organize nuclear operations to limit damage liability are somehow barred. Unregulated utilities would find it technically feasible to establish separate corporations for each unit. The political difficulties these actions would provoke would be a powerful incentive to avoid them. Cooperative insurance schemes are more likely to emerge. If they do not, then the government could take appropriate action.

There are major transitional problems in moving toward this option. To begin with, the federal government has imposed legal limits on the damages companies can be liable for. In the prevailing anti-nuclear climate, removing those limits federally could lead to punitive state requirements. Thus we must devise some means of combining removal of federal liability limits with restrictions on state intervention in nuclear power. This done, the threat of lawsuits should more than suffice to insure that utilities make strenuous efforts to keep nuclear power safe.

Conversely the post mortems following the Three Mile Island accident were the quintessence of the usual moderate approach criticized above. The presidential commission headed by John Kemeny, then president of Dartmouth College, uncovered drastic defects in the NRC. The dual role of the commissioners as the nominal heads of the agency and the final board of review led to disastrous consequences. The commissioners feared being too closely involved in management because their integrity as a board of appeals might be compromised. Thus no one led.[30]

The result was regulation that stressed accumulating data without developing any satisfactory way to analyze it. It has often been noted in the literature that another nuclear plant with the same design as that of Three Mile Island experienced the same mechanical failure that produced the accident; this problem was reported to the NRC, but its system was unable to react by making the information available in a way to insure action. After the Three Mile Island accident, the

---

30. U.S. President's Commission on the Accident at Three Mile Island, *Report of the President's Commission on the Accident at Three Mile Island, The Need for Changing the Legacy of TMI*, (Washington, D.C.: U.S. Government Printing Office, 1979.)

prime NRC spokesman issued incorrect statements that were a major cause of the resulting apprehension. That official, nevertheless, was lauded. Since the accident, the NRC seems to have moved to correct, indiscriminantly, every problem it even suspects might become serious.

The Kemeny Commission clearly recognized the grave deficiencies of the NRC. As one would expect from such a consensus-oriented group, it dared only propose that the NRC be reformed. The defects of the magnitude they noted, however, justify abolishing the NRC.

Still another area for reform is air-pollution regulation, which has been heavily and validly criticized for adopting inappropriate means.[31] Complex regulatory limits on pollution are cumbersome; they overly centralize decision making and encourage litigation and other forms of foot dragging. A preferred enforcement means are taxes on polluters. Such taxes would impose unrelenting pressures on the polluting firm, which is best equipped with its superior knowledge of the costs and choice of compliance options to remedy the situation.

A less well recognized problem is the fragile basis for present regulations. The present rules were greatly influenced by Lave and Seskin's estimates of air-pollution-induced mortality. Subsequent observers, notably Ramsay, believe these figures significantly overestimate harm.[32] Others, such as Wilson, Colome, Spengler, and Wilson, warn that since pollutants appear together, we cannot be sure which is the true cause. Wilson et al. fear that it is not the sulfur oxides but instead small accompanying particles that are the culprits. Some practices adopted under pollution-control regulations—notably encouraging shifts to lower sulfur—but higher particulate, coal may have increased hazards.[33]

The acid-rain debate at first seemed an effort to find new reasons for control once the old ones had weakened. Apparently this is not the case. Evidence is mounting that acid raid is essentially only a new

31. The literature on this subject is enormous and growing. Of the numerous items in the bibliography, Edwin S. Mills, *The Economics of Environmental Quality* (New York: W. W. Norton, 1978) is particularly lucid and forceful.

32. See William Ramsay, *Unpaid Costs of Electric Energy: Health and Environmental Impacts from Coal and Nuclear Power* (Baltimore: Johns Hopkins University Press for Resources for the Future, 1979). The major presentation of the Lave and Seskin work is Lester B. Lave and Eugene P. Seskin, *Air Pollution and Human Health* (Baltimore: Johns Hopkins University Press for Resources for the Future, 1977).

33. Richard Wilson, Steven D. Coloame, John D. Spengler, and David Gordon Wilson, *Health Effects of Fossil Fuel Burning, Assessment and Mitigation* (Cambridge, Mass.: Ballinger Publishing Company, 1980).

term to describe previously recognized issues. This argument was understandably first made by representatives of those most likely to bear the costs of the regulation. A 1984 Office of Technology Assessment report on acid precipitation has, however, largely confirmed this impression. The OTA report even reiterated the Lave and Seskin numbers and ignored subsequent criticisms.[34] The call for legislation is simply an argument that past action was inadequate. No one seems able to explain the justification for more stringent rules when new research suggests the problems were less serious than first assumed.

Public power policy also needs radical change. At a minimum, the low-interest loans granted through the Rural Electrification Administration have never been economically rational and should be abolished. So should other low-interest loans to utilities including air-pollution bonds for private utilities.

It would be desirable to ultimately transfer as much public power as possible to the private sector. Public power has not made any contribution that justifies its perpetuation. Moreover it is those public-power ventures that historically seemed most justified—hydroelectric dams allegedly serving public as well as private purposes—that are now the prime targets for privatization.

The prior discussion of Bonneville indicates a widespread problem with such dams—the disposal of the economic rents that their low costs generate. Endless bickering occurs over who should get the benefits. Sale would provide an allocation once and for all. The sale should realize the present value of the rents; then they could be distributed as the government thought appropriate. Subsequently the private owner could sell the electricity at its social value. These changes should probably follow deregulation, however. The considerably greater freedom from regulatory constraints enjoyed by public power and publicly funded cooperatives provides an escape valve that might be retained until other reforms are effected.

CONCLUSIONS ON ELECTRICITY REGULATION

This paper suggests that the malaise of the electric utility industry reflects the increasing stringency of regulations at precisely the mo-

---

34. Among the first published statements of this sort I was aware of was that by Eugene Trisko, "Speaking Out—Acid Rain Remedies and Clean Air Act Revisions," *Inside EPA Weekly Report,* 23 March 1984. Trisko writes on these matters frequently under the aegis of the Stern brothers with West Virginia business interests. On the appraisal, see U.S. Congress, Office of Technology Assessment, *Acid Rain and Transported Air Pollutants: Implications for Public Policy.* (Washington, D.C.: U.S. Government Printing Office, 1984.)

ment in the industry's history when changing circumstances necessitated greater flexibility. A clear need exists to move radically to alter this problem. Reforms are needed in all the major regulations affecting electric utilities.

Some easy starting points—at least according to a consensus among informed observers—are to repeal the Public Utilities Holding Company Act and to shift air-pollution regulation toward use of pollution fines. Only those totally opposed to nuclear power would deny that reform of the NRC is needed. Its abolition appears to be the best reform, but established intellectual sloth precludes debate on the subject.

State energy planning is a demonstrated failure and clearly should cease. Siting probably should be made an exclusively local concern.

It is increasingly apparent that democratic governments—as well as autocrats—can benefit from Machiavelli's advice to act quickly and decisively in dealing with difficult issues. Reform of electric utility regulation will be a monumental task whether it involves trying to insure—which probably cannot be done—that the present system is managed well or, better, to make substantial changes.

The relevant choices are total deregulation or separating generation from transmission and distribution and deregulating generation. As previously indicated, a compromise must be made between the need to act and the uncertainties about the effects of actions. Thus what is provided here should be considered a best estimate, subject to correction by informed criticism.

Total deregulation has only one drawback, but it is a defect that could have greater costs than the several limitations of reorganization. With total deregulation, we risk exercise of significant monopoly power by retail distributors.

Separation and deregulation of generation avoids unregulated distribution monopolies but could leave the possibly more inefficient system of regulated retail rates. Advocates of reorganization argue that the inefficiencies of rate-making are less than those of an uncontrolled market or that with lesser responsibilities regulators can do a better job of retail rate setting. This comes at the cost of reorganizing a complex industry. As suggested, these might largely involve the fees for reincorporation, but even these could be substantial. On balance, total deregulation seems more attractive than restructuring.

SELECTED BIBLIOGRAPHY
PART IV

Ackerman, Bruce A., and William T. Hassler. *Clean Coal/Dirty Air*. New Haven, Conn.: Yale University Press, 1981.

Alexander, Tom. "The Surge to Deregulate Electricity." *Fortune* 104 (13 July 1981): 98–105.

"Are Utilities Obsolete?" *Business Week* (21 May 1984): 116–29.

Bailey, Elizabeth. "Contestability and the Design of Regulatory and Antitrust Policy." *American Economic Review* 71 (1981): 178–83.

Baumol, William J. *Economics, Environmental Policy, and the Quality of Life*. Englewood Cliffs, N.J.: Prentice-Hall, 1979.

Baumol, William J., and Wallace E. Oates. *The Theory of Environmental Policy: Externalities, Public Outlays, and the Quality of Life*. Englewood Cliffs, N.J.: Prentice-Hall, 1975.

Baumol, William J.; John C. Panzar; and Robert D. Willig. *Contestable Markets and the Theory of Industry Structure*. New York: Harcourt Brace Jovanovich, 1982.

Behling, Burton N. *Competition and Monopoly in Public Utility Industries*. Urbana: University of Illinois Press, 1938.

Bellamy, Jan. "Two Utilities Are Better Than One." *Reason* 13 (October 1981): 23–30.

Berlin, Edward; Charles J. Cicchetti; and William J. Gillen. *Perspectives on Power: A Study of the Regulation and Pricing of Electric Power*. Cambridge, Mass.: Ballinger Publishing Co., 1974.

Bohn, Roger E. "Spot Pricing of Public-Utility Service." Cambridge: Massachusetts Institute of Technology Energy Laboratory. MITEL-82-031 and Ph.D. thesis in Applied Economics, 1982.

Bohn, Roger E.; Michael C. Caramanis; and Fred C. Schweppe. "Optimal Spot Pricing of Electricity: Theory." Cambridge: Massachusetts Institute of Technology Energy Laboratory Working Paper. MITEL-081-008WP, 1981.

Bohn, Roger E.; Bennett W. Golub; Richard D. Tabors; and Fred C. Schweppe. "Deregulating the Generation of Electricity Through the Creation of Spot Markets for Bulk Power." *Energy Journal* 5 (April 1984): 71–91.

———. "Deregulating the Electric Utility Industry." Cambridge: Massachusetts Institute of Technology Energy Laboratory Working Paper. MITEL-82-003, 1982.

California Energy Commission. *1979 Biennial Report.* Sacramento: California Energy Commission, 1979.

———. *Energy Tomorrow: Challenges and Opportunities for California, 1981 Biennial Report to the Governor and to the Legislature.* Sacramento: California Energy Commission, 1981.

———. *Securing California's Energy Future, 1983 Biennial Report to the Governor and to the Legislature.* Sacramento: California Energy Commission, 1983.

Chadwick, Edwin. "Results of Different Principles of Legislation and Administration in Europe; of Competition for the Fields as Compared With Competition Within the Field of Service." *Royal Statistical Society Journal* 22 (1859): 381–420.

Clark, John M. *Competition as a Dynamic Process.* Washington, D.C.: Brookings Institution, 1961.

Coase, Ronald H. "The Nature of the Firm." *Economica* New Series 4 (1937): 386–405. Reprinted in K. Boulding and G. Stigler, eds., *Readings in Price Theory,* pp. 331–51. Homewood, Ill.: Irwin, 1952.

———. "The Problem of Social Cost." *Journal of Law and Economics* 3 (October 1960): 1–44.

Cohen, Linda. "A Spot Market for Electricity: Preliminary Analysis of the Florida Energy Broker." Santa Monica, Calif.: Rand Corp., 1982. (Mimeo.)

Cook, Franklin H. "Comparative Price Economies of Combination Utilities." *Public Utilities Fortnightly* 79 (1967): 34–36.

Crain, Mark, and Robert Ekelund, Jr. "Chadwick and Demsetz on Competition and Regulation." *Journal of Law and Economics* 19 (1976): 149–62.

Crain, Mark, and Robert Tollison. "Constitutional Change in an Interest-Group Perspective." *Journal of Legal Studies* 8 (1979): 165–75.

Demsetz, Harold. "Why Regulate Utilities?" *Journal of Law and Economics* 11 (1968): 55–65.

Dorfman, Joseph. *The Economic Mind in American Civilization.* Vol. 1. New York: August M. Kelley, 1966.

Edison Electric Institute. *Deregulation of Electric Utilities: A Survey of Major Concepts and Issues.* Washington, D.C.: Edison Electric Institute, 1981.

———. *Alternative Models of Electric Power Deregulation.* Washington, D.C.: Edison Electric Institute, 1982.

———. *Deregulation in the Electric Power Industry Conference Proceedings.* Washington, D.C.: Edison Electric Institute, 1983.

———. *Regional Regulation of the Electric Power Industry: Major Concepts and Issues.* Washington, D.C.: Edison Electric Institute, 1983.

Ekelund, Robert Jr., and Richard Saba. "Human Capital and Incumbent Advantages." *Southern Economic Journal* 47 (1980): 100–109.

———. "A Note on Politics and Franchise Bidding." *Public Choice* (1981): 203–8.

Ekelund, Robert Jr., and Richard Higgins. "Capital Fixity, Innovations, and Long-Term Contracting: An Intertemporal Economic Theory of Regulation." *American Economic Review* 72 (1982): 32–46.

Farris, Martin T., and Roy J. Sampson. *Public Utilities: Regulation, Management, and Ownership.* Boston: Houghton Mifflin, 1973.

Furubotn, Eirik G., and Svetozar Pejovich, eds. *The Economics of Property Rights.* Cambridge, Mass.: Ballinger Publishing Co., 1974.

Goldberg, Victor. "Regulation and Administered Contracts." *Bell Journal of Economics* 7 (1979): 426–48.

———. "Protecting the Right to Be Served by Public Utilities." *Research in Law and Economics* 1 (1979): 145–55.

———. "Relational Exchange: Economics and Complex Contracts." *American Behavioral Scientist* 23 (1980): 337–52.

Golub, Bennett W., and Leonard S. Hyman. "Financial Problems in the Transition to Deregulation." In J. Plummer, T. Ferrar, and W. Hughes, eds., *Electric Power Strategy Issues,* pp. 93–115. Arlington, Va.: Public Utility Reports, 1983.

Golub, Bennett W.; Richard D. Tabors; Roger E. Bohn; and Fred C. Schweppe. "An Approach for Deregulating the Generating of Electricity." In J. Plummer, T. Ferrar, and W. Hughes, eds., *Electric Power Strategy Issues,* pp. 59–92. Arlington, Va.: Public Utility Reports, 1983.

Gordon, Richard L. "Optimization of Input Supply Patterns in the Case of Fuels for Electric Power Generation." *Journal of Industrial Economics* 23 (September 1974): 19–37.

———. *Reforming the Regulation of Electric Utilities: Priorities for the 1980s.* Lexington, Mass.: Lexington Books, 1982.

———. "Resource Procurement: A Case Study of U.S. Electric Utilities." In D. Pearce, H. Siebert, and I. Walter, eds., *Risk and the Political Econ-*

omy of Resource Development, pp. 319–37. London: Macmillan, 1984.

Gray, Horace M. "The Passing of the Public Utility Concept." *Land Economics* 16 (1940): 8–20.

Hay, Donald A., and Derek J. Morris. *Industrial Economics: Theory and Evidence.* Oxford: Oxford University Press, 1979.

Hayek, Friedrich A. *The Constitution of Liberty.* Chicago: University of Chicago Press, 1960.

————. *Law, Legislation and Liberty.* 3 vols. Chicago: University of Chicago Press, 1973, 1976, and 1979.

Hellman, Richard. *Government Competition in the Electric Utility Industry: A Theoretical and Empirical Study.* New York: Praeger Publishers, 1972.

Hollas, Daniel R., and Thomas S. Friedland. "Price Discrimination in the Municipal Electric Industry." *Research in Law and Economics* 2 (1980): 181–98.

Hughes, David. "The Potential Federal Role in Deregulation." In J. Plummer, T. Ferrar, and W. Hughes, eds., *Electric Power Strategy Issues,* pp. 119–26. Arlington, Va.: Public Utility Reports, 1983.

Joskow, Paul, and Richard Schmalensee. *Markets for Power: An Analysis of Electric Utility Deregulation.* Cambridge: MIT Press, 1983.

Kahn, Alfred E. *The Economies of Regulation: Principles and Institutions.* Vol. 2. New York: John Wiley & Sons, 1971.

Kneese, Allen V., and Charles L. Schultze. *Pollution, Prices and Public Policy.* Washington, D.C.: Brookings Institution, 1975.

Landes, William, and Richard A. Posner. "The Independent Judiciary in an Interest Group Perspective." *Journal of Law and Economics* 18 (1975): 875–901.

Lave, Lester B., and Gilbert S. Omenn. *Clearing the Air: Reforming the Clean Air Act.* Washington, D.C.: Brookings Institution, 1981.

Lave, Lester B., and Eugene P. Seskin. *Air Pollution and Human Health.* Baltimore: Johns Hopkins University Press, for Resources for the Future, 1977.

Leibenstein, Harvey. "Allocative Efficiency vs. 'X-Efficiency'." *American Economic Review* 56 (June 1966): 392–416.

Mills, Edwin S. *The Economics of Environmental Quality.* New York: W. W. Norton, 1978.

Moore, Thomas G. "The Effectiveness of Regulation of Electric Utility Prices." *Southern Economic Journal* 36 (1970): 365–75.

National Association of Regulatory Utility Commissioners. *Annual Report on Utility and Carrier Regulation.* Washington, D.C.: National Association of Regulatory Utility Commissioners, annual.

Nelson, Randy A., and Walter J. Primeaux, Jr. "An Examination of the Relationship Between Technical Change and Regulatory Effectiveness." December 1983. (Unpublished.)

Owen, Bruce M. "Monopoly Pricing in Combined Gas and Electric Utilities." *Antitrust Bulletin* 15 (1970): 713–26.

Owen, Bruce M., and Ronald Braeutigam. *The Regulation Game: Strategic Use of the Administrative Process*. Cambridge, Mass.: Ballinger Publishing Co., 1978.

Peacock, Alan, and Charles Rowley. "Welfare Economics and the Public Regulation of Natural Monopoly." *Journal of Public Economics* 1 (1972): 224–27.

Peltzman, Sam. "Toward a More General Theory of Regulation." *Journal of Law and Economics* 19 (August 1976): 211–40.

Phillips, Charles F. *The Economics of Regulation: Theory and Practice in the Transportation and Public Utility Industries*. Homewood, Ill.: Irwin, 1969.

Plummer, James L. "A Different Approach to Electricity Deregulation." In J. Plummer, T. Ferrar, and W. Hughes, eds., *Electric Power Strategy Issues*, pp. 45–57. Arlington, Va.: Public Utility Reports, 1983.

Plummer, James L.; Terry Farrar; and William Hughes, eds. *Electric Power Strategy Issues*. Arlington, Va.: Public Utilities Reports, and Palo Alto, Calif.: QED Research, 1983.

Posner, Richard A. "Natural Monopoly and Its Regulation." *Stanford Law Review* 21 (1969): 548–643.

Primeaux, Walter J., Jr. "A Reexamination of the Monopoly Market Structure for Electric Utilities." In A. Phillips, ed., *Promoting Competition in Regulated Markets*, pp. 175–200. Washington, D.C.: Brookings Institution, 1975.

———. "An Assessment of X-Efficiency Gained Through Competition." *Review of Economics and Statistics* 59 (1977): 105–8.

———. "The Effect of Competition on Capacity Utilization in the Electric Utility Industry." *Economic Inquiry* 16 (1978): 237–48.

———. "Some Problems With Natural Monopoly." *Antitrust Bulletin* 24 (1979): 63–85.

———. "Deregulation of Electric Utility Firms: An Assessment of the Cost Effects of Complete Deregulation vs. Deregulation of Generation Only." Chicago: University of Illinois, 1982. (Mimeo.)

———. "Estimate of the Price Effect of Competition: The Case of Electricity." *Resources and Energy* (in press).

———. *Direct Electric Utility Competition: The Natural Monopoly Myth*. New York: Praeger Publishers, 1986.

Primeaux, Walter J., Jr., and Mark Bomball. "A Reexamination of the Kinky Oligopoly Demand Curve." *Journal of Political Economy* 82 (1974): 851–62.

Primeaux, Walter J., Jr.; John E. Filer; Robert S. Herren; and Daniel R.

Hollas. "Determinants of Regulatory Policies Toward Competition in the Electric Utility Industry." *Public Choice* (in press).

Primeaux, Walter J., Jr., and Patrick C. Mann. "A Seemingly Unrelated Regression Analysis of Regulator Selection and Electricity Prices." Chicago: University of Illinois, 1984. (Mimeo.)

Primeaux, Walter J., Jr., and Randy A. Nelson. "An Examination of Price Discrimination and Internal Subsidization by Electric Utilities." *Southern Economic Journal* 47 (1980): 84–99.

Ramsey, William. *Unpaid Costs of Electric Energy: Health and Environmental Impacts from Coal and Nuclear Power*. Baltimore: Johns Hopkins University Press, for Resources for the Future, 1979.

Scherer, Frederic M. *Industrial Market Structure and Economic Performance*. Boston: Houghton Mifflin, 1980.

Schultz, Walter. "Conditions for Effective Franchise Bidding in the West German Electricity Sector." In B. Mitchell and P. Kleindorfer, eds., *Regulated Industries and Public Enterprise*, pp. 57–69. Lexington, Mass.: Lexington Books, 1979.

Schumpeter, Joseph. *Capitalism, Socialism and Democracy*. 3d ed. New York: Harper & Row, 1950.

Scranton, William W. "Reforming and Improving Electric Utility Regulation." *Public Utilities Fortnightly* (4 April 1983): 19–23.

Shaker, William H., ed. *Electric Power Reform: The Alternatives for Michigan*. Ann Arbor: University of Michigan, 1976.

Shepherd, William G., and Thomas G. Gies, eds. *Utility Regulation: New Directions in Theory and Policy*. New York: Random House, 1966.

Smith, Adam. *An Inquiry Into the Nature and Causes of the Wealth of Nations*. New York: The Modern Library, 1937.

Stigler, George J. "The Division of Labor Is Limited by the Extent of the Market." In *The Organization of Industry*. Homewood, Ill.: Irwin, 1968.

———. "The Theory of Economic Regulation." *Bell Journal of Economics and Management Science* 2 (Spring 1971): 3–21.

Stigler, George, and Claire Friedland. "What Can Regulators Regulate? The Case of Electricity." *Journal of Law and Economics* 5 (October 1962): 1–16.

Sunset Task Force on Utility Regulatory Reform: Final Report to the Governor. State of Illinois, 1984.

Telser, Lester G. "On the Regulation of Industry: A Note." *Journal of Political Economy* 17 (1969): 937–52.

U.S. Federal Energy Regulatory Commission (FERC). "Opinion No. 203. Opinion and Order Finding Experimental Rate to be Just and Reasonable and Accepting Rate for Filing." Washington, D.C.: Federal Regulatory Commission, 1983.

U.S. Office of Technology Assessment. *Acid Rain and Transported Air Pollutants: Implications for Public Policy*. Washington, D.C.: Government Printing Office, 1984.

U.S. President's Commission on the Accident at Three Mile Island. *Report of the President's Commission on the Accident at Three Mile Island, The Need for Changing the Legacy of TMI*. Washington, D.C.: Government Printing Office, 1979.

Waddell, Thomas G. *The Economic Damages of Air Pollution*. Washington, D.C.: Government Printing Office, 1974.

Weiss, Leonard W. "Antitrust in the Electric Power Industry." In A. Phillips, ed., *Promoting Competition in Regulated Markets*, pp. 135–73. Washington, D.C.: Brookings Institution, 1975.

Weitzman, Martin L. "Prices vs. Quantities." *Review of Economic Studies* 41 (October 1974): 477–91.

Williamson, Oliver E. *Markets and Hierarchies: Analysis and Antitrust Implications, A Study of the Economics of Internal Organization*. New York: Free Press, 1975.

———. "Franchise Bidding for Natural Monopolies—In General and With Respect to CATV." *Bell Journal of Economics* 7 (1976): 73–104.

Wilson, Richard; Steven D. Colame; John D. Spengler; and David Gordon Wilson. *Health Effects of Fossil Fuel Burning, Assessment and Mitigation*. Cambridge, Mass.: Ballinger Publishing Co., 1980.

INDEX

impact of taxation on, 107–127
passim
inducement of, by regulatory
revision, 419–420
marginal, in entrepreneurial
decision-making, 368–369
in monopolistic environment,
37–38
of peak-load pricing, 323–327
of pooling, 91
and pricing, 55–58
and rate of return, 8
and rate structure, 9–10
and recovery of operating
expenses, 47–48
and taxation of natural
monopolies, 104
Effluent charges, 217
Eisenhower, Dwight D., 228, 236
Ekelund, Robert B., Jr., 393
Electricity, imports of, 226, 227
(table)
Electric Power Research Institute,
315–316, 356
Electric Reliability Council of
Texas, 453–454
El Paso Electric, 453, 457
Embedded debt costs, 50, 322, 328
Emergency Petroleum Allocation
Act (1973), 229
Emissions standards, 187. *See also*
National ambient air-quality
standards (NAAQS); New-
source performance standards
Employment Retirement Income
and Securities Act, 345
Endangered Species Act (1966),
184n. 2, 188n. 22
End-use tax and efficiency of
resource use, 107, 108
Energy and Environmental Policy
Center, Harvard University, 350
Energy audits, 256–257
Energy broker system, 414–415
Energy Conservation and Policy
Act (1978), 256
Energy crisis, 1, 23
and concern with energy
efficiency, 107
Energy markets, interdependence
of, 219, 221–223, 225–228

Energy Security Act (1980), 257n.
17
Energy Supply Act (1975), 230
Entitlements program, 229
Entrepreneurship
marginal efficiency of, 368–369
misapprehension of, as
monopoly power, 367–368
Entry, market
and access to transmission, 92
and challenges to natural
monopoly, 38
fixed v. sunk costs and, 443–
444
promotion of competition
through, 377, 378
regulatory control of, 295, 402,
403
and sustainability of natural
monopolies, 18–19
Environmental impact statements
(EIS)
circulation of, 187
and licensing requirements, 186
Environmentalism
impact of, on regulatory
environment, 337–338
political strategy of, 212–214
public policy impact of, 183–
185
as stimulus to regulatory-reform
debate, 448
Environmental Protection Agency
(EPA), 14, 15, 108, 188n. 22,
212, 216, 217n. 125, 267, 338
and air-quality enforcement, 195,
198, 200, 202–203
and water-quality enforcement,
203–204, 206
Environmental regulation
alternatives to command-and-
control method of, 216–217
circumscription of utilities'
decision-making by, 185–188
costs of, 14–16, 185, 197–198,
200, 202–203, 206–207, 214–
216
and fuel substitution, 231–232
impact of, 212–218
and income redistribution, 267–
269

ABOUT THE EDITOR

John C. Moorhouse is professor of economics at Wake Forest University. He received the A.B. degree from Wabash College and the Ph.D. from Northwestern University. Dr. Moorhouse has been a Woodrow Wilson Fellow and an Earhart Fellow. His research interests include applied price theory, regulation, and law and economics. His articles have appeared in the *American Mathematics Monthly, Cato Journal, Journal of Political Economy, Public Choice, Quarterly Review of Economics and Business, Reason Papers, Southern Economic Journal,* and other scholarly journals.

ABOUT THE AUTHORS

Craig J. Bolton is an associate of the Phoenix law firm Snell and Wilmer. Previously he was a John M. Olin Fellow at the Law and Economics Center at Emory University, and a member of the economics faculty at the University of Dallas. He received his B.A. from the University of Arizona, his Ph.D. in economics from Texas A&M University, and his J.D. from Emory University. Dr. Bolton's research interests are in law and economics and the history of economic thought.

Dr. Bolton is the author of articles that have appeared in *History of Political Economy* and *Bankruptcy Developments Journal.*

Robert B. Ekelund, Jr. is Lowder Professor of Economics at Auburn University, and was previously professor of economics at Texas A&M University. Dr. Ekelund received his B.B.A. and M.A. from St. Mary's University in San Antonio, Texas, and his Ph.D. from Louisiana State University.

He is the author of *A History of Economic Theory and Method* (with R. F. Hebert) and *Mercantilism as a Rent-Seeking Society* (with R. D. Tollison). His articles have appeared in the *American Economic Review, Bell Journal of Economics, Economic Inquiry, Economica, Journal of Law and Economics, Journal of Political Economy, Quar-*

511

terly Journal of Economics, Southern Economic Journal, and other scholarly and popular publications.

Richard L. Gordon received his A.B. in economics from Dartmouth College, and his Ph.D. from the Massachusetts Institute of Technology. He is professor of mineral economics at Pennsylvania State University.

Professor Gordon's articles have appeared in a number of scholarly publications including *Canadian Journal of Economics and Political Science, Energy Journal, Energy Policy, Energy Systems and Policy, Journal of Industrial Economics, Journal of International Law, Journal of Political Economy, Materials and Society, Natural Resources Journal, Quarterly of the Colorado School of Mines, Regulation,* and *Science.*

Professor Gordon is also the author of *Coal and Canada—U.S. Energy Relations, Coal in the U.S. Energy Market, Coal Industry Problems, An Economic Analysis of World Energy Problems, The Evolution of Energy Policy in Western Europe, Federal Coal Leasing Policy: Competition in the Energy Industries, Historical Trends in Coal Utilization and Supply, Marketing Prospects for Western Coal, Problems of Coal Supply Modeling: An Appraisal of Existing Studies, Reforming the Regulation of Electric Utilities, The Steel Industry and U.S. Business Cycles,* and *U.S. Coal and the Electric Power Industry.*

Thomas Grennes is associate professor of economics at North Carolina State University. He received his B.A. from Indiana University, and his M.A. from the University of Wisconsin. He is the author of *International Economics* and *The Economics of World Grain Trade* (with P. Johnson and M. Thursby). Professor Grennes' articles have been published in *American Journal of Agricultural Economics, Challenge, Current History, Journal of International Money and Finance, Journal of World Trade Law,* and the *Southern Economic Journal.*

Claire Holton Hammond received her B.A. from Mary Washington College and her Ph.D. from the University of Virginia. She is currently assistant professor of economics at Wake Forest University. In 1984 she was co-winner of the Irving Fisher Award for best dissertation in the United States. Dr. Hammond has done research on housing economics and is the author of the forthcoming *The Benefits of Subsidized Housing Programs: An Intertemporal Approach.*

Gregg A. Jarrell received his B.S. from the University of Delaware and his M.B.A. and Ph.D. from the University of Chicago. He has taught at the University of Rochester and the University of Chicago, and he has received a University of Chicago Fellowship and an Earhart Fellowship. He is presently at the Office of Chief Economist with the U.S. Securities and Exchange Commission and is a member of the U.S. Securities and Exchange Commission Advisory Committee on Tender Offer Policy. He is a member of the American Economic Association and the Financial Management Association. Dr. Jarrell has served as consultant to the Federal Trade Commission on antitrust cases.

Dr. Jarrell's articles have appeared in *Journal of Accounting and Economics, Journal of Finance, Journal of Law and Economics, Journal of Political Economy, New York University Law Review, The Supreme Court Economic Review,* and other scholarly publications.

Milton Z. Kafoglis is John H. Harland Professor of Business Administration at Emory University. He received his Ph.D. from The Ohio State University, and has served on the faculties of the University of Florida, University of South Florida, University of Tennessee and The Ohio State University. Dr. Kafoglis has also served as senior economist at the Council on Wage and Price Stability. His articles have appeared in the *American Economic Review, Bell Journal, Land Economics, National Tax Journal,* and other professional publications.

Robert E. McCormick is Professor of Economics at Clemson University. He received his B.A. and M.A. in economics from Clemson, and his Ph.D. from Texas A&M University. Professor McCormick was formerly an instructor for the Federal Trade Commission, senior visiting research fellow at the Center for the Study of Public Choice at Virginia Polytechnic Institute and State University, and assistant professor at the University of Rochester.

Professor McCormick's articles have appeared in *American Economic Review, International Review of Law and Economics, Journal of Business, Journal of Economic Behavior and Organization, Journal of Law and Economics, Journal of Political Economy, Public Choice,* and the *Southern Economic Journal.*

Roger E. Meiners received his B.A. from Washington State University, his M.A. from the University of Arizona, Ph.D. from Virginia Polytechnic Institute and State University, and his J.D. from the University of Miami. He is currently professor of economics and director of the Center for Policy Studies at Clemson University. He served as director of the Atlanta Regional Office of the Federal Trade Commission (1983–1985), and as professor at the University of Miami, Emory University, and Texas A&M University. Professor Meiners has been the recipient of a John M. Olin Fellowship, Mont Pelerin Society Fellowship, Institute for Humane Studies Fellowship, and the Outstanding Research Award from Texas A&M University.

Professor Meiners is the author of *Legal Environment of Business* (with A. Ringleb), *Barriers to Corporate Growth* (with B. Baysinger and C. Zeithaml), *Victim Compensation: Economic, Legal and Political Aspects, Intermediate Microeconomics* (with R. L. Miller), and *Distortions in Official Unemployment Statistics* (with K. Clarkson). His articles have appeared in popular and professional journals such as *Academy of Management Journal, American Spectator, Business Horizons, International Review of Law and Economics, Journal of Social and Political Studies, Policy Review, Public Choice, Public Finance Quarterly*, and *Social Science Review*.

Peter Navarro is professor of economics at the University of California at San Diego School of Business. He received his B.A. from Tufts University, an M.A. in public administration from the John F. Kennedy School of Government at Harvard University, and subsequently, an M.A. and Ph.D. in economics from Harvard University.

Mr. Navarro's articles have been published in a number of scholarly and popular publications such as *Bell Journal of Economics, Boston Globe, Boston Herald American, Boston Phoenix, Business Week, Chicago Tribune, Christian Science Monitor, Energy Law Journal, Harvard Business Review, Industrial and Labor Relations Review, Los Angeles Times, Miami Herald, National Review, New York Times, Public Interest, Public Policy, Public Utilities Fortnightly, Regulation, Urban Land, Wall Street Journal, Washington Post*, and the *Washington Star*. He is the author of two books, *The Dimming of America* and *The Policy Game*.

Ernest C. Pasour, Jr. received his B.S. and M.S. from North Carolina State University, and his Ph.D. from Michigan State University. He received appointments from the National Science Foundation at the University of Missouri and the University of Chicago. He is professor of economics and business at North Carolina State University.

Professor Pasour's articles have appeared in popular and professional journals such as *Agricultural Economics Research, The Alternative, The American Economist, American Journal of Agricultural Economics, Cato Journal, The Freeman, The Intercollegiate Review, Journal of Libertarian Studies, Journal of Post Keynesian Economics, Journal of Public Finance and Public Choice, Journal of Social, Political and Economic Studies, Land Economics, Manhattan Report, Modern Age, National Tax Journal, Public Choice, Reason, Southern Economic Journal,* and *Wall Street Journal.*

Walter J. Primeaux, Jr. is Professor of Business Administration at the University of Illinois at Champaign-Urbana. He received his B.A. from the University of Southwestern Louisiana and his M.A. and Ph.D. degrees in economics from the University of Houston. He has served as a consultant to numerous private firms and government agencies. He is currently a vice president of the Association of Managerial Economists and is an associate editor of *Managerial and Decision Economics.*

Professor Primeaux is the author of *Direct Electric Utility Competition, Foundations of Business Economics: The Contributions of Joel Dean, The Effect of Price and Other Selected Variables on Water Consumption* (with K. Hollman), *Personal Income Estimates of Mississippi Counties* (with N. Waller, M. Beuchner, and R. Curtis), and editor of *Essays in Business and Economics.* His articles have appeared in *Alabama Law Review, Denver Law Journal, Economic Affairs, Economic Inquiry, Energy Journal, Journal of Business of the University of Chicago, Journal of Law and Economics, Journal of Political Economy, Land Economics, Managerial and Decision Economics, Monthly Labor Review, Mississippi Law Journal, Public Choice, Public Finance Quarterly, Public Utilities Fortnightly, Quarterly Review of Economics and Business, Resources and Energy, Review of Economics and Statistics, Southern Economic Journal,* and *Western Economic Journal.*

Al H. Ringleb received his Ph.D. in economics from Kansas State University and his J.D. from the University of Kansas. He is assistant professor of business and management at Texas A&M University.

Dr. Ringleb's articles have been published in *Columbia Journal of*

Environmental Law, Houston Law Review, Journal of Energy Law and Policy, Oil and Gas Tax Quarterly, and *Pacific Law Journal.* He is the author of several books, including *The Legal Environment of Business* (with R. Meiners).

Richard P. Saba received his B.A. and M.B.A. from the University of Dallas and his Ph.D. from Texas A&M University. He is currently assistant professor of economics at Auburn University. His articles have appeared in *Journal of Financial Research, Public Choice, Quarterly Review of Economics and Business,* and the *Southern Economic Journal.*

John T. Wenders is professor of economics at the University of Idaho. He received an A.B. degree from Amherst College, an M.A. from the University of Hawaii, and an M.A. and Ph.D. from Northwestern University. He has been on the faculties of the Panahou School, Northwestern University, Middlebury College, and the University of Arizona.

Professor Wenders' articles have appeared in *Antitrust Bulletin, Arizona Review, Bell Journal of Economics, Electric Ratemaking, Energy Economics, Energy Journal, Journal of Economic Issues, Journal of Law and Economics, Journal of Industrial Economics, Journal of Natural Resources, Journal of Political Economy, Public Utilities Fortnightly, Southern Economic Journal, Telecommunications Policy, Water Resources Research,* and *Water Engineering and Management.*

Asghar Zardkoohi is associate professor of business in the Business and Public Policy Group in the Department of Management at Texas A&M University. He received his Ph.D. in economics from Virginia Polytechnic Institute and State University, and was previously on the faculty at Auburn University.

Professor Zardkoohi's articles have appeared in *American Economic Review, Atlantic Economic Journal, Economic Inquiry, Journal of Law and Economics, Kyklos, Public Choice,* and the *Southern Economic Journal.*

The Pacific Research Institute for Public Policy is an independent, tax-exempt research and educational organization. The Institute's program is designed to broaden public understanding of the nature and effects of market processes and government policy.

With the bureaucratization and politicization of modern society, scholars, business and civic leaders, the media, policymakers, and the general public have too often been isolated from meaningful solutions to critical public issues. To facilitate a more active and enlightened discussion of such issues, the Pacific Research Institute sponsors in-depth studies into the nature of and possible solutions to major social, economic, and environmental problems. Undertaken regardless of the sanctity of any particular government program, or the customs, prejudices, or temper of the times, the Institute's studies aim to ensure that alternative approaches to currently problematic policy areas are fully evaluated, the best remedies discovered, and these findings made widely available. The results of this work are published as books and monographs, and form the basis for numerous conference and media programs.

Through this program of research and commentary, the Institute seeks to evaluate the premises and consequences of government policy, and provide the foundations necessary for constructive policy reform.

PACIFIC STUDIES IN PUBLIC POLICY

FORESTLANDS
Public and Private
Edited by Robert T. Deacon and M. Bruce Johnson
Foreword by B. Delworth Gardner

URBAN TRANSIT
The Private Challenge to Public Transportation
Edited by Charles A. Lave
Foreword by John Meyer

POLITICS, PRICES, AND PETROLEUM
The Political Economy of Energy
By David Glasner
Foreword by Paul W. MacAvoy

RIGHTS AND REGULATION
Ethical, Political, and Economic Issues
Edited by Tibor M. Machan and M. Bruce Johnson
Foreword by Aaron Wildavsky

FUGITIVE INDUSTRY
The Economics and Politics of Deindustrialization
By Richard B. McKenzie
Foreword by Finis Welch

MONEY IN CRISIS
The Federal Reserve, the Economy, and Monetary Reform
Edited by Barry N. Siegel
Foreword by Leland B. Yeager

NATURAL RESOURCES
Bureaucratic Myths and Environmental Management
By Richard Stroup and John Baden
Foreword by William Niskanen

FIREARMS AND VIOLENCE
Issues of Public Policy
Edited by Don B. Kates, Jr.
Foreword by John Kaplan

WATER RIGHTS
Scarce Resource Allocation, Bureaucracy, and the Environment
Edited by Terry L. Anderson
Foreword by Jack Hirshleifer

LOCKING UP THE RANGE
Federal Land Controls and Grazing
By Gary D. Libecap
Foreword by Jonathan R. T. Hughes

THE PUBLIC SCHOOL MONOPOLY
A Critical Analysis of Education and the State in American Society
Edited by Robert B. Everhart
Foreword by Clarence J. Karier

RESOLVING THE HOUSING CRISIS
Government Policy, Decontrol, and the Public Interest
Edited with an Introduction by M. Bruce Johnson

OFFSHORE LANDS
Oil and Gas Leasing and Conservation on the Outer Continental Shelf
By Walter J. Mead, et al.
Foreword by Stephen L. McDonald

ELECTRIC POWER
Deregulation and the Public Interest
Edited by John C. Moorhouse
Foreword by Harold Demsetz

TAXATION AND THE DEFICIT ECONOMY
Fiscal Policy and Capital Formation in the United States
Edited by Dwight R. Lee
Foreword by Michael J. Boskin

THE AMERICAN FAMILY AND THE STATE
Edited by Joseph R. Peden and Fred R. Glahe
Foreword by Robert Nisbet

DEALING WITH DRUGS
Problems of Government Control
Edited by Ronald Hamowy

CRISIS AND LEVIATHAN
Critical Episodes in the Growth of American Government
By Robert Higgs
Foreword by Arthur A. Ekirch, Jr.

FORTHCOMING

THE NEW CHINA
Comparative Economic Development in Hong Kong, Taiwan, and Mainland China

POLITICAL BUSINESS CYCLES
The Economics and Politics of Stagflation

RATIONING HEALTH CARE
Medical Licensing in the United States

HEALTH CARE IN AMERICA: PUBLIC AND PRIVATE

CRIME, POLICE, AND THE COURTS

MYTH AND REALITY IN SOCIAL WELFARE

RENT CONTROL IN SANTA MONICA

UNEMPLOYMENT AND THE STATE

For further information on the Pacific Research Institute's program and a catalog of publications, please contact:

PACIFIC RESEARCH INSTITUTE FOR PUBLIC POLICY
177 Post Street
San Francisco, California 94108